Social Ecology

M.I.T. STUDIES IN COMPARATIVE POLITICS

Under the general editorship of Harold D. Lasswell, Daniel Lerner, and Ithiel de Sola Pool.

The Emerging Elite: A Study of Political Leadership in Ceylon, Marshall Singer, 1964.

The Turkish Political Elite, Frederick W. Frey, 1965.

World Revolutionary Elites: Studies in Coercive Ideological Movements, Harold D. Laswell and Daniel Lerner, editors, 1965.

Language of Politics: Studies in Quantitative Semantics, Harold D. Lasswell, Nathan Leites, and Associates, 1965 (reissue).

The General Inquirer: A Computer Approach to Content Analysis, Philip J. Stone, Dexter C. Dunphy, Marshall S. Smith, Daniel M. Ogilvie, 1967.

Political Elites: A Selected Bibliography, Carl Beck and J. Thomas McKechnie, 1968.

Force and Folly: Essays on Foreign Affairs and the History of Ideas, Hans Speier, 1968.

Quantitative Ecological Analysis in the Social Sciences, Mattei Dogan and Stein Rokkan, editors, 1969.

Social Ecology

edited by
Mattei Dogan and Stein Rokkan

THE M.I.T. PRESS
Massachusetts Institute of Technology
Cambridge, Massachusetts, and London, England

First MIT Press paperback edition, April 1974

Library of Congress catalog card number: 68–21558

ISBN 0 262 54022 3

Foreword

THE PRESENT volume brings into the M.I.T. Studies in Comparative Politics explicit consideration of an important range of issues which concern policy scientists everywhere. That the volume is the product of an International Symposium involving the participation of social scientists from many different disciplines and many different lands enhances its contemporary interest and, we believe, its lasting importance.

Among the many merits of the volume is the fresh focus it brings to the analysis of trends. Disciplined knowledge of the past is basic to the analysis of conditions under which historical turning points have occurred and to the projection of alternatives under which future turning points consonant with our preferred values may be helped to occur. We especially welcome, therefore, the studies of trends presented as "historical dimensions of ecological analysis" (Part Five).

The analysis of conditions under which trends occur — the "manifold of events," in Whitehead's phrase, which produces what we are calling a "turning point" in any particular time-space configuration — has concerned social scientists over many years. Indeed, there are some who consider this the proper business of social science *qua* science. In this context we welcome the businesslike studies gathered under "multivariate analysis in political ecology" (Part Three) as well as "factor analysis and ecological typologies" (Part Four).

Consideration of typologies usually leads social scientists to rethink the fundamental structure of empirical social research. The participants in this co-operative enterprise have chosen, again wisely, to make their rethinking of these issues explicit and public. The chapters subsumed under "the logic of ecological inference" (Part One) are a valuable contribution to the continuous rethinking of fundamentals, which is indispensable to the scientific enterprise. Equally important for any student of the effort to shape the "behavioral sciences" over the past two decades so that they can deal with political and other "systems" is the group of studies concerned with "individual behavior and collective properties" (Part Two).

Among the high hopes of social scientists in recent years is the creation of a "world observatory." This requires social research to become "cumulative" in order that statements about different time-space configurations of individual and social behavior may become genuinely "comparative." The construction of "operational indices," upon which these high hopes depend, can proceed only in the measure that we build data banks in such a way that observations made in different places at different times can be ordered as "functional equivalents" and thus can be collated and compared. The chapters concerned with "organization of ecological data archives" (Part Six) provide a reasoned response to these high hopes and the associated demands that social scientists have put upon themselves and each other.

We welcome, in short, a volume of studies that respond to the real needs of "comparative politics" in our time — a volume that, in so doing, may help to build the developing science of democracy throughout the world.

May 1968   Harold D. Lasswell
                                            Daniel Lerner

Preface

THIS VOLUME is an outgrowth of a long history of exchange and co-
operation among European and American social scientists. The core of
this movement was made up of electoral analysts: social psychologists,
sociologists, and political scientists eager to apply the latest techniques
of data collection and statistical analysis in the study of modes and
trends of mass politics in the advanced democracies of the West. This
group never reached the stage of formal organization but maintained
frequent and fruitful contacts through a circuit of overlapping memberships in such bodies as the Research Committee on Political Sociology
of the International Sociological Association and the Standing Committee of the International Social Science Council; various joint
publications in the field of comparative political analysis testify to the
strength of these ties.

The Europeans in this core group were torn between two styles of
political research: they were attracted by the great potentialities of the
sample survey developed to such a high level of precision by their American colleagues but at the same time felt heavily committed to the older
European tradition of *geographical-ecological analysis* expressed in such
admirable works as André Siegfried's *Tableau Politique de la France de
l'Ouest* (1913) and Herbert Tingsten's *Political Behaviour* (1937). The
sample survey appealed to them because of the greater wealth of
variables and the directness of the analysis. The Siegfried-Tingsten
style of analysis limited itself to a smaller range of variables but allowed
detailed exploration of variations in geographical and historical depth:
through the collection, unit by unit, of data from official statistical
sources it was possible not only to identify local deviations from

national and regional averages but also to *go further back in time* than any sample survey would allow, back to the earlier phases of democratization and party formation.

The balance between these two styles of research was deeply affected by changes in the technology of analysis. The sample survey came in with the sorter-counter and the tabulator. This equipment fitted the requirements of straightforward survey analysis very well but did not prove very helpful in work with data for ecological units. With the arrival of the electronic computer all this changed: the greater capacity of these machines obviously had its effects on the level of sophistication of survey analysis, but the impact on ecological work was much more profound. The earlier attempts at ecological differentiation had been excessively simplistic: percentage and decile distributions, crude typologies, calculations of differences on dependent variables. The electronic computer opened up a vast range of further analysis options for ecologists: correlation matrices, regression and covariance analysis, factor analysis, causal path analysis, calculations of systems of simultaneous equations in the econometric style. The decisive change in the balance between the two traditions of research came between 1960 and 1965: even the most ardent believers in the survey techniques found themselves attracted by the possibilities of longitudinal analysis opened up through the establishment of large-scale files of aggregate data for computer analysis. It is deeply significant that it was that great Mecca of the American survey tradition, the Center at Ann Arbor, that took the initiative which led to the establishment of a computer archive for historical ecological data for the United States.

One consequence of this change in the technological conditions of research was a realignment of scientific alliances. During the era dominated by the survey technique, the analysts of elections tended to maintain their closest links with social psychologists and students of social stratification and mobility. With the arrival of the data archive for aggregate statistics a new set of alignments began to take form: on one side, the analysts of elections found themselves less and less attracted by the cartographic concreteness of the school of electoral geography; on the other, they became increasingly aware of their intellectual affinities with the *urban ecologists* and the econometricians of the *regional science* movement. As soon as the analysts of electoral behavior moved into the computerization of their data for local units, they discovered that a number of their analytical problems had already been thoroughly dissected by sociologists and economists working on spatial variations for purposes of urban and regional planning. Their dependent variables differed, but their analytical procedures had a number of features in common.

The present volume represents a step in this spelling out of new convergencies in the study of territorial and spatial variations. In our joint Introduction, we have tried to sketch some of the background of these trends. The chapters in Part One focus on the crucial issue in the debate between the sample survey enthusiasts and the *aficionados* of the ecological method: *the level-of-analysis fallacies*. The chapters in Part Two concentrate on the concrete possibilities of level-to-level linkage through contextual analysis and the development of joint "macro-micro" designs. Parts Three, Four, and Five offer illustrations of the wide range of analysis options in ecological research: the various techniques of multivariate regression, covariance, and linear causal analysis now used in political research, the factor analytical techniques used by urban ecologists and geographers, and the newer methods of time series analysis currently explored in historical studies of demographic, economic, and political change. The final section of the volume concentrates on the concrete and practical tasks of *ecological data archiving*: this shows how the arrival of the "third generation" computers opened up extraordinary possibilities of expansion, both back into history and across a variety of distinct files, and how work has moved ahead in country after country, not only in the United States but in several European countries and in Latin America.

This volume could not have been assembled without the generous help of several organizations, research centers, and individual scholars. Drafts of about half of the chapters were originally presented at a symposium organized by the International Social Science Council with the assistance of UNESCO, the Ecole Pratique des Hautes Etudes, and the Direction de la Coopération of the French Ministère de l'Education Nationale. We are greatly indebted to these organizations for their generous support and are particularly grateful to Kazimierz Szczerba-Likiernik and Clemens Heller of the International Social Science Council and to Samy Friedman of UNESCO for their help and their patience.

We wish to record our thanks to Daniel Derivry of the Centre National de la Recherche Scientifique in Paris for his contribution to the organization of the symposium.

Finally we are both happy to acknowledge our lasting indebtedness to the research institutions where this volume was planned and organized: the Centre National de la Recherche Scientifique and the Centre d'Etudes Sociologiques in Paris, the Chr. Michelsen Institute in Bergen, and the Center for Advanced Study in the Behavioral Sciences at Stanford. We do not hold any of these institutions or individuals responsible for errors or omissions in this volume, but we do want to make it clear that this volume would never have seen the light of day without their generous support.

Paris   Mattei Dogan
October 1967   Stein Rokkan

List of Contributors

Hayward R. Alker, Jr.   Yale University, Department of Political Science; Massachusetts Institute of Technology, Department of Political Science

Erik Allardt   University of Helsinki, Institute of Sociology

Jane H. Bayes   University of California (Los Angeles), Department of Political Science

Vittorio Capecchi   Universita Commerciale Luigi Bocconi, Istituto di Statistica, Milan

Philip E. Converse   University of Michigan, Survey Research Center

Kevin R. Cox   The Ohio State University, Department of Geography

Karl W. Deutsch   Yale University, Department of Political Science; Harvard University, Department of Government

Mattei Dogan   Centre National de la Recherche Scientifique, Centre d'Etudes Sociologiques

Giorgio Galli   Istituto di Studi e Ricerche Carlo Cattaneo, Bologna

Jorge Garcia-Bouza   Center for Social Research, Torcuato Di Tella Institute, Buenos Aires

Wolfgang Hartenstein   Dokumentations- und Ausbildungszentrum für Theorie und Methode der Regionalforschung, Bad Godesberg

Nigel Howard   University College London, Center for Urban Studies

Carl-Gunnar Janson   University of Stockholm, Institute of Sociology

Jean A. Laponce   The University of British Columbia, Department of Political Science

Peter Laslett	University of Cambridge, Trinity College
Klaus Liepelt	Institut für angewandte Sozialwissenschaft, Bad Godesberg
Juan Linz	Colombia University, Department of Sociology
Duncan MacRae, Jr.	University of Chicago, Department of Political Science
Dwaine Marvick	University of California (Los Angeles), Department of Political Science
James A. Meldrum	Northern Illinois University, Department of History (retired)
Marshall W. Meyer	Harvard University, Department of Social Relations
Warren E. Miller	Inter-University Consortium for Political Research, Ann Arbor
Peter Norman	University of Glasgow, Department of Social and Economic Research
Stein Rokkan	University of Bergen, Institute of Sociology
Erwin K. Scheuch	University of Cologne, Institut für international vergleichende Sozialforschung
David R. Segal	University of Michigan, Department of Sociology
Rodney Stiefbold	The University of Wisconsin, Department of Political Science; University of California, Berkeley, Department of Political Science
Frank L. Sweetser	Boston University, Department of Sociology and Anthropology
Tapani Valkonen	University of Helsinki, Institute of Sociology

Contents

xiii

MATTEI DOGAN AND STEIN ROKKAN

Introduction

BACKGROUND

SINCE 1962 the International Social Science Council has concentrated its efforts on the advancement of the theory and methodology of comparative cross-national and cross-cultural research. Steps have been taken to ensure broad international confrontations of techniques and experiences in the analysis of data for different political and cultural units and from different types of sources.

Major emphasis in the program has been given to the possibilities and limitations of *quantitative* comparisons across different types of units and to the examination of alternative ways of improving the data bases for such comparisons.

Until 1966 the work within the program was focused on data from *sample surveys*[1] and on *aggregate national statistics*.[2] Experts on cross-national research assembled for a Round Table Conference in Paris in April 1965, recommended a broadening of the program, and urged the planning of co-operative work on the cross-national archiving and analysis of other types of data.[3]

Among such new lines of activity one was given a particularly high priority: international co-operation in the organization of facilities and the development of techniques for *quantitative analysis of cross-local variations.*

[1] See the reports in the special issue on "Data in Comparative Research," *International Social Science Journal, 16* (1964), pp. 2–97.

[2] See R. L. Merritt and S. Rokkan (eds.), *Comparing Nations* (New Haven: Yale University Press, 1966).

[3] See S. Rokkan, "Trends and Possibilities in Comparative Social Science," *Social Science Information, 4* (1965), pp. 139–165.

1

The need for concerted effort to advance such cross-national "ecology" had already been spelled out in some detail at the large-scale International Conference held at Yale University in 1963; the discussion of the archiving and analysis of aggregate *national* statistics naturally led to an examination of the possibilities of systematic studies of *within-nation* variations, not just at the level of the individual or the household, but quite particularly at the level of the *constituent territories and communities.*[4]

Statistical studies of local and regional variations have been part of the stock in trade of the social sciences for more than a century, but the vast majority of these studies were limited to the single countries; only a scattering of attempts had been made at quantitative comparisons *across* several nations of the directions and ranges of such variations. By the late 1950's, however, the accelerating demand for research on the conditions for economic growth and social and cultural modernization had added new dimensions to such studies of within-nation variations and prompted a variety of methodological innovations. The great technical novelty of the 1930's and 1940's, the systematic sample survey, had proved of immense value in the study of sociocultural variations, but the samples generally allowed only few and very crude breakdowns by region and type of community. The greatest resource for systematic research on local variations was still clearly the continuously accumulating masses of data from official enumerations and bookkeeping operations. The spread of electronic computing facilities made it increasingly tempting for a variety of social scientists to delve into these data masses and to test new methods of analysis. The result was a mushrooming of quantitative studies of cross-local variations during the late fifties and early sixties and a number of efforts to set up facilities for further analyses in the form of data archives.[5]

Statistics by locality had for decades been studied from a wide variety of perspectives: by social and economic historians, geographers, economists, anthropologists, sociologists, and political scientists. Highly divergent approaches had developed in the study of local

---

[4] See, particularly, the papers by Allardt, Linz and de Miguel, Rokkan and Valen, and Scheuch in Merritt and Rokkan (eds.), *op. cit.*

[5] On archives for data by locality see the paper by Allardt and Riihinen in S. Rokkan (ed.), *Data Archives for the Social Sciences* (Paris: Mouton, 1966), and the article by R. Bisco, "Social Science Data Archives: A Review of Recent Developments," *American Political Science Review, 60* (1966), pp. 93–109. For a broader treatment of the issues in the handling of official statistical data masses see J. Beshers (ed.), *Computer Methods in the Analysis of Large-Scale Social Systems* (Cambridge, Mass.: The M.I.T. Press, 1968).

variations: historians and geographers gave priority to cartographic methods; anthropologists collected information about the "fit" between the natural habitat, the state of technology, and the organization of society; economists developed techniques for the study of variations in physical and labor force resources, in distance to markets, in the localization of industries; sociologists studied dimensions of differentiation among rural, suburban, and urban communities and among sectors and zones of the metropolitan areas; political scientists focused on territorial variations in the size and complexity of administrative structures, in the entrenchment and activity of parties and interest organizations, in the behavior of the citizenry at the polls, in referenda or in strikes and demonstrations. There was very little co-operation across these divergent intellectual disciplines, and the debates among the practitioners of these differing approaches often tended to generate confusion rather than promote clarification.

LEVELS AND DIRECTIONS OF "ECOLOGICAL" RESEARCH

Some of the confusion in these debates across the disciplines is reflected in the multiple usages of the term "ecology."

The original usage is quite clear: Ernst Haeckel introduced the neologism as a term for the study of the influence of the physical and biological environment on the behavior and development of organisms.[6] Haeckel had confined his research to *plants*, but essentially the same perspective was soon to be applied in the study of *animals*.

A distinctive school of *human* ecology first developed within the sociology of urban communities,[7] but similar approaches to

---

[6] Ernst Haeckel, *Natürliche Schöpfungsgeschichte* (1867); for further discussion of the historical context see R. C. Stauffer, "Haeckel, Darwin, and Ecology," *Quarterly Review of Biology, 32* (1952), pp. 138–144.

[7] The first to extend the ecological perspective to the study of human communities and behaviors were the Chicago sociologists Robert E. Park and Ernest W. Burgess; see their *Introduction to the Science of Sociology* (Chicago: University of Chicago Press, 1921), Chapters III and VIII. The central texts of this tradition are R. D. McKenzie, *The Metropolitan Community* (New York: McGraw-Hill, 1933); M. Alihan, *Social Ecology* (New York: Columbia University Press, 1939); A. Hawley, *Human Ecology: A Theory of Community Structures* (New York; Ronald Press, 1950). For a broader selection of texts illustrating these developments see G. A. Theodorsen (ed.), *Studies in Human Ecology* (Evanston: Row, 1961). A useful discussion of the linkages between plant, animal, and human ecology is O. D. Duncan, "Social Organization and the Eco-system," Chapter 2 of R. E. L. Faris (ed.), *Handbook of Modern Sociology* (Chicago, Rand McNally, 1964), pp. 37–82.

the study of environmental influence on human institutions and human behavior soon developed within cultural and social anthropology.[8]

The term "ecology" soon won general acceptance in the social sciences, although usage varied from discipline to discipline. In its broadest sense "ecology" was used to cover all varieties of research on the adjustment of human beings to their environments. A recent reader in human ecology has chapters on the climate and the soil as well as on the sociocultural community contexts of behavior; it even includes a discussion of man's possibilities of adjustment in entirely new environments, such as the depths of the ocean and outer space.[9] In a narrower sense "ecology" has tended to be used of a wide variety of approaches to the study of *spatial* and *territorial* environments of human activity, whether defined in smaller surface units, such as tracts of agricultural land, villages, neighborhoods, blocks or precincts, or in larger administrative units, such as communes, cantons, counties, constituencies, or even entire national polities.

Even in the narrower sense the term "ecology" has been applied to a wide variety of approaches to the study of the spatial-territorial environments of human behavior. These divergencies can be mapped along several dimensions: the levels of variation distinguished, the direction of the explanatory efforts, the availability of data level by level, and the techniques used in handling the data. All ecological studies focus attention on variations among units at some level above the individual actor; the studies differ from each other in their choices of dependent variables and in their strategies of data collection and data handling.

To simplify, let us assume only *two* levels of variation: variations among *individuals* (on variables such as sex, age, education, religious affiliation, party preference) and variations among *proximal territorial units* (villages, rural communes, and precincts or wards within urban areas).

The data available at each level will either be *primary* (originating at the given level) or *derived* (deduced from characteristics of the subordinate or the superordinate units). This

---

[8] See the review of such trends in J. Helm, "The Ecological Approach in Anthropology," *American Journal of Sociology, 67* (1962), pp. 630–639.

[9] M. Bressler (ed.), *Human Ecology: A Collection of Readings* (Cambridge: Addison-Wesley, 1965).

gives the four possibilities shown in the accompanying table.[10]

	Primary Data	*Derived Data*
Individuals	*Personal* attributes (sex, age, etc.) or behavior characteristics (church attendance, voting)	*Contextual* data: membership of, exposure to, territorial unit of given global or aggregate attribute
Territorial units	*Global* attributes characterizing unit as a whole, not derivable from data on individuals in the unit	*Aggregate* data: unit characteristics derived from distribution of individual attributes or behaviors

In practice, data in one or the other of the four cells may not be at hand: they may be impossible to obtain for political-administrative reasons, and it may be too late to resort to any "direct" methods of data collections.

There may be data for *individuals* across a range of areal units but no way of identifying the characteristics of the proximal community contexts of their behavior. This is frequently the case in secondary analyses of nationwide sample surveys; for reasons of secrecy, or economy, or sloppy administration, there may no longer be any possibility of allocating individual respondents to any known set of primary sampling units.

The contrary situation is even more frequent: no individual data are at hand, but *aggregate* distributions have been established for territorial units at different levels. This is the case for a wide variety of official

[10] For early statements of the level-of-analysis logic see P. L. Kendal and P. F. Lazarsfeld, "Problems of Survey Analysis," in R. K. Merton and P. F. Lazarsfeld (eds.), *Studies in the Scope and Method of "The American Soldier"* (Glencoe: Free Press, 1955), and the chapter on "Formal Aspects of Research on Human Groups," in P. F. Lazarsfeld and M. Rosenberg (eds.), *The Language of Social Research* (Glencoe: Free Press, 1955). For an application to political statistics see S. Rokkan, "The Comparative Study of Political Participation," in A. Ranney (ed.), *Essays on the Behavioral Study of Politics* (Urbana: University of Illinois Press, 1962), pp. 47–90. For further development see J. A. Davis *et al.*, "Analyzing Effects of Group Composition," *American Sociological Review, 26* (1961), pp. 215–225, and R. Boudon, "Propriétés individuelles et propriétés collectives," *Revue française de sociologie, 4* (1963), pp. 275–299, and Chapters II and V of his *L'analyse mathématique des faits sociaux* (Paris: Plon, 1967); see also J. Galtung, *Theory and Methods of Social Research* (Oslo: Universitetsforlaget, 1967), Chapter 2.

statistics: the primary individual data have either been kept secret from the outset, as in elections or referenda, or cannot be made available for administrative or economic reasons, as will often be the case for census data, school grades, tax records, criminal statistics.[11]

What are the typical strategies in the face of such difficulties of data access? There are essentially four options. On the one hand, a social scientist may choose to focus his study on the explanation of variations at the level of the *individual,* or he may aim at the explanation of variations at the level of the *territorial* unit. On the other hand, he may wish to limit his research to *one level at a time,* or he may be more ambitious and consider the *processes of interaction between the two levels.* These options can be presented as shown in the accompanying table.

LEVEL OF DEPENDENT VARIABLE	FOCUS OF ANALYSIS	
	One Level	*Interaction of Two Levels*
Individual	I. *Either*: individual data (e.g., from surveys) treated without reference to territorial contexts *Or:* territorial aggregate data used to analyze individual variations	III. *Either*: individual data used jointly with contextual data for territorial units *Or:* aggregate/global data used to test *interaction* between levels
Territorial unit	II. Aggregate/global data for territorial units used to describe and account for variations at territorial level	IV. *Either*: joint use of individual/aggregate/global data to test *sources of change* in territorial structure *Or*: aggregate/global data used to test *interaction* between levels

[11] For a historical perspective on the importance of secrecy in the organization of political statistics see S. Rokkan, "Mass Suffrage, Secret Voting and Political Participation," *European Journal of Sociology, 2* (1961), pp. 132–152. For a discussion of the arguments against uncontrolled linkage of official records, see E. S. Dunn, Jr., "The Idea of a National Data Center and the Issue of Personal Privacy," *The American Statistician, 21* (1967), pp. 21–27. Dunn's distinction between *intelligence systems* (data about individuals *as* individuals) and *statistical information systems* (data about individuals as members of aggregates) is of basic importance in the discussion of the pros and cons of ecological analysis.

A few concrete examples may help to clarify the differences between these four approaches:

Type I

Your primary interest may be to explain individual political choices, and you want to find out how the type of dwelling unit (for example, rented apartment versus rented semidetached house versus family-owned house) affects voting for Socialist parties. Suppose you do not have access to individual data (no survey carried out for the given period, or the surveys available do not cover the variable in which you are interested), but you have access to data from a housing census and from an election for the same territorial units. Using the two sets of marginal figures for the territorial units, you proceed to calculate correlations and to derive regression coefficients. You use your aggregate figures to establish equations for the likelihood of the occurrence of a particular individual behavior (voting Socialist).

Type II

You may not be interested in individual behavior at all but in mapping the characteristics of territorial units (neighborhoods, *quartiers,* census tracts). You will then need data on types of housing or of shops, value of land, age, sex, and marital status of the population, rates of in-and-out migration, etc. You may even add such typically individual variables as religious participation, party choice, and suicides, but these only add to the characterization of the area and are not interesting in themselves. Your task is to map the dimensions of such variations among territorial units and to test models of explanation. Typically, these efforts at accounting will focus on straight physical factors such as type of soil and land contours or on such basic features of human settlement as distances from transportation facilities, centers of production, markets, and entertainment areas.[12]

Type III

You may have retained an interest in the sources of variations at the individual level but have become increasingly aware of the possibilities of error in inferences from aggregated territorial data; you have been alerted to the need to guard against the "ecological fallacy." You are then faced with two options: *either* you go out to collect information on individual variations (the optimal procedure would be to organize

[12] For examples see the papers on urban ecology in Part Four of this volume.

sample surveys in a stratified sample of ecological contexts varying along the dimensions you want to study) and proceed to analyze individual behaviors as a function of their spatial-territorial context,[13] *or* you continue to stick to data at the aggregate/global level but develop statistical models for the exploration of alternative linkages between individual distributions and higher unit characteristics.[14] You may, for example, have established a correlation between aggregate percentages of rented apartments and Socialist votes, but you do not feel confident that you can infer from this correlation any statement about the distribution of individual votes by type of dwelling. You may be able to specify upper and lower limits to your estimates for each cell in the "black box," but to increase the precision of your analysis, either you will have to invest in some direct field work, or you will have to go further in the specification of your model and bring in more aggregate/ global variables (percentages of municipally versus privately controlled apartment houses, the party or parties in control of municipal government, the degree of class homogeneity within the territory, etc.) to test the alternative expectations against the observed aggregate distributions.

Type IV

You may finally opt for a "micro-macro" design: your dependent variables are the characteristics of the territorial social systems, but you seek your explanatory variables not only at the global/aggregate level (such as geographical configurations, concentration factors, distance factors) but at the level of *individual decisions*. There is an interesting parallel here between the work of political sociologists and urban ecologists. In the field of electoral ecology there is a clear need for a continuous shuttle between the "macro" and the "micro" levels. The behavior of the citizens cannot be understood without knowledge of the ecological alternatives set for them by parties, electoral arrangements, and so on, but at least some of these alternatives (such as the mainten- ance of a party list as an alternative) are, in turn, dependent on the behaviors of individuals. In the field of urban ecology the "macro" characteristics of each unit establish a variety of constraints on and alternatives for individual behavior. Thus to take only one sector, the age, quality, size, and cost of the dwellings and the social characteristics

---

[13] For examples of such procedures see the chapters by Juan Linz and Erwin Scheuch in Part Two of this volume.

[14] For an excellent example see G. Carlsson, "Partiförskutningar som tillväkst- processer," *Statsvetenskaplig tidskrift, 66* (1963), pp. 172–213.

of the current occupants set alternatives for in-migrants seeking housing, but the character of these alternatives is in itself a function of a wide variety of past individual decisions and will be affected in the future by the current decisions. The urban ecologist may be content to develop typologies of dwelling areas and leave it to others to study differential behavior across the different types of areas (this would be a Type II study in our scheme), but there will always be the temptation to go one step further toward the study of the *interaction* of "micro" and "macro" variations in processes of structural change in territorial units.

This fourfold typology tells only part of the story. There have been even wider divergencies in the actual *method of analysis* used in dealing with data at the one level or the other.

In his classic study of the ecology of that intensely individual variable *suicide*, Durkheim proceeded again and again by simple typologies of available units and straightforward contrasting of resultant distributions. One of his best-known tables, for suicide rates in Switzerland, simply looks like this:[15]

	Suicides per Million Inhabitants	
	French Cantons	Alemannic Cantons
Catholic	83	87
Protestant	453	293

The pioneer of political ecology, André Siegfried,[16] did not even go that far toward the establishment of general propositions. He used the local statistics he could find for occupational structure, size of land-holdings, religious divisions, and voting to establish *concrete contrasts* between adjacent areas rather than to test general propositions about the consequences of variations in community structure. The great French school of human geography concentrated attention on concrete variations in economic, social, cultural, and political conditions but was committed primarily to the description of unique locations and constellations; the idea of treating each locality as a cluster of statistical characteristics for purposes of regression analysis was essentially alien to this tradition. Correlations between territorial traits and aggregated individual behaviors tended to be studied by the juxtaposition of *maps*. This was a source of great strength but obviously also limited the *range*

[15] E. Durkheim, *Le suicide* (Paris: Alcan, 1897), p. 152.
[16] *Tableau politique de la France de l'Ouest* (Paris: Colin, 1913).

of variables considered and restricted the *number* of variables taken into account in any one analysis. Variables tended to be judged by their immediate graphical covariation with the dependent variable rather than by their share in the total variance: there is no obvious cartographic equivalent of the partial correlation.[17] The reduction of territories to points in a scattergram or units in a statistical calculation clearly cuts the analyst off from a variety of rich spatial-cultural cues to an understanding of the processes at work but at the same time forces him to clarify the logic of his reasoning and specify the evidence for his conclusions.

For a variety of reasons the devotion to social, cultural, and political cartography was particularly stubborn in France. The German and the American attempts to develop a "statistical geography" did not find much response there until well into the fifties. This was not a methodologically unified movement. Several parallel efforts were pursued in isolation from each other: there were attempts to refine the early work by Durkheim on the ecology of deviant behavior and mental disease;[18] there was a continuous movement toward greater statistical refinement in the study of urban development and urban structure;[19] there were signs of increasing interest in the construction of multivariate typologies of areal units, whether cities or rural units;[20] and there was a great variety of efforts to build the foundations for a discipline of *political*

---

[17] For a general discussion of maps versus correlation techniques in research on local variations, see H. H. McCarthy and N. E. Salisbury, *Visual Comparison of Isopleth Maps as a Means of Determining Correlations between Spatially Distributed Phenomena* (Iowa City: State University of Iowa, 1961). The current trend in statistical geography is toward a stepwise alternation between multivariate analysis, mapping of areas of "consistent residuality," and the addition of further variables to reduce the residual variance; see Kevin R. Cox, *Regional Anomalies in the Voting Behavior of the Population of England and Wales: 1921–1951* (Urbana: Department of Geography, University of Illinois, 1966).

[18] See, especially, Ruth Cavan, *Suicide* (Chicago: University of Chicago Press, 1928), and R. E. L. Faris and H. W. Dunham, *Mental Disorders in Urban Areas* (Chicago: University of Chicago Press, 1939). On the methodology of such studies, see Otis D. Duncan, R. Cuzzort, and B. Duncan, *Statistical Geography* (Glencoe: Free Press, 1960).

[19] For the earlier literature on urban ecology see Paul K. Hatt and A. J. Reiss, Jr. (eds.), *Cities and Society* (Glencoe: Free Press, 1954). For further developments see James Beshers, *Urban Social Structure* (New York: Free Press, 1962), and Leo F. Schnore, *The Urban Scene* (New York: Free Press, 1965). A useful review of current trends is Peter Orleans, "Robert Park and Social Area Analysis: A Convergence of Traditions in Urban Sociology," *Urban Affairs Quarterly, I* (1966), pp. 5–19.

[20] A major example is C. A. Moser and W. Scott, *British Towns: A Statistical Study of Their Social and Economic Differences* (Edinburgh: Oliver and Boyd, 1961). For further developments of "principal components analysis" see the papers by Howard and Norman in this volume.

ecology at the crossroad of geography, sociology, and political science.[21] By the fifties increasing emphasis was also given to the *temporal* dimensions of such research. The great wave of studies of developmental processes — whether economic, cultural, or political — had tempted a number of scholars to try out new approaches to the analysis of local variations: geographers such as Torsten Hägerstrand,[22] economists such as Walter Isard, [23] and political scientists such as Karl Deutsch,[24] had all in their various styles suggested ways of formulating models for the spread of items of "modernity" (production facilities, consumption habits, vocabularies, skills, occupations, styles and norms of living) from central to peripheral areas and proposed techniques for the statistical study of such processes of change in space and in time. By the 1960's these striking convergencies of orientation across traditionally very distinct disciplines had created much ferment in the advanced countries and tempted an increasing number of scholars to explore new models and new techniques in the study of time-space variations at different levels of the society and the polity.

THE EVIAN SYMPOSIUM: OBJECTIVES, ISSUES, PERSPECTIVES

It was against this background of long-standing intellectual concerns and exciting theoretical and methodological innovations that the International Social Science Council took steps to prepare a first *Symposium on Quantitative Ecological Analysis* in 1966.

[21] Kevin Cox, *op. cit.,* discusses the differences between geographical and politico-sociological approaches to the study of territorial variations and reserves for "electoral geography" the task of identifying, describing, and analyzing *"the distinctive regional associations of variables at the subuniverse level"*; in practice, this amounts to saying that the geographer's task begins when the standard analyses of sociologists or political scientists have identified the areas that *deviate most consistently* from the mean expectation within the given territorial universe. This is hardly a stable demarcation of the discipline: the boundary is a function of the number and sophistication of the variables brought into the multiple regression equations.

[22] T. Hägerstrand, *Innovationsförloppet ur korologiskt synspunkt* (Lund: Gleerup, 1951); *The Propagation of Innovation Waves* (Lund: Lund Studies in Geography Ser. B., No. 4, 1962); "A Monte Carlo Approach to Diffusion," *Archives européennes de sociologie, 6* (1965), pp. 43–67; "Quantitative Techniques for Analysis of the Spread of Information and Technology" in C. A. Anderson and M. J. Bowman (eds.), *Education and Economic Development* (Chicago: Aldine, 1965).

[23] W. Isard *et al., Methods of Regional Analysis: An Introduction to Regional Science* (New York: Wiley, 1960).

[24] K. Deutsch, "Social Mobilization and Political Development," *American Political Science Review, 55* (1961), pp. 493–514.

The objectives of this initial international gathering were formulated as follows:

1. To provide an opportunity to discuss in some detail experiences in the planning, organization, and operation of *ecological data archives* and to examine plans for joint international action to ensure accelerated development of such facilities

2. To ensure effective confrontations of differing *substantive emphases and methodological traditions in the use of quantitative data* for localities and to examine the pros and cons of alternative designs of analysis

3. To review the possibilities of *joint strategies at several levels of aggregation*, particularly the possibilities of combining sample surveys of variations at the level of the individual with ecological analyses of the proximal contexts of such variations

4. To examine recent experiences in the *development of ecological analyses in historical depth*, particularly through the organization of data files for local and regional variations *before* the decisive break-through to economic growth and *during* the subsequent processes of urbanization, mobilization, and modernization

On each of these points a great variety of efforts have been registered at the *national* level, but very little has as yet been done to ensure effective *international* co-operation.

The International Social Science Council has taken a first step toward the organization of regular interchanges among *archives of ecological data*.[25] It has established a Standing Committee on Social Science Data Archives and has set up under this committee a "task force" to look into the possibilities of joint action on technical and methodological problems in the accumulation, storage, and retrieval of data for localities.[26]

A first round of discussions of *the logic of aggregate analysis* was organized at the Yale conference in 1963; the comparison of aggregate statistics for *nations* confronted the social scientists with essentially the same issues as the comparison of aggregates for *regions or communities*.[27] At the Evian symposium these issues were at the heart of the

[25] For details see S. Rokkan (ed.), *Data Archives for the Social Sciences, op cit.*

[26] See R. Bisco, "Social Science Data Archives: Progress and Prospects," *Social Science Information, 6* (1967), pp. 63 and 67–68.

[27] For details see the papers by Erik Allardt and Erwin Scheuch in Merritt and Rokkan (eds.), *Comparing Nations, op. cit.,* and the further reflections by Hayward Alker, a leader in the Yale efforts of cross-national comparison: "Regionalism versus Universalism in Comparing Nations," pp. 322–340, of B. M. Russett *et al., World Handbook of Political and Social Indicators* (New Haven: Yale University Press, 1964); cf. Alker's *Mathematics and Politics* (New York: Macmillan, 1965), Ch. 5.

debate; there was abundant evidence that the early attacks on the "ecological fallacy"[28] had given way to serious efforts to spell out the assumptions and the limitations of inferences from one level of description to another and to develop better tools for the handling of aggregate data.[29] The field is in a great ferment, and there is a definite need to develop better channels of communication among all social scientists currently engaged in the analysis of ecological data masses.

The Evian symposium also offered a first opportunity for detailed discussions concerning analysis techniques and research strategies. The experts gathered for the symposium unanimously agreed to recommend that such exchanges be followed by the organization of international work teams to test alternative procedures on several bodies of national data. It was strongly recommended that "data confrontation seminars" be organized for ecological data along the lines currently tried for survey data: experts on ecological analysis would bring their data with them to an analysis center and work out joint analysis programs through detailed discussion of data characteristics, techniques of data handling, and models of explanation. A plan for seminars of this type has since been presented to UNESCO, and the first in the series is likely to take place in 1969.

The International Social Science Council has also given consideration to the planning of comparative research on *local time-lags in processes of historical change* and has been concerned with enlisting the co-operation of historians in such research. At the Evian symposium one session was focused on problems and potentialities in the development of comparative historical ecology. This is a field where the French schools of historical demography and regional history have made particularly important contributions.

At the Evian symposium the principal concern was with local variations in economic, social, and cultural conditions *before* the decisive thrust or urbanization and industrialization in the nineteenth

[28] The initial statement of the fallacy of reference from ecological to individual correlations is due to W. S. Robinson, "Ecological Correlations and the Behavior of Individuals," *American Sociological Review, 15* (1950), pp. 351–357. For further discussion see the papers by Alker, Allardt, and Valkonen in Part One of this volume.

[29] Major contributions to this literature include: Leo Goodman, "Some Alternatives to Ecological Correlation," *American Journal of Sociology, 64* (1959), pp. 610–625; O. D. Duncan *et al., Statistical Geography*; R. Boudon, "Propriétés individuelles et propriétés collectives," *Revue française de sociologie, 4* (1963), pp. 275–299; H. M. Blalock, *Causal Inferences in Non-Experimental Research* (Chapel Hill: University of North Carolina Press, 1964), pp. 97–114; and Donald Stokes, "A Variance Components Model of Political Effects," in *Mathematical Applications in Political Science* (Dallas: Arnold Foundation, 1965), pp. 61–85.

century. Peter Laslett set out the work of the Cambridge Group currently endeavoring to establish benchmark data for the study of changes in demography and social structure in England during the seventeenth and the eighteenth centuries; this represented an attempt to apply to available English records of the techniques of family reconstruction from parish registers developed with such success by the French school directed by Louis Henry.[30] The French historian Emmanuel LeRoy Ladurie, himself a leading analyst of seventeenth- and eighteenth-century developments, showed how the data on regional and local variations in the early phases of nation building could be linked to corresponding information on the acceleration of these processes of change in the nineteenth century. He did this with the aid of a large collection of maps for regional variations in France, some of them based on records and estimates for the *ancien régime*, others taken from an extraordinarily interesting volume from 1836, d'Angeville's *Essai sur la statistique de la population française.*[31]

The International Social Science Council hopes to link up these French efforts with similar projects in other countries. The recent scholarly discussions of dimensions of political development have led to increased interest in the possibilities of establishing local variations in *rates of change* during the nineteenth and the twentieth centuries. In these further efforts it will be essential to link up the work of "pre-take-off" conditions with analyses on the variations in the rates of change during the decisive periods of cultural, social, and political mobilization. To cite a recent example, the great strength of Charles Tilly's study of the ecology of the Vendée during the French Revolution is that it ties in so closely with, and adds further perspective to, André Siegfried's classic study of the political divisions of the West of France a hundred years later.[32]

Plans for further work along these lines have already been discussed with UNESCO and will be worked out in further detail during the next year or two. One line of activity focuses on the organization of a network of *historical data archives.* An initiative in this direction has already been taken by the DATUM organization at Bad Godesberg and will, it is hoped, be linked up with similar efforts in the United States

---

[30] See Chapter 19 of this volume.

[31] E. LeRoy Ladurie, "Introduction cartographique à une écologie quantitative de la France traditionelle (XVIIe–XIXe siècles)," a paper for the Symposium on Quantitative Ecological Analysis in the Social Sciences, Evian, September 1966. This collection of maps will be published separately in the near future.

[32] Charles Tilly, *The Vendée* (London: Arnold, 1966).

under the aegis of the American Historical Association and the Inter-University Consortium. The standing committee of the International Social Science Council will have an important role to play in these developments. Perhaps the most interesting proposal to come out of these international discussions is the idea of *data confrontation seminars* for historical ecological data; these go beyond the traditional discussions of already "frozen" national analysis toward joint computer processing of the raw data brought together by the participants from each country. This innovation in the organization of international research co-operation will be tried out for post–World War II data by the Inter-University Consortium at Ann Arbor in 1969. Once the technical difficulties of such joint processing operations have been solved, it is expected that this style of co-operation will assume increasing importance in comparative research on national developments.

Closely linked with these efforts of historical data archiving are the plans for the preparation of *Guides to Data for Comparative Research.* The initial work undertaken in the field of electoral statistics[33] will, we hope, be followed up by parallel efforts to account for variations in the availability of historical statistical indicators by locality for a selection of countries. A trend report and selected bibliography on ecological analysis are being prepared.

Finally, a third set of plans focuses on the systematic exploration of *alternative models of nation building and center-periphery contrasts.*[34] A first conference of historians and social scientists interested in the comparative study of processes of change during the crucial periods of centralization, urbanization, mass education, and democratization from about 1750 to 1914 will, it is hoped, be organized some time during 1970 and should, if the necessary finance can be found, make it possible for the International Social Science Council to launch a longer-term program of co-operation between statistically oriented historians and developmentally oriented social scientists.

[33] See S. Rokkan, "The Comparative Study of Electoral Statistics," *Social Science Information, 5* (1966), pp. 9–19. The first volume of the *International Guide to Electoral Statistics* is scheduled to appear in 1969.

[34] For a review of research in this field and a set of suggestions about possible steps in the organization of international co-operation see S. Rokkan, "Models and Methods in the Comparative Study of Nation-Building," *Acta sociologica* (in press, 1969).

PART ONE

The Logic of
Ecological Inference

These four chapters constitute our entrée en matière: *they seek to clarify the methodological contexts of the current efforts to make fuller and more meaningful use of the vast bodies of available statistics by territorial units.*

Karl Deutsch sets the general framework for the further discussion. Having made signal contributions to quantitative analysis at the levels of individuals and localities as well as at the levels of national polities and regional political systems, he is in a better position than any other social scientist to map the territories for promising advances and to place the contributions of the ecologists in a broad theoretical perspective.

The other three chapters all focus directly on the ecological fallacy: *they constitute so many commentaries on the classical article by W. S. Robinson. Hayward Alker generalizes the Robinson argument and shows how the ecological fallacy fits into a broader system of level-to-level shortcuts in analytical procedure. The two representatives of the great Finnish school of social ecology, Erik Allardt and Tapani Valkonen, take up the challenge of the Robinson article and raise important issues of research strategy: the old warning against inference from ecological to individual covariations should not just be treated as another "red light" in the control of the research traffic but should be used as a springboard for the development of new methods of two-level analysis. The level-by-level discrepancies in the direction and strength of correlations constitute an* important field of research *in its own right: individual behaviors do not just vary directly with ecological characteristics, they* interact dynamically *with them. What Robinson did was simply to point to the problem: the next step is to develop a strategy for research on these processes of level-with-level interaction. The 1950 warning weighed heavily with the generation of research workers brought up in the tradition of the test and the sample survey: it kept them from the rich body of ecological information produced by the governmental bookkeeping machineries. The current generation of social scientists has been freed from the pressures of this academic superego: to them Robinson does not set a barrier but poses a problem for serious research.*

I

KARL W. DEUTSCH

On Methodological Problems of Quantitative Research*

I HAVE GENEROUSLY been allotted the task of illuminating the general methodological context of quantitative research: one of those neat, sharply defined topics. I propose to examine three major functions of quantitative methods and data in the social sciences, and will later proceed to a discussion of some of the implications for the next steps in our work.

THREE MAJOR TASKS OF QUANTITATIVE METHODS

The first of the major functions is the elaboration and specification of existing theories and existing sociological knowledge. The second is the generation of heuristic suggestions about new phenomena, new relations, new questions, and new theories. This involves the development of our powers of recognition and our tools of recognition for new phenomena. Then, in the third place, we shall deal with the use of quantitative data and methods for deciding particular theoretical questions through processes of strong inference; and, insofar as this is successful, we shall consider the possibility of a substantial general acceleration of the growth of knowledge which is both nontrivial and at least partially verified. From a general discussion of these three functions, I would then like to go on to their implication for some of the next practical steps which social scientists could take.

* Research utilized in this paper was supported in part by the Carnegie Corporation and in part by the National Science Foundation and by the National Institutes of Health through the Mental Health Research Institute at the University of Michigan.

Making Existing Theories Richer and More Precise

Let me begin with a discussion of the first point: the elaboration and specification of existing theories and existing knowledge. Here, I must go back to what looks like a very abstract philosophical question, namely, what, for our purposes, is meant by *knowledge*. At this point, I have to take issue with the philosophy of Sir Karl Popper, who has, I fear, obscured this subject.

Existential Statements and Discoveries. As I see it, knowledge involves first of all a collection of *existential statements*, that is, precisely the kind of statements Sir Karl Popper thinks are of only secondary importance.[1] An existential statement is a statement that has the logical form of "there is": for instance, "there is a continent west of the Atlantic Ocean." Existential statements are the very essence of discovery. Discovery usually leads to new existential statements. "There is a planet Neptune" and "*X* has the property *Y*" are logical forms of existential statements. An existential statement is a discovery either of a thing or of a relation. If you discover a relation, the statement has the form of "if . . . then," such as "if amber is rubbed with dry cloth, then it will attract lint," which is one of the existential statements that led to the discovery of electricity.

In either case, the existential statement can be verified not only by one operation that can be reproduced but by many different kinds of operations that are all reproducible. As more and more kinds of these different but confirmatory operations are discovered, there comes a point at which scientists tend to accept the former construction as an existential statement. What was once a hypothesis is now accepted as a fact. And to accept it as a fact is to ascribe to it *reality*, that is, to predict that additional confirmation for the existence of this fact will be discovered and that the class of such possible operations may be treated as inexhaustible. After its acceptance and multiple confirmation as factual, of course, every existential statement may serve as a building block for new theories and as a stepping stone to new discoveries.[2]

An existential statement can take the form of an invention. We can

---

[1] Cf. Karl R. Popper, *The Logic of Scientific Discovery* (London: Hutchinson, 1959), pp. 68–70. For a gentle but penetrating criticism, see Paul Bernays, "Reflections on Karl Popper's Epistemology," in Mario Bunge (ed.), *The Critical Approach to Science and Philosophy* (New York: Free Press, 1964), pp. 32–44.

[2] Cf. James B. Conant, *Science and Common Sense* (New Haven: Yale University Press, 1951), pp. 32–37, 262–265; Robert Cohen, "What Is Physical Reality?" paper presented at conference of American Academy of Arts and Sciences, Boston, 1955; K. W. Deutsch, "On Theories, Taxonomies and Models as Communication Codes for Organizing Information," *Behavioral Science*, *11*:1 (1966), pp. 1–17.

say not only "there is" but also "there can be." A proposition of the form "There can be a machine that flies, and that is heavier than air, and though it has not yet been built, it could be built" was one of the crucial intellectual steps which led to the invention of the airplane.

Not only can existential statements be disconfirmed in principle, but they can be confirmed positively. Sir Karl Popper has made a great deal of the argument that *constructs*, the more abstract and not immediately verifiable concepts of scientific theory, are susceptible to disconfirmation but not to confirmation. Indeed, he has denied that they can ever be confirmed.[3] Existential statements, on the other hand, are susceptible to positive confirmation. We can build the airplane. We can see whether the continent of America exists. We can repeat these operations, and so can others.

Even more extended conceptual schemes can be turned into existential statements. We may have many scattered geographical data and organize them into a conceptual scheme of the flat and bounded earth, although at the time when it was constructed no individual had ever traversed this flat earth to its supposed limits. Another theory or conceptual scheme was then developed, picturing the earth as round. This was done at a time when no one had circumnavigated the world. At that time, the globe was only a conceptual scheme, and if Sir Karl Popper had been alive in the thirteenth century, he would have argued that it could only be disconfirmed, but not confirmed, because it was a theory. However, in the fullness of time, the earth was circumnavigated by Magellan in three years, and more recently by satellites in eighty minutes. What had been a conceptual scheme became an existential statement.

One of the most important processes of science is exactly, therefore, the turning of conceptual schemes into existential statements. The physicist P. W. Bridgman has spent some time in explaining how the concept of the electron in the 1890's was a "construct" and, presumably in Popper's sense, only susceptible to radical disconfirmation. However, in time, as cumulative evidence built up, physicists came to the conclusion that "there was something there." They now treated the electron as a concept that had proved fruitful and for which there was some direct evidence; and eventually, on the strength of still more evidence, they attributed reality to it. This was exactly the difference between the ether concept, which could never by turned into an existential statement, and the electron concept, which could be transformed in

---

[3] Cf. Popper, *op. cit., passim.*

that sense.[4] Popper's view — that there is nothing in science, natural or social, but theoretical constructs, susceptible to nothing but discon- firmation — ignores this crucial contribution of existential statements and discoveries. It is the philosophy of a philosopher who has never made an empirical discovery in his life and who, perhaps, would not even like one if he saw it. It is, in this sense, a serious obstacle to the growth of scientific knowledge in the social sciences.

Knowledge, then, is first of all a collection of existential statements, of statements capable of positive confirmation. But it also consists of theories. We may define *theory* as an information code for the storage, retrieval, and processing of new items of information, and for the search for new items of information.[5]

Theories can be disconfirmed in their predictive dimension, and this is the element of truth in Popper's arguments. But theories can also, in part, be confirmed positively as to their relative *truth content* in terms of the collection of verified existential statements that they encode. These existential statements, then, would also have to be included (at least most of them) in their successor theories.

In this sense, the succession of theories is not arbitrary or accidental. We can predict of any theory that, when and if it is overthrown, all or most of the existential statements that it encoded will have to be included in its successor theories, if these successor theories are not to be con- sidered a backward step in knowledge.

The Impact of Quantitative Data. Quantitative data and methods in any field of science add a great deal to the specificity and richness of the existential statements in our knowledge. Therefore, they increase the demands and the tests of verification confronting our theories. In this sense, the introduction, on a very broad front, of quantitative methods and of quantitative data is of decisive importance in making our social science theories more scientific.

Let me give a few examples of the specific use of such existential statements in the testing and development of theories. One is the existential statement that in West German opinion polls for more than a decade, national issues as a primary topic of saliency or attention have outweighed issues of European integration, usually by a ratio of ten to one or fifteen to one. That is, typically, 51 per cent of voters consider national issues as deserving primary attention, while only 3

---

[4] P. W. Bridgman, *The Logic of Modern Physics* (New York: Macmillan, 1946), *passim.*

[5] See references in footnote 2.

per cent or 5 per cent put European integration first. This is an existential fact, and it tells us something about politics at a certain time and place. Or here is an existential statement for a slightly longer period: It is possible to show, on the one hand, increases in certain quantitative indicators of European integration all the way from 1913 to the early 1950's or to the mid-1950's, as well as the rise and growth of a wide variety of European political institutions; but these indicators fail to show any further structural integration of Western Europe after 1959. That is, although we have a fairly stable increase from 1913 to 1955–1959, we find that after 1959 Western European structural integration has halted.[6] Another existential finding shows that French mass opinion began to diverge radically from the Western European consensus on such important issues as attitudes toward the Soviet Union as early as 1955, that is, preceding the accession to power of General de Gaulle. It was not President de Gaulle who produced the French attitudes; the change in French attitudes preceded General de Gaulle. Similarly, there is substantial evidence of a relative withdrawal of the French economy from international integration. The economies of Germany, Italy, and Britain today have roughly similar ratios of foreign trade to gross national product as they had in 1928. The French economy has a substantially smaller ratio — about a third less of it.[7] France has become, in many ways, more self-sufficient in the long run. This fact may be changing in the late 1960's, and we can interpret this in different ways, but there is no denying the fact itself, once it has been discovered and put into significant context.

I have given a number of examples from some recent research we have done on European integration. There is the gap, let us say, in the mass opinion both in Germany and in France, between expression of mutual sympathy and indications of trust. Usually we find about three Frenchmen expressing sympathy or "good feelings" about Germany for one Frenchman willing to express trust. The same seems true of German mass opinion.[8] Other facts bearing on the probability of lasting political integration among nations are the ten-to-one preponderance of domestic mail over foreign in most advanced countries, including small countries with reputations for internationalism, such

---

[6] The indicator figures are based on reproducible facts. The inferences of their significance are, of course, hypotheses based on our conceptual scheme of integration. Cf. K. W. Deutsch, L. J. Edinger, R. C. Macridis, and R. L. Merritt, *France, Germany and the Western Alliance* (New York: Scribner, 1967).

[7] *Ibid.*, pp. 230–255.

[8] *Ibid.*, *passim.*

as Switzerland, the Netherlands, Britain, or France, in contrast with colonial countries, where foreign mail predominates over domestic mail.[9] Other such facts are the declining rate of foreign trade both with time and with the size of the country (on which we have a great quantity of data), and the near symmetry of the indices of relative acceptance in transaction flow and their correlation with empire or past memories of empire.

Another existential statement of theoretical relevance is the large variability of indices of income inequality. Some of the work of Hayward Alker and Bruce Russett produced data which seem incompatible with the theories of Vilfredo Pareto, namely, the view that income inequality was supposed to be independent of social change or political revolution. Pareto's view turned out to be false.[10] There is now a possibility of getting quantitative indicators of social mobility in different countries, thanks to the work on matrix analysis by Harrison White, I. Richard Savage, and Leo Goodman.[11] Or it turns out that in a comparison among 53 countries in the 1950's, the frequency of political violence changes with the level of income: political violence increases with income over low-income ranges but stays roughly unchanged over an intermediate range, and it decreases with income over high-income ranges.[12]

All these are examples of existential statements which ought to be accommodated, which put demands and pressures on the theoretical

[9] K. W. Deutsch, "Shifts in the Balance of International Communication Flows," *Public Opinion Quarterly, 20*:1 (1956), pp. 143–160.

[10] Bruce M. Russett and Hayward R. Alker, Jr., in R. L. Merritt and Stein Rokkan (eds.), *Comparing Nations* (New Haven: Yale University Press, 1966), pp. 349–372; Bruce M. Russett, Hayward R. Alker, Jr., K. W. Deutsch, and Harold D. Lasswell, *World Handbook of Political and Social Indicators* (New Haven: Yale University Press, 1966), pp. 237–240, 243–247.

[11] A technical description of the method is given in I. Richard Savage and K. W. Deutsch, "A Statistical Model of the Gross Analysis of Transaction Flows," *Econometrica, 28* (1960), pp. 551–572; and a computer program has been published by Hayward R. Alker, Jr., in *Behavioral Science, 7*:4 (1962), pp. 498–499. For suggested improvements in the method, see Leo A. Goodman, "Statistical Methods for the Preliminary Analysis of Transaction Flows," *Econometrica, 31* (1963), pp. 197–208; and "A Short Computer Program for the Analysis of Transaction Flows," *Behavioral Science, 9*:2 (1964), pp. 176–186. See also Harrison C. White, "Cause and Effect in Social Mobility Tables," *Behavioral Science, 8*:1 (1963), pp. 14–27; Karl W. Deutsch, "Toward an Inventory of Basic Trends and Patterns in Comparative and International Politics," *American Political Science Review, 54* (1960), pp. 34–57, esp. pp. 46–48; Hayward R. Alker, Jr., and Donald A. Puchala, "Trends in Economic Partnership in the North Atlantic Area," in J. David Singer (ed.), *Quantitative International Politics* (New York: Free Press, 1967), pp. 287–316.

[12] Russett *et al., World Handbook, op. cit.,* pp. 306–307, 319–321.

structures that we have before us. Many other facts are pressing on our theories. The expansion of middle-class jobs, the changes in the structure between skilled and unskilled labor and between white-collar and blue-collar jobs — all these facts have been well known. Nevertheless, their cumulative pressure on social science theories has become great, and our social science theories have not been accommodating them.

Heuristic Suggestions for New Inquiries

The specification of our theories leads almost immediately to heuristic suggestions. Here I would like to say something about heuristic suggestions in regard to the search for the turning points and the limits of processes and relationships. Classic Aristotelian thinking seeks the *limits* of regularities in social behavior and tends to point out the limits in order to urge the social scientist or philosopher to keep away from them because all excess is to be avoided. Pragmatic thinking, very widespread in social science in the United States, happily ignores such limits. It works with the here and now, and it does not often raise the question: "How far can this thing go, and at what point will it break down?" Marxist thinking selects certain types of limits and then emphasizes where some dialectic change ought to be expected. Usually, however, Marxist thinking only points out that some particular change will happen, but it does not investigate in detail just how it works; and other limits which are not highlighted in classic Marxist theory are very often not studied, or their study is delayed. (It may be that we in the West are not informed enough about the development of Marxist social science, but my impression is that while most of the limits pointed out fifty years ago in the Marxist classics may have been studied, only very few new limits or new qualitative changes have attracted the attention of our colleagues in the countries that we sometimes inaccurately call "the East.") The need in all these matters is for more scientific thinking, for more attention to the limits of relationships and to the points where things break down. In that sense, the work of the late V. O. Key, Duncan MacRae, Philip Converse, and others on critical elections and basic realignments is of real interest.[13]

In the future before us, we may have a period of far more careful studies of just where the regularities that we observe change and just

[13] V. O. Key, Jr., "A Theory of Critical Elections," *Journal of Politics 17* (1955), pp. 1–18; Philip Converse, "Survey Research and the Decoding of Patterns in Ecological Data," Chapter 17 in this volume; Duncan MacRae, Jr., and James A. Meldrum, "Factor Analysis of Aggregate Voting Statistics," Chapter 18 in this volume.

where the thresholds come. We may need, in this respect, a better theory of national and supranational integration; the first five existential statements of which I gave examples were all taken from this area. In another area, we may need a better theory of the limits of privileges — social, political, and economic — and the limits of equalization. We have only a very rough knowledge that there is some extent of income equality that seems essential for maintaining material incentives for efforts, and we know rather vaguely that there are, on the other hand, some limits of inequality beyond which "excessive" inequality tends to destroy social cohesion and the capacity of co-operation in a society. But we do not have a very good theory for this. We have bits and pieces, and we have arguments about them, but there has not been any coherent theory of the balance between the incentive function of income equalization, whether in collectivistic economies or in so-called private enterprise economies.

We also lack a theory of the future of violence in relation to rising income levels. All past history deals with situations where most incomes were so low that the marginal utility of an increment in income was high enough to offer reinforcement for the learning of violent habits, or of violent action for or against change. We do not know in practice, but we must assume, in theory, that there could be income levels where the marginal utility of an additional increment in economic income might be lower than the individual and social costs of violence. We do not know just how high this "peace level" of income is, but we have some theoretical reasons to believe that there ought to be such a level, unless we throw out the complete principle of declining marginal utility of economic goods. We may then find, at the peace level of income, that psychological or cultural reasons for violence might still persist. But we shall then have removed the *economic* causes, and we shall therefore reach a situation different from any other we have ever known.[14]

We know from experience in the United States that from the 1880's to the 1930's, when American per capita income developed from about $700 to $1,500 in modern money, labor conflicts in the United States were accompanied by substantial loss of life. We know that nowadays, and from the 1950's on, when American incomes ranged between $2,000 to $3,000 per capita, American labor disputes were being carried

[14] This argument is pursued a bit further in K. W. Deutsch, "Nation and World," in Ithiel de Sola Pool (ed.), *Political Science and Political Philosophy* (New York: McGraw-Hill, 1967), pp. 204–227.

on without loss of life, even in the New York newspaper industry. There may be very prolonged strikes, but there is no longer loss of life. Wage increases are no longer a killing matter. The only economically tinged disputes in which lives are lost in the 1960's occur in the slums of our Negro minority; we know that the Negro per capita income in the mid-1960's averaged 60 per cent of the white income, that is, in the $1,500 to $1,800 range, which seems well below the peace level range.

If we add a substantial safety factor, we could therefore predict that quite conceivably the economic reinforcement of violence might disappear in the world and in international relations if we could increase world income to $4,800 per capita, which is eight times the present $600 average world income per capita. This would require an eightfold increase of the per capita income of the world and can be attained within about seventy years by means of a 3 per cent growth rate of per capita income, which was the average income growth rate per capita for 68 countries in the 1950's, and which is similar to the past per capita growth rate of between 2 and 3 per cent which we have known in recent decades.[15] That is, we could reach it in just about the time that the world population growth would increase fourfold, which is just about the limit we can handle on this planet more or less conveniently.

To be sure, world peace probably will also require a substantial reduction of the present extreme degree of inequality of incomes among countries, as well as within many of them. Such income inequalities will be less strongly defended, however, as average incomes rise; thus resistance in the United States and in many other advanced countries declined as average incomes rose.

In other words, we find that we get projections that, though they seem fantastic from one point of view, are very much in line with what we have found to be manageable based on the experience of modern technologies in the last fifteen or twenty years. Such considerations also can give us a new approach to the old question of the persistence and the limits of class politics in highly developed countries. Additional relevant data and projections on these problems could be obtained on the inequality issue and on the job structure issue. Thus we can use our quantitative data to increase our ability to recognize crucial variables

---

[15] The average per capita growth rate for 68 countries in 1950–1960 was 2.99 per cent, the median rate was 2.55. Russett *et al., World Handbook, op. cit.*, p. 160. For earlier long-term growth rates, see Simon Kuznets, *Modern Economic Growth — Rate, Structure and Spread* (New Haven: Yale University Press, 1966), pp. 64–71.

and strategic points that may lead us into very large theoretical issues.

We need perhaps even more badly to develop a skill as social scientists that will give us greater powers of recognition in regard to numbers. Any mother of a family in an advanced Fahrenheit-oriented country knows the difference between 99 and 101 degrees in her child's temperature (or between 37 and 41 degrees in a centigrade-oriented country). Every long-surviving automobile driver knows the difference between driving 40 miles per hour and 70 miles per hour. But very few social scientists know the meaning of the difference between an assimilation rate of one tenth of one per cent a year and one half of one per cent a year, or between the social mobilization rate of one tenth of one per cent and one per cent a year. We need a generation of social scientists to whom percentage ratios of social change, or the difference between the upper middle class of 21 per cent of the work force and of 5 per cent of the work force, is as intuitively obvious and familiar as miles per hour and acceleration rates are to drivers and temperature levels are to housewives. In other words, we need an intuitive familiarity with figures that will make them as familiar to the social scientists as sand is to the Arab and snow to the Eskimo. Such familiarity will lead to a better understanding of subtle changes, and to a greater awareness of where the changes and choice points come.

For these reasons, the kind of work done by such social scientists as Duncan MacRae and Philip Converse leads us from the tactics of better surveys and analysis to the grand strategy of social science. We find that better tactics of social research transform the strategy of grand theorizing. In very many ways there is now a steady pressure from the better quantitative tactics which we are getting from the leaders in this field to the transformation of grand theory. We have, however, a second possibility. We have neglected the complementary activity to this, namely, to use deliberately the resources of grand strategy and theory to accelerate and to develop new tactics. By grand strategy, I mean the development of strong inference and the development of decidable questions in social science.

Strong Inference: Making Questions of Theory Decidable

Let me describe very briefly what is meant by *strong inference*. I am using the term as it is used by the biologist and physicist John Platt in a recent book of his, *The Step to Man*.[16] To use the technique of strong inference means to formulate a problem in a field of science as a

---

[16] John Platt, "Strong Inference," *The Step to Man* (New York: Wiley, 1966).

preshaped sequence of logical alternatives among divergent and mutually contradictory hypotheses, leading from choice point to choice point, and eliminating at each choice point large classes of alternatives so as to narrow down rapidly the search for a solution. This procedure requires that we can devise or discover for each choice point a crucial experiment or crucial set of data or observations that will permit us, at this choice point, to make a decision with a high degree of reliability. To make questions decidable thus requires finding techniques or empirical evidence that will help us to decide them.

It might also require, and this I would like to add to John Platt's paradigm, that after every choice point, or after every few choice points, we get some confirmatory feedback in terms of new existential statements, new observations, and discoveries. Quite possibly we might also require from time to time some indication whether the particular strategy or sequence of choice points which we have been following also shows some heuristic effectiveness.

The questions I would like to put before us are: Which questions are decidable? Why is it that certain questions are decidable and certain sciences have been successful in this, and others are not? Which problems can be encoded in such a manner as to permit their treatment by methods of strong inference?

So far as I can see, the applicability of strong-inference methods requires at least four necessary conditions.

1. All variables relevant to the theory to be tested must be not only clearly recognized but delimited with high reliability, so that we can get statistical universes with sharply bounded limits.

2. Each variable must be relatively uniform, so that its distribution over the universe concerned is likely to be well represented by samples of limited size.

3. The relevant correlations must be relatively exhaustive; that is, they must account for a large part of the variance to be explained.

4. The relevant correlations must be relatively stable over time, so as to permit good prediction across all relevant periods. These points must be elaborated.

With regard to the first condition, a question becomes decidable, in the sense of strong inference, if all or most of the members of the relevant class of phenomena or variables can be clearly recognized and delimited by standardized operations, and if the presence or absence of an item, or any relevant state of a variable, can be clearly recognized. This criterion excludes, therefore, the *thematic* dimension of social science —

what Gerald Holton has called "perennial themes"[17] or others have called the "haunted house" doctrines,[18] in which at least one variable, for instance, "economic cause," has no clearly defined limit. If we say that every political event has an economic cause, it is very hard to find out what would *not* be an economic cause. The universe, the statistical ensemble, of socioeconomic causes is so loosely defined that we cannot find any reliable frequency distributions. Therefore, we cannot make here any statistical statements, and we cannot draw strong inferences. We need narrower definitions. If the variable is to be used in formulating decidable questions, then the presence or absence of any crucial item must be clearly established. That was the first demand.

The second requirement is that of relative uniformity. This condition requires that the variance of the class of phenomena we are using must be relatively limited, so that a tolerably small sample, a sample small enough that we can afford it with the limited research budget available to us, is truly representative. Remember that if the class has very high variance, then even a sample with a large number of items in it will not be highly representative of the class as a whole. Therefore, the more uniform the class, the smaller will be the size of the smallest acceptable sample; and the size of samples we can work with is limited by our time and resources. But the size of samples we can afford will necessarily limit the classes of phenomena, and the ranges of their states, about which we make general statements which are valid and not trivial. We can draw strong inferences only about phenomena that are sufficiently homogeneous, so that their distribution curve has such a shape that the samples we can handle will tell us something about the class. It is possible that there are classes of phenomena in the world that are so diverse and have such a high variance and such an unfavorable distribution that the sample sizes we can handle today are inadequate for giving us confirmed statements about the class. But if our students, or the students of our students, can handle sample sizes twice or ten times the size of sample sizes we handle today, or if they increase their capabilities for analyzing more difficult statistical distributions, then classes with much greater intrinsic variance, classes that we cannot handle today, will become

[17] Gerald Holton, "Scientific Research and Scholarship: Notes Toward the Design of Proper Scales," *Daedalus, 91* (Spring 1962), pp. 363–399, and "Science and New Styles of Thought," *The Graduate Journal* (The University of Texas), 7: 2, pp. 394–422.

[18] I am indebted to Hayward Alker for having drawn my attention to this nice term for them.

accessible to them. There is, therefore, a historic dimension in the statistics that we can deal with at any particular time.

The third point is the degree of exhaustiveness of a correlation. If we want to make a problem decidable by methods of strong inference, we shall need variables that will account for such a large part of the total variance that we can account for most of the variance of the phenomena relevant to the theory concerned. If we find that we have even quite good and statistically acceptable data, concerning some conditions or background factors or determinants, which account for 10 per cent of the variance but leave 90 per cent in the realm of ignorance or in the realm of pure chance, we cannot pretend to have decided a scientific question by methods of strong inference. If, on the other hand, we can account for two thirds, three fourths, or nine tenths of the variance, the claim of strong inference will be considerably more plausible, and it will be much better founded. This is what I meant by the relative exhaustiveness of the relevant data and their correlations. We can be sure we can never completely exhaust the variance observed in many phenomena, but we should like to be able to account for at least more than one half of the variance. Once we have reached that level, our inferences can begin to become strong.

Fourth, and finally, the correlations, the probabilities, and the distributions we are dealing with must all not change too erratically during the time of observations or during the time relevant for our inferences to be drawn from them. The statistics of the behavior of caterpillars permit few if any strong inferences about the behavior of butterflies. This may exclude certain phenomena of evolution, rapid change, or nonconverging feedback, where the occurrence of certain phenomena will increase or decrease the probability of their own recurrence. If these changes occur at time scales which are not critical for the observations on which the theory is to be based, strong inference should be possible, but if they occur at faster rates, it is not.

Within the limits of these four conditions, however, quantitative data can be used in aiding strong-inference methods to turn philosophical problems of men's social behavior into decidable questions of social sciences. There are many examples of this possibility. Karl Marx and John Stuart Mill assumed that the world was getting more international, that the world economy and world culture were growing faster than national economies and national cultures. Werner Sombart assumed the opposite, and Sir Norman Angell in 1940 assumed that the growth was at identical rates. This question is decidable for particular times and places by means of quantitative evidence. It happens that in the case of

Britain, which may be typical for some other countries, Marx and Mill
were right for the middle decades of the nineteenth century, from about
1830 to 1870. It turns out, however, that for Britain in the period 1871
to 1914, Sir Norman Angell's view was most realistic, and that during
the period 1914 to the 1960's, the Sombart theory of the faster growth
of national economies and of national communities seems to be true for
Britain, as well as for many other countries. (What this tells us for the
future is, of course, another question.)

There are many problems in social science for which we can draw
strong inferences, at least for periods of half centuries. In such cases,
we can use strong-inference procedures for deciding among alternative
lines of theory and research at each further step, and we need, therefore,
relevant empirical data series over time and across nations.

We also need to a much greater extent a study of existing theories.
We have neglected to study the stock of classic major social science
theories so as to try to recode them into propositions suitable for study
by strong-inference methods. We need a reformulation, then, of these
existing theories, and of any new or emerging theories, so as to recast
them into terms testable by quantitative evidence, and we need to test
them for their ripeness for treatment by strong-inference methods. As
the era of quantitative research and of mathematical analysis is getting
under way, the era of serious and strong theory construction will be
beginning.

Substantive Theories versus *Perennial Themes and Languages*

This involves an understanding of the distinction and contrast between quickly evolving substantive theories and long-lasting philosophical themes and languages. A substantive theory involves specific
predictions of just what is likely to happen precisely there and precisely
then, and at what rates. A philosophical theme, or philosophical
language, on the other hand, tells us what is interesting, what is relevant,
and what is worth looking for.

To some extent, whenever a theory becomes perennial, that is, when
a theory lasts over a long period of discoveries, it turns into a theme,
or a collection of themes, or into a language. This has, to some extent,
been observably true of Marxism as well as of Thomism, and of many
other philosophies.[19] For instance, when Marxism argued that matter
was very important, the content of the word "matter" changed from

[19] See Philip Frank, *Relativity: A Richer Truth* (Boston: Beacon Press, 1950), pp.
78–82.

the chemistry of the nineteenth century to the physics of the time when Lenin wrote his famous article on materialism for the *Karat Encyclopaedia* in 1914, and it changed again at the time when Soviet physicists began to work with splitting the atom as other physicists did in the 1930's, 1940's, and 1950's. But while the *content* of the word "matter" thus changed a very great deal, the *theme* that matter is important and therefore worth putting into the thought of Marxist philosophers has remained persistent among all of them. It is important to remain aware of this distinction between the rapidly changing and quickly evolving substantive theories, on the one hand, and the relatively slow-changing or long-lasting philosophical themes, on the other. It is possible, then, that we will much more often find a convergence of our findings on substantive theories, even if, for political and cultural reasons, the themes and the language that we use are different.

SOME PRACTICAL IMPLICATIONS FOR THE DEVELOPMENT OF SOCIAL SCIENCE

From these lines of thought, what priorities could be suggested for our work? First, we need not merely data libraries, which we call archives, but we also need program libraries for computer routines and mathematical models.

A Survey of Models and Applications

Ideally, I imagine that we shall eventually try to work toward a survey of types of such mathematical models and of fields and classes of cases for their application. Let us assume, and this is a gross simplification, that we could use a row for each mathematical model of a paradigm. We would put next to each other those models which are only minor variations of each other and put further apart those models which are radically different from each other; for instance, models involving probability are distinct from those which do not and thus constitute a different class of models. Then let us have columns for the different fields of application: sociology, economics, political science, and so on. There would be subcolumns within those fields for particular problems. It might turn out, for instance, that a stochastic process model can be used for research on elections, or on aerial warfare, or on civil wars, or that a matrix analysis of the type that Richard Sprague, Leo Goodman, and Harrison White have been working on can be used for international trade as well as for social mobility inside particular countries.[20]

In this simple scheme, the rows will show the range of applications and hence the generality of each type of model. On the other hand, the columns will show that a particular substantive problem can be, or has been, handled by two or several radically different mathematical models. It will thus show the multiplicity of effective approaches to each problem. It would be convenient to put the most frequently used mathematical models into our top rows and to list the least frequently used models toward the bottom. Similarly, in our columns, the problems that are most often quantitatively treated these days should be put into the left-hand columns; and the problems which are least often so treated should go into the right-hand columns. In this arrangement the density, so to speak, or the current saliency of mathematical approaches to social science problems would fall off along the main diagonal. In time, of course, the matrix would become larger, but we could still explore it quickly because the most important and relevant areas would always be found near the top left-hand corner. We could then work out a reasonably serious survey of all the different models, or of most of them, that are now being used and of all or most of the problems to which they apply. This would also help us to find out, better than we know now, how many of these models are genuinely different from each other and how many of them are simply different packagings of the same or nearly the same mathematical pattern. This kind of work would probably require a division of labor and of team work between mathematicians, on the one hand, and substantive social scientists, on the other, but it would help us a great deal in finding out what we are doing.

Specialized Computer Programmers and Programs for Social Science

I am suggesting this not just as a project. I am suggesting that something of this sort will eventually give rise to libraries of models which, then, will give rise to libraries of program routines which could then, ideally, be exchanged on tape or on cards or their equivalents between different countries

A part of this general need will be the development of programs

---

[20] T. W. Anderson, "Probability Models for Analyzing Time Changes in Attitudes," in Paul F. Lazarsfeld (ed.), *Mathematical Thinking in the Social Sciences* (New York and Glencoe: Free Press, 1954), pp. 17–66; for the survey data used, see also Paul F. Lazarsfeld, Bernard Berelson, and Hazel Gaudet, *The People's Choice* (New York: Columbia University Press, 1948). For matrix analysis, see references made in footnote 11.

specifically fitted to social science theories and the generation of a new career (there is a bit of applied sociology involved), namely, the new profession of social science programmers for electronic computation. There already are today some computer programmers who are motivated and skilled in developing program routines in computer analysis specifically suited to social science. If we do not create careers attractive to such people, we shall get a horrible mixture of inefficiency and snobbery (if we are not getting some of it already). Some good people will go into this kind of work only to find themselves looked down upon in the caste hierarchy of academic establishments, and they will quickly flee from it, so that all their experience and skills will have to be learned by others over and over again. We have to create a respected and rewarding profession for such social science computer programmers, with its own career lines similar to those of university administrators, or librarians or research specialists, that will give stability and cumulative growth to this vital type of knowledge.

Public and Private Formats for Computer Programs

We also need an agreement, if possible, on combating the formation of local dialects among computer centers and social scientists. The general mathematical pattern, the mathematics of the tower of Babel, let us say, is very simple. If communication within a group is very much higher than communication between two groups, then the slight changes in the communication code within each group will persist and lead to the formation of dialects. This is observable in the dialects of the Tyrolean mountain valleys and also within the local operating conventions of computer programmers at different computer centers in the United States. If, on the other hand, communication across group boundaries is much higher in terms of a signal-to-noise ratio than it is within groups, then the uniform code persists easily. If the in-group communication is the signal and the cross-group communication is mere noise, we get dialects. If the cross-group communication is the signal and the in-group communication is mere noise, we can maintain a uniform, standardized communication code. If neither of the two is clearly the signal or clearly noise, then we get a situation where everybody is marginal all the time. Such a situation is frequent but highly unstable.[21] Knowing that we cannot abolish the development of dialects, so to speak, or of special notations and conventions, because they are

[21] This argument is pursued further in Deutsch, "On Theories, Taxonomies and Models as Communication Codes. . .," *op. cit.* (footnote 2).

a function of the facts of life, we could try to make our computing programs and our centers bilingual. By degrees, we could try to put all computer routines into two formats. One would be a private format for the men who invented it, their private language, their cherished conventions, just as they like it and feel most comfortable with it. The second would require extra budgetary appropriations from the science foundations and from the computing centers for hiring translators and for putting into a public format any routine that has turned out to be reasonably important. We might have general rules, supplemented by screening committees of experts, to decide which program routines are worth this expenditure. To some extent, of course, the University of Michigan is doing this with survey data when a deck is cleaned up and double punches and other abominations which make it hard to use the deck again are taken out. But this should be done for all our computer routines which are of any great interest, so that we can have public formats that can, ideally, be exchanged around the world.

The Growth of Secondary Data: Budgeting of Funds and Time

We need, further, a series of decisions based on a better awareness of the point which our data libraries will reach when they will come to contain more secondary data than primary data. Most of our information about the world is contained, not in the raw data, but in the relations among them. Ratios and rates of change are of as much, and often of more, interest than the raw data are. We need to preserve the raw data, of course, in order to make our work reproducible. But we also need to reproduce, store, and communicate the relevant ratios and rates of change which we have discovered and computed — all the many secondary data that come out of our working on primary data. The growth of total data in our data libraries, therefore, will be proportional not merely to the influx of raw data but more likely to some power of those data. It might be as high as the square of the data that are coming in. I do not know how high this will go, but we must be prepared to budget for it, and we must already count on this very large growth of secondary data.

The same will hold for the budgeting of both staff time and scholars' time. In most universities, we still expect our doctoral candidates to spend much more time on gathering the data than on analyzing them. Historians, in particular, are famous for this practice, and the same is true in many other fields. We may eventually find that data processing, elaboration, and analysis may take as much time as data gathering, and perhaps later more time. This is characteristic, of course, of the development of all industries. In the primitive tribe, looking for flint took much longer than chipping flint into a stone ax. In making Swiss watches, finding iron ore is the least of the trouble. It is the fabrication from ore to steel to watches that takes long. I would assume that the industrialization of the production of knowledge will show the same tendency toward increasing roundabout production that all industrial processes have shown. There is no need to become afraid of this. As in all industries, in the end the unit costs go down as the process, though longer, becomes more powerful.

New Kinds of Data

What kinds of data shall we want? At the moment, we are still collecting mostly input data of the political and social process. That is, we should like to find determinants of political results, but we know little about the output of the political system. We know that we need more relevant quantitative political and social output data. What kinds of social, economic, and political decisions are being produced? How does a society perform? How many kinds and instances of penalties and of rewards does it produce? What kinds of distribution of values, rewards, and penalties does a society or a social group or a social pattern produce? Much more often than in the past, we shall now find that the same data can be used as output and as input data. This will force us to develop more elaborate models of the social process.

We shall want to get whole new classes and new lines of fruitful secondary data. We should like to have *innovation curves* showing what percentages of a certain activity are transformed by technical innovation and at what points in time. An innovation curve would therefore involve percentages of cases of a particular practice, such as the ratio of newspapers set by linotype machines against total circulation. The percentage of copies produced by the new method could be put on the vertical axis of a diagram, and years put on the horizontal axis. Such a diagram could show the rise of a new practice of automatic printing of newspapers, or the use of the linotype machine, or automatic typesetting, say, from 10 per cent in one year to 20 per cent in the next. The innovation curves might be convex or concave, and their shapes and slopes could be compared by countries, periods, industries, forms of ownership, or types of public policy. We might also want to know what are the curves for political innovation and change. To put this slightly differently, we may ask: What is the half life of a prejudice? Given a certain conservative attitude, how many years does it take until the number of people holding a prejudice has been cut in half?[22] It is my guess that, in modern society, it is about 25 years. I am thinking, in the field of American politics, about the dwindling of the opposition to the St. Lawrence Seaway and of the opposition to equal rights and integration for Negroes. But this is, as you see, a desperately rough guess. Our survey research specialists could find much better figures on the period it takes to reduce a substantial prejudice and under what conditions it is reduced. What, here, are in each case the critical areas and proportions? And what are the relevant signal-to-noise ratios and their equivalents in social processes?

Cumulative Effects of Visibility and Speed of Intellectual Communication

Finally, as the last point, what can we do to make more of our data visually perceptible? This is not a matter of showmanship; nor is it a minor matter. Hayward Alker succeeded, as many others have, in making visible certain relations in the voting of nations in the United Nations Assembly by means of factor and proximity analysis. By showing clusters of issues or factors in two-dimensional space, he makes it possible for people to see at once something of what goes on. This is why Mattei Dogan's work on making changes in Communist regions visible is not trivial.

Let us recall a very basic analogy. In driving an automobile through a city, the delays at every street corner can be very small, but the cumulative effect of these delays or risks is crucial for the performance of the traffic system as a whole. In using our telephone, the slight delays or small chances of inaccuracy in dialing every digit of the number we are calling seem trivially small; together, they are crucial for the performance of the telephone system. In the collective thinking of social scientists around the world, the delays in getting from one man's foibles, or special language or code or data, to another's and in translating data from columns of figures into a visual image may seem trivial. But they may be utterly critical for the emerging new level of speed and power of the invisible communication system which has constituted the collective thought, the collective social science, of mankind.

[22] "Conservative" is taken here in its traditional sense, as a preference for conserving rather than changing existing practices and institutions, and as a preference for low risks over high risks and for low rates of change over higher ones. Edmund Burke, Benjamin Disraeli, and Otto von Bismarck, in their day, were conservatives in this sense. Persons in international politics favoring a deliberate policy of high risk of nuclear war are not conservatives in this meaning of the term, even though they may claim this label.

Data gathering, data processing, data transmission — if we improve their methods even to a small degree — can add new powers to this collective thinking of mankind. In the field of quantitative ecology, that is, in the study of the interplay of man and his environment in space and time, and at the level of individuals, groups, nations, and the international system, we can apply these methods and search for new and more powerful ones. In our age of unprecedented dangers, these new powers are urgently needed.

2

ERIK ALLARDT

Aggregate Analysis:
The Problem of Its Informative Value

THE CONVENTIONAL QUESTION regarding ecological analysis is: What kind of inferences can one safely make on the basis of ecological or, more generally, aggregate data? The aim of this paper is to discuss whether the persistent focus on this problem has hindered discussions of other matters of at least equal importance.

As a point of departure it may be contended that ecological analysis has been sometimes put under more severe restrictions than other forms of analysis. Historically the first restricting factor was created by the early discussions of the ecological fallacy which culminated in Robinson's famous paper.[1] Today it seems fair to say that everybody agrees with Robinson's contention that an ecological correlation is usually not equal to its corresponding individual correlation and, accordingly, that ecological correlations cannot be used without strict qualifications as substitutes for individual correlations. There also seems to be agreement on the fact that Robinson went too far in stating that ecological correlations are used simply and only as substitutes for individual correlations and that ecological correlations consequently are less valuable than individual ones. Almost equally well known as Robinson's paper is Menzel's comment in which, on the basis of Robinson's own examples, he went on to show that ecological correlations may retain their validity even after it has been shown that the

[1] William S. Robinson, "Ecological Correlations and the Behavior of Individuals," *American Sociological Review, 15* (1950), pp. 351–357.

ecological and individual correlations clearly differ.[2] Ecological correlations may tell something about territorial units, which can be used as contextual properties explaining the variations in the correlated variables. Scheuch's formulation, that one cannot argue in principle against the statement that individual and ecological correlations usually will not coincide but that one cannot rest with such an observation, appears as an authoritative assertion of the present-day position. Not only are territorial units important in their own right but there are also methods for estimating the size of error when ecological data are used for inferences about individual units.[3]

DELIBERATE USES OF THE "ECOLOGICAL FALLACY"

Considering the actual practices in social science, one is tempted to defend not only ecological correlations but also what could be labeled the "deliberate use of the ecological fallacy" as well. Even if it is assumed that ecological correlations are seldom the same as their corresponding individual correlations, one may ask whether demonstration of individual correlations is the prime objective in sociological and political studies. Certainly not! The main objective is causal explanations, not demonstrations of correlations.

Even taking into consideration the serious and promising work that is going on today in finding precise criteria and procedures for causal inferences in nonexperimental research, one may safely say that most causal explanations in today's social science rest heavily on some form of speculation. Since "speculation" in some quarters is considered a dirty word, one usually speaks of *causal interpretations*, which are to be distinguished from *causal inferences*. If we say that A is the cause of B, we have to know at least three things: (1) that A and B tend to appear together; (2) that A precedes B in time; and (3) that the relation between A and B is not a result of their common relation to a third variable. The first requirement can be demonstrated by reliable statistical analysis, but the other conclusion can be drawn with reasonable certainty only through experiments. One can start an argument as to whether a causal relation can ever be demonstrated empirically, but the

[2] Herbert Menzel, "Comment on Robinson's 'Ecological Correlations and the Behavior of Individuals,' " *American Sociological Review, 15*: 5 (1950), p. 674.

[3] Erwin K. Scheuch, "Cross-National Comparisons Using Aggregate Data: Some Substantive and Methodological Problems" in R. L. Merritt and Stein Rokkan (eds.), *Comparing Nations: The Use of Quantitative Data in Cross-National Research* (New Haven: Yale University Press, 1966), pp. 148–156.

fact remains that the logic of casual inference is heavily tied to the classical experimental procedure. In other words, it is only in experimental research that we can make causal inferences, and causal inferences are, so to say, defined by the classical experimental procedure. It is typical of survey studies — which are often contrasted with ecological analysis — that we cannot draw causal inferences with any reasonable degree of certainty. We can, however, on the basis of experience, existing explanatory hypotheses, and other available information, make causal interpretation. In practically all survey studies, for instance, of political behavior, the analyst is in a situation where he cannot positively infer that one variable has preceded another variable in time. Neither can he be sure that the association between two variables is not a result of their relation to a third variable. Nevertheless, the analysis would be uninteresting if the analyst had only demonstrated the existence of individual correlations.

The common practice in making causal interpretations may be labeled "soft," but it does not need to be arbitrary. Usually the analyst draws upon a wealth of both theoretical and empirical material before he makes his causal interpretations. What does it mean when an analyst of, for instance, political behavior makes a causal interpretation to the effect that A is the cause of B? One can, of course, say that the analyst has to make simplifying assumptions about the time order of A and B and about disturbing influences of other variables. However, one does not make simplifying assumptions just like that. The crucial point in making causal interpretations is that the analyst tries to describe and pin down the intervening processes by which a factor A affects a behavior B. Let us suppose that the task is to study how division of labor affects political radicalism. In such a case the researcher tries to describe the mechanisms and perhaps the psychological processes that in the *routine or normal case* are the result of different degrees of division of labor. It is not just a question of introducing a specific intervening variable into the statistical analysis. Only if the analyst succeeds in making the description of the intervening processes understandable are we satisfied with his causal interpretation. In experimental research the experimenter is usually able to observe directly how and by what process A affects B. This is generally not the case in nonexperimental research. Therefore, the researcher has to go through great pains in order to specify the psychological processes and mechanisms that in the normal or routine case are intervening between cause and effect.

The moral of the preceding discussion, in the first place, is that it is rather unreasonable to maintain that ecological research should be restricted to the demonstration of ecological correlations. However, we may go further than that. In a survey analysis, in which the analyst is making statements about the behavior of individuals on the basis of variables denoting individual properties, the force and power of the analyst's presentation will rest very much on his skill in making the causal interpretation, in other words, his description of the intervening mechanisms. In survey analysis — as in other nonexperimental work — there will be not only an apparent but also a strategically important speculative or interpretive element. Causal interpretations will always be hypothetical; and we may say that in making causal interpretations it is not a question of valid demonstration but rather a matter of presenting fruitful hypotheses. As an old rule says, the way of invention (finding hypotheses) is definitely something other than the way of demonstration. In making inventions or finding hypotheses the researcher may use whatever he has in his power — of course, with some ethical limitations — in order to proceed. Turning to "the deliberate use of the ecological fallacy," one may contend that the analysis of ecological data and correlations may indeed for some researchers in some circumstances be a powerful tool in making statements about individual behavior. It may be that the ecological data facilitate fruitful causal interpretations better than the corresponding individual data, if such are available. Now it may be argued that in such a case ecological correlations have actually been used as substitutes for individual correlations. One may of course argue in this fashion, but this kind of counterargument certainly introduces strong restrictions on actual research. Ecological data may fit some researchers' temperaments better than individual data, and as far as inventions, hypotheses, and causal interpretations are concerned, temperamental differences really count. Hence, it is here contended that the use of simple ecological data and correlations for arriving at statements about individuals may be a fruitful way to proceed.

This kind of argument introduces, of course, some kind of immorality in a serious discussion about quantitative ecological analysis. A true methodologist may frown, or at least feel irritated. If the methodologist's irritation is strong enough, the author of this paper may retreat and say that the intention is not to present any programmatical arguments but rather just to describe actual research practices. In any case, there exist deliberate but fruitful uses of ecological correlations for arriving at statements about individuals.

The true methodologist may, however, still ask: What is the use of presenting or defending methodologically loose research practices? The present author's answer would be that it is often important to analyze liberal-mindedly the prevailing research practices and to ask why they prevail. The deliberate users of ecological correlations for making conclusions about individuals may have had some other scientific criteria in mind than did the discussants of the quantitative ecological method. The former would probably stress something that for the time being could be labeled fruitfulness, while the latter focus on the question of how safe and probable is the evidence. The contention here is that discussions on quantitative ecological analysis should not only deal with the problem of what inferences are allowed on the basis of aggregate data but should also be forcefully directed toward the question on the fruitfulness of ecological data.

This discussion has a rather old-fashioned flavor. The real issue in methodological discussions of today does not seem to be the ecological fallacy but rather the techniques used in analyzing data from many levels of social organization. It has also been shown, for instance by Scheuch, that there are also individualistic fallacies, that is, invalid inferences about territorial units on the basis of individual data,[4] and a systematic treatment of possible fallacies has been presented by Alker.[5] Nevertheless, the discussions in terms of fallacies has tended to divert the attention from asking questions about fruitfulness. Of course, the question of evidence is central, but in the following section we shall discuss problems in terms of fruitfulness.

DIFFERENT FOCUSES FOR ANALYSES OF SOCIAL SYSTEMS

In order to proceed, we require a simple classification about types of analysis that differ according to the level of a social and political system they refer to. Instead of dealing mainly with ecological data, we shall consider the more general case of grouped or aggregate data. A simplified classification has been presented by Matilda White Riley, who distinguishes between four types of analysis:[6]

1. The first type is group analysis, in which the data deal entirely with

[4] Scheuch, *op. cit.,* pp. 158–164.

[5] Hayward R. Alker, Jr., *Mathematics and Politics* (New York: Macmillan, 1965), pp. 80–88.

[6] Matilda White Riley, "Sources and Types of Sociological Data" in R. L. Faris (ed.), *Handbook of Modern Sociology* (Chicago: Rand McNally, 1964), pp. 1014–1020.

properties of the groups and aggregates and the conclusions also focus on the group. As an example Riley mentions Kingsley Davis and Hilda Golden's result, according to which there is a negative correlation between agriculturalism and urbanization in different countries of the world.

2. In structural analysis the data and conclusions also focus on the group, but individual variables are used either for specifying the result or for checking its validity. Riley's example is taken from Faris and Dunham's famous study of the relation between mental illness and social disorganization. In order to check that their main finding concerning the relationship between rates of mental illness and patterns of social disorganization in different zones of the city was valid, Faris and Dunham compared segments or groups of the several zones in which individuals were alike with respect to an individual characteristic.

3. Another type is contextual analysis, which differs from structural analysis in that the main focus is on individuals, but individual relationships are checked or specified by accounting for differences between the groups to which the individuals belong. An example is provided by James Davis' examination of the relationship between the degree of activity and the tendency to drop out of the group. Here the role volume or the proportion of group members who are active role players appears to be an important contextual characteristic.

4. The fourth type is individual analysis, of which there is, of course, an abundance of examples. We have learned in voting studies that, for example, exposure to mass media and political activity tend to be positively correlated or that early deciders tend to be politically more interested than other voters.

There are, of course, additional types. Riley does not differentiate between group variables obtained by summing up individual characteristics and group variables that are clearly global. The statement "There are more murderers in countries with a death penalty than in countries without death penalty" is different from Davis and Golden's type of group analysis. We may, however, here rest with Riley's classification.

Provided that proper controls have been made, all four types of analysis seem to be legitimate means of obtaining evidence about social phenomena. The question here, however, is whether all four types of analyses are equally interesting or fruitful. Intuitively at least, one would be strongly inclined to say that types 2 and 3, structural and contextual analysis, appear as more fruitful than types 1 and 4, group and individual analysis. The selection of examples might, of course, be very unfair, but an inspection of the examples presented seems to support the contention that structural analysis and contextual analysis are more fruitful. In the group analysis case of the negative correlation between agriculturalism and urbanization one has at least a feeling that there is a tautological element in the finding. This feeling is even stronger in the examples selected from voting surveys. To be exposed to mass media is already a symptom of political activity, and to be an early decider during an election campaign is, if anything, a symptom of political interest. At least the examples from both the group and the individual analysis appear as decidedly trivial compared to the examples from structural and contextual analysis.

Many researchers have felt strongly for some time that the most fertile uses of ecological or generally aggregate data are those in which it is possible to combine both aggregate and individual data.[7] This belief has been based mostly on intuition or on the experience of simultaneously working with method and theory. In the following section I shall attempt to show why the combination of aggregate and individual data is particularly fruitful.

THE INFORMATIVE VALUE OF AGGREGATE DATA

The concept of fruitfulness has hitherto not been specified, and here, too, it will be exchanged for another concept, namely that of informative value. Among contemporary sociologists few have given so much explicit attention to the question of informative value as has Hans Zetterberg, who also asserts that sociologists have given much less attention to the question of informative value than to the question of evidence.[8] The notion of informative value has been put forward particularly by Karl Popper, who also speaks of the empirical or informative content of scientific statements. The empirical content of a statement increases with its degree of falsifiability:[9] the larger the number of ways in which a statement can be proved false, the greater its empirical content (the higher its informative value). Formulating it in a more popular way, one could also say that the greater variety of events a statement accounts for, the higher its informative value. According to Popper, "science does not aim, primarily, at high probabilities. It aims at high informative content, well backed by

[7] Scheuch, *op. cit.,* p. 166.

[8] Hans L. Zetterberg, *On Theory and Verification in Sociology* (Totowa, N.J.: Bedminster Press, 1965).

[9] Karl R. Popper, *The Logic of Scientific Discovery* (London: Hutchinson, 1959), pp. 119–121.

experience. But a hypothesis may be very probable because it tells us nothing, or very little."[10]

Statements with low informative value are what we call trivial, and, with regard to the empirical content, the most trivial of all statements are, of course, the tautological ones. Triviality is a matter of degree. One sometimes has the feeling that many sociological and political science statements are close to tautologies without being so completely. The earlier-mentioned result from voting surveys, according to which those who are more interested in politics make their decision to vote earlier than those who are less interested in politics, is an example of such a statement. It is close to being a tautology because early decisions may on the theoretical level very well be seen as a symptom of political interest, and in many studies one may actually use the time of the voting decision as an indicator or an operational definition of political activity. Nevertheless, such statements are often presented as empirical findings, and the analyst would, if he is questioned, usually reply that the time of the voting decision and political interest are operationally defined independently of each other. This is a standard reply, for example, when survey analysts are questioned about the triviality of their results. Apparently, the matter of informative content cannot be discussed without going into the problem of operational definitions. Any kind of thorough analysis cannot be attempted here. In making some suggestions we can heavily rely on Ilkka Heiskanen,[11] who has made a detailed analysis of the problem.

We can start from the generalization presented earlier, that "the more people are interested in politics, the earlier they tend to make their voting decision," and characterize it as a generalization with one generalizing term (interest in politics) and one predicate (the time of voting decision). Why is it so trivial and almost tautological? In the first place, we may say that the generalization is on a very low level of abstraction. It applies only to election campaigns. We could also say that the generalization is trivial because the generalizing term must be operationalized in such a way that it expresses a predisposition toward the predicate in terms of all our common-sense notions. Interest in politics is a disposition that is likely to be released in an early voting decision. In such a case the number of potential ways in which the

[10] Karl R. Popper, "Degree of Confirmation," *British Journal for the Philosophy of Science, 5* (1954), p. 146.

[11] Ilkka Heiskanen, "Theoretical Approaches and Scientific Strategies in Administrative and Organizational Research: A Methodological Study," *Commentationes Humanarum Litterarum. Societas Scientiarum Fennica, 39* (1967), pp. 20–39.

generalization can be falsified is indeed small, or, as also can be said, the number of potential falsifiers is very small.

It is important to note that the narrow scope of such dispositional generalization leads also to a sort of arbitrariness or instability in the use of operational definitions. If one operational definition of the generalizing term, such as the attendance at a political meeting, fails or does not confirm the generalization, it is easy to switch to another operational definition, such as the reading of political information, and hope for better luck. When a generalization is very narrow in scope and accordingly not too tied to other and different phenomena, there are actually no guides and few restrictions on how operational definitions should be chosen. We may conclude that if in a generalization the generalizing term and the predicate concern very similar phenomena, there is both a great likelihood for arbitrary adjustments of the operational definitions and very few potential falsifiers. Already this contention speaks for the value of generalizations containing variables from different levels, for instance, variables from both the group and the individual level. The use of variables from different aggregate levels will decrease the likelihood that they concern the same type of phenomena and will increase the likelihood of results of high informative value.

The case can be put more strongly by considering the procedure of specification. There is generally a feeling that two-variable relationships seldom are interesting in sociology and politics. There are, of course, also good grounds for such a feeling. If generalizations are to be theoretically relevant, they must be specified, that is, their conditions of validity must be assessed. In the elaboration of social science data specification usually means that the generalizations are formulated in terms of at least three variables. In general, specification tends both to increase the number of potential falsifiers and also to eliminate arbitrariness in the choice of operational definitions, since the specifiers indicate the potential connections of the operational definitions with other phenomena. If we could specify our generalization by saying that "the more people with a high education are interested in politics, the more they tend to delay their voting decision, whereas the more people with a low education are interested in politics, the earlier they tend to make their voting decision," we have certainly added to the empirical content and increased the number of potential falsifiers. Here we may return to Riley's four types of analysis and say that already the fruitfulness of specification is one reason why structural or relational analysis is often more interesting than simple group or individual analysis. Structural and contextual analyses involve in practice a systematic specification.

Structural and contextual analyses, however, also differ from group and individual analyses in that they involve variables from both group and individual levels. The fruitfulness of specification rests, of course, on the nature of the specifiers used. If the body of variables (theory) from which the specifier has been selected concerns the same type of phenomena as the generalization to be specified, there is a danger that the specification will not increase the degree of falsifiability. There is likewise the risk that there will be much arbitrariness in selecting operational definitions. If the body of variables from which the specifier has been selected deal with clearly different subject matter than the generalizations to be specified, the arbitrary adjustment of operational definitions becomes difficult. Of course, for a specifier to be fruitful it also has to be related via theory or generalizations to other phenomena on its own aggregate level. In any case, if the specifier and the generalization to be specified are from different aggregate levels, there is great likelihood that they will deal with clearly different subject matter and also great likelihood that the specified generalization will be of high informative value. This is also why generalizations in psychology often appear particularly interesting when they contain references to either physiological or sociological theory. One cannot, of course, rule out the fact that specifications can be interesting even when the specifier and the generalization are of the same aggregate level. They can be so, provided that they really deal with sufficiently different subject matter. However, one may say that crossing different aggregate levels either through structural or contextual specification is an extremely powerful tool in aiming at generalizations with high informative content.

SUMMARY

The main contentions may be summed up in a few short statements.

1. Discussions of the ecological method tend to focus almost entirely on the problem of what kind of inferences are permissible on the basis of ecological data (the problem of evidence), but discussions of the fruitfulness of generalizations based on ecological data would be of equal importance (the problem of informative value).

2. The discussions about the ecological and other fallacies have — their great importance notwithstanding — diverted the attention too much from questions about informative value. The persistent existence

of the ecological fallacy may be taken as an indication of strivings for results of high informative value through speculations and interpretations. There exist deliberate and cold-blooded uses of the ecological fallacy.

3. When the informative value of a statement is defined by the number of ways it can be proved false, it appears that generalizations containing variables dealing with entirely different subject matters or chosen from different theoretical systems are most likely to have high informative value. Generalizations containing variables from different levels of a social system (different aggregate levels) are likely to have high informative content and also likely to restrict arbitrariness in the selection of operational definitions. On the other hand, generalizations containing variables that all concern the same type of phenomena are usually trivial.

4. When generalizations are specified, the most fruitful specifications are those in which the specifying variable is chosen from a clearly different area from the generalization to be specified. Again, the selection of variables from different aggregate levels serves as a powerful safeguard against both triviality and arbitrariness with operational definitions.

5. For the reasons given earlier structural analysis (the generalization is on the group level but the specifier on the individual level) and contextual analysis (the generalization is on the individual level but the specifier on the group level) will be extremely useful tools in arriving at generalizations with high informative content.

6. Of course, it cannot be asserted that all generalizations containing variables from the same aggregate level are trivial. Triviality, however, is a matter of degree. Structural and contextual generalizations tend as a rule to be less trivial than generalizations based either entirely on grouped or entirely on individual data.

3

TAPANI VALKONEN

Individual and Structural Effects in Ecological Research

ONE APPROACH to the methodological problems of ecological research is to ask: What kinds of inferences are permissible when using aggregate data[1] or, more specifically, how can inferences about the behavior of individuals be made on the basis of such data?[2] This paper also deals with these kinds of methodological problems. The point of departure is not, however, the nature of data generally used in ecological research. To solve problems associated with the use of ecological data it seems necessary to examine the sociological meaning of areal units and the kinds of effects their properties may have on the behavior of individuals.

Ecological analysis can be carried out by taking the areal units as wholes in their own right.[3] In most cases, however, the units are collectives, the properties of which are obtained by aggregating properties of smaller units (e.g., of individuals), and if one wants to make causal interpretations of the observed relationships among variables, the multiple-level nature of the phenomena must be taken into account.

---

[1] See Erwin Scheuch, "Cross-National Comparisons Using Aggregate Data: Some Substantive and Methodological Problems," R. Merritt and S. Rokkan (eds.), *Comparing Nations* (New Haven: Yale University Press, 1965), pp. 148–167.

[2] See, e.g., Leo A. Goodman, "Some Alternatives to Ecological Correlation," *American Journal of Sociology, 64* (1959), pp. 610–625; O. D. Duncan, R. P. Cuzzort, and B. Duncan, *Statistical Geography* (Glencoe: Free Press, 1961), pp. 68–80; and Raymond Boudon, "Propriétés individuelles et propriétés collectives: un problème d'analyse écologique," *Revue française de sociologie, 4* (1963), pp. 275–299.

[3] Cf. Paul F. Lazarsfeld and Herbert Menzel, "On the Relation between Individual and Collective Properties," in A. Etzioni (ed.), *Complex Organizations* (New York: Holt, Rinehart, & Winston, 1961), p. 425.

The situation is then a special variant of the type of sociological research in which there are units and variables from many levels of social organization. Although much confusion over the conceptual definitions of the levels and their relationships still exists and few appropriate research methods have been worked out,[4] an attempt will be made here to examine ecological research as a type of multiple-level research.

To make the matter concrete, let us cite an example in which we are studying the modernity of farming practices in a rural area. The area can be divided into smaller areas, for instance, villages. An average describing the modernity of all the farmers is calculated for every village. These averages might be means of some kind of modernity scores of farmers or percentages showing the proportion of farmers who have adopted a given farming practice. The question is: What is the sociological meaning of the differences in modernity among villages, and what kinds of causal processes can give rise to the differences?

SOME MODELS EXPLAINING ECOLOGICAL VARIATION

First, there is the possibility that the differences are random. If the variance in individual modernity scores for the whole population and the sizes (number of farmers) of the areas are known, the expected variance of the averages of the areas, that is, the expected ecological variance, can be calculated, assuming the differences are random.[5] The areal units used in ecological research are usually so large that the averages of the areas would be practically equal. Sociologically, that means that no properties of the areas and no individual variables with nonrandom ecological variance would have an effect on the behavior under study.[6] From the point of view of ecological research, such a situation is quite uninteresting. Such sociological variables whose ecological variances can be totally explained by random factors are, however, uncommon in practice. In psychological research one could expect to find such variables more often.

If the averages of the areas differ from each other significantly in a statistical sense, the simplest explanation would be that an individual-

[4] M. W. Riley, *Sociological Research, a Case Approach* (New York: Harcourt, Brace & World, 1963), pp. 642–739.

[5] This is based on the same statistical theory as one-way analysis of variance.

[6] There is, however, the possibility that the nonexistence of significant differences is analogous to "spurious zero-correlation" in survey research: the opposite effects of two factors eliminate each other.

level variable x, which has ecological variance, has an effect on the dependent variable y. If y is the modernity of farmers, x could be, for example, education, if the inhabitants of the villages differ in average education. In this case, y would also have nonrandom ecological variance because of the individual-level relationship. If no other ecologically relevant independent variable has influence upon y, the slope of regression of the y-averages on x-averages is equal to the slope of regression of the respective individual variables. In addition to the individual-level slope calculated for the whole population, slopes can be calculated separately within each area. All these slopes should be at least approximately equal, if the assumption of only one ecologically relevant effect is valid. The ecological correlation and the individual correlation in the whole population or within areas are not equal. The size of the difference is dependent on the ratios of the ecological variances of the two variables to the individual variances. The correlation coefficients within different areas are also unequal, if the within-area variances of x are not equal.[7]

The case in which the ecological correlation is only a reflection of an individual-level relationship has received special attention because it is possible to approximate the individual correlation by means of ecological data using the equality of individual and ecological slopes or their analogies.[8] If the ecological variation of y can be explained by the ecological variation of x, a new question may arise: How then can the ecological variation of x be explained? The explanation could be found in new individual variables that have ecological variance. However, in some phase of the causal chain there apparently must be a global-type variable characterizing the areas as wholes and explaining the differences in the compositions of the populations of the areas.

In most cases, it is not realistic to assume that the ecological variation of y can be explained by only one independent individual variable. In practice usually there would be several ecologically relevant independent variables. The situation is, however, in principle, the same as with one independent variable: the ecological relationships are only reflections of individual-level causal processes. From the point of view of the

---

[7] These conclusions are based on Hubert M. Blalock, Jr., *Causal Inferences in Nonexperimental Research* (Chapel Hill: University of North Carolina Press, 1961), pp. 95–126, and Duncan *et al., op. cit.,* pp. 68–80, especially the equation on page 66: $b_T = b_w + E^2{}_{zA} (b_b - b_w)$, where b_T is the individual slope for the whole population, b_w is the average within-area slope, b_b is the ecological slope, and $E^2{}_{zA}$ is the correlation ratio of the independent variable x on the area.

[8] See Goodman, *op. cit.* and Boudon, *op. cit.*

sociological meaning of ecological units, these kinds of processes are not very interesting. In the explanation of the phenomenon under study no proper ecological effects have to be taken into account. Situations in which the properties of areas affect the behavior and properties of individuals are ecologically more interesting.

Contextual analysis has been the approach by which the effects of the properties or groups of collectives on individuals have been studied.[9] In the methodological discussions especially a variant of contextual analysis appears to have been given considerable attention, namely the variant dealing with so-called structural effects[10] or compositional effects.[11] The properties describing the collectives in this kind of analysis are analytical variables formed from the properties of members of the collectives. The variables, in addition, usually also have purely individual-level effects on the dependent variable.

Davis, Spaeth, and Huson have made an attempt to classify different types of compositional effects, mainly according to their mathematical forms.[12] The first criterion is the linearity or nonlinearity of the compositional effect. The second classification criterion is whether the compositional property of the collective has a direct effect on the individual-level dependent variable or on the relationship between the dependent and independent individual-level variables. The direct-effect models of Davis, Spaeth, and Huson can be formalized by the following regression equation:

$$\hat{y}_{ij} = a + b_1 \bar{x}_j + b_2 x_{ij} \tag{1}$$

Here $\hat{y}_{ij}$ is the expected value of the dependent variable of the individual i living in the area j and having the value x_{ij} of the independent variable; $\bar{x}_j$ is the average of the independent variable in the area j and a, b_1, and b_2 are constants.[13] If y is modernity of farming practices, the

[9] See, e.g., David L. Sills, "Three 'Climate of Opinion' Studies," *Public Opinion Quarterly, 25* (1961), pp. 571–573, and Riley, *op. cit.* Riley considers contextual analysis as a partial form of a more general approach which he calls social system analysis.

[10] Peter M. Blau, "Structural Effects," *American Sociological Review, 25* (1960), pp. 178–193, and Arnold S. Tannenbaum and Jerald G. Bachman, "Structural versus Individual Effects," *American Journal of Sociology, 69* (1964), pp. 585–595.

[11] James A. Davis, Joe L. Spaeth, and Carolyn Huson, "A Technique for Analyzing the Effects of Group Composition," *American Sociological Review, 26* (1961), pp. 215–225.

[12] *Ibid.,* pp. 218–222.

[13] Davis, Spaeth, and Huson do not use regression models in this way when representing their models; Tannenbaum and Bachman, *op. cit.,* p. 591, suggest multiple-regression technique as a method of analysis.

individual-level variance of it in the whole population would be explained, according to the model, by the education of the individuals ($b_2 \neq 0$) and, additionally, by the average education in the areas ($b_1 \neq 0$). If b_1 and b_2 have the same sign, as seems natural, both individual-level education and ecological-level education have an effect in the same direction. If b_1 and b_2 have different signs, the variables on the two levels have opposite effects. Davis, Spaeth, and Huson[14] give an example of this seemingly improbable situation.

In addition to the complete models already mentioned, the equation can describe three incomplete models corresponding to three types of effects dealt with by Davis, Spaeth, and Huson: if $b_1 = 0$ and $b_2 = 0$, there is no nonrandom effect at all; if $b_1 = 0$ while $b_2 \neq 0$, there is only an individual-level effect, and if $b_1 \neq 0$ and $b_2 = 0$, there is only a compositional effect. In the last case, education would affect the behavior of individuals only through the average education of the areas.

As was the case with the reflections of individual-level relationships, it is probably unrealistic to assume that just one variable would have a compositional effect on the behavior under study. Therefore, several independent variables must again be taken into account. Some of them may have effects at both the ecological and the individual level, and some at only one or the other.

A model in which the ecological variable, instead of having a direct effect on the dependent variable, has an effect on the relationship between the independent and the dependent variable can be represented formally as follows:

$$\begin{aligned} \hat{y}_{ij} &= a + b_j x_{ij} \\ b_j &= c + d\bar{x}_j \end{aligned} \tag{2}$$

The individual-level slopes of regression of y on x are not equal in all areas, as was assumed in the preceding case. The steepness of the slope is now a linear function of the area averages of the independent variable. If, for example, d were negative, the education of a farmer would not have as strong an effect on his modernity in an area of high average education as in an area of low average education. The most usual case of this kind of interaction is probably "weak" interaction, where the sign of the slope remains the same in all areas. It is possible, however, that the slope is near to zero at either end of the ecological variable or that it actually has different signs within different areas.[15]

[14] Davis et al., op. cit., p. 220.
[15] These types of effects are dealt with in ibid., pp. 217–221.

In the model represented by Equations 2, the variable affecting the slope b_j is the ecological counterpart of the variable that explains y at the individual level. Other ecological variables, too, can have effects on the slope. In addition, the strengths of the effects of a number of individual-level variables may be functions of contextual variables.

It has been assumed, up to this point, that all effects are linear. A large number of new models can be formed if nonlinear relationships are allowed. Davis, Spaeth, and Huson mention some examples, in which the effects of group-level variables on individual-level variables are nonlinear, and it is easy to construct other types of nonlinear models.

In all the preceding cases the ecological variables have been measured analytically and thus have a counterpart at the individual level. The situation does not change formally if the ecological variables are global measures. A global variable can also, for example, have an effect either on the individual-level variable or on the relationships between individual-level variables. In the discussion of structural or compositional effects, only analytical group-level variables are usually considered. This is apparently due to the fact that only the existence of the same variables on both levels has posed special problems of analysis. The distinction between analytical and global variables may be, however, useful for the interpretation of the results.

The effects have been introduced here by means of regression models explaining the behavior of individuals only formally, without discussing the sociological processes giving rise to the effects. Knowledge of these processes is important for ecological research. When the models are complex and include nonlinear effects and interactions, it may, however, be very difficult to discover the processes. Only the simplest models will be examined next from this point of view.

SOCIOLOGICAL INTERPRETATIONS OF STRUCTURAL EFFECTS

Let us consider the simplest structural effect mentioned before, namely $\hat{y}_{ij} = a + b_1\bar{x}_j + b_2x_{ij}$, where b_1 and b_2 have same signs. One process that can give rise to this effect is the following: in the areas where the average education of individuals is high, the value system and norms are more modern than in the areas of low average education, and the value system and norms have an effect on the behavior of individuals independent of their own education. Similarly, in areas where workers are in the majority, a "political climate" favoring leftist voting may exist. Concepts like value systems, norms, or climates describe areas as wholes and are "conceptually global" properties of areas. It is not meaningful to speak of value systems or norms if they exist only internalized by individuals. In this kind of explanation an analytical measure is thus used to measure a conceptually global property.[16]

The existence of structural effect can be interpreted in another way, too. Campbell and Alexander give an example of it.[17] In studies of high-school students, a structural effect has been found: the larger the proportion of middle-class students in a high school, the greater the likelihood that students of a given socioeconomic stratum have high educational aspirations. This result can now be interpreted by means of differing value systems in the schools: the average socioeconomic status of its students determines the value system of a school, and the students orient themselves toward the expectations constituted by the school-wide value system. Campbell and Alexander, however, show that the structural effect can be explained without using variables that characterize the whole collectivity. They assume a two-step causal process. The first step is based on the social-psychological theory presented, for example, by Festinger and Homans, according to which persons feeling attraction to one another are likely to become similar in their values and behavior. As the second step of the explanation it is assumed that in every school the friendship relations of the individuals are distributed randomly, without regard to socioeconomic status. The friends of students in schools having high average socioeconomic status are then, on the average, from higher strata than the friends of students in other schools. As friends are likely, because of the social-psychological process mentioned before, to become similar to each other, it follows that the average socioeconomic status of the school has an effect independent of the properties of the individuals. When in the empirical study by Campbell and Alexander the average socioeconomic status of the two closest friends of high-school students was controlled, the differences in the socioeconomic status of schools no longer explained the differences in educational aspirations of the students. The status of friends was, on the other hand, clearly related to the status of the school.[18]

The article by Campbell and Alexander has been quoted rather

---

[16] Tannenbaum and Bachman, *op. cit.*, p. 594, emphasize this distinction using the terms "structural concept" and "structural measure."

[17] Ernest Q. Campbell and C. Norman Alexander, "Structural Effects and Interpersonal Relationships," *American Journal of Sociology, 71* (1965), pp. 284–289.

[18] *Ibid.*, p. 287.

extensively, because the "contagion" or learning effect[19] it deals with seems to be highly relevant to research using areal units. People living near each other have many contacts and mutual friendship relations. Similarity of behavior and attitudes is to be expected as a result. It can be assumed that some learning or contagion will take place without special attractions between people, if only because of daily interaction. If the contagion process is usual, as seems likely, a structural effect caused by interaction and friendship relations will always be found when the ecological variance of a variable having an individual-level effect is not small.

A consequence of the contagion model with several independent individual-level variables can be stated as follows: If there are data on the composition of areas by individual-level variables and on the relationships among the variables at the individual level, it is possible to calculate, assuming no structural effects, the expected ecological value of the dependent variable in each area. The slope of regression of the observed ecological values on the expected values is then greater than one. The observed values thus are greater than the expected ones in areas where the expected values are above the average of all areas, and lower in areas where the expected values are below the average.[20]

Although it is conceptually possible to make the distinction between the effects of value systems and the effects of interpersonal contacts, it is in practice difficult to draw firm conclusions about them, if there are no independent data on the system-wide values and norms.[21] It is possible, too, to think of a third type of effect associated with the composition of the collectives. This effect is more clearly "global" than the others. For example, the high average education of farmers in an area might result in farmers' organizations and co-operatives being strong and active and farmers with low education also adopting new methods. In a similar way, in areas where the proportion of workers is high, the local organization of leftist parties may be stronger than in other areas. As it is not usually so difficult to get data on a certain kind of organized activity as on prevailing values or norms, a study of this type of variable might give interesting results.

Besides effects associated with the composition of the areas there are

[19] James S. Coleman, in his *Introduction to Mathematical Sociology* (Glencoe: Free Press, 1964), constructs some mathematical models describing processes related to this kind of effect and labels them with the term "contagious processes."

[20] Duncan *et al., op. cit.,* pp. 99–128, give an empirical example of this case.

[21] Cf. Campbell and Alexander, *op. cit.,* pp. 109–111.

"pure" global effects. These kinds of effects are interesting and important, especially for practical applications of sociological knowledge, like
planning purposes. If changes in the circumstances in certain areas are
desired, global properties of the areas are usually changed first: new
administrative organizations, local chapters of associations, schools,
and factories are founded. These global property changes then change
the analytical properties of the areas. On the other hand, if one wants to
know how the areal differences in the activities of an agricultural
extension organization affect farming practices, one must control for
the areal differences caused by composition and the effects associated
with it.

THE NATURE OF AREAL UNITS AS ANALYTICAL UNITS

When dealing with structural effects, as has been done here, no
strict distinction is made between "natural" social systems (schools,
associations, etc.) and areal units. From the point of view of ecological
research, it is important to know in what ways these two situations
differ from each other. A difference between areal units and other
types of collectives used in contextual analysis seems to be that areal
units are, as a rule, "modifiable units": a set of areas is not the only
possible one, but the aggregates can also be constructed in other ways.
In typical contextual analysis, the units can be defined more clearly.
What is then the significance of the modifiability of the units for the
effects dealt with in this paper? If the ecological variance of the dependent variable can be explained by merely individual-level relationships,
or, in other words, if the properties of areal units have no effect,
the same results are obtained whatever units are used, assuming,
of course, that the independent variable has some ecological
variance. Be the units smaller or larger administrative areas or
even arbitrarily limited squares of a map, the individual-level slope
of the population as a whole is equal to those calculated within
every area and, additionally, to the ecological slope. The difference
between the ecological correlation and the individual correlation is a
function of the sizes of the areas and the ecological variance of the
independent variable: the larger the areas and the larger the ecological
variance, the higher the ecological correlation as compared with the
individual correlation.

The question of appropriate areal units is more complex when one
is dealing with contagion effects. It seems likely that these effects become

most apparent when one uses units within which the populations are completely intermixed, that is, when contacts and friendship relations are random, at least in regard to the phenomena under study.[23] In the example given by Campbell and Alexander, the units are schools, and there the assumption of random interaction probably is approximately valid. In ecological research the interaction areas of different individuals are not the same but overlapping. One can imagine that in a rural area, where the population is concentrated in small villages isolated from one another, each village might be an area within which the majority of the interaction of the inhabitants would take place. Usually, however, areal units are considerably larger than the areas of interaction of individuals. In addition, the contacts of individuals are not distributed randomly among the people living in the ecological unit, and the contacts are not limited to those living in the same unit. It is thus difficult to say how the manifestations of the contagion effect vary when different kinds of areal units are used. The effect is probably rather clear when most of the interaction of the individuals takes place within their own areas and the areas are small.

When dealing with global effects, the areal units that are most relevant are those to which the global phenomena in question apply. If the effects of properties of communal administration on political behavior are studied, there are no alternatives in choosing the analytical unit. The question of the "best" or "natural" unit of an ecological study can thus be illuminated by examining what types of units have relevant global properties. Sometimes there may be global properties at more than one level.[24]

The question of global properties is made more complex by the nonsociological differences among areas. In a way, practically all types of areas have global properties associated with, for example, geographic and climatic factors. Although these properties are not sociological, they seem to explain many of the sociological differences of the areas. Differences caused by nonsociological factors are often accepted as given, and only the relationships among sociological variables are studied. This may sometimes be fallacious, because nonsociological factors can give rise to spurious correlations between sociological variables.

---

[23] In most of the contagious processes presented by Coleman, *op. cit.,* Chaps. 10 and 11, an analogous assumption is made.

[24] Cf. Lazarsfeld and Menzel, *op. cit.,* p. 425.

STRUCTURAL EFFECTS WITH INDIVIDUAL AND
AGGREGATE DATA

In contextual analysis, as a rule, data from both the individual and the group level can be used. In ecological research, on the contrary, the most usual type of data are aggregate data — a fact which changes the basic situation. Some analytical problems will be examined here, first in studies with data from both levels and then in studies with only aggregate data.

To isolate structural effects, Blau used a technique[25] that can be presented by the following example. To find out if education has, besides an individual effect, a structural effect on farmers' modernity, the areas studied are divided into two subgroups: those of high average education and those of low average education. Within these subgroups the individuals in their turn are divided into two groups according to their education. If individuals with low education are more modern in areas of high average education than similar individuals in areas of low average education and if the same thing holds true for individuals with high education, a kind of structural effect has been found, according to Blau. The technique presented by Davis, Spaeth, and Huson is based on the same principle, but the areas are divided into more than two subgroups.[26]

Tannenbaum and Bachman show, however, that both Blau's technique and the technique of Davis, Spaeth, and Huson are incorrect, and at least some of the structural effects observed are probably not genuine. The error is caused by the fact that if two classes are used when dividing individuals into subgroups, although the independent variable is not really dichotomous (like sex) but quantitative (like education), the properties of individuals are not controlled strictly enough.[27]

Several partial solutions to this problem have been proposed by Tannenbaum and Bachman. Some are based on the use of more exact classifications and some on correlational methods. One of the correlational methods is multiple-regression analysis,[28] which in this paper has been used to formalize the models. In it, the variance of the individual-level dependent variable is explained by independent variables, some of which are properties of individuals and others analytical or

[25] Blau, *op. cit.*

[26] Davies *et al., op. cit.*

[27] Tannenbaum and Bachman, *op. cit.*, pp. 585–588.

[28] *Ibid.*, p. 591, Goodman, *op. cit.*, Duncan *et al., op. cit.*, and Boudon, *op. cit.*, use multiple-regression analysis in studies with aggregate data in a related way.

global contextual variables measuring properties of the areas. As the slopes in multiple-regression analysis are in a way analogous to partial correlations, the existence of structural effects is shown if the slopes of contextual variables differ from zero. When using this technique or others based on correlations, one must make sure that all the effects are approximately additive and linear. If they are not, more complex models can be applied.

Compared to cross tabulation, correlational methods have several advantages: data can be used more effectively so that more independent variables can be taken into account at the same time, the fallacy shown by Tannenbaum and Bachman is avoided, and, relevant to the topic of this paper, the models and results will be more easily comparable to those of ecological analysis using aggregate data. The dichotomous or qualitative nature of some of the variables is not an insurmountable obstacle to the use of correlational methods, as such variables can be taken into the analysis as "dummy" variables.[29] If one is content to make inferences without the aid of exact statistical tests, assumptions about the distributions of variables are not necessary.

When isolating structural effects there is a difficulty analogous to the one shown by Tannenbaum and Bachman which cannot, however, be solved by merely adopting a correlational technique. If one would observe, for example, that the larger the proportion of workers in an area, the larger the percentage of both workers and the other inhabitants voting for leftist parties, he might have found a true structural effect. It is as likely, however, that workers living in middle-class areas are wealthier and more similar to middle-class people in other ways than workers living in working-class areas. Middle-class people living in poor areas are likely to differ from those living in rich areas in an analogous way. To separate a genuine structural effect from this kind of spurious effect, the classification of occupations must contain more than two classes, or there must be a control variable, such as income.

Another cause of spurious structural effects may sometimes be selective migration.[30] If the same structural effect as that given before is observed, one explanation would be that people with conservative sympathies, whatever their social class, do not feel at home in working-class areas and are more apt to move to other areas. This kind of

---

[29] See, e.g., Hayward R. Alker, Jr., *Mathematics and Politics* (New York: Macmillan, 1965), 80–88.

[30] Cf. Tannenbaum and Bachman, *op. cit.,* p. 593. Scheuch, *op. cit.,* p. 155, also gives an example of the possible fallacy caused by selection.

phenomenon may be general, especially in areas where migration is considerable. These cases are interesting in their own right, but they are not similar to the structural effects proper.

Selvin and Hagstrom try to solve another problem of contextual analysis.[31] This problem is caused by the confounding of the effects of variables correlated with each other. In nonexperimental research the collectives cannot be manipulated in a way that allows the study of the effects of one collective property controlling for the others. As the number of collectives is often small, it is difficult to carry out the cross tabulations needed to separate the effects. The solution proposed by Selvin and Hagstrom is the use of factor analysis. Using it and taking collectives as observations, they reduce the number of variables to a few (in the example, to five). Selvin and Hagstrom take into factor analysis only analytical or, in their terminology, aggregative measures. Global measures could probably also be included. Selvin and Hagstrom make use of the results of factor analysis to classify collectives by means of factor scores into four subgroups, which are then used in contextual analysis. A more effective way seems to be to use the factor scores of collectives as contextual properties of individuals and then to use correlational techniques. If an orthogonal rotation is applied, the factor scores will be relatively uncorrelated with each other. This makes it easier to separate the effects of the factors. Instead of factor scores, a set of the original variables could be used to characterize the collectives. A variable that has a high loading on the factor and is meaningful in other ways is chosen to represent each factor. This makes the analysis less cumbersome and less abstract.

Like most other sociological research, multiple-level analysis is usually based on nonexperimental research design. It is therefore exposed to all the usual sources of errors due to difficulties in determining the direction of causal relationships and in controlling for all relevant factors. The multiple-level approach, however, makes it easier to avoid two kinds of fallacies of a more theoretical nature, which Riley calls "psychologistic fallacies" and "sociologistic fallacies." A psychologistic fallacy is committed if the researcher, when explaining individual behavior, looks only at the facts about each separate individual, disregarding factors such as the character of the community context. The danger of a sociologistic fallacy is present if the individual-level processes are disregarded when one is interpreting relationships

[31] Hanan C. Selvin and Warren O. Hagstrom, "The Empirical Classification of Formal Groups," *American Sociological Review, 28* (1963), pp. 399–411.

between variables describing collectives.[32] These fallacies are not necessarily due to the use of a certain type of data but are rather associated with the researcher's theoretical frame of reference. Although working with aggregate data, one can at least try to have regard for individual- and collective-level relationships, as well as for the relationships between collective and individual variables.

PROBLEMS OF ANALYSIS USING ONLY AGGREGATE DATA

All the technical pitfalls dealt with previously are, of course, still present when one has to be content with aggregate data, as is usually the case in ecological research. In addition to them, there are then the special difficulties caused by a lack of information about individual-level relationships. The best-known fallacy associated with the use of aggregate data is the so-called ecological or aggregative fallacy.[33] Since the article by Robinson and the discussion following it, this naïve assumption, according to which the ecological correlation as such could be used as an approximation of the individual correlation, is no longer likely to be made. A more sophisticated version of this fallacy is committed, however, if the ecological slope and the individual slope or their analogies are incorrectly supposed to be equal.

Eight types of possible fallacies have been defined by Alker by means of the covariance theorem dividing the total individual covariance into within-subgroup and between-subgroup covariances.[34] Some of the fallacies are especially relevant to research using aggregate data. One is, of course, the usual ecological fallacy; of the others the most important one is perhaps the "contextual fallacy," in which the individual relationship is incorrectly assumed to be equal in all areas.

It is easy to see that the types of fallacies mentioned by Alker are not the only possible ones, if it is taken into consideration how insufficient

[32] Riley, op. cit., pp. 707–709. Scheuch, op. cit., p. 158, uses the term "individual-istic fallacy" meaning "the negation of the usefulness of an explanation that treats the collectivity as collectivity," which is closely related to the idea of psychologistic fallacy. His "group fallacy" is much like the sociologistic fallacy, although he puts more emphasis on the nature of data making the group fallacy a generalization of the ecological fallacy.

[33] See, e.g., William S. Robinson, "Ecological Correlations and the Behavior of Individuals," American Sociological Review, 15 (1950), pp. 351–357, and Riley, op. cit., pp. 704–706.

[34] Alker, op. cit., pp. 102–106. It seems that it might be more appropriate to define the fallacies in terms of slopes instead of covariances as "it is the regression coefficients which give us the laws of science" (Blalock, op. cit., p. 51).

aggregate data are for describing complex ecological phenomena. Some authors have, however, made attempts at developing methods to draw conclusions and to avoid the pitfalls. Goodman has presented some techniques for estimating individual correlations on the basis of ecological data, using both qualitative and quantitative variables.[35] In most of the models treated by him, it is assumed that the ecological relationship is only a reflection of an individual-level relationship, in which case the ecological slope can be used as an estimate of the individual slope. Boudon has dealt with the same types of problems, also examining models containing structural effects. Boudon presents further a general strategy for making inferences on the basis of aggregate ecological data.[36] These important techniques are not treated here in detail; but some comments will be made.

Boudon examines the shapes of the models to determine whether the ecological regression of the dependent variable on the independent variable is linear or nonlinear and divides them accordingly. If the regression is linear and certain other conditions are met, it is inferred that no contextual effects are present and the ecological correlation is merely a reflection of the individual correlation. It seems, however, that the conditions presented in addition to linearity are not always sufficient to separate all kinds of structural effects from the assumed reflection of an individual correlation.

One way of making erroneous inferences from the linearity of an ecological regression is associated with the direct structural effect (type III effect by Davis, Spaeth, and Huson), which does not influence the regression between individual variables and does not cause statistical interaction. This model has been presented as follows (see Equation 1):

$$\hat{y}_{ij} = a + b_1\bar{x}_j + b_2x_{ij}$$

When the areal averages are calculated, the following equation is arrived at:

$$\hat{\bar{y}}_j = a + b_1\bar{x}_j + b_2\bar{x}_j$$

or

$$\hat{\bar{y}}_j = a + (b_1 + b_2)\,\bar{x}_j$$

It can be seen that the ecological regression is linear but the slope is steeper than the individual slope (assuming that b_1 and b_2 have same

[35] Goodman, *op. cit.*, and "Ecological Regression and Behavior of Individuals," *American Sociological Review, 18* (1963. pp. 663–664. The discussion by Duncan *et al., op. cit.*, pp. 68–80, is based largely on these papers by Goodman.
[36] Boudon, *op. cit.*

signs). Without additional assumptions it is not possible to estimate the relative strengths of individual and structural effects.[37] It is sometimes possible in these cases to demonstrate the existence of a structural effect, as by means of the additional criteria mentioned by Boudon, but the problem may not be easy to solve in a general way.

Boudon presents a model with dichotomous variables (model B) with a structural effect almost similar to the one just treated.[38] In his model, the ecological regression, however, is not linear. This is caused by the fact that Boudon uses two parameters to describe the structural effect. One of them can be interpreted as showing a direct structural effect analogous to b_1 already given, and the other showing an interactive effect: the within-area individual slope is thus assumed to be a function of the composition of the areas. This model may often be more realistic than the model with one parameter describing the contextual effect. The latter should be, however, fitted first because it is simpler.

There are so many sources of errors in aggregate analysis that it is very difficult to make inferences correctly using just one type of analysis. It thus seems necessary to use flexibly various methods and the partial controls given by the authors mentioned earlier. New kinds of controls should also be developed. The areas can be, for example, divided into subgroups, within which separate analyses are made. In addition to grouping by proximity, as proposed by Goodman and Boudon, other criteria like size and density of population seem relevant.

It is important for ecological reasearch that our knowledge of the general multiple-level analysis and of the special nature of areal units as collectives increase. Methods and principles appropriate for ecological research are perhaps not developed in the best way by traditional research using only aggregate data. In studies with systematic data from both the individual and ecological level, for example, the nature of contextual effects and their generality could be examined.[39] The problems and costs of data collection are, of course, much greater for this kind of research. However, the trouble is worthwhile, because no other way of developing and, especially, of testing methods of aggregate ecological analysis seems as effective.

---

[37] Cf. Goodman, "Some Alternatives to Ecological Correlation," *op. cit.*, p. 623.

[38] Boudon, *op. cit.*, pp. 293–295.

[39] Scheuch, *op. cit.*, pp. 164–167, also recommends the combination of individual measurements and aggregate data.

4

HAYWARD R. ALKER, JR.

A Typology of
Ecological Fallacies

MANY YEARS have passed since W. S. Robinson startled, dismayed, and even infuriated many users of ecological data with his demonstration and "proof" that statistical associations for aggregated populations might differ in magnitude and even in sign from those for individual population members.[1] Now we are more clearly aware of the inferential limitations and the conceptual advantages of ecological data, and alternative ways of using such data to infer individual behavior have become available. But if it is a measure of Robinson's success that his findings have now become methodologically commonplace or even passé, his original article is still worth reading — largely because of his incisive and exemplary use of simple statistical tools objectively to illuminate value-laden political discourse.

Starting with Robinson's well-known interpretations of the covariance theorem, can we find other inferential fallacies equally tempting to hasty researchers? Might not other statistical tautologies be similarly subject to methodologically and substantively relevant interpretations? It is this path of generalizing on Robinson's procedure that I should like to take, seeking also to follow up the more negative implications

---

[1] "Ecological Correlations and the Behavior of Individuals," *American Sociological Review*, *15* (1950), pp. 351–357. More recent reactions or extensions are discussed in Leo A. Goodman, "Some Alternatives to Ecological Correlation," *American Journal of Sociology*, *64* (1959), pp. 610–625; O. D. Duncan, R. P. Cuzzort, and B. Duncan, *Statistical Geography*: *Problems in Analyzing Areal Data* (Glencoe: Free Press, 1961); and Raymond Boudon, "Propriétés individuelles et propriétés collectives: un problème d'analyse ecologique," *Revue française de sociologie*, *4* (1963), pp. 275–299.

of a typology of ecological falacies with some more positive thoughts on how to explore the very questions that we sometimes try too immoderately to answer. For if we really know that certain ecological associations are false or misleading or spurious, then logically we need only to rearrange our knowledge in order to discover the direction in which truth might be found.

SOME STATISTICAL PRELIMINARIES

Mathematical reasoning can only add empty, tautological form to the content of our arguments. Nevertheless, the clarity, the certainty, the abstract generality, and the potential for complexity of such a form of expression often lead to, or help convey, surprising and worthwhile discoveries.

In order to discuss a variety of potentially fallacious ecological inferences, I find it convenient to use several versions of the well-known covariance theorem of elementary statistics. From a mathematical point of view, once notational conventions are established, these theorems combine an elegance of form with a simplicity of derivation. Empirically, they suggest and help us to organize our thinking about a whole range of obvious and not-so-obvious relationships among statistical associations defined at different levels of analysis.

Notationally, let us direct our discussion to variables, such as X, Y, and Z, defined for a universe of N "units." Exhaustive subsets of these units with sizes N_r, form various disjoint "regions" r, of which there are a total of R ($r = 1, 2, \ldots, R$). Each observation X_{ir}, Y_{ir}, etc., on unit i in region r will be assumed to occur at time t; usually observations will be considered available for every one of T different (and consecutive) times. Because the "units" involved may already reflect considerable aggregation, we have at least definitionally avoided calling a "unit" an "individual." Nonetheless, it will now be our frequent practice to describe X_{irt} as the X value in year t for individual i belonging to regional collectivity r.[2]

Various averages, taken over individuals, regions, or times can easily be defined. Using the "dot" notation to represent such averages, we

---

[2] More generally, if time units were to be broken down into periods in the same way as individuals, the notation X_{irtp} might be used to indicate the X value of unit i in region r at time t in period p. Despite persuasive arguments by Karl Deutsch as to the generalizability of this approach, I have here refrained from such an elaboration. Both he and Duncan MacRae are to be thanked, however, for their efforts in improving the symbolic notations used throughout the present paper.

can summarize formulas for $X_{\cdot rt}$, $X_{\cdot \cdot t}$, $X_{i\cdot}$, and $X_{\cdot \cdot}$ in rows A1 through A6 of Table 1.

Table 1

STATISTICAL ELEMENTS OF COVARIANCE THEOREMS

Symbol	Definitional Formula	Interpretation
(A1) X_{irt}, Y_{irt}	$(i = 1, \ldots, N; r = 1, \ldots, R;$ $N_1 + \ldots + N_r + \ldots + N_R = N;$ $t = 1, 2, \ldots, T)$	The value of variable X (or Y) at time t for unit i belonging to region r
(A2) $X_{\cdot rt}$	$\dfrac{1}{N_r} \sum\limits_{i \in r}^{N_r} X_{irt}$ Where N_r is the number of units i in region r	The average value of X at time t for all N_r units i belonging to region r
(A3) $X_{\cdot \cdot t}$	$\dfrac{1}{N} \sum\limits_{i=1}^{N} X_{irt}$	The average value of X at time t for all N units
(A4) $X_{i\cdot}$	$\dfrac{1}{T} \sum\limits_{t=1}^{T} X_{irt}$	The average value of X for all times t of a particular unit i
(A5) $X_{\cdot r\cdot}$	$\dfrac{1}{TN_r} \sum\limits_{t=1}^{T} \sum\limits_{i \in r}^{Nr} X_{irt}$	The average value of X for all units i belonging to region r and all times t
(A6) $X_{\cdot\cdot}$	$\dfrac{1}{TN} \sum\limits_{t=1}^{T} \sum\limits_{i=1}^{N} X_{irt}$	The average value of X for all units i and times t

Formulas exactly parallel to A2 through A6 old for $Y_{\cdot rt}$, $Y_{\cdot t}$, $Y_{i\cdot}$, $Y_{\cdot r\cdot}$, and $Y_{\cdot\cdot}$.

(B1) $C_{XY;t}$	$\dfrac{1}{N} \sum\limits_{i=1}^{N} (X_{irt} - X_{\cdot t})(Y_{irt} - Y_{\cdot t})$	The universal variance of X and Y for all units i (at time t)
(B2) C_{XY}	$\dfrac{1}{TN} \sum\limits_{t=1}^{T} \sum\limits_{i=1}^{N} (X_{irt} - X_{\cdot\cdot})(Y_{irt} - Y_{\cdot\cdot})$	The universal covariance of X and Y for all i and all t
(B3) $C_{XX;t}$	$\dfrac{1}{N} \sum\limits_{i=1}^{N} (X_{irt} - X_{\cdot t})^2$	The universal variance of X for all units i (at time t)

(A similar expression, with double sums and deviations about $X_{\cdot\cdot}$, gives C_{XX})

Table 1—continued

Symbol	Definitional Formula	Interpretation
(B4) $WC_{XY;t}$	$\dfrac{1}{N} \sum\limits_{i=1}^{N} (X_{irt} - X_{\cdot rt})(Y_{irt} - Y_{\cdot rt})$	The within-region co-variance of X and Y (at time t)

(Similarly, with double sums, etc., we can define WC_{XY})

(B5) $C_{XYr;t}$	$\dfrac{1}{N_r} \sum\limits_{i \in r} (X_{irt} - X_{\cdot rt})(Y_{irt} - Y_{\cdot rt})$	The covariance of X and Y within a particular region r (at time t)
(B6) $EC_{XY;t}$	$\dfrac{1}{N} \sum\limits_{i=1}^{N} (X_{\cdot rt} - X_{\cdot\cdot t})(Y_{\cdot rt} - Y_{\cdot\cdot t})$	The between-region or "ecological" covariance of X and Y (at time t)

(Similarly, we may define, EC_{XY})

(B7) TC_{XY}	$\dfrac{1}{TN} \sum\limits_{t=1}^{T} \sum\limits_{i=1}^{N} (X_{\cdot\cdot t} - X_{\cdot\cdot\cdot})(Y_{\cdot\cdot t} - Y_{\cdot\cdot\cdot})$	The between-times or "trend" covariance or X and Y
(B8) $WC_{XX;t}$	$\dfrac{1}{N} \sum\limits_{i=1}^{N} (X_{irt} - X_{\cdot rt})^2$	The "within-region" variance of X (at time t)

(Similarly, with double sums and deviations about $X. r.$ define WC_{XX})

(B9) $EC_{XX;t}$	$\dfrac{1}{N} \sum\limits_{i=1}^{N} (X_{\cdot rt} - X_{\cdot t})^2$	The between-regions or "ecological" variance of X (at time t)

(Similarly, define EC_{XX})

Formulas analogous to B3, B8, and B9 hold for $C_{YY;i}$, $WC_{YY;\,t}$, $EC_{YY;\,t}$, and C_{YY}, WC_{YY}, EC_{YY}.

(C1) $E^2_{XR;t}$	$\dfrac{EC_{XX,t}}{C_{XX;t}}$	The correlation ratio of X and R (at time t)
(C2) $E^2_{YR;t}$	$\dfrac{EC_{YY;t}}{C_{YY;t}}$	The correlation ratio of Y and R (at time t)
(D1) $R_{XY;t}$	$\dfrac{C_{XY;t}}{\sqrt{C_{XX;t}} \ \sqrt{C_{YY;t}}}$	The universal correlation of X and Y (at time t)
(D2) $WR_{XY;t}$	$\dfrac{WC_{XY;t}}{\sqrt{WC_{XX;t}} \ \sqrt{WC_{XY;t}}}$	The within-region correlation of X and Y (at time t)

Table 1—continued

Symbol	Definitional Formula	Interpretation
(D3) $ER_{XY;t}$	$\dfrac{EC_{XY;t}}{\sqrt{EC_{XX;t}}\ \sqrt{EC_{YY;t}}}$	The between-region or "ecological" correlation of X and Y (at time t)

After time-averaging, formulas D1 through D3 give R_{XY}, WR_{XY}, or ER_{XY}.

To generate covariance theorems, we need only to define and algebraically to manipulate several simple tautologies. Which tautologies we choose depends, of course, on the kinds of relationships we are interested in studying. In particular, the expression

$$(X_{irt} - X_{\cdot t}) = (X_{irt} - X_{\cdot rt}) + (X_{\cdot rt} - X_{\cdot t}) \tag{1}$$

or its slightly more complex version,

$$(X_{irt} - X_{\cdot\cdot}) = (X_{irt} - X_{\cdot rt}) + (X_{\cdot rt} - X_{\cdot t}) + (X_{\cdot t} - X_{\cdot\cdot}) \tag{2}$$

gives us a suggestive time-specific "decomposition" of the moment of X_{irt} in terms of within-region, across-region, and universal deviations in X.[3]

An attractive property of Equations 1 and 2 is that summing them over t gives a simple and meaningful result:

$$(X_{i\cdot} - X_{\cdot\cdot}) = (X_{i\cdot} - X_{\cdot r\cdot}) + (X_{\cdot r\cdot} - X_{\cdot\cdot}) \tag{3}$$

In more familiar form, ignoring time, this becomes

$$(X_i - X_{\cdot}) = (X_i - X_{\cdot r}) + (X_{\cdot r} - X_{\cdot}) \tag{3a}$$

[3] Although most of the ecological studies we shall cite use the conceptual distinctions suggested by Equations 1 and 2, these Equations do restrict our modeling possibilities by omitting differences like $X_{irt} - X_{i\cdot}$, $X_{\cdot rt} - X_{\cdot r}$, $X_{\cdot r\cdot} - X_{\cdot\cdot}$, and $X_{i\cdot} - X_{\cdot\cdot}$. MacRae and Meldrum, however, have used the first of these expressions in their investigation of critical election deviations in Democratic voting. Thus, the tautology, somewhat like Equation 2,

$$(X_{it} - X_{\cdot\cdot}) = (X_{it} - X_{i\cdot}) + (X_{i\cdot} - X_{\cdot t}) + (X_{\cdot t} - X_{\cdot\cdot})$$

can be used to define a residual deviation RX that they subject to direct principal component analysis:

$$RX_{it} = (X_{it} - X_{i\cdot}) - (X_{\cdot t} - X_{\cdot\cdot})$$

The second term, in effect, sums over i in the first parentheses, so that the result controls for both individual and temporal averages. See D. MacRae, Jr., and J. A. Meldrum, "Critical Elections in Illinois: 1888–1958," *American Political Science Review*, 54 (1960), pp. 669–683.

Again we see how an over-all deviation can be decomposed into an individual one and a regional one.[4]

Covariances are average products of the deviations in two variables about their means. In various ways the preceding tautologies can be multiplied by an equivalent equation in Y, averaged, and simplified, to give a relationship among covariances of the expressions in parentheses. Options include whether to average over i or t or both, and the choice of initial tautology (see expressions B1 through B9 in Table 1). Simplifications of an algebraic and conceptual sort are possible, largely because so many of the parenthetical expressions have means of zero.

The first such covariance theorem we shall present derives from

---

[4] In fact, subtracting Equation 3 from 1 and rearranging the result gives a more complex tautology:

$$(X_{irt} - X_{i\cdot\cdot}) = [(X_{irt} - X_{\cdot rt}) - (X_{i\cdot\cdot} - X_{\cdot r\cdot})] + [(X_{\cdot rt} - X_{\cdot\cdot t}) - (X_{\cdot r\cdot} - X_{\cdot\cdot\cdot})]$$
$$\text{total trend} \qquad\quad \text{individual trend} \qquad\qquad\quad \text{regional trend} \qquad (4)$$
$$+ [(X_{\cdot\cdot t}) - (X_{\cdot\cdot\cdot})]$$
$$\text{universal trend}$$

Starting from the right, notice how each of the terms in this expression subtracts "constant" or "timeless" deviations from universal, regional, and individual time-specific ones. The resulting terms associated with each of these three different levels of analysis we have called "trend "components.

Further rearrangements are also possible. In a fascinating paper on the locus of political "left-right" and turnout phenomena, Donald Stokes has described such data in terms of variable and constant national, state, and (Congressional) district effects. To derive his model, first note in Equation 4 that summing the three signed "constant" expressions in the second set of parentheses in each square bracket gives $-X_{i\cdot\cdot}$, which also appears as the second term in the leftmost expression. (Stokes calls these three "constant" or "timeless" expressions A_i, B_i, C_i, respectively.) Expanding the $-X_{i\cdot\cdot}$ on the left as $-\alpha - \beta - \gamma$ and moving it to the right of the equals sign would indicate that X_{irt} equaled the sum of the three "trend" components already there *plus* three new "timeless" ones ($\alpha + \beta + \gamma$). Second, one might want to rewrite each of the trend expressions so that each pair of parentheses contained both temporal and timeless terms. Stokes symbolizes the resulting national, state, and district effects as A_t, B_t, and C_t:

$$A_t = (X_{\cdot\cdot t} - X_{\cdot\cdot\cdot})$$
$$B_t = (X_{\cdot rt} - X_{\cdot r\cdot}) - (X_{\cdot\cdot t} - X_{\cdot\cdot\cdot})$$
$$C_t = (X_{irt} - X_{i\cdot\cdot}) - (X_{\cdot rt} - X_{\cdot r\cdot})$$

Thus Equation 4 is equivalent to an even more complex tautology:

$$X_{irt} = \quad \alpha \quad + \quad \beta \quad + \quad \gamma \quad + \quad A_t \quad + \quad B_t \quad + \quad C_t \qquad (5)$$
$$\quad\;\; \text{national} \quad \text{state} \quad \text{district} \quad \text{national} \quad \text{state} \quad \text{district}$$
$$\quad\;\; \text{effect} \qquad \text{effect} \quad \text{effect} \qquad \text{effect} \qquad \text{effect} \quad \text{effect}$$
$$\underbrace{\qquad\qquad\qquad\qquad\qquad} \qquad \underbrace{\qquad\qquad\qquad\qquad\qquad\qquad}$$
$$\qquad\quad \text{constant terms} \qquad\qquad\qquad \text{mixed time-specific terms}$$

Equation 1.[5] Multiplying corresponding expressions for $(X_{irt} - X_{\cdot t})$ and $(Y_{irt} - Y_{\cdot t})$ and averaging over all units in all regions gives:

$$\frac{1}{N} \sum_{i=1}^{N} (X_{irt} - X_{\cdot t})(Y_{irt} - Y_{\cdot t}) = \frac{1}{N} \sum_{i=1}^{N} (X_{irt} - X_{\cdot rt})(Y_{irt} - Y_{\cdot rt})$$

$$+ \frac{1}{N} \sum_{i=1}^{N} (X_{\cdot rt} - X_{\cdot t})(Y_{\cdot rt} - Y_{\cdot t}) + \frac{1}{N} \sum_{i=1}^{N} (X_{irt} - X_{\cdot rt})(Y_{\cdot rt} - Y_{\cdot t})$$

$$+ \frac{1}{N} \sum_{i=1}^{N} (X_{\cdot rt} - X_{\cdot t})(Y_{irt} - Y_{\cdot rt})$$

Fortunately, multiplying out and then summing the resulting terms tells us that the last two terms on the right of the equals sign, or the "cross-level" covariances, cancel each other out. (In showing this cancelation, it is helpful to remember that the r subscripts refer to various specific subsets of i, and that averages over all i are equivalent to proportionally weighted combinations of "dot-r" averages.) In terms of the covariance notation and definitional formulas B1, B4, and B6 given in Table 1, the remaining terms of the preceding equation indicate that

$$C_{XY;t} = WC_{XY;t} + EC_{XY;t} \qquad (6)$$

Equation 6 shows how the covariance of X and Y for N individuals i at a particular time t can be thought of as the sum of a within-region covariance and a between-region, ecological one for the same time t. Either from the preceding derivation or the definitional formula it should be clear that the ecological covariance is a population-weighted average product of *regional* deviations in X and Y. Similarly, the within-region covariance can be thought of as a population-weighted sum over all regions of the covariances of individual X and Y values within each of the regions.

A slightly more complex (and less familiar) form of this covariance theorem comes from a similar treatment of Equation 2. Let us first speculate about and then state the results. Taking expressions for $(X_{irt} - X_{\cdot\cdot})$ and $(Y_{irt} - Y_{\cdot\cdot})$ and averaging them over *both* the individual units i and times t should give something like Equation 6. Perhaps it will be extended to include another term related to the $(X_{\cdot t} - X_{\cdot\cdot})$ type of expression that makes Equation 2 more complex than Equation 1.

---

[5] Since the t subscript in the Covariance Theorem of Equation 6 enters its derivation in only a trivial way, it should be clear that using either Equation 3 or 3a with any subdivisions of t gives a result essentially similar to Equation 6.

Such a "trend covariance" term does result, and the various other covariances vanish. Using again the notion and formulas of Table 1, after considerable simplification, we get

$$C_{XY} = WC_{XY} + EC_{XY} + TC_{XY} \tag{7}$$

Each term in Equation 7 corresponds to a similar one in Equation 2. Like the result of Equation 6, Equation 7 "decomposes" the covariance over i and t of X_{irt} and Y_{irt} into a set of distinct and exhaustive components: temporally averaged within- and between-region terms and an over-time or trend component.[6]

Finally, we are in a position to derive the correlational version of the covariance theorem that Robinson himself used.[7] The switch from covariances to correlations and correlation ratios is quite simple. When we divide covariances by standard deviations, we of course get correlations. As indicated in rows C1 and C2 of Table 1, correlation ratios, denoted $E^2_{XR;t}$ and $E^2_{YR;t}$, are nothing more than ratios of ecological (between-region) variances to total variances.

Dividing Equation 6 by $\sqrt{C_{XX;t} \ C_{YY;t}}$ changes $C_{XY;t}$ into $R_{XY;t}$. Similar divisions of EC_{XY} and WC_{XY} by the relevant standard deviations also turn these covariances into ecological and within-region correlations (ER and WR as defined in D2 and D3 of Table 1). Making the relevant multiplications to preserve the equality in Equation 6 and dropping the t's after the C's for convenience gives:

$$R_{XY} = \frac{WC_{XY} + EC_{XY}}{\sqrt{C_{XX} \ C_{YY}}} = \frac{WC_{XY}}{\sqrt{WC_{XX} \ WC_{YY}}} \cdot \sqrt{\frac{WC_{XX} \cdot WC_{YY}}{C_{XX} \ C_{YY}}}$$
$$+ \frac{EC_{XY}}{\sqrt{EC_{XX} \ EC_{YY}}} \cdot \sqrt{\frac{EC_{XX} \cdot EC_{YY}}{C_{XX} \ C_{YY}}}$$

[6] A *variance components* interpretation of Equations 6 and 7 is possible in the special case when $Y = X$. In the notation of Table 1, Equation 7, for example, becomes

$$C_{XX;t} = WC_{XX;t} + EC_{XX;t} + TC_{XX;t} \tag{8}$$

Leslie Kish has used equations like Equation 8 to considerable advantage in locating at what level of a social system the greatest inequalities or homogeneities exist. See his imaginative "A Measurement of Homogeneity in Areal Units," *Bulletin de l'Institut International de Statistique*, 33e Session (Paris, 1961). Stokes's work, which uses a similar variance component model, differs in that not all the cross-level covariance terms vanish. As in our own Equation 2, MacRae and Stokes, but not Kish, are concerned with only "partially nested" levels of data aggregation.

[7] Our derivation follows the extremely clear exposition of Duncan *et al., op. cit.*, Chapter 3. They too are responsible for the elegant and simple formula relating ecological and individual *regression* coefficients given in footnote 8.

Substituting WR_{XY} and ER_{XY} for their formulas will help a lot to simplify the preceding expression: the EC/C ratios of the last square root are obviously correlation ratios. Continuing to ignore time-specific subscripts and recalling that $WC_{XX} = C_{XX} - EC_{XX}$ and that $WC_{YY} = C_{YY} - EC_{YY}$, we may introduce correlation ratios for all remaining C terms. Making these substitutions gives the last version of the covariance theorem we shall consider:

$$R_{XY} = WR_{XY} \sqrt{1 - E^2{}_{YR}} \sqrt{1 - E^2{}_{XR}} + ER_{XY} E_{YR} E_{XR} \qquad (9)$$

Equation 9 is the one cited in Robinson's original article on the ecological fallacy.[8]

FALLACIES OF ECOLOGICAL INFERENCE

Having now retraced, and to some extent generalized, the logical foundations of Robinson's argument, we are in a better position to explore whether or not other fallacies of ecological inference may have occurred. This must seem a thankless and destructive task to those who in the interests of a universal behavioral science seek to establish generalizations valid at many different levels of analysis. Similar covariances or correlations *can* occur at different levels of analysis, but the cogency of any *inference* from one such association to another remains unestablished until such time as the intriguing logical and empirical interdependencies of our concepts are more fully understood. Furthering this goal does not seem unworthy of the scientific investigator.

The cross-level covariance and correlation relationships of Equations 6, 7, and 9 suggest a number of such risky or unproved inferences.

[8] A detailed review and extension of the discussion of ecological regressions will not be given here. Nevertheless, Duncan *et al.* present and prove with such simplicity an obviously relevant equation relating individual and ecological regressions that it deserves to be mentioned. Using simple notational extensions and B's to label regression slopes, they obtain this result:

$$B_{YX} = WB_{YX} + E^2{}_{XR} (EB_{YX} - WB_{YX}) \qquad (10)$$

It follows directly from Equation 6 using the definition of $E^2{}_{XR}$ and the formulas defining regression slopes as ratios of a covariance to a variance.

A further body of related literature has existed in the econometrics area. For some time, in their characteristically constructive fashion, such scholars have focused their attention on the conditions under which misspecification errors at the individual level can be detected from aggregate data, as well as the conditions necessary for correct cross-level inferences; see, for example, H. A. J. Green's *Aggregation in Economic Analysis* (Princeton: Princeton University Press, 1964).

We may call inferences from higher levels to lower levels fallacies of "decomposition" or "disaggregation." The practice of assuming between-region (ecological) correlations to equal individual-level correlations, stigmatized by Robinson, would be an obvious example. Similarly, inferences incorrectly increasing their level of analysis might be labeled fallacies of "aggregation." Fallacies of inference from one subpopulation to another at the same level of analysis remain the third general possibility.

The Ecological Fallacy

In particular, Equation 6, or its correlational form Equation 9, shows why Robinson could find ecological correlations so different from universal individual ones. The effects of the regional grouping variable R and the within-region covariations both interfere with this relationship. That is why a small Negro-illiteracy individual correlation of .20 can be magnified by spurious ecological effects to a fantastic .95 magnitude when aggregated data for a small number of regions are analyzed.

The Individualistic Fallacy

Let us reverse the direction of Robinson's concern. Do people ever confuse relationships among individuals with those governing aggregates? Certainly they do, as when ideologically motivated social scientists try to generalize from individual behavior to collective relationships. Should we believe, for example, that because laborers tend to be socially radical, there will be an equally high tendency to express radical opinions in those economically advanced states with high proportions of laborers in their populations? Or do laborers in the more economically advanced states become politically conservative? Whether or not states should be treated as mere aggregations of individual units, correlations between economic indebtedness and political power, to cite another example, may well be very different for an international universe of citizens than for a congerie of nation states within which citizens are indebted to each other.

Using Figure 1, we can see how both these fallacies are aggregative or disaggregative attempts to equate universal and ecological covariances. Further patterns of plausible but logically unproved inference may be illustrated if we decompose within-region covariance into population-weighted covariances within particular regions (denoted in formula B5 of Table 1 as C_{XYr}). Expanding the WC_{XY} term of Equation

6 in this fashion into a weighted combination of R such terms ($r = 1, \ldots R$) gives:

$$WC_{XY} = \sum_{r=1}^{R} \frac{N_r}{N} \, C_{XYr} = \sum_{r=1}^{R} \frac{N_r}{N} \sum_{i \in r} \frac{(X_{irt} - X_{\cdot rt})(Y_{irt} - Y_{\cdot rt})}{N_r} \quad (6a)$$

When particular weighting coefficients, N_r proportions, have been omitted in Figure 1, a special addition sign, $\oplus$, has been used. Note also that time-specific subscripts have again been removed.

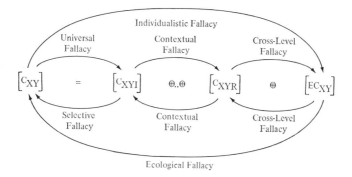

Figure 1

A TYPOLOGY OF ECOLOGICAL FALLACIES

The basis of this figure is Equations 6 and 6a. A slightly different version of this figure is given and discussed in my *Mathematics and Politics* (New York: Macmillan, 1965), pp. 102–105.

Cross-Level Fallacies

Perhaps the most obnoxious fallacies of aggregation have been false generalizations from individual relations within a single region to a universe of intercollectivity relationships. The most striking example in the eyes of some, in this regard, concerns giving to states the attitudes, the responsibilities, and the allegiances due to individuals — not all individuals, but some of them within a particular state.

After critically discussing work by Kaplan and Deutsch and other advocates of a general systems approach, Harold and Margaret Sprout have recently argued as follows:

> . . .the issue remains whether one derives clearer and richer insight into the operations of political organizations by endowing them even metaphorically with pseudo-biological structures and pseudo-psychological functions. . . .
>
> [The use of such psychoecological terms] tends to reify abstractions and to divert attention from the human persons who ultimately decide what is to be undertaken. In the case of the state, reification buttresses ethnocentric values and images which characterize so much of the discussion of foreign policy, military defense, and international politics in general.[9]

Cross-level inferences raise a problem for any general systems theory. For even if all "regions of data" obey the same set of relationships, the schema of Figure 1 shows how, even in a simple logical fashion, aggregated, higher-order systems may evidence different associations.[10] The most enduring debates along these lines continue to be about the similarities and differences of individual, community, and national models of social and political systems.

The Universal Fallacy and the Selective Fallacy

Closely related to the problem of making valid cross-level inferences are the problems of generalizing relationships from subsamples and of representing in one particular subsample a universally true relationship. If the subsamples are randomly extracted, only ordinary problems of statistical inference exist, but nonrandomly selected subgroups raise the likelihood that other variables, perhaps associated with the partitioning relationship, destroy any such easy correspondences.

[9] Harold and Margaret Sprout, *The Ecological Perspective on Human Affairs: with Special Reference to International Politics* (Princeton: Princeton University Press, 1965), pp. 208–210.

While disassociating myself from the view that human psychological and biological metaphors do not add rich insights into the behavior of "healthy" or "pathological" states, I do accept the charge that humanly described states appear to be beyond the control of individual human actors as a serious problem. But it is important to distinguish the analytical problem of correctly discovering relationships among states and connecting these relationships to those among individuals from the normative questions of the obedience and responsibility due to reified and personalized collective authorities.

[10] The fact that associations at two levels are, in general, unequal when the high-level variable is an aggregate of the lower one suggests but does not prove that similar generalizations might hold for a large number of structural variables that are not "mere" aggregations. The fact that some of these examples do refer to such cases suggests that these inferences are equally difficult. Similarities or differences may well be closely related to problems of context, to be discussed shortly. Erwin Scheuch has helpfully emphasized these points in commenting on my paper.

Popular discourse is full of such inferences — for example, that the universal positive (and weak?) relation between ability and success means that within every group those most successful are those most able. And anyone can select a few cases that "prove" a general point.

More methodological issues arise when universal correlations are published for data compendiums such as Banks and Textor's *Cross-Polity Survey* and the Yale Data Program's *World Handbook of Political and Social Indicators*. Apparently, the assumption that universal correlations hold in geographically or sociologically defined data subsets is as empirically risky as the opposite assumption. Thus the null hypothesis of *no* universal relationship between McClelland's need for achievement measure and economic development is roughly confirmed by a look at European data, disconfirmed in a *positive* direction (as McClelland might theorize) among more traditional Latin American states, and disconfirmed in a *negative* direction among recently colonized Afro-Asian states. Or we might note that European nations *avoid* a moderately strong ($R_{XY} = 0.47$) universal relationship between land inequality and domestic group violence.[11]

Contextual Fallacies

Even at the same level of analysis, the preceding examples suggest that context or social structure may dramatically alter the strength or form of causal or merely statistical relationships. What is a well-known fact to sophisticated sociologists apparently has to be rediscovered by statistically minded data analysts who rarely use the relevant interaction-detecting statistical procedures.[12] In the previously cited analysis, for example, the simple European – non-European distinction significantly interacts with the land inequality – domestic group violence relationship: One might attribute the depolarizing effects of European countries to their multiple mobility opportunities. The salutary effect of merely

[11] For other examples of this sort, some evidencing and some not subject to the universal fallacy, see my "Regionalism versus Universalism in Comparing Nations," in B. Russett, H. Alker, K. Deutsch, and H. Lasswell, *World Handbook of Political and Social Indicators* (New Haven: Yale University Press, 1965).

[12] The most interesting schematization of such macro-micro relationships of which I am aware is S. Rokkan, "The Comparative Study of Political Participation: Notes Toward a Perspective on Current Research" in A. Ranney (ed.), *Essays on the Behavioral Study of Politics* (Urbana: University of Illinois Press, 1962), pp. 47–90.

I have tried to suggest a number of multiplicative ways of modeling such contextual phenomena in several places, especially "The Long Road to International Relations Theory: Problems of Statistical Nonadditivity," *World Politics, 18* (1966), pp. 623–655.

increasing incomes in the "culture of poverty" may also be a contextually fallacious assumption. Although the examples become harder
to come by, one can extend such a list almost indefinitely.

The Cross-Sectional and Longitudinal Fallacies

As Duncan and his associates have done, we can interpret Equations
6 and 9 as if temporal "regions" were years, and we can generate time
series correlations from the ecological terms.[13] Then we could interpret
the cross-level links as indicating the unequal relationship between
cross-sectional and longitudinal covariations. Even though the inadequacy in most cases of inferring instantaneous relationships from
longitudinal data or vice versa is well known, the temptation is almost
irresistible. The peculiar advantage of Equations 6 and 7 is that they
show quite precisely why and to what extent such inferences are valid
or invalid.

Rather than present a number of examples, I should like briefly to
discuss Equation 7's expansion of the regional and temporal covariance
into within-region ecological and trend covariances, each of which can
be further broken down into within-year and or within-region terms.[14]
The great merit of this expansion is that it shows simultaneously how
all sorts of fallacious simultaneous cross-level or within-level inferences
can be further confused when longitudinal data is considered.

The simplest form of mechanistic assumption we can make about
human behavior is that it obeys linear additive determinative relationships — in fact, we assume this, at least approximately, every time we
calculate a product moment correlation coefficient and impute to it
causal significance. Much more closely corresponding to the insights

[13] Duncan *et al.*, *op. cit.*, Chapter 3, and "Regionalism versus Universalism,"
op. cit. These sources give empirical evidence on when and where cross-sectional
and longitudinal covariances have and have not corresponded.

[14] An analytical technique making use of these kinds of problems and taking
account of within-region and between-region differences is Gibson's continuous
variable extension of Lazarsfeld's "Latent Class Analysis," which he calls "Latent
Profile Analysis." The algebraic tautologies from which model equations are derived
are not unlike those given earlier. Their distinctive feature, however, is the use of
triple products of the form

$$(X_i - X.) (Y_i - Y.) (Z_i - Z.)$$

which are assumed to be equal to zero. "Regions" are constructed as subgroups
within which regular and triple-product covariances disappear. See P. Lazarsfeld
and N. Henry, "The Application of Latent Structure Analysis to Quantitative
Ecological Data," in F. Massarik and P. Ratoosh (eds.), *Mathematical Explorations
in Behavioral Science* (Homewood, Ill.: Irwin Press, 1965).

of biological and cybernetically orientated theorists is the idea of contextually contingent determinative relationships, which themselves may evolve or devolve through time as the result of certain feedback processes. For example, explicitly temporal models allowing for regionally or contextually nonadditive effects help us better to model the often delayed impact of fluid social structures on the class-to-party or ethnic-to-party voting relationships that we sometimes associate with V. O. Key's concepts of a critical election. If the most interesting social and political phenomena are those in which the rules change from context to context, then statistical formulations that do not allow for such processes are painfully irrelevant.

FROM ECOLOGICAL FALLACIES TO CROSS-LEVEL HYPOTHESES

It may seem paradoxical to say that the discovery of error is the beginning of wisdom, but this is, in one sense, an implication of Herbert Simon's brilliant algebraic treatment of causal inference problems in "Spurious Correlation: A Causal Interpretation."[15] In a similar fashion, does not Robinson's demonstration of the existence of a "fallacious" ecological correlation point toward the discovery of the true pattern of ecological relationships?

Recall Robinson's examples. Individually, Negroes showed only a small tendency ($R_{XY} = .20$) to be more illiterate than whites; ecologically, however, the tendency appeared extremely strong ($ER_{XY} = .95$). The result provides almost unavoidable political ammunition for segregationist arguments — unless the ecological fallacy argument can be made credible. Less likely to appear in campaign oratory is the pro-immigration argument that foreign-born Americans are much less likely to be illiterate than native-born ($ER_{XY} = .62$); but even this, too, is an ecological fallacy ($R_{XY} = .12$).

Let us speculate about these results, especially the politically loaded one. Our liberal sensibilities make us feel that, even for 1930 data, the ecological Negro-illiteracy correlation is a false one. Moreover, some knowledge about the different areas of the United States of the 1930's in which Negroes and illiteracy were concentrated, those that were least

[15] Reprinted in *Models of Man* (New York: Wiley, 1957). The implications of Simon's insights have been more fully brought out in Hubert Blalock, Jr., *Causal Inferences in Nonexperimental Research* (Chapel Hill: University of North Carolina Press, 1964), and A. Ando, I. M. Fisher, and H. A. Simon, *Essays on the Structure of Social Science Models* (Cambridge: M.I.T. Press, 1963).

urbanized and industrialized, suggests that the ecological grouping variable probably hides the causal effects of urbanization, bringing about less illiteracy and the tendency toward the exclusion (in Robinson's prewar data) of Negroes from industrial opportunities. If there is a real but small correlation of Negro race and illiteracy, as Robinson observed, we might say that even this small association, when all effects of ecological groupings are taken into account, is spurious. Thus we should expect that WR_{XY}, for small and homogeneous enough regions, would be even closer to zero than R_{XY} for individuals!

Using the correlational version of the covariance theorem, the argument might go like this:

$$.20 = \sqrt{1 - E^2_{YR}} \sqrt{1 - E^2_{XR}} \, WR_{XY} + .95 \, E_{XR} \, E_{YR}$$

For the reasons given, we should expect much — say half — of the variance in X (being Negro) and Y (being illiterate) to be ecologically determined, that is, EC_{XX}/C_{XX} and EC_{YY}/C_{YY} would be about .5. But then the preceding equation becomes

$$.20 = .75 \, WR_{XY} + .24$$

from which it appears that $WR_{XY} = .05 \approx .0$. (In fact, for the four macroregions that Robinson does publish within-region data, the average within-region correlation is considerably smaller than .20.) Now what does it mean that WR_{XY} is approximately zero? From our previous formulations, especially Equation 6a, we know that we can think of WR_{XY} as an average of within-region correlations. Also, we have argued that the *nominal* regional grouping variable R acted something like industrialization and/or urbanization in its decreasing effect on illiteracy and something like traditional ruralism in its depressant effect on Negro educational aspirations and opportunities. Therefore, treating the regional distinction R as an aggregate interval scale index of industrialization and urban opportunity leads us to interpret $WR_{XY} \approx 0$ as meaning that R somehow accounts for, averages over, or "partials out" whatever real correlation there is between X and Y. That is, in partial correlational language:

$$R_{XY \cdot R} \approx 0$$

This result is, in turn, Simon's causal prediction equation associated with the cross-level hypothesis of a spurious causal relationship between X (Negro race) and Y (illiteracy) controlling for R (industrial opportunity):

In summary, we have expanded the ecological fallacy argument into two stages to show how ER_{XY} is totally misleading, R_{XY} less so, and WR_{XY} least of all. The first stage, reducing the significant correlation from .95 to .20, was the one suggested by Robinson; the second stage, reducing it further to about .05, seems to follow from and complete the intentions of his original data analysis and methodological orientation. But, in fact, it derives from what has come to be called the "Simon-Blalock causal modeling" tradition.[16]

One begins to wonder about the extent to which the literature of ecological analysis might develop along different lines if all investigators were always aware of both kinds of fallacies — those of aggregation and those of spurious correlation. If we were to continue to develop this line of reasoning, we might possibly benefit from our previous discussion in two significant ways.

First of all, modeling cross-level processes would more naturally be assumed to be of significant theoretical interest. When, for example, do national and/or regional factors dominate election behavior? And when do they reflect, via aggregation, the summation of local and individual decisions? Variance components models such as Equation 4, 5, or 8 help us to begin to locate effective political decision making (unfortunately, we cannot empirically choose among these models, at least until additional variables are introduced). Causal modeling with different levels of expression, such as $(X_{.i} - X_{..})$ and $(Y_{irt} - Y_{.rt})$, should help us move further in this direction; and it should benefit from a knowledge of the logical relationships that might exist among such terms.

But the preceding analysis, particularly of contextual differences and effects, leads me to expect that nonlinear causal models will be necessary

[16] See, for example, Blalock, *op. cit.*, Chapter 5, where in making causal inferences he uses higher levels of aggregation to cancel out processes that are random *between* regions. I have summarized and applied some of the relevant literature on recursive and nonrecursive causal models in "Causal Inference and Political Analysis" in Joseph Bernd (ed.), *Mathematical Applications in Political Science* (Dallas: Southern Methodist University Press, 1966).

if we are fully to take into account the rich variety of effects due to geopolitical context and the socioecological environment. This second implication of this reanalysis also remains to be explored.[17]

[17]Since this was written, R. Boudon, *L'analyse mathématique des faits sociaux* (Paris: Plon, 1967), has made a number of impressive contributions along these lines. See also A. L. Stinchcombe, *Constructing Social Theories* (New York: Harcourt, Brace & World, 1968).

Individual Behavior and Collective Properties

The five papers presented in Part Two focus on a crucial question of research strategy: the optimal "mix" between stratified sample surveys of the national population and ecological analyses of data for a wide range of territorial units within each country.

The typical sample survey concentrates on individual-level variables such as age, sex, education, denomination, occupation and adds very little information about the social and cultural environment within which each individual pursues his activities. But it is well known that the behavior of an individual is rarely a direct function of his abstract position but is heavily conditioned by his immediate social context. It makes a great deal of difference to the cultural or the political behavior of an individual whether he or his household is in a minority or a majority position within the given social context: the Catholic tends to behave in one way in a predominantly Protestant milieu, in another in a thoroughly secularized environment, and again in another in a homogeneous context of like-minded people; similarly, an office employee's behavior is quite different in a working-class district from his behavior in an upper-middle-class area.

The papers by Juan Linz, Erwin Scheuch, Kevin Cox, Jean Laponce, and David Segal and Marshall Meyer all offer a variety of examples of the influence of the ecological context on the behavior of individuals and, in fact, constitute a powerful critique of the "atomizing" model underlying the standard nationwide survey.

This, of course, does not imply any rejection of the sample survey as a technique of data gathering. To the contrary, the papers all call for surveys but in a new sampling frame: *they call for* ecologically controlled surveys *instead of* "atomistic" *ones. In his rich and suggestive paper Juan Linz sorts out with admirable clarity the pros and cons of the two competing methods: the nationwide* sample and the analysis of aggregate data by locality. He does not end up with a final verdict for or against any one of these but argues persuasively for the joint use of the two procedures: for the organization of surveys within a wide range of culturally, socially, and/or politically distinct ecological contexts.

The papers by Cox and by Segal and Meyer offer examples of ecological controls in survey analysis: Cox shows how information about the majority-minority balance in each precinct adds a decisive dimension to the analysis of the flow of political communication; Segal and Meyer demonstrate the importance of ecological variables in the reanalysis of survey data.

There has been much emphasis during the last ten to fifteen years on the dangers of the ecological fallacy: the papers by Alker, Allardt, and Valkonen in Part One remind us forcefully of this issue. But it is time that we react with equal insistence against the opposite error, the individualist fallacy, the tendency to generalize findings for individual behavior without controlling for the characteristics of the immediate social, cultural, or political contexts. The five contributors to Part Two all agree on this point: they all reject the assumption of the "individualist survey." Erwin Scheuch has perhaps gone further than anyone else in this direction; his initial denunciation of the individualist fallacy in his contribution to the volume Comparing Nations has been widely quoted as a sign of a change in the trend of research. In his paper in this volume he formulates his position with great succinctness: "In ordinary survey research the individual is usually treated, albeit by implication, as an atom. Just adding atoms does of course not make for molecules."

Jean Laponce adds a further indictment against the indiscriminate nationwide survey: he underscores the dangers of handling national averages for countries marked by strong regional contrasts. In countries such as Canada, France, Italy, Spain, India, or Mexico, any attempt to draw conclusions from nationwide sampling will be highly hazardous without built-in controls for regionally specific contexts. In these countries the correlations between sociocultural characteristics and political variables tend to wash out within the total national sample. The correlations come out differently for each region because the sociocultural characteristics and the political restrictions both take on different concrete meanings according to the geographical, and therefore historical, context. It does not mean the same politically to be a peasant or a worker in Tuscany as in Calabria, in Andalusia as in Catalonia, in the Pas-de-Calais as in the Limousin. In France there are, in fact, cases where the differences between social classes within a region are smaller than the differences among regions for the same sociocultural category. This, of course, does not mean that sociocultural differences do not count within each region; the categories simply take on different meanings from context to context.

The need for contextually controlled surveys tends to be particularly urgent wherever the primary sector still weighs heavily in the balance of political forces —

in fact, in all countries with markedly underdeveloped regions. The same goes for countries with a history of territorial-cultural oppositions. Standard nationwide surveys of the United States tended to treat the South as if it were just another region; the recent attempts to oversample the South and to stratify by the local Negro-white balance testify to the inadequacy of this procedure.

For all these reasons direct comparisons of nationwide survey data will tend to lead one astray. In many cases the better strategy will prove to be in the direction of cross-regional *surveys across several countries — surveys conducted in regions at similar levels of development in several countries, for example, Tuscany in Italy, Andalusia in Spain and the Limousin in France, or the Finnmark in Norway, the Norrland in Sweden, and the Lappland in Finland.*

In sum, this section of our volume pleads for ecological *surveys against* individualist *surveys, for* cross-regional *analyses* against *cross-national. The survey-ecology polarity seems to us profoundly false. What is needed is a strategy of systematic linkage: a deliberate effort to merge information for several levels of variation.*

5

JUAN J. LINZ

Ecological Analysis and
Survey Research

INTRODUCTION

IF WE TURN to the history of research in diverse fields of sociological
inquiry and to the emphases of the different centers of learning, we
discover that ecological analysis and survey research have developed
separately, even when they have studied fairly similar if not identical
problems. Sociological ecology has a longer history than the sample
survey. But the dominance of the latter type of research in recent times,
particularly in the United States, might give the erroneous impression
that it would ultimately displace ecological analysis. The argument of
this paper is that both methods have advantages and disadvantages for
the study of certain problems and that in many cases the two could
complement each other and be combined in a fruitful way. Theoretical
and practical considerations make such a marriage of methods desirable.
But — as we shall see at length — such a combination of methodologies,
with their traditions and distinctive requirements, is not without strain.
An awareness of the difficulties may contribute toward preventing a
quick divorce after a hasty and unpremeditated union based on a rosy
vision of the future.

The scarcity of studies combining both approaches[1] can be attributed not only to the separate intellectual traditions but to the fact that at an early stage of our knowledge each of those methods could by itself contribute much to our findings. To mention one example, any reader of the reviews of research in the field of political behavior is well aware that the same propositions or generalizations are documented by reference to both survey and ecological studies.[2] André Siegfried (1913), followed by R. Heberle and the early more quantitative studies of W. F. Ogburn, Stuart Rice (1924, 1928), and their students at Columbia, H. Gosnell at Chicago, Samuel Eldersveld, and particularly V. O. Key are quoted simultaneously with the survey studies of the Bureau of Applied Social Research by P. F. Lazarsfeld and his collaborators, and those of Angus Campbell and his group at the Survey Research Center of the University of Michigan. Also cited are the findings of European survey research organizations such as IFOP, DOXA, DIVO, the *Institut für Demoskopie, et al.* In fact, scholars like V. O. Key turned from ecological to survey data in the course of their own work.[3] However, no major work published to date (except some work in progress at the Survey Research Center and some articles of the regional panel project at the Bureau of Applied Social Research) has combined both ecological analysis and survey research systematically in the same study.[4]

[1] Among the exceptions we may mention: Henry Valen and Daniel Katz, *Political Parties in Norway: A Community Study* (Oslo: Universitetsforlaget, 1964), a study that combines attention to the ecological context with the analysis of survey data, Stein Rokkan and Henry Valen, "Regional Contrasts in Norwegian Politics: A Review of Data from Official Statistics and from Sample Surveys," in Erik Allardt and Yrjö Littunen (eds.), *Cleavages, Ideologies and Party Systems. Contributions to Comparative Political Sociology* (Helsinki: Westermarck Society, *10*, 1964), pp. 162–238, see especially pp. 187–201. The classification of communities by the availability of the party press serves as context for the analysis of voting behavior in S. Rokkan and Per Tarsvik, "Der Wähler, der Leser und die Parteipresse," *Kölner Zeitschrift für Soziologie und Sozialpsychologie, 12* (1960), pp. 278 ff. Norman M. Bradburn and David Caplovitz, *Reports on Happiness: A Pilot Study of Behavior Related to Mental Health* (Chicago: Aldine, 1965), pp. 1–5, selected as the context for their survey communities differently affected by economic depression.

[2] Paul F. Lazarsfeld, S. M. Lipset, Allen Barton, and J. Linz, "The Psychology of Voting: An Analysis of Political Behavior," in G. Lindzey (ed.), *Handbook of Social Psychology, 2* (Cambridge: Addison-Wesley, 1954), pp. 1124–1170.

[3] V. O. Key, Jr., *Public Opinion and American Democracy* (New York: Knopf, 1961), after his monumental *Southern Politics* (New York: Knopf, 1949).

[4] Warren E. Miller, "Majority Rule and the Representative System of Government," in Allardt and Littunen, *op. cit.*, pp. 343–376, relates data obtained by interviews with legislators, a sample of the electorate in their constituencies, with the roll-call behavior of representatives taking into account the safe or marginal character of the district determined on the basis of voting statistics. The studies of the Survey

The main questions we can raise are:

1. Are the two methods interchangeable in their results, and if so, why should we prefer one to the other?

2. If the findings are not always interchangeable, which would be the intellectual rather than the strictly practical advantages and disadvantages of each?

3. Granted that they are not interchangeable and both have distinctive contributions to make, is there any particular advantage in combining their use in a single research design?

4. If one assumes valid theoretical and practical reasons for combining the two approaches, the infrequency of this combination suggests that there must be certain difficulties involved. What are those difficulties, and how could we attempt to circumvent them?

SITUATIONS FAVORING ECOLOGICAL APPROACHES

Certainly there are problems for which both methods can be used and in which the choice will depend largely on strictly practical considerations and/or the personal preferences of the researcher. But in other cases one or the other method will have distinct advantages and will impose itself. Of course, to estimate the political preferences of broad strata of society — such as the working class Catholics in Germany (see the excellent early study by Johannes Schauff)[5] — both

---

Research Center of the University of Michigan have, on occasion, tabulated data from surveys using characteristics of the county or community as a context, for example, when they tabulate awareness of candidate information by the fact that the incumbent lives in the same community (leaving aside large urban centers), as in Donald E. Stokes and Warren E. Miller, "Party Government and the Saliency of Congress," in Angus Campbell, Philip E. Converse, Warren E. Miller, and Donald E. Stokes, *Elections and the Political Order* (New York: Wiley, 1966), pp. 208–209, or when in studying the "Economic Antecedents of Political Behavior" they relate the percentage of unemployed in a country to the attitudes toward governmental guarantees of full employment, as in A. Campbell *et al.*, *The American Voter* (New York: Wiley, 1960), pp. 383–384. See also Philip H. Ennis, "The Contextual Dimension in Voting," in William N. McPhee and William A. Glaser (eds.), *Public Opinion and Congressional Elections* (Glencoe: Free Press, 1962), pp. 180–211; for a more extended version see his unpublished Columbia University Ph.D. dissertation in sociology, 1961.

[5] Johannes Schauff, *Die deutschen Katholiken und die Zentrumspartei. Eine politisch-statistische Untersuchung der Reichstagswahlen seit 1871* (Köln: J. P. Bachem, 1928). It should be noted that Schauff in the absence of survey data, wanting to know how many Catholics voted Zentrum, developed a methodology very similar to the one used by Mattei Dogan (without knowledge of this work) in his article "Le vote ouvrier en France: analyse écologique des élections de 1962," *Revue Française de Sociologie*, 6 (1965), pp. 435–472.

approaches can and have been used. In the case of more specific
population groups like the "occupational communities" of miners,
fishermen, etc., living in distinctive communities, or even neighborhoods
(such as dock workers), ecological data offer a more economical way to
obtain the same information.[6] National sample surveys generally would
have too few cases in such numerically small but sociologically and
politically interesting groups. However, sample surveys among such
groups, in such constituencies, once identified by ecological research,
would have the advantage of allowing us to inquire into the motivations
of the voters and to use other "intervening variables" in the analysis.
It would allow us to use the panel method to study turnover and to
check the "ecological fallacy" in its crudest form, as pointed out by
Robinson (even when survey analysis has its homologous fallacies).[7]

The impossibility of using survey techniques, owing to the lack of
organization of or freedom to use them or a high rate of refusals or
nonresponse on certain questions (such as on Communist voting in
France and Italy) may force us back to using ecological data. (See, for
example, the ecological studies of leftist voting in France and Italy, by
Mattei Dogan.)[8] Also in the case of numerically small social groups
living in distinct areas, ecological data would allow us to reach generalizations that numerically extensive sampling would make too costly.

In an exploratory and descriptive study, an ecological analysis can
also be extremely fruitful in pointing to the variables that might be
important in an explanatory analysis using survey techniques that the
researcher unfamiliar with the phenomenon he intends to study may
not have considered. To profit from this advantage of ecological approaches, attention should be centered not only on the correlations but
also on the clusters of deviant cases we are likely to find in a scatter
diagram of the relationship between two variables. An analysis of the
characteristics of those units — departments, cities, etc. — for which
the over-all relation does not hold can be helpful in locating additional
explanatory variables. Often the hypothesis derived in this way from
the ecological analysis will be testable only through survey data.

[6] See for many examples S. M. Lipset, *Political Man* (Garden City: Doubleday, 1960), *passim*.

[7] See the paper by Hayward R. Alker, Jr., in this same volume.

[8] See Mattei Dogan's chapter on the social bases of parties, "La stratificazione sociale dei suffragi in Italia," in A. Spreafico and J. LaPalombara (eds.), *Elezioni e comportamento politico in Italia* (Milano: Comunità, 1963), pp. 407–474. See also his "Les clivages politiques de la classe ouvrière," in L. Hamon (ed.), *Les nouveaux comportements politiques de la classe ouvrière* (Paris: Presses Universitaires de France, 1962), pp. 101–143.

Ecology and the Study of Rural Society

The characteristic dispersion of relatively small numbers of people in rural societies and the wide variety of social characteristics over many easily identifiable and often fairly homogeneous administrative (and therefore statistical) units make the ecological approach particularly useful in the study of rural society. In fact, only with extremely large samples (without previous ecological information) and in only a few homogeneous societies would it be possible to represent and identify adequately all the types of rural social structure and class relations. The dimensions that have to be taken into account in the study of rural society are so numerous, their combinations are so complex, while their geographic distribution is so far from random that a normal survey may miss many of them. Dimensions like patterns of land tenure (property, tenancy, and other agrarian contracts), settlement patterns, types of crops and their rotation, agricultural density, incidence of economic crises due to climate or market conditions permit many combinations that determine differences in attitudes and political behavior. The wealth of statistical data and maps for all these indicators for small, relatively unpopulous administrative units permits us to identify a great number of such types in a way that the data from a national sample survey, without many sampling points and a very large sample, never would permit.[9]

Furthermore, in contrast to the urban social structure, in a rural community the various strata and social groups are visible to each other; therefore the particular mix of systems of land tenure, etc., is much more likely to have a "compositional effect"[10] on people who occupy comparable, if not identical, socioeconomic positions in villages of very different social structure. The aggregation in survey analysis of such

[9] Folke Dovring, *Land and Labor in Europe, 1900–1950: A Comparative Survey of Recent Agrarian History* (The Hague: Martinus Nijhoff, 1956); Wilbert E. Moore, *Economic Demography of Eastern and Southern Europe* (Geneva: League of Nations, 1945); Pitirim Sorokin and Carle C. Zimmerman, *Principles of Rural-Urban Sociology* (New York: Holt, 1929); Arthur L. Stinchcombe, "Agricultural Enterprise and Rural Class Relations," *American Journal of Sociology*, 67; 2 (1961), pp. 165–176.

[10] Patricia Kendall and Paul F. Lazarsfeld, "Problems of Survey Analysis," in Robert K. Merton and Paul F. Lazarsfeld (eds.), *Continuities in Social Research: Studies in the Scope and Method of "The American Soldier"* (Glencoe: Free Press, 1950), pp. 187–196. Paul F. Lazarsfeld, "Problems in Methodology," in Robert K. Merton, Leonard Broom, and Leonard S. Cottrell, Jr. (eds.), *Sociology Today* (New York: Basic Books, 1959), pp. 39–78; see especially pp. 69–73. The same ideas were developed further in P. F. Lazarsfeld and H. Menzel, "On the Relation Between Individual and Collective Properties," in Amitai Etzioni (ed.), *Complex Organizations* (New York: Holt, Rinehart & Winston, 1961), pp. 422–440. Among the articles on

people without reference to the community context may be thoroughly fallacious. For example, in Spain a poor peasant owner in a small Galician hamlet finds himself in a completely different context from a man classified in the same way living in a large Andalusian village dominated by large landowners and with large numbers of farm laborers.[11] The social context of the village becomes a prime determinant of the occupants' different political and social behavior. In a national sample survey it seems improbable that the data would permit easy identification of such social structural contexts, while they are obvious to anyone at all familiar with the wealth of available ecological data.

In this perspective it is not surprising that in the past, national censuses in semideveloped or underdeveloped countries have been less satisfactory for describing the rural than the urban social structure. However, the combination of census data with the data of agricultural statistics, land registers, tax records, historical data on property relations, etc., facilitates the study of rural society in a way that national surveys would not. It is no accident that ecological research has contributed much more to our knowledge of rural politics and social structure than has survey research.[12] Certainly it cannot exhaust the topic, but anyone attempting to use survey research in this area would be ill advised if he were to start his study without an effort first to consider all available ecological data and to design his survey taking them into account.

We must add practical reasons to those derived from the nature of rural society based on the diversity of soils, climate, and the history of rural property relations, which are less subject to evolutional change

---

methodological problems in the study of "structural" or "compositional" effects, see Peter M. Blau, "Structural Effects," *American Sociological Review, 25* (1960), pp. 178–193. James A. Davis, Joe L. Spaeth, and Carolyn Huson, "A Technique for Analyzing the Effects of Group Composition," *American Sociological Review, 26* (1961), pp. 215–225. Arnold S. Tannenbaum and Jerald G. Bachman, "Structural versus Individual Effects," *American Journal of Sociology, 69* (1964), pp. 585–595, take issue with some points in the previously mentioned article.

[11] See J. Díaz del Moral, *Historia de las agitaciones campesinas andaluzas — Córdoba* (Madrid: Revista de Derecho Privado, 1929) for a description of such social structures and their political implications.

[12] Carl J. Friedrich, "The Agricultural Basis of Emotional Nationalism," *Public Opinion Quarterly, 1* (1937), p. 50 ff; Rudolf Heberle, *Landbevölkerung und National-sozialismus: Eine soziologische Untersuchung der politischen Willensbildung in Schleswig-Holstein 1918 bis 1932* (Stuttgart: Deutsche Verlagsanstalt, 1963). See also the bibliography in Gordon Wright, *Rural Revolution in France: The Peasantry in the Twentieth Century* (Stanford: Stanford University Press, 1964), pp. 258–259. Philip Converse, "Agrarian Political Behavior," in Campbell *et al.*, *The American Voter, op. cit.*, Chap. 15, pp. 402–440.

than are class relations derived from acquisitive processes in the market or the occupational sphere. (This distinction was made by Max Weber when he spoke of *Besitzklassen*, propertied classes, and *Erwerbsklassen*, or money-earning classes).[13] The costs of interviewing people dispersed over large areas and the difficulties of making random choices when the number of interviews per community becomes too small lead survey researchers to concentrate their efforts on a smaller number of sampling points. This is not likely to affect the national findings seriously, particularly when the rural population is a small proportion of the total population. But in view of the nonrandom dispersion of relatively homogeneous types of rural social structure, it can affect seriously the representativeness of such samples of the types of rural social structure. If we note also the great instability of rural political choices in certain countries (noted by Lipset, Converse, and others),[14] when we use small national samples, we would never be sure whether the different results of two studies were due to such changes in political preference in response to changed conditions or to the fact that they actually were samples representing different populations — different types of rural society — even when the occupational or income distributions in both were comparable. Furthermore, numerically less important types of rural social structure easily identified by ecological methods may be of great theoretical interest since they may allow crucial comparisons. But these would be missed in a survey type of study design.

The advantages we have just mentioned may be greater in under-developed or semideveloped societies than in highly advanced Western societies in which the countryside is increasingly populated by a mixture of people active in agriculture, industry, or services like tourism, or in combinations of these,[15] or who commute between the country and the city. Such mixed communities, particularly frequent in Central Europe, obviously represent the danger of the ecological fallacy.

Historical Analysis and Ecology

An area of research in which ecological data are indispensable is *historical sociology and research* in general, insofar as it wants to include

[13] Max Weber, *Wirtschaft und Gesellschaft, Grundriss der Verstehenden Soziologie, I* (Tübingen: J. C. B. Mohr, 1956), 4th ed., prepared by J. Winckelmann, pp. 177–178.

[14] P. Converse, in A. Campbell *et al.*, *The American Voter, op. cit.*, pp. 404–408, 416–425. S. M. Lipset, *Political Man, op. cit.*

[15] The German rural sociologists have paid particular attention to this problem. See particularly the reports on research of the Institut für Agrarsoziologie, Universität Giessen: H. Kötter, *Die Landbevölkerung im sozialen Wandel* (Düsseldorf-Köln, 1958).

in its analysis the behavior of the anonymous masses rather than to limit itself to that of the elites who have left us personal documents. Voting records, police reports, parish registers, property deeds, tax records, etc., allow us to reconstruct the relationships between different aspects of the social structure — political behavior, violence, religiosity, family structure, and the class structure — for periods long past. These data are forever out of reach of the interviewer of the individuals whose thoughts are not recorded like those of their governors, priests, or intellectuals. To mention some specific data relevant for the political sociology of societies that made the transition to modernity in the nineteenth and early twentieth centuries, we have relevant data on voting, violence, strikes, political crimes, party and trade union membership, as well as data on the social structure from censuses, official social surveys, tax, educational, and religious statistics, etc. The possibilities for correlational analysis, ecological estimates, analysis of variance, factor analysis, etc., for data extending over a period of 100 or more years are practically unlimited for most Western countries. The study of strikes in Britain by Knowles[16] and a pioneer article by Hobsbawm[17] show the range of generalizations that could be based on such data. Such an analysis combined with the study of trends for such ecologically defined units over long periods of time would permit us to study more efficiently the processes of social change, tracing (for selected districts) the relationships between behavioral and attitudinal changes, and structural changes like urbanization, industrialization, the opening to communications, increases in literacy, economic crises, and the diffusion of ideas from the center to the periphery (as suggested by the work of Stein Rokkan).[18] Such a correlational analysis would allow us to discover the *time gaps* between structural and "superstructural" changes (along the lines suggested by Marxist theory or the "cultural lag" theory of Ogburn), or situations like that described by K. Mannheim in his essay on Conservative thought:[19] the diffusion of ideologies (or

[16] Kenneth Knowles, *Strikes: A Study in Industrial Conflict, with Special Reference to British Experience between 1911 and 1947* (Oxford: B. Blackwell, 1952).

[17] E. J. Hobsbawm, "Economic Fluctuations and Some Social Movements Since 1800," in *Labouring Men: Studies in the History of Labour* (London: Weidenfeld & Nicolson, 1964), pp. 126–157.

[18] Stein Rokkan and Henry Valen, "The Mobilization of the Periphery," in Stein Rokkan (ed.), *Approaches to the Study of Political Participation* (Bergen: The Michelsen Institute, 1962); S. Rokkan and H. Valen, "Regional Contrasts in Norwegian Politics," in Allardt and Littunen (eds.), *op. cit.*

[19] Karl Mannheim, "Conservative Thought," in Paul Kecskemeti (ed.), *Essays on Sociology and Social Psychology* (New York: Oxford University Press, 1953), pp. 74–164; especially see pp. 120–125.

institutions) before the structure to which they should respond has actually developed. The latter situation may be quite frequent in some latecomers to modernity.

Using such ecological units it would be possible to develop a kind of ecological panel following the model of the work of Lipset on voting in Southern counties in the United States before the Civil War,[20] in the secession referenda and afterward. In this way it is possible to apply to ecological units the logic of panel and multivariate analysis and to explore the impact of great historical events and crises on communities or districts of different predispositions, at the same time taking into account their social structure.

The "contemporaneity of history" that social scientists often discover belatedly in their research makes this advantage particularly important. *If the research on contemporary behavior and social structure cannot ignore the weight of history, it cannot ignore ecological data.*

Ecological data acquire particular relevance for *cross-national* comparisons of sequences of social and political development. Over-all national comparisons suffer from the disadvantage that few, if any, countries as a whole find themselves at the same stage of social and economic development in a comparable historical context, while particular regions or communities within several countries may find themselves in a similar situation. Therefore comparing the impact of different institutional arrangements (political, legal, and religious systems) in corresponding social structures would be possible.

Such cross-national comparisons of smaller units, as well as comparisons of intranational differences of several nations,[21] would contribute more substantially to our knowledge of social change than comparisons between nations as a whole. Such a comparative ecological approach to the social, economic, and political history of France, Italy, Spain, and Portugal — countries that share such a large historical and

---

[20] S. M. Lipset, "The Emergence of the One-Party South: The Election of 1860," in *Political Man, op. cit.,* Chap. XI, pp. 344–354.

[21] J. Linz and Amando de Miguel, "Within-Nation Differences and Comparisons: The Eight Spains," in Richard L. Merritt and Stein Rokkan (eds.), *Comparing Nations: The Use of Quantitative Data in Cross-National Research* (New Haven: Yale University Press, 1966), pp. 267–319. Also Erik Allardt, "Implications of Within-Nation Variations and Regional Imbalances for Cross-National Research," in *ibid.,* pp. 337–348, for examples of how "contingency"— in terms of different sociogeographic contexts — effects are ignored or relationships misinterpreted using national averages. See also the section on ascertaining the limits of universality, in Hayward R. Alker, Jr., "The Comparison of Aggregate Political and Social Data: Potentialities and Problems," in Stein Rokkan (ed.), *Comparative Research Across Cultures and Nations* (Paris: Mouton, 1968).

institutional heritage, but whose development, both economic and political, proceeded at such different paces — would destroy many myths derived from over-all cross-national comparisons.

A particular problem revealed by survey studies that could be clarified by ecological research concerns the continuities and discontinuities in *party identification* as a determinant of political attitudes and behavior, independently from initial or subsequent changes in the social structure. Such identifications of many districts were made in particular historical crises and have persisted ever since. The problem of such *continuities* and *discontinuities* in some districts, which at first sight seem to have a similar social structure, has intrigued social scientists. (This has been noted, for example, by Key and Munger[22] as a factual basis for questioning some of the more simplistic social determinism that has crept into voting research using survey techniques.) Only long-term ecological research can contribute to our knowledge of the problem of continuity and change in politics. This knowledge would be crucial to an understanding of the politics of countries in which the democratic political process is interrupted for a long period of time or of situations in which some districts respond quickly to changed political appeals by parties and leaders while others remain loyal to their first love, even when either party or leadership composition and/or the political appeals have changed.[23]

In such cases of continuity in political loyalties, the question that ecological data will allow us to pose more adequately is: Why did forces dominant in large parts of a country persist in some places, while in others they were displaced or absorbed by new movements and parties? The comparison could contribute to a better understanding of the original strengths and weaknesses of a movement that is being reduced to marginal survival, as well as of the factors underlying its persistence. The ecological data can give us important leads on how to explore the conditions for local fractionalization of politics versus nationalization of politics through absorption of marginal elements by dominant parties. Such patterns also can tell us much about the social structure of a country, its cultural and social integration, later to be explored more intensively by survey data. The one-sided focus on class cleavages, which certainly are dominant in modern societies, has led to a neglect of

[22] V. O. Key, Jr., and Frank Munger, "Social Determinism and Electoral Decision: The Case of Indiana," in Eugene Burdick and Arthur J. Brodbeck (eds.), *American Voting Behavior* (Glencoe: Free Press, 1959), pp. 281–299.

[23] On such continuities and discontinuities in political behavior, see Lazarsfeld *et al.*, "The Psychology of Voting," in Lindzey, *op. cit.*

vertical cleavages, often corresponding to (or strongly correlated with) spatial alignments. Ecological data covering a long time span can give us many cues for the study of the factors that determine traditionalism in a changing society and that are likely to be related to patterns of social integration,[24] organizational strength, etc., but are often neglected in survey research.

SITUATIONS FAVORING SURVEY RESEARCH

Survey research has the unique advantage that it allows us to obtain much information about the *same* individual, rather than only about aggregates of individuals, and to group those individuals according to our interests rather than in a predetermined way as in much of the precollected ecological data for administrative units. Furthermore, surveys permit us to introduce a large number of *intervening variables,* particularly psychological variables that we never would have in ecological studies, between the information about the social position and the recorded behavior. The relationship between independent and dependent variables does not have to be inferred indirctely by the researcher but can, at least in part, be ascertained directly by using the information the respondent gives us about his attitudes or predispositions, his perceptions of the reality affecting his behavior, his motives as he sees them, the inferences he himself makes about the relationships between his position and his behavior. Not only can we relate the information about his position to that about his behavior, but we can study to what extent the perception of that social position accounts for his behavior. To put it graphically, with ecological data it would be almost impossible to study "false consciousness."

The subjective reality — what is real in the minds of people — is also real in its consequences, and that reality will generally escape us when we use exclusively the usual aggregate data about people on which ecological analysis is based. Certainly survey research may miss the unconscious motives of people, or their subjectively honest rationalizations, to which psychoanalysis has called our attention. But these are even more likely to be neglected in ecological approaches. Often the

[24] For example, it would be possible to relate the data on the size of "social isolates," defined by the frequency of consanguineous marriages, using the methods of G. Dahlberg, *Mathematical Methods for Population Genetics* (London: Interscience Publishers, 1948), and J. Sutter and L. Tabah, "Les notions d'isolat et de population minimum," *Population,* 6 (1951), pp. 481–489, relating them to acceptance or resistance to change, i.e., to continuities and discontinuities in political loyalties.

comparison between ecological data for aggregates and those for individuals in those aggregates inevitably points to psychological intervening variables that force us to modify the inferences we would be tempted to make on the basis of ecological data. For example, if we have a region with a high per capita income in a country in which the income has been rising but we do not find this reflected in answers to questions about improvement in standard of living over the last years, we can suspect that the perception of reality is affected by frames of reference, reference groups, etc., which in turn may be related to the ideological orientations of people. Such variables would explain why inferences about economic improvement and change in political behavior may be misleading. The empirical test of such theoretical constructs, however, will be possible only through the use of survey data.

In the majority of cases the inferences based on survey data are at least as good as or generally better than those a social scientist can make about the relationship between social position and behavior on the basis of ecological correlations. Certainly those inferences are less likely to be vitiated by a rationalistic bias than those based on ecological data. Often the same objective (in the view of an outside observer), social position, is differently perceived by those in the specific social position, and those differences in perception account for differences in behavior that generally would elude ecological explanation.

The direct rather than the inferential linkage between individual social position and behavior is the great advantage of survey research over ecological analysis. The exclusive reliance on objective data characterizing aggregates without intervening subjective variables that underlies the inferences based on ecological data makes them particularly susceptible to the dangers of the ecological fallacy, even when the inferences based on aggregations of survey data are subject to comparable fallacies.

We have already noted the possibility of using ecological units for a kind of panel analysis of aggregate data to explore problems of change over time. (In fact, the first long-term attitude change studies, by Newcomb, of classes of Bennington College girls were based on turnover tables of data on aggregates rather than individuals, and in this they were very similar in their logic to ecological panels.)[25] One of the difficulties with such comparisons along the time dimension of ecological data is that they assume a certain continuity in the composition of

[25] Theodore M. Newcomb, *Personality and Social Change* (New York: Dryden Press, 1943).

the population of the units under analysis, either of the individuals or of some characteristics of the population, if they extend over more than one generation.

The relationship between predispositions as well as the exposure to events or stimuli and changes in attitude or behavior is possible to assess only with surveys made at two points in time. Only the availability of records with information about the same individuals at two points in time (such as registration of voters, academic records, etc.) would allow a comparable study of change to the panel analysis of survey data.

Survey data are undoubtedly threatened by the possibility of dishonesty among the respondents and those collecting the information. However, in most cases this problem can be exaggerated in dealing with large aggregates of randomly selected respondents. More than outright lying, the problem is evasive responses. The no answers, no opinions, refusals to be interviewed, when they exceed a certain level, have to be treated as distinctive responses that may often stand for quite well-defined attitudes discernible by relating them to other responses in which people did not feel the same need to be cautious or reticent. For some patterns of behavior about which we have both survey and ecological data, the discrepancy in itself can be an important factor for research and contributes to our understanding of the phenomenon. Certainly, if in a country we find communities where the officially recorded Communist vote is much higher than the number of voters who, in a survey, are willing to admit having voted Communist, while in other towns the two sets of data coincide, we may ask ourselves: What distinguishes the confessed and the discreet supporters of the party? Probably the significance of being a Communist is not the same in those two types of community. In this case the data alert us to the existence of different types of Communist voters. The comparison of both types of communities will tell us something either about the probable characteristics of those voters — their occupation, their religion, their past voting, etc. — or about the community structure — the milieu in which those voters live — and thereby about characteristics affecting their responses, such as the importance of social controls and pressures for concealing an unpopular choice or loyalty to party instructions not to answer. We would expect the first in small rural communities, areas of strong religious and clerical tradition, and the second in strongly Communist urban industrial districts.

Finally, let us note that the same dangers of dishonesty threaten the original ecological data. These data, after all, are often collected by government agencies, using methods no different from those of polling agencies. Often the methods are relatively unsophisticated and cause the respondent to feel even more strongly that his responses may have negative consequences for him, particularly in the form of taxation. Government agencies cannot always be trusted more than private organizations or social scientists in collecting accurate information.

CIRCUMSTANCES FAVORING EITHER METHOD IRRESPECTIVE OF ADVANTAGES IN PRINCIPLE

Sample surveys are subject to a number of practical difficulties that may force us to turn back to an ecological analysis, even when they would provide us with more and better information. We have already dealt at length with the case of historical data and the study of rural social structure. To those categories we have added all the societies in which there are no competent survey research organizations or which would not allow the researcher to carry out surveys but which have published a wealth of data for relatively small administrative units. If we were to rely only on survey research, we would be obliged to leave out of comparative social research many countries and problems that otherwise can be studied, even though to a limited extent.

Survey research, for reasons intrinsic to the technique itself and connected with the organization and financing of research, often cannot be used to study the impact of certain events or crises. But often ecological data become available to reflect such impact. There are also certain social changes that occur so slowly, almost imperceptibly, that even a panel analysis would not be able to pin them down. But long-term ecological data would clearly reflect them. We have the feeling that some of the changes in demographic behavior in the last decade would fall into this category. This probably would be the case with fertility patterns of different social groups.

There are also data that the individual with the best intentions could not give us with exactitude because the information is not available to him, though official records contain it. An example would be a study of the health conditions of a population where the morbidity and health statistics and the records of hospitals and doctors may give us better information than individuals or their families and where many of the factors accounting for the situation (such as number of doctors available, health insurance affiliation, number of beds, and economic conditions affecting health) are easily available for aggregate units.

Ecological correlations for such data may be the most helpful in an exploratory study.[26]

A problem not easy to solve is the case where in addition to attitude data we would like to use a large number of precise data of a census type difficult to obtain because of the time it would take. For example, in a study of rural social structure we would like to relate sociological data and attitude information with very exact data on land use, crop rotation, machinery used, labor inputs, cattle, production, etc., of the type collected in the lengthy questionnaires of the agrarian census or tax records. The combination of both sociological and agroeconomic data in the same questionnaire-interview becomes *practically* impossible. Often these data are available in public records, official statistics, or specialized surveys. With some indicators of that type in the survey (asked in a form identical to that of the official statistics) and data for small enough ecological units, it might be possible to circumvent this difficulty to some extent.

Ideally we should be able to combine the information obtained from attitude surveys, which are focused on more strictly sociological problems, with the more exact records that different administrations carry about those same individuals. A certain limiting case is not likely to occur in the immediate future in "liberal" societies because of public resistance, and probably not in planned societies because of bureaucratic competition. In this case it would be possible to accumulate all the sociologically, economically, and otherwise relevant information on any single individual (or organization such as the business firm or the hospital) under a single number. We can dream of and fear a situation in which it would be possible to put together on an IBM tape all the population census information, the social security administration data (with the complete employment record), the income tax statements, health data, military records, as well as academic career data, including those of psychological tests administered in the course of the individual's life. It requires little imagination to realize the studies of social mobility that this would make feasible. If, then, we would ask in survey studies on politics, values, etc., for the identification number, there would be no difficulty in combining both sets of data and exploring with incredible

[26] For an example see Fundación Fomento de Estudios Sociales y de Sociológia Aplicada, *Informe sociológico sobre la situación social de España* (Madrid: Euroamerica, 1966), realized by DATA S.A. under the direction of Amando de Miguel, F. Andres Orizo, and M. Gomez-Reino, Madrid, Part III, "Sociológia de la sanidad." In that study, fifteen indicators of socioeconomic development, organization of health services, social security affiliation rates, and health conditions are correlated. Some of those data then are related to those obtained from a national sample survey.

precision hypotheses like those about the difference between class and status politics or status inconsistencies. Technically, such a dream is within our reach: in the United States the social security number that serves to record all changes in employment is now used in all income tax statements (which include information on savings, investments, certain types of expenditures, etc.), and great universities have begun to use the same number to keep academic records. The interviewers in attitude studies could probably obtain that same number and make the combination suggested.

However, in the immediate future such data from public records will be available only in aggregate form, assuring the anonymity of individuals, either for certain strata or for ecological units or, most frequently, a combination of both. The smaller such units (occupational, income, and age groups) and the ecological units (cities, counties, census tracts, etc.) are, the greater the possibility of combining them with the data from surveys for individuals. In some countries (like the United States) the social scientist not only will depend on the published data but will have access to the original IBM cards (without identification of individuals) or to samples of such data to do his own analysis. Certainly such data analyzed for ecological units in a way comparable to the survey data will facilitate their combination. This will not allow the matching of individuals in the official records and those interviewed in attitude surveys of a private character. But certainly the combination of aggregate data from both sources will become increasingly feasible. However, this will require important changes in the design of survey research and the construction of questionnaires.

An effort could and should be made to obtain data from government and other records to combine them with those — generally attitude data — acquired by academic social scientists through surveys. This would require certain safeguards, like eliminating from the newly created record (tape or IBM card) any information that could lead easily to the identification of the person, as well as agreeing not to make the attitude data available to those agencies that might take advantage of the records. Limitations like those restricting the publication of statistics for groupings of less than a certain number of firms should be established in these cases to protect the rights of individuals or organizations.

In this changing context the researcher accustomed to working with attitude surveys, particularly those coming from a psychologically oriented tradition, will have to pay more attention to the work of human ecologists, urban and rural sociologists (human geographers in many European countries), demographers, and economists. A thorough knowledge of government records, population censuses, and other official statistics, the methods used in their collection, and their serious weaknesses for sociological analysis will become more important. It should not be forgotten that the official character of such data, the fact that they are based on enumeration rather than sampling, is no guarantee of their reliability and validity and that before using them one should be aware of their limitations as the experienced survey researcher is aware of the limitations of his data.

THEORETICAL REASONS FOR COMBINING ECOLOGICAL AND SURVEY DATA

The combination of both types of data grows not only out of the complementarity and the need for a better use of available information about most societies but out of an important change in theoretical orientation in sociology. The advance in knowledge, partly due to the accumulation of data, as well as of cross-national research, has made us aware of the need to specify further many of our generalizations by taking into account contextual variables, milieu, institutional settings, absolute and relative rates of change, reference groups, membership groups, etc., in understanding individual attitudes and behavior. *Structural-functional* analysis, on the one hand, and the emphasis on *social interaction,* on the other, have stressed that the individual and his behavior cannot be studied in isolation from his social context[27] and from his interaction with others. Sociometric data allow us to place the individual in a network of social interactions, but they do not take care of the more diffuse influences of the milieu[28] or of global properties[29] of the milieu, of whose influence the individual might not be aware even when they affect his attitudes and behavior. Persons in apparently the same "objective" situation — in terms of occupation, skill, income, education, social origin, religion, etc. — will think differently about their position and react to it differently depending on the social context. Context is defined by attributes such as whether those so placed are in a majority or a minority in their community, whether they work in large

[27] Robert K. Merton, *Social Theory and Social Structure* (Glencoe: Free Press, rev. ed., 1957), see Chap. 1: "Manifest and Latent Functions," pp. 19–84, with a bibliographical postscript on structural-functional analysis. See pp. 72–73 on "structural context."

[28] On the concept of reference group, milieu, etc., see "Contributions to the Theory of Reference Group Behavior," and "Continuities in the Theory of Reference Groups and Social Structure," in *ibid.*, pp. 281–386. See p. 304 on milieu.

[29] See references in footnote 10.

or small plants, whether they are present in different proportions, and whether they interact or are isolated. To emphasize this contextual element in social reality was one of the great contributions of Émile Durkheim's *Suicide*.[30] Such a context can affect the attitudes of people consciously or without their awareness, a difference that often will coincide with the interaction with others as a mediating factor or a more indirect influence of the milieu.

In the case of interaction with others and awareness of the impact of that interaction, we speak of "interpersonal influence," "opinion leadership," "pressure toward conformity," etc. These are likely to be revealed by survey research in a community context, particularly when sociometric techniques are used. The situations where there is interaction but no awareness of influence on particular attitudes or behaviors are often more surprising to the social scientist but no less important. The concept of reference group is often useful in accounting for these situations.

The situations where there is no direct interaction also are generally those where the individual is not aware of how the social, institutional, and organizational context, and even the physical setting of his life affect his attitudes. Obviously there are situations in which the individual can be aware of how he reacts to his environment without forming his opinions through interactions with others in it. Ecological data are likely to reveal such compositional effects but unlikely to distinguish these four kinds of situations. Ecological approaches therefore are more likely to point toward the need to search for structural effects than to account for their presence.

Even the fact itself — independently of the awareness of it — that a great majority or a small minority in a community (or organization) holds the same opinions will affect the social relations of those holding them and their "way of holding" their opinions: degree of conviction, resistance to change, etc. In other cases the social context, of which the ecological context is a particular case, will allow us to redefine "apparently" equal social positions as different, without the need for many additional questions. For example, a railroad worker of the SNCF of the same category, income, age, marital status, etc., in its Western or its Southern division is basically in the same social position as his counterpart in another division but in a different context. This will be reflected

---

[30] Hanan C. Selvin, "Durkheim's *Suicide* and Problems of Empirical Research," *American Journal of Sociology*, 63 (1958), pp. 607–619. Also see S. M. Lipset and Neil J. Smelser, *Sociology. The Progress of a Decade* (Englewood Cliffs, N.J.: Prentice-Hall, 1961), pp. 132–145.

in his vote. But the Andalusian farm laborer and the one living in Castille are really in two basically different social positions, masked only by a superficial classification based on occupation and income. We should be clear when we are speaking of context in a strict sense and when we use it as a shorthand to define more precisely different social roles that are only apparently identical in a standard national sample survey.

In practice, the distinction we just made often is very fluid, and to decide whether we are confronted with one or the other case might not always be important. Confronted with the second case, we shall have to use more refined categories, additional information for the individuals studied, in future research when we might not have contextual information (for example, ecological data) to correct our overly simple categorization of social reality. It might serve as a rule of thumb that when the differences in attitudes or behavior in different contexts of those classified in a certain category are much greater than those between categories (such as broad occupational groups), we may want to redefine the classifications used. Strictly defined contextual effects should generally be minor. We are more likely to be confronted with them when we find differences in the same direction in all or most groups in the same contexts, even when they are also situations where contingent effects are involved.

The information about the social context, including the ecological context, can be derived either from prepublished data (censuses, statistics) that we combine with the survey data (on the basis of the selection of sampling points within such contexts or b your knowledge of the location of those points) or from the aggregation of the data on the basis of the interviews made within units or communities we want to consider as a context.[31] In both cases we can use averages as well as

[31] In a study of Spanish businessmen by Juan J. Linz and Amando de Miguel, we characterized the business community of different industrial centers as more or less socially integrated — we could also say cohesive — by the proportion of entrepreneurs who claimed that the majority of their friends were businessmen. The attitudes and behavior of the men of affairs in those communities were different, even among those who themselves had a similar proportion of friends in business among their five best friends. See Juan J. Linz and Amando de Miguel, *Los Empresarios ante el Poder Público: El Liderazgo y los Grupos de Interéses en el Empresariado Español* (Madrid: Instituto de Estudios Políticos, 1966), pp. 277–279, for a list of articles based on this study in which comparisons often are made between entrepreneurs in different cities or industrial regions. For a specific example of how the integration affects the perception of the prestige of five elite occupations, including that of the important businessman, see J. J. Linz and A. de Miguel, "El prestigio de profesiones en el mundo empresarial," *Revista de Estudios Políticos, 128* and *129–130* (1963).

measures of dispersion to characterize the climate of opinion or the
social structure that we want to consider as a context. Certainly the
information obtained by both methods can be used to estimate some of
the same characteristics and their correlation might be worth studying
to gain better insight into the milieu. Sometimes a discrepancy might
force us to question the validity of one or the other, and in other cases it
might suggest a discrepancy between the "more objective" ecological
indicators and their "subjective" perception or description by respondents. For example, we may characterize a community by the
inequality in the distribution of land ownership and at the same time by
the perception of that inequality by a sample of farmers. Both data do
not have to coincide, since for a number of reasons the discernibility of
the inequality might be different. A particular way to characterize a
community is by the perception of consensus or dissensus and to
compare that perception with the results of the actual responses on the
same issues (for example, the agreement with certain measures like land
consolidation by farmers) in that community — in other words, by
assessing its climate of opinion.

As another example, the crime rate for a district does not have to
coincide with the perception of the frequency of crime by those living
there. Areas with equal crime rates might be characterized by very
different perceptions. To account for them would be important, and
without doubt the perceptions are likely to have an impact on politics
if crime becomes an issue.

Let us emphasize that ecological data (from precollected sources,
mainly official ones) and survey data are not always interchangeable in
defining an ecological context.[32] This might well be the case with the
"latent" memories of the past, which are not easily verbalized or
forgotten but affect present politics, such as the areas of Finland where
Communists were shot by the White Guards (used by Allardt),[33] or
areas where the Depression hit strongly, or which had a particularistic
past of anti-Prussianism in Germany, etc. It would be interesting to
compare to what extent, in such ecologically defined areas, the memories
of the past have survived and to act upon the present through awareness
of that past. Historical ecologists have pointed to the second approach,
but its delimitation from the first is possible only by the use of survey
data. Certainly there will be cases in which the "weight of the past" will

[32] Paul F. Lazarsfeld and Wagner Thielens, Jr., *The Academic Mind* (Glencoe:
Free Press, 1958), pp. 402–407, discuss this problem of interchangeability of indices.

[33] Erik Allardt, "Patterns of Class Conflict and Working Class Consciousness in
Finnish Politics," in Allardt and Littunen (eds.), *op. cit.*, p. 123.

become evident only through ecological analysis, while in others the *mémoire collective* is also an individual memory.

Another example of a situation in which ecological and survey data are not interchangeable but complementary is in the study of deviance and normative behavior. In this area survey data and official data, often in ecological form, would give us very different pictures, either because of evasion of responses or because of the importance of differences in perception in cases of conflict of interests. For example, the number of labor law violations, conflicts between workers and employers about wages, etc., in different districts can give us some interesting information about labor relations. Undoubtedly, on the basis of their own experience, businessmen cannot generally give us adequate information about the proportion of cases before the labor courts that are decided favorably or unfavorably for either businessmen or workers. They can tell us their own experience (often too limited and distorted by their feelings) and, what is almost more interesting, their perception of those decisions. The comparison between those perceptions and the actual data for ecological units would reveal situations of discrepancy in both directions.[34] The situation where many businessmen believe that the courts are overwhelmingly pro-labor when they are not is certainly not the same as when, with an identical pro-con ratio, they believe that the courts are fair. Labor relations that objectively may be similar are likely to have, in both cases, very different political consequences.

EXAMPLES OF ECOLOGICAL CONTEXT DATA IN ANALYSIS OF SURVEY DATA

Let us exemplify our discussion with some data from a recent national sample survey in Spain.[35] In it we have the responses of men in different occupational groups that reflect the class differences in the society. The combination of these survey data with the information

[34] For example, see the attempt to compare survey and ecological data on Labor Court decisions in Spain: Juan J. Linz and Amando de Miguel, "El empresario ante los problemas laborales," *Revista de Politica Social, 60* (Madrid, 1963), pp. 5–105; see especially pp. 93–101; and on attitudes toward labor representatives in the enterprises and participation in trade union elections, the same authors: "La representación sindical vista por los empresarios," *Fomento Social, 78* (1965), pp. 115–147.

[35] These data were made available to the author by the courtesy of Fundación FOESSA (Fomento de Estudios Sociales y de Sociologia Aplicada) and of Dr. Amando de Miguel, Director of DATA S.A., who directed the study and whose co-operation is gratefully acknowledged. Neither of these sources is responsible for the interpretation given here to the data.

about the economic development of the province of residence, as indicated by the provincial per capita income data,[36] allows us to begin to test propositions about the consequences of modernization in attitudes, values, and behavior. One characteristic of a modern society — almost irrespective of political system — is increasing equality of the citizens before the law. Another is the greater emphasis on achieved rather than ascribed qualities, on universalism rather than particularism, on the greater predictability of life and consequently less feeling that success depends on luck.

These propositions would lead us to expect different responses to questions touching on these dimensions among men in comparable occupations in provinces of high and low per capita income. In the following tables (Tables 1 and 2) we have divided the respondents into seven occupational groups by their residence in provinces of low, medium, and high income. In general we can expect some kind of linear relation between provincial economic development and attitudes within each of the seven occupational groups. (Incidentally, such contextual effects may not always be linear, particularly when we can distinguish clearly some of the more extreme contexts in which other factors may become relevant, producing a U-shaped pattern or a reversal in certain groups at the extremes.) The data presented (Table 1) show that provincial wealth is associated in all occupational strata (if we compare low- and high-income provinces) with a larger number of people feeling that they would receive equal treatment by the police in an incident such as a traffic violation.[37] As a matter of fact, in five

---

[36] The classification of the provinces by per capita income is based on the study of the Banco de Bilbao, *Renta Nacional de España y su distribución provincial 1962* (Bilbao, 1963), p. 16. The provinces in the low-income group are all the Andalusian except Sevilla, Estremadura, two of the south central meseta, and three of Galicia. The high-income provinces are Madrid, Barcelona, and Gerona in Catalonia, Vizcaya, and Guipuzcoa in the Basque country and the Baleares. In this case operationally defined units coincide largely with actual geographically contiguous provinces.

[37] The question was taken with a slight modification — leaving out the second example, or a "minor violation" — from the five-nation study by Gabriel A. Almond and Sidney Verba, *The Civic Culture: Political Attitudes and Democracy in Five Nations* (Princeton: Princeton University Press, 1963). See pp. 106–114 for a comparative analysis of the findings. The percentages expecting equal treatment in Italy among those with no education and with some university education were 27 and 74, and 68 among those with some secondary education; in Mexico the proportions, respectively, were 14, 51, and 54. The no-education and university-educated can probably be compared with the farm laborers and free professionals in Spain. In the United Kingdom those with primary education or less were 88 per cent, those with some university education, 96 per cent; in West Germany they were, respectively, 70 and 88 per cent.

Table 1

EXPECTATION OF EQUAL TREATMENT BY POLICE, ACCORDING TO OCCUPATION AND ECONOMIC DEVELOPMENT OF PROVINCE.

Occupation	Per Capita Income in Province (Pesetas)	Expectation of Treatment (%)			Don't Know and No Answer	Number in Group
		Better	Equal	Worse		
Farm laborers	17,000 or less	6	76	10	8	(182)
	17,000–26,000	2	90	4	4	(52)
	26,000 or more	0	100	0	0	(36)
Manual workers	17,000 or less	5	78	9	9	(204)
	17,000–26,000	6	83	3	8	(180)
	26,000 or more	5	84	8	3	(170)
Farmers	17,000 or less	7	78	6	9	(188)
	17,000–26,000	4.5	83.5	4	8	(176)
	26,000 or more	4.5	91	0	4.5	(22)
Small business and self-employed workers	17,000 or less	10	81	4	5	(155)
	17,000–26,000	8	87	1	4	(78)
	26,000 or more	1	94	0	5	(67)
White-collar workers (including civil servants and managerial)	17,000 or less	16	76	2	6	(147)
	17,000–26,000	22	69	4	5	(88)
	26,000 or more	11	85	3	1	(143)
Large and medium businessmen	17,000 or less	11	85	0	4	(26)
	17,000–26,000	12	81	0	7	(52)
	26,000 or more	0	100	0	0	(18)
Free professionals	17,000 or less	32	60	0	8	(37)
	17,000–26,000	19	69	3	9	(32)
	26,000 or more	6	94	0	0	(34)
Total	17,000 or less	10	77	6	7	(939)
	17,000–26,000	9	82	3	6	(622)
	26,000 or more	6	89	4	2	(490)

groups the relationship is a linear one. If we had the data only by occupation, we could not be sure that they would not be due to the different proportions of those engaged in them who live in developed and underdeveloped regions. If we had only the data for men living in regions of unequal development (see bottom of the tables), we could never be sure whether they were due to the different proportions of privileged or underprivileged strata living in them. The data as presented allow us to state that both occupation and economic development are related to the perception of equality before the law in Spanish society. Certainly in some strata the expectation of being treated unequally is an expectation of disadvantage, in others one of privilege. (We may note that in such an underprivileged stratum as the farm laborers in the underdeveloped areas a larger minority expects favorable treatment, perhaps counting on the weight of particularistic friendship ties.) Among free professionals, small businessmen, self-employed workers, and farmers, their status in the less developed provinces seems to assure them a more privileged position. The same is true for white-collar workers and civil servants and bigger businessmen, if we compare their responses in low- and medium-income provinces with those in the most developed ones. Another indication of the importance of the contextual factor is the minimal proportion without an opinion on the question in developed Spain and the almost consistently higher proportion in the low-income provinces.

It might be argued that some of the contextual effects that this combination of ecological and survey data has allowed us to discover would disappear if we redefined the occupational groups with greater precision. Certainly the categories "farm laborer" and "farmer" comprise, in different regions of Spain, people who should not be included in the same occupational grouping. With more cases in each group we might have gone a step further by taking within the 21 groups we are considering only those with an almost identical income. However justified this may be in analytical terms, by doing so we risk losing sight of the social reality that these different provincial milieus represent, even when they in turn are a reflection of the different occupational structure that is associated with economic development, as revealed by the absolute figures in parentheses, on which the percentages are based. In underdeveloped Spain, fewer people in all strata believe in full equality before the law, but the larger proportion (19 per cent) of underprivileged farm laborers in it must contribute to that climate of opinion and to the police mores that the answers may more or less accurately reflect.

Quite consistently with the basic homogeneity of industrial society and the great heterogeneity of rural social structures we find that the differences by context among manual workers are relatively small compared with those among farm laborers and farmers. The great differences in the expectations of free professionals — an occupationally relatively homogeneous group — in different social contexts is particularly noteworthy. Certainly the elite position of the professional in a semideveloped society, as the poorer provinces of Spain can be considered, becomes apparent from the data, and we may add that they support our image of the professions as part of a premodern society compared to the business bourgeoisie.[38]

Let us stress that these findings would not have been possible without combining the survey data with ecological data since it would have been difficult if not impossible to derive the economic development of each province (or better, sampling point) from averaging the responses on income of the respondents in them. Naturally, there are situations in which the contextual variablesc an be derived from the data of the survey, particularly in studies of people in organizations, work groups, or elites. But this is not likely to be the case in national sample surveys.

The question concerning equality of treatment by the police probably reflects in part the reality, in part differences in values affecting expectations, and it is likely to be somewhat affected by political attitudes (as the slight increase of the "worse" response among workers in the developed regions suggests). Another question[39] about the factors accounting for success is even more likely to reflect differences in values between a developed, mainly industrial society and a more traditional, rural one.

Before we enter into a detailed analysis, it might be noted that despite the differences in economic development (see last three rows of Table 2) there is an over-all national pattern of response. Luck still occupies an important place, though most marked among the less privileged, particularly for the rural population for whom irregular crops due to the

---

[38] On this point — the distinction between a bourgeoisie based on a modern economy and the middle classes (*clases medias*) — whose existence and growth is largely independent of economic development, see Juan J. Linz and Amando de Miguel, "Within-Nation Differences and Comparisons: The Eight Spains," in Merritt and Rokkan (eds.), *op. cit.*, pp. 285–295.

[39] This question is a modified version of the one used in a study of values of college students. See Rose K. Goldsen, Morris Rosenberg, Robin M. Williams, Jr., and Edward Suchman, *What College Students Think* (Princeton: Van Nostrand, 1960), p. 18. The same question has been asked in Spain in a National Youth Study and in studies of secondary school and university students.

Table 2

FACTORS FOR SUCCESS, BY OCCUPATION AND PROVINCIAL PER CAPITA INCOME*

Occupation	Per Capita Income in Province (Pesetas)	Luck (%)	Adapt- ability (%)	Acquaint- ance with Influential People (%)	Capacity to Get Along (%)	Pleasant Personality (%)	Hard Work (%)	Intel- ligence (%)	Number in Group
Farm laborers	17,000 or less	30	4	14	3	5	15	16	(182)
	17,000–26,000	42	6	14	0	2	15	21	(52)
	26,000 or more	22	0	8	0	0	36	31	(36)
Farmers	17,000 or less	39	3	77	2	3	17	23	(188)
	17,000–26,000	17	1	55	1	3	36	30	(176)
	26,000 or more	14	0	5	0	0	32	46	(22)
Manual workers	17,000 or less	32	4	14	3	3	12	24	(204)
	17,000 –26,000	28	5	10	4	5	24	23	(180)
	26,000 or more	28	2	19	7	4	11	27	(170)
Small business and self-employed workers	17,000 or less	26	5	10	1	8	20	25	(155)
	17,000–26,000	19	6	10	4	12	13	35	(78)
	26,000 or more	24	2	16	3	13	33	16	(67)
White-collar workers (including civil servants and managerial)	17,000 or less	14	7	7	2	13	14	39	(147)
	17,000–26,000	17	5	7	3	10	8	50	(88)
	26,000 or more	14	6	14	3	9	15	40	(143)
Large and medium businessmen	17,000 or less	15	4	14	4	19	27	31	(25)
	17,000–26,000	6	6	14	6	25	19	25	(52)
	26,000 or more	6	0	8	6	11	17	56	(18)
Free professionals	17,000 or less	8	3	16	0	14	24	30	(37)
	17,000–26,000	6	0	3	3	9	47	31	(32)
	26,000 or more	6	3	6	6	12	18	50	(34)
Total	17,000 or less	28	4	11	2	7	16	25	(939)
	17,000–26,000	22	4	8	3	6	24	30	(622)
	26,000 or more	20	3	13	4	7	18	33	(490)

* First factor mentioned when asked "Which of the qualities in this list do you believe lead most rapidly to success today?"

Spanish climate make this a not-so-unrealistic answer. The two most clearly universalistic criteria; hard work and intelligence, even in a semideveloped society, are already prominent (41 per cent of the responses in the low-income and 51 per cent in the high-income provinces). The most particularistic response; the reliance on "pull," acquaintance with people of influence and power, the patronage so important in traditional societies (and so often noted as an evil by critics of Spanish society), is important but not more so than qualities that involve an element of "other-orientedness."[40]

The basic pattern of regional differences is reproduced with relatively few reversals in all occupational groups. Luck, independently of economic development, is more important for farmers and farm laborers, but it is less important even for them in the more developed areas. It is also more important for manual workers than for other urban occupational groups, particularly upper middle- and upper-class strata. The relatively small differences among workers by economic development may be due to the large proportion of rural migrants among the workers in the most developed parts of the country. At the other extreme we find that the importance of intelligence increases with economic development in almost all occupations. (The only significant reversal is among small business people and independent workers, where luck and hard work seem to be more important in the most developed areas of Spain.) It is noteworthy that while the importance of work increases from the low-income to the medium-income provinces (among farmers, manual workers, free professionals) and among some groups continues to increase from medium to high income, there is a significant number of cases in which it is emphasized less in the developed regions, particularly among the free professionals and the medium and larger business men. It seems as if these groups would consider intelligence — and probably education — as more important, with hard work considered to be a traditional, petit bourgeois virtue. We would not mention this finding if a study of Spanish businessmen, employing over fifty workers, had not shown the same pattern by region and size of business.[41]

[40] Obviously, the response to the question is only indicative of qualities that might be described by this term as used by David Riesman, in collaboration with R. Denney and N. Glazer, *The Lonely Crowd: A Study of the Changing American Character* (New Haven: Yale University Press, 1950).

[41] The emphasis on hard work is a typical response of small businessmen (54 per cent of those employing 50 to 100 workers mention it among five qualities for success) while among the heads of large enterprises (1,000 or more workers) only 26 per cent mention it, stressing more "thinking ahead" and "getting along" with others. Data are from a forthcoming study by Juan J. Linz and Amando de Miguel on the Spanish businessman.

As in the case of a national sample, study of youth and relationship between development and particularism are not as clear as the writings of Talcott Parsons as many students of social change would lead us to expect. The same response seems to have a different meaning for various occupational groups in similar contexts. Among rural groups knowing a "patron" seems more important in the poorer parts of the country. At the other extreme of the stratification system — free professionals and businessmen — we also find the greatest emphasis on particularism in the underdeveloped areas (where they also more often expected favorable treatment by the police). It is among the urban lower and lower-middle classes that we find the unexpected reversal: particularism is perceived as more important in the developed provinces. We can only speculate about this response. It might be a result of the recent migration to the cities of rural people who substitute the belief in luck — inappropriate to an urban context — for a more predictive trust in protection, a belief that also would protect their egos from being hurt by having to attribute failure to lack of hard work or intelligence. Or it might be that the response reflects the disappointments suffered in relation to their expectations of rewards for achievement in a society where particularism is still important: the larger proportion mentioning it reflects, not a greater rate of particularism in the society, but a greater sensitivity to it.[42] The low emphasis on luck and pull among the most privileged in the developed areas may reflect, not reality, but their greater commitment to the values of achievement and universalism, as well as the psychological need, under those circumstances, to attribute their own privileged social position (indirectly) to their own efforts. As Max Weber and Robert Merton have stressed, the successful also want to feel that they have a moral right to their privileged position.[43]

Let us stress the methodological implications of the preceding analysis. Without the contextual variable (in this case derived from ecological data) we would not have been able to go beyond the impact of occupation on the perceptions of the social system. We would not have discovered that the value system that seems to dominate in a society changes with economic development, even for those who do not occupy directly the positions resulting from that change. The change is one of

[42] The problem of particularism versus universalism in Spanish culture, society, and attitudes has been studied, using data from a national sample study of Spanish youth by Amando de Miguel, "Estructura social y juventud española: normas institucionales," *Revista del Instituto de la Juventud, 1* (Madrid, 1965), pp. 111–144. See also articles by the same author in numbers *0* (1965), *5*, and *6* (1966) based on the same national survey.

[43] "Social Structure and Anomie," in Merton, *op. cit.*, pp. 148–149.

milieu. But such a contextual analysis alerts us to the fact that similar responses may, in different contexts, result from different motivations or mean different things, and in this our data point beyond our previous example. Some of the reversals in the high-income provinces and the different patterns in various occupational strata in those provinces point in that direction. (We would not be giving such emphasis to this finding if we had not encountered similar patterns in two other independent studies.) Here we are dealing with what Peter Blau has called contingency effects,[44] a type of structural effect that he describes as cases where the structural effects, "instead of having an effect on a third variable that is independent of the individual's value orientation, may determine whether the individual's value orientation and a third variable are related or how they are related." In the case we are discussing the individual's value orientation — for which we have no information — is his own attitude toward the universalism-particularism dimension, his valuation of its legitimacy, that may be different among people in the same occupation in different regions.

If we wanted an example of how basic social positions have a different subjective meaning in different contexts, the data about subjective class identification (Table 3) of seven occupational groups in three types of provinces by economic development would be sufficient. The most striking difference can be found in those from the lower-income and lower-status occupations who identify themselves as "poor" rather than "working"-class. Certainly a farm laborer or manual worker who calls himself "poor" is likely to have a different view of society and politics than the one who calls himself working-class. Leaving aside those who are nothing but poor in a strict sociological sense, that is, those without an occupation, the poorly paid have the choice of seeing themselves as poor or working-class; as poor or as workers, their expectations and demands are likely to be quite different. Undoubtedly, the long-time weakness of the Spanish Socialist Party in areas with a large proletariat and its strength among workers in developed and semideveloped areas are not unrelated to this subjective perception of class position. The proportion of those in the more privileged strata who are willing to consider themselves "working-class" also increases with economic development. These findings about the greater willingness to identify oneself as working-class with economic development is an intranation replication of the same finding when we compare the answer to an identical or similar question in nine Western countries — with 93 per

44 Blau, *op. cit.*, pp. 183–185.

Table 3

SUBJECTIVE CLASS IDENTIFICATION BY OCCUPATION AND PROVINCIAL PER CAPITA INCOME*

Occupation	Income (Pesetas)	Alta (%)	Media Alta (%)	Media Baja (%)	Trabajadora (%)	Pobre (%)	Number in Group
Farm laborer	17,000 or less	0	0	4	55	41	(181)
	17,000–26,000	0	0	6	69	25	(52)
	26,000 or more	0	0	0	97	3	(35)
Farmer	17,000 or less	0.5	3	21	67	7	(188)
	17,000–26,000	2	10	26	53	9	(179)
	26,000 or more	0	0	14	86	0	(22)
Manual worker	17,000 or less	0	0.5	7	76.5	16	(204)
	17,000–26,000	0	2	10	76	12	(181)
	26,000 or more	1	1	6	85	7	(170)
Small business and independent	17,000 or less	1	10	24	55	10	(155)
	17,000–26,000	0	2	10	45	4	(78)
	26,000 or more	0	13	22	60	2	(67)
White-collar and managerial people	17,000 or less	1	26	31	34	7	(148)
	17,000–26,000	2	23	40	33	2	(88)
	26,000 or more	1	29	38.5	28	3	(143)
Larger and medium businessmen	17,000 or less	0	48	36	12	0	(25)
	17,000–26,000	0	56	25	19	0	(16)
	26,000 or more	6	50	17	28	0	(18)
Free professionals	17,000 or less	3	43	43	11	0	(37)
	17,000–26,000	16	44	28	13	0	(32)
	26,000 or more	0	53	32	15	0	(34)
Total	17,000 or less	0	9	18	56	16	(938)
	17,000–26,000	2	13	22	54	9	(626)
	26,000 or more	1	16	20	59	4	(489)

* The question asked was "Of these five social classes to which would you say your family belongs?" And the alternatives were: upper, upper-middle, lower-middle, working, and poor.

cent of Dutch workers so identifying themselves, 57 per cent of a Mexican sample, and 85 per cent among Spaniards.[45]

In the examples presented we used an ecological variable as a variable in the analysis of survey responses, but there is also the possibility of analyzing ecological data on the basis of information derived from surveys. In a study of Spanish businessmen[46] we obtained the prestige ranking of five elite occupations and calculated the average rank of each among the businessmen in a number of provinces. From various sources — biographical data, lists of civil servants, census data — we were able to obtain the proportion of members of the elites born in different provinces and calculated the extent to which those born in them were over- or underrepresented in relation to the population of those provinces at the time of their birth. This allowed us to correlate the ranking of provinces in terms of prestige assigned to various occupations and their ranking in terms of their recruitment. This effort to relate ecological data to survey data served to test the hypothesis that prestige and recruitment into occupations are closely related. Certainly data on the recruitment of elites cannot always be obtained by surveys, particularly national sample surveys, but they are available in many sources giving the place of birth. On the other hand, the prestige of occupations in different milieus cannot easily be assessed except by survey data. Bringing both together permits us to reach new conclusions. Survey analysts should therefore be more concerned about the type of ecological data that would allow them to test additional hypotheses for which they might not have data in their surveys. To give another example, it would be difficult to obtain in surveys information on violations of norms; but it is not difficult to obtain opinions about the legitimacy of norms, about the degree to which norms hurt the interests of people, the extent to which people would condone violations or be punitive toward violators, would fear punishment, or would favor change in the norms. It seems obvious that we could more often design research about deviance from norms relating such attitudes to the actual rates of deviance recorded by the police, the courts, or administrative agencies for the same groups in specific communities or administrative units. What better test is there of the significance of attitudes toward labor legislation than the number of violations in industrial communities where different attitudes predominate? Such studies could better

[45] Data quoted in Fundación FOESSA, *Informe sociologico sobre la situación social de España, op. cit.*

[46] Linz and Miguel, "El prestigio de profesiones en el mundo empresarial," *op. cit.,* pp. 56–64.

determine the importance of various attitudes in encouraging or deterring from deviance.

PROBLEMS IN THE COMBINED USE OF ECOLOGICAL AND SURVEY DATA

If the advantages just mentioned are convincing, the usefulness of combining both types of data should not make us overly optimistic about the feasibility of doing so in many cases and about the difficulties involved. Certainly both the orthodox survey design and the normal construction of questionnaires will have to be modified, and the more refined ecological analysis may have to be modified to an extent that many ecologists will find disappointing.

Generally, randomly selected sampling points proportional to population will not be adequate to represent ecological areas defined by social, economic, and other characteristics, particularly if some of the most distinctive ones are sparsely populated. On the other hand, some heavily populated ecological types would be more than adequately represented in a national sample. An oversampling of the first and an undersampling of the second might be the answer, with a weighting of interviews to obtain, at the same time, a representative national sample.

The oversampling of certain areas and types of communities will always be necessary if we want to analyze the impact of ecologically defined contexts on the attitudes and behavior of individuals or organizations located in them. (The only other alternative would be extremely large samples.) This need becomes even greater when we want to explore structural effects in a particular community with its global properties (for example, the long-time leadership of a particular politician) or properties derived from attitude distributions within the community (the "climate of opinion"). If that information is to be obtained in the same survey, it should also, in principle, be a sample representative of the community. These difficulties will be compounded if through sociometric techniques we attempt to go beyond an imputed climate of opinion (derived from the attitude distributions within the community or organization) to the interaction system of the individual by interviewing also those persons he mentions as friends, opinion leaders, reference groups, etc., since in that case the original sample will be expanded in an initially undetermined way.[47] The study of attitudes

[47] Elihu Katz and Paul F. Lazarsfeld, *Personal Influence: The Part Played by People in Flow of Mass Communications* (New York: Free Press, 1964); see pp. 149–161 on designators, influentials, and influences (Part II, Chap. 1) and the Technical Appendixes.

and behavior in ecologically defined contexts by survey methods, particularly in a specific set of individually defined communities rather than merely a type of community, is not easy within the framework of a more comprehensive (national or regional) survey without loss of statistical representativeness by either. This dilemma cannot be dismissed since without an adequate knowledge and understanding of the over-all basic relation between the variables we cannot be sure that the differences observed between communities are due to compositional effects. In addition, it would generally be illegitimate to derive statements about the larger universe if the selection of such sampling points has been made on the basis of ecological (often purposive) criteria rather than randomly, or if, for the sake of concentrating the interviews in those places where we expect interesting compositional or general structural effects, certain types of areas are omitted as sociologically or demographically less interesting. The discussion of theoretical advantages of the combination of ecological and survey data can ignore these practical problems. But unless endowed with an unlimited budget, any attempt to make use of their combination has to take such problems into consideration (as I quickly discovered when planning a research design for an OECD study of Andalusia).[48] Several possibilities for circumventing this dilemma are open:

1. One could use in the ecologically based studies questions from nationally representative samples that could serve as a "base line."

2. One could execute simultaneously with many identical questions a representative sample survey of the larger unit and the context-oriented sample surveys.

3. In the case of cumulative research by the same organization or researcher, the information about the climate of opinion in particular units derived from intensive research could be treated as a global property in the analysis of a smaller number of respondents in the same community found in a national representative sample.

4. The partial duplication of previous surveys in ecologically defined contexts would allow improvement of the representativeness of the national survey for them, with the addition of new problems particular to a new study of those units. It would be best to place the findings in a national or larger context without the costs of a new national study.

All these approaches involve uneasy compromises. The choice to be

[48] Study of Institutional and Social Obstacles to Economic Development of Andalusia (Spain) by a team of experts of the OECD.

made will be more or less satisfactory for either the ecologically based contextual analysis or the more descriptive (and/or analytical) study of the larger unit, particularly of the whole society. For instance, in the Andalusia study the surveys in a small number of communities selected within socioeconomically typical areas will be particularly useful for the community power and development aspects and for the rural sociologist but considerably less so for the member of the research group interested in describing, interpreting, and predicting migration and labor force trends for the region. I believe that most compromise solutions between the traditional representative sample survey and the ecologically context-oriented surveys will have to use in the analysis *types* of ecologically defined areas (grouping communities and sampling points) rather than focus on *individually identifiable contexts* in which the individuals interviewed would be actually interacting socially or be exposed to identical global effects. This means that in most cases we shall be dealing with some kind of abstract structural effects rather than with actual compositional effects.

The problems of combining survey research techniques with ecological analysis become compounded when we consider the secondary analysis of already collected data or the use of the national sample surveys of public opinion research organizations, which cannot devote so much effort to planning ecologically based studies or designing such complicated samples as suggested earlier. In this case we have to limit ourselves to asking for much more adequate reporting on the IBM cards for secondary analysis of the sampling points so that we shall be able to make our own combinations in view of the ecological analysis.

An effort to improve the representativeness of the samples for regions, size of community, types of socioeconomic areas, etc., by stratifying the sample by such criteria would be useful. In this case an attempt to code in the original study basic ecological information would help secondary analysis. The availability for each country of a data bank for minor administrative units[49] (municipalities, cantons, even departments) whose information would automatically be added to every interview would be ideal. (With the use of electronic tapes this should be neither difficult nor costly.) Even so, an ecologically oriented secondary analysis

[49] Such a file exists in a number of countries. For Finland, see Allardt, in Merritt and Rokkan (eds.), *op. cit.*, pp. 338–339, for the variables included in a file for the 550 Finnish communes. For Norway, see Stein Rokkan and Henry Valen, "Archives for Statistical Studies of Within-Nation Differences," in *ibid.*, pp. 412–418, and E. Allardt, "Social Sources of Finnish Communism: Traditional and Emerging Radicalism," *International Journal of Comparative Sociology*, 5 (1964), pp. 49–72.

of ordinary survey data will always encounter the difficulty of lack of representativeness and small size of any part of a national sample for distinctive areas or communities. Only the accumulation of several national samples would bypass this difficulty. This, in turn, would require that such national samples be drawn the same way, using the same background characteristics (with the same coding) and at least a minimum of strictly identical questions over a relatively short period of time. Such an approach, incidentally, would also facilitate trend studies. (Marked changes over time naturally would make the accumulation of interviews for the same ecological areas of dubious validity.)

My feeling is that social research could make greater advances if all concerned would more often sacrifice the desire to be original, always to ask new questions and to obtain as many attitude data as possible, but rather would repeat more often those questions already used in the past or in another country and obtain more detailed "background variables." The accumulation of interviews for ecological analysis would require this, particularly since for the exploration of "compositional effects" it is essential to be able to control for a number of background variables simultaneously (occupation, education, income, length of residence, social integration, organizational memberships, etc.). Otherwise it would be impossible to know whether the discrepancies found between those living in different social contexts are due to their differences as people (either by background or by self-selection) or fundamentally to the fact of living in a different context or milieu. If in Spain, for example, we want to compare the attitudes of native Catalan and Basque workers in those regions with immigrant workers from other parts of Spain and with each other, we would, ideally, make the comparison between workers with similar occupational skills, incomes, working in similar plants, etc., to make sure that we do not attribute to the "climate of labor relations" in each region differences due to the position of the workers studied in the social and economic structure of each region. Those differences in position exist and naturally contribute to the "climate of labor relations." But the componential effects can be isolated only by analytic study of those groups not contributing to them, that is, by comparing metalworkers in both areas, even when the milieu of Barcelona is shaped by the dominant workers employed in family textile enterprises.[50] It should be noted that studies focused

[50] For examples see the articles based on the study of the Spanish businessman, particularly: Linz and Miguel, "El empresario ante los problemas laborales," op. cit., pp. 20–27, 72–76.

on structural effects may be highly misleading as descriptive studies, since groups central to the analysis may well be numerically, socially, or politically unimportant.

The refinements of survey and ecological analysis combined will often advance social science knowledge, the formulation of propositions and the testing of hypotheses. But it also may lead to a certain neglect of reality. An occasional glance at the absolute figures for the populations represented by those sampled in the survey would easily make us aware of the actual significance of groups whose analytical significance is unquestionable. For example, the few peasant owners of olive groves in small West Andalusian communities are important for sociological analysis. But this should not make us forget that olive cultivation predominates on large nonpeasant farms, in larger communities, etc., and that it is this dominant social structure that characterizes Western Andalusia. This difference in perspective is not unimportant in accounting for a certain dissatisfaction of policy makers or even of those of us attempting to describe a total national society with much of the knowledge accumulated by sophisticated studies.

The combination of ecological and survey research, particularly if data from government records (censuses, labor force surveys, social security data, immigration statistics, special surveys, etc.) become available for secondary analysis, will require the survey researcher to make his questions more comparable with those used in collecting these kinds of information. The census-type questions will have to be asked and coded in identical ways, something not always satisfactory since the manner of asking them in official forms is often unsatisfactory in the interview situation (for example, it may require the respondent to fill in tables or give data with a precision obtainable only if the trust in or the power of a government is absolutely assured). The experience of survey researchers could certainly be used to make official agencies more conscious of the shortcomings of their questionnaires from the point of view of the interview situation (that is, their inclusion of tables to be filled by the census taker without any actual wording of the questions asked by him).

In the preceding pages we have emphasized changes, and often sacrifices, that the traditional survey research approach will have to make in its marriage with ecological research. But as in all happy marriages, both sides will have to make some sacrifices. The ecologist is tempted to stress the uniqueness of certain regions as geographicosocial units or, if he has a historical bent, to stress the influence of history on socio-structurally identical areas, or, if he attempts to develop typologies of socioeconomic regions of a certain homogeneity (particularly agricultural regions combining crop data with land tenure systems and demographic change data), to arrive at a relatively large number of such units. If we consider that those ecological units have to serve in designing samples for survey analysis and that samples, to be representative, cannot be below a certain size irrespective of the size of the population sampled, it becomes apparent that the natural (and basically justified) tendency to multiply the units of ecological analysis becomes a source of strain between the research and the colleague who is planning a survey on the basis of his efforts.

To avoid the divorce of the two methods, a compromise is needed. One possible solution is to recombine the more adequate and refined ecological area types into broader ones defined only by the main variables. Another is that the survey analyst might convince the ecologist that, within any given budget, he can represent adequately only some types of areas, ignoring others either in terms of their demographic and thereby electoral, political, social importance or in terms of their strategic research interest irrespective of demography. The methods of areal representation used by ecologists coming from human geography often make the first approach difficult since only cumbersome calculations can transform areas that appear so distinctive on the maps into data on population. We have the impression that ecological data can serve as a basis for designing a survey only after their transfer from maps to IBM cards so that types can be selected at will by using different dimensions simultaneously and so that rapid estimates of their demographic significance can be obtained. Practically, this means that the data from maps or census-type statistics have to be coded or classified in intervals and that the cards have to include the absolute population figures.[51] Obviously, the inclusion of other absolute figures would allow us to obtain an important "by-product": the averages on other variables for the types selected (which sometimes could be compared with averages obtained by survey methods from respondents living in those areas). A fruitful by-product of this marriage of the two methods would be to make the ecologist more aware of the logic of social typologies so central to modern survey analysis and to make the survey researcher more conscious of the complex combinations in which the variables he uses analytically are found in social reality. It would also make him

[51] In comparisons over time the relative figures can be misleading, for example the per cent of men active in agriculture in a district may decrease census after census while the absolute number engaged in farming may be increasing with the consequent pressures on the land resources and resulting social conflicts.

more sensitive to the demographic significance of the groups he is used to seeing only analytically rather than as numbers of actual people.

It is probable that the use of the ecological data now in statistical yearbooks or on maps as the basis for the design of survey studies would greatly accelerate their transfer to IBM cards and tapes and would initiate data banks of a type that was not necessary as long as ecological analysis relied mainly on correlations or averages for a limited number of types of areas. Experimenting with different typologies of social structure in the process of defining ecological areas for sampling will require such data banks and will give the ecologist a new perspective.

In some areas like political sociology, survey research in the last decades has become increasingly cross-national (producing studies like those of Lipset, Alford, Almond, and Verba, and others).[52] The question may be raised as to whether the more contextual orientation derived from a combination with ecology and the various methodological adaptations (many of a practical nature) previously discussed will not limit cross-national comparability. My feeling is that this may happen, but it does not have to happen. In fact, an intelligent use of an ecological approach could improve much cross-national research. The logic of *internation* comparisons of *intranation* comparisons[53] relies on the collection of data on a cross-national basis with an ecological perspective in mind. This requires the selection of samples within countries that are not fully comparable but relatively similar, in geographical or institutional settings that are highly comparable, on the basis of information obtained a priori on an aggregate basis. The impact of the different institutional (democracy versus dictatorship, industrial versus semi-industrial, socialist versus capitalist) and historical factors characterizing total social systems on the attitudes and behavior of persons placed similarly in the social structure (as individuals living in similar social contexts, communities, regions of similar economic development, working in similar organizations, etc.) can then be studied much better. Cross-national studies of similar social strata or elites in comparable ecological settings could certainly contribute to comparative sociology as much as do present research designs. For example, the comparative study of elites in Rome, Madrid, and Lisbon, on the one hand, and in Milano-Torino-Genoa, Barcelona-Bilbao-Oporto, on the other (with

[52] S. M. Lipset, *op. cit.*, Almond and Verba, *op. cit.*, Robert Alford, *Party and Society: The Anglo-American Democracies* (Chicago: Rand McNally, 1963).

[53] Linz and Miguel, "Within-Nation Differences and Comparisons: The Eight Spains," in Merritt and Rokkan (eds.), *op. cit.*, pp. 267–272.

the consequent oversampling in some of those cities),[54] would certainly provide better insights into the elites and the social structure of these three areas than one designed to obtain just a representative sample of the elites, ignoring the distinctive role of those types of cities.

In general, an approach oriented toward developing *types* of ecological areas and aiming at representative samples of such areas rather than toward representing *distinctive communities* as such would be particularly fruitful for cross-national comparisons. The focus on actual compositional effects in this sense could be slightly detrimental to over-all international comparative research if no attempt is made to link such surveys with national survey data. However, as I noted before, any tendency to study particular ecological contexts without reference to the total national context is undesirable, on strictly theoretical grounds, in the study of community climates of opinion and other structural effects. Ecologically oriented survey research can be an advantage, not a detriment, to comparative research.

SUMMARY

While theoretical considerations—the awareness of context and structural effects — and the immense advantage of using the store of social and economic data accumulated by most societies strongly urge us to combine ecological and survey research methods, our discussion has brought out some of the many practical difficulties in doing so. The solutions required (unless the research should have at its disposal budgets far beyond what is usual in social research) will, I fear, not be fully satisfactory to the survey analyst and even less so to his statistical adviser, and it will distress the ecologist intimately familiar with the spatial distribution of social phenomena. The need to obtain representative samples of reasonable size, to accumulate data over time, to combine national with regional or local studies, to facilitate a certain degree of cross-national comparability will oblige us to pay much more attention to theoretically sound and empirically usable typologies of social structure,[55] using the most salient dimensions of social systems and

[54] For an example of a paper bringing together data characterizing the social structure of a city and province in a national context, see Amando de Miguel and Juan J. Linz, "El papel de Barcelona en la estructura social española," in *La Provincia: Dimensiones económica, informativa y sociológica* (Barcelona: Instituto de Ciencias Sociales. Diputación Provincial de Barcelona, 1966), pp. 243-254.

[55] For an initial list of dimensions to be used in developing such a typology, see Linz and Miguel, "Within-Nation Differences and Comparisons: The Eight Spains," in Merritt and Rokkan (eds.), *op. cit.*, pp. 279–282.

disregarding some of the uniqueness that the ecological approach would force upon us. In contrast to much of the traditional survey research that grew out of a sociopsychological perspective with an individualistic and rationalistic bent, the approach advocated here would have to turn more to macrosociological perspectives. Certainly such simple continua, like *Gemeinschaft* versus *Gesellschaft*, folk versus urban, rural versus urban, peasant versus feudal or neofeudal, class versus status-oriented, tradition versus modern, industrial versus non-industrial, developed versus underdeveloped, would quickly prove insufficient if not misleading. To consider them as continua rather than as dichotomies would be helpful. But we suspect that more refined theoretically and empirically meaningful types of social structure are needed and can be developed.

We are all aware of a number of dimensions, neither small nor unlimited, that we can use to characterize a society or unit within a society. We should make an effort to agree on a limited number of such dimensions and then decide on certain cutting-off points to place societies or units within the resulting typology. (Certainly the classifications in each specific case could be quite refined, but there should be a possibility of combining them into a more limited number of categories for comparability.) My feeling is that it would be easiest to progress in this direction by limiting our attention to countries within the same cultural area, with relatively similar degrees of economic, social, and/or political development. For cross-national research it would be ideal to be able to sample representatively regions, provinces, or communities falling into each of the "boxes" of such a typology, as long as the population falling into each was of a certain minimal numerical importance. By such a combination of ecologically defined units with sample surveys we could make more cross-national comparisons holding constant a relatively large number of variables and more comparisons of intranation differences — two types of comparison that are difficult to make today by using national samples. Another gain would be to discover the absence of certain types of social structure in some societies. We could start doing this on a limited number of dimensions (between five and ten) for half a dozen countries, using the data for provinces and major cities and taking the information from published data. On each of those dimensions we could use more or less complex classifications or one based on their positions with respect to the national average or to that of the countries being studied. By classifying each administrative unit and adding up their populations, we could estimate what proportion of the population lives in each "structural context." By doing this for a number of census years, we would be able to describe more accurately the social changes that have taken place and their direction.

In summary, we believe that an effort to combine ecological data and methods with survey research will contribute, indirectly but considerably, to macrosociology.

6

ERWIN K. SCHEUCH

Social Context and
Individual Behavior

BACKGROUND OF THE PROBLEM

THEORIES AND *ad hoc* explanations in the social sciences tend to be of greater interest when they link phenomena at different levels. However, in sociological and social psychological publications that are based on empirical research a different kind of theorizing has been common: relating two or more variables at the same level of reality. Of course, there has also been a tradition of cross-level theorizing in the social sciences, especially for topics with political implications. Although these types of statements have a greater inherent relevance, they have usually been based on inadequate empirical measures. This paper is a plea for combining the greater relevance of cross-level theorizing with the greater rigor of so-called direct measurement. The main obstacles to such a combination (which has become technically feasible) are (1) a lack of theoretical formulations that relate both levels as interacting realities and (2) certain intellectual traditions.

Whenever social scientists have been their own recorders of sense observations (for example, via controlled observation or interviews), they have preferred to use data on individual behavior (such as mobility aspirations) to account for higher-order phenomena (such as rigidity of a status system). For social psychologists, and also for many sociologists, it has accordingly been usual to "explain" higher-order phenomena by means of relative frequencies observed at a lower level of a social system,[1] either in terms of a partial explanation or with a reductionistic intent.[2] In European political science more often higher-order properties (such as stability of political preferences in counties) have been interpreted as if they were expressions of individual behavior (such as stability of an individual's political preference).[3]

Implicit in such substitutions for direct measurement is, in many cases, the assumption that occurrences at one particular level have a "higher" degree of reality. Thus individual behavior may be treated as being the only real phenomenon, while system properties are abstractions, or individual behavior may be viewed as a mere reflection of the only reality, namely structural properties — as some Marxist-inspired writings assert. Naturally, such orientations are rarely defended as explicit theoretical positions. And often the substitution for direct measurement is an accommodation to past necessities that turned into a tradition.[4]

In cross-level explanations our chains of inference are often frightfully long, in spite of the verbal respect that in empirical social science is paid to Robert Merton's notion of "theories of the middle range." We are so conditioned to this practice that we do not consider it outrageously bold when direct equivalences are posited between presumed personality properties in a population (such as authoritarianism) and

[1] A major example of the "individualistic fallacy" is Gabriel Almond and Sidney Verba, *The Civic Culture* (Princeton: Princeton University Press, 1963).

[2] Most versions of a reductionistic orientation are related to the ontological conceptions of Auguste Comte, namely that higher-order phenomena are just combinations of lower-order phenomena; accordingly, there should be a hierarchy of science where each preceding science in this hierarchy "explains" the phenomena of the subsequent via a reduction to its own level of observation. Thus, chemistry could be "reduced" to nuclear physics, psychology to neurophysiology. Reductionism in the social sciences usually takes the form of "explaining" sociological statements with reference to psychological variables and laws. This is the explicit program of George C. Homans, e.g., in his *Social Behavior in Its Elementary Forms* (New York: Harcourt, Brace & World, 1961). In the form of a reduction of sociology to psychology, reductionism seems intuitively plausible. Nevertheless, reductionism as a general stance is logically untenable; cf. Ernest Nagel, *The Structure of Science* (New York: Harcourt, Brace & World, 1961), especially chapters 11 and 14.

[3] Cf. the conception of "climate of opinion" in B. Berelson, Paul F. Lazarsfeld, and W. MacPhee, *Voting* (Chicago: University of Chicago Press, 1954).

[4] The clearest example is probably the school of *géographie electorale* in France. The logic of procedure is basically still the same as in André Siegfried's *Tableau politique de la France de l'Ouest sous la Troisième République* (Paris: Colin, 1913). For a critical evaluation see Austin Ranney (ed.), *Essays in the Behavioral Study of Politics* (Urbana: University of Illinois Press, 1962), pp. 91–102; see also Erwin K. Scheuch, "Cross-National Comparisons Using Aggregate Data," in Richard L. Merritt and Stein Rokkan (eds.), *Comparing Nations* (New Haven: Yale University Press, 1966), pp. 131–168.

the character of a polity.[5] Perhaps the chains of inferences are so long and so tenuous because the data we work with leave us so much freedom to organize findings in a variety of ways. Especially when we work with data from only one level of observation, the data put few restrictions on the fertile mind of a social scientist — and this is naturally an appealing condition.

Today most of our empirical knowledge in industrialized countries is based on surveys or other recordings of the verbal behavior of individuals. A check of a recent attempt to inventorize our social science knowledge confirmed this impression.[6] This check also showed how extensively we have neglected what Stein Rokkan termed "process-produced" data and have failed to take advantage of the fact that few things occur in developed societies that do not leave a trail of paper and numbers.[7] Not only do social researchers prefer to collect their own data at the expense of other available information, but they are also inclined to be monomaniacal with respect to techniques of data collection.

This description characterizes the situation in Anglo-Saxon countries, Scandinavian nations, and Central Europe. In some other countries, notably the Latin societies and Eastern Europe, social scientists more often prefer to work with one type of process-produced data: official statistics. This is especially true for political behavior. In addition, in most of Europe election returns and census data are the kind of data that the mass media and the politicians accept most readily as "hard evidence." Since in all Continental countries the fate of social science as a branch of learning, as well as the fate of individual social scientists, is more influenced by the reaction of mass media and the intelligentsia in general than by fellow social scientists, this veneration of "official

[5] This type of reasoning was very popular immediately following World War II in attempts to account for the development of totalitarian regimes in Germany and Japan. Theodor Adorno, Bertram Schaffner, and David McClelland (for Germany) and Ruth Benedict (for Japan) are authors whose explanations gained a good deal of credence and even fame. A popularized version of the reasoning is found in the writings of Geoffry Gorer. If the object of explanation were not a nation but rather a factory, it would be much less plausible if an author were to argue that the specific character of the Renault versus the Peugeot factories and their products was due to a personality trait common to the workers in one but not in the other factory. Explanations of political systems with reference to personality traits of their members are plausible only because they tend to rephrase in an acceptable terminology what is already known by way of national stereotypes.

[6] Cf. Bernard Berelson and Gary A. Steiner, *Human Behavior — An Inventory of Scientific Findings* (New York: Harcourt, Brace & World, 1964).

[7] Compare Stein Rokkan (ed.), *Data Archives for the Social Sciences* (Paris: Mouton, 1966).

data" is one important stimulus for basing cross-level analyses on one-level (aggregate) data; and this kind of audience for the social scientist also provides a largely uncritical market for one-level theorizing.[8]

The audience for social science research, and specifically for politically relevant writings, accounts just as much for national continuities in data use and in theorizing as any inherent need or any intellectual tradition could possibly do. Traditions are undoubtedly important, too, and the present interest of Continental sociologists and political scientists in aggregate data is still a consequence of the fact that in the nineteenth century data from the official bookkeeping of bureaucracies were available before social scientists became their own data collectors; in the United States the reverse tended to be true.

The most important type of data from official "social bookkeeping" are so-called ecological data, that is, data aggregated for territorial units. In the United States the use of such data has become an object of a much-justified criticism.[9] Insofar as these data are employed as indicators for individual behavior, they give rise to the "ecological fallacy."[10] If a direct measurement for lower-level units (such as individual voters) is available, the use of ecological data for statements about individual behavior is obviously either poor research strategy or a regrettable adjustment to one's limited resources. The same is, in principle, true for other kinds of grouped data, such as information aggregated according to school classes, army units, or hospitals.[11]

In all these instances the chances of becoming the victim of an ecological fallacy, or of other versions of the "grouped data fallacy,"

[8] The consequences of the societal and institutional settings in which social research is carried out, and specifically the impact of different kinds of audiences on the style of social science are analyzed in Erwin K. Scheuch, "Sozialforschung und sozialer Wandel," *Kölner Zeitschrift für Soziologie und Sozialpsychologie, 17* (1965), pp. 1–48.

[9] For example, see Austin Ranney, "The Utility and Limitations of Aggregate Data in the Study of Electoral Behavior" in Ranney (ed.), *op. cit.*; Roy G. Francis, "On the Relations of Data to Theory," *Rural Sociology, 22* (1957), pp. 258–266.

[10] See William S. Robinson, "Ecological Correlations and the Behavior of Individuals," *American Sociological Review, 15* (1950), pp. 351–357; Herbert Menzel, "Comment," *American Sociological Review, 15* (1950), p. 674; Erwin K. Scheuch, "Cross-National Comparisons Using Aggregate Data" in Merritt and Rokkan (eds.), *op. cit.*, pp. 131–167.

[11] Another example is the erroneous use of statistics in the controversy about whether Thalidomide caused malformations in newborns. Intake of medicaments containing Thalidomide occurred in terms of millions of units, malformations in thousand of cases — a "classical" situation for committing ecological fallacies. A fuller discussion will be found in Erwin K. Scheuch, "Zur Methodik und Statistik der Dysmelie-Forschung," *Wiener Medizinische Wochenschrift, 117* (1967), pp. 402–414.

is a function of the degree to which the marginals of a contingency table also control the within-cell variation.[12] The dangers are, *ceteris paribus*, especially great when one tries to explain from variations observed on higher-order units (like counties) the changes in the behavior of rare lower-level units (like individual voters for small parties).

Of course, Herbert Menzel is right in emphasizing that ecological data (or other grouped data) are not always employed as a substitute for a more direct measurement on a lower level but are used as descriptors for groups or areas.[13] Many of the practical interests that applied research serves are of this type, as when politicians are interested primarily in numbers of votes regardless of who may have cast a particular ballot. Also, a direct measurement may not in all cases be the most reliable or even the most valid indicator of behavior, as in some areas of consumer behavior. There are, in addition, various techniques to obtain under some conditions an approximate expression of the size of the ecological fallacy. Essentially, these techniques consist of cross-cutting sub-divisions of grouped material while observing the stability of the regressions across the different partitions of the material.[14]

Thus there are instances where ecological or group indicators are either the most direct or even the relatively most precise measure. In general, however, we recommend as a rule in choosing indicators what could be termed "the principle of direct measurement": the measurement that requires the shortest chain of inference is generally to be preferred. This principle of direct measurement does not, however, imply a recommendation to avoid using ecological (or grouped) data; rather it points to specific usages of grouped data that have so far been neglected.

[12] Cf. Otis D. Duncan and Beverly Davis, "An Alternative to Ecological Correlations," *American Sociological Review, 18* (1953), pp. 665–666; Leo A. Goodman, "Ecological Regressions and the Behavior of Individuals," *American Sociological Review, 18* (1953), pp. 663–664. Since these earlier publications there has been little progress in discussing the determinants of the ecological fallacy, until the very important contribution by Hayward R. Alker, "A Typology of Ecological Fallacies," Chapter 4 of this volume. See also Paul F. Lazarsfeld and N. Henry, "The Application of Latent Structure Analysis to Quantitative Ecological Data" in Fred Massarik and Philburn Ratoosh (eds.), *Mathematical Explorations in Behavioral Science* (Homewood, Ill.: Irwin Press, 1965).

[13] Cf. Menzel, *op. cit.,* p. 674. There is, of course, nothing inferior about ecological or other grouped data; what is at issue when working with ecological data is in each case the relation of the criterion, according to which units are grouped, to the types of inferences intended when using the results of aggregated units.

[14] Discussions of techniques to estimate and control the ecological fallacy will be found in Duncan and Davis, *op. cit.*; Lazarsfeld and Henry, in Massarik and Ratoosh (eds.), *op. cit.*; and Alker, *op. cit.*

DANGERS OF THE INDIVIDUALISTIC FALLACY

The ecological fallacy (or group fallacy) has come under sufficient scrutiny that we can now consider most of the problems raised as intellectually settled, even though in practical research these errors continue nearly unabated. The reverse fallacy, to infer incorrectly from observations on lower-level units the condition of higher-order systems, is rarely treated in methodological literature. This type of fallacy has been termed the "individualistic fallacy."[15] In many cases there will not even be a suspicion of a fallacious reasoning, probably because of the greater control over the individual case and the greater sense of reality when dealing with individual units.

The criticism that Hegelians of all known varieties, and in general European culture critics, level against survey research expresses a feeling of uneasiness, couched in philosophical terms, about an often real misuse of empirical evidence. It is argued and widely believed among the European elite that social research (which incorrectly is equated with survey research) just registers man's subjective reflection of or unwitting adjustment to reality instead of catching the real determinants of behavior or the character of social systems. Social research is accused of reinforcing an already false consciousness by publishing facts about mere epiphenomena.[16] In itself this argument is nothing but a contemporary version of Feuerbach's notion of *Verdoppelung des Scheins*. As an objection in principle against social research, this reduces itself either to some sort of theology inspired by a revelation about the true nature of things, or to solipsism; as a corrective for a prevailing hack use of survey research and other kinds of individual measurements this is a very useful critique.

In the course of another project we inspected a large number of publications based on survey research. We found that in terms of the uses made of individual questions — that is, in their function as indicators — they could be classified as follows:

a. Ego's responses are the observable phenomenon itself. This is true for the usual opinion questions in surveys, for many psychological tests, or for scales that use statements. Provided we abstract from such disturbing factors as response sets,[17] the problem of the permissible inferences is shifted largely from the phase of using data to the act of

[15] Cf. Scheuch, in Merritt and Rokkan (eds.), *op. cit.,* pp. 158–164.

[16] See especially Theodor W. Adorno, "Der Begriff der Gesellschaft," in *Evangelisches Staatslexikon,* index word: *Gesellschaft* (Stuttgart: Kreuz-Verlag, 1966).

[17] There exists a vast literature on response sets. The *locus classicus* is Lee J. Cronbach, "Response Sets and Test Validity," *Educational and Psychological*

constructing the instruments. Typically, the unit of measurement and the unit of analysis are indentical.

b. Ego's responses are treated as self-observations. This tends to be a characteristic of what are called behavior questions in surveys. What kinds of inferences are legitimate is determined mainly by the degree of congruence between responses and actual behavior. Again, the unit of measurement and the unit of analysis are usually identical.

c. Ego's responses are treated as an observation of one's environment. Examples are such frequently used questions as "What does your family . . . " or "How often do people here. . . ." In these cases the unit of analysis is often the behavior of persons or group outside the dyadic relationship between researcher and research subject.

d. Ego's responses are treated — albeit very often unwittingly — as expert judgments. Examples are "What do you think is most important to get ahead in your company?" or "Do teen-agers in your neighborhood cause more problems than they did five years ago?" — provided these questions are used as indicators for determinants in upward mobility or as evidence for changes in the behavior of teen-agers.

Like all classification systems that the human mind imposes upon reality, this one too simplifies the actual complexities in using verbal behavior in social research. Behavior questions such as "How often do you listen to the radio?" may be used as indicators for attitudes toward the mass media; and opinion questions such as "Do you believe most people here work as hard as they can?" may be employed as indexes of behavior.[18] Secondary analysis has caused us to become more conscious of the autonomy of uses that we have already practiced if we compare the actual use of indicators to their manifest meaning. Important in this context, however, is only the relation that the type *c* and *d* uses of questions have to the manifest meaning of indicators.

It is the type *c* and *d* of indicators that comes in for the kind of criticism mentioned earlier. We shall mention but two examples: (1) speaking with all members of a family would give us better data for processes that concern the family as a unit than the usual substitute

---

Measurement, 6 (1946), pp. 475–494. A summary of the findings since then will be found in Lee J. Cronbach, *Essentials of Psychological Testing* (New York: Harper, 1962). A taxonomy of indicator uses in their relation to the validity of inferences is given in Erwin K. Scheuch, "Das Interview," in René König (ed.), *Handbuch der empirischen Sozialforschung, 1* (Stuttgart: Enke Verlag, 2nd ed., 1967), pp. 707–715.

[18] Daniel Lerner has made extensive use of behavior questions as indicators for attitudes. See especially his book *The Passing of Traditional Society* (Glencoe: Free Press, 1958), Chapter 3.

measure, namely the report of just one family member;[19] and (2) compiling data from groups of workers in the same shop about their employment history would be a more reliable basis for analyzing factors in promotion than the opinions of isolated respondents. Yet in both instances interviews with individual respondents are vastly more economical than the "best measure," provided this is technically feasible.

We have now become alerted to the problems accompanying the use of ecological data; but we still need to realize that the social scientist using survey research or other techniques of individual measurement is often dealing with indirect measures, too. Calling attention to the principle of direct measurement works both ways — not merely as a caveat against an uncritical use of grouped data but equally as a plea to realize that individual data can be indirect measures as well.

The problems associated with type d indicators are compounded if individual responses are combined to represent measures of higher-level properties. "Do most people who work hard and have a bit of luck get ahead?" is already a difficult enough indicator to interpret for one individual; the national averages of those replying in the affirmative is then certainly a dangerous measure to express differences in chances for upward mobility in various countries. Incidentally, using the average responses to such a question as indicating the differences in mobility between the United States and France happens not only to be dangerous in principle but to be empirically wrong as well.[20]

[19] Dan Cahalan and his Audience Research Bureau have shown to what extent husbands and wives disagree in describing their consumer behavior. By and large, reports differed most when they required from the respondent that he should summarize a large number of behavioral acts, as in a question like "Who has changed most in ideas and attitudes since you were married?" By implication a question like this really asks the respondent to perform as an expert witness. While Cahalan's results remained largely unpublished because of commercial reasons, results of the "difference reveal technique" — interviews in which husbands and wives were confronted with their conflicting statements — were more widely published (Fred Strodtbeck; Urie Bronfenbrenner). Ernest Burgess interviewed husbands and wives simultaneously but separately over a number of years, and our as-yet-unpublished secondary analysis of data showed considerable disagreements between the spouses even about such "hard" facts as length of betrothal.

[20] In an internationally comparative study Alex Inkeles found an especially low percentage of belief in chances for upward mobility in France, and a prevailing belief in chances for mobility in the United States. As Hall and Ziegel showed in David Glass (ed.), *Social Mobility in Britain* (London: Routledge, 1954), actual mobility rates are not very different. Chances for intergenerational mobility from manual to nonmanual were even a bit better in France than in the United States. The contradiction between perceived chances and actual chances in two polities provides, however, interesting raw material for describing subjective arrangements within objective contexts.

Almond and Verba asked cross sections of the populations of various nations about what one is proud of in one's own country, and the between-nation differences in responses were used as expressing stability of political institutions; certainly such answers are mainly reflections of collective properties in the minds of respondents.[21] In the same internationally comparative study, cross sections of respondents were asked to name what they considered to be successful forms of protests against bureaucratic measures; again, these aggregated opinions are most certainly not the most direct measure of citizens' ability to influence authorities. Aggregating individual responses as a measure of the "climate" of opinion in a community is equally problematic; while there is reason to believe that something like the "breakage effect" of Lazarsfeld and Berelson does exist as the property of a district, an aggregation from the responses of a small sample of individuals is hardly its best measure.[22]

In ordinary survey research the individual is usually treated — albeit by implication — as an atom. Merely adding atoms of course does not make for molecules. To continue with the same metaphor, just how one represents "social" molecules if the interrelation of atoms as part of a molecule is what one is interested in happens to be largely unexplored. It is this kind of interrelation between the character of individual units and the character of higher-order units that the group of social scientists in the Bureau of Applied Social Research of Columbia University has studied.

CONTEXTUAL AND RELATIONAL ANALYSIS

Lazarsfeld and his collaborators have attempted to develop procedures that provide direct expressions for some kinds of interaction between properties of individuals and properties of groups and in-

---

[21] Cf. Almond and Verba, *op cit.*

[22] The procedures to which we refer are described in Bernard Berelson *et al., Voting* (Chicago: University of Chicago Press, 1954); compare also Paul F. Lazarsfeld *et al., The People's Choice* (New York: Duell, 2nd ed., 1949). A more refined attempt to account for the continuity of voting in local communities is described in David R. Segal and Marshall W. Meyer, "The Social Context of Political Partisanship," Chapter 9 of this volume. The most differentiated attempt to relate individual and contextual properties is Hans D. Klingemann, *Bestimmungsgründe der Wahlentscheidung im Bundestagswahlkreis Heilbronn: Eine regionale Wahlanalyse* (Meisenheim a. G.: Anton Hain, 1968).

stitutions.[23] Stouffer had observed that soldiers' attitudes toward promotion can best be explained by relating them to relative opportunities for actual promotion within given military units. For an approach that in this way relates individual attitudes and properties of a group Lazarsfeld coined the term "contextual analysis."[24] Contextual analysis is then the description of a member of a collectivity by using properties of the collectivity.

Soon it became apparent that in relating units to collectivities (or finite sets) indicators of different types were used, and this in turn reflected the differences in the type of explanations for the unit as part of a collectivity. Closest to the usual orientation is the so-called "relational analysis," which characterizes an individual relative to other individual units of the same set of persons.[25] Describing a pupil's grade as "B" and also as "second quartile" is an example: the first grade denotes an ability as an absolute property, that is, independent from the specific class to which he belongs, while the second attribute expresses performance relative to the distribution of abilities in a specific set. In this way, the individual is accounted for as member of a group, but the group is treated only as an aggregate of specific individuals.

Indeed, for many aspects of behavior this representation of an individual's environment is appropriate, but not for all aspects. Thus, a chance for upward occupational mobility is a consequence not just of an individual's relative ability but also of changes in the mix of jobs in the economy at large. The latter type of attribute of a set is called a "global

[23] Cf. Paul F. Lazarsfeld and Herbert Menzel, "On the Relation between Individual and Collective Properties," in Amatai Etzioni (ed.), *Complex Organizations* (New York: Holt, Rinehart, & Winston, 1961), pp. 422–440; see also James S. Coleman, "Relational Analysis" in the same volume. Further discussion will be found in Hanan C. Selvin and Warren O. Hagerstrom, "The Empirical Classification of Formal Groups," *American Sociological Review, 28* (1963), pp. 399–411; Ernest Q. Campbell and C. Norman Alexander, "Structural Effects and Interpersonal Relationships," *American Journal of Sociology, 71* (1965), pp. 284–289; Leo Meltzer, "Comparing Relationships of Individual and Average Variables to Individual Responses," *American Sociological Review, 28* (1963), pp. 117–122; Erwin K. Scheuch, "Entwicklungsrichtungen bei der Analyse sozialwissenschaftlicher Daten" in König (ed.), *op. cit.,* pp. 655–685, especially pp. 670–677.

[24] Examples of uses of contextual properties in empirical research that influenced Lazarsfeld's methodological orientation are: Samuel A. Stouffer *et al., The American Soldier, 1* (Princeton: Princeton University Press, 1949), pp. 256 ff., *passim*; Seymour M. Lipset *et al., Union Democracy* (Glencoe: Free Press, 1956), especially Appendix I; Herbert Menzel and Elihu Katz, "Social Relations and Innovation in the Medical Profession," *Public Opinion Quarterly, 19* (1966), pp. 337–352.

[25] Cf. James S. Coleman, "Relational Analysis — the Study of Social Organizations with Survey Methods," *Human Organization, 17* (1958/59), pp. 28–36, and also in Etzioni (ed.), *op. cit.*

property," that is, a property that exists for all units independent of the composition of the group. The term "contextual analysis" is now used primarily for an analysis that relates global properties to individual attributes. Examples of this type of analysis are as yet quite rare, and for ecological data as a form of global properties there are exceedingly few examples.

So far, contextual analysis and relational analysis are largely attempts to overcome some of the limitations of ordinary cross-sectional surveys. This methodological approach proceeds from a more realistic assessment of an individual's cross-pressures rather than from reflections about the structure of collectivities.[26] However, we do note the beginning of a realization that in many of our observations on the level of individual actors we do not really take seriously the fact that there is something like social structure. Hence there has been the tendency to proceed immediately from observations on the level of individuals to statements about the character of higher-order units, and hence the inclination to equate observations of individual attributes with the state of the polity. This tendency is, however, due not merely to a particular blindness of empirical researchers but also to a gap in theorizing. Good substantive theory would need to specify the intervening processes and structures, and if this were done more explicitly, it would also be easier to develop appropriate measures.

At this point in the line of arguments it is possible to relate the discussion of research methodology to the initial statement: that explanations are more interesting when they connect phenomena on different levels. Together with the principle of direct measurement this connection has implications for research design and for theorizing:

1. A research design becomes more powerful when it provides for direct measurements of phenomena on different levels.

2. Theories in the social sciences that maintain a dependency between the state of a higher-order collectivity and the characteristics of the units within the collectivity should specify the processes of interchange between system levels.[27]

According to this perspective, the controversy between advocates of

[26] Most of the methodological discussion and the majority of the important examples in empirical work are accounts of the political behavior of individuals. Voting behavior appears to be especially suited to permit the development of models since the number of alternatives is limited.

[27] The notion of "interchange" is that of Talcott Parsons, as developed by him in *Family, Socialization and Interaction Process* (Glencoe: Free Press, 1955), and in *Economy and Society* (London: Routledge & Kegan Paul, 1957), especially Chapter II.

ecological measures and those preferring individual measurement becomes a spurious issue. If it is easier and often less risky to infer
structural properties from survey data than to derive statements about
individual behavior from ecological data, this is due primarily to practical difficulties rather than a matter of principle.[28] It so happens that
ecological data as a main form of "process-produced data" are organized
according to administrative concerns rather than research interests.
And because of this particular difficulty in working with ecological data,
grouped data in general have come under unnecessary criticism.

From this analysis one may conclude that cross-level measurements
will become more common within the near future. The methodological
discussion will help to overcome some of the reservations that exist
toward the use of one or the other kind of data, and data banks as a new
type of facility in the social sciences will increasingly store several kinds
of data in an easily accessible format.[29] The main handicap is probably
still the lack of explicit conceptual orientations for relating data from
different levels.

In the remainder of this contribution we shall suggest such a conceptualization for relating individual properties to data for collectivities
and shall then give some examples of the usefulness of combined cross-
level measurements and cross-level theories. Our particular notion has
been influenced by Max Weber's conceptualization of social action
(*soziales Handeln*) and to some degree by George H. Mead. Of course,
this is just one attempt among other possible approaches. It is made in
the expectation that at this particular point in the development of
empirical research new conceptualizations and examples of successful
usage will stimulate methodological discussion, which, left to itself,
remains at present preoccupied with details of the research process.

THE USES OF OPTIONS ANALYSIS

The higher level of any two-level measurement or explanation can be
conceptualized as the "environment" of the lower-level units. Let us
assume that the higher-order unit combines lower-level units that have

---

[28] As an example of an attempt to infer structural properties from opinion ques-
tions, see E. K. Scheuch: "Die Sichtbarkeit politischer Einstellungen im alltäglichen
Verhalten," in E. K. Scheuch and R. Wildenmann, *Zur Soziologie der Wahl* (Opladen:
Westdeutscher Verlag, 1965).

[29] Cf. Rokkan (ed.), *Data Archives in the Social Sciences, op. cit.*; Rokkan,
"Comparative Cross-National Research," in Rokkan and Merritt (eds.), *op. cit.*, pp.
3–26.

some heterogeneity or that the higher-order unit is homogeneous merely with respect to the characteristic(s) that define(s) its boundaries. We may now postulate that this environment will be reacted to differentially by lower-level units that have different locations relative to the points in the distribution of characteristics of the higher-order unit. The different locations of lower-level units in the set that makes up the higher-level unit can thus be represented by distinguishing several subsets. If we denote every lower-level unit by a combination of several characteristics, the subsets have to be conceptualized as constituting relatively homogeneous but partially overlapping "selective" environments for the lower-level units. In our particular approach, which we term "options analysis," a subset can be thought of as a selective environment for a group of lower-level units in the sense that for each particular subset the higher-level unit is a combination of characteristics with different values.

Let us interpret lower-level units to be persons and higher-order units to be some collectivity with which they are in immediate interchange, such as the community. For any given group of actors, defined by a common position, the community can be viewed as a "raw material." In other words, for every group the community is a different constellation of "objective" characteristics. The constellation of objective characteristics that is unique to a group of persons with a given position should be understood as the "subjective environment of that group." Conversely, the combination of values in the higher-order set y_i that forms the subjective environment for a group with the characteristics x_i should be predictable from its position within the larger context y_i.

For a graphic representation let us first assume that the higher-order units $y_{i \ldots n}$ are factories. The left-right dimension represents the distance of departments or working groups (or any other smallest subdivision of the personnel) from the act of selling the product, while the up-down (north-south) dimension represents status within the company. The subdivisions of y_i represent the departments $x_{ii \ldots in}$, and the individual workers are represented by subscripts in arabic numerals $x_{ii_1 \ldots n}$. (See Figure 1.)

The mathematics of this notion has not been worked out, but there is no doubt that it can be formalized in some sort of topological language. Apart from this, however, some implications for analysis across levels of observation should be fairly obvious.

In research about motivations to work the level of the factory as a unit in which work is performed is obviously important and needs to be represented via direct measurement of its properties. This graphic

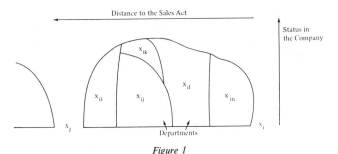

Figure 1

GRAPHIC PRESENTATION OF THE RELATIONSHIP BETWEEN LOWER- AND
HIGHER-LEVEL UNITS

representation shows that in some respects a breakdown of workers'
responses (or other attributes) by factories will not be the most efficient
strategy; what a factory means as a constraint on behavior or as an
economic unit differs according to the location of the employees within
the factory. Accordingly, the properties of the higher-level-unit factory
should be assigned with different combinations of weights to the
departments and to the individuals within the department — depending
on their location in a two-dimensional space. In the same manner one
can represent the subjective (or selective) meaning of a geographic unit
or a social organization.

From the earlier statements it follows that the greater the homogeneity of a higher-level unit y_i, the smaller will be the differences between the subjective and the objective environment. In addition to the
within-unit variability the predictive or explanatory power of using
descriptors for higher-level units is a function also of between-unit
variability; this the greater the between-unit variability the greater is,
ceteris paribus, the usefulness of higher-order units $y_{i...n}$ as an independent level of observation.

As Valkonen has rightly pointed out, a unit is constituted by the
variable under consideration.[30] However, just as some variables (such
as age, sex, and occupation) happen to determine a variety of behavior
and can thus be understood as "general determinants," there are some
kinds of units (or more precisely, variables that define units) which are
levels of integration for a variety of behavior. The greater the number of

[30] Tapani Valkonen, "Individual and Structural Effects in Ecological Research,"
Chapter 3 in this volume.

variables for which the same type of higher unit is the level of integration (or has an influence in its own right on the behavior of lower-order units), the more we are justified in treating its effects as "structural." The notion of looking at a higher-order unit as an objective environment for lower-level units is, *ceteris paribus,* most appropriate for such structural units.

From this observation it follows that the notion of options analysis — a technology and a perspective of treating higher-level units as an environment — is fruitful only for specific types of units. In addition, a technical prerequisite for it is a "multiple measurement," preferably a combination of individual and global properties. Provided these conditions are met, it is necessary to compute "clusters" of lower-level units or subsets. These subsets are then related to their higher-order unit by denoting (according to their relative position) the subsets with different values for the higher-order unit (see Figure 1). An alternative procedure, and one that is closer to the original notion, is the computation of the differing degree of determination of clusters of lower-level units from characteristics of the higher-order units. Still another variant of this analysis emphasizes the differences in explanatory power for configurations of attributes of the higher-order unit; this is the most direct expression of a "subjective environment."

We shall give but one technically simple example. We may observe a general correlation between the level of economic development by areas, on the one hand, and family composition and family stability, on the other. Provided we observe that with a very high level of economic development several forms of the family coexist, we would interpret this as a reduction of constraints on the family which permit a greater number of options. The "cost" of these options would then be determined by analyzing indexes of family stability for families with different member compositions.

The notion of a subjective use of an objective environment had been first invoked ex post facto to help solve some problems in a cross-level analysis. The substantive problem was then to account for the effects of some kinds of communities on voting behavior: some communities appeared to have an influence on voting in addition to the usual individual properties, while others did not. We then remembered Uexküll's distinction between an objective *Umgebung* and an *Umwelt* which differed according to the needs of the various species. This notion from biological ecology seemed one possible way to explain the varying strengths of relationship between system levels. In addition, this dichotomy also appeared related to one perspective in sociology that was expressed by Max Weber as the task of *soziales Handeln deutend zu verstehen.*[31]

Subsequently, this approach guided a number of empirical studies, and it became possible to include appropriate features in the design. Among those were an investigation of differences in primary group influence on voting behavior and a study of returnees from Germany to their native Greece and Turkey. The latter may be helpful in indicating some of the consequences for research design. The problem formulation itself was one calling for cross-level analysis in that the interaction between levels of social reality was the major independent factor for the phenomenon of readjustment: The character of the native environment could be expected to have different consequences depending on the attributes of the individual returnee. However, merely comparing the influence of large contexts such as the nation-states of Turkey or Greece would be too gross a description of environmental effects; for the individual returnee Turkey and Greece were, in part, abstractions that exert influences only through several mediating institutions. Therefore, extensive use was made of descriptors for such immediate environments as the larger family, the peer group, and the work setting. While the factory can be understood as one setting in which Turkey or Greece as economies become concrete for the individual returnee, the factory in turn is an individual unit influenced by the economic organization of the nation-state. In this way, the influence of the nation-state is filtered through many intermediary steps down to the individual. The fact of "filtering" phenomena in turn gives opportunities to the individual returnee to choose work settings of different character where he experiences the effects of an abstraction such as national economy in different ways.

"SUBJECTIVE ENVIRONMENT" IN STUDIES OF VOTING BEHAVIOR

The notion of "subjective environment" and the formalization of this notion were first used in an analysis of election data to account for the stability of voting in some communities of Southwest Germany. This stability is in itself a well-known phenomenon, but in attempts to give an explanation we came across some other curious regularities. In small

[31] Max Weber, "Begriff der Soziologie und des 'Sinnes' sozialen Handelns," *Wirtschaft und Gesellschaft, 1* (Cologne: Kiepenheuer u. Witsch, Studienausgabe, 1964).

communities with a high stability of election returns there were also sometimes abrupt switches in voting, and the new pattern then tended to exhibit considerable stability. A breakdown of community size by degree of political homogeneity revealed a monotonic but strongly curvilinear distribution somewhat related to a hyperbolic curve. Most puzzling at first were the strong contrasts in voting behavior between neighboring communities for which there were no obvious explanations by community characteristics. All these observations confirmed that communities as such sometimes had a strong influence on voting behavior, in addition to the usual individual characteristics.

Of course, there were labels to attach to this observation, such as "climate of opinion" and "breakage effect," which Lazarsfeld and Berelson had coined.[32] However, these terms are merely descriptive and not explanatory. The one explanation sometimes given in this connection, that voting patterns are determined by the principle of inertia, namely that once established they will continue, would not be specific for a collective such as a community; also, it agreed with only some of the acts. Fortunately, the design of our main empirical study, the 1961 election study, permitted further analyses.[33]

The *Bundestagswahlstudie 1961* combined three national sample surveys at three points in time with constituency panels that were interviewed in four waves; special attention was paid to interpersonal processes. The interview data were then supplemented by a program of systematic field observations, by content analyses of newspapers and television coverage, and by a collection of ecological data for communities and within larger communities for census tracts. Thus, various forms of "direct measurement" for phenomena at different levels of the political process were available. Here only the cases of the constituencies of Heilbronn and München-Land will be reported — two units with quite different objective characteristics and with contrasting political histories.[34]

The varied forms of measurement were essential for the later attempt to give the notion of a "breakage effect" in part a real explanatory meaning. When working with voting statistics for different types of

[32] Berelson *et al., Voting, op. cit.,* pp. 98 ff. *passim.*

[33] Scheuch and Wildenmann, *op. cit.,* Chapter 1.

[34] A detailed description of the raw data and several ecological analyses are given in the following two dissertations, both based on the "Wahlstudie": Franz U. Pappi, *Das Wahlverhalten im Bezugsrahmen der politischen Kultur: Eine soziologische Analyse der politischen Kultur in Deutschland unter besonderer Berücksichtigung von Stadt-Land Unterschieden* (Munich, 1967), and Klingemann, *op. cit.*

subdivisions of the large constituencies (more than 100,000 persons), it could be observed that some of the strongest differences between small ecological units occurred when these units were adjacent. However, this regularity seemed to hold only for rather small communities (definitely below about 500 inhabitants, and sometimes up to 1,000), and it mostly disappeared for larger towns and cities. In the more populated geographical units voting behavior varied in the expected way with the relative frequency of demographic characteristics, and it was also of usual heterogeneity.

To account for these observations it was postulated that social characteristics that are perceived by the actors as antagonistic express themselves also as differences in voting behavior. This statement implies that one main orientation in casting a ballot is the confirmation of group "belongingness;" in an earlier analysis it had already been demonstrated that the voters treat parties largely as reference groups.[35] This generalization of social differences into equivalent differences in voting behavior was presumed to be strongest for social characteristics of general relevance (operational definition: generality of relevance equals the number of situations for which quasi-group characteristics determine behavior). Belonging to a community can be shown to mean for actors a quasi-group characteristic such as age or occupation.[36] Let us now introduce the following as an additional proposition: the smaller the community and the more homogeneous the environment, the stronger is the effect of belonging to a community as a quasi-group membership. Therefore, in small and relatively homogenous communities voting should have the function of affirming community distinctiveness; in larger communities the equivalent function should be served by voting according to membership in antagonistic quasi groups. This mechanism leads to stability of voting behavior over time and manifests itself in phenomena called the "climate of opinion" in a community.

To test this line of reasoning as explaining differences in voting behavior between geographical and social subdivisions, we determined in the first step those communities that displayed a distinctive voting pattern (operational definition; clear majorities for any one party). In the second step we selected communities that were unusually

---

[35] Scheuch, "Die Sichtbarkeit politischer Einstellungen im alltäglichen Verhalten," *op. cit.*

[36] In a pre-election survey in North Rhine-Westphalia in 1962 we asked respondents to imagine themselves in a foreign country having a casual conversation in a restaurant and being asked to explain who they are. A majority included a community indentification in their description of self.

homogeneous with respect to the following characteristics: (1) occupational composition; (2) religious denomination. The communities that had been identified in this way were then plotted on a map; this made it easier to identify proximity as one major variable in our theory of "habitually antagonistic voting behavior."

The following notion could now be empirically tested: Distinctiveness of voting behavior is a function of physical proximity of communities with opposing sets of characteristics. The greater the homogeneity (within-class differences) of adjacent communities with differing characteristics, the greater the chance that these communities would show mirror images of voting results. Physical proximity of communities can be considered as a rough index of social contacts between these higher-order units. From studies of social class we knew that antagonism was greatest between those groups on a scale of social prestige which were either adjacent or at the two extremes of the total distribution; the latter were safe hate objects, while adjacent groups just tended to "rub" each other more in daily contacts.[37] The analogous phenomenon in voting behavior by ecological units would be intensity of social contacts as transforming difference into antagonism. This effect would sometimes be strong enough to reverse the correlations between group membership and voting behavior that are usual in the society at large. For most communities or ecological units below 500 inhabitants, and for many between 500 and 800 inhabitants, this conceptualization could account for a large number of deviant election results if we understand by deviant a change from the normal relation between group membership and voting.

The notion of "climate of opinion" can now be restated as an explanation of phenomena instead of merely as a label. Thus the "climate of opinion" is the generalization of a distinct pattern (or configuration) of historical and/or social characteristics of a territorial unit which include voting behavior, together with the continued assertion of this distinctness in voting patterns. If one substitutes for the term "territorial units" the term "groups," the preceding statement becomes a general explanation of "deviant" voting, that is, of voting behavior that does not follow in the usual way from a combination of group characteristics. In a short form the phenomenon of "climate of opinion" can be restated as an "assertion of a generally deviant or marginal position of a group vis-à-vis its neighbors by means of voting behavior."

[37] Erwin K. Scheuch (with Hans J. Daheim), "Sozialprestige und soziale Schichtung," *Kölner Zeitschrift für Soziologie und Sozialpsychologie, 13* (1961), special issue no. 5, pp. 65–103, especially pp. 69–82.

An essential condition for this mechanism to operate is a high degree of internal homogeneity, with a relatively (that is, in relation to within-group heterogeneity) strong difference from other groups. The effect is strongest if there are both internal homogeneity for several characteristics at once and low spatial and/or social distance from other groups. For groups with deviant social characteristics this condition is found most often in classical minority group situations, while for territorial units it tends to occur only when such areas are rather small. In this way, the often observed long-term traditions of voting behavior in minority groups, the stability of voting in some territorial units, and even the continuity of election results in societies with strong social cleavages can be explained by the same mechanism.[38]

The conditions that have just been described imply that for persons within these groups or territorial units, subjective and objective environment would coincide more than can be expected. Accordingly, for larger communities and for heterogeneous territorial units a different kind of cross-level explanation appeared indicated, as well as a different technology in tracing the interaction between levels. If indeed subjective and objective environment differ from each other, independent measures for the phenomena at different levels are required.

To increase the contrast with the conditions that we previously examined, we selected in the next step of this analysis the largest cities of several constituencies. Special attention was given to the cities of Heilbronn (in Southwest Germany) and Freising (in Bavaria near Munich). A breakdown of election results into precincts again showed stronger differences in voting behavior than could be expected from the differences in social composition. Again we found in a number of precincts that an unusual homogeneity of voting behavior continued over long periods, even though the original population had in part been replaced by new inhabitants. These stable political units had remained stable with respect to one social characteristic as well, in spite of the exchanges of population with other areas: namely continuation of a population with an extreme social status position. For the population in those areas, the city as a unit had a limited relevance, and voters tended to assert their marginal positions by means of voting behavior — just like the population in "marginal" small communities. In general, however, surveys showed the expected pattern of a moderate association

[38] Examples are the stability of voting behavior for a period of more than fifty years in such countries as Austria, the Netherlands, and Belgium; cf. G. Vidick, "Le système électoral belge: démocratie ou oligarchie?" Res Publica, 9 (1967), pp. 353–367.

between group characteristics and electoral behavior, with the various territorial subdivisions having little predictive value.

An analysis of voting results for Freising demonstrated surprising irregularities of election results in various areas. Ecological data did not lead to any explanation, but survey data did. Freising is within commuting distance of Munich as the economic center of the whole region. It was natural, therefore, to analyze the effects of commuting or non-commuting on voting behavior, holding membership in quasi groups (like occupation or age) constant. In many social groups commuters voted as their counterparts in the metropolitan city voted; this is especially true for skilled workers. In other cases the commuters adopted the voting pattern of their bedroom community Freising; this is sometimes the case with white-collar workers. Which territorial unit had an influence on voting (or rather can be treated as a reference area in accounting for election results) varies by social group — a variation that can be explained only by using survey data.

Still another group of data needs to be considered before a summarizing statement for the interrelation between higher-order units and individual characteristics can be attempted: data for intervening institutions. This can be demonstrated by the failure of either aggregated individual observations or ecological data to account for two phenomena: (1) variations in the success of the new radical party, the NPD and (2) dramatic shifts in voting that occur in small communities.

In communities of less than 800 inhabitants long periods of stable voting behavior may be interrupted by sudden reversals of political preferences, resulting in a new stable voting pattern, or by equally sudden and then persisting splits within a unit hitherto characterized by high political homogeneity. A number of such dramatic changes could be observed in small communities of the Saarland. A more detailed observation of these communities revealed that straight reversals of established political preferences in the electorate were usually accompanied by switches in the party allegiance of local leaders. Two conditions had to coincide in order to produce the phenomenon of reversals: small size of community plus relatively great homogeneity and a change in the party preference of leaders. Surveys confirmed that in these very small communities participation in politics is not behavior functionally differentiated from other behavior. Under such conditions voting for an opposition can be looked upon as a form of deviant behavior. This particular deviance is meant to be made easy by the secret ballot, but surveys again showed that voting is not thought to be completely secret (villagers make quite accurate guesses about who votes against the majority), and even that rather painless deviance still re-quires a little extra effort on the part of the deviating person. Under those conditions a survival of an older and general pattern in homogeneous local units occurs: the ability of leaders — typically they are functionally unspecific leaders — to count on the general loyalty of their local groups.

The sudden splitting of votes in small communities amounts to a breakdown of this order and occurs usually either when there is a split in a previously monolithic leadership or when the leadership allies with a party that to the villagers represents an "outside" world hostile to them or when a new functionally specific leadership for politics moves into the community. Again we can rely on surveys to confirm what an analysis of ecological descriptors leads us to suspect, namely that even in small communities the social heterogeneity is often greater than the heterogeneity of voting behavior. This general heterogeneity does not become political pluralism, however, unless there is some support via intermediary institutions or persons. According to survey figures and ecological data, social heterogeneity is translated into political pluralism if the deviant political behavior receives outside support, and unionized commuters are often the first group to import the prevailing political culture at their place of work into their villages. This observation can be generalized: Whenever a person is moving in more than one environment, he is likely to vote independently of the local majority; and whenever in this or any other way a threshold of "exemplary heterogeneity" in voting is reached, the previously controlled social cleavages tend suddenly to express themselves fully in political pluralism.

The surprising success of the new radical party of the right, the *Nationaldemokratische Partei Deutschlands* (NPD), even in the 1965 federal elections and subsequently in *Länder* elections, affords us an opportunity to demonstrate the need for a joint use of separate indicators for several aspects of reality. A first analysis of ecological data had led most commentators in Germany to conclude that the sudden increase in votes for the NPD was due largely to the refugees. Indeed, there were quite strong correlations between the high percentage of refugees in a constituency and the successes of the NPD. However, survey figures gave only an extremely weak correlation between refugee status and the tendency to vote for the NPD.[39] A more complete

[39] Discussed in detail in Erwin K. Scheuch and Hans D. Klingemann, "Die Flüchtlinge und die Versuchung des Rechtsradikalismus" in *Materialien zum Phänomen des Rechtsradikalismus in der Bundesrepublik* (Cologne: Institut für vergleichende Sozialforschung, 1967).

analysis of constituency characteristics revealed that this contradiction between survey and ecological analyses was not just another instance of the ecological fallacy.

The percentage of refugees in a constituency (or territorial subdivision) had a real influence on the tendency of individuals to vote for the NPD but in a more indirect way than had been assumed in the first explanations. Refugees had been, in general, much less extreme in their political views than the pronouncements of refugee organizations — a usual phenomenon if one considers refugee organizations as pressure groups with a weak mass basis yet deriving their effectiveness from claiming mass support. The NPD, on the other hand, had to rely for propaganda on word-of-mouth contacts plus old-fashioned tools of political propaganda (such as leaflets and local rallies), since it had little money and no real access to the mass media. In view of these conditions the correct causal chain was: (a) the higher the percentage of refugees in a territorial unit, the stronger were organizations of political extremists; (b) the stronger the organization of political extremists, the greater was the success of the NPD.

Hence, the percentage of refugees in a constituency had a causal influence on the effectiveness of local political propaganda, instead of being an indicator of the tendency of refugees as individuals to vote for political extremists.

7

KEVIN R. COX

The Spatial Structuring of Information Flow and Partisan Attitudes[1]

AWARENESS of the limitations of cross-sectional studies in describing social processes over time is widespread in the behavioral sciences.[2] In many areas this is reflected in the construction of more dynamic models, either by replicating social process in simulations or by cross-sectional analysis containing variables describing change in the observational units. One aspect of this concern for process in political science is interest in information flow. This is seen in studies using survey data, such as those by Converse[3] and Putnam,[4] and in studies using coarser aggregate data, such as the recent attempts of Alker[5] and of McCrone and Cnudde[6] to model political modernization.

This emerging concern among political scientists coincides with a similar development in human geography. In this field much interest is

[1] The research on which this paper is based is supported by a grant from the National Science Foundation; this support is gratefully acknowledged.

[2] See, for example, Otis Dudley Duncan, Ray P. Cuzzort, and Beverly Duncan, *Statistical Geography* (Glencoe: Free Press, 1961), pp. 160–161.

[3] Philip E. Converse, "Information Flow and the Stability of Partisan Attitudes," *Public Opinion Quarterly, 26* (1962), pp. 578–599.

[4] Robert D. Putnam, "Political Attitudes and the Local Community," *American Political Science Review, 60* (1966), pp. 640–654.

[5] Hayward R. Alker, "Causal Inference and Political Analysis" in Joseph L. Bernd (ed.), *Mathematical Applications in Political Science, II,* Arnold Foundation Monographs, *16* (Dallas: Arnold Foundation, Southern Methodist University, 1966), pp. 7–43.

[6] Donald J. McCrone and Charles F. Cnudde, "Toward a Communications Theory of Democratic Political Development: A Causal Model," *American Political Science Review, 61* (1967), pp. 72–79.

centering on the diffusion of innovations over space; Hagerstrand, for example, has examined the diffusion of subsidized pasture and of certain religious groups in Sweden and of Rotary Clubs in Western Europe,[7] and Morrill has examined the expansion of the Negro ghetto in American metropolitan areas.[8] In these studies the role of social relations over space and the impact of distance upon the probability of social relations has been emphasized as crucial to explaining the flow of information preceding adoption of innovations. Further, there is some good evidence for such spatial diffusion movements in the literature of political sociology. Rokkan and Valen[9] have described the narrowing of Norwegian urban-rural political participation differences over time, and Myron Weiner has examined the spatial extension of elite recruitment into rural areas in Bengal.[10]

This developing body of empirical studies and related theory suggests that a spatial approach toward information flow and political behavior or attitudes might help resolve some currently vexing problems. In particular, certain contradictions already appearing in the literature of contextual analysis may be resolved by examining the areal scale at which the networks connecting individuals to contexts operate.

This paper has two aims: first, to identify certain contentious issues in recent contextual analyses of political behavior and to suggest some alternative interpretations and solutions; second, five hypotheses summarizing these new interpretations and solutions will be presented and tested using data collected in the Columbus metropolitan area of Ohio.

CONTEXTUAL ANALYSIS

Contextual analysis attempts to explain an individual behavior pattern in terms of the social context or milieu in which the individual

[7] Among other papers by Torsten Hägerstrand, see "Quantitative Techniques for Analysis of the Spread of Information and Technology," in C. Arnold Anderson and Mary Jean Bowman (eds.), *Education and Economic Development* (Chicago: Aldine Publishing Company, 1965), and "Aspects of the Spatial Structure of Social Communication and the Diffusion of Information," *Papers and Proceedings, Regional Science Association, 16* (1966), pp. 27–42.

[8] Richard L. Morrill, "The Negro Ghetto: Problems and Alternatives," *Geographical Review, 55* (1965), pp. 339–361.

[9] Stein Rokkan and Henry Valen, "The Mobilization of the Periphery: Data on Turnout, Party Membership and Candidate Recruitment in Norway," *Acta Sociologica, 6* (1962), Fasc. 1–2.

[10] Myron Weiner, "Changing Patterns of Political Leadership in West Bengal," *Pacific Affairs, 32* (1959), pp. 277–287.

lives when certain of his own social or other personal attributes are held constant.[11] Although a sizable literature concerned with the identification of such effects is developing, technical concerns will not be the focus of interest here;[12] rather, we shall be concerned with the development of the contextual model as providing evidence for a political information transmission and influence process.

Coleman has identified the contextual model as a social relational model, basing its conclusions on assumptions of personal influence.[13] More specifically, a recent paper by Putnam exemplifies the information flow interpretation of the contextual model and illustrates the type of conclusion possible from such contextual analysis.[14] Putnam is most interested in the effects of political context — measured by the per cent Democratic at the county level — upon political behavior. He finds first that community influence is mediated largely through friendship groups and that members of secondary associations are more susceptible to community influence than are nonmembers. He goes on to demonstrate that friends in secondary organizations are more representative of community opinion and that people who belong to such organizations are not only more likely to have friends typical of the community as a whole but also more sensitive to the opinions of their friends. His paper has gone a long way toward establishing the promise of this area for further investigation.

The contextual model, as developed thus far, contains certain weaknesses. First, in its present form it is not able to discriminate between senders and receivers. We are unable to offer any improvement in this direction. Second, implicit in much of the work using the contextual model is the assumption that the individual who is being affected by the context via an influence process confines his friends and associational contacts to the ecological unit chosen for analysis. Yet intuitively one knows that is not necessarily so; not only will the number of external

[11] For example, see Warren E. Miller, "One-Party Politics and the Voter," *American Political Science Review, 50* (1956), pp. 707–725 and Philip H. Ennis, "The Contextual Dimension in Voting," in William N. McPhee and William A. Glaser (eds.), *Public Opinion and Congressional Elections* (Glencoe: Free Press, 1962), pp. 180–211.

[12] For example, see James A. Davis, Joe L. Spaeth, and Carolyn Huson, "A Technique for Analyzing the Effects of Group Composition," *American Sociological Review, 26* (1961), pp. 215–225 and Arnold S. Tannenbaum and Jerald G. Bachman, "Structural versus Individual Effects," *American Journal of Sociology, 69* (1964), pp. 585–595.

[13] James S. Coleman, "Relational Analysis: The Study of Social Organization with Survey Methods," *Human Organization, 17* (1958–1959), pp. 28–36

[14] Putnam, *op. cit.*

contacts increase with decreasing areal size of ecological unit but those having contacts outside the ecological unit are less likely to be influenced by information biased by the context within the ecological unit. Third, the model has not yet incorporated a measure of political susceptibility to information flow. Interpretations of contextual effect assign a conversion or support role to information, but the resistance of different individuals to the partisan cues inherent in much information has yet to be evaluated. Fourth, and most importantly, the contextual model does not examine receivers before and after receipt of information in order to determine the behavioral impact of that information flow. If individuals are influenced to change their partisan attitudes or to strengthen them, what evidence do we have that this takes place as a function of the political context? Each of these points will be considered in turn and suggestions made for incorporating more realistic assumptions into the contextual model.

If we examine the second problem from the spatial viewpoint, it seems clear that it can partially be solved by examining formal and informal networks at areal levels or scales other than that of the locality. Like most students of contextual effects, Putnam works at one areal level — in his case, the county level. He assumes that all the individual's formal links take place within the county unit while informal links take place at lower levels and are likely to provide the individual with information unrepresentative of the county as a whole.[15] Yet in reality the friendships of people and their more formal links take place at a variety of areal levels: some confine their friendships to the immediate neighborhood, while others have friends at some distance from their home. Furthermore, some voluntary organizations give their members scope to come into contact with other members of very diverse areal origins, while others confine their memberships to the immediate locality. Recognition of these facts demands that we attempt to specify the spatial characteristics of informal and formal links more carefully and that theory be formulated regarding their effects on partisan attitudes.

Formal and informal groups can be arrayed on at least three spatial dimensions: (1) the areal extent of the hinterland of one branch or meeting place in the system of formal or informal links; (2) the degree of centralization within an organization or the degree to which branches or individual nodes look to some central policy making or administrative body — of either a formal or informal nature — for information, advice, orders, or propaganda; (3) the connectivity between those branches or

---

[15] *Ibid.*

meeting places (by "connectivity" is meant the degree to which all nodes in a network are connected one with another). Thus, labor unions are characterized by branches with areally large hinterlands and with strong connections with a central co-ordinating agency publishing union news and views. Parent-teacher associations, on the other hand, have areally very restricted hinterlands and low levels of connectivity between branches. The three dimensions are not necessarily correlated: Jewish and Roman Catholic churches, for example, like Protestant churches, have areally limited hinterlands: but, unlike Protestant churches, they also have relatively strong central co-ordination and circulation of propaganda. Likewise, though the areal extents of the information catchment areas of Protestant and Catholic families are likely to be very much the same — other things being equal — minority group Roman Catholics are likely to be much more interconnected via marriage ties and attendance at the same church.

The recognition of a series of information fields or personal information catchment areas varying along these dimensions is implicit in the work of Putnam[16] and of other workers such as Segal and Meyer,[17] but their failure to apply it has led in at least one instance to a curious contradiction between their findings. Segal and Meyer both examine the effects of contexts at the city and ward level and both draw attention to the effects of different religions in integrating the individual into networks of greater or lesser connectivity over the nation as a whole. They find, for example, that the more cohesive religious groupings of Roman Catholics and Jews are considerably less affected in their political behavior by the social milieu of the ward than are Protestants.[18] Putnam, likewise, recognizes that "obviously 'community environment' could be defined at any number of levels ranging from the state down to the precinct," though exigencies of data force him to work at the county level. Again, like Segal and Meyer, he finds that members of minority religious groups are much less affected by the political context than are Protestants, ascribing this to the reduced social interaction of the minority religious groups with the remainder of the community.[19] The contradiction in their work arises in their treatment of the effects of voluntary group membership. At the ward level, Segal and Meyer find that those belonging to more voluntary organizations are less affected

[16] *Ibid.*
[17] David R. Segal and Marshall W. Meyer, "The Social Context of Political Partisanship," in this book, Chapter 9.
[18] *Ibid.*
[19] Putnam, *op. cit.*, p. 648.

by the milieu than are those who belong to fewer organizations.[20] At the county level, Putnam finds that those belonging to more voluntary groups are more affected by the milieu.[21] Although Segal and Meyer are dealing with a milieu defined in socioeconomic terms while Putnam is examining the effects of political context, quite possibly the contradiction is due to the different levels of analysis that the two authors use. People belonging to more organizations seem likely to have their additional affiliations outside the voting ward but largely within the county.

This paper is concerned primarily with the variation in areal size of information fields defined in terms of formal or informal affiliations. Thus, contextual effects on those with local friends or those with nonlocal friends will be examined separately. We also consider the impact of the context on those belonging to voluntary groups, the cells of which have memberships that are areally intensive compared with those belonging to voluntary groups the cells of which have areally extensive memberships.

One criticism that we made earlier against the contextual model was its failure to take into account individual variations in susceptibility to flows of information. In fact, resistance does seem to vary greatly according to demographic or psychological characteristics. Rokkan and Valen, for example, have documented the resistance of rural women in Norway to stimuli encouraging them to more active political participation.[22] Likewise, other data from the United Kingdom have shown the greater resistance of older age groups and women to the adoption of Labour Party preferences when social class is held constant.[23] While it is true that political sociology has succeeded in discriminating conceptually between access to information and susceptibility, it has not yet succeeded operationally in isolating susceptibility from more subtle psychological aspects of accessibility such as interest in politics. The principal contribution in this area has been that of Philip E. Converse,[24] and, in lieu of a more appropriate model, certain hypotheses that we shall test are based on his work.

Converse argues that the probability of any given voter being sufficiently deflected in his partisan momentum to cross party lines in a

---

[20] Segal and Meyer, *op. cit.*, pp. 222–224.

[21] Putnam, *op. cit.*, pp. 646–648 n.

[22] Rokkan and Valen, *op. cit.*

[23] See Kevin R. Cox, "Regional Anomalies in the Voting Behavior of the Population of England and Wales: 1921–1951" (unpublished Ph.D. dissertation, Department of Geography, University of Illinois, 1967).

[24] See Converse, *op. cit.*

specified election varies directly as a function of the strength of short-term forces toward the opposing party and varies inversely as a function of the mass of stored information about politics. Moreover, the short-term forces that either reinforce partisanship or deflect the voter from his normal partisan course depend on the flow of current information. The strength of current information flow will affect the magnitude of deflection from different parties at an election:

> If the flow of information is strong, no particular prediction is safe, in the sense that the partisan valences of the incoming information may be so varied that net pressures toward change are weak or in the sense that other cancelling processes may arise between individuals whose current reactions polarize. If the flow of information is weak, however, very potent limits on defections and vote oscillation are established.[25]

In the light of the postulated biasing effect of a context on the partisan character of information, however, we would argue that where information flow is strong, defection will be influenced by any bias inherent in that information.

The information intake of the voter is limited by two factors: (1) the output of the system of communication in society; (2) the interest of the individual or his motivation to attend to information once some flow exists. Further, Converse claims that interest shows a correlation with stored information, but its variation across individuals is much greater than that of current information intakes. Converse suggests that a minimum interest level is required before information flows affect the individual's partisan attitudes. At the lowest levels there is insufficient interest to attend to current information flow; at higher levels the individual is "protected" from the impact of current information flows by his relatively large mass of stored information. Converse postulates and demonstrates a parabolic relationship between partisan instability and access to information, with the least accessible and the most accessible being the most resistant to current information flows. In this paper a measure of access to political information will be employed in order to identify contextual effects upon individuals of varying susceptibility to the biased information flows of the locality.

A final critical omission of the contextual model has been its failure, thus far, to examine the behavior of individuals vis-à-vis their local ambiences over time. If there is a flow of information which leads to the partisan conversion or reinforcement of individuals, then such attitudinal change ought to be revealed in panel studies over an appropriate

[25] Converse, *op. cit.,* p.585.

length of time. In current contextual analyses it is exceedingly difficult to discriminate between (a) a case of information flow leading to partisan conversion or reinforcement and (b) a case of homopolitical selectivity. "Homopolitical selectivity" is a term suggested by Ulf Himmelstrand and refers to the tendency for like individuals consciously to seek each other out for formal and informal interaction.[26] Himmelstrand defines homopolitical selectivity for both senders and receivers of political information as the tendency of a sender (receiver) to orient himself mainly to receivers (senders) who are known to have the same political stand as himself. However, a political selection process might also result from the application of a social criterion to choice of friends; the findings of political sociology suggest that a selection on the basis of social affinity would also be politically selective.

With cross-sectional data, an alternative approach, operating within the assumptions of the contextual model regarding the biasing of an individual's information field by the political milieu of a district, is to examine individuals who have lived in that neighborhood and have been exposed to that milieu for varying lengths of time. The changing effects of a milieu with length of residence in that milieu are open to speculation. There are two possibilities: (1) that the increasing time spent in particular political contexts leads to increasing integration into informal groups and formal organizations in that area and hence to an increasing contextual effect via a flow of information with time spent in an area; (2) that an individual moving into a new locality searches that locality for individuals and organizations of similar ideology and viewpoint to himself. This search procedure is a trial-and-error process, and early results are likely to be much more biased by the nature of the political context than are later outcomes. Indeed, probability theory demonstrates that under perfectly random conditions where an individual is exposed to a number of alternatives the expected wait or number of unsuccessful exposures before a given alternative is presented to an individual equals the probability of not being exposed to that alternative on any one trial divided by the probability that exposure will occur on any one trial.[27] Thus, in this particular case, let Pd equal the probability of being exposed to a Democrat as determined empirically by the per cent Democratic in a precinct; and let Qd equal the probability of being exposed to a Republican as determined empirically by the per cent

[26] Ulf Himmelstrand, *Social Pressures, Attitudes and Democratic Processes* (Stockholm: Almquist and Wiksell, 1960), pp. 399–408.

[27] William Feller, *An Introduction to Probability Theory and Its Applications* (New York: Wiley, 2nd ed., 1957), p. 210.

Republican in a precinct; then in a completely two-party situation, in which all individuals identify with either of the two parties,

$$E(x) = \frac{Qd}{Pd}$$

that is, the expected number of unsuccessful exposures required before the individual contacts a Democrat. So in a precinct that is 90 per cent Republican, assuming randomness of contact and confinement of contacts to the precinct, an individual would have to undergo, on the average, nine exposures before contacting a Democrat. In a precinct that is 50 per cent Republican, however, an individual would have to have only one exposure before contacting a Democrat. Nevertheless, little is known about space-searching procedures in geography or in other social sciences,[28] and the area is entered with an almost complete innocence regarding possible relationships.

SOME HYPOTHESES

The critical discussion of the contextual model just outlined has many implications, only a few of which can be considered here. The hypotheses selected for initial investigation are, however, central to further inquiry along the lines previously suggested on theoretical grounds:

H. 1. Those belonging to informal social networks at the local level will be much more influenced in their partisan attitudes by the political milieu at the local level than will be those belonging to informal social networks at the extralocal level.

H. 2. Those belonging to formal social networks at the local level will be much more influenced in their partisan attitudes by the political milieu at the local level than will be those belonging to formal social networks at the extralocal level.

H. 3. The effects of the local political milieu will be increased for those initially establishing new links in a locality over and above the contextual effects present for those who have long since established such links.

H. 4. The effects of the political milieu will be greatest neither for the least involved nor for the most involved but for an intermediate

[28] See, for example, the review of this literature in Peter R. Gould, "Space Searching Procedures in Geography and the Social Sciences," Working Papers, No. 1, Social Science Research Institute: (Honolulu: University of Hawaii, 1966).

group that has relatively low levels of current political information
but sufficient interest to be susceptible to the biased political stimuli
of the local environment.

DATA AND METHOD

The dependent variable employed throughout this study is party
identification. This is an ordinal variable consisting of seven categories
with three gradations of identification allocated to Democrats and
Republicans, respectively, and an intermediate category to Independ-
ents. The local political context is measured at the precinct level for a
random sample of 604 respondents in the Columbus metropolitan
area.[29] We have differentiated six categories of political context:
0–25 per cent, 26–37 per cent, 38–49 per cent, 50–61 per cent, 62–73 per
cent, 74–100 per cent. Other variables employed in this analysis are
discussed where necessary as testing of the individual hypotheses
proceeds.

The method of testing for contextual effects and for comparing the
varying contextual effects to which different subgroups are subject is
that recently employed by Putnam.[30] The independent variable per
cent Democratic in the precinct is related to the dependent variable
party identification using Kendall's τ_c. As Putnam has described it,
"this statistic can be interpreted as a measure of the gradient in the
percentage of the Democratic votes among respondents as we move
from strongly Republican to strongly Democratic counties."[31] Thus,
when the social group is held constant, the magnitude of the coefficient
can be interpreted as a measure of the sensitivity of a group to the
political milieu, and the comparative sensitivities of different subgroups
can be evaluated. One of the problems associated with Kendall's τ_c is
that, although it is possible to test for the significance of any one τ_c
coefficient, it is impossible to test for the significance of a difference
between two such coefficients. Indeed, in many cases, where cross-
tabulations involve four or five variables, sample sizes are reduced to
dangerously low magnitudes. In almost all cases, however, the pattern

[29] The best available sampling frame was the *Haines Columbus City Directory,*
which proved a reasonably reliable listing of the city population. Students from
classes in Public Opinion, Metropolitan Politics, and Political Behavior were used as
interviewers. All classes were given several days' instruction in interviewing technique.
Extensive telephone checking of interviews revealed no cases of fabrication. Somewhat more than 80 per cent of the interviews attempted were completed.

[30] Putnam, *op. cit.*

[31] *Ibid.,* p. 642.

of findings is highly consistent and the differences between coefficients clear cut. Furthermore, the percentages appearing in the bodies of the accompanying tables refer to the proportions identifying with the Democratic Party but ignoring gradations of intensity within those identifiers; needless to say, the τ_c coefficients have been computed on the basis of all seven party identification categories.

TESTING OF THE HYPOTHESES

H. 1. Those belonging to informal social networks at the local level will be much more influenced in their partisan attitudes by the political milieu at that local level than will be those belonging to informal social networks at the extralocal level.

As Table 1 and the accompanying values of τ_c indicate, the partisan attitudes of those with local friends do seem to vary more as a function of the political context than do the partisan attitudes of those with nonlocal friends. The difference in the values of τ_c, however, is a small one. If this difference is a reflection of a converting or supporting effect of biased political information within a context, then the difference would be intensified when we turn our attention to those who discuss politics — that is, those most accessible to that information, be it biased or unbiased by the local political context.

Presumably, the difference in the contextual effect upon those with local and nonlocal friends, respectively, would be greatest for those who discuss politics. One can imagine four kinds of respondents in our sample:

(1) those who discuss politics with local friends; (2) those who don't discuss politics with local friends; (3) those who don't discuss politics with nonlocal friends; (4) those who discuss politics with nonlocal friends. Hypothetically, if there is a transmission of information biased by the political context, one would expect the contextual effect to be most intense for those who talk politics with local friends and to be least for those talking politics with nonlocal friends, while those who don't talk politics should occupy intermediate positions. As can be seen from Table 2, this is not the pattern that emerges in the case of informal contacts. Indeed, instead of finding the greatest contextual effect for those who discuss politics with local friends and the weakest contextual effect for those who discuss politics with nonlocal friends, the greatest difference in the τ_c coefficients occurs for the two groups who do not discuss politics at all.

KEVIN R. COX

Table 1

CONTEXTUAL EFFECTS AND FRIENDSHIP GROUPS

	Precinct Per Cent Democratic, 1964						Kendall's τ_c
	0–25%	26–37%	38–49%	50–61%	62–73%	74–100%	
Local friends	10.0% (10)	30.7% (39)	42.8% (28)	47.1% (53)	46.7% (15)	72.7% (33)	.265 (N = 178)
Nonlocal friends	7.1% (14)	37.8% (66)	46.4% (56)	50.0% (68)	48.5% (33)	74.6% (63)	.231 (N = 300)

Table 2

CONTEXTUAL EFFECTS, FRIENDSHIP GROUPS, AND DISCUSSION OF POLITICS

	Precinct Per Cent Democratic, 1964						Kendall's τ_c
	0–25%	26–37%	38–49%	50–61%	62–73%	74–100%	
Local friends:							
Discuss politics	0.0% (6)	31.1% (16)	24.9% (16)	38.9% (18)	20.0% (5)	55.5% (9)	.186 (N = 70)
Do not discuss politics	25.0% (4)	30.4% (23)	72.8% (11)	60.0% (34)	66.6% (9)	81.8% (22)	.298 (N = 103)
Nonlocal friends:							
Discuss politics	9.1% (11)	21.4% (28)	44.4% (27)	30.7% (26)	40.0% (10)	66.7% (21)	.255 (N = 123)
Do not discuss politics	0.0% (3)	50.1% (38)	48.2% (29)	61.9% (42)	52.1% (23)	78.6% (42)	.168 (N = 177)

The burden of the evidence presented here suggests that the areal scale of informal groups does not have a differential converting or supporting effect on those belonging to local and nonlocal informal groups respectively via a biased flow of information. Not only is the difference in the contextual effect upon local and nonlocal groups very small, but holding discussion of politics constant does not lead to the anticipated intensifier effect.

H. 2. Those belonging to formal social networks at the local level will be much more influenced in their partisan attitudes by the political milieu at the local level than will be those belonging to formal social networks at the extralocal level.

The testing of this hypothesis poses two operationalization problems. First, there is the problem of identifying a defensible allocation of voluntary groups to a scale of areal extent in branch catchment areas. Second, any one individual may belong to organizations differing sharply in areal extent. Here, in lieu of detailed knowledge about the organizational characteristics of interest, voluntary organizations are classified into these two categories:

1. Areally Intensive: parent-teacher associations, church groups, local service groups.

2. Areally Extensive: labor unions, fraternal organizations, veterans' associations, political clubs, sports groups.

Then, if an individual belongs to any of the areally extensive groups, he is allocated to the areally extensive category. This does not preclude the possibility that the same individual might also belong to an areally intensive group, but this would be of no significance in categorizing an individual who belongs to an areally extensive group also. If, however, an individual belongs only to areally intensive groups, he is allocated to that category.

As Table 3 shows, those belonging to areally intensive organizations are characterized by much greater contextual effects than is true of those with areally extensive affiliations. Moreover, the difference in these contextual effects is much greater than was true of the differences in the τ_c coefficients for those with local and nonlocal friends, respectively. However, if we hypothesize a contextual effect by which information is passed between individuals leading to conversion or support, we must first establish the relationships between context and partisan attitude for those who don't talk politics and for those who do, controlling for areal intensiveness or extensiveness.

Table 3

CONTEXTUAL EFFECTS AND ORGANIZATION MEMBERSHIPS

	Precinct Per Cent Democratic, 1964						Kendall's τ_c
	0–25%	26–37%	38–49%	50–61%	62–73%	74–100%	
Areally Intensive	0.0% (12)	28.0% (57)	43.7% (32)	40.3% (42)	40.0% (15)	81.4% (43)	.342 (N = 201)
Areally Extensive	24.7% (12)	32.7% (55)	41.7% (48)	49.2% (69)	58.6% (29)	63.8% (47)	.178 (N = 260)

Table 4

CONTEXTUAL EFFECTS, ORGANIZATION MEMBERSHIPS, AND ORGANIZATION DISCUSSION OF POLITICS

	Precinct Per Cent Democratic, 1964						Kendall's τ_c
	0–25%	26–37%	38–49%	50–61%	62–73%	74–100%	
Areally Intensive:							
Discuss politics	0.0% (9)	15.3% (26)	66.7% (6)	43.7% (16)	33.3% (6)	69.3% (13)	.380 (N = 76)
Do not discuss politics	0.0% (2)	38.4% (26)	47.6% (21)	28.5% (21)	42.9% (7)	84.6% (26)	.271 (N = 103)
Areally Extensive:							
Discuss politics	25.0% (8)	25.8% (31)	36.9% (27)	36.6% (30)	40.0% (10)	59.1% (22)	.156 (N = 128)
Do not discuss politics	25.0% (4)	40.0% (20)	47.4% (19)	63.3% (30)	70.6% (17)	70.6% (17)	.208 (N = 107)

Table 5

CONTEXTUAL EFFECTS, ORGANIZATION MEMBERSHIPS, AND DISCUSSION OF POLITICS WITH FRIENDS

	Precinct Per Cent Democratic, 1964						Kendall's τ_c
	0–25%	26–37%	38–49%	50–61%	62–73%	74–100%	
Areally Intensive:							
Discuss politics	0.0% (11)	22.2% (36)	39.1% (23)	41.7% (24)	37.5% (8)	78.2% (23)	.385 (N = 125)
Do not discuss politics	0.0% (1)	38.1% (21)	55.5% (9)	35.3% (17)	50.0% (6)	85.0% (20)	.280 (N = 74)
Areally Extensive:							
Discuss politics	27.3% (11)	30.3% (43)	44.5% (36)	36.2% (47)	56.1% (16)	54.1% (24)	.144 (N = 177)
Do not discuss politics	0.0% (1)	41.7% (12)	33.3% (12)	77.3% (22)	61.6% (13)	76.2% (21)	.193 (N = 81)

If formal groups do exert a biasing effect on the political content of one's information intake in such a manner as to lead to conversion or support of one's partisan attitudes, then the contextual effect should be greatest for those who discuss politics and belong to areally intensive organizations. This can be tested for two cases: (1) discussion of politics with group members; (2) discussion of politics with friends. The results for these two analyses are presented in Tables 4 and 5, respectively.

The hypothesis is clearly upheld in this case. There is a remarkable congruence between these two tabulations in the magnitudes of the analogous τ_c coefficients and in the rankings of the coefficients: intensive–discuss politics, intensive–don't discuss politics, extensive–don't discuss politics, extensive–discuss politics. Therefore, thus far, there is far greater evidence to support the idea of transmission of information in the case of formal organizations than in the case of informal organizations.

Indeed, it is possible to rank formal and informal organizations in terms of the contextual effects upon partisan attitudes as evidenced by the τ_c coefficients (see Table 6). Table 6 suggests the existence of a

Table 6

τ_c COEFFICIENTS FOR FORMAL AND INFORMAL CONTACTS
INSIDE AND OUTSIDE THE LOCALITY

	Kendall's τ_c
Areally intensive organizations	.342
Friends in the local area	.265
Friends outside the local area	.231
Areally extensive organization	.178

continuum with areally intensive organizations showing the greatest contextual effect, areally extensive organizations showing the least contextual effect, and local and nonlocal friendships falling into intermediate positions. This continuum agrees intuitively with one definable in terms of the degree to which affiliations in the different groups are representative of the political context. Putnam has suggested at the county level that informal friendship groups are likely to be far less representative of the political context in terms of their political complexion than formal groups;[32] this appears to be true at the precinct level also. Moreover, outside the precinct, informal groups appear more

[32] *Ibid.*, p. 648.

representative of their precinct of residence than do formal groups. This is impressive because it stresses the degree to which the contacts induced by formal groups are involuntary and therefore likely to bring the respondent into contact with a different range of political opinions than he might choose of his own accord.

H. 3. That the effects of the local political milieu will be increased for those initially establishing new links in a locality over and above the contextual effects present for those who have long since established such links.

It will be recalled that in our discussion of the contextual model and problems in its application thus far it was suggested that length of residence could have two possible impacts: (1) with increasing length of residence in an area the individual becomes increasingly integrated into the formal and informal networks of the locality, resulting in increased exposure to, and increased probability of conversion or support by, political information biased by the locality; (2) with increasing length of residence in an area the individual broadens the political range of his informal and formal contacts, a range which is likely to be highly restricted in the early stages of space searching in a biased political environment. This second possibility resembles Hypothesis 3. In the tabulations that follow, these ideas will be tested by using a dichotomous definition of length of residence: two years or less in one's current residence or more than two years.

Tables 7 and 8 suggest that for the local contacts of either a formal or informal character, recent residents are more influenced by the context than residents of long standing, in support of the second possibility; while for nonlocal contacts the contextual effect seems to increase with length of time resided in a precinct, in support of the original hypothesis and the first possibility. This is perfectly feasible if one interprets those with nonlocal contacts as being in a situation that protects them initially from the biased space-searching procedures to which those with only local contacts are subjected; that is, the process of making initial contacts is much slower than for those who confine their contacts to the locality.

Moreover, if the τ_c coefficients are rearranged as in Table 9, further relationships become evident. First, it is clear that the ranking of formal and informal organizations at different areal levels in terms of contextual effects upon partisan attitudes is apparent for both recent and nonrecent residents. Second, there appears to be a homogenization or convergence effect for those contextual effects over time; there is a

Table 7

CONTEXTUAL EFFECTS. ORGANIZATION MEMBERSHIPS, AND RECENCY OF RESIDENCE

	Precinct Per Cent Democratic Vote, 1964						Kendall's τ_c
	0–25%	26–37%	38–49%	50–61%	62–73%	74–100%	
Areally Intensive:							
Recent	0.0% (6)	29.2% (24)	50.0% (14)	35.3% (17)	50.0% (4)	87.0% (23)	.377 (N = 88)
Nonrecent	0.0% (6)	27.3% (33)	38.9% (18)	44.0% (25)	36.4% (11)	75.0% (20)	.311 (N = 113)
Areally Extensive:							
Recent	0.0% (3)	38.0% (21)	33.4% (24)	39.1% (23)	49.9% (14)	63.6% (22)	.101 (N = 107)
Nonrecent	33.3% (9)	29.4% (34)	50.0% (24)	54.3% (46)	66.7% (15)	64.0% (25)	.225 (N = 153)

Table 8

CONTEXTUAL EFFECTS, FRIENDSHIP GROUPS, AND RECENCY OF RESIDENCE

	Precinct Per Cent Democratic Vote, 1964						Kendall's τ_c
	0–25%	26–37%	38–49%	50–61%	62–73%	74–100%	
Local friends:							
Recent	0.0%	12.5%	54.6%	31.6%	60.0%	70.0%	.303
	(4)	(8)	(11)	(19)	(5)	(20)	(N = 67)
Nonrecent	16.7%	35.5%	35.3%	56.0%	40.0%	61.6%	.233
	(6)	(31)	(17)	(34)	(10)	(13)	(N = 111)
Nonlocal friends:							
Recent	12.5%	42.1%	39.2%	44.2%	28.5%	83.3%	.225
	(8)	(38)	(28)	(32)	(14)	(30)	(N = 150)
Nonrecent	0.0%	32.1%	53.5%	55.5%	63.2%	66.7%	.231
	(6)	(28)	(28)	(36)	(19)	(33)	(N = 150)

Table 9

τ_c Coefficients for Formal and Informal Contacts, Inside and
Outside the Locality for Recent and Nonrecent Residents

	Recent	Nonrecent
Areally intensive organization	.377	.311
Friends in the local area	.303	.233
Friends outside the local area	.225	.231
Areally extensive organization	.101	.225

decreasing variance in the values of the coefficients as one moves from
recent to nonrecent residents, although the mean varies hardly at all.
Third, the differential in contextual effect between those with local and
nonlocal contacts, respectively, is obliterated for those with informal
links with increasing length of residence but remains intact — though
reduced — for those with formal links at different areal scales.

If these relationships for those with local contacts and nonlocal
contacts, respectively, are indicators of a political influence process,
then they ought to be intensified when the degree to which individuals
discuss politics is taken into account. Thus, the partisan attitudes of an
individual who has just moved into an area and who makes local
contacts and discusses politics ought to be much more affected by the
context than someone who does not discuss politics. Likewise, the
partisan attitudes of a respondent who is a recent resident with nonlocal contacts ought to be much less affected by the political context
if he discusses politics than if he doesn't. Further, the rank ordering
of the τ_c coefficients for the four groups defined in terms of locale of
contacts and discussion of politics ought to be preserved over time.
In order of descending magnitude this order should be: local–discuss
politics, local–do not discuss politics, nonlocal–do not discuss politics,
nonlocal–discuss politics.

Table 10 presents the cross tabulation for informal contacts, and it
can be seen that these expectations are not entirely borne out. If a
political influence process was at work concurrent with the space-
searching procedures suggested earlier, there should be a decrease in
the value of the τ_c coefficients with increased length of residence for
those who discuss politics with local friends. In fact, there is an increase.
Likewise, for residents of long standing the highest τ_c coefficient should
be for those with local contacts who discuss politics, and the lowest
should be for those who discuss politics with nonlocal friends. The
table indicates that the latter coefficient is, in fact, greater than the

Table 10

CONTEXTUAL EFFECTS, FRIENDSHIP GROUPS, RECENCY OF RESIDENCE, AND DISCUSSION OF POLITICS

	Precinct Per Cent Democratic Vote, 1964						Kendall's τ_c
	0-25%	26-37%	38-49%	50-61%	62-73%	74-100%	
Recent:							
Local friends:							
Discuss politics	0.0% (2)	33.3% (3)	0.0% (3)	20.0% (5)	66.6% (3)	66.6% (3)	.286 (N = 19)
Do not discuss politics	20.0% (0)	0.0% (1)	75.0% (4)	25.0% (8)	0.0% (0)	100.0% (6)	.293 (N = 19)
Nonlocal friends:							
Discuss politics	20.0% (5)	39.9% (15)	54.6% (11)	23.6% (17)	20.0% (5)	77.7% (9)	.144 (N = 62)
Do not discuss politics	0.0% (0)	66.6% (9)	0.0% (2)	57.2% (7)	33.4% (6)	100.0% (6)	.155 (N = 31)
Nonrecent:							
Local friends:							
Discuss politics	14.3% (7)	30.4% (23)	43.7% (16)	46.1% (26)	20.0% (5)	66.7% (12)	.220 (N = 89)
Do not discuss politics	0.0% (1)	33.3% (12)	50.0% (4)	69.3% (13)	66.6% (6)	70.0% (10)	.298 (N = 46)
Nonlocal friends:							
Discuss politics	0.0% (8)	23.9% (29)	40.7% (27)	48.3% (29)	50.0% (14)	65.4% (26)	.277 (N = 133)
Do not discuss politics	0.0% (1)	46.2% (13)	56.2% (16)	80.0% (15)	75.0% (8)	77.3% (22)	.190 (N = 75)

former. For informal relations, therefore, the τ_c coefficients do not reveal the pattern required to sustain the hypothesis of changing political influence patterns as a function of space-searching procedures.

Tables 11 and 12 present the results for formal contacts: Table 11 treats those organization members who discuss politics with their friends, and Table 12 examines those organization members who discuss politics with other group members. In these tabulations the hypothesized rank ordering is validated much more clearly than was true for informal links. While the pattern is blurred slightly in the case of discussing politics with friends, it is very clear in the case of discussing politics with organization members. Those recent residents with local contacts who discuss politics are much more affected by the biasing effects of the political milieu as they search space for secondary links than are those who do not discuss politics. Likewise, those recent residents who discuss politics with nonlocal contacts are very much sheltered from influence by the local political milieu. Furthermore, the convergence in the values of the coefficients over time is much greater for those who discuss politics than for those who don't; thus in Table 12, while the values of the τ_c coefficients for those who discuss politics decrease from .413 to .160 over time (a difference of .253), they decrease from .163 to .038 (a difference of .125) for those who don't discuss politics. Thus, not only are the apolitical who belong to areally intensive groups less affected by the political milieu, but they are also less affected by the biasing effects of the milieu on space searching. It is similar for the apolitical among those in areally extensive groupings — they are more affected by the political milieu but less affected by the need for search for local contacts.

In summary, it appears that for those belonging to areally intensive organizations, the original space-searching hypothesis is validated: recent residents are more biased by the milieu. For those belonging to areally extensive organizations, on the other hand, it appears that contextual influence starts at a low level and increases over time as a result of a retarded local space-searching procedure in which the individual is sheltered from the impact of the biased information encountered in the early stages of the space search. For informal groups, on the other hand, the pattern of the τ_c coefficients, as with the testing of other hypotheses, is far too distorted to provide evidence for the postulated process.

H. 4. The effects of the political milieu will be greatest neither for the least involved nor for the most involved but for an intermediate group that has relatively low levels of current political information

Table 11

CONTEXTUAL EFFECTS, ORGANIZATION MEMBERSHIPS, RECENCY OF RESIDENCE, AND DISCUSSION OF POLITICS WITH FRIENDS

	Precinct Per Cent Democratic Vote, 1964						Kendall's τ_c
	0-25%	26-37%	38-49%	50-61%	62-73%	74-100%	
Recent:							
Areally Intensive:							
Discuss politics	0.0% (4)	42.9% (7)	40.0% (5)	33.4% (6)	100.0% (2)	85.7% (7)	.420 (N = 31)
Do not discuss politics	0.0% (0)	33.4% (6)	0.0% (0)	28.6% (7)	0.0% (1)	100.0% (4)	.311 (N = 18)
Areally Extensive:							
Discuss politics	0.0% (0)	30.0% (10)	30.0% (10)	18.2% (11)	33.3% (6)	50.0% (4)	.031 (N = 41)
Do not discuss politics	0.0% (0)	100.0% (3)	33.3% (6)	57.2% (7)	75.0% (4)	71.5% (7)	—.030 (N = 27)
Nonrecent:							
Areally Intensive:							
Discuss politics	0.0% (7)	17.2% (29)	38.9% (18)	44.4% (18)	16.7% (6)	74.9% (16)	.366 (N = 94)
Do not discuss politics	0.0% (1)	40.1% (15)	55.5% (9)	40.0% (10)	60.0% (5)	81.2% (16)	.261 (N = 56)
Areally Extensive:							
Discuss politics	27.3% (11)	30.4% (33)	50.0% (26)	41.7% (36)	70.0% (10)	55.0% (20)	.176 (N = 136)
Do not discuss politics	0.0% (1)	22.2% (9)	33.3% (6)	86.6% (15)	55.5% (9)	78.6% (14)	.299 (N = 54)

Table 12

CONTEXTUAL EFFECTS, ORGANIZATION MEMBERSHIPS, RECENCY OF RESIDENCE, AND ORGANIZATION DISCUSSION OF POLITICS

	Precinct Per Cent Democratic Vote, 1964						Kendall's τ_c
	0–25%	26–37%	38–49%	50–61%	62–73%	74–100%	
Recent:							
Areally Intensive:							
Discuss politics	0.0% (3)	33.4% (6)	100.0% (2)	40.0% (5)	0.0% (0)	100.0% (3)	.439 (N = 19)
Do not discuss politics	0.0% (0)	42.9% (7)	0.0% (1)	16.7% (6)	50.0% (2)	87.5% (8)	.300 (N = 24)
Areally Extensive:							
Discuss politics	0.0% (0)	60.0% (5)	28.6% (7)	16.7% (6)	25.0% (4)	40.0% (5)	.016 (N = 27)
Do not discuss politics	0.0% (0)	42.9% (7)	33.3% (9)	50.0% (8)	66.7% (6)	100.0% (5)	.137 (N = 35)
Nonrecent:							
Areally Intensive:							
Discuss politics	0.0% (6)	10.0% (20)	50.0% (4)	45.5% (11)	33.3% (6)	60.0% (10)	.358 (N = 57)
Do not discuss politics	0.0% (2)	36.8% (19)	50.0% (20)	33.4% (15)	40.0% (4)	83.3% (18)	.269 (N = 79)
Areally Extensive:							
Discuss politics	25.0% (8)	19.2% (26)	40.0% (20)	41.7% (24)	50.0% (6)	64.7% (17)	.198 (N = 101)
Do not discuss politics	25.0% (4)	38.5% (13)	60.0% (10)	68.2% (22)	72.8% (11)	58.3% (12)	.231 (N = 72)

but sufficient interest to be susceptible to the biased political stimuli of the local environment.

Thus far we have suggested that those belonging to areally extensive organizations are far less subject to the political influence of the local political milieu than are those belonging to areally intensive organizations. Further, we have found that these relationships change over time in relation to different stages in the space-searching process. The hypotheses regarding informal contacts, however, have not been sustained. If the political milieu does exercise a converting or supporting effect upon the partisan attitudes of those belonging to voluntary organizations at different areal scales, who are the most resistant, and who are the most susceptible?

As set forth earlier, Converse has suggested that it is neither those who are most informed about politics nor those who are least informed who demonstrate the greatest susceptibility to partisan change under the impact of current information flows but an intermediate group — a group that has sufficient interest to attend to current flows of information but insufficient stored information with which to defend itself against the persuasiveness of such contemporary material.[33]

In this paper an attempt has been made to operationalize Converse's current information continuum in terms of a Guttman scaling of certain items thought to be indicative of political involvement;[34] in his original statement, Converse did use attention to actual media as his index of current information intake, but such data are not available for our Columbus sample. Certainly, however, as shown in Table 13, the same pattern of greatest partisan instability for the intermediate group does seem to reveal itself. In this case, the measure of partisan instability is provided by τ_c coefficients between the respondent's partisan attitude and his party preference in 1960 and the party identification of his father, respectively.

As Table 14 indicates, it is indeed in the groups of medium political involvement that the contextual effect is greatest when the areal level

[33] Converse, *op. cit.*

[34] These items were the responses to the following questions, in order of increasing hardness: (1) "When you talk with your friends do you ever talk about public problems, that is, what's happening in this country or in this city?" (2) "About how often do you get into a conversation about politics?" (3) "Compared with people you know, are you more or less likely than any of them to be asked your views about politics?" (4) "Have you tried to convince anyone of your political views in the last week or so?" This produced a five-point scale of political involvement. It was found, however, that relatively few respondents were allocated to the first three categories; these were therefore combined.

Table 13

τ_c COEFFICIENTS FOR PARTY IDENTIFICATION AND PARTY PREFERENCE
1960, AND FATHER'S PARTY IDENTIFICATION, CONTROLLING FOR
POLITICAL INVOLVEMENT

	Low Involvement	*Medium Involvement*	*High Involvement*
Party preference, 1960	.500 ($N = 128$)	.485 ($N = 193$)	.569 ($N = 94$)
Father's party identification	.355 ($N = 124$)	.259 ($N = 204$)	.319 ($N = 79$)

of voluntary groups is held constant; indeed, for areally intensive groups the value of the τ_c coefficients is particularly high, accounting for much of the difference in the τ_c's for areally intensive and areally extensive groups, respectively.

From Table 15, however, it is again clear that this pattern is not repeated for more informal groupings. While for those with nonlocal links the expected pattern is confirmed, such is not the case for those with local contacts.

CONCLUDING COMMENTS

This paper has four noteworthy empirical conclusions. First, it seems that formal contacts much more than informal contacts act as the channels along which political influence flows. While predicted differences in contextual effect have appeared for both informal and formal groups at different areal levels, these differences are intensified in magnitude and direction only when discussion of politics is held constant for formal groups. The respective cross tabulations in which length of residence and susceptibility are held constant also strengthen these arguments. This is an important conclusion since previous work, particularly that of Putnam, assigned almost equivalent and complementary roles to formal and informal organizations as channels for information flow.[35] Clearly, this contradiction needs to be taken up in further empirical work.

Second, this flow of political influence has a spatial component, so that for any precinct of residence those individuals who belong to

[35] Putnam, *op cit.*, pp. 650–651.

Table 14

CONTEXTUAL EFFECTS, ORGANIZATION MEMBERSHIPS, AND POLITICAL INVOLVEMENT

	Precinct Per Cent Democratic Vote, 1964						Kendall's τ_c
	0-25%	26-37%	38-49%	50-61%	62-73%	74-100%	
Areally Intensive:							
Low involvement	33.3%	30.6%	39.3%	41.2%	66.7%	57.8%	.168
	(9)	(36)	(28)	(34)	(12)	(19)	(N = 138)
Medium involvement	0.0%	22.2%	41.2%	29.5%	60.0%	81.1%	.412
	(9)	(27)	(17)	(17)	(5)	(16)	(N = 91)
High involvement	25.0%	60.0%	50.0%	58.4%	20.0%	100.0%	.184
	(4)	(5)	(8)	(12)	(5)	(7)	(N = 41)
Areally Extensive:							
Low involvement	0.0%	41.7%	30.0%	73.1%	60.4%	72.7%	.171
	(1)	(12)	(10)	(23)	(12)	(22)	(N = 80)
Medium involvement	0.0%	35.0%	55.5%	42.9%	42.9%	84.2%	.295
	(1)	(20)	(9)	(14)	(7)	(19)	(N = 70)
High involvement	0.0%	80.0%	62.5%	88.9%	50.0%	81.6%	.256
	(1)	(5)	(8)	(9)	(4)	(11)	(N = 38)

Table 15

CONTEXTUAL EFFECTS, FRIENDSHIP GROUPS, AND POLITICAL INVOLVEMENT

	Precinct Per Cent Democratic Vote, 1964						Kendall's τ_c
	0–25%	26–37%	38–49%	50–61%	62–73%	74–100%	
Local Friends:							
Low involvement	0.0% (1)	25.0% (12)	62.5% (8)	61.1% (18)	57.2% (7)	74.9% (16)	.310 (N = 62)
Medium involvement	12.5% (8)	34.7% (23)	37.5% (16)	37.5% (24)	60.0% (5)	69.3% (13)	.266 (N = 89)
High involvement	0.0% (1)	25.0% (4)	25.0% (4)	45.5% (11)	0.0% (3)	75.5% (4)	.026 (N = 27)
Nonlocal Friends:							
Low involvement	0.0% (1)	54.5% (22)	47.1% (17)	72.7% (22)	54.6% (11)	85.7% (28)	.190 (N = 101)
Medium involvement	9.1% (11)	29.4% (34)	42.9% (28)	39.4% (33)	46.7% (15)	70.8% (24)	.251 (N = 145)
High involvement	0.0% (2)	30.0% (10)	54.6% (11)	38.5% (13)	42.9% (7)	54.6% (11)	.158 (N = 54)

areally more extensive organizations are likely to be exposed to political opinion different from that to which members of intensive organizations are exposed. It is probably for this reason that Putnam and Segal and Meyer obtained conflicting results in their respective examinations of contextual effects on groups varying in their number of secondary affiliations. Certainly, the more contacts an individual has, the more likely some of them will be outside the immediate locality.

Third, there appears to be a space-searching stage in the individual's socialization into a community. This is a stage in which the individual is trying to find agreeable contacts of a formal or informal nature in the local area and during which he is more likely to be exposed to radically different opinions than later in this trial-and-error process. All we have provided in this paper, however, are some indications that space searching is involved in the socialization of an individual into a new community; applications of learning theory here might provide more definitive conclusions in the future.

Finally, we have attempted to incorporate Philip Converse's measure of partisan instability into our contextual analysis. While the surrogate scale for information intake employed in our testing of Converse's hypothesis is not the most desirable, the parabolic relationships identified between partisan instability and current information intake are clearly reflected in the relationship between contextual effect and political involvement scale for formal groups at different areal levels.

An attempt has been made in this paper to provide more definitive conclusions on the basis of a contextual model than have been provided hitherto. By examining individuals characterized by varying lengths of residence, we have tried to minimize the dangers of inferring fallacious influence flows where a more realistic interpretation would be in terms of homopolitical selectivity. Retrospectively, controlling for discussion of politics has performed a similar function. Unfortunately, there is very little literature on the problem of contextual effects as a reflection of an influence flow process and/or as an indication of a selection process in the choice of friends. Yet the problem of evaluating influence flow as opposed to homopolitical selectivity is not likely to be a difficult problem to resolve and should occupy a high priority in the research of those concerned with explaining variations in political behavior.

8

J. A. LAPONCE

Ethnicity, Religion, and Politics, in Canada: A Comparative Analysis of Survey and Census Data

IN ITS MORE common usage "ecological" describes the study of inter-actions between individuals and their environment. In a more technical sense it also describes the use of aggregate statistics obtained for comparable territorial units in order to determine individual behavior. It is, then, a sort of hide-and-seek game one plays with obscure data, usually for lack of better information, sometimes for the pleasure one gets from drawing maps and from relating people and territory.

Taken in its narrow technical sense, the ecological method is only one application of the use of aggregate to reach individual characteristics. These "individual characteristics" need not be "individuals";[1] they may be traits contained within an individual, individuals contained within a group, or a series of subgroups contained within a larger group — a territory, for example. There is no necessary opposition between ecological and survey research. As a territory is the environment of individuals, an individual is the environment of traits, and to relate these traits through material obtained by interview leads to the same difficulties as the attempt to reach the individual through census data. Whatever difference there may be between the use of survey and of

[1] The language is treacherous — one slips easily from the notion of "individual" meaning "indivisible unit of analysis" to the notion of "individual" meaning "people." H. R. Alker does it in his excellent summary of the arguments against ecological analysis. See his *Mathematics and Politics* (New York: Macmillan, 1965), p. 62.

187

census data will come from the definition of our units of observation and analysis, of our definition of what is container and what is content, of where the fish begins and where the fishbowl ends.[2]

To contrast, as we propose to do, findings obtained from Canadian poll surveys with those obtained from the census is not to oppose survey and census per se but simply to compare the advantages and drawbacks of each kind of data for our very specific intent, which is to relate the religious denomination and the ethnic origin of Canadians to politics. Since our unit of analysis is the individual, the survey will give us individual statistics, while the census, most of the time, will yield only aggregate statistics.

THE DATA USED

The choice of the election of 1963 as the pivot of our analysis needs to be justified. The national surveys available to us spanned the years 1953–1963; all had been taken on the occasion of a federal election. Two of them, those of 1958 and of 1962, would have been closer to the time of collection of the census (1960). The election of 1958 was ruled out as a clearly deviant case; it marks the only time in Canadian history when a single party obtained over 75 per cent of the seats in Parliament. In that year, partly as a result of the electorate's desire to give a majority to a party that had governed with a minority in the House, the Conservatives progressed suddenly from their 30–35 per cent norm of the popular vote, a norm they had maintained since 1935, to a high of 53 per cent of the electorate. That this election was a deviant case is shown by the elections that followed (1962, 1963, 1965). In 1962 the two major parties, Conservatives and Liberals, were at a balance point, each with 37 per cent of the votes; in 1963 the Liberals had regained a more "normal" lead of 40 per cent to 30 per cent over the Conservatives, and this is the justification for our choice.

The poll survey used is that taken by the Canadian Institute of Public Opinion (CIPO), an affiliate of Gallup, before the election of April 1963. It has the advantage of providing a relatively large number of cases ($N = 2,710$, of which 2,157 are originals and 553 duplicates); it suffers, however, from the disadvantages associated with the area-quota type of sampling and from the further disadvantage of using categories

---

[2] For a summary and further discussion of the "Aggregation problem" in the social sciences see O. D. Duncan, R. P. Cuzzort, and B. Duncan, *Statistical Geography: Problems in Analyzing Areal Data* (Glencoe: Free Press, 1961).

of classification often badly adapted to the Canadian scene. For example religious affiliation is given for Protestant, Catholic, and Jew, a traditional United States classification. But the Jewish classification is practically useless, even in a sample of that size, because there are too few Canadian Jews. Inversely, the Protestant classification is too broad. The Anglicans, at least, should have been singled out; though they are not an established church as in Great Britain, they have maintained much of the social and psychological attitudes that result from a priviliged link with the Crown.

The census material we used is not available in the printed publications of the Dominion Bureau of Statistics (DBS) but can be obtained from them in the form of computer printouts, which provide some demographic statistics by electoral district. The usual demographic charactersitics were not all available in this special report; there were none, for example, on profession. This imposed some restrictions on our choice of variables. But even if all the usual information had been available, the census would still have frustrated us by its usual limitations. The categories it uses to segregate individuals are evidence of the concern of economists and of bureaucrats in the hospital and coroners' services rather than of sociologists. It is unfortunately as unacceptable for a census taker to ask "What political party do you prefer?" or "How often do you go to church?" as to have him say "I shall read you two jokes; you tell me which one, on the whole, you like best."

Of the electoral statistics used little need be said. They were taken from the 1963 Chief Electoral Officer's report; its only claim to distinction is that for the first time in Canada it mentioned the political party of the candidates. Although, as in the United States or Britain, voting is, on the whole, either for a party or for a national leader, Canada continues to adhere officially to the theory that electors vote for individuals rather than for the groups that sponsor them. But the party names that appeared for the first time in 1963 in the election reports have still to appear on the ballots.

THE VARIABLES

We propose to relate ethnicity and religion (a) to a social hierarchy measured by the level of education and (b) to the left and right continuum as indicated by party preference.

We expect, of course, to disprove the null hypothesis that ethno-religious groups are found in equal proportions at all levels of the

educational hierarchy and among all political electorates. Beyond dis-
proving the null hypothesis, we expect also to be able to measure the
relative position of the groups we have selected in these educational and
political dimensions.

Dependent Variables

To measure level of education, we shall use only two variables,
describing the two extremes of the pyramid: (a) primary school education and (b) university education.

The politial variables are given by the five parties represented in the
Parliaments of the 1960's: the New Democratic Party (NDP), the
Liberals, the Conservatives, the Social Credit Party and the Créditistes.
The NDP is Canada's socialist party; it combines rather than blends
an agrarian tradition in the West and a Fabian–trade-unionist movement in the major English Canadian cities. The Liberals can be best
compared with the Swiss Radicals, or the French Radicals of the
Third Republic; they are the "governmental" party, *par habitude* if not
par excellence. The Conservatives, like the Socialists, have also a western
agrarian antibank, anticity stronghold tradition but remain linked as
well to the city business interests—a link that has weakened somewhat
under the leadership of John Diefenbaker. The two Social Credit parties
can be best compared to the French Poujadists; they have, however,
the embryo of an economic doctrine, a poor man's version of Keynes.

Independent Variables

The Canadian population can be divided roughly into three major
ethnic categories, if we define ethnicity by the country of origin of a
person or of his ancestors on the father's side. There are 44 per cent
British, 31 per cent French, and 23 per cent "other Europeans," who
are sometimes described as "New Canadians" in contrast to the two
"founding races." The remaining 2 per cent, which comprises Indians,
Eskimos, and Asians, will be left outside the scope of this study.

Religiously, Canada is almost equally balanced between Protestants
and Catholics, so well balanced that the immigration authorities have
ceased to publish and, theoretically, also to record the religion of new
immigrants. As in Lebanon, official ignorance of changes in a contentious and precarious situation is thought politically advisable.

If the major Protestant denominations are counted separately, the
Roman Catholics dominate with over 45 per cent of the population, the

two numerically nearest competitors have only 20 per cent (the United Church)[3] and 13 per cent (the Anglicans).

If we go beyond this gross classification and relate religion to country of origin, we see the ethnic-religious mosaic so characteristic of North America. Table 1 gives the percentage of the total population of each of the 168 ethnic-religious groupings recognized by the census. Only three groups have more than 10 per cent: French Catholics (29 per cent), British Anglicans (11 per cent) and British United Church (15 per cent). British Catholics, with 8 per cent, are the only other group having more than 5 per cent. Thus four ethnoreligious groups account for 63 per cent of the total population. The remaining 37 per cent are divided among a large number of small and very small groups.

Among major religious and ethnic groups reciprocal overlap is the rule, with one important exception. A few statistics will illustrate the rule. Only 84 per cent of Anglicans are British, and only 25 per cent of British are Anglicans; only 84 per cent of Presbyterians are British, and only 8 per cent of British are Presbyterians. Only 25 per cent of Lutherans are Scandinavians, and only 38 per cent of Scandinavians are Lutherans. Over 10 per cent of Poles belong to denominations other than Catholic, Jewish, or Lutheran. The exception is that of French Canadians. If only 63 per cent of Catholics are French, 96 per cent of French are Catholics. This is a striking measure of the lack of penetration of the Protestant denominations into French Canadian society — an indication of the success of the "besieged fortress" mentality adopted by French Canadian society since the conquest. If one considers the size of both the Protestant and the French Canadian groups and the statistical chances of social contact between the two groups in cities such as Montreal or Ottawa, the French Canadian Protestant is as odd as the Chinese Jew.

The CIPO poll survey did not allow much choice in the selection of ethnic and religious variables. We shall use its "Protestant" and "Catholic" categories and its ethnic-linguistic definitions of "English," "French," "Others (New Canadians)," which are based on the language spoken in childhood and still understood. The census classifications are more refined; we shall use only some of them (see Table 2).

The two instruments of research at our disposal have different qualities. The survey has the great advantage of giving us individual statistics but has only gross and limited categories. The census has a

[3] The United Church is the result of a merger of Methodists, Congregationalists, and a majority of Presbyterians.

Table 1

Percent Distribution of Ethnoreligious Groups in Canada

	Anglican	Baptist	Greek Orthodox	Jewish	Lutheran	Mennonite	Pentecostal	Presbyterian	Roman Catholic	Ukranian Catholic	United Church	Other	Totals
British	11.13	2.36	0.01	0.04	0.35	0.02	0.53	3.81	7.75	0.02	15.64	2.15	43.81
Dutch	0.18	0.11	**	**	0.06	0.33	0.03	0.10	0.44	**	0.58	0.58	2.41
French	0.45	0.09	**	**	0.04	0.01	0.03	0.09	29.11	0.01	0.49	0.14	30.46
German	0.38	0.29	**	0.01	1.61	0.41	0.08	0.15	1.42	0.01	1.03	0.41	5.80
Italian	0.04	0.01	**	**	0.61	**	0.01	0.01	2.33	**	0.07	0.02	2.50
Jewish	**	**	**	0.93	**	**	**	**	**	**	**	0.01	0.94
Polish	0.07	0.02	0.05	0.15	0.06	0.06	0.01	0.02	1.17	0.06	0.14	0.05	1.80
Russian	0.03	0.02	0.08	0.14	0.04	0.01	0.01	0.01	0.10	0.01	0.09	0.12	0.71
Scandinavian	0.19	0.07	**	**	0.80	0.02	0.04	0.06	0.15	**	0.62	0.16	2.10
Ukranian	0.10	0.01	0.66	**	0.04	0.01	0.02	0.03	0.44	0.87	0.33	0.08	2.59
Other European	0.15	0.05	0.47	0.12	0.58	0.01	0.02	0.10	1.84	0.07	0.36	0.12	3.89
Asiatic	0.06	0.01	0.03	**	**	**	**	0.04	0.10	**	0.21	0.25	0.70
Native Indians and Eskimo	0.30	**	**	**	**	**	0.01	0.02	0.69	**	0.14	0.04	1.20
Other and not stated	0.19	0.16	0.06	0.01	**	**	0.02	0.08	0.27	**	0.42	0.11	1.32
Totals	13.27	3.20	1.36	1.40	3.59	0.86	0.81	4.52	45.81	1.05	20.12	4.24	100%**

* Error due to rounding = 0.23 per cent.
** Less than 0.01 per cent.
Source: *Census of Canada, 1961*, Vol. I, Part 3.

Table 2

ETHNIC AND RELIGIOUS CATEGORIES USED FOR
THE DEFINITION OF THE INDEPENDENT VARIABLES

CIPO Categories	*Census Categories*
Ethnic (language spoken in childhood)	*Ethnic* (language spoken in childhood)
English	English
French	French
Other	Other
	Ethnic (country of origin)
	British Isles
	France
	Germany
	Scandinavia
	Ukraine
Religious	*Religious*
Protestant	Anglican
Catholic	United Church
Jew	Lutheran
	Baptist
	Catholic

refined classification but most of the time will give us only aggregate statistics. Since in the balance of advantages and disadvantages the survey appears the better tool, we shall proceed from the survey to the census, taking the survey as far as possible; then we shall seek to duplicate its findings by the ecological method and should the duplication be made — an intuitive reassurance of its soundness — use it to try to go further than the survey could have gone because of its categorical limitations.

ETHNICITY, RELIGION, AND THE EDUCATION HIERARCHY

Combining the sample linguistic and religious categories gives five major groupings: English Protestant, English Catholic, French Catholic, "New Canadian" Protestant, "New Canadian" Catholic.[4] For

[4] Studies of the association of religion and ethnicity are strangely lacking in Canada. This lack is all the more surprising since, when studied separately, ethnicity and religion are shown to be excellent social discriminators. A limited attempt to relate the two, and to control each when studying their interaction with other variables, has been made in John Porter, *The Vertical Mosaic, an Analysis of Social Class and Power in Canada* (Toronto: University of Toronto Press, 1965). See in particular p. 101 and Chapter IV. This work is also of specific interest because it makes abundant use of the ecological method.

each of these categories let us determine the proportion of respondents
with at least one year of university training, a proportion that could also
be read as the observer's chances of being right in saying that an English
Protestant or a new immigrant Catholic has university training. (See
Figure 1.)

The trees of university training and low educational achievement
presented by Figures 1 and 2 indicate first the differences between urban
and rural areas, then for each side of the tree the differences between
linguistic groups, and finally differences between linguistic-religious
groups. The percentage in the upper left corner of Figure 1 indicates
that 10 per cent of adult English Protestants in nonmetropolitan areas
have entered a university. The sample percentages for French Canadians
have been multiplied by 1.75 to account for the fact that the first three

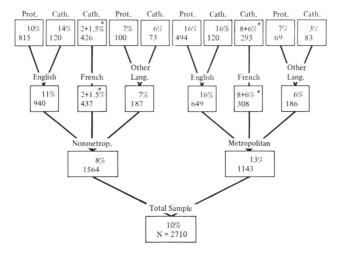

*The French Canadian sample percentage has been multiplied by 1·75 to account
for the difference between English and French universities.

Figure 1

TREE OF UNIVERSITY EDUCATION (PERCENTAGES)

This figure is based on CIPO survey No. 302, 1963.

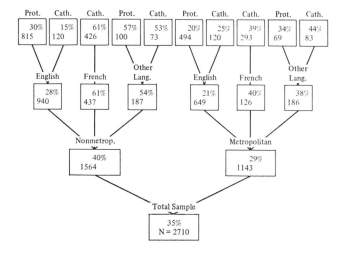

Figure 2

TREE OF POOR EDUCATION (LESS THAN EIGHT YEARS OF SCHOOLING)

This figure is based on CIPO survey No. 302, 1963.

years of university by English Canadian definition are obtained in French Canada in schools outside the university.[5]

The division between metropolitan (over 100,000 people) and non-metropolitan (rural–small town) was put at the base of the tree since it was found to be a better discriminator than either sex or socioeconomic status (SES).[6] But either sex or SES would have given a pattern of differences between ethnoreligious groups similar to the one presented.

On either side of the tree the English appear as better educated than French and "New Canadians." In the metropolitan areas the difference between French and English Canadians is not great at the university level, but twice as many French as English Canadians failed to go be-

[5] The 1.75 multiplier was obtained from the figures given in DBS, *Census 1961*, Vol. I, Part 3, "Schooling by Age Group."

[6] An analysis of the weak social-class cleavages in Canada as compared to Australia, Great Britain, and the United States, has been made, on the basis of survey material, in Robert Alford, *Party and Society* (Chicago: Rand McNally, 1963).

yond primary school.[7] In the small-town and rural areas the difference between the two "founding races" is even greater. On the whole, French Canadians appear closer to the "New Canadians" than to the dominant English group. That ethnicity rather than religion is the factor causing these differences is indicated by the facts that in the metropolitan areas English Catholics and English Protestants have the same percentage of university-trained people and that the Catholics do slightly better in the rural areas. Among "New Canadians" there is a marked tendency for Protestants to rank higher than Catholics; but, here again, very likely religion disguises an ethnic difference between the immigrants from Northern and Central Europe.

In an English-speaking country, one would naturally expect individuals whose mother tongue is not English to find educational and social upgrading more difficult. That there is a wide gap between English and "new Canadian immigrants" is thus not surprising; more interesting is that the French of Quebec rank so low compared to the relative standing of the French in other provinces.

A comparison of the two major Canadian provinces, Quebec and Ontario, confirms our previous observations (see Table 3) but might lead one to think that the educational dominance of the English in Quebec is compensated by the dominance of the French in Ontario. The 2–1 ratio in favor of the English of Quebec is almost reversed in favor of the French in Ontario.

However, while the educated French Canadians of Ontario are concentrated in Ottawa and serve in a federal civil service that is theoretically bilingual but is in fact almost entirely English-speaking, the English Canadians of Quebec are concentrated in Montreal; they are business executives or managers and need not work through the language of the host community. The French are in Ottawa as civil "servants"; the English are in Quebec as business "dominants." In Toronto, the major English Canadian metropolitan center, only 3 per cent of the population spoke French as their mother tongue, while in Montreal, the major French Canadian metropolis, 24 per cent spoke English.[8]

At this point in our analysis we need to measure each linguistic

[7] Compulsory education from the age of six to fourteen in rural areas and from six to sixteen in urban centers, was finally introduced in Quebec in 1942. See C. E. Phillips, *The Development of Education in Canada* (Toronto: W. J. Gage, 1957), p. 188.

[8] For studies on the history of economic development in Quebec see, among others, the contributions by A. Faucher, M. Lamontagne, and Falardeau in J. C. Falardeau (ed.), *Essais sur le Québec Contemporain* (Québec: Les Presses de l'Université Laval, 1953).

Table 3

PERCENTAGE OF PEOPLE IN SELECTED ETHNORELIGIOUS GROUPS
WITH UNIVERSITY TRAINING IN METROPOLITAN
ONTARIO AND QUEBEC

	Ontario	*Quebec*
English Protestants	17	24
English Catholics	12	*
French Catholics	26	11**
"New Canadian" Protestants	8	*
"New Canadian" Catholics	7	3

* Too few cases (less than 25).
** After correction (see note to Figure 1).
Source: CIPO poll No. 302, April 1963.
Note: In each cell the maximum is 100%.

group's resistance to assimilation by the other, since we have anticipated our findings by assuming that the French become assimilated (at least linguistically) in Ontario, but that the English do not become assimilated in Quebec, or at least not to the same extent.

Since the survey lacks the data on which to base such an analysis, we shall use the census, and since the census fails to correlate mother tongue and the official language spoken, we must compare aggregates.

Before doing so, let us seek to duplicate part of our survey observations. In order to find out whether ethnic and religious groups are so distributed that individuals may be described by their social environment within the bounds of the electoral districts, we shall correlate the percentage of university-trained in each district with selected ethnic and religious variables.

For the metropolitan areas of Quebec (see Table 4) the simple correlation of each ethnic and religious variable with university education clearly indicates that the French and consequently the Catholic stand apart by their high negative scores; they are the only variables with negative signs. With few exceptions, the other variables have such high positive single correlations (see Table 5) that it is impossible to sort out the new immigrants from the British, or the Protestant denominations among themselves.

One could try, of course, to isolate the "New Canadians" from the British at a smaller territorial level, something that can be done more easily for linguistic than for denominational groups. Our purpose is,

Table 4

ETHNICITY, RELIGION, AND UNIVERSITY EDUCATION
IN METROPOLITAN QUEBEC*

Ethnic (national origin)		*Religion*	
British	.66	Anglican	.69
French	−.76	Baptist	.61
German	.87	Lutheran	.85
Scandinavian	.77	Catholic	−.82
		United Church	.69
Ethnic (mother tongue)			
French	−.76		
Other than			
French or			
English	.47		

* Simple correlation of selected ethnic and religious groups with the percentages of university-trained per electoral district. Only correlations over .40 are given.

however, fulfilled by drawing from the correlations both a confirmation and a warning. We find it confirmed that English Canadians have a distinctly higher educational ranking than French Canadians. The warning is that the "New Canadians" settle, within the French host society, alongside the British, and that when the percentage of British increases, the percentage of "New Canadians" tends also to increase. Thus whenever we compare "French" and "British" districts, we should endeavor to control for the "New Canadians."

Measures of Linguistic Assimilation

To measure assimilation or resistance to it, we shall use two different ratios: (*a*) mother tongue to ethnic origin and (*b*) official language to mother tongue. We want to know, for example, how many of those who spoke English as their mother tongue are of British origin and how many of those listing it as their official language spoke it in childhood. Similar data for the French will give a comparative measure of both the resistance to assimilation and the success in assimilating others.

The mother tongue–ethnic origin ratio for the French of metropolitan Quebec is 1.01; for the British it is 1.12. If we assume that the English linguistic group has kept nearly all its original members or their descendants, a reasonable assumption, it has expanded 12 percentage points beyond its base; but the French have progressed hardly at all. A few French Canadians of non-French origin are well known — the former Prime Minister of Quebec and leader of the *Union Nationale,*

Table 5

SIMPLE CORRELATIONS BETWEEN THE VARIABLES USED IN TABLE 4

	British	French	German	Scandinavian	French Language	"Other Language"	Anglican	Baptist	Lutheran	Catholic
British										
French	-.83									
German	.74	-.90								
Scandinavian	.92	-.81	.85							
French language	-.85	.99	-.90	-.83						
"Other language"	.27	-.73	.65	.34	-.71					
Anglican	.98	-.84	.78	-.96	-.86	.31				
Baptist	.95	-.84	.74	.87	-.86	.36	.94			
Lutheran	.79	-.91	.98	.89	-.91	.62	.84	.79		
Catholic	-.84	.97	-.93	-.84	.97	-.65	-.85	-.84	-.94	
United Church	.95	-.80	.74	.92	-.81	.24	.94	.86	.78	-.83

Daniel Johnson, for example — but they remain striking exceptions. The French Canadian milieu has remained a very closed society.[9] The "New Canadians" have assimilated into English culture rather than into French culture, even in Quebec. For the whole of Canada the ratios, as one should expect, are even more unfavorable to French Canadians; the French ratio is a low 0.92; the English ratio is 1.33.

The ratio of official language to mother tongue should measure more contemporary trends. Its use is complicated, however, by the fact that the census, in addition to the categories "French" and "English", uses also "bilingual." We shall assume that all those who listed themselves as speaking "French only" had French as their mother tongue. The bias introduced by this assumption favors a high ratio of French Canadian resistance to linguistic assimilation since it implies that no "English" born would have given French as his sole official language, which is probably very close to the truth, but it implies also that no "New Canadian" immigrant would have listed French to the exclusion of English. Since we want to show that the French have a low degree of resistance to linguistic assimilation, the bias can only make the figures obtained more convincing. The correlation between the ratio of resistance to linguistic assimilation and the percentage of French Canadians in the electoral districts of urban Quebec is given by Figure 3. The ratio of resistance to linguistic assimilation through bilingualism is negatively correlated to the percentage of English people. Not even Quebec City, which is geographically isolated from any large English settlement escapes this trend. Factors other than the number of English settlers are, of course, responsible for the correlation: upward social mobility, education and wealth in particular. Thus the better-educated, the wealthier the French Canadian, the more likely he is to have acquired English and to live in the same suburbs as English Canadians.

To reduce the disturbing effect of "New Canadian immigrants" who often list English as their sole official language, we shall restrict the

[9] One of the consequences of this inward-looking and defensive attitude has been that for French Canadian scholars, analysis has, by and large, meant self-analysis. English Canadians have studied French Canada, but not vice versa, as if the study and the understanding of the dominant group by the minority involved a difficult reversal of psychological attitudes. The result is that we are relatively well provided with studies on French Canada. As guides through the social science and historical literature on Quebec, see in particular Marcel Rioux and Yves Martin, *French-Canadian Society, Sociological Studies* (Toronto: McClelland & Stewart, 1964), and Falardeau (ed.), *op. cit.* While Ontario receives about 50 per cent of all immigrants to Canada, Quebec receives only about 20 per cent. According to recent estimates made by the Quebec Cultural Affairs Ministry, 90 per cent of immigrants to Quebec seek assimilation into the British rather than into the French group.

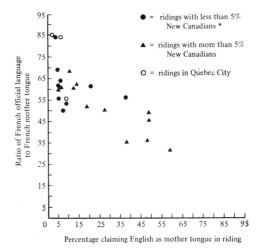

* "New Canadian" is used to describe the respondents who indicated a mother tongue other than French or English.

Figure 3

RESISTANCE OF FRENCH CANADIANS TO LINGUISTIC ASSIMILATION

analysis of the ratio of English resistance to assimilation to the electoral districts with less than 5 per cent of "New Canadians" in their population. Although the number of cases remaining is small, the indication is clearly given by Figure 4 that the ratio of English resistance is much higher than the French and hardly affected by the size of the "opponent." It is only when the French Canadians in the district are more than 90 per cent of the population that the ratio falls under 0.75, and even then it falls only to about 0.50, a level obtained with far less English population pressure in the case of the French.

ETHNORELIGIOUS GROUPS RELATED TO POLITICAL PARTIES

The reinforcement of the major linguistic and religious divisions by educational and geographical differences would seem to predispose Canada to a communal as well as regional party system, a system where the major ethnoreligious communities would anchor their claims in

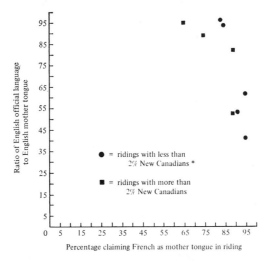

* "New Canadian" is used to describe the respondents who indicated a mother tongue other than French or English.

Figure 4

RESISTANCE OF ENGLISH CANADIANS TO LINGUISTIC ASSIMILATION
(IN RIDINGS WITH LESS THAN 5% NEW CANADIANS)

different parties. One might expect there to be a major French and a major English party, since it is between these two groups that there is the least amount of linguistic, religious, and geographical overlap. However, despite the growing economic and political conflicts between Quebec and Ottawa, the party system, though affected, has maintained, on the whole, its multiethnic characteristics. The heightening during the past ten years of the Franco-English opposition has strained the constitutional and party structures but has not thus far fundamentally altered them.

French Canadians have found sufficient protection in the federal system to continue to support federal parties, although the latter are led by and from English Canada, even when a French Canadian is at the head. Only one of the five parties fails to link at least two of the major ethnoreligious groups. The Quebec Créditistes are exclusively French and consequently Catholic.

What is the ethnoreligious balance of each of the five electorates? How does each of the major ethnoreligious groups split its votes between these parties? The two questions must be answered. Even if we were to find that a given party is the sole microcosm of the nation, we still could not conclude that it is the best political agency of ethnic and religious conciliation unless we know its size as related to the size of the groups it mirrors.

The Internal Ethnoreligious Balance of Canadian Parties

At the outset of this analysis, it is important to recall that the definition of ethnicity we derived from the survey is purely linguistic. "English" and "French" categories refer to those who spoke either English or French as their mother tongue. "New Canadian" immigrant describes those who had a mother tongue other than French or English.

The degree of under- or overrepresentation within each party is given by Table 6. The index of support of a party by a given ethnoreligious group is a ratio of party to national percentages. For example, the New Democratic Party has among its supporters 58 per cent English Protestants, compared with 52 per cent of English Protestants in the sample. The index of English Protestant representation in the NDP electorate is thus $(58 \times 100)/52 = 111$.

We may arbitrarily decide to consider as not underrepresented any group that scores at least 80 (shaded areas on Table 6).

The Liberal Party, the major center party, is weak only in its share of Protestant new Canadians ("other language" groups), while the Conservatives have low scores in the whole Catholic column. The NDP and

Table 6

INDEX OF REPRESENTATION WITHIN EACH CANADIAN PARTY OF SELECTED ETHNORELIGIOUS GROUPS

	NDP		Liberals		Conservatives		S. Credit (Eng. Canada)		S. Credit (Quebec)	
	Cath.	Prot.	Cath.	Prot.	Cath.	Prot.	Cath.	Prot.	Cath.	Prot.
French	52		114		59		17		384	
English	90	111	155	88	52	130	89	133	0	0
Other language	173	159	121	36	57	125	158	277	0	0

Source: CIPO poll No. 302, April 1963.

the Social Creditors are well balanced between English and new Canadians, whether they are Catholic or Protestant, but they are both very weak in their representation of the most important minority group, the French Canadians. The Liberals are thus the only party to come close to being the microcosm of the nation; they underrepresent only the "new Canadian" Protestants, who account for only 6 per cent of the sample.

The Political Preference of Ethnoreligious Groups

The prime importance of the Liberal Party as an agent of ethnic and religious aggregation appears even more clearly from the study of the balance of political preferences among the ethnoreligious groups considered (see Table 7).

Neither of the two major parties receives less than 15 per cent support from any of the groups, a level that is rarely reached by the smaller parties; both major parties can thus qualify as political agencies of aggregation and conciliation if not integration. But again the Liberal Party is the only one not to be unbalanced; it alone obtains massive support from both the French and English communities.

Ethnic and religious conciliation is thus a characteristic of the political center. As one moves toward the extremes, the parties take a more specific ethnoreligious form.

Schematically we can represent the Canadian party system as a bell-shaped curve skewed to the right of the ideological center. Close to that ideal center we find the point of greatest electoral support, the "traditional" government party and the point of greatest political conciliation and amalgamation of the various religious and ethnic communities.

Table 7

PERCENTAGE OF SUPPORT GIVEN BY SELECTED ETHNORELIGIOUS GROUPS TO CANADIAN PARTIES

	NDP		Liberals		Conservatives		S. Credit (Eng. Can.)		S. Credit (Quebec)		Totals (rounded)	
French	4		47		23		1		26		100	
English	11	13	64	37	17	42	6	8	0	0	100	100
Other language	19	20	50	22	18	40	11	18	0	0	100	100
	Cath. Prot.		Cath. Prot.		Cath. Prot.		Cath. Prot.		Cath. Prot.		Cath. Prot.	

Source: CIPO poll No. 302.

As one moves toward the extremes, one finds parties (*a*) weaker in their electoral support and thus less likely to form or control the government and (*b*) less likely to link together the major ethnoreligious groups (see Figure 5).

The division between Catholics and Protestants, though weak in the large cities because of the wide appeal of the Liberals, remains marked in the nonmetropolitan areas. (See Table 8.) Even if the Conservatives were to regain the votes they lost to the Social Credit (Créditistes) in French Canada, the contrast, though attenuated, would remain.

The Metropolitan-Nonmetropolitan Variations

To further this analysis, let us now turn to the census data, and in order to match as nearly as possible our survey definition of metropolitan

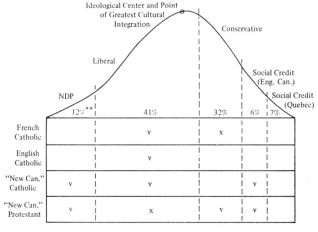

** Votes obtained in 1963.

** Votes obtained in 1963.

Figure 5

SCHEMATIC REPRESENTATION OF THE CANADIAN PARTY SYSTEM SHOWING
ETHNORELIGIOUS GROUPS LINKED TO THE ENGLISH PROTESTANT
DOMINANT GROUP BY EACH PARTY

(*v* = very strong link; *x* = weaker link)

Table 8

Parties Supported by Selected Ethnoreligious Groups in the Order of Preference (Percentages)

	1st Preference		2nd Preference		3rd Preference		4th Preference		Total
Small-Town and Rural Areas									
Eng. Protestants	Cons.	47	Liberals	33	NDP	10	S. Credit	8	100
Eng. Catholics	Liberals	62	Cons.	24	S. Credit	7	NDP	6	100
French Catholics	Liberals	41	Créditistes	31	Cons.	23	NDP	4	100
Other language — Protestants	Cons.	48	S. Credit	21	Liberals	17	NDP	12	100
Other language — Catholics	Liberals	49	Cons.	25	NDP	17	S. Credit	7	100
Metropolitan Centers (over 100,000)									
Eng. Protestants	Liberals	41	Cons.	33	NDP	17	S. Credit	6	100
Eng. Catholics	Liberals	67	NDP	15	Cons.	11	S. Credit	4	100
French Catholics	Liberals	57	Créditistes	20	Cons.	12	NDP	9	100
Other language — Protestants	Liberals	30	NDP	28	Cons.	26	S. Credit	13	100
Other language — Catholics	Liberals	50	NDP	23	S. Credit	13	Cons.	11	100

areas, let us separate the 77 most urban districts from the others.[10] In both areas let us determine for each party the most relevant ethno-religious variables by means of a stepwise regression analysis. At each step the variable added to the equation was that which caused the greatest increase in the coefficient of determination (R^2) — in other words, the variable that had the highest partial correlation on the dependent variable partialed on the variables already in the equation. The variables tested were the following (they all refer to the percentage of people described by that variable in each electoral district):

Religious
   Anglican
   Baptist
   Lutheran
   United Church

Ethnic (defined by the nationality of origin)
   British
   French
   German
   Scandinavian
   Ukrainian

Ethnic (defined by the mother tongue)
   French
   Other language

Immigration
   Postwar immigrant

Education
   Less than five years of formal education
   University education

We retained only the variables that produced at least a 2 per cent point increase in the R^2 or had a significant change in R^2 (we used a 0.05

[10] In the order in which they are listed by the Chief Electoral Officer's report the metropolitan districts are as follows:
   British Columbia: 1, 2, 4, 6, 12, 16, 17, 18, 19, 20, 21, 22.
   Alberta: 5, 6, 7, 8, 9. *Saskatchewan:* 11, 14. *Manitoba:* 10, 11, 12, 13, 14.
   Ontario: 6, 19, 20, 21, 22, 34, 42, 43, 44, 47, 54, 68, 69, 70, 72, 73, 74, 75, 76, 78, 79, 80, 81, 82, 83, 84, 85. *Quebec:* 19, 27, 35, 37, 38, 57, 58, 59, 60, 61, 62, 63, 64, 65, 66, 67, 68, 69, 70, 71, 72, 73, 74, 75.
   Nova Scotia: 7.

significant level in the F test). The variables retained are presented in the order in which they appeared in the equation for metropolitan and nonmetropolitan areas studied separately (see Tables 9 to 12).

Table 9

MULTIPLE STEP-BY-STEP REGRESSION OF NDP ELECTORS (IN %) ON PERCENTAGE OF SELECTED ETHNIC AND RELIGIOUS GROUPS PER ELECTORAL DISTRICT*

Metropolitan Districts ($N = 77$)

---

a. Regression equation (nonstandardized):
   % NDP = 36.67% $-$ (.24) (% Catholic) $-$ (1.89) (% university education)
b. Regression equation (standardized):**
   NDP = 3.13 $-$ .62 (Catholic) $-$ .48 (univ. educ.)
c. Order in which the variables entered the equation with R^2 and F values at each step:
   1st step = Catholic ($F = 24.9$); $R^2 = .25$
   2nd step = Catholic ($F = 50.3$) + univ. educ. ($F = 29.6$); $R^2 = .46$
d. Simple correlation of each variable in the equation with party:
   Catholic = $-$.50; univ. educ. = $-$.40

Nonmetropolitan Districts ($N = 188$)

---

a. Regression equation (nonstandardized):
   % NDP = 60.98% $-$ .58 (% University education) $+$ .38 (% Anglican) $-$ (.98) (% postwar immigrant)
b. Regression equation (standardized)**
   NDP = 2.05 $-$ .68 (univ. educ.) $+$ .28 (Anglican) $-$ .39 (postwar immig.)
c. Order in which the variables entered the equation with F and R^2 values at each step:
   1st step = univ. educ. ($F = 162.4$); $R^2 = .46$
   2nd step = univ. educ. ($F = 272.4$) + postwar immig. ($F = 64.4$); $R^2 = .60$
   3rd step = univ. educ. ($F = 195.1$) + postwar immig. ($F = 77.8$) + Anglican ($F = 35.1$); $R^2 = .66$
d. Simple correlations of each variable with the party:
   Univ. educ. = $-$ .68; postwar immig. = $-$ .14; Anglican = .51

---

* We stopped entering variables in the equation when the R^2 stopped increasing by more than .2 or when the F value of the variable to be entered was not significant at the 0.05 level.

** In the standardized equation the variables are measured in units of their own standard deviations.

Source: Census data 1961 and election data 1963.

Table 10

MULTIPLE STEP-BY-STEP REGRESSION OF LIBERAL ELECTORS (IN %) ON PERCENTAGE OF SELECTED ETHNIC AND RELIGIOUS GROUPS PER ELECTORAL DISTRICT*

Metropolitan Districts (N = 77)

---

a. Regression equation (nonstandardized):

% Liberal = 41.78 − 3.76 (% Scandinavian) + 3.7 (% university education) − 1.02 (% German) + .22 (% other language)**

b. Regression equation (standardized):***

Liberal = 1.13 − .68 (Scand.) + .49 (univ. educ.) − .37 (German) + .25 (other lang.)

c. Order in which the variables entered the equation with F and R^2 values at each step:

1st step = Scand. $(F = 58.5)$; $R^2 = .44$

2nd step = Scand. $(F = 120.5)$ + univ. educ. $(F = 35.6)$; $R^2 = .62$

3rd step = Scand. $(F = 51.3)$ + univ. educ. $(F = 35.9)$ + German $(F = 4.8)$; $R^2 = .65$

4th step = Scand. $(F = 47.3)$ + univ. educ. $(F = 45.1)$ + German $(F = 13.0)$ + other lang. $(F = 10.4)$; $R^2 = .69$

d. Simple correlations of each variable with the party:

Scand. = − .66; univ. educ. = .40; German = − .58; other lang. = − .03.

Nonmetropolitan Districts (N = 188)

---

a. Regression equation (nonstandardized):

% Liberal = 8.91 + .87 (% French) − .86 (% university education) + 252.9 (% Ukrainian)

b. Regression equation (standardized):***

Liberal = .24 + .90 (French) − .22 (univ. educ.) + .14 (Ukrainian)

c. Order in which the variables entered the equation with F and R^2 values at each step:

1st step = French $(F = 1034.7)$; $R^2 = .84$

2nd step = French $(F = 1444.7)$ + univ. educ. $(F = 96.3)$; $R^2 = .89$

3rd step = French $(F = 1652.0)$ + univ. educ. $(F = 97.0)$ + Ukrainian $(F = 24.6)$; $R^2 = .91$

d. Simple correlations of each variable with the party:

French = .92; univ. educ. = .86; Ukrainian = .04

---

* We stopped entering variables in the equation when the R^2 stopped increasing by more than .2 or when the F value of the variable to be entered was not significant at the 0.05 level.

** Mother tongue other than French or English.

*** In the standardized equation the variables are measured in units of their own standard deviations.

Source: Census data 1961 and election data 1963.

Table 11

MULTIPLE STEP-BY-STEP REGRESSION OF CONSERVATIVE ELECTORS
(IN %) ON PERCENTAGE OF SELECTED ETHNIC AND RELIGIOUS
GROUPS PER ELECTORAL DISTRICT*

Metropolitan Districts ($N = 77$)

---

a. Regression equation (nonstandardized):
   % Conservative = 5.59 + .84 (% United Church) + .96 (% low education)** − 2.95 (% Scandinavian) + .88 (% German)
b. Regression equation (standardized):***
   Conservative = .54 + 1.02 (United Church) + .41 (low educ.) − .61 (Scand.) + .37 (German)
c. Order in which the variables entered the equation with F and R^2 values at each step:
   1st step = United Church ($F = 30.5$); $R^2 = .29$
   2nd step = United Church ($F = 39.0$) + low educ. ($F = 9.3$); $R^2 = .37$
   3rd step = United Church ($F = 60.6$) + low educ. ($F = 17.3$) − Scand. ($F = 15.8$); $R^2 = .48$
   4th step = United Church ($F = 35.1$) + low educ. ($F = 10.5$) + Scand. ($F = 24.7$) + German ($F = 8.9$); $R^2 = .54$
d. Simple correlations of each variable with the party:
   United Church = .54; low educ. = − .19; Scand. = .19; German = .50

Nonmetropolitan Districts ($N = 188$)

---

a. Regression equation (nonstandardized):
   % Conservative = 10.89 + .38 (% postwar immigrant) + 2.73 (% not born in Canada) + 200.9 (% Ukrainian) − .08 (% French) − .13 (% Anglican) − .16 (% Baptist)
b. Regression equation (standardized):***
   Cons. = .92 + .38 (postwar immig.) + .24 (not born Can.) + .34 (Ukrainian) − .26 (French) − .24 (Anglican) − .22 (Baptist)
c. Order in which the variables entered the equation with F and R^2 values at each step:
   1st step = postwar immig. ($F = 79.3$); $R^2 = .29$
   2nd step = postwar immig. ($F = 82.9$) + not born Can. ($F = 47.2$); $R^2 = .43$
   3rd step = postwar immig. ($F = 75.2$) + not born Can. ($F = 68.7$) + Ukrainian ($F = 44.9$); $R^2 = .54$
   4th step = postwar immig. ($F = 72.4$) + not born Can. ($F = 39.8$) + Ukrainian ($F = 41.5$) + French ($F = 16.1$); $R^2 = .58$
   5th step = postwar immig. ($F = 82.8$) + not born Can. ($F = 24.7$) + Ukrainian ($F = 44.2$) + French ($F = 26.4$) + Anglican ($F = 11.5$); $R^2 = .61$
   6th step = postwar immig. ($F = 66.9$) + not born Can. ($F = 21.8$) + Ukrainian ($F = 34.7$) + French ($F = 23.5$) + Anglican ($F = 21.1$) + Baptist ($F = 18.0$); $R^2 = .64$

Table 11 (continued)

d. Simple correlations of each variable with the party:
   Postwar immig. $= .54$; not born Can. $= .43$; Ukrainian $= .38$;
   French $= - .44$; Anglican $= - .04$; Baptist $= - .44$

---

* We stopped entering variables in the equation when the R^2 stopped increasing by more than .2 or when the F value of the variable to be entered was not significant at the 0.05 level.

** Percentage of adults with less than Grade Five education.

*** In the standardized equation the variables are measured in units of their own standard deviations.

Source: Census data 1961 and election data 1963.

Table 12

MULTIPLE STEP-BY-STEP REGRESSION OF SOCIAL CREDIT ELECTORS
(IN %) ON PERCENTAGE OF SELECTED ETHNIC AND RELIGIOUS
GROUPS PER ELECTORAL DISTRICT*

Metropolitan Districts West of Ontario ($N = 23$)

---

a. Regression equation (nonstandardized):
   % Social Creditor $= - 9.77 + 5.04$ (% Baptist) $+ 1.87$ (% French)
b. Regression equation (standardized):**
   Social Creditor $= - 1.46 + .67$ (Baptist) $+ .37$ (French)
c. Order in which the variables entered the equation with R^2 and F values at each step:
   1st step $=$ Baptist ($F = 9.9$); $R^2 = .32$
   2nd step $=$ Baptist ($F = 14.9$) $+$ French ($F = 4.4$); $R^2 = .44$
d. Simple correlation of variable with party:
   Baptist $= .56$; French $= .15$

Nonmetropolitan Districts West of Ontario ($N = 47$)

---

a. Regression equation (nonstandardized):
   % Social Creditor $= 16.6 + 2.5$ (% Baptist) $+ .3$ (% postwar immigrant) $- .7$ (% Anglican) $- .3$ (% Catholic)
b. Regression equation (standardized):**
   Social Creditor $= 1.60 + .26$ (Baptist) $+ .40$ (postwar immig.) $- .37$ (Anglican) $- .25$ (Catholic)
c. Order in which the variable entered the equation with R^2 and F values at each step:
   1st step $=$ Baptist ($F = 11.4$); $R^2 = .20$
   2nd step $=$ Baptist ($F = 6.9$) $+$ postwar immig. ($F = 4.0$); $R^2 = .27$
   3rd step $=$ Baptist ($F = 8.6$) $+$ postwar immig. ($F = 9.1$) $+$ Anglican ($F = 5.8$); $R^2 = .35$
   4th step $=$ Baptist ($F = 4.1$) $+$ postwar immig. ($F = 11.4$) $+$ Anglican ($F = 8.3$) $+$ Catholic ($F = 5.0$); $R^2 = .42$

Table 12 (continued)

d. Simple correlation of variable with party
Baptist = .45; postwar immig. = .39; Anglican = − .03; Catholic =
− .36

Metropolitan Districts in Quebec ($N = 25$)

---

a. Regression equation (nonstandardized):
% Social Creditor = − 8.74 + .40 (% French)
b. Regression equation (standardized):**
% Social Creditor = .72 + .79 (French)
c. and *d.* *F* value = 40.5; R^2 = .63; simple correlation $(r) = .79$

Nonmetropolitan Districts in Quebec ($N = 50$)

---

a. Regression equation (nonstandardized):
% Social Creditor = − 9.4 + .47 (% French)
b. Regression equation (standardized):**
Social Creditor = .67 + .44 (French)
c. and *d.* *F* value = 12.1; R^2 = 20; $r = .44$

---

* We stopped entering variables in the equation when the R^2 stopped increasing
by more than .2 or when the *F* value of the variable to be entered was not significant
at the 0.05 level.
** In the standardized equation the variables are measured in units of their own
standard deviations.
Source: Census data 1961 and election data 1963.

On the whole, the regression analysis confirms the survey findings.
The NDP's success is negatively correlated in the metropolitan centers
to Catholicism and to university education. A regional analysis shows
that the negative correlation with Catholics remains in Ontario but
disappears in British Columbia and Alberta, a qualification that also
confirms the survey data. (See the appendix to this chapter.)

In the metropolitan centers the Liberals are positively correlated with
university education but negatively correlated with Protestant "new
Canadian" ethnic groups (the Scandinavians appear first in the equation).
In the nonmetropolitan areas Liberals are highly correlated with the
percentage of French people.

The association of Conservatives with Protestants and "new
Canadians" is confirmed. The equation indicates in particular that in
the rural areas the Ukrainians, a non-Protestant "New Canadian"
group, are positively correlated with that party.

The variable "French" alone explains 63 per cent of the Social
Créditistes variance in the urban areas of Quebec and 20 per cent in the
rural and small-town areas; this indicates that the support for Social

Credit in the metropolitan centers was among French Canadians more evenly distributed geographically than in the rest of the province.[11]

The fact that in the western English Canadian provinces Baptists enter the Social Credit equation first, in metropolitan as well as non-metropolitan areas, confirms the link between religious fundamentalism and the western brand of Social Credit. The negative correlation of Social Creditors with Catholics is a further indication of the homogeneous Protestant character of that party in the West, at least in the rural areas.

Among the correlations presented in Table 11 one claims special attention because it was not anticipated. Where we had expected "Anglicans" to score in the Conservative column, "United Church" appeared. We hypothesized that this might have been due to the weight of Western Canada and that if we were to analyze separately Ontario and the West, we would find Anglicans a better predictor of a Conservative vote in Ontario and United Church in the West. The hypothesis was not substantiated. The correlations with "Anglican" were not significant in the West; they became positive in Ontario but remained insignificant. The United Church, on the contrary, had a high positive correlation in Ontario (.63). Maybe the territorial distribution of the two religions is such as to tempt us to accept an "ecological fallacy."[12] We feel reluctant to accept the suggestion that United Church membership is a better predictor of a Conservative vote than is Anglican Church membership. But it may well be that the folklore is out of date on this point. Two of three small-scale surveys made in recent years have shown

[11] For an ecological study of the Social Credit vote in Quebec in 1962 and 1963, see Vincent Lemieux, "Les dimensions sociologiques du vote créditiste au Québec," *Recherches Sociographiques, 6*: 2 (1965), pp. 181–195. The Social Credit success appears linked to the size of the community, its votes being the highest in communities of 1,000 to 5,000 inhabitants. See also M. Pinard, "Political Factors in the Rise of the Social Credit in Quebec" (paper presented to the 1964 meeting of the Canadian Political Science Association), and V. Lemieux, "The Elections in the Constituency of Lévis" in J. Meisel (ed.), *Papers on the 1962 Election* (Toronto: University of Toronto Press, 1964).

[12] Nor should one be tempted to accept without caution the high correlations obtained in our analysis, which was intended simply to identify the major variables. As Robinson pointed out, ecological correlations tend to exaggerate the correlations obtained between demographic variables at the level of individuals. See W. S. Robinson, "Ecological Correlations and the Behavior of Individuals," *American Sociological Review, 15* (1950), pp. 351–357. For suggested corrections of this bias, see Leo A. Goodman, "Ecological Regressions and the Behavior of Individuals," *American Sociological Review, 18* (1953), pp. 663–664; also see a discussion and application in A. R. Baggally, "Religious Influence on Wisconsin Voting, 1928–1960," *American Political Science Review, 56* (1962), pp. 66–70.

a slightly greater support of the Conservative party by the United Church than by Anglicans: John Meisel's study in Kingston (Ontario) and that of Grace Anderson in Hamilton (also in Ontario).[13] In both cases the authors felt reluctant to generalize from local observations, but it is possible that the local situations evidenced an evolution that has affected not only the Conservatives but the Canadian party system generally — a movement of the Anglicans toward the center.

Should further research establish that the traditional link between Conservatives and Anglicans has been replaced, even in Ontario, by a preferred link between United Church and Conservatives, we would have to revise our bell-shaped model of the Canadian party system. Close to the ideological center, which cuts through the Liberal Party, we would locate the ideal point of better representation of the "historical" churches, the Anglicans and the Catholics; moving toward the extremes, we would then see a greater saliance of the more recent denominations. Admittedly, the Quebec Créditistes would not fit within such a model. But in Quebec as in France, the Poujadists are not expected to last. Should they last, however, or should French Canada develop other specifically French parties, it might become increasingly difficult to use the same model of explanation for the link between ethnoreligious groups and political parties in both Quebec and English Canada.

Our hesitation to accept the suggestions offered by the ecological analysis, or our reluctance to explain the individual by the group when so doing violates the folklore, is evidence of the serious limitations of the method used. But it could be argued also that, had we not tried this method, unsatisfactory as it is, we might have not met the problem at all.

[13] The expected high correlation between Anglicans and Conservatives is reported in a systematic sample survey made by P. Regenstreif, "Some Aspects of National Party Support in Canada," *Canadian Journal of Economics and Political Science* (*CJEPS*), *29* (1963), pp. 59–74; higher support by the United Church is reported in John Meisel, "Religious Affiliation and Electoral Behavior," *CJEPS, 22* (1956), p. 486, and in Grace M. Anderson, "Voting Behavior and the Ethnic-religious Variables," *CJEPS, 32* (1966), pp. 29–37. For a discussion of the religious factor in the 1957–1963 elections, see P. Regenstreif, *The Diefenbaker Interlude* (Toronto: Longmans, 1965), Chapter V. For a historical analysis see S. D. Clark, *Church and Sect in Canada* (Toronto: Toronto University Press, 1948).

Appendix

SUPPORT GIVEN BY SELECTED ETHNORELIGIOUS GROUPS TO CANADIAN PARTIES — BY REGION AND BY METROPOLITAN, NONMETROPOLITAN AREAS*

	NDP		Liberal		Conservative		Social Credit	
	Metro.	Nonmetro.	Metro.	Nonmetro.	Metro.	Nonmetro.	Metro.	Nonmetro.
The West								
English Prot.	13	16	37	20	37	45	12	35
English Cath.	10	0	55	71	—	23	—	5
French Cath.	—	—	—	—	—	—	—	—
O-L Prot.	10	13	40	8	20	51	20	27
O-L Cath.	25	18	29	36	—	33	—	15
Area average	(13)		(31)		(37)		(17)	
Ontario								
English Prot.	18	9	38	32	27	45	3	3
English Cath.	16	8	60	63	7	15	0	10
French Cath.	3	—	50	33	11	4	0	9
O-L Prot.	48	11	8	38	24	38	4	7
O-L Cath.	11	15	48	54	7	18	0	0
Prov. average	(14)		(39)		(30)		(3)	
Quebec								
English Prot.	9	—	68	—	22	—	0	—
English Cath.	14	—	57	—	12	—	0	—
French Cath.	9	2	53	40	12	23	22	33
O-L Prot.	—	—	—	—	—	—	—	—
O-L Cath.	29	—	58	—	11	—	17	—
Prov. average	(6)		(47)		(18)		(25)	

Appendix (continued)

	NDP		Liberal		Conservative		Social Credit	
	Metro.	Nonmetro.	Metro.	Nonmetro.	Metro.	Nonmetro.	Metro.	Nonmetro.
Maritimes								
English Prot.	16	2	27	48	—	46	5	2
English Cath.	6	3	66	51	—	41	0	3
French Cath.	—	0	—	60	—	20	—	20
O–L Prot.	—	—	—	—	—	—	—	—
O–L Cath.	—	—	—	—	—	—	—	—
Area average	(3)		(49)		(41)		(5)	
Canada								
English Prot.	17	10	41	33	33	47	6	8
English Cath.	15	6	67	62	11	24	4	7
French Cath.	9	4	57	41	12	23	20	31
O–L Prot.	28	12	30	17	26	48	13	21
O–L Cath.	23	17	50	49	11	25	13	7
Nat'l. average	(12)		(42)		(32)		(13)	

— = under 25 cases. O–L = mother tongue other than French or English.

* In each row, the four metropolitan classifications add up to 100 per cent, as do the nonmetropolitan classifications. Metropolitan means those areas having more than 100,000 inhabitants; nonmetropolitan is the residual.

Source: CIPO Survey No. 302, April 1963.

9

DAVID R. SEGAL AND MARSHALL W. MEYER

The Social Context of
Political Partisanship

BETWEEN THE INDIVIDUAL and the society of which he is a member, there exists a multitude of primary and secondary social groupings that define his place in the social order and demand certain behaviors of him. Thus conceived, primary and secondary group memberships at once condition a person's relationships with others — affecting the choice of his associates and the roles he takes — and at the same time exert a normative influence by requiring certain attitudes and actions and proscribing others. These mediating groups serve several integrative functions for the individual and society. First, they integrate the individual into society by placing constraints on his behavior. Durkheim showed, for example, that members of cohesive mediating groups — such as married people and members of the Catholic Church — were less susceptible to suicidal currents at the societal level than nonmembers or members of more loosely knit collectivities — unmarried individuals and Protestants.[1] Second, mediating groups with overlapping memberships may serve to integrate society as a whole by limiting cleavages along class, sectional, or ideological lines. Simmel, Coser, and Coleman have explored this issue in their discussions of primary, formal organizational, and community structures.[2]

---

[1] Emile Durkheim, *Suicide* (Glencoe: Free Press, 1951), p. 145.

[2] Georg Simmel, *Conflict and the Web of Group Affiliations* (Glencoe: Free Press, 1955); Lewis A. Coser, *The Functions of Social Conflict* (Glencoe: Free Press, 1956); James Coleman, *Community Conflict* (Glencoe: Free Press, 1957).

KORNHAUSER AND SHILS ON POLITICAL PARTICIPATION

William Kornhauser has suggested that a diversity of mediating organizations may be necessary for the maintenance of the political integration of society. Where such organizations do not exist, he argues, the public is available to manipulation by the elite, and a state of mass apathy and lack of participation exists. Such conditions are definitive of mass society in Kornhauser's formulation.[3] A somewhat different view of mass society is suggested by Shils, who feels that mass society can provide the conditions for increased political involvement by diversifying the potential bases for political participation.[4] The present paper suggests that each theory has its element of truth. We propose that the juxtaposition of Shils's notion of diversified bases of involvement with Kornhauser's concept of mediating organizations presents a more realistic and less pessimistic view of mass society than Kornhauser suggests, while not refuting his basic hypothesis.

In terms of Kornhauser's formulation, a strong intermediate group structure is necessary to preserve pluralism in society. Lacking such a strong intermediate structure, the individual becomes responsive to manipulation by the elite through political organization and the mass media.

Kornhauser conceives of intermediate structures for the most part as voluntary organizations. Differentiation of the labor force, he argues, is such that union and professional groups are now needed to fill the integrative function formerly accomplished by informal work associations. In the same manner, the complexity of the modern community is such that only organized and vocal interest groups can prevent accessibility of nonelites to elites.[5] In more operational terms, we interpret Kornhauser as saying that individuals who lack attachment to voluntary organizations are open to political control and domination by the national political elite. The unattached person is viewed as rootless, devoid of ties to any political community, and of transient and inconsistent beliefs. Kornhauser, then, portrays the unattached person as the apolitical man.

It is our contention that this is not the case. While we do not mean to refute Kornhauser's basic hypothesis that the absence of mediating

[3] William Kornhauser, *The Politics of Mass Society* (Glencoe: Free Press, 1955), pp. 60–73.

[4] Edward A. Shils, "A Theory of Mass Society," *Diogenes, 39*.

[5] Kornhauser, *op. cit.,* pp. 76–77.

associations leads to apathy, we reject his limited operational definition of mediating association and argue that forms of social relationship besides voluntary organizations may serve this mediating function.

OTHER THEORIES OF PARTICIPATION

It has been demonstrated that diverse kinds of nonpolitical organizations can serve to integrate the individual into the political community.[6] Several studies have indicated the importance of primary group relationships in the formation of political attitudes. These findings show that people in large measure pattern their political beliefs after those of their friends, family, and coworkers.[7]

A major preoccupation of research into American political behavior has been the relationship of social class and political partisanship. Surveys of national samples of the electorate have consistently shown that, although there are regional differences, people of high socioeconomic status tend to support the Republican Party, and persons of low socioeconomic status tend to support the Democratic Party.[8] Similarly, people who perceive themselves as middle (or upper) class tend to call themselves Republicans in much greater proportion than those who identify with the working (or lower) class.[9] We do not intend to discuss at length the connection between social class and political choice. It will suffice to note that either self-interest or class interest may explain the relationship between low socioeconomic class standing and preference for "left" political parties, as well as its converse, the relationship between high social class position and "right" political preference. These studies drawn from national samples have identified a number of individual-level correlates of political choice — for instance, age and religion. But national surveys, by drawing from a very dispersed sample of respondents (a few respondents at each of the great number of sampling points), have been unable to account systematically for the effects of the social context in which a person finds himself, his immediate environment, on his political choices. The effects of local community structure or locally based formal organizations cannot be deduced

[6] See Scott Greer and Peter Orleans, "The Mass Society and the Parapolitical Structure," *American Sociological Review, 27* (1962), pp. 634–646.

[7] See, for example, Bernard Berelson, Paul F. Lazarsfeld, and William N. McPhee, *Voting* (Chicago: University of Chicago Press, 1954), Chapter 6.

[8] See Angus Campbell, Philip E. Converse, Warren E. Miller, and Donald E. Stokes, *The American Voter* (New York: Wiley, 1960).

[9] Richard Centers, *The Psychology of Social Class* (Princeton: Princeton University Press, 1949).

from data that ignore these variables. Other studies of political behavior have concentrated in single communities. While such designs allow analysis of the effects of organizational membership, cross-community comparisons have not been possible. Thus, the authors of *Voting* hypothesize a "breakage effect" — that is, all other things being equal, people will tend to vote for the party supported by the climate of opinion of the communities in which they live.[10] But the fact that this effect is observed in Elmira, New York, does not allow us to generalize it to the whole of American politics.

Another approach has received a great amount of attention in the study of voting behavior in the United States. In the absence of individual data on social status, regional aggregate statistics have been used to describe characteristics of voters.[11] While we recognize the shortcomings of inferences from ecological correlations, two benefits can be derived from these studies.[12] First, they take into account the local context of partisanship *on a comparative basis*. Second, they demonstrate that a strong relationship exists between the social status of aggregate groups and political partisanship.

NEIGHBORHOOD AND INDIVIDUAL SOCIOECONOMIC INFLUENCES

It is our contention that such findings are meaningful though we do not assume that the characteristics of the community reflect the characteristics of any given individual in that area. We hypothesize that the local community can serve as an important means of political orientation for a person, regardless of whether or not he shares the social status of his neighbors. That is, we are suggesting that the community is one of the bases of political diversity discussed by Shils and is therefore a functional alternative to voluntary association membership in terms of Kornhauser's model.

Our data are drawn from a study conducted in 1963 by the Bureau of Applied Social Research in nine towns in northeastern United States. A total of 1,382 respondents were interviewed on a block probability basis. For purposes of our analysis, 127 respondents have been omitted because we could not judge their socioeconomic status. We have

[10] Berelson *et al., op. cit.*, p. 98.

[11] See, for example, V. O. Key, Jr., *Southern Politics in State and Nation* (New York: Knopf, 1949).

[12] W. S. Robinson, "Ecological Correlations and the Behavior of Individuals," *American Sociological Review, 15* (1950), pp. 585–595.

defined neighborhoods in each town along lines of voting wards, though we recognized the possibility that local definitions of neighborhood may differ from our own. Each neighborhood is described by the mean score on our index of socioeconomic status (SES) of respondents living in it, excluding, of course, those for whom we could not compute a score. In addition to this index of neighborhood SES, we have a measure of neighborhood homogeneity; this is the standard deviation of SES scores within each community.

Table 1 shows the relationship between the respondent's SES, neighborhood SES, and party choice. Among low-SES respondents, 27 per cent in low-SES neighborhoods and 47 per cent in high-status communities consider themselves Republicans, a difference of 20 percentage points. Among high-SES respondents, 40 per cent in low-SES neighborhoods and 66 per cent in high-status neighborhoods choose the Republican label, a 26 percentage point difference. Not only does neighborhood class composition influence people's political choices, but by comparing percentage point differences, we can see that the effect of neighborhood does not represent a spurious structural effect.[13]

Table 1

PERCENTAGE REPUBLICAN BY RESPONDENT'S SES AND
NEIGHBORHOOD SES

Respondent's SES	Neighborhood SES	
	Low	High
Low	27%	47%
Total number	(460)	(110)
High	40%	66%
Total number	(194)	(278)

NEIGHBORHOOD STRUCTURE AS AN INFLUENCE

If neighborhood class structure is strongly linked to a local climate of opinion that influences political partisanship, then we should expect to find that communities with homogeneous status structures exhibit greater political consensus than more heterogeneous neighborhoods. Thus, we should predict that among residents of low-status neighborhoods,

[13] For a discussion of which types of apparent structural effects may be spurious, see Arnold S. Tannenbaum and Jerald G. Bachman, "Structural versus Individual Effects," *American Journal of Sociology, 69* (1964) pp. 585–595.

those living in more homogeneous areas tend to be Democrats in greater proportion than those in heterogeneous neighborhoods. In the same manner, there should be proportionally more Republicans in homogeneous than in heterogeneous high-status communities. Table 2 shows that this is, in fact, the case for both low- and high-status respondents, although we cannot make a definitive conclusion about how SES affects individuals in high-SES areas for lack of sufficient respondents on which to base a reliable percentage.

So far, we have established that neighborhood structure does significantly influence political behavior. We can thus conceptualize the local community as one of the several bases of political diversity in the United States. Such a notion provides an adequate description of what is seen in our data, but it does not provide an explanation of the processes at work there. One possible explanation is that community structure, as measured by our variable of neighborhood SES, is only an index of the extent to which the organization of one party or the other has penetrated the community. We do not have data with which to test this possibility, but Putnam's study has indicated that party organization in the community has little influence on political choices when other variables are taken into account.[14] A second possibility is that neighborhood structure is reflected in the kinds of formal associations into which a person enters and that what we observe as an effect of neighborhood is but an artifact of voluntary organization membership patterns. This explanation is, in fact, equivalent to Kornhauser's

Table 2

PERCENTAGE REPUBLICAN BY RESPONDENT'S SES,
NEIGHBORHOOD SES, AND NEIGHBORHOOD HOMOGENEITY

Respondent's SES	Neighborhood SES*			
	Low Homo-geneous	Low Hetero-geneous	High Hetero-geneous	High Homo-geneous
Low	25%	32%	48%	41%
Total number	(276)	(184)	(93)	(17)
High	33%	44%	63%	71%
Total number	(79)	(115)	(125)	(80)

* In order of hypothesized increasing Republicanism.

[14] Robert D. Putnam, "Political Attitudes and the Local Community," *American Political Science Review, 60*:3 (1966), pp. 640–654.

hypothesis, for it requires that the effect of community structure on partisanship be shown to be spurious when we control for organizational participation. We wish to challenge this hypothesis, and we shall present the appropriate data presently. A third possible explanation is that community socioeconomic structure is reflected in primary group associations. Let us assume for a moment that a person's primary associations in the local community are selected more or less randomly. This may not be true, but it is a useful working assumption. Let us also assume that persons of low SES are predisposed to be Democrats and individuals of high SES are predisposed to be Republicans. It is obvious that, if one accepts assumption of random association, the mean SES of the primary groups is the mean SES of the neighborhood in which they are formed. But when we ask which political party has a majority in these primary groups formed by random association, an interesting pattern emerges. By calculating binomial probability distributions, we can see that in an area where there is a majority of either high- or low-status people, and thus by assumption a preponderance of either Republican or Democratic sentiment, the likelihood that primary groups will be dominated by members of the majority party is *higher* than the proportion of adherents to that party in the community. For instance, Table 3 shows that if 60 per cent of the people in a neighborhood are of high status and are thus predisposed to be Republicans, 65 per cent of the three-person primary groups and 68 per cent of the five-person groups will have a majority of Republicans, if we assume random association. In other words, the majority sentiment in the community is accentuated in primary groups. Social psychological theory tells us that there exist strong pressures toward similarity of attitudes in small groups; this notion and the calculation of some

Table 3

PROBABILITY THAT PRIMARY GROUPS WILL HAVE REPUBLICAN MAJORITY
(PERCENTAGE)

	Proportion of High SES Persons* in Neighborhood						
	20	*30*	*40*	*50*	*60*	*70*	*80*
Three-person group	10	22	35	50	65	78	90
Five-person group	6	16	32	50	68	84	94

* All assumed to be predisposed to Republicans.

probabilities can tell us how a small majority can influence the minority far out of proportion to its numbers. These calculations are based on the assumption of random association. If, as seems to be the case, individuals within a community strive for acceptance by the dominant group and therefore bias their social contacts in that direction, this effect will be accentuated. It is a matter of semantics to argue whether the neighborhood or the primary group is "really" responsible for the differences in partisanship that we see, for the composition of informal primary groups is largely an artifact of community structure. We should note that this intensification of majority sentiment — this "halo effect" — applies to all kinds of groups, not only to neighborhoods. Religious bodies, voluntary organizations, and whole cities, in fact, can exert the same influence, which is disproportionate to the size of the majority, and act as equally effective bases of political stability.

THE EFFECTS OF THE TOWN POLITICAL CLIMATE

If neighbors serve as important reference points for a person's political orientations, we might want to know how the political climate of the town affects this process. In making this analysis, we shall follow the broad outlines of the model that Durkheim presented. Assuming that the greater political consensus in a town, the more integrated that town's political structure, we can immediately speculate that the less consensus in a town, the greater will be the effects of interpersonal processes at the neighborhood level on partisan choice. Our model, then, posits that the town climate of opinion conditions the relationship of neighborhood pressures to political behavior, just as Durkheim saw certain primary and secondary affiliations intervening between suicidal currents at the societal level and the individual.

Table 4 shows the effect of neighborhood class composition on political party preference when we take into account variations in town political climates. We need look only at the summary statistics at the bottom of the table to understand its implications. In towns we characterize as Democratic, neighborhood SES results in an average of 14 percentage points difference in proportions of Republicans. In dissensus towns, the effect of community structure increases to 29 percentage points; and in Republican towns, neighborhood SES produces a 21 percentage point difference. The first conclusion is obvious but important: the effects of neighborhood class structure persist when we take town climate into account. The second and more interesting finding is that neighborhood composition exerts the most influence in

Table 4

PERCENTAGE REPUBLICAN BY RESPONDENT'S SES, NEIGHBORHOOD SES, AND TOWN CLIMATE

	Democratic Town Neighborhood SES		Dissensus Town Neighborhood SES		Republican Town Neighborhood SES	
	Low	High	Low	High	Low	High
Respondent's SES						
Low	16%	29%	20%	43%	49%	67%
Total number	(148)	(31)	(178)	(40)	(134)	(39)
High	22%	36%	31%	65%	65%	89%
Total number	(60)	(77)	(68)	(89)	(89)	(112)
Effect of neighborhood, in percentage points	14		29		21	

towns without a clear political tradition or leaning. The effects of neighborhood SES, then, are somewhat mitigated by political forces at the town level; the local community most effectively directs the partisanship of its members where neither party commands the partisan allegiance of the town. In this sense, strong partisan traditions at the town level and the same sentiments at the neighborhood level may be seen as functional substitutes for each other.

THE EFFECTS OF RELIGION

In the same manner as we have examined the effects of town political climate on the relationship between neighborhood structure and partisan choice, we should investigate how membership in a religious community impinges on this relationship. For our purposes, a person's religion rather than his religiosity is most important to us. We shall assume, on the basis of Lenski's findings, that a person's associations with his coreligionists rather than his formal ties with his church are most important in forming his political sentiments.[15] We shall also assume Durkheim's conclusion that members of the Catholic Church and Jews are more integrated as groups than are members of Protestant denominations. Following Durkheim's logic again, we should predict that members of more cohesive religious groups — Catholics and Jews — are most immune to political currents in the local community. An additional factor impinging upon this relationship is that the Jews and Catholics have more deeply entrenched political cultures than does the more socially heterogeneous Protestant group. Both Catholic and Jewish traditions favor support of the Democratic Party.[16] Table 5 shows how neighborhood SES affects party preference when we hold constant the respondent's religion. The data clearly show how religious background is a strong determinant of political choice. Regardless of their own SES and regardless of their neighbor's SES, Protestants are consistently Republicans in greater proportion than are Catholics or Jews. But our main concern is with the effect of neighborhood composition when we hold constant the religious factor, and the summary percentage point differences at the bottom of the table show a significant

[15] Gerhard Lenski, *The Religious Factor* (New York: Doubleday Anchor, 1961), pp. 174 ff.
[16] Robert R. Alford, *Party and Society* (Chicago: Rand McNally, 1964), p. 241; Lawrence H. Fuchs, *The Political Behavior of American Jews* (Glencoe: Free Press, 1956); Raymond E. Wolfinger, "The Development and Persistence of Ethnic Voting" *American Political Science Review, 59* (1965), pp. 896–908.

Table 5

PERCENTAGE REPUBLICAN BY RESPONDENT'S SES, NEIGHBORHOOD SES, AND RESPONDENT'S RELIGION

	Non-Protestant Neighborhood SES		Protestant Neighborhood SES	
	Low	High	Low	High
Respondent's SES				
Low	16%	36%	36%	61%
Total number	(196)	(61)	(261)	(49)
High	27%	42%	53%	85%
Total number	(92)	(123)	(99)	(149)
Effect of neighborhood, in percentage points	18		29	

difference here. Among Catholics and Jews, neighborhood SES accounts for an average of 18 percentage points difference in proportions of Republicans. Among Protestants, neighborhood class composition results in 29 percentage points difference in partisan affiliation.

The difference between Protestant and non-Protestant responsiveness to neighborhood influences is even greater when we look at votes cast in a specific election rather than at party affiliation. As Table 6 shows, for the 1960 presidential election, neighborhood SES made a 7 percentage

Table 6

PERCENTAGE OF TWO-PARTY VOTE FOR NIXON IN 1960 ELECTION BY RESPONDENT'S SES, NEIGHBORHOOD SES, AND RESPONDENT'S RELIGION

	Non-Protestant Neighborhood SES		Protestant Neighborhood SES	
	Low	High	Low	High
Respondent's SES				
Low	11%	16%	38%	59%
Total number	(174)	(56)	(189)	(46)
High	23%	32%	51%	80%
Total number	(91)	(123)	(91)	(143)
Effect of neighborhood, in percentage points	7		25	

point difference for non-Protestants — a much smaller figure than that obtained for party affiliation — and a 25 percentage point difference among Protestants. Protestants, then, are clearly most sensitive to the politics of their neighbors. Stated in more general terms, we can say that members of more cohesive religious groups are least affected by political pressures at the neighborhood level. One of the elements of such cohesion is subscription to a common set of subcultural values, one of which may dictate a preference for one or another political party, as was the case with Catholics and Jews. Membership in a cohesive religious group, then, can serve in part as a focus of orientation to the larger political order.

We shall now turn to an examination of Kornhauser's premise that the proliferation of intermediate voluntary organizations is necessary for the maintenance of pluralistic society. Just as Kornhauser has argued that the presence of such organizations is necessary for the political integration of society as a whole, other analysts have found that membership in such voluntary organizations helps integrate the individual into the political order. Thus, Almond and Verba, controlling for both education and the respondent's nationality, have found that members of voluntary organizations feel a greater sense of political competence than do nonmembers.[17] We do not wish to challenge this finding, and, in fact, we cannot do so within the scope of our data. We wish to show only that in the absence of participation in voluntary organizations the neighborhood or local community strongly influences the political behavior of its residents and thus renders them less available to manipulation by a national political elite.

An index of organizational participation was constructed by combining the number of organizations of which the respondent was a member with the number in which he took an active role. If we assume that the greater an individual's participation in organizations, the more integrated he is in groups outside of his local community, we should find that organizational participation diminishes the effects of neighborhood structure on party preference. Table 7 demonstrates how organizational participation is related to the effects of neighborhood SES on party choice. The table shows, first, that people who participate in voluntary organizations are more likely to be Republicans than others who do not participate, regardless of their own socioeconomic status or neighborhood SES. This finding has been clearly documented

[17] Gabriel Almond and Sidney Verba, *The Civic Culture* (Princeton: Princeton University Press, 1961), Chapter X.

Table 7

PERCENTAGE REPUBLICAN BY RESPONDENT'S SES, NEIGHBORHOOD SES, AND RESPONDENT'S ORGANIZATIONAL PARTICIPATION

	No Participation Neighborhood SES		Low Participation Neighborhood SES		High Participation Neighborhood SES	
	Low	High	Low	High	Low	High
Respondent's SES						
Low	23%	43%	31%	51%	44%	54%
Total number	(269)	(54)	(159)	(43)	(32)	(13)
High	30%	60%	42%	65%	68%	76%
Total number	(86)	(115)	(86)	(101)	(22)	(63)
Effect of neighborhood, in percentage points		25		22		9

elsewhere, and we need not labor the point.[18] The table also shows, as indicated by the summary percentage point differences at the bottom, that the effects of neighborhood on partisan choice decrease as organizational participation increases. Among respondents who take part in no organizations, neighborhood class composition accounts for an average of 25 percentage points difference in proportions of Republicans. Among those whose participation is low — the marginally involved — neighborhood SES produces a 22 percentage point difference. And among high participators — those most committed to formal, voluntary organizations — neighborhood class structure results in only 9 percentage points difference in proportion of Republicans. The greater the extent to which a person is involved in voluntary organizations, the less sensitive he is to local neighborhood pressures in the formation of his political attitudes. This is merely a special case of the more general proposition that we have now established: the more a person is integrated into the political order by secondary group ties outside the local community — attachments to the sentiments of his town, to his coreligionists, and to voluntary organizations — the less the local community in which he lives influences his party choice. Conversely, those who are least integrated into other secondary groups are most swayed by partisan currents at the neighborhood level.

SUMMARY OF FINDINGS

A short recapitulation of our findings may be in order here. We find, first, that neighborhood socioeconomic status exerts a powerful effect on people's political party choices. This effect of neighborhood SES is, in fact, greater than that of a person's own socioeconomic class standing. We find, second, that the magnitude of the effect of neighborhood class composition on party choice is inversely proportional to the extent to which a person is integrated into the political structure by other secondary groups. Political pressures in the local community can be said to operate as functional substitutes for other means of integrating the individual into the political order. It may be argued that those local political party organizations are strongest which best represent the economic interests of the majority of residents in a community, and that because of their superior organization, they may influence members of the community who represent minority economic interests. This line of reasoning is questionable in the light of Levin's finding regarding

[18] Berelson *et al., op. cit.,* p. 52.

the party choices of high school students. His study revealed that high school students are influenced by the partisan climates of their neighborhoods regardless of the party choices of their parents.[19] Surely, it would be difficult to explain how party organizations influence adolescents without influencing their parents. This explanation, then, must be rejected. It might also be argued that our findings are the result of social mobility. The community effects persist, however, when mobility is controlled.

Our data do suggest that there are diverse bases of political partisanship in America but that underlying these is a unique form of status politics, where social status is measured, not in terms of occupation,[20] but rather in terms of association.

These findings bear some implications for mass society theories. We challenge Kornhauser's contention that only formal, voluntary organizations can render nonelites unavailable to elites. We argue instead that many forms of association, but especially residence in the local community, can serve to integrate the individual into the political structure and thus provide bases for diversity which are absent from Kornhauser's model of mass society. We further contend that the importance of the neighborhood as a basis for political pluralism increases as an individual's integration into the political order by means of other associations becomes more tenuous. Although Wilensky sees a diminution, which our data do not reveal, of the importance of the local community in integrating the individual into mass society, we find ourselves generally in agreement with his assumption that the social bonds embedded in traditional forms of social relationships are not weakening, although the quality of such relationships may be changing. "In much of the discussion of 'mass' society or 'totalitarian' society, the persistence and stability of such ties are underestimated. The masses have nowhere in any developed country been kept 'atomized,' 'available,' 'unattached,' 'in motion.' "[21]

The fact that partisan forces in the local community exert so powerful an influence on a person's political choice argues for the essential stability of American politics. Americans may not be inclined to radical

[19] Martin L. Levin, "Social Climates and Political Socialization," *Public Opinion Quarterly, 25*:4, pp. 596–606.

[20] See Richard F. Hamilton, "Skill Level and Politics," *Public Opinion Quarterly, 29*:3, pp. 390–399.

[21] Harold L. Wilensky, "Mass Society and Mass Culture," in Bernard Berelson and Morris Janowitz (eds.), *Reader in Public Opinion and Mass Communications* (New York: Free Press, 1966), p. 297.

ideologies or sudden shifts in party loyalties because intermittent persuasion cannot overcome the way a person's social setting structures his political beliefs. Our data add to the already substantial body of evidence that people do not make their political choices — or, for that matter, any other kinds of decisions — as isolated, atomized individuals.

PART THREE

Multivariate Analysis in
Political Ecology

The papers in this part of our volume focus on the two countries in Europe which offer perhaps the greatest temptations for the political ecologist: France and Italy. Both these Latin countries are characterized by marked and persistent contrasts among historically and culturally distinct regions and have always manifested great varieties of local political configurations. Both countries offer vast masses of official data at various levels of aggregation, and these have in many cases been successfully matched with private data from parties, unions, and church organizations. In addition, and this is important for an understanding of developments in academic research, the standard nationwide surveys carried out in these countries have not met the needs of the political analyst: the very high percentage of refusals, especially among the Communists, has made it difficult to obtain reliable maps of the sociocultural bases of political behavior through the survey method, and the simple stratification design of most sample surveys has rarely allowed realistic analyses of the many regional contrasts in the two countries.

The papers included in Part Three show how far it is possible to go in ecological analysis without direct recourse to survey data. Capecchi and Galli report on their attempt to use Blalock-Boudon-style path analysis in the study of causal structures in ecological data. In the broader study from which this paper has been extracted,[1] they have tried out a variety of other methods: transition matrices, correlation

---

[1] V. Capecchi *et al.*, *Il Comportamento Elettorale in Italia* (Bologna: Mulino, 1968). For an example of another type of analysis applied to provinces and communes in Italy, see Corrado Barberis and Guido Corazziari, "Strutture economiche e dinamica elettorale," in M. Dogan and O. M. Petracca (eds.), *Partiti politici e strutture sociali in Italia* (Milano: Comunità, 1968); it is noteworthy that the general results reached by this study turned out to be very similar to those of Capecchi and Galli.

matrices, regression equations, analyses of residual variances. But they have clearly found linear causal modeling the most effective of these procedures: this method offers a variety of significant cues for theorizing and allows flexible testing of alternative interpretations.

In his painstaking analysis of data for the rural cantons of France, Mattei Dogan has also underscored the need for methodological flexibility. In his earlier work he proceeded descriptively through the use of simple models of the likely sources of strength for each party: by assuming alternative levels of working-class support for the Communist and the Socialist parties, he was able to generate highly suggestive hypotheses about the sources of regional variation in France.[2] In his later work he has explored a broad range of statistical procedures: the paper in this volume offers detailed results of an attempt at an analysis of covariance. The extraordinary richness of the French data has not yet been exhausted, but it is clear already that it is not possible to get much further in the explanation of the total variance on the basis of aggregate data alone. To push further toward the explanation of the residual variance, it will no doubt be necessary to organize ecologically controlled sample surveys in each of the politically distinct regions of France: an attempt in this direction is already under way and should add further to the model of explanation suggested through the analysis of the aggregate data available.

The French and the Italian political ecologists have gone further than anyone else in Europe and have worked out models of analyses well worth testing in the other countries. A great deal can still be done in France and Italy on the extensive backlogs of historical ecological data, and it is not inconceivable that a concerted attack on the development of typologies of early political constellations in each locality will pay off even in the explanation of post-1945 variances:[3] this is a subject to which we shall return in Part Five.

[2] See especially his chapter on France and Italy in S. M. Lipset and S. Rokkan (eds.), *Party Systems and Voter Alignments* (New York: Free Press, 1967), pp. 129–195.

[3] Cf. the very interesting Italian comparisons of continuities in voting strength, from 1919 to 1946, in Capecchi, *op. cit.*, pp. 21–52.

IO

VITTORIO CAPECCHI AND GIORGIO GALLI

Determinants of Voting Behavior in Italy: A Linear Causal Model of Anlyasis[1]

WHEN ONE considers the great socioeconomic transformations of the period 1946–1963, it is remarkable that the Italian electorate has been characterized by such a high degree of stability. Socioeconomic evolution has certainly produced factors of change in our electoral situation, but precisely what is their influence? One method of appraising the ecological data is by means of indices of correlation, which have been applied in this study.

In these indices, the political vote has always been considered as a variable dependent on other factors. The number of factors, as in all ecological analysis, is limited by the availability of both electoral data and the multiple elements that can be correlated with the vote. The unavailability of quantitative information on the communes makes this kind of analysis particularly difficult in Italy.

As a consequence of this limitation, therefore, we decided to integrate these indices of correlation, constructed from data on the Italian communes, with other indices, constructed on the basis of provincial data. These data have been used in cases in which such data were lacking

[1] The research for this essay was carried out by the Istituto Carlo Cattaneo of Bologna with a Twentieth Century Fund grant. The analysis of Italian political participation covers the years 1946–1963 and is based on data at the commune and provincial level.

Italy is administratively divided into 19 regions, 92 provinces, and 8,035 communes. In this research we have excluded the provinces of Aosta, Bolzano, Gorizia, and Trieste for lack of homogeneous data. The total number of communes analyzed was 7,144.

at the commune level. The analysis of this material, therefore, will be divided into two main parts. In the first, we shall examine the correlations at the provincial level, and in the second, the correlations at the commune level.

CORRELATION AT THE PROVINCIAL LEVEL

Eighty-eight territorial units were used for the construction of these indices; four Italian provinces, Aosta, Bolzano, Gorizia, and Trieste were excluded for lack of homogeneous data. Indices relating to the 1953 and 1963 elections were constructed with statistical data from the 1951 and 1961 census. The 1961 agricultural census was used for 1963 agricultural data. Indices relating to income were constructed on the basis of data assembled by G. Tagliacarne. It was also possible to compare factors regarding economic management, in spite of the absence of professional classification data, such as for wage earners, *mezzadri* (sharecroppers), and farmers, in the 1961 general census. These data had been available in the 1951 census, and for 1961 we substituted data relating to area under cultivation by *mezzadria*, direct farming, or the employment of wage earners. Data relating to parties, parapolitical organizations, and press circulation were provided directly by the respective parties and organizations.

Since we were limited as to time and finances, we were not able to calculate correlations for each of the eight national parties. Individual correlations were calculated only for the two parties that were largest at the time of the research, the DC (Democrazia Cristiana) and PCI (Partito Comunista Italiano), and the others were classified as either non-Communist Left or Right.

The Communist Vote

For each of the major parties, we have prepared a table of significant indices of correlation. It should be remembered in the appraisal of these indices that, on a basis of eighty-eight units, the correlation has significance only from the 0.25 level upward, even if the lower indices constitute a useful point of reference. In the following chart, the factors positively correlated with the Communist vote in 1963 are listed in order of diminishing significance:

Members of the party	.822
Members of CGIL (Confederazione Generale Italiana del Lavoro)	.722

Circulation of *L'Unità*	.636
Mezzadria (sharecropping) area	.530
Vote for the Republic in 1946	.449
Participation (percentage of voters)	.310
TV licenses, 1962	.282

The factors positively correlated with the Communist vote in 1953 were as follows:

Members of the party	.841
Members of CGIL	.718
Circulation of *L'Unità*	.629
Participation (percentage of voters)	.451
Vote for the Republic in 1946	.439
Mezzadri (sharecroppers)	.434

The permanence and stability of factors positively correlated with the Communist vote are confirmed by the maintenance of positive correlations for the two years at the same, or nearly the same, level. Foremost, they are organizational factors, such as party and trade union membership and newspaper circulation. There is also, however, the factor of left-wing tradition, the vote for the Republic in the referendum of 1946. Tradition has always been an important element of influence in the Italian political system. The only economic activity that was significantly correlated with the Communist vote and that also identifies a social category is that of the *mezzadri*.

Since the censuses have not provided data relating to the provincial distribution of industrial workers and we have preferred not to use data from other sources that appeared somewhat uncertain, we lack at this time information relating to the social category of the Communist vote. However, by establishing a correlation between degree of industrialization and voting behavior with its first term the total population working in industry, we know that the Communist vote is negatively correlated with this index of correlation.

Among the factors positively correlated with the Communist vote, besides organization and left-wing tradition, which we have already mentioned, we find electoral participation, expressed by the percentage of the population which casts a vote. This factor requires some explanation.

In Italy a higher percentage of the electorate goes to the polls than in any other advanced industrial country with a democratic system of government. In the first political elections of 1946, this was in part due to the "novelty" of voting after twenty years of Fascist rule; in 1948, the Catholic organizations actively encouraged everyone to vote, popularizing the slogan "Vote for whom you like, but vote." A high percentage of the electorate has continued to vote in the subsequent elections, although to a diminishing degree.

This tendency has been considered to be an element favoring the non-Communist vote. In other words, it is held that the Communist voters, who are more "faithful," committed, and active, always go to the polls, whereas the non-Communists, who are often not strongly committed or involved, might forego their vote. But if these persons were to vote, they would, in general, vote for a moderate party.

This popular assumption, however, seems to be refuted by the positive correlation between the Communist vote and electoral participation. It seems that in areas in which the highest percentage of citizens vote, the Communist and left-wing vote in general is increased. This also corresponds, as we shall see, to a negative correlation between this same participation and the Christian Democrat and right-wing vote.

Another popular assumption that must be modified on the basis of our positive correlations relates to the spread of television. It is commonly believed that exclusion of the PCI from the control of television because it is an opposition party has had a negative electoral effect on the PCI. However, we find a positive correlation between television and the Communist vote which corresponds, as we shall see, to a negative correlation between the exposure to television and the Christian Democrat vote. It seems that the Communist Party, with its secular traditions, is better adapted to mass culture and television, its principal medium, than the Catholic-inspired movement.

This conclusion must be accepted with great caution, however. Although television is a particularly powerful means of breaking down cultural barriers and diffusing new behavioral and political models, there may be other elements that are affecting the correlation and should be considered.

Television was first introduced into the economically more advanced sections of the country, sections that have been traditionally Socialist. The working classes of these areas, which had achieved a higher standard of living, accepted and adapted quickly to new mass-communication media, including television.

In spite of this reservation, however, the positive correlation between television and the Communist vote, and the negative correlation between television and the Christian Democrat vote are too constant and general not to be significant, as we shall see when we examine the correlations at the commune level and for each area. At the provincial level, for example, this correlation is more significant than the income correlation.

To complete this summary of factors positively correlated with the Communist vote, we should indicate two factors immediately below the level of significance, about the .20 level: income and strike hours. The Communist electorate has been positively influenced by both economic development and the active efforts of the working class to improve their economic and social conditions.

We may now consider the factors that are to a significant degree negatively correlated with the Communist vote. The situation in 1963 was as follows:

Spoiled (invalid) votes	.330
Members of CISL (Confederazione italiana sindicati lavoratori)	.307
Members of the Christian Democrat Party	.305
Area of peasant small holdings	.296

In 1953 the situation was as follows:

Farmers working own land	.492
Invalid votes	.410
Members of the Christian Democrat Party	.334
Members of ACLI (Azione Cattolica Lavoratori Italiani)	.290

The factors listed here are of the same type as the positive ones; they relate to organization and apply to a rural social category.

According to our chart, the Communist vote is negatively correlated with the degree of organization of its major antagonist, the Catholic movement (the CISL, ACLI, and Christian Democrats). It is also negatively correlated with the rural social category organized by the Catholics, that is to say, the farmers working their own land. Spoiled votes provides another negative correlation. These spoiled votes are positively correlated with the vote for other parties, but not the PCI. It seems that the Communist electorate is better educated in voting procedure, and consequently its votes are not annulled; in this sense, the absence of spoiled votes is also related to organization.

The educational level of the Communist vote is positively correlated with illiteracy, whereas the Christian Democrat correlation is negative in this respect (this applies to 1953; the value was insignificant in 1963). The Christian Democrat electorate has a higher level of primary education than the Communist electorate. Theoretically, it would seem that the elector with a primary education would have some knowledge of voting procedure, sufficient to avoid the annulment of his vote. The Christian Democrat vote, however, is positively correlated with spoiled votes. According to this information, it seems that the spoiled votes are the votes of moderate electors, from the Christian Democrats to the right wing, whose parties have not taught them to vote with the same care as the PCI teaches its voters. However, this supposition needs further substantiation in the perspective of the entire political and sociocultural context.

Immediately below the level of significance in 1953 we find the variable of women working in industry ($-.224$). This indicates that women generally do not vote for the PCI even when they work in an industrial environment. In 1963 this variable was somewhat less ($-.136$); ten years later, there were slightly more women who voted for the PCI.

The Left-Wing Non-Communist Vote

In 1963 the significant factors that influenced the left-wing non-Communist vote (Partito Socialista Italiano, Partito Socialista Democratico Italiano, and the Partito Repubblicano Italiano) were as follows:

Primary education	.604
Vote for the Republic	.553
Industrial population	.551
Income	.543
Participation	.473
Strike hours	.440
Blank votes	.437
Radio-TV licenses 1962	.430
Secondary education	.415
Women working in industry	.392
Circulation of L'Unità	.306
Population working in commerce	.300
Members of CGIL	.262

In 1953 the situation was as follows:

Votes for the Republic	.743
Blank votes	.606
Primary education	.596
Members of CGIL	.590

rculation of *L'Unità* .469
Mezzadri (sharecroppers) .330
Illiterates .279
Agricultural laborers .259

As surprising as it may seem, the chart shows that the DC electorate was more left-wing in character in 1953 than in 1963. In 1953 there was no correlation at a significant level between the vote for the Republic and the Christian Democrat vote (the correlation is − .135), and this has been one of the constant factors in the DC vote. This was presumably the result of the more right-wing sectors of the DC electorate's
tion toward the PNM (Monarchist Party), which was then at the
of its expansion. But, in fact, the negative correlation between
t-wing vote and the vote for the Republic was higher in 1963
1953 (− .688 and − .870). If the MSI (Movimento Sociale
is excluded, the correlations are slightly lower (− .500 and
urthermore, in 1953 there was a significant negative correla-
n illiteracy and the DC vote, which by 1963 had practically
. These two facts, however, can be reconciled.
the DC lost votes to the right wing primarily in southern
. These were the votes of an electorate with a low educational
monarchical orientation. In 1963, on the other hand, the DC
of its votes to the right in the northern cities. These were votes
I (Partito liberale italiano) from an electorate with a higher
al level which was not necessarily monarchical. In fact, there
gative correlations in 1963 between the DC electorate and
ry and university education.
3, besides the previously mentioned correlations relating to the
te tradition, educational level, and the organizing force of the
ere were other indices in negative correlation with the DC vote.
related specifically to the diffusion of television, income level, and
ation working in commerce, which are all typical phenomena
ng to the emergence of an industrial society. We have already dealt
he other phenomena negatively correlated with the 1963 DC vote
ur dicussion of their significance in relation to the left-wing vote.
t seems then that in 1963 the Christian Democrat vote, insofar as
concerned a series of correlations relating to tradition and organiza-
n, was the exact opposite of the Communist vote. Furthermore, it
ears to have been a vote negatively correlated with the phenomena
ted to industrialization. It is a vote that is characteristically anti-
munist and linked to those sectors of society less affected by the

75
.534
.443
.417
.399
.367
.352
.331

Income .541
Circulation of *L'Unità* .514
Participation .457
Members of PCI .453
Population working in industry .388
Secondary education .366

These correlations relate primarily to three factors: (1) educational level, or the percentage of the population which has completed primary and secondary education; (2) the level of economic development, or the percentage of population working in industry and commerce; and (3) income. In other words, in terms of education, economic growth, and income, the left-wing non-Communist vote has been positively in-fluenced by the development of modern industrial society.

Although the non-Communist left-wing electorate reflects a develop-ing industrial society better than the PCI, it shares with the Communist electorate, but to a greater degree, the data relating to participation and the influence of television.

There is also an high correlation between the left-wing vote and blank votes. It may be suggested, however, that the blank vote, as opposed to a spoiled vote, results from a "conscious" act, not from ignorance or inability to vote correctly. It expresses a refusal on the part of the elector to choose between the various left-wing parties with which he is presented on the ballot. However, it is also known that some of the blank votes result from the ignorance of the elector, whereas votes are spoiled because of writing on the ballot. These votes may indicate, not voting ignorance, but very definite political opinions.

As we have pointed out, the left-wing non-Communist electorate is more characteristic of a developing industrial society than is the Communist electorate. Even the correlation of their vote with the num-ber of hours on strike is higher than for the PCI. From this we can conclude that the strike is not an indication of radicalism; it is a means by which workers can effectively exert pressure on the industrial community.

It now remains to make some comments on the influence of organ-izational factors. In 1953, the non-Communist left wing was still significantly influenced by the PCI organization through both member-ship in the party or the CGIL and circulation of *L'Unità*. Two thirds of the electorate was affiliated with the PSI. By 1963 the situation had somewhat changed: there was no longer a positive correlation with membership of the PCI, but there remained, though to a greatly reduced degree, the positive correlations with the CGIL membership and with the circulation of the Communist paper. The first factor can be easily explained. The CGIL of Italy has been the trade union of the left-wing Socialist tradition, even though it has been more important electorally to the PCI than to the non-Communist left wing. The second factor, however, is more difficult to explain, as *L'Unità* heavily criticized the non-Communist left-wing in the years immediately preceding the 1963 electoral campaign and even during the campaign itself.

In our opinion, the interpretation of the correlation is the following. During these years, there was a reduction in the size and distribution of the non-Communist left-wing press. *La Giustizia* disappeared, *La Voce repubblicana* was reduced in size, and the *Avanti!* declined. The democrats and socialists who had read these papers, however, maintained their attitude of resentment or reserve toward the "independent" press, which reflected moderate and conservative opinions. Therefore, *L'Unità*, which is the only national "people's" newspaper, became more popular with the left-wing non-Communist sectors of the population. On the other hand, these sectors have attained an educational and cultural level that permits them to evaluate critically the editorializing of the Communist press, and the reading of the newspaper is not necessarily followed by an acceptance of its political bias.

These situations should be clarified by further research. There is a need for data regarding newspapers with different orientations so that they may be compared, as well as research other than of the ecological type. This need for further classification, however, in no way invalidates our ascertainment of the basic characteristics of the left-wing non-Communist electorate. In terms of economic activity, income level, and educational level, it is comprised of the upper stratum of the emerging modern industrial society.

The Christian Democrat Vote

The DC voting patterns further clarify the general electoral situation. The significant factors that positively influenced the DC vote in 1963 were as follows:

Members of the DC	.496
Spoiled votes	.359
Members of CISL	.312
Members of ACLI	.293

The situation in 1953 was as follows:

Farmers working own land
Primary education
Members of ACLI
Members of DC
Women in industry
Population working in industry

As in the case of the PCI, there is a prevalence of organizational. The predominance of these data, as compared to social factors, m the DC electorate the direct opposite of the PCI.

There are also some significant changes in the electorate of t years. The positive correlation with the population and women w in industry which was present in 1953 had reached almost the zer ten years later. The two important pieces of "social" data of 1 level of primary education and influence among farmers worki own land, were a little below the level of significance (about .20 In this regard, the difference in kinds of information on which relating to direct farm management was constructed should mind.

On the other hand, there is a negative correlation above of significance between the DC electorate and the developing i society. The situation in 1963 was as follows:

Members of CGIL
Members of PCI
Circulation of *L'Unità*
TV licenses 1962
Income
Vote for the Republic
University degrees
Mezzadri (sharecroppers)
Participation
Strike hours
Secondary education
Population working in commerce
Blank votes

The situation in 1953 was as follows:

Members of CGIL
Members of PCI

The situation in 1953 was as follows:

Farmers working own land	.448
Primary education	.368
Members of ACLI	.359
Members of DC	.324
Women in industry	.275
Population working in industry	.253

As in the case of the PCI, there is a prevalence of organizational data. The predominance of these data, as compared to social factors, makes the DC electorate the direct opposite of the PCI.

There are also some significant changes in the electorate of the two years. The positive correlation with the population and women working in industry which was present in 1953 had reached almost the zero point ten years later. The two important pieces of "social" data of 1953, the level of primary education and influence among farmers working their own land, were a little below the level of significance (about .20) in 1963. In this regard, the difference in kinds of information on which the index relating to direct farm management was constructed should be kept in mind.

On the other hand, there is a negative correlation above the level of significance between the DC electorate and the developing industrial society. The situation in 1963 was as follows:

Members of CGIL	.702
Members of PCI	.688
Circulation of *L'Unità*	.675
TV licenses 1962	.534
Income	.443
Vote for the Republic	.417
University degrees	.399
Mezzadri (sharecroppers)	.367
Participation	.352
Strike hours	.331
Secondary education	.319
Population working in commerce	.283
Blank votes	.255

The situation in 1953 was as follows:

Members of CGIL	.720
Members of PCI	.609

Circulation of *L'Unità*	.469
Mezzadri (sharecroppers)	.330
Illiterates	.279
Agricultural laborers	.259

As surprising as it may seem, the chart shows that the DC electorate was more left-wing in character in 1953 than in 1963. In 1953 there was no correlation at a significant level between the vote for the Republic and the Christian Democrat vote (the correlation is $-.135$), and this has been one of the constant factors in the DC vote. This was presumably the result of the more right-wing sectors of the DC electorate's orientation toward the PNM (Monarchist Party), which was then at the height of its expansion. But, in fact, the negative correlation between the right-wing vote and the vote for the Republic was higher in 1963 than in 1953 ($-.688$ and $-.870$). If the MSI (Movimento Sociale Italiano) is excluded, the correlations are slightly lower ($-.500$ and $-.841$). Furthermore, in 1953 there was a significant negative correlation between illiteracy and the DC vote, which by 1963 had practically disappeared. These two facts, however, can be reconciled.

In 1953, the DC lost votes to the right wing primarily in southern rural areas. These were the votes of an electorate with a low educational level and a monarchical orientation. In 1963, on the other hand, the DC lost most of its votes to the right in the northern cities. These were votes for the PLI (Partito liberale italiano) from an electorate with a higher educational level which was not necessarily monarchical. In fact, there were negative correlations in 1963 between the DC electorate and secondary and university education.

In 1963, besides the previously mentioned correlations relating to the moderate tradition, educational level, and the organizing force of the PCI, there were other indices in negative correlation with the DC vote. These related specifically to the diffusion of television, income level, and population working in commerce, which are all typical phenomena relating to the emergence of an industrial society. We have already dealt with the other phenomena negatively correlated with the 1963 DC vote in our dicussion of their significance in relation to the left-wing vote.

It seems then that in 1963 the Christian Democrat vote, insofar as it concerned a series of correlations relating to tradition and organization, was the exact opposite of the Communist vote. Furthermore, it appears to have been a vote negatively correlated with the phenomena related to industrialization. It is a vote that is characteristically anti-Communist and linked to those sectors of society less affected by the

Income	.541
Circulation of *L'Unità*	.514
Participation	.457
Members of PCI	.453
Population working in industry	.388
Secondary education	.366

These correlations relate primarily to three factors: (1) educational level, or the percentage of the population which has completed primary and secondary education; (2) the level of economic development, or the percentage of population working in industry and commerce; and (3) income. In other words, in terms of education, economic growth, and income, the left-wing non-Communist vote has been positively influenced by the development of modern industrial society.

Although the non-Communist left-wing electorate reflects a developing industrial society better than the PCI, it shares with the Communist electorate, but to a greater degree, the data relating to participation and the influence of television.

There is also an high correlation between the left-wing vote and blank votes. It may be suggested, however, that the blank vote, as opposed to a spoiled vote, results from a "conscious" act, not from ignorance or inability to vote correctly. It expresses a refusal on the part of the elector to choose between the various left-wing parties with which he is presented on the ballot. However, it is also known that some of the blank votes result from the ignorance of the elector, whereas votes are spoiled because of writing on the ballot. These votes may indicate, not voting ignorance, but very definite political opinions.

As we have pointed out, the left-wing non-Communist electorate is more characteristic of a developing industrial society than is the Communist electorate. Even the correlation of their vote with the number of hours on strike is higher than for the PCI. From this we can conclude that the strike is not an indication of radicalism; it is a means by which workers can effectively exert pressure on the industrial community.

It now remains to make some comments on the influence of organizational factors. In 1953, the non-Communist left wing was still significantly influenced by the PCI organization through both membership in the party or the CGIL and circulation of *L'Unità*. Two thirds of the electorate was affiliated with the PSI. By 1963 the situation had somewhat changed: there was no longer a positive correlation with membership of the PCI, but there remained, though to a greatly reduced degree, the positive correlations with the CGIL membership and with the circulation of the Communist paper. The first factor can be easily explained. The CGIL of Italy has been the trade union of the left-wing Socialist tradition, even though it has been more important electorally to the PCI than to the non-Communist left wing. The second factor, however, is more difficult to explain, as *L'Unità* heavily criticized the non-Communist left-wing in the years immediately preceding the 1963 electoral campaign and even during the campaign itself.

In our opinion, the interpretation of the correlation is the following. During these years, there was a reduction in the size and distribution of the non-Communist left-wing press. *La Giustizia* disappeared, *La Voce repubblicana* was reduced in size, and the *Avanti!* declined. The democrats and socialists who had read these papers, however, maintained their attitude of resentment or reserve toward the "independent" press, which reflected moderate and conservative opinions. Therefore, *L'Unità*, which is the only national "people's" newspaper, became more popular with the left-wing non-Communist sectors of the population. On the other hand, these sectors have attained an educational and cultural level that permits them to evaluate critically the editorializing of the Communist press, and the reading of the newspaper is not necessarily followed by an acceptance of its political bias.

These situations should be clarified by further research. There is a need for data regarding newspapers with different orientations so that they may be compared, as well as research other than of the ecological type. This need for further classification, however, in no way invalidates our ascertainment of the basic characteristics of the left-wing non-Communist electorate. In terms of economic activity, income level, and educational level, it is comprised of the upper stratum of the emerging modern industrial society.

The Christian Democrat Vote

The DC voting patterns further clarify the general electoral situation. The significant factors that positively influenced the DC vote in 1963 were as follows:

Members of the DC	.496
Spoiled votes	.359
Members of CISL	.312
Members of ACLI	.293

dynamics of industrialization and urbanization. This situation presents significant analogies to the right-wing vote.

The Right-Wing Vote

In order to assess possible differences, we have distinguished in our analysis between the vote of the entire right wing, the liberals, monarchists, and MSI, and that of the non-Fascist right wing.

There are some major differences in the organization of the Right during the period under discussion. In 1953, the strongest right-wing party was the PNM, which was particularly strong in what might, from a socioeconomic point of view, be called the "backward" parts of Italy. In 1963, on the other hand, the strongest right-wing party was the PLI, which was strongest in the socioeconomically "advanced" parts of Italy. In both years, however, the MSI seems to have been the most backward sector of the right wing, as may be measured in terms of income, educational level, and population working in industry. In fact, all the relative indices are higher for the right wing as a whole than for the right wing with the exclusion of the MSI vote.

In order to clarify the relationship between the moderate electorate, the Christian Democrats, and the Left, given the previously mentioned differences in the formation of the Right in 1953 and 1963, we shall confine ourselves to pointing out the factors significantly correlated with the vote of all parties to the right of the Christian Democrats in 1963. The positive correlations are as follows:

Spoiled votes	.413
Illiteracy	.329
Area of small holdings	.328
University degrees	.310

It can be seen that the positive correlation with the members of the DC (.211) is just below the significance level; in 1953 the positive correlation was .44. The correlation with membership of CISL is practically equal to zero, although still positive. Clearly negative, however, is the correlation with ACLI membership (.394).

The negative correlations were as follows:

Vote for the Republic	− .688
Primary education	− .552
Members of the PCI	− .458
Participation	− .410

Members of CGIL	— .410
Members of ACLI	— .394
Mezzadri (sharecroppers)	— .374
Circulation of *L'Unità*	— .322
Blank votes	— .319
Population working in industry	— .248

From these correlations it is clear that the right-wing vote is primarily correlated with conservative, monarchical tradition. It is the same positive correlation that generally appears for the DC to a significant degree whether at the provincial or commune level, with the single exception of the 1953 elections analyzed at the provincial level.

Furthermore the right-wing vote is negatively correlated with the level of elementary education and positively correlated with illiteracy. This is the major difference between the right-wing and the DC electorates, and it seems to be the educational level that transfers the moderate vote from the Right to the DC. This is even clearer at the university level, but the correlation concerns only about one per cent of the population, usually from the privileged high-income groups. In general, however, with this one exception, the right-wing vote is negatively correlated with income, an element that is analogous to the DC electorate. The positive correlation of the right-wing vote with diffusion of peasant small holdings also indicates an analogy between the two electorates.

With regard to negative correlations, the most significant, as we have seen, relate not to organizational factors, as in the DC and PCI electorates, but to traditional and educational factors. In this sense, the right-wing electorate is in diametrical opposition to the non-Communist left-wing electorate.

We also find, of course, that the organizational strength of the PCI negatively influences the right-wing vote; and other factors positively correlated with the left-wing vote, such as level of participation, number of blank votes, and extension of métayage area, act in the same way. But the organizational strength of the PCI positively influences the DC vote to a much greater degree than the right-wing vote. It is very significant that the membership of ACLI, which is the left wing of the Catholic parties, negatively influences the right-wing vote almost as much as the number of members of CGIL, and to a greater degree than the circulation of *L'Unità*.

As we have pointed out, there are several sectors of convergence between the Christian Democrat and the right-wing electorates, and there are also two fundamental factors of differentiation: education and income. The DC electorate is better educated than the right-wing electorate, but it is also poorer. But in this regard it is interesting to note that the situation in 1963 was the reverse of the one in 1953. The correlations between income and vote were as follows:

	1953	1963
Right wing	− .453	− .085
DC	− .080	− .443

We believe that this situation is related to the modifications that occurred in the strongest right-wing party between the two elections. As we have said, the right wing of 1953, led by the PNM, was predominantly a poor, subproletarian and monarchical electorate. On the other hand, the right wing of 1963, led by the PLI, was middle-class and not necessarily monarchical. In both of these instances the Right took votes away from the DC in the corresponding sectors of the electorate.

It should also be noted that there is a nonsignificant correlation, but only slightly below the level of significance (− .184), with the number of strike hours. As we have seen, it was at a significant level with regard to the DC (− .331), which indicates a less conservative orientation.

The Circuits of Correlation

Although the tables of the previous sections indicate the relative influence of different variables, they do not clarify the relationships between these variables. For this purpose we have constructed causal linear circuits based on the coefficients of correlation.

For the methodological significance of the causal linear circuits, we have used the suggestions set forth by Raymond Boudon in recent contributions.[2] With this type of analysis we can generally determine whether variables have a direct or indirect influence, and the causal relations by which these influences are determined. In other words, given a dependent variable, which in this case is the vote, we can identify the variables that influence it and determine whether these influences are direct or indirect.

For example, if we examine the circuits of Figure 1, we can see that income does not directly influence the vote. It is mediated by the variable of education, which, in turn, is sometimes mediated by the variable of tradition and organization.

[2] Raymond Boudon, *L'analyse mathématique des faits sociaux* (Paris: Plon, 1967).

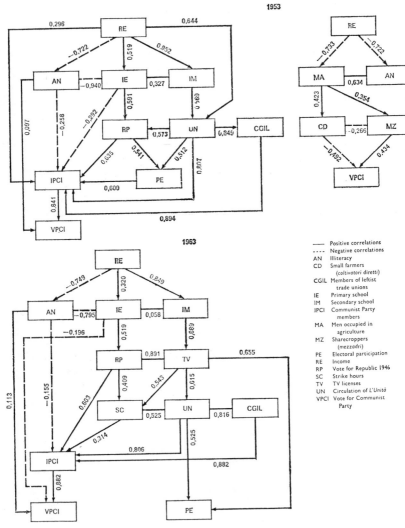

Figure 1

CAUSAL MODELS OF COMMUNIST VOTE IN 1953 AND 1963,
AT PROVINCIAL LEVEL, FOR ALL OF ITALY

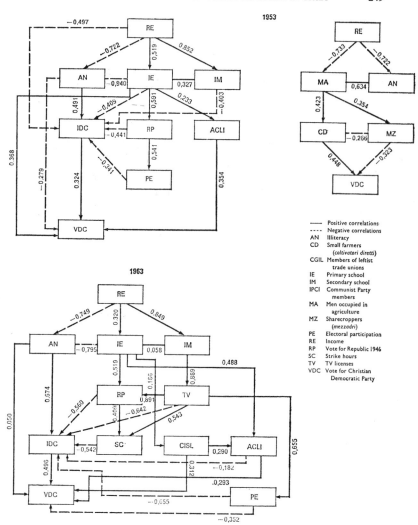

Figure 2

CAUSAL MODELS OF CHRISTIAN DEMOCRATIC VOTE IN 1953 AND 1963,
AT PROVINCIAL LEVEL, FOR ALL OF ITALY

1953

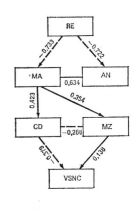

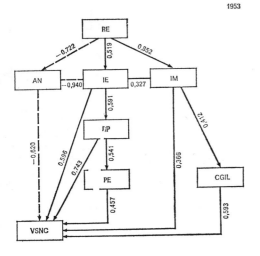

1963

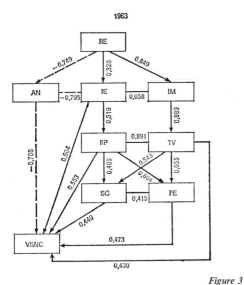

---- Positive correlations
- - - - Negative correlations
AN   Illiteracy
CD   Small farmers
        (coltivatori diretti)
CGIL Members of leftist
        trade unions
IE   Primary school
IM   Secondary school
IPCI Communist Party
        members
MA   Men occupied in
        agriculture
MZ   Sharecroppers
        (mezzadri)
PE   Electoral participation
RE   Income
RP   Vote for Republic 1946
SC   Strike hours
TV   TV licenses
VSNC Vote for Socialist
        Parties (Leftist vote
        without Communist
        Party)

Figure 3

CAUSAL MODELS OF SOCIALIST VOTE IN 1953 AND 1963,
AT PROVINCIAL LEVEL, FOR ALL OF ITALY

For each party or group under consideration we have constructed two types of circuits at the provincial level which are presented in Figures 1, 2, and 3. The first type is of a general character, whereas the second is more limited, relating only to agriculture.

A well-known index of economic development in a country is the average income of its population. In Italy this figure almost doubled between 1950 and 1963. From our tables we know that high income is positively correlated with a vote for the non-Communist Left, the PCI, and the nonextremist Right, whereas it is negatively correlated with the DC. Upon examination of the circuits, however, it may be seen that income exerts an indirect influence on the vote. Immediately connected with income in the circuit chain is the level of education, and successive links are represented by such factors as tradition (indicated by a vote for the Republic), social commitment (indicated by the number of strike hours), spread of mass culture (as measured by the number of television licenses), and party membership. These positive-influence circuits have been marked in white, whereas the negative-influence circuits are in black.

Careful examination of the correlations will show that there are no significant variations within the respective circuits of the Left, PCI, and DC for 1953 and 1963. There are, however, significant variations in the Right causal circuit, in both configurations, with or without the MSI.

We find in the circuit of the PCI that illiteracy and primary education negatively influence PCI membership, which is the final link in the chain leading to the vote. Primary education, however, is also positively correlated with the left-wing tradition, and through this mediation it enters the causal chain that leads to the vote. Secondary education as well is indirectly related to PCI membership. It is linked with the circulation of *L'Unità*, which, in turn, is linked with membership in CGIL and with political participation. While reading the party newspaper and membership in the trade union directly favor the Communist vote, participation also favors this vote through membership in the party. (See Figure 1.)

This causal circuit for the PCI is practically the same for 1963. In the latter year, however, as can be seen in the diagram, the spread of television and number of strike hours form a perfect link in the circuit. The former is positively correlated with the latter (which, in turn, influences PCI membership) and with participation and the circulation of *L'Unità*.

These two variables, television and strike hours, are always correlated with the Communist vote. This fact contradicts the generally held opinion that television only reduces social tensions. As it is the means by which people inform themselves about social reality, it is also the means by which these tensions may be intensified. It serves a double function, which consequently favors the left more than the right.

With regard to the Christian Democrat circuit, it can be seen that primary education negatively influences DC membership, even though it positively influences the vote. Illiteracy, on the contrary, negatively influences the DC vote, but it may have a positive influence when mediated by party membership. Secondary education is negatively correlated with both the Christian Democrat vote and party membership. It is worth noting, however, that, in 1963, although primary education did not favor DC membership, it did favor CISL and ACLI membership, and that there is a positive correlation between these two factors. Although neither CISL nor ACLI membership favors DC membership and there is a negative correlation between ACLI and DC membership, they both lead directly to voting for the DC, bypassing party membership.

It seems that party membership is a filter for the votes of illiterates. Membership in the CISL and the ACLI, on the other hand, constitutes a filter for persons with primary education. In a similar way participation in the various forms of the Catholic organizations appears to converge in favor of the DC vote. There are other factors in the circuit, however, which act against the DC vote. The left-wing tradition, secondary education, television, and strike hours, both directly and through the party, function in this way.

The causal circuits of the non-Communist left wing and the right wing form an antithetical pair. The circuit that leads to the left-wing vote — primary and secondary education, republican tradition, and participation, with the addition, in 1963, of the spread of television and strike hours — is the antithesis of that leading to the right-wing vote: all these factors act negatively, whereas illiteracy is positively correlated with the vote.

As we can observe in the diagrams, there was no significant variation between 1953 and 1963 for the Left, the PCI, or the DC. But as we have already indicated, there was for the Right. The situation changes with regard to only the 1963 circuit relating to the right wing without the MSI. This is fundamentally the liberal Right (7 per cent of national votes as against 1.7 per cent of the Partito democratico italiano di unità monarchica). In this last circuit, the left-wing tradition, strike hours, and participation continued to influence the right-wing vote negatively. Secondary education, however, either directly or filtered by television, positively influenced the right-wing vote and correlated negatively to a significant degree (— .329) with illiteracy. This moderate right wing of 1963, which had become more northern-based and urban, more closely resembled the moderate Left from the sociological-electoral point of view.

As can be seen, these circuits do not indicate any economic evolution, represented by the percentage of the population working in industry or commerce as compared with agriculture. It has been found, however, that the industrialization factor is interchangeable with that of income and could serve, but without adding anything, as the first link in the causal chain.

Besides the four circuits just described, we have constructed two minor integrative circuits for the agricultural professions. Since relevant census data was available only for 1953, the circuits could be constructed only for that year. One circuit shows the factors that lead to the Communist and the non-Communist left-wing vote; the other shows the factors that lead to the Christian Democrat and right-wing vote, with or without the MSI. In the first case, the final link is represented by the prevalence of agricultural workers, the *mezzadri*; in the second, the final link is represented by the prevalence of farmers cultivating their own land.

These circuits further clarify the relationship between economic structure, which is in the process of rapid evolution, and Italian electoral behavior, which is relatively stable. These factors of change — the development of industry and commerce, rising educational and income levels, political social participation, and the extension of mass culture — are positively correlated, either singly or in an organic causal circuit, first with the non-Communist, second with the PCI, and in order of diminishing influence, with the non-Fascist Right, the DC, and the Fascist Right.

Although the socioeconomic structure of society favors the moderate left wing, there are other factors favoring the PCI and accounting for its position as second. The most important of these factors is its politico-social organization. The PCI institutions, the party, trade union, press, etc., direct what might be considered as a natural tendency to vote for the Left toward a vote for the PCI. It should be noted that even in the causal circuits there does not appear to be any mediation between the level of illiteracy and the Communist vote. It seems, however, that there may be a positive influence that is not included among the ones indicated, and, in our opinion, this could be the PCI political machine. Voluntary party workers, who are nonprofessional and nonbureaucratic, seem to be the channel through which general information and Communist propaganda reach the illiterate section of the population.

With regard to the right-wing or moderate electorate, the only evolutionary factor that clearly favors the majority party is that of elementary education, but even this factor favors the non-Communist Left more than it favors the DC. This characteristic can be explained by the Catholic bias of elementary schooling in Italy. In general, the effect of education favors the Left, but this tendency is sometimes redirected by the religious orientation of Italian education.

As with the PCI vote, the Christian Democrat vote depends largely on organizational factors. As in the former case, the party is a means by which the illiterate vote is collected, and the CISL and ACLI accumulate the vote of those with primary education. Also its influence on the organization of farmers working their own land explains the Christian Democrat prevalence in this sector in spite of its circuit identity with the Right.

The relationship between the Right and certain evolutionary factors, such as secondary education, spread of television, and income, has already been indicated. In 1963 these factors tended to favor a moderate and conservative Right, as represented by the PCI, and not an extremist element, such as the PNM in 1953 and primarily the MSI in both 1953 and 1963.

THE CAUSAL CIRCUITS AT THE COMMUNE LEVEL

The causal circuits at the commune level were constructed on the basis of the same criteria as the analogous circuits at the provincial level. With these circuits, however, a greater number of units were considered. On the one hand, this rendered all the correlations practically significant and, on the other, permitted comparisons of the circuit at the national level with the six historically important areas. These zones have been characterized in terms of the predominance in each of the Communist and Christian Democrat Party subcultures.

Zone I (Northwest Italy) includes Piedmont, Liguria, and Lombardy, excluding the provinces of Bergamo, Brescia, Mantua, and Piacenza. In the late nineteenth century socialism was introduced into this zone.

Zone II (Northeast Italy) includes the provinces of Bergamo and Brescia in Lombardy, the province of Trento, the province of Udine, all of Veneto with the exception of the province of Rovigo. This is a zone outside the industrial concentration of the Turin-Genoa-Milan triangle, where clerical influence is considerable. In other words, it is a "white" zone.[3]

Zone III (Central Italy) includes the provinces of Mantua, Rovigo, Viterbo, the whole of Emilia except for the province of Piacenza, Tuscany, Umbria, and the Marches except for the province of Ascoli Piceno. This is the zone in which Mazzinian, anarchist, and socialist movements occurred successively in the nineteenth century. These movements took place within an exclusively agricultural society and were strongly anticlerical. It is then a "red" zone.

Zone IV (Southern Italy) includes the provinces of Ascoli Piceno, Lazio, with the exception of the province of Viterbo, Campania, Abruzzi e Molise, Apulia, Basilicata, and Calabria. There was no widespread cultural, political, or trade union movement before the Fascist period in this zone, neither Socialist nor Catholic. Such movements are found in isolated areas in which semifeudal conservatism has been maintained.

Zone V consists of Sicily, and *Zone VI* of Sardinia. Although these regions share a movement toward autonomy, each has clearly defined and individualistic historical characteristics.

As the data regarding income were not available at the commune level, the index of industrialization, expressed by the percentage of the population working in industry, was used as the first link in the chain. As we have already pointed out, this factor is interchangeable with the income indicator. The correlation with agriculture, therefore, does not appear in the circuit as it naturally correlates negatively with industry in almost perfect symmetry ($-.935$ in 1953; $-.914$ in 1963).

In order to illustrate the position of persons working in agriculture in the circuit, we have considered the *mezzadri* in 1953. With regard to the two categories thus excluded, paid laborers and farmers working their own land, it should be noted that in 1953 the variable expressed by the former was to a high degree positively correlated with illiteracy (.482) and therefore with the vote for the PCI and the right-wing parties. In 1963, on the other hand, the variable expressed by agricultural concerns employing paid laborers showed no significant correlation. The variable "farmers cultivating their own land" is, for both 1953 and 1963, positively correlated with elementary education and negatively

---

[3] The provinces of Aosta, Bolzano, Gorizia, and Trieste have been ignored as there is no comparable data over time for them. The conditions under which the 1919 elections took place in these provinces were very special since they had been recently annexed and contained a high proportion of non-Italian ethnic groups.

correlated with secondary education. It positively influences the Christian Democrat vote and, to a lesser degree, the right-wing vote.

The causal circuits for all of Italy are shown in Figures 4, 5, 6, and 7. The similarity of these circuits to those at the provincial level confirms the patterns already presented. With level of industrialization as the starting point in the causal chain, the antithetical relationship between the PSI and the right wing is confirmed. In the first instance, the percentage of persons working in industry has a positive influence; in the second, the same factor has a negative influence. An analogous situation exists for the DC and the PCI. Although industrialization has an indirect influence on both, upon examination of the mediating factors in this influence, we find that they are antithetical as well: that which favors the DC, particularly primary education, negatively affects the PCI. On the other hand, those factors which support the Communist vote — secondary education, though this is of little weight, illiteracy, progressive tradition, number of voters, spread of television, and the marginal factor of *mezzadri* — all have a negative effect on the DC vote. In effect, the mediation of primary education is necessary in order for industrialization to influence the Christian Democrat vote positively, whereas the mediation of secondary education and of the spread of television is necessary in order for the Communist vote to be influenced.

There are several factors that are always positive for the PSI apart from the aforementioned direct influence of industrialization. Both primary and secondary education exert an indirect influence. These two educational factors were both negative for the right wing in 1953, but in 1963 the former was positive and the latter negative, and the positive influence, in this case, was also direct. This variation was evidently a consequence of the already described liberal leadership of the right wing in 1963, which reduced the positive influence of illiteracy on the right-wing vote. Conversely, the negative influence of illiteracy on both the Christian Democrat and Socialist vote was reduced, whereas its positive influence on the Communist vote increased.

In the commune-level circuits, the factor of tradition, indicated by a vote for the Republic in the referendum of 1946, remained decisive. With regard to the DC, this factor maintained its position between industrialization and level of education in the causal chain but increased in significance. This was also the case with the Right, in which the electorate is more "cultured" but nonetheless conservative.

The circuit of the PCI remained practically unchanged. The progressive tradition served as a filter between the vote and elementary education both in 1953 and 1963, but in the former year it had less influence.

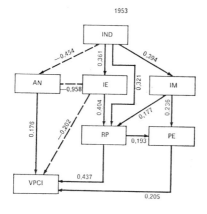

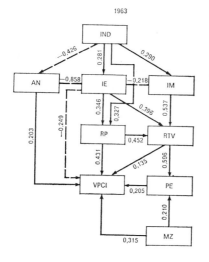

——— Positive correlations
- - - - Negative correlations
AN   Illiteracy
IE   Primary school
IM   Secondary school
IND   Industrialization
MZ   Sharecroppers
        (mezzadri)
PE   Electoral participation
RTV   Radio-television
RP   Vote for Republic 1946
VPCI Vote for Communist
        Party

Figure 4

CAUSAL MODELS OF COMMUNIST VOTE IN 1953 AND 1963 IN ITALY

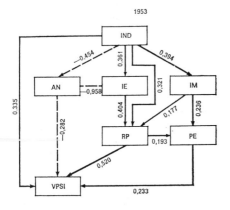

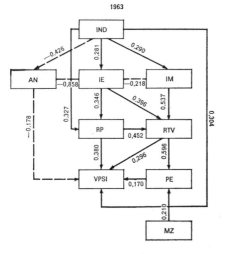

—— Positive correlations
- - - - Negative correlations
AN   Illiteracy
IE   Primary school
IM   Secondary school
IND   Industrialization
MZ   Sharecroppers
        (*mezzadri*)
PE   Electoral participation
RTV   Radio-television
RP   Vote for Republic 1946
VPSI Vote for Socialist Party

Figure 5

CAUSAL MODELS OF SOCIALIST VOTE IN 1953 AND 1963 IN ITALY

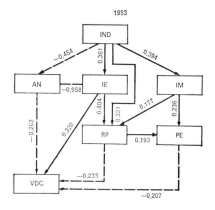

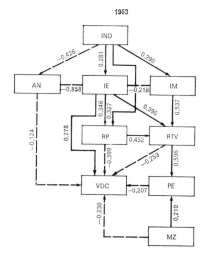

————	Positive correlations
- - - -	Negative correlations
AN	Illiteracy
IE	Primary school
IM	Secondary school
IND	Industrialization
MZ	Sharecroppers (mezzadri)
PE	Electoral participation
RTV	Radio-television
RP	Vote for Republic 1946
VDC	Vote for Christian Democratic Party

Figure 6

CAUSAL MODELS OF CHRISTIAN DEMOCRATIC VOTE
IN 1953 AND 1963 IN ITALY

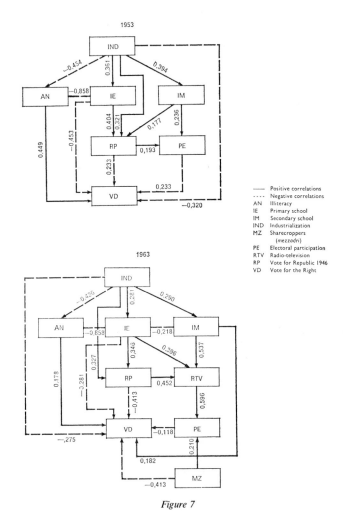

Figure 7

CAUSAL MODELS OF RIGHTIST VOTE IN 1953 AND 1963 IN ITALY

The PCI shared with the PSI the positive influence of television; it acted in the causal chain as a filter between education level and the vote.

This was the general situation on a national scale. Now we can compare it with the six areas.

The Industrial Triangle (Zone I)

The industrial triangle varies significantly from the national situation, as can be seen from the circuits of Figures 8, 9, 10, and 11. The industry of the area exerts a greater direct positive influence on the Socialist vote than is generally the case, and this influence increased between 1953 and 1963. Correspondingly, there is a higher index of negative correlation between industrialization and the right-wing vote, although this index decreased between 1953 and 1963.

Heavy industrialization also has a special effect on the composition of the Communist vote. There is a positive correlation between the Communist vote, illiteracy, and republican tradition, a combination that is not typical of the PSI. Correspondingly, the correlation between illiteracy and the right-wing vote becomes negative. If one considers, however, that the other constant social and professional component of the Communist vote, the rural middle classes, does not operate in this area, it is clear that the basic component of the Communist vote in the area is the lower stratum of social classes involved in the industrialization process. It is a class with little culture but with a left-wing tradition.

In addition to this component, there is also another, which reaches the vote through the channel of secondary education and television. It may be supposed that the organizational factor, the presence of institutions and Communist activism, which we were unable to check at the commune level, is an important link in the chain. It leads to the vote of the illiterate in the absence of other means of communication and in the presence of a progressive tradition.

Secondary education as usual, however, appears as a positive influence in the left-wing circuit; in 1963, as a result of PLI prevalence, it appears in the right-wing as well. But it always has a negative influence on the Christian Democrat vote. This relationship between the right wing and secondary education could probably be clarified by data, which we have not included, relating to the circulation of the nonparty press. It could serve as a filter between the given cultural level, the conservative tradition, and the right-wing electoral choice. In that the republican tendency, in comparison with the national situation, favors the Left to the disadvantage of the Right, it might also confirm the

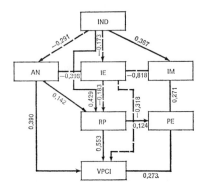

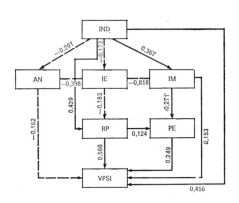

Figure 8

CAUSAL MODELS OF COMMUNIST AND SOCIALIST
VOTE IN 1953 IN THE "INDUSTRIAL" ZONE

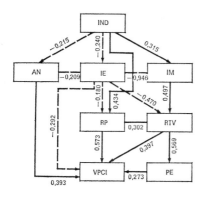

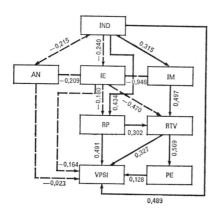

—— Positive correlations
- - - - Negative correlations
AN   Illiteracy
IE   Primary school
IM   Secondary school
IND   Industrialization
PE   Electoral participation
RTV   Radio-television
RP   Vote for Republic 1946
VPCI   Vote for Communist
       Party
VPSI   Vote for Socialist Party

Figure 9

CAUSAL MODELS OF COMMUNIST AND SOCIALIST
VOTE IN 1963 IN THE "INDUSTRIAL" ZONE

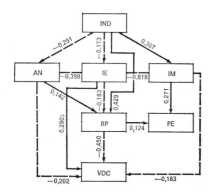

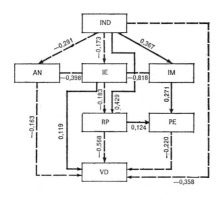

—— Positive correlations
- - - Negative correlations
AN   Illiteracy
IE   Primary school
IM   Secondary school
IND   Industrialization
PE   Electoral participation
RP   Vote for Republic 1946
VDC   Vote for Christian
      Democratic Party
VD   Vote for the Right

Figure 10

CAUSAL MODELS OF CHRISTIAN DEMOCRATIC VOTE
AND THE RIGHTIST VOTE IN THE "INDUSTRIAL" ZONE

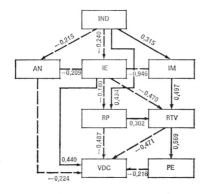

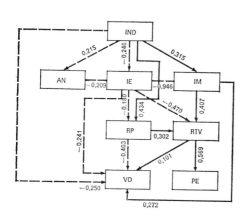

Figure 11

CAUSAL MODELS OF CHRISTIAN DEMOCRATIC VOTE AND THE
RIGHTIST VOTE IN 1963, IN THE "INDUSTRIAL" ZONE

"moderating" role played by the nonparty press, which is read primarily by those persons who have attained the secondary level of education.

In the case of the Christian Democrats, the level of primary education remains the central link of the chain leading to the vote. In this area it is primary level of education, and not illiteracy on the national scale, which is positively correlated with the moderate political tradition. This double component, primary education and moderate political tradition, is the basis of the Christian Democrat vote in the industrial areas.

Party organization, the nonparty press, and Catholic organizations are also important factors of the DC vote in the industrialized zone. Television is characteristically a negative correlation with the vote.

The White Zone (Zone II)

The correlation circuits for this zone also show significant differences from the national situation, although less important than those in the industrialized area. They may be seen in Figures 12, 13, 14, and 15.

In this zone the circuit variables that always favor the Left — progressive tradition and percentage of voters — maintain their role, but with smaller indices. In other words, there are some weaker links in this causal chain whereby it can be more easily broken. Even industrialization does not exert such a strong direct influence on the Left, specifically the PSI.

In the case of the DC vote, however, the central link in the chain, primary education, is particularly strong in this zone. But it varies from the national situation because of its connection with political tradition. Furthermore, unlike the national scale, it is negatively correlated with illiteracy. This characteristic was also found in the industrial area, but in this case it was also negatively correlated with elementary education. The only positive correlation of the progressive political tradition is with secondary education.

In this area with its pronounced Catholic hegemony, the conservative political tradition is filtered by both the absence of education and primary level of education. It is only at the level of secondary education that culture does not act as a filter for this tradition. In fact, this educational level serves a role in the left-wing, particularly the PSI, circuit. Television also plays this role, as it has a positive correlation with the progressive tradition in the left-wing circuit.

It should also be noted that in 1963, secondary education and radio-television had the same position in the circuit leading to the right-wing vote as they had in the circuit leading to the left-wing vote. As has

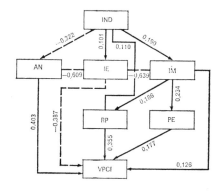

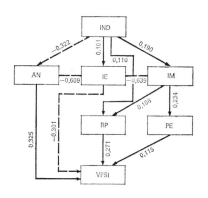

Positive correlations
---- Negative correlations
AN   Illiteracy
IE   Primary school
IM   Secondary school
IND   Industrialization
PE   Electoral participation
RP   Vote for Republic 1946
VPCI Vote for Communist
       Party
VPSI Vote for Socialist Party

Figure 12

CAUSAL MODELS OF COMMUNIST AND SOCIALIST
VOTE IN 1953 IN THE "WHITE" ZONE

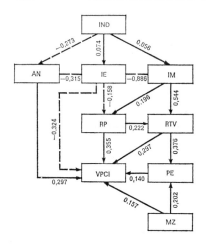

---- Positive correlations
- - - - Negative correlations
AN   Illiteracy
IE   Primary school
IM   Secondary school
IND   Industrialization
MZ   Sharecroppers
      (mezzadri)
PE   Electoral participation
RTV   Radio-television
RP   Vote for Republic 1946
VPCI Vote for Communist
      Party
VPSI Vote for Socialist Party

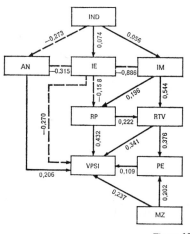

Figure 13

CAUSAL MODELS OF COMMUNIST AND SOCIALIST
VOTE IN 1963 IN THE "WHITE" ZONE

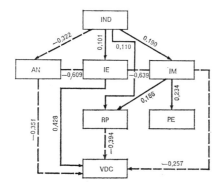

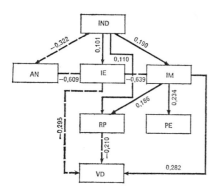

Positive correlations
- - - - Negative correlations
AN   Illiteracy
IE   Primary school
IM   Secondary school
IND   Industrialization
PE   Electoral participation
RP   Vote for Republic 1946
VDC   Vote for Christian
       Democratic Party
VD   Vote for the Right

Figure 14

CAUSAL MODELS OF CHRISTIAN DEMOCRATIC VOTE AND
THE RIGHTIST VOTE IN 1953 IN THE "WHITE" ZONE

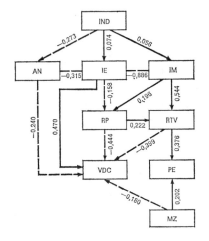

- —— Positive correlations
- ---- Negative correlations
- AN   Illiteracy
- IE   Primary school
- IM   Secondary school
- IND   Industrialization
- MZ   Sharecroppers
-        (mezzadri)
- PE   Electoral participation
- RTV   Radio-television
- RP   Vote for Republic 1946
- VDC   Vote for Christian
-        Democratic Party
- VD   Vote for the Right

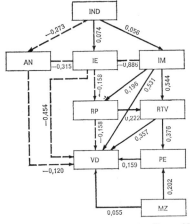

Figure 15

CAUSAL MODELS OF CHRISTIAN DEMOCRATIC VOTE AND
THE RIGHTIST VOTE IN 1963 IN THE "WHITE" ZONE

already been explained, this phenomenon is related to the secular, middle-class character of the Right in an area in which the conservative tradition is predominantly Catholic and rural. The moderate character of the Christian Democrat electorate in the white zone is quite clear from the causal circuit.

The Red Zone (Zone III)

The circuits for Zone III are shown in Figures 16, 17, 18, and 19. In appraising these circuits, it should be remembered that the PCI has a particularly strong organization in this zone. Rather than a party of political participation, in this case it is a party of social integration.

The presence of this organizational factor, which could not be quantified at the commune level, is the key to the interpretation of all the circuits. It provides a link in the causal chain which filters all the other factors, with the single exception of elementary education. This is the only element that is negatively correlated with the Communist vote and, conversely, positively correlated with the Christian Democrat vote.

In all of the circuits of the red zone, industrialization does not directly influence the vote. One link is the educational factor, or primary and secondary education, and others are progressive political tradition and percentage of voters. The latter factors are also found on the national scale in favor of a left-wing vote, but in this case they have higher indices and are of greater significance.

At this point the link or filter represented by the PCI organization can be clearly understood: it strengthens the positive variables of tradition and participation and draws into the causal chain variables that are in themselves an indifferent influence upon political forces, such as industrialization, secondary education, and illiteracy. Radio-television also fits perfectly into this causal circuit and is already negatively correlated with the Christian Democrat vote. Furthermore, the positive correlation of the socioprofessional *mezzadria* variable confirms this situation; it is even correlated negatively with the other left-wing party, the PSI. Presumably, this is a result of powerful political and para-political organizations of the PCI, such as the Federation of *Mezzadri* and the CGIL.

The South (Zone IV)

Figures 20–23 show the circuits for Southern Italy. As is generally known, there have been many important political changes in the South

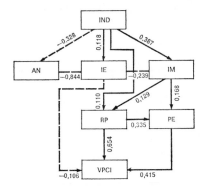

--- Positive correlations
- - - - Negative correlations
AN   Illiteracy
IE   Primary school
IM   Secondary school
IND   Industrialization
PE   Electoral participation
RP   Vote for Republic 1946
VPCI   Vote for Communist
        Party
VPSI   Vote for Socialist Party

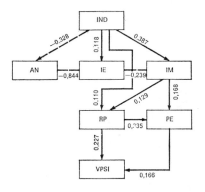

Figure 16

CAUSAL MODELS OF COMMUNIST AND SOCIALIST
VOTE IN 1953 IN THE "RED" ZONE

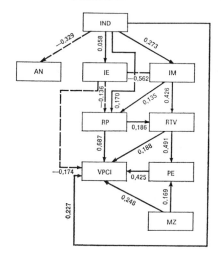

Positive correlations
---- Negative correlations
AN   Illiteracy
IE   Primary school
IM   Secondary school
IND   Industrialization
MZ   Sharecroppers
         (*mezzadri*)
PE   Electoral participation
RTV   Radio-television
RP   Vote for Republic 1946
VPCI Vote for Communist
         Party
VPSI Vote for Socialist Party

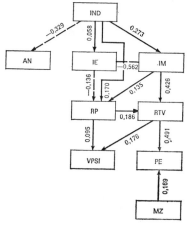

Figure 17

CAUSAL MODELS OF COMMUNIST AND SOCIALIST
VOTE IN 1963 IN THE "RED" ZONE

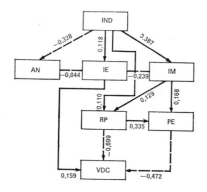

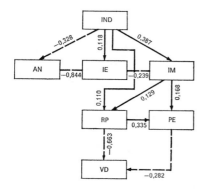

——— Positive correlations
- - - - Negative correlations
AN Illiteracy
IE Primary school
IM Secondary school
IND Industrialization
PE Electoral participation
RP Vote for Republic 1946
VDC Vote for Christian
      Democratic Party
VD Vote for the Right

Figure 18

CAUSAL MODELS OF CHRISTIAN DEMOCRATIC VOTE
AND THE RIGHTIST VOTE IN 1953, IN THE "RED" ZONE

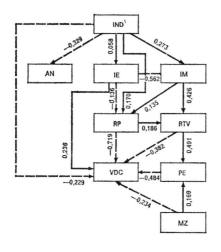

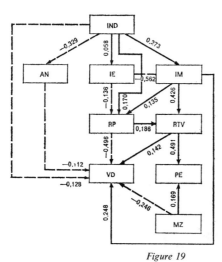

Legend:

————— Positive correlations
- - - - Negative correlations
AN   Illiteracy
IE   Primary school
IM   Secondary school
IND   Industrialization
MZ   Sharecroppers
      (mezzadri)
PE   Electoral participation
RTV   Radio-television
RP   Vote for Republic 1946
VDC   Vote for Christian
      Democratic Party
VD   Vote for the Right

Figure 19

CAUSAL MODELS OF CHRISTIAN DEMOCRATIC VOTE
AND THE RIGHTIST VOTE IN THE "RED" ZONE IN 1963

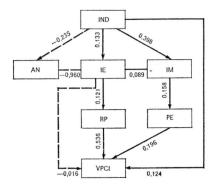

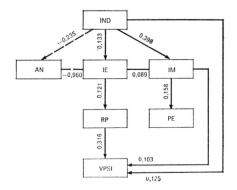

Figure 20

CAUSAL MODELS OF COMMUNIST AND SOCIALIST
VOTE IN 1953 IN THE "SOUTH" ZONE

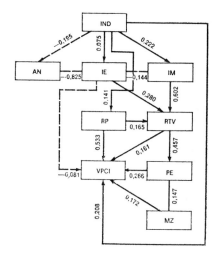

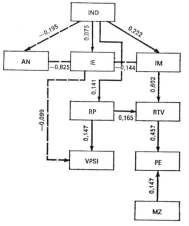

Legend:

—— Positive correlations
- - - - Negative correlations
AN   Illiteracy
IE   Primary school
IM   Secondary school
IND   Industrialization
MZ   Sharecroppers
      (mezzadri)
PE   Electoral participation
RTV   Radio-television
RP   Vote for Republic 1946
VPCI Vote for Communist
      Party
VPSI Vote for Socialist Party

Figure 21

CAUSAL MODELS OF COMMUNIST AND SOCIALIST
VOTE IN 1963 IN THE "SOUTH" ZONE

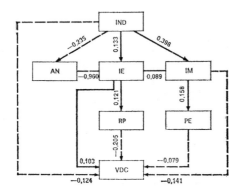

— Positive correlations
- - - Negative correlations
AN   Illiteracy
IE   Primary school
IM   Secondary school
IND Industrialization
PE   Electoral participation
RP   Vote for Republic 1946
VDC Vote for Christian
         Democratic Party
VD   Vote for the Right

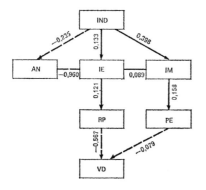

Figure 22

CAUSAL MODELS OF CHRISTIAN DEMOCRATIC VOTE
AND THE RIGHTIST VOTE IN 1953 IN THE "SOUTH" ZONE

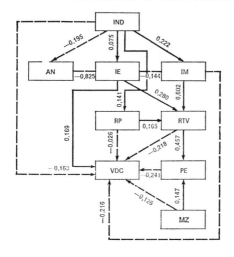

— Positive correlations
- - - Negative correlations
AN   Illiteracy
IE   Primary school
IM   Secondary school
IND Industrialization
MZ   Sharecroppers
     (mezzadri)
PE   Electoral participation
RTV Radio-television
RP   Vote for Republic 1946
VDC Vote for Christian
     Democratic Party
VD   Vote for the Right

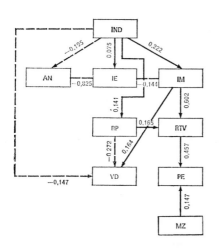

Figure 23

CAUSAL MODELS OF CHRISTIAN DEMOCRATIC VOTE
AND THE RIGHTIST VOTE IN 1963 IN THE "SOUTH" ZONE

since 1946. Most of them, however, were before 1950, which was about the time the industrialization of the area began.

We find in this area that industrialization has a more direct influence on the vote and that it influences the PCI positively and the DC and Right negatively. On the other hand, this variable has practically no influence on the PSI; it is not favored by participation, which is usually the case with the Left. Other factors that are usually connected with the Socialist vote, such as primary and secondary education, also have a minimum weight in this circuit. Progressive political tradition remains influential but decreasingly so. Although the paths that lead to the Communist vote are quite clearly indicated by the circuit, the Socialist vote seems to be somewhat more fluid and difficult to classify. This gives us the impression that whereas the Communist vote is relatively consolidated, the Socialist vote is still in the process of consolidation.

With regard to the DC, elementary education remains the central link in the chain leading to the vote, and it is only through this factor that the negative influence of illiteracy, secondary education, and radio-television is mediated and reduced. The other link in the chain that reduces the negative influence of industrialization and thereby favors the Christian Democrat vote is the conservative political tradition.

The circuit of the Right is analogous to that of the DC, with the single exception that the role of elementary education in favor of the DC vote is assumed by secondary education in the case of the Right.

Sicily (Zone V)

The situation is different in Sicily. Industrialization has had little direct influence on the vote, and this influence decreased between 1953, when it affected the PCI positively and the DC negatively, and 1963. Correspondingly, education has become a more important link in the chain, and it serves as a filter, as already observed on the national scale, for a variety of other factors: illiteracy for the Left, elementary education for the DC, and secondary education for the Right. This circuit, however, differs from the national circuit because there is a strong correlation between illiteracy and the left-wing tradition (.224 in 1953 and .326 in 1963). As a result, illiteracy more frequently leads to a vote for the Left than was the case in the other areas of the southern peninsula and islands. Conversely, secondary education clearly favors the right-wing vote, particularly in 1963, and exerts no positive influence on that of the left wing, even on the Socialist vote. Not even the *mezzadria* serves as a link in the chain.

We also find that the Socialist vote differs the most in Sicily from the national situation also with regard to factors other than level of education. In 1953 the vote was positively related not only to the number of voters, which is not uncommon, but also to the factor of farmers farming their own land, which indicates the moderate character that socialism is assuming. In 1963, on the other hand, the participation factor no longer entered into the circuit leading to the Socialist vote. In this respect the PSI was similar to the Right, although the two could be differentiated by means of other factors, such as political tradition, the persistence of illiteracy, and less extensive secondary education. These factors accentuate the "popular" connotations of the Socialist electorate and perform a role contrary to that of the participation factor.

Sardinia (Zone VI)

In this area we find that industrialization once again has a direct influence on the vote, even though it decreased between 1953 and 1963. This influence favored the Left and worked to the disadvantage of the DC and Right. The only difference from the South lies in its influence on the Left and the Socialist vote. All other factors operated in their usual way: the *mezzadria* supported the Communist Left, and farmers working their own land favored the DC. Elementary education remained the decisive, positive link for the Christian Democrat vote and a negative factor for the Communist vote. Secondary education, in a circuit including radio-television and participation, remained the connecting link between industrialization and the right-wing vote. Radio-television also functioned positively in the circuit that led to the Communist vote.

With regard to the PSI, the positive role of progressive tradition and primary education in 1963 remained unchanged. As in Sicily, participation did not enter into the causal chain that led to the Socialist vote, nor was television a decisive factor. The consequences of this break in the circuit were reduced by both the positive, direct influence of industrialization on the Socialist vote and the indirect influence of elementary education and the progressive tradition.

The National Circuit and the Area Circuits

Now that we have examined the situations for the individual areas, we can compare them with the situation on the national scale.

In all of Italy political tradition emerges as a decisive factor. With the single exception of the PSI in the red zone, in which there was a Communist hegemony, it serves as a link in the causal chain. In this case it was possible to collect most of the progressive political tradition under the PCI banner; all other political forces tended to be moderate. With this exception, which is nevertheless a significant one, political tradition, as it is transmitted through the family, leaders of opinion, and political or nonpolitical associations, enters into the causal circuit that leads to a left-wing, either Socialist or Communist, vote.

The role of elementary education is also clear at both the national and commune level. At the commune level, primary education emerges as the decisive link in the chain leading to the Christian Democrat vote. Although at the national level (which is based on provincial data, thereby attenuating local, regional, and areal differences) primary education appears to be a factor more favorable to the non-Communist Left, there can be no doubt that at both the national and areal level this factor is a link in the causal chain that leads to the Christian Democrat vote. Thus we can deduce that it is this level of education, particularly in the smaller communes, which favors a Christian Democratic electoral orientation.

As one would expect, illiteracy acts in the opposite way, and it never enters the causal chain leading to the Christian Democrat vote. It does, however, have a positive effect with regard to the Communist and the right-wing votes and, in Sicily, to the Socialist vote. Other characteristics in the chain, however, vary from area to area.

The position of illiteracy is particularly important in the causal chain leading to the Communist vote in the industrial zone, Sicily, and Sardinia. South of the peninsula, however, industrialization is of greater weight; in the white zone, the important link is the level of secondary education; and in the red zone, as may be expected, it is the organization factor. Even for the Right the role of illiteracy varies from area to area, depending upon the strength of the PCI organization. Its weight is less in the industrial area, Sicily, Sardinia, and also in the white zone, in which, as has been seen, it may tend toward the Christian Democrat vote.

With regard to the DC, secondary education plays an even more negative role than illiteracy, on the same level as radio-television. Whereas illiteracy can be a filter in the white zone for even the DC vote, secondary education and radio-television are never links in the chain leading to the DC vote.

Secondary education and radio-television generally perform a similar role, but their influence on the left-wing or right-wing vote varies from area to area. In the Veneto and the Islands, these factors favor the right; in the industrial area they support the PSI. Invariably they enter the causal chain leading to the Communist vote, but they have relatively little influence.

From our analysis of the correlations in the circuit, we can make certain conclusions about political forces. The greatest differences from area to area seem to be within the PSI, whereas the DC appears to be the most constant. The Right and the PCI are also relatively constant, although with certain areal differences, primarily in the "advanced" character of the right-wing electorate in the white zone and the more "industrial" character of the Communist electorate in the south of the peninsula.

As we have said, it is the Socialist electorate that appears to be the most varied. In the first two areas, the industrial and white zones, it is typically industrial, cultured, and progressive; in Sardinia, it is cultured; but in the red zone, it is moderate. In the south of the peninsula and in Sicily it is difficult to classify, as there are links that are not always analogous in the causal chain leading to the Socialist vote.

One important element that plays an ambivalent role, however, is level of education. It does not act as a filter toward socialism in the south of the peninsula, and it favors the Right at the level of secondary education in Sicily.

With the exception of the organization factor, which we were not able to examine, it is our general conclusion that the process of industrialization influences the vote almost exclusively through the filter of the educational level. The progression from illiteracy to elementary education tends to favor the DC, to the disadvantage of the PCI and the Right. There is also, however, the filtering function performed by political tradition, either moderate or progressive, which tends to counterbalance the level of education. At a further stage, the progression from elementary education to secondary education, combined with the spread of mass culture, primarily through radio and television, tends to favor the Left, primarily its Socialist component, and the liberal component of the Right, to the disadvantage of the DC. In this case as well, however, there will presumably be a limit to the contraction of the DC and the expansion of the others through the filtering function performed by political tradition.

On the whole, the basic causes that orientate the Italian electorate seem to balance and compensate for one another. This may be seen in terms of both space (in areal differences) and time (the process of industrialization and the increase of culture). This balancing effect favors an increasingly stable Italian electorate.

II

MATTEI DOGAN

A Covariance Analysis of
French Electoral Data*

A REGRESSION ANALYSIS concerning 2,477 cantons, the results of which were presented at the Symposium on "Quantitative Ecological Analysis" in September 1966,[1] demonstrates the importance of the religious factor in the electoral behavior of the French. One can ask, however, whether this religious factor does not conceal the influence of other factors, notably social class. One of the best methods for measuring the influence of other factors, by neutralizing the influence of religion, is *covariance analysis*; this method appears to be of methodological relevance only if seen as an extension and a complement of regression analysis. By eliminating the effects of the religious factor, the role of social class in the determination of the vote can be explored. This was the first objective of the covariance analysis attempted on the data for 1956.

The second objective was to explore the influence of the regional context. Multiple regression analysis had demonstrated how correlations between party, religion, and class vary from one region to another. But we were not able to measure the weight of "region" taken as an independent variable or to situate it in relation to other explanatory variables. Consequently, we have established a second factorial plan,

* We are very grateful to Daniel Derivry (Centre National de la Recherche Scientifique) for his kind co-operation in this research. He and Alain Degenne (C.N.R.S.) have prepared the program of covariance analysis by computer. We are also grateful to Hayward Alker (Massachusetts Institute of Technology) and René Bassoul (C.N.R.S.) for their comments on an earlier draft of this paper.

[1] The paper on regression analysis is being revised by the author and will be published at a later date.

285

which utilizes, on the one hand, a nominal variable, the region, and holds constant, on the other hand, different types of social structure.

CONSTRUCTION OF THE FACTORIAL PLAN

By means of covariance analysis the "disturbing" effect of a variable can be eliminated. It is thus a sophisticated technique of investigation. Nevertheless, it has rarely been employed in electoral sociology because the quantified data are not always appropriate to the construction of an orthogonalized plan, and the statistical distributions are often "abnormal."[2] We have, however, a sufficient number of cases (2,477 cantons) to surmount the difficulties.

First, we have retained as independent variables the proportion of workers in industry and the proportion of electors belonging to the middle classes. After a cross tabulation between the two variables, we have drawn for each of them two cut points, which permit us to distinguish a total of nine categories of cantons. These cut points have been determined in such a way that the number of units is "maximized" for the less numerous categories. From this we have obtained the distribution shown in Table 1.

From each category 100 units were randomly sampled, and for each

Table 1

DISTRIBUTION OBTAINED IN COVARIANCE ANALYSIS OF FRENCH ELECTORAL DATA FOR 1956*

Proportion of Electors from Middle Classes	Proportion of Industrial Workers		
	Less than 15.4%	Between 15.5 and 22.4%	More than 22.5%
Less than 20.9%	684	143	101
Between 21 and 24.4%	180	129	179
More than 24.5%	106	230	725

* Based on a total of 2,477 cantons. Of the 3,000 cantons in France, 2,477 were chosen for analysis; these are defined as "rural" because they do not contain any city of more than 20,000 inhabitants.

[2] "In order for covariance analysis to apply, certain conditions must be satisfied: normality of distributions, homogeneity of variance . . . " Cf. René Bassoul, "Analyse de covariance et méthodes des résidus en sociologie," *Revue Française de Sociologie, 1* (1960), pp. 445–453.

of them the curve of the distribution was controlled. Since the distribution was normal, it was not necessary to transform it. By the construction of this factorial plan, we have been able to retain a little more than a quarter of the cantons: 900 out of 2,477. If the categories had been multiplied (twelve or fifteen instead of nine), we would have been obliged to retain a smaller sample of cantons. One can see that even with 2,477 cantons, it has not been easy to construct the factorial plan. The alternative is to introduce only one intervening control variable: the proportion of workers in industry, since the proportions of middle-class inhabitants constitute, in the final analysis, only an indicator of urbanization. We could thereby multiply the categories of cantons and conserve the totality of the universe. By doing this, we can expect that the influence of the "social class" variable would be increased.

REGIONAL FACTORIAL PLAN

From the group of 2,477 cantons, we isolated 880, corresponding to the three regions already distinguished in our regression analysis: West (386 cantons), North (165 cantons), and Center (329 cantons). An effort was made to get the best stratified sample, and we have obtained the classification presented in Table 2. For each of the categories, 30 cantons have been retained, which is a total of 270 cantons, less than a quarter of the population (880 cantons).

The analysis has been done by the Control Data 3600 computer of the Centre National de la Recherche Scientifique with a B.M.D. program[3] (analysis of covariance for factorial design). This program

Table 2

REGIONAL FACTORIAL ANALYSIS OF FRENCH ELECTORAL
DATA FOR 1956*

Proportion of Industrial Workers	West	North	Center
Less than 19.9%	274	30	252
Between 20 and 25%	40	30	39
More than 25%	72	105	38
Total	386	165	329

* Based on the population of 880 cantons.

[3] *Biomedical Computer Programs* (Los Angeles: University of California, 1966), pp. 511–524.

furnished a complete analysis of the variance of the religious factor and the political vote, and the covariance between the two.

THE "RE-EMERGENCE" OF SOCIAL CLASS BY COVARIANCE ANALYSIS

By the F test (the relation between the variance of each variable and the residual variance), the different covariance tables indicate the actual effect of each independent variable, observed after the elimination of the religious factor.

It has been confirmed, for rural France in its entirety, that the proportion of electors belonging to the middle classes has no tangible effect on the vote. Thus, as the effects of religion have been neutralized, the "middle class" variable does not appear to have any more weight than in the regression analysis. This is, without doubt, due in part to the imprecise character of this variable, referring as it does to a socially heterogeneous population: all the social categories with the exception of the industrial workers and persons occupied in agriculture.

On the other hand, covariance analysis indicates for the working class a degree of influence which was not fully recognized by multiple regression analysis. All of the Snedecor F are significant, and they are higher for the Communist vote than for the group of leftist parties. Covariance analysis does not contribute anything really new on this point, but it assigns a greater significance to such phenomena than does regression analysis.

By regression analysis we have obtained a correlation coefficient of .28 between the percentage of industrial workers and the proportion of Communist votes in the legislative elections of 1956; a coefficient of .21 between workers and Communist-Socialist votes; and a coefficient of .13 between workers and votes for the Left (Communist, Socialist, and Radical). For the covariance analysis the F is respectively: 19.6, 9.79, and 3.90.

Covariance analysis has permitted not only a clearer perception of the role of the working class in the determination of the vote, but also the measurement of the differentiated influence of this variable on the Communist, Socialist, and Radical votes.

The effect of the interaction of the two variables (workers and middle classes) cannot be established at the level of rural France as a whole. If the combination of these two variables has no influence on the vote, one can rightfully conclude that the variable "population occupied in agriculture," which is the complement of the other two, also does not exercise any perceptible influence on the political attitudes at the level of aggregate data on the national scale. (The influence of the religious factor has, of course, been neutralized.)

It is by introducing the nominal variable "region" that covariance analysis assumes its greatest significance. In effect, "region" influences the three dependent variables much more than the working-class variable. This result brings out clearly the importance of social context. It has been found that the influence of the working-class proportion is not only weaker than the influence of region, but also, for each region, weaker than the weight of the working-class variable established for all of rural France. In other words, the proportion of workers influences the proportion of Communist, Socialist, or Radical votes less in the regional contexts than for all of France. In the regional framework, the working class exercises a greater influence on the combined Communist-Socialist vote than on the Communist vote alone. In compensation, the effect is nil for the total of leftist votes. This last fact is easily explained by the great number of small farmers and electors belonging to the middle classes who vote Radical.

The interaction of the working-class and region variables exercises an influence on the Communist and the Left votes. This signifies that, in addition to the respective effects of region and class, there is a specific effect that results from the interaction of these two variables.

In short, if the religious factor is held constant, the regions maintain their distinct characters, a fact which demonstrates very well the importance of social and political context.

GRAPHIC REPRESENTATION OF THE COVARIANCE ANALYSIS

Covariance analysis permits the calculation for each of the dependent political variables, and in each of the categories distinguished by the plan of analysis, a new mean that one can call a "corrected mean" after the elimination (or rather the neutralization) of the effect of religious practice.

For each of the dependent political variables it is possible to represent graphically:

1. The effects of each of the two independent variables retained in the factorial plan before (that is, at the level of variance) and after (at the level of covariance) the neutralization of the religious variable.

2. The effects of the two variables with and without the religious factor. There is no doubt that the construction of such graphs is

meaningful only if one can establish by means of covariance analysis a significant effect for one of the two variables or their interaction. Those significant results, tested by the F of Snedecor, are reassembled in Table 3.

The resulting statistics confirm our hypotheses:

1. Liberated from the effects of the religious "supervariable," social class intervenes in a very positive manner for rural France as a whole. This is just what we expected. In effect, regression analysis poses a problem. Thus, for the Communist vote we have been able to establish that the multiple correlation coefficient with the independent variables of "religious practice" and "industrial workers" was .64, whereas the correlation coefficient with the single religious variable was .59, and it fell to .25 for the "worker" variable. This divergence was verified for all the political variables. Apparently, the preponderance of the religious factor concealed, at the ecological level, the effect of social class. Although the correlation coefficients between these two variables are weak, one can suppose that there is a certain interaction between them which produces a confusion of effects.

By holding the religious factor constant, the variations in the vote for the different proportions of workers are accentuated. Certainly the differences between the results of variance analysis and those of covariance analysis are not considerable, but it is necessary to emphasize that even before the religious variable was neutralized, the variations of the vote according to the proportion of workers was also weak. They

Table 3

COVARIANCE F TEST

	$PC*$	PC and $SFIO*$	$Total\ Left**$
Rural France:			
Middle classes	—	—	—
Workers	19.60	9.79	3.90
Interaction	—	—	—
Regional Analysis:			
Region	19.39	50.84	20.04
Workers	10.39	11.52	—
Interaction	4.30	—	6.76

* PC is the Communist Party and SFIO the Socialist Party in France.
** Communist, Socialist, and Radical Parties.

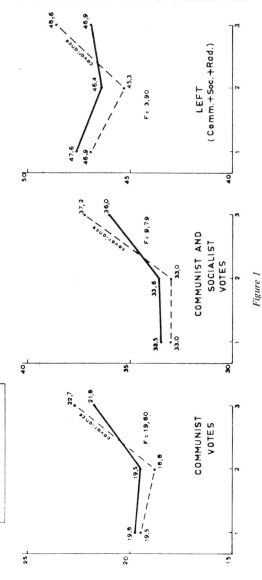

Figure 1

"Liberation" of the Effect of Social Class on the Vote after Neutralization of Religious Incidence (Rural France)

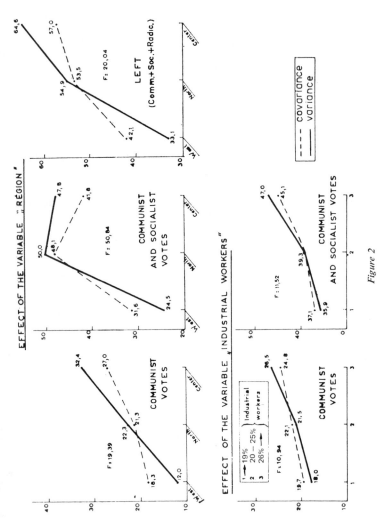

Figure 2

REGIONAL CONTEXTS AFTER NEUTRALIZATION OF RELIGIOUS INCIDENCE

are 2.3 points for the Communist vote, 4.2 for the Communist-Socialist vote, and 3.3 for the Communist-Socialist-Radical vote. Such differences are significant.

It should also be noted that the curves are perceptibly the same for the three political variables. For the first two levels of workers, the "corrected" mean is always weaker than the normal mean. In other words, with "religiosity" equal, the proportion of Communist, Communist-Socialist, or leftist votes in those cantons with few workers is clearly weaker. The religious factor weighs heavily on political behavior: where religious practice is strong, it constitutes a dam for the parties of the left; where it is weak, these political tendencies are free to develop. The first two levels in the proportion of workers are essentially represented in the agricultural cantons. Here the Communist, Socialist or Radical vote is always bound up with dechristianization. It is clear that the religious factor is more important in an agricultural milieu than in an industrial milieu. This appeared even in the regression analysis, since the correlation between the Communist vote and religious practice was .66 for the cantons in which the active population was more than 75 per cent agricultural, whereas it was only .59 for the less agricultural cantons (less than 25 per cent of the people occupied in agriculture).

The fact that with the religious variable constant the leftist vote is weaker in those areas in which there are few workers, and stronger in those areas in which workers are numerous, provides evidence of the sociopolitical context of the leftist vote everywhere.

2. The "region" variable remains the most important even after the elimination of the influence of religion. Thus, because of the significance attributed to the religious factor in the regression analysis, it seems that the regional differences are based upon the different levels of religious practice; the notion of context may be considered as a "regionalization" of religious practice.

Although the elimination of the religious factor reabsorbed some of the differences between the three regions, the strong contrasts remain. The regional context is certainly determined by the religious factor, but it is not confined to this single factor. Regional context is not unidimensional. As regression analysis has shown and covariance analysis has confirmed, the social and political context is a very complex phenomenon. Subsequent investigation, in particular "contextual surveys," will enable us to differentiate its components better.

It can be seen that the contours of the curves in the graphs are the same. The elimination of religion has appreciably augmented the means of the different political variables for the West, where religion is strong.

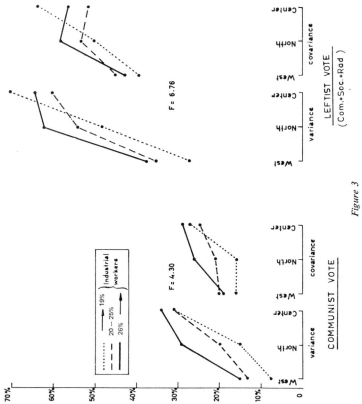

Figure 3

INTERACTION OF THE VARIABLES "WORKERS" AND "REGIONS" IN REGIONAL CONTEXTS

It scarcely intervenes for the North, the region of moderate religious practice, and it significantly lowers the vote for the parties of the Left in the dechristianized Center.

In other words, if the level of religious practice were the sams for all of France, the West would vote more for the leftist parties and the Center less, but the two regions would remain politically distinct.

In the regional framework, social class clearly plays a lesser role if religion is eliminated. In other words, it seems that in the different regions, there was a very clear interaction between the religious factor and the social class factor. The social variable has its role, but to a large degree only if the religious variable permits. In this sense, religion serves as a kind of catalyst.

Table 4

SOCIAL CLASS AND POLITICAL PARTIES
COVARIANCE ANALYSIS FOR ENTIRE RURAL FRANCE

(Elections of 1956)

1. Variance of Religious Practice

Source of Variation	Degrees of Freedom	Sum of Squares	Mean Squares	F
Middle class	2	13,304	6,652	15.5*
Workers (industrial)	2	4,735	2,367	5.51**
Interaction	4	2,053	513	1.19
Residual	891	382,341	429	
Total	899	402,435	447	

2. Variance of the Communist Vote

Source of Variation	Degrees of Freedom	Sum of Squares	Mean Squares	F
Middle class	2	1,200	600	4.98**
Workers (industrial)	2	1,001	500	4.15***
Interaction	4	89	22	1
Residual	891	107,250	120	
Total	899	109,542		

* Significant at 1 per 1,000.
** Significant at 1 per cent.
*** Significant at 5 per cent.

Table 4 (continued)

3. *Covariance between Religious Practice and the Communist Vote*

Source of Variation	Degrees of Freedom	Sum of Squares	Mean Squares	F
Middle class	2	265	132	1.642
Workers	2	2,720	1,360	16.9*
Interaction	4	267	66	1
Residual	890	71,760	80	

4. *Variance of the Communist and Socialist Vote*

Source of Variation	Degrees of Freedom	Sum of Squares	Mean Squares	F
Middle class	2	1,658	829	3.37***
Workers (industrial)	2	1,048	524	2.13
Interaction	4	115	28	1
Residual	891	218,818	245	
Total	899	221,639	246	

5. *Covariance between Religious Practice and the Communist and Socialist Vote*

Source of Variation	Degrees of Freedom	Sum of Squares	Mean Squares	F
Middle class	2	215	107	1
Workers (industrial)	2	3,478	1,739	9.79*
Interaction	4	342	85	1
Residual	890	159,075	177	

6. *Variance of the Vote of the Left (Communist, Socialist, and Radical)*

Source of Variation	Degrees of Freedom	Sum of Squares	Mean Squares	F
Middle class	2	2,811	1,405	4.19***
Workers (industrial)	2	205	102	1
Interaction	4	393	98	1
Residual	891	298,798	335	
Total	899	302,208	336	

7. *Covariance belween Religious Practice and the Vote of the Left*

Source of Variation	Degrees of Freedom	Sum of Squares	Mean Squares	F
Middle class	2	192	96	1
Workers (industrial)	2	1,649	824	3.90***
Interaction	4	177	44	1
Residual	890	187,888	211	

* Significant at 1 per 1,000.
** Significant at 1 per cent.
*** Significant at 5 per cent.

Table 5

SOCIAL CLASS POLITICAL PARTIES AND REGIONAL CONTEXT

1. Variance of Religious Practice

Source of Variation	Degrees of Freedom	Sum of Squares	Mean Squares	F
Regions	2	58,033	29,016	162.66*
Workers	2	4,852	2,426	13.60*
Interaction	4	1,236	309	1.73
Residual	261	46,558	178	
Total	269	110,681	411	

2. Variance of the Communist Vote

Source of Variation	Degrees of Freedom	Sum of Squares	Mean Squares	F
Regions	2	18,599	9,299	142.89*
Workers	2	3,164	1,582	24.31*
Interaction	4	902	225	3.46**
Residual	261	16,985	65	
Total	269	39,650	147	

3. Covariance between Religious Practice and the Communist Vote

Source of Variation	Degrees of Freedom	Sum of Squares	Mean Squares	F
Regions	2	1,781	890	19.39*
Workers	2	1,005	502	10.94*
Interaction	4	790	197	4.00**
Residual	260	11,940	45	

4. Variance of the Communist and Socialist Votes

Source of Variation	Degrees of Freedom	Sum of Squares	Mean Squares	F
Regions	2	32,693	16,346	148.44*
Workers	2	5,011	2,505	22.75*
Interaction	4	708	177	1.60
Residual	261	28,741	110	
Total	269	67,153	249	

* Significant at 1 per 1,000.
** Significant at 1 per cent.
*** Significant at 5 per cent.

Table 5 (continued)

5. *Covariance between Religious Practice and the Communist and Socialist Vote*

Source of Variation	Degrees of Freedom	Sum of Squares	Mean Squares	F
Regions	2	8,807	4,403	50.84*
Workers	2	1,997	998	11.52*
Interaction	4	593	148	1.71
Residual	260	22,518	86	

6. *Variance of the Vote of the Left (Communist, Socialist, and Radical)*

Source of Variation	Degrees of Freedom	Sums of Squares	Mean Squares	F
Regions	2	46,691	23,345	144.03*
Workers	2	1,859	929	5.73**
Interaction	4	4,273	1,068	6.59*
Residual	261	42,302	162	
Total	269	95,127	353	

7. *Covariance between Religious Practice and the Vote of the Left*

Source of Variation	Degrees of Freedom	Sums of Squares	Mean Squares	F
Regions	2	4,953	2,476	20.04*
Workers	2	237	118	1
Interaction	4	3,346	836	6.76*
Residual	260	32,131	123	

* Significant at 1 per 1,000.
** Significant at 1 per cent.
*** Significant at 5 per cent.

PART FOUR

Factor Analysis and
Ecological Typologies

This part goes one step further in technical refinement and presents a variety of examples of the use of factor analysis in the handling of multiple data files for territorial units. Techniques for the extraction of common factors from multivariate correlation matrices were originally developed by differential psychologists but have since been found useful in the treatment of a wide variety of other social science data. In his opening paper the Swedish ecologist Carl-Gunnar Janson shows the extraordinary range of uses found for these techniques in the study of urban structure. This is the field where the factor analytic techniques have so far proved most useful in the mapping of dimensions of ecological variation. Janson does, it is true, point to a few factor analytic studies of variations across wider ranges of local communities — rural, suburban, as well as urban — but so far most of the work in this field has made use of simpler statistical procedures such as regression analysis and analysis of variance. It is indeed significant that all the examples of ecological factor analysis assembled in this volume focus on variations among areas within metropolitan cities: the availability of extensive files of statistics for very small units of territory offers great temptations to the factor analyst and opens up intriguing possibilities of theory construction. Three of the papers deal with one of the largest metropolitan areas in the world: Greater London. The geographer Kevin Cox analyzes the distribution of votes in the London suburbs, and the sociologist Peter Norman and the mathematician Nigel Howard report on progress in the development of factor analytical typologies of census tracts in London. The fourth paper, by the American urban sociologist Frank Sweetser, opens up a comparative perspective: he reports on a study of the ecological structure of two historically and topographically very different cities, Boston and Helsinki, and points to interesting similarities and contrasts.

In the discussions of these papers at the symposium at Evian, a number of participants felt very uneasy about factor analysis as a method: one of them went so far as to characterize factor analysis as a "sledgehammer approach," while others called for further tests of the interpretation of the factors extracted through the rotation of the matrices.

There was consensus, however, that factor analysis constituted a powerful tool in the initial mapping of the covariations in large data files and could serve admirably in the construction of typologies of ecological contexts: in fact, there was general agreement that principal component procedures of the type used in the London study ought to be introduced wherever possible as a basis for the construction of sampling frames for "ecological surveys."

We are still far from any general consensus on optimal strategies in ecological research. The factor analysts have made important contributions and will, no doubt, go still further as the large-scale computers allow more and more complex analyses. But it is also clear that the results of factor analysis will be easier to interpret if they are subject to further treatment through broader batteries of statistical techniques. Kevin Cox's study is of particular interest in this perspective: he first proceeds by factor analysis and then checks some of his findings through the testing of a causal model along the lines of the Blalock-Boudon schema. This would seem to be a procedure well worth testing on a variety of ecological data.

12

CARL-GUNNAR JANSON

Some Problems of
Ecological Factor Analysis

1. BRIEF REVIEW OF FACTOR ANALYSES IN
HUMAN ECOLOGY

1.1. Introduction

Recently factor analysis has been much in demand within human ecology and has almost become a controversial fad. Although there are a few early examples, even before World War II, the bulk of ecological factor analyses belong to the latest ten or fifteen years.

Naturally, the short review of ecological factor analytical studies given here is intended not as a comprehensive bibliography but as a highly selected series of illustrative examples, the selection being made with a heavy Scandinavian, American, sociological, and egocentric bias. However, the review is intended to illustrate the kinds of applications of factor analysis to ecological problems and the kinds of results they have produced. The technical solutions employed and the problems involved will be discussed in later sections.

From the areal units the analyses are divided in two categories: (1) those concerned with variations within communities, actually intra-city variations, that is, aspects of urban spatial structure, and (2) those concerned with variations among communities or other units, such as communes, counties, and countries, that is, intercity variations and regional structure in a broad sense. Within each category studies may concentrate on a specific variable or aspect or be of a more general kind.

It should be pointed out that "factor analysis" in this paper is taken to include also "component analysis."

1.2. *Factor Analyses of Urban Spatial Structure*

1.2.1. *Studies Concentrating on Specific Aspects.* Some factor analyses of spatial urban patterns concentrate on, or pay special attention to, a specific variable or aspect, often delinquency and crime, following an old sociological tradition. However, also other aspects have been treated.

Back in the 1930's Gosnell and Schmidt (1936) made a factor analysis of 17 voting or environmental variables in Chicago. Later Holzinger and Harman picked 8 of the variables of this study to give one of their well-known examples, in this case of the principal factor solution, with "Traditional Democratic Vote" as the first of two principal factors (Holzinger and Harman 1941, pp. 177–179, oblique solution on pp. 260 f.; cf. Harman 1960, pp. 177–179, 287 f., 332 f.).

A recent example of an ecological factor analytical study of voting within an urban community is provided by Cox (1966). He was interested in the political differences between suburbs and central city. He used 20 demographic, housing, socioeconomic, and migration variables assumed to be politically relevant for 69 areal units of the London metropolitan area in 1951. In a preliminary stage to further analysis Cox extracted 4 principal components accounting for 89.2 per cent of the total variance of the matrix. After rotation to new orthogonal dimensions according to the varimax principle, the factors were named "Social Rank," "Suburban–Central City," "Commuting," and "Age." Measures of them were computed and used as variables in a linear regression causal model of the Simon-Blalock type (cf., e.g., Blalock, 1961, Chap. 3) together with "Participation" and "Conservative Vote" variables, which were not included in the matrix analyzed.

In 1964 Wiseman and Warburton reported three factor analyses of educational and environmental variables from 1951 and 1957 in the Manchester area, using wards or schools as units. The first analysis of the 1951 data in 26 wards in Manchester used 6 educational and 10 environmental variables. Four orthogonal factors were extracted and rotated according to the quartimax method. After rotation they contributed 32.5 per cent, 19.1 per cent, 9.3 per cent, and 8.4 per cent, respectively, of the total variance. The first three factors were interpreted in order, as a genetic (*sic!*) factor of social "Disorganization," "Economic Background," and "Lack of Parental (or Maternal) Care." Three measures of intellectual and educational backwardness were heavily loaded on the first factor. The second analysis used the same 6 educational variables and 6 environmental ones for 48 schools in Salford. It resulted in three rotated orthogonal factors, contributing 24, 18, and 7 per cent, respectively, of the total variance. They were interpreted as

"Socioeconomic Status," "School Atmosphere," and "Good Teaching Conditions," with backwardness now closely related to the second factor. The third analysis concerned the 1957 data, employed 9 educational and 20 environmental variables, and gave 6 rotated orthogonal factors with a total contribution of 77 per cent and with the educational loadings mostly in the first factor, "General Educational-Social," and next in factors of "Lack of Maternal Care," psychological, and physical, respectively (Wiseman, 1964).

Lander (1954, Chap. 5) in a well-known study on Baltimore data made a factor analysis of juvenile delinquency and seven presumably criminologically relevant variables. From two centroid factors accounting for 94.7 per cent of the total variance he got two rather strongly correlated (0.68) factors, which he interpreted as "Socioeconomic" and "Anomic" factors, with delinquency belonging to the anomically loaded variables.

Bordua (1959) in a similar study of juvenile delinquency in Detroit used 11 variables and extracted three orthogonal factors accounting for 74.4 per cent of the total variance. The first factor was said to describe "clearly deteriorated areas of high nonwhite settlement." The second factor was interpreted as "Socioeconomic Status" and the third one as a "Poverty and Social Disorganization" factor. Juvenile delinquency was loaded almost equally but not very strongly on the first and the third factors.

Chilton (1964) re-examined Lander's and Bordua's variables and added data of his own from Indianapolis. The same 8 variables were analyzed in each city, with principal factors and varimax rotation of four factors, covering around 90 per cent of the total variances. In each case "Delinquency" had its heaviest loading on the same factor as "Owner-Occupied Dwelling Units," one of the measures of "Anomie." There was some support of an Anomic factor in Baltimore but not much of it in the other cities. Also, further variables as measures of "Socioeconomic" and "Anomic" factors were added in Detroit (2 variables) and Indianapolis (2 and 11 variables) and the extended matrices of 10, 10, and 19 variables, respectively, were analyzed. Clear anomic factors, as distinct from socioeconomic ones, did not emerge. The factors with a high loading on "Delinquency" also had marked socioeconomic elements.

When the data given by Sainsbury (1955) were divided in two similar sets of 11 and 12 variables, respectively, two slightly correlated factors were extracted from matrices of rank correlations, when boroughs were used as units. The factors corresponded roughly to Lander's factors, but this time "Juvenile Delinquency," which was included in both sets, belonged more to the socioeconomic group of variables (Janson, 1960).

In Helsinki, Grönholm (1960) analyzed seven indices of disorganization and six other background variables with the 21 city wards as units. By the centroid method he got three factors, which he rotated graphically to new orthogonal factors, covering 71 per cent of the total variance. Juvenile delinquency had some loadings on each of them. The highest one, although rather modest (0.59), was on the first factor, which Grönholm interpreted as an "Urbanization" or "Metropolitan" factor, not to be confused with the Shevky-Bell "Urbanization" but here connected with shunning of work, suicide, mental disorder, nonresidential buildings, loneliness, and divorce. The second factor was clearly connected with "Socioeconomic Status," while the third one was ambiguous, with loadings on loneliness, poverty, and divorce.

Ecological studies of delinquency and crime usually deal with the residential distribution of the offenders, not with the distribution of places where offenses were committed. Recently, however, Schmid (1960) analyzed the distribution of crime against property, including robbery, and of suicide, according to places of occurrence, together with the residential distribution of drunkenness, disorderly conduct, vagrancy, and sex offenses. His data refer to Seattle around 1950. He used 20 crime variables and 18 social, economic, and demographic variables for 93 census tracts. Eight principal factors were extracted and rotated orthogonally. They accounted for 86.6 per cent of the total variance. One factor was ambiguous. Six others were interpreted by means of the "background" variables, although two of them, "Low Family and Economic Status" and "Population Mobility," had their highest weights on crime variables. Residential crime variables dominated the former factor, occurrence variables the latter one. Two occurrence variables had substantial loadings on the "Race" factor, and there were scattered crime weights on "Low Family Status" and the ambiguous factor, whereas "Low Occupational Status" and "Low Mobility Groups" had small crime weights only. Finally one factor with three crime weights had no weights on background variables and was labeled "Atypical Crime Pattern."

Boggs (1965) analyzed 17 crime occurrence and criminal offender rates in St. Louis (1960). She discussed four orthogonal varimax rotated factors which accounted for 70 per cent of the total variance.

1.2.2. *General Factor Analyses.* More general factor analyses have also been published. Some of them have taken the Shevky-Bell conceptual scheme or typology as their point of departure. (The Shevky-Bell scheme was first published in Shevky and Williams, 1949; for a later version, see Shevky and Bell, 1955). The scheme was supported by a cluster analysis of the San Francisco Bay Region by Tryon (1955) and by factor analyses of the same region and of Los Angeles by Bell (1955).

Both analyses of the seven component variables resulted in three oblique factors with correlations consistent with the scheme. One factor had considerable loadings on the three components of "economic status" but small weights on the other variables; the others had high loadings only on the "family status" components and the "ethnic status" measure, respectively. Thus they were easily identified as the three dimensions of the scheme.

Anderson and Bean (1961) analyzed the six components, rent excluded, of the three dimensional measures together with seven other variables in Toledo, Ohio, with 55 census tracts as units. They extracted four centroid factors, which after rotation to simple structure were interpreted according to the Shevky-Bell scheme with the exception that "urbanization" was divided into two dimensions, called "Urbanization" and "Family Status," the latter with a high weight on the fertility ratio only. The factors together accounted for 82.6 per cent of the total variance and were kept orthogonal, as oblique rotations were no improvement.

In another study the six components of the scheme's three dimensions, rent again excluded, were factor-analyzed in ten cities. The multiple group method was used for factorizing. For each city the factor matrix was rotated to a least-squares approximation of a matrix according to the Shevky-Bell scheme. In four Southern or border state cities "Fertility" could be equally well or better fitted to "Social Rank" as compared to "Urbanization." In Providence, the same was true for "One-Family-Dwelling Units." Moreover, the correlations between "Segregation" and the other oblique dimensions varied somewhat between cities (Van Arsdol, Jr., Camilleri, and Schmid, 1958).

Additional studies have approached the urban structure in other frames of references, such as Schmid and Tagashira (1964) in analyzing Seattle. Sets of 42, 21, 12, and 10 variables were used, a larger set containing all smaller ones. A considerable amount of redundancy in the largest set was gradually reduced in the smaller sets. Various numbers of principal factors were extracted and rotated according to a modified varimax criterion. Eight factors of the largest set accounted for 88.0 per cent of the total variance, but not all of them were easily interpreted. The first three sets yielded four clearly defined factors, "Family Status," "Economic Status," "Ethnic Status," and "Maleness," of which the latter was eliminated in the fourth set. Other factors varied or were not easily interpretable. Finally, measures of the three main factors were computed, mapped, and discussed.

Sweetser analyzed Helsinki and Metropolitan Boston thoroughly and reported the results in a series of papers. He used principal factors, but computed them with communality estimates, and varimax rotation to new orthogonal dimensions.

First, sets of twenty variables were prepared in Helsinki with 70 areal units and in Metropolitan Boston with 441 units and made as similar as possible. A second set in Helsinki had 6 variables in common with the basic Finnish set and 14 substitute variables. The two Helsinki sets resulted in three dimensions that, in order of importance, were labeled "Socioeconomic Status," "Progeniture" or "Young Familism," and "Urbanism" in both cases. The loadings were very similar for the sets, with coefficients of congruence (Harman, 1960, p. 257) of 0.995, 0.933, and 0.902, respectively, for the three factors. Also the Boston matrix produced three dimensions, which were correspondingly named. The congruence between the Helsinki basic set and the Boston set was substantial but clearly less than between the two Finnish matrices, particularly in the loadings of "Urbanism," with coefficients of congruence of 0.744, 0.792, and 0.480, respectively, for the factors. In Boston, "Urbanism" was associated with surplus of men and with housing defects but in Helsinki with surplus of women and with lack of housing defects (Sweetser, 1965a).

Then, in Helsinki a set of 42 variables, containing 17 of the basic set variables, was compared with the basic set. After the rotation of seven principal factors the six strongest ones were interpreted. They accounted for 76.4 per cent of the total variance of the larger set. "Socioeconomic Status" remained the most important dimension, "Progeniture" the second strongest with approximately unchanged loadings. "Urbanism" now corresponded to a "Career Women" dimension. A fourth dimension of "Residentialism" was similar to a possible fourth dimension of the smaller set of variables. Coefficients of congruence for the four factors were 0.998, 0.932, 0.931, and 0.826. Two dimensions from the later stages of the family cycle, "Established Familism" and "Postgeniture," were added (Sweetser, 1965b).

In Boston, a 34-variable set was analyzed. It was similar to the larger Finnish set but had less redundancy and included some variables concerning families; day population and land use were excluded, but measures of income and migration were added. Again six dimensions were taken out, with "Socioeconomic Status" as the most important one. The next to strongest factor was interpreted as "Familism." There were also two dimensions of migration and two ethnic ones called "Irish middle class" and "Nonwhite/Italian" (Sweetser, 1965c).

Comparing the large-set analyses, Sweetser finds matching dimensions of socioeconomic status, child-centered familism, and residential status. The Boston "Familism" factor then corresponds to "Progeniture" and "Established Familism," the Helsinki "Residentialism" factor to the two migration factors. There are also distinctive factors, "Career Women" and "Postgeniture" in Helsinki and the ethnicity dimensions in Boston (Sweetser, 1966).

Factor scores of the six Helsinki factors were computed and their spatial distribution examined. A mainly sectorial pattern was found for "Socioeconomic Status," mainly zonal patterns in the others with sectorial tendencies also for "Progeniture" and "Residentialism" (Sweetser, 1966).

As seen in his paper in this volume, Sweetser (1968) also studied the factors involved in zones and sectors of Helsinki and Boston. In an earlier paper differential change in importance of factors in suburb and core also was studied for Boston 1950–1960 (Sweetser, 1964).

In Copenhagen, Pedersen analyzed sets with 14 variables each, referring to 1950 and 1960. Three orthogonal dimensions, interpreted as "Urbanization," "Socioeconomic Status," and "Growth and Change" were found to account for 84 to 92 per cent of the total variances of the matrices, partly because of a limited and somewhat redundant selection of variables (Pedersen, 1967).

In a study of the City of Newark, New Jersey, six orthogonal (principal) dimensions accounted for 71.4 per cent of the total variance of 48 demographic, social, economic, housing, location, and land use variables. After varimax rotation the strongest dimension was interpreted as a "Segregation" or "Racial Slum" dimension, another one as "Social Rank," whereas two further dimensions were related to the middle stages of the family cycle and tentatively called "Residentialism" or "Familism" and "Middle Age." Two weak dimensions were labeled "Mobility" and "Density." Factor scores were computed. Within the central city the familism, social rank, segregation, and density dimensions showed concentric tendencies, whereas sectorial tendencies were seen mostly in the social rank dimension but to some extent also in the segregation, middle age, and density aspects of the structure (Janson, 1968).

Several factor analytical studies of the urban spatial pattern have recently been reported or are under way, for example, of Manhattan

(Carey, 1966). The Center for Urban Studies in London has been analyzing London and other British cities according to the 1961 Census of
Population and Housing, as could be read in Norman's paper in this
volume (Norman, 1968). The component analysis used in a preliminary
step toward a multiple classification of urban areal units means a
further development and an application on another problem of the
classificatory techniques referred to here in the next section (see also
Scott, 1964). The British Inter-Universities Census Tract Committee
has co-ordinated factor analytical and classificatory studies of other
British conurbations, such as Southampton, Merseyside, and South-East
Lancashire (Gittus, 1964).

The biggest Swedish cities are now being studied by the Swedish
Building Research Institute, Stockholm.

1.3. *Intercity and Regional Factor Analyses*

1.3.1. *Studies Concentrating on Specific Aspects.* Just as some analyses
concentrated on the intracity variation of specific variables, the variation
of special phenomena between other areal units has been studied by
factor analytical methods. Perhaps Hofstaetter's (1952) reanalysis of
Thorndike's *Your City* (1939) can be included among this type of studies,
as its 23 variables concentrated on the specific aspect of "goodness" or
"moral integration" in intercity variation. Of works using other units,
Cattell's study (1949) of nations may be mentioned.

Olsen and Garb (1965) selected ten American states with a relatively
high level of per capita income, industrialization, and technologically
advanced agriculture for a factor analysis of 49 variables, mostly of an
economic character. The analysis was compared with another one of the
same variables for the ten states of the American "South," thus providing a means for describing the South in comparison to the ten first
"standard" states. Five centroid factors were used in the comparisons
after quartimax rotation. In the standard states "Urbanization" and
"Suburbanization" were the most important factors, of which the second one was virtually absent in the South. There "Urbanization" and
a factor representing the presence of a lower-income group of unskilled
labor were the strongest factors.

Some regional factor analyses of the specific aspect type specialize in
political behavior. Recently the factor analytical approach has been
tried out rather extensively in this field. As non-American examples,
the Finnish studies by Allardt (1964*a* and *b*) may be mentioned. There
the regional distribution of Communist votes was analyzed with communes as units. The communes were divided into five categories. Cities

and towns constituted one category, whereas the rural communes made up the other four types: those with Swedish-speaking population, southern and western communes, eastern communes, and communes in northern Finland. For each set of communes 37 normalized social and political variables were analyzed. Seven principal factors were extracted in each case and rotated according to an oblique method invented by Ahmavaara and Markkanen. Also, centroid factors were computed and rotated according to the varimex principle to new orthogonal factors. The two solutions gave mutually consistent results. In the North, but not in the other areas, Communist strength was found to be associated with social change and insecurity. This result supports the view of "Backwoods Communism" as a reaction to alienation. (For Finnish regional studies see also Allardt and Riihinen, 1966).

In Sweden, Janson (1961, pp. 216 f.) used the 28 Swedish constituencies in an analysis of Social Democratic and Communist vote in 1948 and 20 normalized social, economic, and demographic variables by means of the centroid method. Three factors were extracted and slightly rotated.

Original approaches are provided by Alker, Jr. (1964), and by MacRae and Meldrum (1968) in this volume. Alker analyzed roll calls in the UN General Assembly 1961–1962 separately for economically developed countries and underdeveloped countries and for all countries together. (See also Alker, 1966.) MacRae and Meldrum use deviations from election and county means in various Illinois elections as variables in principal factor analysis on a county basis to reveal "critical elections."

1.3.2. *General Factor Analyses.* Another series of studies, however, aim at a general descriptive and/or classificatory scheme for areal units with the factors as basic descriptive dimensions. Often the units are cities, for which factor analysis offers an alternative approach to the usual aprioristic, geographical, and economic classification systems for cities according to functional criteria.

As early as 1942, Price analyzed 15 variables for 93 cities. Applying Thurstone's centroid method, he extracted four factors, which after rotation were interpreted as "Population Size," "Occupational Structure" (service center if there is no industry), "Level of Living," and "Per Capita Trade Volume."

Kaplan (1958) sampled 370 out of 484 cities with over 25,000 population in the United States. Two analyses were made, employing the centroid method. First, 10 variables expressed in absolute numbers — that is, not proportions, means, or ratios — were analyzed together with 22 variables expressed as relative numbers. Five factors resulted, the first of which was obviously a "Total Population Size" dimension. Then "population size" and the 22 relative variables of the first set were analyzed together with 24 other variables of the same relative type. In addition to size the variables concerned demographic, social, economic, educational, locational, occupational, housing, administrative, and other conditions. Four factors rather closely corresponding to the four remaining dimensions of the first analysis resulted. They were labeled "Socioeconomic Status," "Population Stability," "Ethnic and Racial Homogeneity and Strong Residential Area Orientation," and "Age-Sex Structure" dimensions. Kaplan then went on to measure the dimensions by means of simple scales with the highest loaded variables as items; thus he could list the cities characterized by the various combinations of factor scores. Many categories of the list showed marked regional homogeneity.

Hadden and Borgatta (1965) carried out eight analyses of 644 out of 674 cities of the United States with 25,000 or greater population in 1960. The 65 variables measured population size and changes, other demographic, economic, educational, occupational, housing, functional, locational, and regional aspects, most variables being percentages, means, or values per capita. One analysis covered all cities, but the cities were also divided into categories according to size or metropolitan status and separate analyses made for each category. According to size the cities were classified as "town-cities" below 50,000, "small cities" between 50,000 and 75,000, "intermediate cities" of 75,000 to 150,000, and "large cities" over 150,000. Of 679 listed cities the categories contained 344, 150, 106, and 79, respectively. The three remaining analyses concerned 246 "central cities" (that is, "principal political or administratively defined cities" in Urbanized Areas or Standard Metropolitan Statistical Areas of the 1960 census), 227 "suburbs" in such areas, and 171 "independent cities."

In each analysis 15 principal factors, accounting for at least 90 per cent of the total variance, were isolated and rotated according to the varimax criterion. Six of the dimensions were given parallel interpretations in all analyses, although there were some, mostly minor, variations in loadings between analyses. The dimensions were named "Socioeconomic Status Level," "Age Composition," "Educational Center," "Residential Mobility," "Population Density," and "Wholesale Concentration." Four more dimensions, "Total Population," "Manufacturing Concentration," "Durable Manufacturing Concentration," and an unnamed dimension pivoted by "Percent employed in public administration," were identified in all but one analysis, whereas "Non-white," "Communication Center," and a dimension pivoted by "Percent in high school" were missing in two analyses.

Finally the profiles of cities were represented as deciles on two composite indices and ten single variables, selected as measures or part measures of dimensions or, in one case, as a theoretically important variable, which was split into several factors.

Moser and Scott (1961) analyzed 57 variables for 157 English and Welsh administratively defined cities having at least 50,000 inhabitants in 1951. The variables covered the fields of population size and structure, population change, households and housing, economic character, social class, voting, health, and education. Four principal components accounted for 60.4 per cent of the total variance. They were interpreted as "Social Class," "Population Change between 1931 and 1951," "Population Change between 1951 and 1958," and "Overcrowding."

The cities were grouped after their factor scores into homogeneous categories. This multiple classification resulted in 14 groups which contained all but two towns, London being one of them. Three groups, totaling 36 cities, were mainly resorts and administrative and commercial centers; five groups, composed of 65 cities, were mainly industrial towns; the remaining six groups held 54 suburbs and suburban-type towns. (For a further development of the technique of multiple classification by Howard, see the paper by Norman in this volume.) Berry (1966) mentioned a classificational study of Indian cities by Ahmad.

Factor analysis of countries and other areal units and subsequent multiple classification has been used to delineate regions of various kinds (cf. Berry, 1966, for a review). From a purely technical standpoint, however, factor analysis is not necessary to precede a multiple classification but may be used to facilitate the grouping or for theoretical reasons. An interesting variant of analysis employed to delineate regions is to use the $n(n-1)$ pairs of areal units as cases and let the variables measure contacts, flows, or interactions between units (Berry, 1966).

Basic dimensions have been developed by means of factor analysis also for units other than cities. Gouldner and Peterson (1964) analyzed 59 variables from the Yale Cross-Cultural Files for 71 primitive or preindustrial societies. They presented 10 orthogonal and 11 oblique factors, four of which in both sets were, according to expectations, called "Linearity," "Sex Dominance," "Level of Technology," and "Apollonianism" or "Norm-Sending." They also made a second-order analysis of the oblique factors and discussed causal priorities of "Level of Technology" and "Apollonianism" especially.

Counties were analyzed by Jonassen (1961), who used 82 variables describing Ohio's 88 counties. He brought out seven orthogonal factors, accounting for 73 per cent of the total variance. He named the factors "Urbanism," "Welfare," "Influx," "Poverty," "Magni-Complexity," "Educational Effect," and "Proletarianism."

Communes were used as units by Riihinen (1965), who analyzed 26 normalized variables for the 548 Finnish communes. He changed the set of variables somewhat to test the invariance of solutions. Principal factors were used and rotated to two separate orthogonal solutions. In one of these, the first factor was rotated so as to be best interpreted according to the theoretical scheme of the study as "Industrialization" or "Division of Labor." The next three factors were rotated according to the varimax principle. The three factors were labeled "Propensity of Economic Disturbance," "Changes in the Per Capita Income," and "Social Disengagement." In the other solution the varimax principle was applied directly on the first five principal factors, which were then interpreted as "Efficiency of the Population," "Pressure toward Conformity," "Narrowing of Differences in the Per Capita Income," "Expansiveness," and "Efficiency of Organization" or "Centrality." Factor scores were computed for both sets of factors and mapped. In another study Piepponen (1961–1962) analyzed Finnish communes.

In Sweden a pilot study of a small sample of 51 communes was analyzed for three sets of variables. Two sets of 45 and 44 had their variables paired to make them as similar as possible and had five variables in common, whereas the third set contained 73 variables, 38 from the first series, 30 from the second one, besides the five variables held in common. The variables were analyzed both before and after normalization. In the larger set 9 factors were extracted, in the others 10 factors. Six dimensions were identified in all six analyses, one more in five of them, and still one more in all nonnormalized sets (Janson, 1965).

Another study aimed at a descriptive scheme for blocks (and buildings) as depicted on maps of detailed urban plans (Fog, Janson, and Lanesjö, 1965).

1.4. *Summary Description*

Factor analysis has been applied in human ecology both to intracity variation and to regional and intercity variation. On both levels specific aspects have been approached, the emphasis within cities being on delinquency, crime, and other social problems and on political behavior. The latter is often treated on the regional level. More general analyses of urban spatial structure often aim at a descriptive scheme, as do the general analyses of cities and regional variation. There also a classificatory system of some kind is often the purpose of the analysis.

Technically, the analyses use as variables mostly averages, including percentages, and quotas. Absolute numbers occur as variables in some cases. Often analyses now include large sets of variables which were not possible to handle before modern computers were available. Principal factors now are frequently computed even for large matrices. However, centroid factors still occur. Rotation to new, mostly orthogonal, axes is common, often according to the varimax principle. There are several cases of oblique solutions. Sometimes factor scores are calculated, occasionally by rather primitive methods, for further study.

As a rule the interpretations are on a descriptive level, and the analysis aims at generalizations essentially as a kind of empirical concept analysis to give basic descriptive dimensions; that is, the "factors" are not interpreted as causal factors behind the manifest variables but as dimensions in terms of which a structure can be described. By selecting as variables what might be considered partial measures, the dimensionality of one or a few concepts is studied.

2. BASIC ASSUMPTIONS OF THE FACTOR ANALYTICAL APPROACH

2.1. Basic Set of Equations

Factor analysis is based on a set of well-known equations that imply certain assumptions concerning the variables to be analyzed. Technically, there are several ways of arriving at solutions with regard to the parameters of this model. These techniques may impose additional assumptions, because they may apply to special cases only of the general model.

Naturally, the application of the basic model poses certain technical difficulties, as the assumptions must fit the actual data reasonably well both theoretically and operationally.

It should be noted that factor analysis is discussed here, except in a part of Section 2.4., as a descriptive tool, not as a causal model. Here, as in the previous section, "descriptive" includes "inferential" as long as the generalizations aimed at in the analysis are noncausal (cf. Hartley, 1954).

The basic equations of factor analysis and their corollaries may be compactly and elegantly stated in terms of matrix algebra, which also has the additional advantage of not being easily understood by every-body, and thus of giving them almost as high a scientific status as differential equations. However, the points to be made seem clearer, at least to me, if the basic equations are simply stated in terms of elementary algebra.

Thus the basic set of equations may be formulated as

$$x_{ikt} = \sum_{j=1}^{p} a_{ij} f_{jk} + b_i s_{ik} + c_i e_{ikt} \tag{1}$$

where

(a) x_{ikt} means the value for unit k at observation t on the manifest variable x_i, with $i = 1, 2, \ldots, m$, and $k = 1, 2, \ldots, N$

(b) f_{jk} means the value for unit k on a *common* factor f_j, with $j = 1, 2, \ldots, p$, and p being not greater than m and the concept of "common factor" applying to all factors occurring in more than one variable x_i

(c) s_{ik} means the value for unit k on a factor, or latent variable, s_i that is *specific* to variable x_i

(d) e_{ikt} means the value for unit k at observation t on a *random* component e_i of the variable x_i, varying between observations

(e) a_{ij} is the weight of factor f_j in variable x_i; b_i and c_i are the weights of s_i and e_i, respectively, in variable x_i.

Usually the number p of common factors is, at least implicitly, assumed to be only a small fraction of the number m of observed variables, although it might be recognized, for example, in the principal factor model, that formally there are as many factors as there are variables. All random components are always assumed to be mutually independent and independent of all other factors, and all specific variables are always assumed to be mutually uncorrelated and uncorrelated to all other factors. The common factors are assumed to be uncorrelated in orthog-onal models but may be correlated in oblique models. Some models contain no specific factors, that is, the b_i-coefficients are all nought, and the principal factor model has neither specific nor random factors. (For a general description and discussion of factor analytical models, see Harman, 1967, and Lawley and Maxwell, 1963; for a discussion of applications of factor analysis, see Henrysson, 1957.)

For simplicity, all variables and factors are here assumed to be standardized, that is, to have mean 0 and standard deviation 1. If so,

$$\sum_{j=1}^{p} a_{ij}^2 + \sum_{j=1}^{p} \sum_{v=1}^{p} a_{ij}a_{iv}\, r_{f_j f_v} + b_i^2 + c_i^2 = 1 \; (j \neq v) \qquad (2)$$

the first two sums together being the *communality* of the variable x_i, that is, the part of the variance of x_i that can be formally accounted for by the variation of the common factors.

The correlation between the variable x_i and the factor f_j is

$$a_{ij} + \sum_{v=1}^{p} a_{iv} r_{f_j f_v} \; (j \neq v) \qquad (3)$$

and the correlation between the variables x_i and x_u is

$$\sum_{j=1}^{p} a_{ij}a_{uj} + \sum_{j=1}^{p} \sum_{v=1}^{p} a_{ij}a_{uv} r_{f_j f_v} \; (j \neq v,\, i \neq u) \qquad (4)$$

The basic set of equations (1) obviously treats each variable as a function of a set of factors. More specifically, each variable is a weighted sum of factors that are seen as underlying or latent.

2.2. *Relation between Factors*

The common factors, as just mentioned, are either allowed to be correlated, in the oblique models, or assumed to be uncorrelated, in the orthogonal models. The assumption of noncorrelation may be sharpened into an assumption of independence in some orthogonal models.

The use of orthogonal dimensions is very widespread. The orthogonal factors seem rather often to be taken, at least implicitly, to be not only uncorrelated but also independent. It has sometimes been argued that the assumption of independence (or, presumably, also of noncorrelation) of factors is principally unreasonable (cf. Coleman, 1964, pp. 20 f.).

Admittedly, it certainly appears that measures of many theoretically important concepts should be correlated. Thus we frequently seem to have a choice between using oblique dimensions and splitting the corresponding concepts so as to obtain uncorrelated (or perhaps independent) dimensions, transferring common components of the concepts to one dimension and keeping the remaining parts as uncorrelated dimensions. The important questions then are, first, whether or not this gives us meaningful and interpretable conceptual units and, second, whether this provides a useful and illuminating analysis of the concepts. It cannot be decided on an a priori basis only that the second

condition is never fulfilled. On the contrary, some of the analyses
mentioned in Section 2.1 might be used as arguments in the opposite
direction.

Furthermore, the oblique dimensions are complicated by the implicit
assumption of some connections between dimensions, whether or not
this problem is just ignored, treated by means of second-order dimensions, or dealt with in some other way, although this is hardly relevant as
a counterargument as far as the unfeasibility of orthogonal factors is
used against factor analysis per se.

It has been suggested that orthogonal factors would be more acceptable with the Q-technique, where correlations are computed for pairs
of cases instead of pairs of variables, as the investigator has control
over the nature of the variables but not over the nature of cases and
thus can select the variables so that statistical independence and meaningful independence do coincide reasonably well (Coleman, 1964, p. 21).

However, this is not a very attractive alternative, as variables should
be selected mainly for relevance and not for such technical reasons. It
is very doubtful that any variables can be found except rather artificial
ones to add to a fairly long list of variables in order to justify the
assumption of uncorrelated weights in many cases.

It seems worth noticing then, first, that some factor analytical models
recognize correlated factors and, second, that even orthogonal factors
are not necessarily independent but just uncorrelated. For example,
in analyzing items of a perfect Guttman scale by the principal factor
method, one will obtain Guttman's principal components as factors,
which obviously are not independent though uncorrelated. So when
factor analysis is sometimes said to imply a principally unreasonable
assumption of independence between factors, this critique can be
directed correctly only against some, though admittedly many, cases of
actual analyses, where the possible unreasonableness should be decided
individually. This holds even if "noncorrelation" is substituted for
"independence."

2.3. *Selection of Variables*

What factors come out of an analysis obviously depends on the
composition and size of the set of variables actually used. The extracted
factors are also roughly interpreted as the aspect common to the
variables that are heavily loaded on them and missing in the variables
with no weights on them. Thus selection of variables is a most important
part of a factor analytical study and should be given the utmost

attention. A deplorable habit of just using whatever variables are available "to see what will happen" puts the famous GIGO (garbage in, garbage out) principle into force and has probably contributed to a certain disrepute of factor analysis.

A careful selection of variables will improve the chances of useful results considerably. In pretests or other exploratory studies the selection will necessarily be rather tentative, but otherwise no variable should be included except for special theoretical or perhaps technical reasons. If definite hypotheses are not tested, implicit hypotheses of relevance or importance of certain fields or aspects to be covered may be followed. If possible, the number of variables from the various fields or aspects should reflect, however vaguely, notions of relative importance of fields and aspects for the problem studied.

In selecting variables the problem of *redundancy* often appears; that is, some variables become related from technical or otherwise trivial and irrelevant causes. This may happen because of careless selection and construction of variables, a limited supply of data, or a very detailed covering of a field.

Most direct redundancy results from one variable, often constructed as a percentage or mean, being literally, in a technical sense, contained in another variable. If n_i is the number of cases belonging to the ith subclass out of a total of a subclasses, together having N members, one variable may be n_1/N and another one $(n_1 + n_2)/N$. Or the first variable may be the mean of the first subclass, the second variable the mean of the first and the second subclass. If so, there is evidently a correlation between the variables, if not confounded by some peculiar compensatory mechanism between the two subclasses. The remarkable result will be the two variables not having a common factor rather than the opposite case. Examples would be "Manufacturing establishments per capita" and "Manufacturing establishments with 20 or more employees per capita."

Sometimes the relation is partially hidden, with the second variable defined as $1 - (n_1 + n_2)/N$ or n_2/N. If $n_1 + n_2$ is rather near N, or if the difference is almost invariant, the two variables will have a strong negative correlation. Thus, there are good reasons to be rather restrictive in including variables n_i/N from the same classificational system simultaneously. If two or only a few variables from such a series are used, not more than one of them should cover a big and varying proportion of cases, and the proportion of cases left out should be big and varying. If several variables from the same series are employed, they may cover all or almost all cases together, but not more than one single variable should alone cover a considerable proportion of cases. Examples of this kind of variables are "Percentage 0–15 years of age of population," "Percentage 15–21 years of age of population," and "Percentage 65 years or more of population."

The redundancy is less direct and, as a rule, smaller if one variable has as numerator a subclass of another variable's numerator but also a different denominator, for example, the variables "Percentage of economically active females of all females 15 years or over" and "Percentage of economically active married females of all married females."

Another indirect, and somewhat less technical, redundancy occurs between variables with the same or almost the same denominator and numerators from different but actually closely related classifications, as between "Percentage of males with college education of all males 25 years or over" and "Percentage of professionals of all economically active males." Here the two variables seem to have a common element more restricted to the two of them than, for example, a factor of social rank (see next section).

Factors with considerable redundancy in their highly loaded variables will appear, to a corresponding degree, as "*artifactors,*" to use the psychologist Charles Leef's expression. Analyses with many of these factors cannot, of course, claim much interest.

On the other hand, factors that may appear to have an artifactorial component may turn out to have a substantive core and remain when the redundancy is eliminated or greatly diminished. Some factors of the large matrix of Schmid and Tagashira may serve as examples. Another can be taken from the study of urban detailed plans by Fog, Janson, and Lanesjö. In the first analysis two variables describing the character of the border of the block were found to be much more strongly correlated than expected. They were constructed as percentages from the same classification and with the same base, and the remaining categories were smaller than expected. The variables defined a dimension of "Border Characteristics," which appeared to be a genuine artifactor, although there were theoretical reasons for a "real" dimension of this kind. In a replication using new data the definitions were changed to reduce redundancy by breaking down the categories into more detailed ones, but a dimension of "Border Characteristics" still resulted, although slightly changed.

Also, redundancy of the last-mentioned indirect kind differs only in degree from substantive and interesting connections between variables. Thus the distinction between redundant and genuine relations is sometimes diffuse.

2.4. *Common Factors*

Because each variable is treated as a weighted sum of certain factors, its variance is formally accounted for by the variation of the factors, as seen in Equations 2. The correlations between variables are correspondingly generated through various degrees of similarities in composition of the variables when the factors vary, as seen in Equations 4.

As much as possible of the information contained in the $n \times N$ matrix of data is transformed to a smaller $p \times N$ matrix of factor scores. The very essence of the analysis seems to be the substitution of a smaller set of factors for a large set of variables. The variables thus are treated as individual items reflecting various aspects of a system. The focus of attention is transferred from the variables to the aspects, or dimensions, of which the variables serve as partial measures.

Some ecologists, however, maintain a keen interest in the special variables and so are not particularly interested in the reduction of data to some basic dimensions. As their orientation seldom makes them deal with very large sets of variables simultaneously, there is rarely reason for them to indulge in factor analysis.

Nevertheless, the common factor model has been challenged as being not only uninteresting but also misleading. The correlations between ecological variables are generally not to be accounted for by common factors, even when the variables are clearly clustered, but by causal relations between the variables themselves in pairs, circles, or chains. Even here the interest in particular variables is retained, and the appropriate technique of analysis would be some variant of path (Wright, 1934) or dependence (Simon, 1954; Blalock, 1961) analysis. (Otis Dudley Duncan and Beverly Duncan are prominent exponents for this line of orientation. Duncan and Duncan, 1955 and 1960, may be seen as typical approaches by them, though not demonstrating path or dependence analysis as in Duncan, 1966.)

As a linear causal model, factor analysis is usually conceived as stating that a system of causally related or unrelated factors influence a set of variables that are not directly related among themselves. Such a model may seem rather special and not to have as wide applicability in human ecology as perhaps in mental testing or attitudinal research. (See, e.g., Blalock, 1961, pp. 167–169).

This conception of the factor analytical model appears to be somewhat unnecessarily restricted. If causal relations are assumed not between the variables but between the variables with the random elements removed, such relations seem to be permitted in certain patterns within the model, the relations going from layers of variables closer to the factors to more remote layers of variables. However, these relations cannot be estimated by the usual factor analytical methods but are included in the loadings of the factors. Thus the weights reflect both direct and indirect influences of the factors on the variables in a more complicated model with increased flexibility but also with correspondingly increased difficulties of interpretations. Even so, it has to be admitted that the factor analytical causal model, thus expanded, will have limited applicability only, as most special models have.

Factor analysis may be useful, however, as would cluster analysis, both technically and theoretically, in order to provide a preliminary grouping of variables in more or less closely connected systems, the causal structure of which could then be further explored by means of the approaches just mentioned. Also, the factors may be entered as variables in a causal system (Cox, Ch. 13 of this book). In fact, this seems very much in line with the main stream of factor analytical research, which aims at developing sets of basic descriptive dimensions. These may be valid regardless of the various possible causal processes underlying them if they are not vested with causal meanings. Furthermore, examples of causal interpretations of ecological correlations given in terms of specific variables instead of factors are not always convincing.

First, the manifest variables are generally seen as fairly reliable and valid measures only of the theoretical variables between which the proposed causal relations will hold; so actually the relations are between components of the variables. Second, the relations sometimes refer to the individual rather than the ecological level. Thus they may be at work for the individual variables, whereas the ecological variables are complicated through additional processes making them react more as measures of some other factors; in other words, the distinction between individual and ecological correlations is not upheld. Third, at times the statements seem to be unduly simplifying a rather complicated situation.

Three examples may illustrate these points, the first and third of which are involved in all of them, though the second point is relevant only to the second illustration. The examples are not intended as elaborations of a position that the factor analytical model always or usually is superior to all other models. On the contrary, the position taken is still, as was earlier stated, that the factorial model of basic dimensions on a descriptive level profitably may be pursued by other, causal models of the particular problem analyzed.

1. In discussing the study by Gouldner and Peterson, Stinchcombe (1964, p. 550) concentrated on the variable "Agriculture." It must have

a direct causal connection with the variable "Use of Grain for Food." It is also the cause of three factors, namely "Level of Technology" and factors described by "Permanency of Residence" and "Private Property in Land," respectively.

If one considers the measuring of variables in four-point scales from dominance or marked elaboration to absence, the rather low correlation of .59 between the two variables, and the possibilities of using grain as object of trade and perhaps also food for domestic animals, it is not entirely unreasonable that approximately half of the correlation between "Agriculture" and "Use of Grain for Food" should be accounted for by the technological factor. With regard to the relation between "Agriculture" and the three factors it is an open question whether Stinchcombe's point of view is more plausible than Gouldner's and Peterson's or vice versa.

2. Instead of introducing a socioeconomic dimension to account partially for correlations between educational, occupational, income, and housing variables, education may be considered to lead to certain occupations and through them to certain levels of income, which makes it possible for some people but not for others to have a house or rent an apartment of a given value and size.

Evidently this point of view has merits on the individual level. However, it is very doubtful that the ecological correlations between the corresponding ecological variables can generally be derived from such simple processes on the individual level. In urban areas with many highly educated people not only these people will provide the area with a great number of high-income families, but also other wealthy families will be attracted by the same qualities of the area, etc.

3. In the study of detailed urban plans one dimension was interpreted as "Block Size." Then the variable "Block Area" might be suggested to generate the other variables of the cluster, such as "Number of Buildings" and "Length of Border." However, "Block Area" is no more an independent variable than are the others, as the size and shape of the block are often manipulated by the planner in designing the area. The variables are thus simply interrelated aspects, among others, of the solution of a planning problem (Fog, Janson, and Lanesjö, 1965).

2.5. *Definition of Factor*

The concept of "factor" in the factor analytical sense is operationally determined through the mathematical procedures in computing the weights and scores of the factors. It has been argued that factor analysis is unfit for detecting basic dimensions of a structure because its factor definition is so broad that "factors" will always result; so no test is provided of the fundamental problem, whether or not there are any common features of the variables studied (Coleman, 1964, p. 20).

This statement needs some qualifications. It is literally true that some factor or factors will always result from a factor analysis. Nevertheless, the outcome may lead to, or make the researcher inclined to, a conclusion of no useful or important basic descriptive dimensions. If a set of randomly generated variables is analyzed, some factors will certainly emerge. But if the observed correlations are based on a reasonably large number of cases, the factors will be weak (unimportant) in terms of the proportion of the total variance accounted for by their variations; that is, the communalities will be low, indicating that most of the variation of the set is uncorrelated with the dimensions, unless we take out a great many dimensions, thus losing sight of the main purpose of the analysis. Also, the factors, or their weights, will be completely unstable from one sample of data to another. Furthermore, even if we get fairly important dimensions in a set, importance still being measured in terms of variances accounted for, we may not be able to make anything out of them, as we cannot interpret them. They may be intelligable after rotation, but as long as we have not found any such rotation, the analysis has not given us a set of basic dimensions (see Section 2.6). Of course, it is not a necessary consequence of the calculations involved in the analysis that the dimensions can always be interpreted.

On the other hand, it must be admitted that the concept of factor in the factor analytical sense is rather weak, not compared to the concept of a unidimensional scale according to Likert or Thurstone, for example, but compared to such a scale according to Guttman. As mentioned, the principal factors of a set of items with a perfect cumulative scale are, by definition, Guttman's principal components. If items from two correlated scales are analyzed together, the two sets of principal components will not emerge as distinctive principal factors. If items measuring the "intensity" of the scale are analyzed together with the items of "content," the resulting principal factors will blur the content and the intensity somewhat. If the principal factors of a perfect cumulative scale are rotated, for example, according to the varimax principle, and factor scores are computed for the new dimensions, none of these will rank the cases perfectly in the order of the original scale (Riley and Janson, forthcoming study).

As it is a reasonable demand of a technique for discovering basic dimensions that it be able to detect possible perfect cumulative scales involved, the stated peculiarities of factor analysis with regard to perfect scales may be seen as more or less serious disadvantages.

2.6. *Nonuniqueness of Solutions*

As has been pointed out many times, the factorization of the variables in Equations 1 is not unique. Any linear set of functions

$$f_{jk} = \sum_{w=1}^{p} b_{jw}g_{wk} \tag{5}$$

transforms the variables to weighted sums of the new factors g_w with the same qualities as the Equations 1 if the g_w factors are standardized and

$$\sum_{w=1}^{p} b^2{}_{jw} + \sum_{w=1}^{p} \sum_{q=1}^{p} b_{jw}b_{jq}r_{g_w\,g_q} = 1 \ (w \neq q) \tag{6}$$

The communalities will be the same as before. Some solutions will be preferable compared to others according to various criteria, but generally no single solution will stand out as the only possible or best one.

This nonuniqueness of factorization has often been held out as a weakness of factor analysis. Clearly, it reduces the value of a negative result. If an expected set of dimensions does not become evident, it might emerge after some rotation (5).

On the other hand, the nonuniqueness may also be seen as a sign of fundamental soundness of the method or at least as having useful aspects. Methods of mathematical and statistical analysis may often conveniently be looked upon as formal and systematic forms of ordinary everyday procedures to draw inferences of the external world from empirical, though perhaps informal and unsystematic, observations.

If this reasoning is applied to factor analysis, the nonuniqueness of solutions reflects the important nonuniqueness of theories and frames of references. If one such conceptual scheme is successfully applied to a matrix of data, this, of course, does not mean that no other schemes will be applicable or fit the data equally well, as they often are at least partially transferable and able to explain similar phenomena but in different ways. This principle then comes out clearly in factor analysis through the infinite number of possible solutions, serving as a practical lesson in scientific tolerance.

3. BASIC TECHNICAL ASSUMPTIONS OF FACTOR ANALYSIS

3.1. Level of Measurement

3.1.1. *Kind of Variables.* Equations 1 and the definitions used there imply that each variable, as a weighted linear sum, is measured at the level of interval scales at least. This, of course, is a very important assumption. However, many variables in ecological theory are defined and used on an ordinal level only, as the reasoning is mostly verbal and often rather vague. A whole set of possible operational definitions of a theoretical variable may give the same rank order of areal units, because any measure in the set is a monotone function of any other measure.

To avoid the assumption of interval scales, a nonmetric (ordinal) analysis may be used. In the selection of an alternative to ecological factor analysis, it is advisable that the quantitative character of the variables be preserved. If the variables are compressed into a few ranked categories, information is lost, and severe new problems are introduced in choosing more or less arbitrary cutting points.

When the original variables themselves are dichotomies or a few ranked categories, such as administrative type of communes or roll-call vote of countries in the UN assembly, it will be easier to find alternatives to factor analysis among the scaling models of social psychology, for example, latent structure analysis or Guttman's cumulative scale analysis (cf. Torgersen, 1958). However, the question of level of measurement does not apply to dichotomies. In ecological factor analysis the question of level of measurement arises mainly in connection with two types of variables. The first type is the ordinary percentage or some other average. For instance, the "Sex Ratio" is often used in theoretical contexts in such a way that a valid measure on rank-order level must arrange the cases according to the proportion $k = W/M$ (not to be confused with the summation index k used in the set of basic equations) of women to men in the adult population. There may be some doubts about what age groups the measure should refer to. If this point has been settled, then all monotone functions $g(k)$ produce the same (or exact opposite) rank order as k, for example, $1/k$, $k/(k + 1)$, $\log k$, e^k, k^2, k^3, $\sqrt{k}$, $1/\sqrt{k}$, $k^2(k + 1)^2$, or $\sqrt{k}/\sqrt{k + 1}$. But they all give different frequency distributions. Usually ecological theory does not demand one particular measure $g(k)$. In that case, there is no reason why any $g(k)$ should be considered a measure on the interval scale level if there are no other criteria to apply. Such possible additional criteria may concern, for example, parsimony, the frequency distribution, or the relations to other variables. Some function $g(k)$ may perhaps have linear regressions to most other relevant variables and so be preferred to those with curvilinear regressions.

For the sex ratio, either the variable $W/(M + W)$ as a simple measure, not so skewed as k and possessing definite upper and lower bounds, or a monotone transformation of k or any monotone function $g(k)$ to a normally distributed variate will show many preferable qualities.

Usually, however, the choice between the many possibilities of interval scales that are equivalent on the ordinal level seems to be largely ignored. Percentages are often used more or less routinely. The correlations between the possible variates on the interval level are generally far from complete because of the nonlinear relations between them. The choice is thus possibly far from unimportant.

Another type of variables is much more infrequent and usually introduced in a set more reluctantly, namely an ordered set of categories with arbitrary values, usually consecutive integers, attached to the categories. To justify such a variable as an interval scale, the numbers should be assigned so as to give "equal intervals" in some sense, as through some judgment technique like the method of paired comparisons with experts as judges. In such a case, the estimates of scores will be subject to some errors, and the simple series of integers may sometimes be considered an approximation to them.

If the set is not too long and the order of the categories is undisputed, the difference between the series of true scores and the series of arbitrary integers may be unimportant with a correlation sufficiently high to justify the use of the latter as an approximation of the former. The parallel between the arbitrary scoring of alternatives of items on a Likert scale and scoring by means of normalization is obvious.

In the study of detailed urban plans by Fog, Janson, and Lanesjö, buildings were classified in six main types according to form of floor area and the types ranked after degree of "closedness" or "shelteredness." The decision on order was unanimous among the experts consulted. The types were assigned numbers from 0 to 5. Various sets of alternative scores considered reasonable instead of the scores 1 through 4 together with various assumptions of distribution of cases gave correlations to the integer series of .90 or more in most instances. The integer series was then considered a rather satisfactory approximation to a wider set of variables among which the "true scores variable" probably could be included.

The average score on "shelteredness" for the block was then used as a variable in the analyses. Another variable of the same type, expressing "openness" of grouping of buildings, was also used with less justification, as its correlation with alternative scoring systems was not studied, although the series of types was longer.

The tentative conclusion, however, is that variables of the ordered categories type can sometimes be treated on the interval level at least as well as the usual percentage or mean variable. This is probably contrary to the opinion of most experts and thus somewhat questionable.

Nevertheless, whatever reason is given for selecting a particular measure from a set of possible measures, the selected variable must be treated as an interval scale.

3.1.2. *Invariance under Selection of Variables.* The procedure of selecting and defining variables for a study can be seen as a process of gradually approaching a degree of specification necessary for the actual calculation of values on the variables. It may take place in stages or steps, with the making of inventories and lists of increasing exactitude. It starts with a list of the general fields or aspects to be covered. Unfortunately, this list often remains implicit. Within the fields or broad aspects more specific aspects are delineated, and this leads to a general, theoretical definition of a variable. Some problems of the process so far were outlined in Section 2.3. Here we are discussing the final step of the procedure, the selection of an operational definition on the interval level from the class of such definitions possible under the chosen theoretical definition, which usually specifies an ordinal measure at most.

If different interval scale definitions lead to practically the same systems of correlations, because they are themselves very highly correlated or for other reasons, then the choice between them literally makes no difference. If various operational definitions do give different matrices of correlations, the choice between them evidently may be important. However, it does not necessarily influence the results decisively.

Suppose a change of variables means a rather regular and proportional shift of the general level of correlations in corresponding arrays of the correlation matrix rather than irregular and spotwise alternations. Then perhaps the differences in results will be limited to changes in communalities with the compensatory changes in loadings of the common factors rather proportional. If these changes concern the whole matrix or if they are restricted to certain arrays but limited in size, the number of factors may be constant, their relative importance approximately unchanged, and the interpretations roughly invariant.

When variables are selected according to theoretically relevant criteria, it is interesting to see what consequences various choices will have. When the choice is a technical question, it ought to have predominantly favorable technical effects, such as enabling the researcher to reach a conclusion otherwise not obtainable. On the other hand, when one disregards changes in technical efficiency, the effects on the substantive results are artifacts. They should be discernible or slight. After due allowance for them the remaining substantive results must show considerable invariance under various technical solutions, in the sense that such solutions must not lead to incompatible conclusions about the subject studied.

When new variables are added to a set of variables, they create possibilities for additional dimensions. If they introduce new fields, the dimensions may reasonably be substantively unrelated to earlier dimensions. If they cover essentially the same aspects as the original variables, they make possible further distinctions among the old dimensions, dividing them into subdimensions and perhaps slightly regrouping a few of them.

If the stress of the variable setup is different because the problem studied differs, then the results of the analysis will naturally be different. On the other hand, if the sets are mainly parallel, with differences consisting mostly of exchanges, or additions, of equivalent variables, the substantive results should be mainly parallel, though more detailed in case of an enlarged matrix, at least when possible expected artifacts are eliminated. Otherwise, factor analysis will not be a useful research tool.

This invariance under selection and definition of variables is expected on various levels down to the purely technical one of deciding on interval scale measures of given ordinal variables.

The invariance of findings over parallel sets of variables of various sizes has been studied in some investigations (Schmid and Tagashira; Sweetser, 1965b; Janson, 1965). The results point to a considerable invariance. The invariance over parallel set of variables with size of set constant was also studied (Sweetser, 1965a; Riihinen, 1965; Janson, 1960, 1965), and Kaplan compared sets with and without variables expressed in absolute numbers included. Here the analyses also showed remarkable invariance. Alternative sets of ecological variables have not yet been analyzed extensively. More studies of this kind should be made, although experiences of factor analysis in other disciplines where it is better established, especially psychology, should be consulted, naturally with due consideration taken of the conditions that may be special to human ecology.

Finally, the possible invariance on the most technical level, that is, when choosing interval scale measures of theoretical ordinal variables, is even less often studied. Nevertheless, it is a problem well worth studying. Very likely it contains aspects special to human ecology; thus the possibility of drawing from other fields of factor analysis decreases. One aspect of the problem will be dealt with shortly in Section 4.1.3.

3.2. *Variables as Linear Sums of Factors*

The fact that the variables are seen as weighted linear sums of factors of course, excludes nonlinear and nonadditive functions of the factors as variables, insofar as they are not transformed to at least an approximately linear sum.

A linear sum may, in some instances and in certain intervals, approximate a more complicated function fairly well. Functions of higher degrees than the first, exponential or logarithmic functions, and products may be transformed into linear functions; for example, the logarithm of a variable can be substituted for the variable itself in the case of a product of various degrees of factors. A higher degree of a factor may come forth as a separate factor if factors are not independent.

Nevertheless, it must be admitted that factor analysis can handle directly only a limited class of functions. Thus interactions between factors are difficult to take into consideration.

Furthermore, in the basic set of Equations 1 it is assumed that the weights are the same for all values of a factor. Thus the case where positive values on a certain factor are important to a given variable but negative values are not is not included. Nor are the cases where only numerically large values of the factor influence the value or where the weight of a factor is a function of another factor.

Under such conditions the estimate of a weight may be seen as an estimate of a kind of mean weight. Compared to "true" weights in a given interval of the factor, the estimates may thus be deflated or inflated. Furthermore, other degrees than the first of the factor may be introduced if dependent factors are permitted. Also, weights of other factors may be influenced. This further underlines the need for careful selection of variables. Again, the problematic assumption might be avoided by choosing another method of analysis (see the discussion of nonadditivity in Alker, 1966).

Within the realm of factor analysis, there are a few steps that may improve the situation somewhat. First, when a variable has a multiplicative factorial element, it may sometimes be eliminated and the residual, approximately additive element of the variable included in the list of variables instead. A *residual factor analysis* may be useful also for other reasons (Tukey, 1962). Second, just as an analysis of variance can be broken down in subanalyses when the interactions are too many or too complicated for easy interpretation, a factor analysis may profitably be divided into several analyses. The variable or variables for which interactions or varying weights are detected or suspected are used to divide the cases into subclasses, and an analysis is made for each class. Interesting differences may be revealed, and the assumption of linear sums may be upheld. The resulting matrices and patterns can be compared by inspection or more formally analyzed, for example, by means of Ahmavaara's and Markkanen's *transformation analysis* (Ahmavaara and Markkanen, 1958, pp. 80–88).

Hadden and Borgatta divided the cities according to size and "metropolitan status." Within the general tendency of similarities between the various classes of cities they also found interesting differences. For instance, for "Large cities" and "Independent cities" the "Nonwhite" factor was fused into the factor of "Socioeconomic Status Level," which was stronger for these cities than for the others. For all cities there was no "Size" factor, but for each subcategory such a factor appeared.

Fog, Janson, and Lanesjö made analyses of detailed urban plans separately for plans concerning the rebuilding of central blocks and for plans of suburban or new blocks. The latter had a "Tallness" factor, which did not appear for the former. Allardt made separate analyses of political behavior, particularly Communist strength, in five categories of Finnish communes and found differences between "Backwoods" and "Industrial" Communism.

3.3. *Uniform Weights of Variables*

Another important assumption of the set of basic Equations 1 is the uniform composition of a given variable. Each variable has the same composition for all units. This means that the random component has the same weight in a variable for all areal units. As a rule, the variable is a function, usually a mean, such as a percentage, of "individual" values. It contains a random element even if all "individual units" (persons, families, dwellings, buildings, enterprises, etc.) within the areas are observed.

First, there is a random element in the mechanisms by which

individual units, within given categories of units, are located in a given area Second, there is often a possibility of observational errors in the observations.

The size of the random element in the ecological variable depends on the number of individual observations on which the values are based. But this number usually varies between areas, and it is often impossible to lower this variation below a rather high level. Furthermore, the random element in the values may vary between areas also because areas differ in degree of homogeneity.

As a rule, the number of observations and the degree of homogeneity cannot be kept sufficiently constant between areas to make the random element of the value on the ecological variable the same in all areas. Instead of a uniform weight c_i for the random component of the ith variable, a series of weights c_{ik} for each case will become operative. This will generate corresponding variation in the other weights as the weights are connected according to Equations 2. The analysis will provide estimates of mean weights c_i, etc., in Equations 1.

A general solution to the problem of a varying random element of given variables will then be to make the relative importance of the random component sufficiently small for the mean weight c_i to be a good approximation to the weights c_{ik}. Evidently, a great relative variation of the weights is not so important for the composition of x_i if the weight c_i of the random factor is small as if the weight is great.

In order to keep the weight of the random factor small enough, rather large and homogeneous areal units should be used. It is especially important to avoid units with very few observations, as their ecological values will contain a considerable random element, even if the areas are homogeneous. With regard to percentages lower limits should be maintained both of the denominator and of the expected value of the numerator under the hypothesis of no systematic variation between areas. Moreover, if the mean size and the lower limit of the number of observations per area are rather small, the variation in size should be restricted. For other reasons this holds under less restricted conditions also, as a systematically uneven size-distribution of units may influence both size and sign of correlations.

Similarly, the limitation of random components naturally has other advantages than making weights uniform. As in other research situations, random elements hamper generalizations in diminishing invariances between samples, whether replicative or systematically varied. Of course, they also may conceal possible "real" differences, as systematic elements are correspondingly weakened.

3.4. *Modifiable Units*

As is well known, the ecological units are *modifiable* in size and shape. Units can be modified in ecological factor analysis as in other analyses to vary the population under study. Sometimes this procedure is motivated from ecological theory, as when Sweetser compared core and suburbs in the Boston metropolitan area and in Helsinki (Sweetser, 1964, and the paper by Sweetser in this volume). At other times the choice of units to study is more of a technical problem. Hadden and Borgatta investigated the consequences of alternatively defined urban units, employing Urbanized Areas, Standard Metropolitan Areas, and politically defined cities as units. They found a considerable, although by no means total, invariance.

In analysis of urban spatial structure the areal units evidently can be delineated and combined in an almost infinite number of ways, as in using blocks conveniently as building stones. Certainly, some sets of units are clearly and uniformly preferable to others, but only exceptionally is one particular set superior to all others according to criteria selected as relevant, such as degree of general or specific homogeneity, character of social subsystem, or spatial distinctiveness. To reduce the class of most preferable sets to a sufficiently limited class among which the choice may be indifferent, it is generally necessary to specify a mean size of units. The question of suitable size is partially technical, as the number of available cases and observations within areal units roughly defines a lower limit on size, whereas requirements on the number of units to study indicate vaguely an upper limit. For instance, census tracts may be generally acceptable as ecological units but may be too small for a reliable estimate of delinquency rates.

Within wide margins the construction of the set of areal units literally is a matter of choice, with a series of seemingly equally possible alternatives. In the case of ready-made units like the American census tracts this may not be so obvious, as the tracts and combinations of them are the only practical possibilities because most of the decisions have already been made when the tracts were constructed.

Nevertheless, the choice of units may influence the outcome of the analysis. The expected size of the correlation between ecological variables tends to increase with the degree of homogeneity of units and with the size of units, measured in number of observations. Thus larger homogeneous units will tend to give a higher mean level of correlations than small homogeneous units. In practice, the influences of homogeneity and size tend to balance each other, as small units are generally more homogeneous than large ones. At any rate, different sets of units

will generally produce different matrices of correlations, but the ecological conclusions reached ought to be invariant under choice of sets
of units if a "good" choice has been made. Naturally, a bad choice of
units can deprive the study of most of its interest. The matrix with the
highest level of correlations generally should be technically most efficient.

Thus, there is a question of invariance involved also in connection
with the selection of areal units. As one way of treating this problem,
it is suggested that ecological factor analysis works with alternative
sets of units in situations where selection of units occurs, as in studies
of urban spatial structure. The study of Swedish cities at the Swedish
Building Research Institute uses two sets of units of different mean
sizes for some cities. Otherwise, such alternative sets are very seldom
used.

4. OTHER TECHNICAL PROBLEMS

4.1. Distributions

4.1.1. *Distributional Assumptions.* In the basic Equations 1, or in
other equations necessary for the factor analysis, there is no assumption
of a specific frequency distribution of factors or of variables. Thus
normal factors or variables are not necessary.

Optional assumptions concerning distributions may, however, be
useful. First, they may add new permissible operations to the analysis.
For example, some tests of significance of weights and of number of
factors have been derived where normality is assumed, although the tests
may have some degree of robustness. Second, additional meanings or
more satisfactory interpretations may be given to operations or results
under assumptions of multinormal distributions. For example, the
principal factors may be identified with the principal axes of ellipsoidal
density surfaces when variables are multinormally distributed. When
uncorrelated factors are multinormal, they are also independent, as is
well known, and that usually makes interpretations much easier. Multinormal factors also generate multinormal variables. When there are
several independent but not normally distributed factors, the distribution of the variables will be somewhat closer to normality than those of
the factors. It should be noticed that the transformation of two variables
separately to one-dimensional normal distributions does not necessarily
produce a bivariate normal distribution. The regression of one transformed variable with regard to the other may even be curvilinear.

4.1.2. *Regressional Assumptions.* The possibility of curvilinear regressions, even if the marginal distributions are normal, certainly is a

complication. However, there is no necessary assumption of linear regression of a given variable on any other variable involved in factor analysis. Nor is there any necessary assumption of linear relations between factors, as the principal factors of the items of a perfect cumulative scale show. But optional assumptions of independent, linearly related, or multinormally distributed factors imply linear regressions between variables. Often they are simplifying and facilitating and thus recommendable. However, they cannot be upheld in the analysis of a set of variables between which curvilinear regressions occur.

Some deviations from linearity in regressions may be removed or diminished by transformations, but not all curvilinear relations can be dealt with in this way. A monotonic transformation to a given distribution may straighten a regression curve, but certainly it cannot be expected to eliminate all bends of the curve.

Here one has to make a choice between certain variables and the assumption that uncorrelated factors also are independent or at least have linear regressions. Some variables of minor importance producing curvilinear regressions may well be dropped without inconvenience. Furthermore, curvilinear regression should be accepted only if it can be derived from meaningful curvilinearity between factors.

For instance, it seems highly probable that various "Familism" factors, referring to different stages of the family cycle, as Sweetser detected them in Helsinki (Sweetser, 1965b), are curvilinearly related when uncorrelated. Low values on a given familism factor may be connected with high or low values on any other familism factor, but high values on the factor should not go together with high values on the others. In this case curvilinear regressions between variables heavily loaded with two different familism factors must be accepted, as familism is an important aspect of the urban areal structure.

4.1.3. *Normalization.* Multinormally distributed variables have certain definite advantages, as was pointed out earlier. Marginally, or unidimensionally, normal variables are considerably less valuable. Nevertheless, transformation to such variables is sometimes made, probably as the best available substitute for the multinormal variables, which are difficult to obtain, and may require reversion of rank orders between units, whereas the easily obtainable marginal normal distributions may increase chances for linear regression and even multinormal distributions. Some Finnish ecological factor analyses are executed with the variables transformed to normal distribution one at a time (Allardt, 1964a and b; Riihinen, 1965; Janson, 1961, also used normalized variables).

Whatever formal reasons there may be for normal variables and however fortunate ecologists would be to have their variables distributed that way, the ecological results should be invariant under transformation of variables unless there are theoretical reasons for preferring one or the other type of variables. Without such reasons, the choice is operational and can be made to increase efficiency and to facilitate the research work but must not otherwise influence the ecological conclusions. On the other hand, if the transformation makes no difference at all, perhaps the original variables can be interpreted in the same way as the transformed ones.

To study the impact of normalization in relation to the study of Swedish communes, three sets of variables were analyzed both before and after normalization of marginal distributions in a pilot study of 51 communes (Janson, 1965). If incompatible results were obtained, they could be treated in either of two ways. Either they might both be dropped, or one version might be kept, if it appeared to be based on a more reasonable version of measures. Convincing reasons why one type of variables should be preferred to the other could be put forward in but one case.

The distributions of "Population" and two closely related variables were originally very skew. They held a concentration of units with small values and even smaller differences between values. When normalizing, these insignificant differences, often random in both size and direction, were given great importance. Here it seemed more reasonable to use a measure of size which allocated approximately the same values for the smallest units of 2,000–3,000 population than to employ a measure that made differences of some ten persons in the smallest communes as important as differences in population between the big cities, say from 250,000 to 25,000. If different results concerning size should appear, it was decided in advance to favor the results from the original, nontransformed series.

Actually, the results were mainly parallel with the exception of a "Size" factor appearing in the original sets but not in the normalized ones, where the clusters of population variables were dissolved and included among the variables of an "Urbanization" factor. It was then decided to drop the normalization in the main study. Instead, other transformations were employed there to reduce curvilinearity and skewness.

4.2. *Invariance between Methods of Computation*

4.2.1. *Computational Solutions.* Evidently, rotations are applied to transform one system of dimensions into another. The nonunique character of dimensional systems, however, does not mean that all systems are compatible. Some systems can be transformed into each other; others cannot. For example, some may account for more of the total variance of the set of variables than other systems. Some may be nearer to theoretical expectations or otherwise easier to interpret. However, insofar as the extracting and rotational techniques aim at the same "simple structure," they may be expected to arrive at rather similar patterns of weights. Gouldner and Peterson and Allardt compared orthogonal and oblique solutions.

Orthogonal and oblique solutions involve different assumptions in their models and so may legitimately seem to be different but still compatible; that is, it should be possible to transform one system into the other both computationally and conceptually.

Obviously, there are several ways of arriving at a solution, and insofar as the techniques are equally efficient, it should not matter which way one chooses. However, when the computational work is manageable, principal factor systems may be generally preferable as a final system or as a preliminary system for further rotation because of their neat mathematical qualities. With regard to rotation, the axes of the new system, whether oblique or orthogonal, may be decided from theoretical expectations that are to be tested by the best possible fit. Otherwise, when clusters are clearly discernible, they may conveniently define the dimensions, in this case more or less oblique. When orthogonal rotation on purely formal grounds is chosen, the varimax principle might be recommended.

In comparing results from analyses of different sets of units or of different sets of variables, one may also compare dimensional systems extracted through the same factorial technique, such as principal axes or dimensions rotated from them according to the varimax principle. Even if two varimax systems could be altered to exhibit marked similarity, the sets of data producing them would have revealed some differences if the dimensional systems are different as they stand. However, the importance of this point may not be easily evaluated.

When a computational technique is used, two questions of invariance remain to be briefly mentioned in the next two subsections, namely the number of factors to be rotated and the communality estimates.

4.2.2. *Number of Rotated Dimensions.* If dimensional systems do not contain the same number of dimensions, they are obviously different, but this may not be very important from an ecological point of view. Some dimensions are often rather weak and can perhaps be disregarded. The degree of similarity for the remaining dimensions may run from practically full equivalence to none at all.

As yet there seems to be no generally accepted and generally applicable way of deciding when to stop factoring, that is, how many dimensions to extract. In general, there are more or less obvious upper and lower limits, but in between there is often some room for discretion; if not, the strictly analytical formulas are thought to apply. Besides, even if the number of significant dimensions has been formally estimated, the last few dimensions may be too weak to be ecologically interesting or even interpreted. Furthermore, different levels of significance may be selected.

In situations where the number of dimensions cannot be decided without ambiguity, it might be interesting to know what degree of invariance the rotations according to a given principle have when the number of rotated dimensions varies. If p principal axes have been extracted, they will not be changed by the extraction of the $(p + 1)$th axis. But if p principal axes are rotated to varimax dimensions, these will hardly be completely stable if instead $p + 1$ axes are rotated. Again, there is a question of invariance. Acceptable modifications would be the split of one dimension in two and perhaps the regrouping of two dimensions into three, but more thorough alterations would make the rotation dubious.

In the study of Swedish cities varimax rotations of 6 and 8 principal factors are compared. In two analyses of detailed urban plans (Fog, Janson, and Lanesjö), 6, 7, 8, and 9 principal axes were extracted and rotated to varimax dimensions. On the whole, the changes were small, and the 6 original dimensions were rather intact also with 9 dimensions. For technical reasons, the 6 of them together accounted for somewhat less variance, but also this change was rather small. Obviously, however, the principal factor solution here has an advantage in its complete invariance under addition of new dimensions (cf. Riihinen).

4.2.3. *Communality Estimates.* The need for inserting communality estimates in the main diagonal of the matrix to start factoring plagued factor analysts for a long time. With the advent of the modern computer equipment, matters improved considerably in this respect. Now the question of communality estimates seems quite unimportant in most cases.

First, efficient estimates from assumptions of a given number of dimensions or from multiple correlations are easily available. Second, iterative methods can readily be applied, with the analysis repeated and with estimates inserted from the earlier round, until stability is eventually reached. Third, with the large matrices often used now more primitive estimates also are satisfactory. Fourth, in large matrices it makes no difference if ones are substituted for the correct, usually rather high, communalities of a carefully selected set of variables, or if rather rough estimates are used. Finally, and most important, now that principal factor solutions can be employed extensively, it can be correctly argued that simply putting ones in the main diagonal is theoretically preferable even to using the communalities, even if known. Thus it is recommended that ones be used when principal factors are extracted.

5. SUMMARY AND CONCLUSIONS

The factor analytical model has limitations. There may be doubts as to the applicability of the concept of factor and the suitability of its implicit definition. Factor analysis is no substitute for a careful theoretical and conceptual analysis of a problem, but it may be a part of such an approach. It is not better equipped for causal interpretations of nonexperimental data than are other correlational and regressional techniques, but it may aid in the interpretations, as it delineates subsystems for further study and helps in testing hypotheses. As Hadden and Borgatta observed, extravagant claims for the technique of factor analysis seem to occur more often in informal comments of critics than in formal presentations of factor analytical applications (Hadden and Borgatta, pp. 18 f., concerning classificational studies by Price, etc.).

Some of the problems in applying the factor analytical model seem to appear almost regardless of the actual field of application, for example those dealt with in Sections 2.2, 2.5, 2.6, 3.2, and most of Section 4. Others are more or less specific to certain kinds of applications, insofar as assumptions of the model are not easily made consistent with theoretical and operational qualities of the substantive variables of the field. Thus problems discussed in Sections 3.3. and 3.4, in Subsection 3.1.1, and to some extent in Sections 2.3 and 2.4 seem to be rather exclusively ecological, or perhaps to be of special relevance in the analysis of aggregate data, whether ecological, time serial, or of other types. The questions presented often contain an ecological element even if not peculiar to ecology, as in Section 2.2 and Subsection 3.1.2. Naturally, also the general questions are seen here in an ecological context.

Used in a rather unpretentious way to bring some order out of chaos on a descriptive level by suggesting basic descriptive dimensions, factor analysis is a very useful research instrument in human ecology insofar as certain technical invariances can be relied on to hold within the class of equivalent but not inferior technical solutions. Of course, lists of such technical invariances, which must be satisfied for the method to be useful in revealing substantive invariances, can be stated for all methods of analysis, although some methods may offer more alternatives of procedures than others.

For factor analysis the invariances concern primarily the following:
a. The number and selection of theoretical variables
b. The operational definitions of variables
c. The definitions of area under study
d. The sets of areal units
e. Certain computational and rotational techniques and number of dimensions.

Not many ecological studies of such invariances have been reported. Thus far, they point at a considerable invariance and tend to support the claims of descriptive and classificational usefulness of factor analysis, provided the method is used with an open mind for its limitations. Thus the not very original conclusion is that more studies are needed but that the evidence presented for the time being is mostly, but not totally, favorable to factor analysis.

Finally, it is suggested here that factor analysis, when used to define basic descriptive dimensions, could conveniently be carried one step further than to the dimensions. It should more often be followed by computation of factor scores, that is, the positions of the units on the dimensions, for further analysis by other methods.

6. REFERENCES

Ahmad, Q. (1965), *Indian Cities. Characteristics and Correlates* (Chicago: University of Chicago); cited by Berry (1966).

Ahmavaara, Y., and T. Markkanen (1958), *The Unified Factor Model* (Helsinki: The Finnish Foundation for Alcohol Studies).

Alker, H. R., Jr. (1964), "Dimensions of Conflict in the General Assembly," *American Political Science Review, 58*, pp. 642–657.

Alker, H. R. Jr. (1966), "The Long Road to International Relations Theory," *World Politics, 18*, pp. 623–655.

Allardt, E. (1964a), "Institutionalized Versus Diffuse Support of Radical Political Movements," *Transactions of the Fifth World Congress of Sociology, 4*, pp. 369–380.

Allardt, E. (1964b), "Patterns of Class Conflict and Working Class Consciousness in Finnish Politics," in E. Allardt and Y. Littunen (eds.), *Cleavages, Ideologies and Party Systems* (Helsinki: Westermarck Society), pp. 97–131.

Allardt, E., and O. Riihinen (1966), "Files for Aggregate Data by Territorial Units in Finland," in S. Rokkan (ed.), *Data Archives for the Social Sciences* (Paris: Mouton).

Anderson, T. R., and L. L. Bean (1961), "The Shevky-Bell Typology: Confirmation of Results and A Reinterpretation," *Social Forces, 40,* pp. 119–124.

Bell, W. (1955), "Economic, Family and Ethnic Status: An Empirical Test," *American Sociological Review, 20,* pp. 45–52.

Berry, B. J. L. (1966), "A Synthesis of Formal and Functional Regions Using A General Field Theory of Spatial Behavior," mimeo.

Blalock, H. M. (1961), *Causal Inferences in Nonexperimental Research* (Chapel Hill: University of North Carolina Press).

Boggs, S. L. (1965), "Urban Crime Pattern," *American Sociological Review, 30,* pp. 899–908.

Bordua, D. J. (1959), "Juvenile Delinquency and 'Anomie': An Attempt at Replication," *Social Problems, 6,* pp. 230–238.

Carey, G. W. (1966), "The Regional Interpretation of Population and Housing Pattern in Manhattan Through Factor Analysis," *Geographical Review, 56,* pp. 551–569.

Cattell, R. B. (1949), "The Dimensions of Culture Patterns by Factorization of National Characters," *Journal of Abnormal and Social Psychology, 44,* pp. 443–469.

Chilton, R. J. (1964), "Continuity in Delinquency Area Research: A Comparison of Studies for Baltimore, Detroit, and Indianapolis," *American Sociological Review, 29,* pp. 71–83.

Coleman, J. S. (1964), *Introduction to Mathematical Sociology* (Glencoe: Free Press).

Cox, K. (1966), "Suburbia and Voting Behavior in the London Metropolitan Area: 1950–51," mimeo; revised version printed in the present volume, Chapter 13.

Duncan, O. D. (1966), "Path Analysis: Sociological Examples," *American Journal of Sociology, 72,* pp. 1–16.

Duncan, B., and O. D. Duncan (1960), "The Measurement of Intra-City Locational and Residential Patterns," *Journal of Regional Science, 2,* pp. 37–54.

Duncan, O. D., and B. Duncan (1955), "Residential Distribution and Occupational Stratification," *American Journal of Sociology, 50,* pp. 493–503.

Fog, H., C.-G. Janson, and B. Lanesjö (1965), "Stadsplaneringens innehåll och omfattning" (Content and Extent of City Planning), mimeo.

Gittus, E. (1964), "The Structure of Urban Areas," *The Town Planning Review, 35,* pp. 5–20.

Gosnell, H., and M. Schmidt (1936), "Factorial and Correlational Analysis of the 1934 Vote in Chicago," *Journal of the American Statistical Association, 31,* pp. 507–518.

Gouldner, A. W., and R. A. Peterson (1964), *Notes on Technology and the Moral Order* (Indianapolis: Bobbs-Merrill).

Grönholm, L. (1960), "The Ecology of Social Disorganization in Helsinki," *Acta Sociologica, 5,* pp. 31–41.

Hadden, J. K., and E. F. Borgatta (1965), *American Cities: Their Social Characteristics* (Chicago: Rand McNally).

Harman, H. H. (1960), *Modern Factor Analysis* (Chicago: University of Chicago Press; second edition, 1967).

Hartley, R. E. (1954), "Two Kinds of Factor Analysis," *Psychometrika, 19*, pp. 195–203.

Henrysson, S. (1957), *Applicability of Factor Analysis in the Behavioral Sciences* (Stockholm: Almqvist & Wiksells).

Hofstaetter, P. R. (1952), "Your City' Revisited: A Factorial Study of Cultural Patterns," *American Catholic Sociological Review, 13*, pp. 159–168; cited by Hadden and Borgatta (1965), pp. 21–24.

Holzinger, K. J., and H. H. Harman (1941), *Factor Analysis* (Chicago: University of Chicago Press).

Janson, C.-G. (1960), "Om stadsbygdens inre differentiering" (On the Inner Differentiation of Urban Settlements), mimeo.

Janson, C.-G. (1961), *Mandattilldelning och regional röstfördelning* (Allocation of Seats and Regional Distribution of Votes) (Stockholm: Idun).

Janson, C.-G. (1965), *Kommunklassificering* (Classification of Communes), (Stockholm: Statens Inst. f. Byggnadsforskning), mimeo.

Janson, C.-G. (1968), "The Spatial Structure of Newark, New Jersey, Part I. The Central City," *Acta Sociologica, 11*, pp. 144–169.

Jonassen, C. T. (1961), "Functional Unities in Community Systems," *American Sociological Review, 26*, pp. 399–407.

Kaplan, H. B. (1958), "An Empirical Typology for Urban Description," unpublished Ph.D. dissertation, New York University.

Lander, B. (1954), *Towards an Understanding of Juvenile Delinquency* (New York: Columbia University Press).

Lawley, D. N., and A. E. Maxwell (1963), *Factor Analysis as a Statistical Method* (London: Butterworths).

MacRae, D. Jr., and J. M. Meldrum (1968), "Factor Analysis of Aggregate Voting Statistics," Chapter 18 in this volume.

Moser, C. A., and W. Scott (1961), *British Towns* (Edinburgh: Oliver & Boyd).

Norman, P. (1968), "Third Survey of London Life and Labor: A New Typology of London Districts," Chapter 14 of this volume.

Olsen, B. M., and G. Garb (1965), "An Application of Factor Analysis to Regional Economic Growth," *Journal of Regional Science, 6*, pp. 51–56.

Pedersen, P. O. (1967), *Modeller for befolkningsstruktur og befolkningsudvikling i storbyområder* (Models of the population structure and development in urban areas) (Copenhagen: Statens byggeforskningsinstitut).

Piepponen, P. (1961–1962), "Suomen kuntien sosiaalisen rakenteen perustekijät," (Dimensions of Ecological Differentiation in Finnish Communes), *The Yearbook of Population Research in Finland, 7*, pp. 34–46.

Price, D. O. (1942), "Factor Analysis in the Study of Metropolitan Centres," *Social Forces, 20*, pp. 449–455.

Riihinen, O. (1965), *Teollistuvan yhteiskunnan alueellinen erilaistuneisuus*, (Regional Differentiation of Industrial Society) (Helsinki: Werner Söderström).

Sainsbury, P. (1955), *Suicide in London* (London: Chapman & Hall).

Schmid, C. F. (1960), "Urban Crime Areas," *American Sociological Review*, *25*, pp. 527–542.

Schmid, C. F., and K. Tagashira (1964), "Ecological and Demographic Indices," *Demography*, *1*, pp. 194–211.

Scott, W. (1964), "Analysis of Census Enumeration District Data," mimeo.

Shevky, E., and W. Bell (1955), *Social Area Analysis* (Stanford: Stanford University Press).

Shevky, E., and M. Williams (1949). *The Social Areas of Los Angeles* (Berkeley and Los Angeles: University of California Press).

Simon, H. (1954), "Spurious Correlation: A Causal Interpretation," *Journal of the American Statistical Association*, *49*, pp. 467–479.

Stinchcombe, A. L. (1964), Review of Gouldner and Peterson (1964) in *American Journal of Sociology*, *69*, pp. 549–551.

Sweetser, F. L. (1964), "Ecological Factors in Suburb and Metropolitan Core: Boston, 1950 and 1960," manuscript.

Sweetser, F. L. (1965*a*), "Factor Structure as Ecological Structure in Helsinki and Boston," *Acta Sociologica*, *8*, pp. 205–225.

Sweetser, F. L. (1965*b*), "Factorial Ecology: Helsinki, 1960," *Demography*, *1*, pp. 372–386.

Sweetser, F. L. (1965*c*), "Factorial Ecology: Zonal Differentiation in Metropolitan Boston, 1960," mimeo.

Sweetser, F. L. (1966), "Helsingin ekologinen erilaistuminen vuonna 1960," "Ekologisk differentiering i Helsingfors år 1960" (Ecological Differentiation in Helsinki, 1960), *Helsinki City Statistical Monthly Review*, *17*.

Sweetser, F. L. (1968), "Ecological Factors in Metropolitan Zones and Sectors," Chapter 16 in the present volume.

Thorndike, E. L. (1939), *Your City* (New York: Harcourt, Brace).

Torgersen, W. S. (1958), *Theory and Methods of Scaling* (New York: Wiley).

Tryon, R. C. (1955), *Identification of Social Areas by Cluster Analysis* (Berkeley: University of California Press).

Tukey, J. W. (1962), "The Future of Data Analysis," *Annals of Mathematical Statistics*, *33*, pp. 1–67.

Van Asdol, M. D. Jr., S. F. Camilleri, and C. F. Schmid (1958), "The Generality of Urban Social Area Indexes," *American Sociological Review*, *23*, pp. 277–284.

Wiseman, S. (1964), *Education and Environment* (Manchester: Manchester University Press).

Wright, S. (1934), "The Method of Path Coefficients," *Annals of Mathematical Statistics*, *5*, pp. 161–215.

13

KEVIN R. COX

Voting in the London Suburbs:
A Factor Analysis and a Causal Model[1]

THE DICHOTOMY of a politically right-wing suburb and a left-wing central city has been a pervasive theme in recent writings on the electoral geography of the United States.[2] Much of the interest in suburban voting patterns accompanied the rapid suburbanization of population which took place after 1945; thus, the phenomenon was first seriously noticed after the 1952 election when 51 of the 67 counties included by the Census Bureau in its classification of the twenty largest metropolitan regions in the United States, went Republican.[3] In England, this feature of electoral geography has attracted less attention, but the Conservative disposition of such suburban constituencies as Solihull, Tynemouth, and Knutsford when compared with the support for the Labour Party

[1] Revised version of an article first printed in the *Annals of the Association of American Geographers, 58* (1968), pp. 111–127. Printed here with the permission of the Association of American Geographers. The original title was "Suburbia and Voting Behavior in the London Metropolitan Area."

An earlier version of this paper was awarded first prize in the Illinois Geographical Essay Awards competition, 1965.

[2] For examples of recent writings on the dichotomy of a politically right-wing suburb and a left-wing central city, see: L. Harris, *Is There a Republican Majority?* (New York: Harper, 1945); W. Whyte, *The Organization Man* (New York: Simon and Schuster, 1956); B. Lazerwitz, "Suburban Voting Trends: 1948–1956," *Social Forces, 39:* 1 (October 1960), p. 29; and F. Greenstein and R. Wolfinger, "The Suburbs and Shifting Party Loyalties," *Public Opinion Quarterly, 22* (Winter 1958–1959), pp. 473–482.

[3] G. E. Janosik, "The New Suburbia: Political Significance," *Current History* (August 1956), pp. 91–95.

in their respective central cities of Birmingham, Newcastle, and Manchester suggests that the dichotomy is not confined to the United States.[4] Certain other evidence suggests that political behavioral differences between central city and suburbs may not be confined to party preference. Thus, recent work by Campbell *et al.* suggests for the United States that there are differences in the level of turnout between central city and suburb, the central city showing markedly lower levels of turnout than the suburbs.[5]

This paper has four purposes:

1. To test the hypothesis that the suburban environment in the London metropolitan area is associated with party preference in a Conservative direction

2. To test the hypothesis that the suburban environment in the London metropolitan area is associated with voter turnout in the direction of greater suburban turnout; and, dependent upon verification of these hypotheses

3. To specify the significance of the suburban context for these two aspects of voting behavior when social contexts other than the suburban-central city dimension are taken into account

4. To draw out the theoretical implications of the results for the study of the geography of intraurban voting behavior.

Beyond the immediate conclusions regarding suburb–voting behavior relationships in the London area, it is hoped that the study will indicate techniques which might be used in the study of these same relationships in other parts of England for comparative purposes. The study universe comprises the Parliamentary constituencies wholly or partly within the London metropolitan area; the only definition of the London metropolitan area is that made by the Metropolitan Police, and this is approximately coincident with the area outlined by Freeman[6] as the London conurbation in 1955 (Figure 1 and Table 1).

[4] Figures of the percentage vote going to the Conservative Party in the election of 1950 in these three central city–suburb pairs are illustrative:

Central City		Suburb	
Birmingham	42.7	Solihull	63.3
Newcastle	42.3	Tynemouth	49.30
Manchester	42.9	Knutsford	49.2

[5] A. Campbell, P. E. Converse, W. E. Miller, and D. E. Stokes, *The American Voter* (New York: Wiley, 1960), p. 464.

[6] T. W. Freeman, *The Conurbations of Great Britain* (Manchester: Manchester University Press, 1959), p. 66.

Table 1

PARLIAMENTARY CONSTITUENCIES OF THE
LONDON METROPOLITAN AREA

* 1. Battersea	35. Hornsey
2. Bermondsey	36. Ruislip-Northwood
3. Bethnal Green	37. Southgate
* 4. Camberwell	* 38. Tottenham and Wood Green
* 5. Chelsea and Kensington	39. Twickenham
* 6. City of London and	* 40. Wembley
City of Westminster	* 41. Willesden
7. Deptford	42. Spelthorne
* 8. Fulham	43. Uxbridge
9. Greenwich	* 44. Croydon
* 10. Hackney and Stoke	45. Kingston
Newington	46. Merton and Morden
* 11. Hammersmith	47. Mitcham
12. Hampstead	48. Richmond
* 13. Holborn and St. Pancras	49. Sutton and Cheam
* 14. Islington	50. Wimbledon
* 15. Lambeth	51. Carshalton
* 16. Lewisham	52. Epsom
* 17. Paddington	53. East Surrey
18. Poplar	54. Esher
19. St. Marylebone	55. Barking
20. Shoreditch and Finsbury	56. Dagenham
21. Southwark	* 57. East Ham
22. Stepney	* 58. Ilford
* 23. Wandsworth	59. Leyton
24. Woolwich	60. Walthamstow
25. Acton	* 61. West Ham
26. Brentford and Chiswick	62. Woodford
* 27. Ealing and Southall	63. Epping
28. Edmonton	64. Beckenham
* 29. Enfield	65. Bexley
30. Finchley	66. Bromley
* 31. Harrow	67. Dartford
32. Hayes and Harlington	* 68. Chislehurst and Orpington
* 33. Hendon	69. Barnet
34. Heston and Isleworth	

* Asterisked constituencies indicate those which consist of two or more constituencies; such amalgamations are due to the lack of socioeconomic data for the original constituencies. The numbers on the left-hand margin indicate the numbers marked on Figure 1.

Source: Compiled by author.

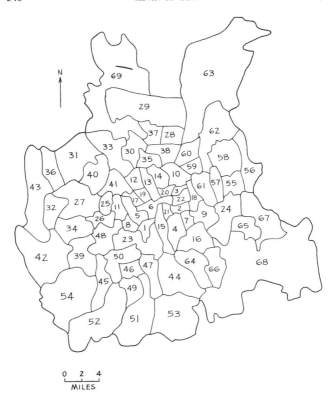

Figure 1

LOCATION OF CONSTITUENCIES

Note: See Table 1 for the key to the names of constituences.

The voting data to be analyzed are for the General Elections of 1950
and 1951, and the dependent variables will be the proportion of the
total vote going to the Conservative Party at a given election and the
proportion of the electorate voting in a given election. The distribution
of the percentage of the total vote going to the Conservative Party in
1951 is presented in Figure 2; the distribution of the percentage of the
electorate participating in that General Election is presented in Figure 3.

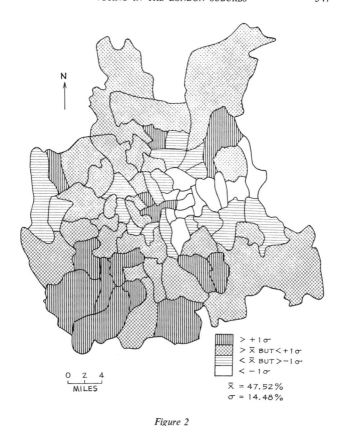

0 2 4
MILES

> + 1 σ
> x̄ BUT < + 1 σ
< x̄ BUT > − 1 σ
< − 1 σ

x̄ = 47.52 %
σ = 14.48 %

Figure 2

PERCENTAGE OF THE VOTERS VOTING CONSERVATIVE IN
THE GENERAL ELECTION OF 1951

The distributions of the dependent variables for the General Election
of 1950 are not presented here, for, as will be noted later, the correlations
between the respective cross sections in time for these variables were
quite high, suggesting very similar distributional patterns for the two
elections. Theoretical considerations relevant to the problem will be
set out initially, and the previous literature will be examined; on the

KEVIN R. COX

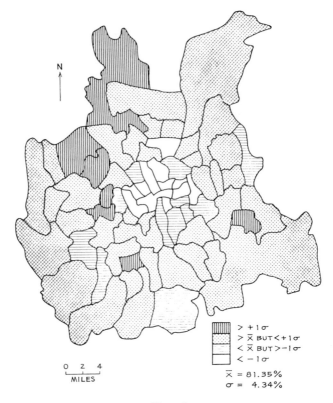

Figure 3

PERCENTAGE OF THE ELECTORATE PARTICIPATING IN THE
GENERAL ELECTION OF 1951

basis of this, one can identify certain problems of research design requiring rectification and can tentatively define suburbanism. Second, a
wide array of socioeconomic variables will be chosen and reduced by
means of principal-axes factor analysis to a much lower number of
dimensions descriptive of the social contexts within which the population of the area votes. Third, the hypotheses will be tested against a
suburban–central city dimension by means of simple correlation.

Fourth, a theoretical model of the interrelationships of different social contexts and voting behavior will be specified and tested. Fifth, the theoretical implications of this model will be discussed.

THEORY, EMPIRICAL INVESTIGATION, AND RESEARCH IMPLICATIONS

In the study of voting behavior, two sets of independent variables have been postulated: the first set of variables refers to the individual characteristics of the voter — his sex, age, and social class; the second set of variables refers to the characteristics of the community or community context in which he lives and works — the suburban context, the colliery village context, and the small town as opposed to the large town. Observed patterns of voting behavior result from the interaction of individual characteristics and contextual characteristics. Thus, Ennis has shown that in certain states of the United States the small-town vote is determined more by the religious characteristics of the individual voters than by their social-class characteristics, and in the case of large towns, the converse is more valid.[7] Clearly, just as there is a variety of individual characteristics that may be true of one person, so a community may be characterized by several different contextual characteristics.[8] Here an attempt is being made to evaluate the effects in the London metropolitan area of one of these contextual variables — the suburban-metropolitan dimension — against the effects of other contextual variables. Ideally, in order to obtain a comprehensive evaluation of the role of suburbanism in voting behavior, it would be desirable to incorporate data on individuals; in the absence of such data, this is not possible.

In empirical studies by American social scientists, three principal theories have been suggested and tested in an effort to account for the effect of suburban residence on party preference.[9] The first argument states, skeptically, that any political conservatism found in the suburbs is a political disposition dependent only upon the social characteristics

[7] P. H. Ennis, "The Contextual Dimension in Voting," in W. N. McPhee, and W. A. Glaser (eds.), *Public Opinion and Congressional Elections* (Glencoe, Illinois: Free Press, 1962).

[8] The problem of aggregate and individual effects in electoral geography is analogous to the problem in economic geography of distinguishing between the effects of economies of concentration and the effect of the characteristics of the individual firm in the evaluation of locational patterns.

[9] Apart from passing reference by Campbell *et al., op. cit.,* footnote 5, p. 464, there are no studies of intraurban variations in political participation to be examined.

of the individual voter and (by tacit assumption) contextual characteristics that show no patterned variation between central city and suburb.
Berger, for example, in a study of a new industrial suburb to the south
of San Francisco, found that central city-to-suburbs residence change
had no effect on the proportion voting Republican.[10] His conclusions
have been supported by a study of a residential suburb of Kalamazoo,
Michigan.[11]

The second theory states that the suburban context exercises a conversion effect, converting erstwhile Democrats or Labor Party supporters from the central city into Republicans or Conservatives when
they move to the suburbs. Greenstein and Wolfinger, for example,
have examined public opinion poll data on individual social characteristics cross-classified with a suburb–central city dichotomy, and they
have found that even when political party identifications are controlled
for education, income, occupation, and ethnic group, the suburban
Republican tendency is not erased.[12]

The third theory states that the right-wing vote of the suburbs is a
result not of conversion but of selective migration of Republicans as
opposed to Democrats from the central city. This is a theory which has
received some confirmation from the work of Campbell.[13]

Examination of the research referred to previously, and of other
literature on the problem of suburban voting behavior,[14] suggests
certain characteristics of previous research design which can be improved in any further testing of hypotheses related to suburban effects
on political behavior. The problems that need attention are as follows:
(1) Suburbanism has not been defined sociologically or economically;
it has been defined as a political unit outside the boundaries of a central
city, and the specific socioeconomic characteristics of suburbanism
have not been rigorously isolated. (2) Suburbanism has been treated as
one part of a suburban–central city dichotomy. In this study, the
assumption will be made that suburbanism lies at one end of a continuum, at the other end of which lie characteristics exclusive to the

---

[10] B. M. Berger, *Working-Class Suburb* (Berkeley: University of California Press,
1960).

[11] J. Manis and L. Stine, "Suburban Residence and Political Behavior," *Public
Opinion Quarterly, 22* (Winter 1958–1959), pp. 483–489.

[12] F. Greenstein and R. Wolfinger, "The Suburbs and Shifting Party Loyalties,"
Public Opinion Quarterly, 22 (Winter 1958–1959), pp. 473–482.

[13] Campbell *et al., op. cit.,* footnote 5, pp. 453–467.

[14] Other material on the relationship between suburban residence and voting
behavior may be found in: Harris, *op. cit.,* footnote 2; Whyte, *op. cit.,* footnote 2;
and R. Wood, "The New Metropolis," *American Political Science Review, 52* (1958),
pp. 108–122.

central city. (3) Most of the previous studies have failed to discriminate between the suburb and other socioeconomic contexts that may be common to both suburb and central city. Boskoff has spelled out objections:[15]

> The lack of definite and meaningful patterns in political affiliation following the suburban move is perhaps best interpreted as a consequence of exploratory investigation and inadequate conceptualization, rather than a reflection of "reality". . . . Furthermore, investigators often proceed on the notion that suburbs are demographically and organizationally interchangeable units wherever they are found. The only exception is a distinction between industrial and residential suburbs.

Similar critical comments have been made by Campbell.[16]

In this study, suburbanism will be defined in the locational, economic, demographic, and social terms in which previous writers have defined it. Economically, the suburb is dependent upon a central city for its economic base. Demographically it is characterized by a relatively low density of population but a rapidly increasing population owing to the addition of migrants from the central city. Socially, the suburb is predominantly middle class, younger rather than older, with high percentages of home ownership and married couples, but with low occupational sex ratios.[17]

The variables from which contextual dimensions have been derived are listed in Table 2. The data for all the variables but one have been derived from the 1951 Census of England and Wales. The final variable — distance from the central business district — is the main road distance in miles from the center of the City of London and City of Westminster constituencies combined to the geographical centers of all the other areal units employed. The variables have been selected on the basis of three criteria: first, their relevance in terms of the theory of voting behavior;[18] second their relevance for the definition of suburbanism; and third, the availability of data. Six variables required

[15] A. Boskoff, "Suburbs, Voting and Style of Life: Clues to Patterns in Voting Shifts" (unpublished manuscript, Department of Sociology, Emory University), p.4.

[16] Campbell *et al., op. cit.,* footnote 5, p. 454.

[17] The criteria employed draw heavily upon definitions suggested in the following works: O. D. Duncan and A. J. Reiss, *Social Characteristics of Urban and Rural Communities, 1950* (New York: Wiley, 1956); S. F. Fava, "Suburbanism as a Way of Life," *American Sociological Review, 21* (1956), p. 35.

[18] For an introduction to the relationships between voting behavior and socioeconomic variables, see: S. M. Lipset, *Political Man* (New York: Doubleday, 1960); or B. Berelson, P. F. Lazarsfeld, and W. McPhee, *Voting* (Chicago: University of Chicago Press, 1954).

logarithmic transformations in order to preserve linearity of association, and these are asterisked in Table 2.

In order to derive contextual dimensions from these variables, inter-correlations were computed, and a principal-axes factor analysis was undertaken. The factors with eigenvalues greater than unity were then rotated to a normal varimax position in order to facilitate empirical interpretation of the factors. Factor analysis is a highly appropriate tool in that it aims at accounting for the variances of the variables in terms of a limited number of factors or indices of the geographical structure. Each variable has a loading or weight on each factor, and this loading is in the form of a correlation coefficient measuring the degree of association between the factor and the variable. The higher the loading for a variable, the higher the degree of association between the respective factor and the variable.[19] Given the theoretical relevance of the variables incorporated into the computations, a rotated principal-axes factor analysis allows one to specify in four continua or dimensions those aspects of the social geography of the London metropolitan area which are relevant to the political behavior of the population of the area and to the definition of suburbanism. For each factor, each areal unit has a factor score. The factor loadings with values greater than 0.3 are shown in Table 3.

The first factor accounts for just less than 36.5 per cent of the variance. In terms of the loadings of the variables on this factor, it may be regarded as a social rank dimension. The two variables loading highest on this factor are the social-class variables. Other indicators of social rank such as years of school education, persons per room, per-centage of occupied males employed in manufacturing, and percentage of occupied males employed in white-collar occupations also load quite high and in the expected directions on this factor. The loading of distance from the central business district of the London metropolitan area — the indicator of the locational attributes of suburbanism — is very low. In terms of ideal polar types, the factor describes areas at one end of the continuum in which the labor force is largely employed in manufacturing, in which mean educational attainment is low, over-crowding is prevalent, low proportions of the population are found in the middle class, and large proportions are found in the lower class. At the other end of the continuum are typically middle-class areas in which educational attainments are generally high, few are employed in

---

[19] An adequate exposition of the principal axes factor analysis can be found in H. H. Harman, *Modern Factor Analysis* (Chicago: University of Chicago Press, 1960), pp. 154–191.

Table 2

The Variables

Variable name	Amplified Description of Variable
* POPCHA.	Population change by migration, 1931–1951
* POPDEN.	Population density
15–44	Percentage of population aged between 15 and 44
OV65	Percentage of population aged 65 and over
SR	Sex ratio
MARR. M.	Percentage of males married
MARR. F.	Percentage of females married
I. II.	Percentage of occupied males aged 15 and over in Social Class I and II†
* IV. V.	Percentage of occupied males aged 15 and over in Social Class IV and V†
EDUC.	Percentage of occupied males aged 15 and over who left school before the age of 15
* PERS. P. RM.	Persons per room
HOS. SHA.	Percentage of households sharing a house
* OCC. SR.	Occupational sex ratio
%SERV.	Percentage of occupied males engaged in service industries
%MANUF.	Percentage of occupied males engaged in manufacturing industries
%WC.	Percentage of occupied males engaged in white collar occupations
* %TRPT.	Percentage of occupied males engaged in transportation
COMEX.	Net outflow of commuters as a percentage of labor force commuting outside constituency of residence
%COM. OUT.	Percentage of occupied labor force commuting outside constituency of residence
%COM. LDN.	Percentage of occupied labor force commuting to the cities of London and Westminster
CBD. DIST.	Distance from the center of the constituency to central business district in miles.

† These variables refer to the definition of social class used by the Census for England and Wales in 1951. The groups are based largely on a prestige ranking of occupations; Social Class I, for example, consists of the highest-ranked occupations, and Social Class V consists of the lowest-ranked occupations.

Source: Compiled by author.

Table 3

SELECTED FACTOR LOADINGS

	I	II	III	IV
POPCHA.	0.4466	−0.7657		
POPDEN.		0.9068		
15–44	−0.3223	0.4535		0.7541
OV65	0.4840	0.4718		−0.6446
SR.	0.8669	0.3814		
MARR. M.		−0.6735	−0.5368	−0.3552
MARR. F.	−0.5524	−0.7045	−0.3546	
I. II.	0.9517			
IV. V.	−0.8214	0.3899		
EDUC.	−0.9627			
PERS. P. RM.	−0.5875	0.4420	0.3717	0.4415
HOS. SHA.		0.8711		
OCC. SR.		0.8782		
%SERV.	0.8507		0.3746	
%MANUF.	−0.8721		−0.3582	
%WC.	0.9247			
%TRPT.	−0.7592	0.5178		
COMEX.			0.9185	
%COM. OUT		0.4333	−0.7122	
%COM. LDN.			0.8074	
CBD. DIST.		−0.9360		
VP*	36.48	30.50	14.57	7.65

* VP is equal to the total contribution of a factor to the variances of all the variables.

Source: Calculated by author.

manufacturing — most are in white-collar occupations — and in which there is very little overcrowding of homes.

The second factor accounts for 30.5 per cent of the variance. In terms of the loadings of different variables on this factor, it may be regarded as a suburban–central city dimension. The loading of distance from the central business district on this factor is very high, suggesting high factor scores on this dimension on the periphery of the metropolitan area as opposed to the center of the metropolitan area. The loadings of population change and population density are also high and are in the direction predicted by tentative notions regarding the characteristics of the suburbs. Loadings are also high and in the predicted direction for the proportion of women in the labor force, the proportions of males and females married, and the proportion of houses shared; this latter variable is a surrogate for home ownership. The ideal-type suburb derived from this analysis is an area located at a considerable distance from the central business district, one with relatively low population densities but high population increase, high proportions of males and females married, a small proportion of women at work, and a low proportion of houses shared.

The third factor accounts for just less than 14.6 per cent of the variance of the variables. The three variables indicative of the magnitudes of commuting to work out of given areal units load highest on this factor. This factor may be regarded as a descriptor of a commuting dimension.

Finally, the fourth factor accounts for just over 7.6 per cent of the variance. Its two highest loadings are descriptive of two aspects of age structure: the proportion of the population in early adulthood has a comparatively high positive loading on this factor, whereas the proportion in the retirement age groups also loads fairly highly but in a negative direction.

CORRELATION DATA AND A CAUSAL MODEL

The computation of correlation coefficients allows one to assess the degree to which the proportion of the electorate voting Conservative and the proportion actually turning out to vote are related, first, to the scores for the suburban–central city dimension and, second, to the scores for other dimensions obtained in the factor analysis. The results are shown in Table 4. Without taking into account relationships with other variables, it can be determined from the table that the suburban–central city dimension accounts statistically for 18.5 per cent and 21.2 per cent of the variation of the Conservative vote, and 49 per cent and 54.8 per cent of the voter turnout for the 1950 and 1951 elections, respectively.

In order to evaluate the degree to which the suburban–central city dimension is associated with these two aspects of voting behavior when other social contexts are taken into account, one could compute partial coefficients of correlation. Computation of partial coefficients of correlation, however, does not allow one to assume asymmetry of relationship. It would be preferable — if it were possible — not only to evaluate the significance of the suburban–central city dimension in correlational terms but also to do so in causal terms. This latter consideration leads to consideration of the work done by sociologists in inferring causal models from correlational data.

Table 4

SIMPLE INTERCORRELATIONS FOR POLITICAL BEHAVIORAL VARIABLES AND SOCIOECONOMIC DIMENSIONS

		1	2	3	4	5	6	7	8
Percentage Conservative Vote, 1950	1.	*							
Percentage Conservative Vote, 1951	2.	0.977	*						
Percentage Participation, 1950	3.	0.519	0.535	*					
Percentage Participation, 1951	4.	0.334	0.343	0.789	*				
Social Rank Dimension	5.	0.916	0.923	0.441	0.225	*			
Suburban–Central City Dimension	6.	−0.432	−0.462	−0.697	−0.740	−0.340	*		
Commuting Dimension	7.	−0.010	−0.001	−0.553	−0.732	0.049	0.573	*	
Age Dimension	8.	−0.692	−0.707	−0.652	−0.586	−0.730	0.582	0.430	*

Source: Calculated by author.

The language of theory and that of empirical research, it must be noted, are quite different and alien one from another. Thus, causal laws assume control of all relevant variables, but such control can never be tested empirically. Likewise, causality involves the notion of production of an effect or asymmetry of relationship; such asymmetry is difficult to formalize in mathematical or logical systems.

Political scientists, sociologists, and economists have attempted to evolve methods of obviating such difficulties of relating empirical research to theory; Blalock, in particular, has done a great deal of work along these lines.[20] He has shown that it is possible to think in terms of causal models of reality that can contain simplifications such as the assumption that neglected factors left outside the system of inter-relationships operate in specified ways. Such models refer to empirical generalizations and not to reality itself, however; a number of alternative models may yield the same predictions, and one can never actually establish a given model. But one can proceed by eliminating or modifying inadequate models that give predictions inconsistent with the data — the models of causal mechanisms that could not create the particular results obtained in the form of correlations. Blalock's technique relies heavily on the use of partial correlation coefficients. In a given causal model, the partial correlation coefficients for variables that are un-related in the causal model are given predicted values of zero; such predicted values can then be compared with actual partial correlations in order to establish the adequacy of different causal links. Moreover, whenever $r_{12 \cdot 3} = 0$, $r_{12} = r_{13} \, r_{23}$.[21] Thus, the causal models to be tested have employed predicted correlations derived from the product of correlation coefficients. For certain other variables that are not causally related via a third variable, the predicted simple correlation will be zero.

There are a number of causal models that could plausibly be postu-lated to relate Conservatism to suburbanism in particular, and to social contexts in general; there are also a number of models that could be suggested to relate voter turnout to social context. However, the voter turnout and the proportion of the voters voting Conservative in an area are so associated ($r^2 = 10.9$ per cent in 1951 and 27 per cent in 1950) that it seems potentially more fruitful to postulate a series of more

[20] For a synthesis and exposition of these ideas see: H. M. Blalock, *Causal In-ferences in Nonexperimental Research* (Chapel Hill: University of North Carolina Press, 1964).

[21] H. A. Simon, *Models of Man: Social and Rational* (New York: Wiley, 1957), Chapter 2.

integrated causal models. Two of the theoretically plausible possibilities are set out in Table 5 together with predicted correlations and observed correlations.

Model I

In the first model (see Table 5) suburbanism has both direct and indirect causal relationships with both party preference and participation. Suburbanism acts indirectly on party preference by affecting social class location; it also acts indirectly on participation by affecting commuter location and hence identification with the community.[22] Age structure can plausibly be regarded as affecting party preference directly — there is a considerable literature on the relationships between old age and political conservatism[23] — and indirectly by affecting social class location: increasing age does tend to be accompanied by upward social mobility in the class structure and accompanying residential change. Some of the predicted relationships are quite accurate in this model; the predicted relationship of .34 between participation and party preference is precisely as expected. Other predicted relationships, however, are wildly inaccurate.

Model II

When faced with such an inadequate causal model as this, Blalock has suggested two rules of thumb for modifying the causal model: (1) make changes where there are the largest discrepancies between actual and predicted values; (2) where possible, make changes first in causal relationships among variables presumed to be operating near the beginning of the causal sequence, that is, those variables that are taken to be the most independent of the others. Both these rules of thumb are satisfied if the direct relationship between age structure and Conservative vote in Model I is erased, and an additional indirect link between suburbanism and party preference is provided by age structure and social class structure in Model II (see Table 5). The discrepancy between predicted and observed for the relationship between age structure and suburbanism — the two most independent variables in Model

---

[22] Commuting is included insofar as it increases or decreases community identification and hence indirectly affects participation; it is theorized that the more time a person spends in his local community, the stronger will be his identification with it. There is ample evidence to suggest that the longer a person resides in a given community, the greater the likelihood of his participating in politics; see Campbell *et al., op. cit.,* footnote 5, p. 464.

[23] See Lipset, *op. cit.,* footnote 18, pp. 231–232.

Table 5

PREDICTIONS AND DEGREES OF FIT FOR MODELS I AND II

Model	Predictions	Degrees of Fit	
		Actual	Expected
Model I			
Commuting ← Suburbanism → Social Rank ← Age (6) / (3) → Conservative Vote (1) / Participation (2) / (4) / (5)	$r_{12} = r_{24}r_{14}$	0.34	0.34
	$r_{15} = r_{14}r_{45}$	0.00	−0.26
	$r_{23} = r_{24}r_{34}$	0.22	0.25
	$r_{26} = 0$	−0.59	0.00
	$r_{35} = r_{34}r_{45}$	0.05	−0.19
	$r_{46} = 0$	0.58	0.00
	$r_{56} = 0$	0.43	0.00
Model II			
Commuting ← Suburbanism → Social Rank ← Age (6) / (3) → Conservative Vote (1) / Participation (2) / (4) / (5)	$r_{12} = r_{24}r_{14}$	0.34	0.34
	$r_{15} = r_{14}r_{45}$	0.00	−0.24
	$r_{16} = r_{13}r_{36}$	−0.71	−0.67
	$r_{23} = r_{24}r_{34}$	0.22	0.25
	$r_{26} = r_{24}r_{46}$	−0.59	−0.43
	$r_{35} = r_{34}r_{45}$	0.05	−0.19
	$r_{56} = r_{45}r_{46}$	0.43	0.33

Source: Calculated by author.

I — is one of the largest; if a causal arrow is drawn between these two variables, it also affects other large discrepancies such as that between participation and age structure. The resultant causal model shows a closer fit between predicted and observed correlations.[24]

In terms of the relationships between suburbanism and other social contexts, on the one hand, and two aspects of the intraurban political geography of the London metropolitan area, on the other hand, this final causal model suggests the following conclusions:

1. Geographical variations of participation have sources dissimilar to the sources of geographical variation in party preference;
2. The social rank and age structures of particular areas affect party preference but not participation;
3. Variations in the magnitude of commuting affect turnout but not party preference;
4. Suburban location affects directly both participation and party preference when other contexts are taken into account;
5. Suburban location is of strategic significance in that it is also related to the political behavioral variables by causal links of an indirect nature.

THEORETICAL IMPLICATIONS

A causal model of suburban–central city political variations has now been elaborated. If it fits at all, how does it fit into broader theory concerning such political differentiation? The two broad streams of thought regarding suburban–central city differences will first be specified in detail, and I shall then try to relate them to the causal model. It should be noted that almost all the work concerned with suburban–central city differentiation has been carried out by American workers within the American context, and hence one must work by analogy between British and American conditions.

Concerning party preference first, there have been two explanations of suburban Republicanism in the United States: the transformation or conversion theory and the transplantation theory. The conversion theory postulates that the new suburbanite is an erstwhile central city Democrat who, upon taking up residence in the suburbs, is subjected to relatively

[24] This closer fit is replicated for the 1950 data, though the discrepancy between predicted value and expected value of correlation is rather higher for the participation–Conservative vote relationship (.30 *versus* .52) and for the participation–social rank relationship (.24 *versus* .44).

new stimuli that may lead him to change his political party identification. These stimuli may be of two types: first, migration to the suburbs involves the novel assumption of property rights and its implications, such as home ownership and the payment of municipal and property taxes (called rates in Britain), which favor identification with the political Right if the individual can perceive the connection between his changed situation and party images. Wood has expressed this line of thought neatly:[25]

> Suburbanites . . . escaping from big city politics are ready converts to the small town set of political values. They may have precious little equity in their houses but they think of themselves — and are thought of — as home owners.

A second novel stimulus affecting conversion may be the climate of opinion. The suburbs are located in areas that were once highly rural and dominated by the right-wing political parties. Because their organization is strong, party workers can be very effective in winning new adherents to the party among the suburbanites. As Wood has written:[26]

> The Republican party lays claim to the suburban vote . . . because it better protects their new interests and status and because it is the political faith of the old-time residents whose friendship is cultivated by the newcomer.

Other workers who have favored the conversion theory have tried to identify the communication process by which conversion takes place. Investigation of the pattern of social contacts in metropolitan areas provides the conclusion that the suburb has a much higher degree of informal social contact or neighboring than the central city. As Van-Duzer has put it:[27]

> The high percentage of married couples with young children, the predominance of middle class status and the homogeneity of the physical siting arrangements which are thought to be characteristic of suburbs are precisely those which are associated with a high rather than a low degree of neighboring.

[25] R. C. Wood, *Suburbia: Its People and Their Politics* (Boston: Houghton Mifflin, 1958), p. 137.

[26] *Ibid.,* footnote 25, p. 137.

[27] E. F. VanDuzer, "An Analysis of the Difference in Republican Presidential Vote in Cities and Their Suburbs" (unpublished Ph.D. dissertation, Department of Geography, State University of Iowa, 1962, p. 17).

This explanation implies that because communication is facilitated, attempted conversion to the dominant opinion of the area encounters little resistance.

Whereas the conversion theory postulates a change in voting behavior after moving to the suburbs from the central city, the transplantation theory argues that changes in the voting behavior of suburban populations observable since 1945 are owing to selective migration from the central city so that the suburbs receive migrants from the central city who already identify with the Republican Party. The most compelling evidence in support of this theory comes from the work done by Campbell and his associates on the Presidential election of 1956. Their analysis points to the following conclusions: (1) Fifty-three per cent of the one-time metropolitan Republicans have moved out of the central city, whereas only 29 per cent of their Democratic Party counterparts have left; this disparity holds true when holding financial ability to leave the central city and intergenerational mobility constant. (2) Emigrants from the metropolitan center and in-migrants to it are arranged in almost identical fashion on the party identification continuum. Members of both groups are dominantly Republican, whereas the lifelong inhabitants of the metropolitan centers constitute a persistent core of Democratic Party support. The reasons for this, the authors speculate, lie in the realm of social values.[28]

In the absence of needed data, we can only speculate about the meaning of these discrepancies in partisan response to intergenerational mobility. It seems likely that fairly basic differences in social values are involved. It may be that the Republicans, despite their own metropolitan origins are more often linked through enduring family ties to ancestral beginnings in small cities, towns, and on farms. Although at least one generation removed, they may reflect the consequences of an earlier era of urbanization and central city growth. With a heritage of values and traditions congenial to nonmetropolitan life they may seize the opportunity created by occupational success and escape from the metropolis. The urban Democrat, on the other hand, may be the child of a thoroughly urban culture. Whether the metropolis of his family line once was Warsaw or Rome or Dublin, or Boston, Baltimore or New York, he may accept more often the way of life of the metropolitan center. For him occupational success may provide the means to exploit and enjoy the treasures of the city, not freedom to leave the familiar for the unknown.

As far as central city–suburban differences in participation are concerned, little work has been done. The only insights come from

[28] Campbell *et al., op. cit.,* footnote 5, p. 467.

Campbell *et al.,* who have cross-tabulated for respondents the voter turnout in 1956 against the place where the respondent grew up and the place where the respondent now lives. One-time rural residents living in the metropolitan centers have the poorest turnout levels, whereas those who grew up in the metropolitan center and still live there and those who grew up in a metropolitan center but have since moved out show the highest turnout levels. Campbell *et al.,* comment:[29]

> The low turnout of former farmers reflects the agrarian political heritage.... It is also consistent with their present relatively low sense of political efficacy. At the same time, the migrant from metropolitan living was supported in his participation by a sense of efficacy commensurate with his objectively demonstrated ability to attain the higher goals among those valued by our society.

The model elaborated in this paper can be compared with previous theory in two respects: (1) the ordering of the different contexts in their relationship with political behavior; (2) the content of the factors in terms of loadings. The latter will be considered first.

The conversion theories tie in ostensibly with the content of the suburban–central city factor. Percentage of houses shared can be taken as a surrogate for the extent of owner occupancy, and the second factor loads heavily on this variable. Further, the content of this second factor lends some support to the "ease of communications in the suburbs" argument: high proportions of men and women in the suburbs, as opposed to the central city, appear to be married, and the occupational sex ratio is low indicating a high proportion of women not going out to work and therefore having more time available for neighboring.

In cause-and-effect terms, the implications of the causal model of suburban voting behavior in the London metropolitan area can be summarized in the following manner:

1. Suburban location influences social rank location, which influences voting for the Conservative Party;

2. Suburban location influences age group location, which influences social rank location, which influences Conservative voting;

3. Suburban location influences both preference for Conservative Party and political participation, but its effects on these two facets of political behavior are independent of one another;

---

[29] *Ibid.,* footnote 5, p. 464.

4. Suburban location influences commuter location, which influences political participation.

It is difficult to relate the form of this model to previous theory. The model is especially weak in three areas: (1) It is based on aggregate data concerning structural effects of social environment on individual political behavior, whereas most previous work on suburban voting behavior has been based on sample survey data for individuals. (2) There are a great many intervening variables that have been omitted owing to lack of data; although one can see that suburbanism affects party preference independent of other contextual factors, one is still left in a quandary as to how this effect occurs; that is, is there a conversion or transplantation effect? (3) Although couched in causal terms, the model fails to look back into the past for factors that might affect the dynamic interrelations of the contexts with political behavior today. The only variable descriptive of change in the social structure incorporated into the factor analytic model is "Population Change 1931–1951." A closer look at possible historical factors is illuminating, however.

In terms of their changes through time, the political and social geography of England are notoriously difficult to manipulate. Thus, in the past fifty years, the boundaries of the Parliamentary constituencies for which voting figures are available have changed out of almost all recognition. Moreover, the boundaries of these constituencies in earlier periods have frequently coincided only poorly with the boundaries of the geographical units for which social data are available. Nevertheless, it is possible to provide some evidence on historical changes in voting behavior in the London metropolitan area in a nonrigorous research design; the answers from such a design as is envisaged, however, can only be suggestive and not conclusive.

Three elections at approximately 25-year intervals — 1895, 1922, and 1950 — have been chosen and the percentage Conservative vote computed for every constituency in the study universe in each election. The London metropolitan area has been divided into four concentric belts, and the mean percentage Conservative vote for each belt for each election has been computed (Figure 4). Although the names of constituencies have in large part retained their identity over time, their boundaries have tended to fluctuate a great deal. The concentric zonation employs the constituencies as they were in the election of 1950 and attempts to group them into zones on the basis of their centers of gravity. Clearly, the centers of gravity for the constituencies in 1895 and

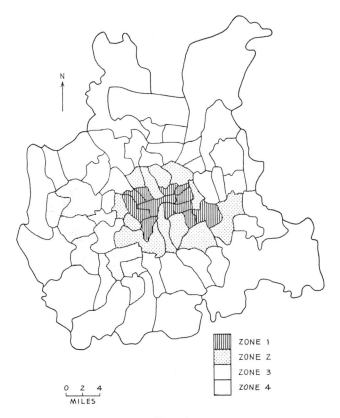

N

ZONE 1
ZONE 2
ZONE 3
ZONE 4

0   2   4
MILES

Figure 4

A CONCENTRIC ZONATION OF THE LONDON METROPOLITAN AREA

1922 differed somewhat, but the limitation to only four zones should minimize inaccuracies inherent in such an areal division. The resultant statistics are tabulated and presented graphically in an attempt to demonstrate the degree to which, and the manner in which, the gradient of political opinion between the central city and the suburbs has changed over time (Table 6 and Figure 5).

In statistical terms, the relevant results of these computations are as

Table 6

MEAN CONSERVATIVE VOTE FOR
CONCENTRIC ZONES, 1895, 1922, AND 1950

	1895	1922	1950
ZONE 1	62.1	56.0	42.0
ZONE 2	62.3	56.6	38.9
ZONE 3	76.9	54.8	44.9
ZONE 4	85.1	67.9	49.7

Source: Calculated by author.

follows: (1) The difference between the percentage Conservative vote in the central city and in the peripheral belts decreases over time. (2) Suburban zones exhibit a tendency over time to approach parity with the central city in terms of the percentage Conservative vote. (3) This tendency toward parity extends itself spatially over time outward from the central city.

In terms of the social geography of voting in the London metropolitan area, these results suggest the following. First, the suburban areas have a heritage of high proportions voting Conservative; these proportions have diminished over time, probably indicating that decreasing numbers of immigrants from the central city have assumed a Conservative Party identification. This is congruent with Lazerwitz' recent findings for a period in the late 1940's and early 1950's in American cities that, far from decreasing, the Democratic vote of recent migrants to the suburbs has actually increased.[30] Second, identification with Left wing political parties has spread outwards from the central city so that although remnants of the Conservative heritage still remain on the outer periphery, they have long since been erased nearer the central city.

The sources of this Conservative heritage are more difficult to identify. To a certain extent, however, it does seem to be independent of social class correlates. Cornford examined certain simple associations for the 1885 election in the Metropolitan constituencies of London; he found:[31]

[30] B. Lazerwitz, "Suburban Voting Trends: 1948–1956," *Social Forces, 39* (1960), p. 29.

[31] J. Cornford, "The Adoption of Mass Organization by the British Conservative Party," in E. Allardt and Y. Littunen (eds.), *Cleavages, Ideologies and Party Systems,* Transactions of the Westermarck Society, 10 (1964), p. 416.

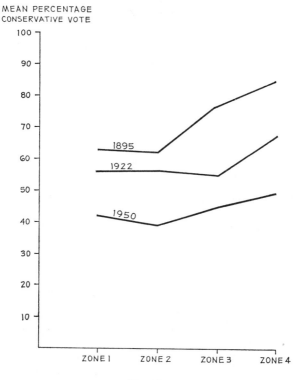

Figure 5

<small>CHANGE IN THE RELATIONSHIP BETWEEN MEAN PERCENTAGE
CONSERVATIVE VOTE AND FOUR CONCENTRIC ZONES: 1895, 1922, AND 1950</small>

1) That there was a high correlation ($+0.74$) between the Conservative percentage of the poll and the prosperity of the constituency, using rateable value per head of population as a measure of prosperity,

and

2) That where two constituencies had the same rateable value per head, the outer and less congested district tended to be more Conservative.

Less evidence is available on the precise nature of the Conservative suburban vote in terms of social sources when social class is held constant. Cornford suggested, however, that[32]

> the outer suburbs, in the county divisions of Middlesex, Surrey, Kent and Essex . . . were still the exclusive preserve of middle class commuters in 1885.

CONCLUSIONS

A firm conclusion that can be derived from this analysis is that suburbanism exercises effects on both party preference and participation independent of other social contexts. Suburbanism also affects political behavior indirectly by influencing social class structure, age structure, commuter locations, but it also has effects of its own.

The nature of these direct effects on party preference is more difficult to specify. Aggregate statistics cannot tell one anything with a great deal of conclusiveness; bearing in mind the constraints on inference implicit in aggregate data, the following statements may be made. It seems that there is evidence for both the transplantation and conversion theories. As far as the conversion hypothesis is concerned, the content of the suburban factor specifies both a stimulus (low proportion of homes shared as a surrogate for low proportion of homes rented) and a higher communication probability (high proportions of men and women are married, and fewer of the women go to work). The additional data on the dynamic component of party preference suggest that the conversion effect is less likely to be political in character as compared with former periods of time. The transplantation hypothesis, on the other hand, is supported by the suburban–age–social rank relationships. It is not difficult to see a relationship between, on the one hand, suburban location affecting age structure location, affecting in its turn social class structure location and, on the other hand, relationships between life cycle, social mobility, residential mobility, and party preference for certain central city elements in the manner inferred by Campbell *et al.*

There seems no good reason why one should choose one theory over the other when taking into account all the available evidence. The Campbell transplantation hypothesis is highly convincing, but it gains part of its conviction from the fact that the argument is presented in either-or terms; either the respondent has a Republican identification or a Democratic Party identification; no allowance is made for variations along the party identification continuum which are known to exist.

[32] *Ibid.,* footnote 31, p. 416.

Hence, if the probability for a central city Republican to migrate to the suburbs is high, and the probability for a central city Democrat to leave the central city is low, then one would tend to allocate a probability intermediate in magnitude to the weakly identified Democrat; these are precisely the persons who would be more likely to be converted in party preference on moving to a suburban location.

The problem of suburban–central city differences in political behavior has now been attacked from two methodological angles: survey data and context; the next stage is to combine both approaches in an effort to resolve the problem of the sources of distinctively suburban political behavior; such analyses are now being initiated with attitudinal and social data for Columbus, Ohio, and with social role data for the London metropolitan area.

14

PETER NORMAN

Third Survey of London Life and Labor:
A New Typology of London Districts*

THE DEFINITION of subareas within a larger urban area may be justified, on practical grounds, as a necessary step toward effective administration at the local level. Indeed, for town planners and local housing authorities, planning could hardly proceed without the framework of land-use zones, neighborhood units, environmental areas, and traffic zones which subdivide the administrative units of local government. For the sociologist, the identification of subareas within the city provides an illuminating and fruitful approach to the study of city life. Whether the aim of the investigator is the validation of generalizations in urban sociology or the development of planning strategy for the allocation of scarce resources, the definition of urban subareas is an important analytical step. The purpose of this brief paper is to outline one method of defining subareas, in this case in Greater London,[1] by using a new form of data and a new procedure of classification.

In the United States the availability of data for census tracts covering a period of twenty years (or longer in some cities) has generated considerable research interest in the empirical subdivision of cities, in which census tracts are used as the basic units. Various methods of

* The research project reported in this paper was conducted at the Centre for Urban Studies, University College London, by Wolf Scott, Nigel Howard, and Peter Norman under the direction of Ruth Glass.

[1] "Greater London," in this paper, means the area covered by the Greater London Council for administrative purposes. "Inner London" is the part of this area which was previously administered by the London County Council; "Outer London" means the remainder of the Greater London Council area.

social area analysis, cluster analysis, scale analysis, and, recently, factor analysis, have been devised and tested for census tract data.[2] Most methods seek to establish the dimensions in which census tracts can meaningfully be differentiated and to allocate them to a number of groups on the basis of scores for each of the important (usually complex) variables.

In marked contrast to the detailed material available in the United States, would-be analysts of urban structure in the United Kingdom have been starved of adequate information. Only very limited data have been produced for areas smaller than the basic administrative units of the country. For censuses prior to that of 1961, data supplied for electoral wards and civil parishes covered only the very basic items of area, enumerated population, and numbers of households and dwellings. A few studies have made use of more detailed census statistics secured by special arrangement with the Census Office,[3] but, on the whole, research has depended on published data for complete administrative units ranging in size from the one million population of Birmingham County Borough to a population of less than 2,000 in some small Urban Districts.[4]

As in so many fields of research, the situation has been radically altered by the advent of the electronic computer. The use of a computer in processing the results of the 1961 census enabled the Census Office to produce a wide range of statistics for the smallest areal unit of the census operation — the enumeration district. An enumeration district is the area covered by a single enumerator during the collection of

[2] Some important references are Robert C. Tryon, *Identification of Social Areas by Cluster Analysis* (Berkeley: University of California Press, 1955); Eshref Shevky and Wendell Bell, *Social Area Analysis,* Stanford Sociological Series No. 1 (Stanford: Stanford University Press, 1955); Calvin Schmid, "Generalisations Concerning the Ecology of the American City," *American Sociological Review, 15* (April 1950); C. Schmid and K. Tagashira, "Ecological and Demographic Indices: A Methodological Analysis," *Demography, 1:* 1 (1964). A brief review of these methods and further references can be found in M. D. Van Arsdol, F. Camilleri, C. Schmid, and McCannell, *Methods of Differentiating Urban Social and Demographic Areas,* papers presented at the Census Tract Conference, December 29, 1958, U.S. Bureau of the Census Working Paper No. 7 (Washington, D.C.: U.S. Department of Commerce, 1959).

[3] See Charles Booth, *Life and Labour of the People in London* (London: Macmillan, 1902); H. Llewellyn Smith, *The New Survey of London Life and Labour* (London: P. S. King, 1930); Ruth Glass, *The Social Background of a Plan, a Study of Middlesbrough* (London: Routledge, 1948).

[4] The administrative areas of England and Wales for which census information was published in 1961 are: 62 administrative counties, 83 county boroughs, 29 metropolitan boroughs, 317 municipal boroughs, 564 urban districts, 474 rural districts.

census information; data covering most of the population and household characteristics investigated by census methods were made available for each of approximately 60,000 such areas in England and Wales, where previously they had been available only for the 1,500 administrative areas of the country. For the convenience of users this material was made available on punched cards or magnetic tape as well as in printed form; therefore, research involving large numbers of enumeration districts was practicable. The project reported here involved processing data, at one stage or another, for approximately 11,000 enumeration districts and 845 electoral wards in Greater London. The project used these data to provide a detailed factual description of the internal variety of London's demographic, housing, ethnic, and class characteristics and to arrive at a general typology of districts which would best define its subareas in terms of these characteristics. Research of a similar nature is taking place in other major cities and conurbations in the United Kingdom.[5]

Analysis of the data for London involved three main phases:

1. The computation and individual analysis of a set of intrinsically interesting variables for enumeration districts and electoral wards

2. Analysis of the interdependence of the variables by correlation methods

3. Classification of enumeration districts and wards into a varying number of types and the further analysis of the typologies.

Each phase will be considered separately.

PHASE 1: COMPUTATION AND ANALYSIS OF INDIVIDUAL VARIABLES

Before proceeding further, it is important to make quite clear the nature of the data. An enumeration district is an area designed primarily for administrative convenience, to provide each enumerator with a clearly defined task and, as far as possible, to ensure that the amount of work involved for each enumerator is roughly the same throughout the country. The variation in population size of enumeration districts is therefore slight, although unusual districts do occur with particularly large or small populations. In London the population of districts ranged from only 70 to over 1,000, with an average size of 660 persons

[5] Similar research projects have been undertaken in particular for Merseyside, the West Midlands, Manchester, Sunderland, and Hampshire.

and 240 households; approximately 90 per cent of enumeration districts lay within the range from 400 to 1,000 population.

The data for each district refer to the population of the district as a whole, and no distinction is possible between the characteristics of particular subsections. Ideally, the analysis was to have covered the population in private households alone, excluding people enumerated in hospitals, hotels, and other institutions, but because of the limitation of aggregate statistics this was not feasible. As an approximation to the ideal, all districts in which the ratio of persons to households was greater than ten to one were excluded from the analysis, the assumption being that the population in these districts lived mainly in nonprivate institutions of one sort or another. Fortunately, large institutions usually make up one complete district and are satisfactorily excluded in this way, but small hotels, children's homes, nursing homes, and other institutions included in an ordinary enumeration district cannot be separately excluded. In Inner London, out of a population of 176,000 living in institutions in 1961, 97,000 were excluded from the analysis by this criterion, the populations of 369 districts.

Some of the most important items of information, relating to socioeconomic status, were collected for only one in ten of the enumerated population. Variables derived from these data are affected by random sampling errors, and scores for particular enumeration districts must be treated with some caution. However, the occurrence of scores differing by more than two standard errors from their true value could be expected not more than one in twenty times. Hence, the over-all geographical configuration of maps based on sample data, and the results of a classification that included sample data as part of the input, could be accepted with some confidence. The data are also affected by an individual enumerator's reliability. Quality is likely to vary from district to district according to the enumerator's precise understanding of working definitions and instructions. But no assessment of each enumerator's results is possible from the edited material, and the data were therefore accepted as presented.

The set of 42 variables computed for each of the enumeration districts are listed in detail in Appendix B. To some extent, the field of "important" or "relevant" variables has already been determined by the process of consultation which precedes the detailed choice of questions by the Census Office. The variables computed for each district covered all fields of the raw data; each variable was assumed to be an intrinsically interesting differentiating dimension between districts, and each was given equal importance in the analysis in the first instance. The variables fell into seven main groups. Those computed from a complete enumeration of the population covered the following:

1. *Population structure:* indices of age structure, marital condition, sex ratios

2. *Household structure:* indices of household size and composition

3. *Housing conditions:* indices of room density, sharing of dwellings and household facilities

4. *Tenure of accommodation:* proportions of households in owner occupation, council tenancies,[6] and private furnished or unfurnished tenancies

5. *Origin:* proportions of residents born in each of seven separate areas or countries outside Great Britain

Variables computed from a sample of one in ten of the population covered the following:

6. *Mobility of the population:* proportions of immigrants into the area during the previous year

7. *Socioeconomic status:* indices of occupational status, educational level, commuting.

As standard procedure, the unweighted means and variances of each variable were computed separately for the districts of Inner and Outer London, and frequency distributions of each variable were drawn up for each sector.

The distributions of individual variables and the geographical locations of districts with particularly high or low scores[7] indicated the extreme complexity and diversity of London, particularly of Inner London. Despite their small size, enumeration districts are rarely homogeneous in population or conditions. There were, in 1961, no districts in which the population was made up entirely of any particular occupational category or immigrant group identified by our variables and few in which the population were all living under the same housing conditions. For example, one might expect that a relatively large number of districts containing only 243 households on the average would contain households from only one of the four tenure categories listed under Group 4. In fact, only 14 per cent of the districts of Greater London had over 90 per cent of households in any of the four tenure categories identified.

---

[6] "Council tenants" are households occupying accommodation supplied by a local administrative authority or by a New Town Corporation.

[7] An "extreme" score is defined in relation to the frequency distribution of each individual variable and will vary as the range of the variable varies.

Similarly, the immigrant composition of districts is best described in terms of a wide range of mixed areas rather than as a polarity of highly segregated, ethnically "pure" districts. In Inner London alone, at one extreme there was only one district analyzed which, in 1961, had no people born outside Great Britain;[8] at the other extreme the heaviest concentration of persons born anywhere outside Great Britain was only 66 per cent. The highest concentration of any immigrant group that we identified was 36 per cent of the population born in the West Indies. Persons born in both parts of Ireland nowhere accounted for more than 30 per cent of the population of an enumeration district.

In terms of occupational status, a simple dichotomy of occupations into manual and nonmanual showed one third of the districts of Inner London with at least 80 per cent of males in one category or the other. But when a more meaningful subdivision was used, separating the professional and managerial from other nonmanual workers and skilled from unskilled manual workers, only 17 districts had 80 per cent or more of males in any category; only 11 per cent of districts in Inner London had 60 per cent or more males in any of the four occupational categories.[9] This does not mean that there was no class segregation; the geographical clustering of districts with relatively large proportions in higher-status occupations shows that there was. The important point is that, although over half of the employers, managers, and professional people of Inner London lived in only 20 per cent of the enumeration districts, they very rarely lived in homogeneous enclaves.

An extensive series of maps, locating districts with extreme scores on particular variables, added further detail to the picture of London's diversity. The most striking feature of the maps in general was the exceptional character of the North-West quadrant of Inner London compared with the rest of Greater London. Many of the maps showed clustering of extreme scores only in this sector. Extreme concentrations of single adults and of furnished accommodation fell entirely in this quadrant; other characteristics, although occurring in extreme form elsewhere, showed their greatest geographical clustering within this sector. Concentrations of children under five, of overcrowded households, and of Irish, West Indian, and Asian immigrants also occurred here. On the other hand, the higher occupational groups, extremes of both high and low average room density and of high and low sex ratios were also concentrated here.

[8] "Outside Great Britain" means anywhere except England and Wales, Scotland, the Channel Islands, and the Isle of Man.
[9] The four occupational categories are defined, in terms of the Registrar-General's socioeconomic groups, in Appendix B — variables 40, 41A, 41B, and 43.

Despite this clustering of many types of extreme districts in the North-West quadrant of London, districts with extreme values of any one index tended to have quite specific and nonoverlapping locations within the sector. Areas with the highest proportion of furnished accommodation occurred immediately adjacent to, but not in, major immigrant areas; single adults were concentrated in districts peripheral to the districts of highest occupational status. Although within this part of London concentrations of some characteristics did coincide, they tended also to occur in isolation elsewhere; in particular, although relatively large proportions of Irish coincided with concentrations of West Indians in North Kensington and with Cypriot areas in Camden Town, the Irish alone were concentrated in Hammersmith, West Indians in Brixton, and the Cypriots in Islington.

In addition to the characteristic geographical distributions of many of the variables just described, there was also a polarity of extremes between the districts at the center and those at the outer edge of the Greater London area. In particular, the proportion of children aged under fifteen and the proportion of households that owned their accommodation were both extremely low in central districts and high in districts at the outer edge of the area.

The geographical distributions of the variables we considered are not easily summarized in terms of some simple dichotomy (for example, between East End and West End). The contrast between suburb and center was only one part of the pattern; equally important was the contrast, at the center, between extreme characteristics of districts lying within a small geographical compass.

PHASE 2: INTERDEPENDENCE OF THE VARIABLES

The second major phase of the analysis investigated the interdependence of each of 38 major variables with every other. A square matrix of product-moment coefficients of linear correlation was computed from the variable scores of all the 4,570 enumeration districts of Inner London excluding variables 4, 25, 31, and 33. (See Appendix B.) The matrix was analyzed by several methods, each of which is reviewed briefly in this section.

The complex geographical distribution of characteristics, as well as the diversity of conditions outlined in the previous section, was reflected in the small size of most of the coefficients in the matrix. As the correlation coefficient is an *average* measure of association, areas in which variables vary together are counterbalanced by areas in which they vary independently of each other. The diverse combinations of characteristics in Inner London therefore exerted an important influence on the values of the matrix; for example, one might, a priori, expect a straightforward relationship between occupational status and housing conditions — between the proportion of males in manual occupations and the proportion of households living in shared dwellings. However, the relationship is not a simple one. In council housing, where the occupational status of tenants is usually lower than average, there is very little sharing of dwellings. At the other extreme, sharing of dwellings is quite common in central areas of high occupational status where it is part of the cost of a central location. In consequence, the correlation between index 18, the percentage of households sharing a dwelling, and index 41, the proportion of males in manual occupations, was only .129. The correlation between index 18 and index 40, the proportion of males in professional and managerial occupations, was only −.141.

This type of complexity resulted in few high correlations among the variables apart from those of a technical nature. Variables that were closely related by definition, particularly indices of sharing of dwellings and facilities and of room density and overcrowding, had high, but trivial, coefficients of correlation among themselves. Apart from correlations of this sort, only two were particularly high; index 2, the proportion of children aged under fifteen, had a correlation of −.800 with index 12, the proportion of households consisting of one or two persons; index 38, the proportion of early school leavers, had a correlation of .827 with index 41, the proportion of males in manual occupations; but even these correlations have an obvious logical explanation. All other nontechnical correlations were smaller than ±.800.

Simple inspection of the coefficients showed that there were several important groupings of variables with relatively high intercorrelation. A first stage in the analysis of these groupings isolated all groups of variables with a minimum correlation between every member of ±.500. Groups isolated in this way ranged in size from 2 to 7 variables, and 31 of the 38 variables fell into one group or another. When the minimum level of intercorrelation was raised to ±.600, the largest group contained only 4 variables, but 23 of the variables still fell in one group or another.

Although many of the groupings were the result of purely technical correlations, a particular set of variables occurred in several of the groupings which could not be explained in this way. At the minimum level of $r = \pm.500$, the following variables occurred together with a minimum intercorrelation of −.523:

Variable No.	*Description*
2	Per cent population aged under 15 (neg.)
9	Per cent single adults
11	Per cent one-person households
12	Per cent one- and two-person households
24	Per cent households renting furnished accommodation
32	Per cent born outside the British Isles and the New Commonwealth
38	Per cent early school leavers (neg.)

At the minimum level of $r = \pm.600$, variables 9, 11 24, and 32 still occurred in one group.

A more rigorous grouping procedure, analogous to the procedure outlined later for classifying enumeration districts, divided all variables with a correlation larger than $\pm.500$ into a number of exclusive sets, each variable occurring in only one of the sets. Thirty-one variables were classified into seven groups such that the average correlation *within* groups was a maximum and that *between* groups a minimum. The results of this grouping procedure indicated that the most important general axes of differentiation between the enumeration districts of Inner London were:

    a. Socioeconomic status, variables 38, 40, and 41

    b. Sharing (of dwellings and household facilities), variables 18, 19, 20, 21, and 30

    c. Room density, variables 14, 15, 16, 22, and 36

    d. Transience, variables 2, 9, 11, 12, 13, 23, 24, 26, 28, 32, and 37

Three minor factors were: (1) fertility, variables 1, 5, 8; (2) the sex ratios, variables 6, 7; (3) and two indices of isolated old people, variables 3 and 27. The variables not included in any group were variables 10, 17, 29, 34, 35, 39, 42.

Another stage involved a principal component analysis of the correlation matrix. The primary aim of the component analysis in this instance was to reduce the computational task of the classification of enumeration districts at the next stage; the first 14 scores of the 38 possible principal components, accounting in all for 84 per cent of the original variance, were used as input for the classification of the 4,570 districts of Inner London in place of the 38 original variable scores, analyzed in the correlation matrix. Although the principal components were regarded primarily as a computational convenience, they also gave an indication of the most important dimensions underlying the variation between enumeration districts. The list of variables most highly correlated with the first principal component included most of the variables associated with socioeconomic status and "transience" (see the variables listed earlier); the first component accounted for exactly one quarter of the total variance. Variables most highly correlated with the second component were the variables of sharing and of room density and accounted for a further 19 per cent of the total variance. The variables most highly correlated with the first two principal components are listed here in rank order.

Component I: Variables Showing the Highest Correlations with Component I in Rank Order

Variable No.	Description	
9	Per cent single adults	− .839
2	Per cent aged under 15	.836
12	Per cent one- and two-person households	− .822
38	Per cent early school leavers	.816
11	Per cent one-person households	− .809
32	Per cent born "elsewhere" outside British Isles and New Commonwealth	− .794
24	Per cent private tenants, *furnished* accommodation	− .783
26	Per cent one-person households with one old person	.709
41	Per cent males in manual occupations	.698
40	Per cent males in professional and managerial occupations	− .653

Component II: Variables Showing the Highest Correlations with Component II in Rank Order

Variable No.	Description	
15	Per cent of all households overcrowded	− .845
20	Per cent households sharing W.C.	− .730
19	Per cent households sharing dwelling, stove, and sink	− .679
21	Per cent households sharing dwelling, stove, sink, and W.C.	− .678
14	Per cent five- or more-person households overcrowded	− .650
16	No. of persons per room	− .629
18	Per cent households sharing dwelling	− .628
1	Per cent aged under 5	− .626
30	Per cent born in British Caribbean	− .601

The results of these analyses are not entirely conclusive. The principal component analysis suggests that the two most general factors of differentiation between districts are an index of "social status" including the elements both of social class and of mobility or "transience," and second, a general index of housing conditions including the elements both of sharing and of room density.[10] Simpler analysis of the correlation matrix suggests that these two general axes are better divided into four. The most interesting feature, however, is the indication that some measure of the mobility of the population, both actual (in terms of length of residence and birthplace) and potential (in terms of marital status, household size, and type of accommodation), is an essential differentiating factor between districts of Inner London, although we do not yet know whether this is so in other British cities.

PHASE 3: A NEW TYPOLOGY OF LONDON'S DISTRICTS — METHOD AND RESULTS

The two phases of the analysis described were, in many ways, only essential preliminaries to the construction of a typology of London's subareas; the features of individual variables and of their interrelationships which have been described were chosen primarily to illustrate the nature of the typological problem. In this section I shall describe the method and results of a classification of the enumeration districts of Inner London and the wards of Greater London into a varying number of groups. The method of classification and the algorithm by which it proceeds were developed by Nigel Howard for this research project (see Chapter 16 of this volume); my description of the method summarizes the main points of his full mathematical exposition, to be published later. From the methodological point of view, the classification of enumeration districts may be regarded as a particular application of a generally applicable method of classification.

A number of previous studies have provided a typology of areas within London. Charles Booth's survey *Life and Labour of the People of London,* produced a series of maps in which all blocks of buildings in the streets of Inner London were allocated to a set of categories according to the social status and income of their inhabitants.[11] Similar maps were produced by the investigators of *The New Survey of London Life and Labour* in the 1930's.[12] A general typology of the wards of the Greater London conurbation, based on census data, was produced by the Census Office in the 1951 report on the conurbations, but the

---

[10] A varimax factor analysis of the correlation matrix for Inner London, computed by Miss Elizabeth Gittus as part of a comparative study of cities co-ordinated by the Inter-Universities Census Tract Committee, gives results similar to the results of principal component analysis.

[11] Booth, *op. cit.*

[12] Smith, *op. cit.*

typology did not follow a rigorous method.[13] A typology restricted to administrative areas as the basic unit is provided in a statement of evidence to the Royal Commission on Local Government in Greater London, presented by the Centre for Urban Studies.[14] The typology reported here departs from its predecessors not only in the use of a new form of data but also in the rigor and flexibility of the results. The method is a development of that used by Moser and Scott in their classification of British towns.[15]

In general, the desirable properties of any classification are that the groups identified should be as homogeneous as possible and that they should be as distinct as possible in respect to all the variables or attributes that are considered relevant to the classification. The problem of classification is not fully defined without, first, a specification of the number of groups to be established and, second, the definition of some measure of the homogeneity of the results. In the classification procedure described here, results were produced for a varying number of groups, ranging from two to thirty; this allowed us to inspect the results and choose the most desirable for any particular purpose.

The measure of homogeneity derives from the analysis of variance; for any individual group of any classification, the measure of its *inhomogeneity* is defined as the sum of the squared distances of every element (in this case every enumeration district) from the mean of its group. Where, as in this case, more than one variable is used, squared distances for each element are summed over all variables used in the classification. Comparability between different measures is achieved by standardizing all scores in units of standard deviation from their original means; this gives each variable a standardized mean of zero and a variance of one.[16]

The *inhomogeneity* of an entire classification is measured by the summation of the inhomogeneity of the individual groups over all groups. Where, as in this case, all variables are measured as deviations

[13] General Register Office, 1951 Census, *Report on Greater London and Five Other Conurbations* (London: H.M.S.O., 1956).

[14] See J. H. Westergaard, "The Structure of Greater London," in *London — Aspects of Change,* edited by Centre for Urban Studies (London: MacGibbon and Kee, 1964).

[15] C. Moser and W. Scott, *British Towns, a Statistical Study of Their Social and Economic Differences,* Centre for Urban Studies Report No. 2. (Edinburgh: Oliver and Boyd, 1961).

[16] Standardization of variables in this way also simplifies the interpretation of results since the total variation of the population, in standard form, is equal to the number of individuals classified, multiplied by the number of variables by which the classification is carried out.

from their respective means in the entire population, the inhomogeneity represents the "within-group variation" in the analysis-of-variance equation:

Total variation = within-group variation + between-group variation

The complementary item of the total variation, that between groups, may therefore be regarded as a measure of the *homogeneity* of the entire classification.

When the homogeneity of a classification is measured in this way, the problem of finding an "optimum" classification is that of delimiting groups so that their total within-group variation is minimal; when this element of the total variation is minimized, the variation between groups is maximized. The computer program for finding an optimum classification works from the principle that a classification that has maximum homogeneity, as defined earlier, also has the property that each element in the population classified is closer to the mean of its own group than to the mean of any other group; the program will "improve" any given classification until it has this property. The algorithm starts with a given classification into P groups and computes the mean vector of each group. The squared distances of each element from the means of each group summed over all the variables are compared; if the squared distance of any element from the mean of its own group summed over all the variables is greater than, or equal to, its squared distance from the mean of any other group, the element is transferred to the group whose mean is closest to it. New means are then computed for the groups involved in any transfers, and a new set of comparisons is made. The process continues until a test shows that every element is closer to its own group mean than to the mean of any other group.

The classification achieved by this algorithm is a "local" optimum in the sense that the homogeneity could not be improved by the transfer of any single element from one group to another. It is not necessarily a "global" optimum in the sense that the homogeneity might not be increased by a different initial starting classification. In any succession of classifications it is therefore important that the algorithm should start with a "good" initial partition of the population. In practice, the computer starts the process by subdividing the population into those elements which lie above and those which lie below the mean of the variable that has the greatest variance. (In the classification of enumeration districts of Inner London, the input data were the first 14 principal component scores derived from the 38 variables of the correlation matrix. The initial partition of the elements was therefore into the group lying above and the group lying below the mean of the first principal component — the component with the greatest variance.) This initial partition is improved until it is optimal. The algorithm proceeds from two to three groups by similarly dichotomizing the group that has the greatest internal variation (the greatest inhomogeneity), and the procedure continues until a sufficiently large number of classifications or a classification into a sufficiently large number of groups has been obtained. For the districts of Inner London, results were produced for classifications into 2 groups, 3 groups, and so on, to 30 groups.

The output of the computer program consists of the following items:

1. An allocation matrix in which each element, identified by a unique number, is listed with the identification number of the group to which that element is allotted in each classification

2. The number of elements allotted to each group in each classification

3. The mean vector of each group in each classification, specified in standard scores above or below the mean of the entire population

4. The total variation within each group of each classification (the inhomogeneity)

5. The total variation within each group of each classification separately for each of the variables used in the classification

6. The proportion of total variation which is taken up by variation *between* the groups of the classification, for each classification (the homogeneity).

In addition to this material, a matrix summarizing the relationships between all the groups of successive classifications shows: (1) the identification numbers of the groups in all other classifications with which each group in any given classification has the largest number of elements in common; (2) a count of the number of elements that do not follow the general pattern of interrelationship between classifications that is shown by the majority of elements.

From this output the results of any classification can be mapped and the groupings interpreted. Obviously, for a project involving the manifold classification of 4,570 enumeration districts, not every classification could be separately mapped and interpreted in full. Technically, the best, but trivial, classification would be one in which every element was in a group on its own (in which case the total variation would be entirely accounted for by variation between groups). In practice, the choice of a classification for further analysis will depend on the particular needs of any inquiry and intuitive preference for a particular number of groups. However, within a given range of possible classifications there are a number of statistical criteria that indicate which classification is preferable to others in the range. In the analysis of Inner London, classifications into two and six groups were selected for most detailed inspection. The purely statistical criteria for this choice may be applied to any typology derived from similar data, but specific intuitive criteria are relevant to this particular study.

The twofold classification was chosen primarily for the intrinsic interest of a simple dichotomy — to test, for example, whether the terms "East End–West End" or "Center" and "Suburb" had any meaning. The sixfold classification involved more complex criteria. The first criterion involves comparison of the measure of homogeneity of any classification with that of its immediate neighbors. As the proportion of total variation accounted for by variation between groups is bound to increase with an increase in the number of groups in the classification, the homogeneity increases with successive classifications. The differences between the homogeneity of each classification and the next show how much is to be gained by going from one classification to the next. Therefore, within a given range, a classification is considered to be a "good" one if the gain in selecting it, rather than the previous classification, is greater than the gain in forsaking it for the classification that follows. Classifications for which this is true are those where the second differences in the original sequence (of proportions of total variation, which is variation between groups) are large, with negative sign. By this criterion, the two-, three-, four-, and sixfold classifications were the best, in that order. However, since the second differences also showed a definite tendency to increase with the number of groups in the classification, a similar argument was applied, treating the second differences as the original sequence of measures; this led to inspection of the fourth differences, which indicated that the sixfold classification was the most satisfactory.

A second important criterion is the inhomogeneity of each of the separate groups of a classification. The total variation within any group, which is part of the program output, is obviously affected by the number of districts in the group. But a measure of homogeneity which is independent of the number in the group is the variance of the group, obtained by dividing the variation by the number of elements in the group. The variance of each group can then be compared with the overall variance of the population and groups with particularly large variances excluded from further analysis. By this criterion we set an upper limit of nine groups; all classifications into ten groups or more included groups with particularly small numbers of districts and with variances as high as four times the variance of the total population.

A third criterion related the results of successive classifications to the analysis of the most important axes of differentiation which were established in Phase 2. The over-all measure of homogeneity, the total between-group variation, can be broken down into the between-group variation of each individual variable. The variables that best distinguish between all the groups are those for which this element of variation is the largest. For all the classifications from the twofold to the sixfold, the most important differentiating variables were those which defined the four basic axes of differentiation outlined earlier under Phase 2; these were Socioeconomic Status, Sharing, Room Density, and Transience. For the sevenfold and subsequent classifications, relatively unimportant differentiating variables, such as the proportion of the population born in Cyprus or in Malta and the ratio of dwellings to buildings, began to play an important distinguishing role. A sixfold classification of the enumeration districts of Inner London was therefore the most detailed classification we could achieve, given the method and input data considered here, which differentiated only according to important general factors of difference.

The classification procedure is based on purely logical considerations. There is no guarantee that the groups of any of the classifications will be meaningful, either geographically or sociologically, since the process is neutral to both geographical and sociological considerations. In this case, the classifications analyzed were meaningful in both respects. A summary of some salient features of the twofold and the sixfold classifications of enumeration districts and of the sixfold classification of all the wards of Greater London occupies the rest of this paper.

Despite the geographical complexity emphasized earlier, the twofold classification of enumeration districts produced a relatively simple geographical pattern. A central group of 855 districts was identified in the North-West quadrant of Inner London. The group was geographically compact and extended to the boundary of the old Administrative County in the North. Apart from this central block, there were a few isolated districts located, in most cases, close to the fashionable commons of South London.

This simple dichotomy, concentric in pattern, isolated the cosmopolitan center from the rest. In the central block occupational status was high and the proportion of early school leavers particularly low — 40 per cent on the average, compared with 80 per cent in the rest of Inner London. The proportions of single adults and of small households were large, and a relatively large proportion of the population was born outside the British Isles and the New Commonwealth (18 per cent). Despite the high status of the center, however, there was little difference between the two sectors in housing conditions.

Subsequent classifications heightened the detail of London's sub-division, but this central block remained until the classification into six groups. In the sixfold classification it was split up (although not in a straightforward way) into a smaller central core and a fringe of districts in which the element of "transience" was much stronger. The high-status districts of the central core were named, for shorthand purposes, the "Upper Class" type (Type 1).

The central core was surrounded by an irregular band of districts in which almost half of all adults were single and 46 per cent of households consisted of only one person. Forty-two per cent of households had furnished accommodations, mobility was high, and the proportion of early school leavers was relatively small. These characteristics, although less strongly marked, were also distinguishing characteristics of the central core, but in this peripheral type, housing conditions were much worse — in particular, there was far more sharing of dwellings and facilities. Because of the pattern of characteristics which these districts showed on average, they were named the "Bed-Sitter" type (Type 2).

Geographically, districts of the "Bed-Sitter" type had a clear concentric relationship to the districts of the central core; they rarely occurred in isolation from the "Upper Class" type, most of them lying immediately adjacent to the central core.

Although none of the remaining types of districts in Inner London had such a strong concentric pattern, the third type described did tend to occur at roughly the same distance from the central group in each direction. This was the "Poor" type of district (Type 3) found in the worst areas of North Kensington, Paddington, Islington, Whitechapel, and Brixton. The distinguishing features of this type were large proportions of households in overcrowded dwellings and sharing domestic facilities, low social status, and relatively large proportions of children under five — amounting to 10 per cent of the population. This type of district included the main areas of West Indian, Cypriot, and Irish immigration.

Compared with the pattern of prewar slums, the "Poor" type of district identified in the sixfold classification occurred in relatively small patches in Inner London. An extensive block of blighted housing which previously ran through the East End and riverside boroughs had, in

1961, been broken up by the slum-clearance efforts of local housing authorities and the effects of bombing during the last war. Few very extensive patches of blight remained, apart from Whitechapel, among the two types of district which then accounted for most of the old slum areas. The "traditional" slum areas were mostly made up of districts that, in terms of our typology, may be called the "Stable Working Class" type and the "Local Authority Housing" type (Types 4 and 5, respectively).

The "Stable Working Class" type was the largest group of districts in the sixfold classification (34 per cent) and may be regarded as the "average" type for Inner London; on none of the variables was this type clearly distinguished from the mean for Inner London as a whole. However, the average district for Inner London was one in which 65 per cent of the population were in manual occupations and three quarters left school before the age of sixteen; almost one third of households shared a dwelling, and one third shared a W.C. This type of district was named "Stable Working Class" because, although housing conditions and social status were comparable to those of the "Poor" type described earlier, the immigrant and recently mobile population was much smaller. It is important here to note the effect of defining all types in terms of their deviation from the London mean; the result is a typology that is not "absolute" because the allocation of individual districts is affected by changes in the size and mean characteristics of the classification universe. If the districts of Inner London had been classified together with those of Outer London and if the mean characteristics of Greater London had been used as the reference, many more districts would have been classified as "Poor" where, in Inner London alone, they were merely "average."

The "Local Authority Housing" type (Type 5), contained 18 per cent of the districts of Inner London but showed no clear geographical configuration. This is not surprising in view of the piecemeal development of public housing and the freedom of public housing authorities from some, at least, of the normal market forces; the main patches of this type of district were the large council estates, mostly close to the boundary of Inner London. A large proportion of children under fifteen, few small and many large households lived in these districts; although average room density was quite high, there was very little actual overcrowding, and sharing of dwellings and facilities was particularly uncommon.

The average characteristics of the "Local Authority Housing" type were apparently straightforward, but closer inspection of the districts revealed, in acute form, one of the difficulties of interpretation of this type of multivariate classification. The shorthand description, "Local Authority Housing," was chosen because, on the average, 75 per cent of households in any district rented their accommodation from a local authority; however, the range was from under 10 per cent to 100 per cent within districts; in four out of five of the other types of district there were individual districts that had 80 per cent or more households in council tenancies. This "overlapping" between types in the classification in terms of a single variable arises because every variable is taken into consideration in the process of classification. Because all the characteristics of the districts were considered in the process at the same time, the classification did not produce results that had a very distinct meaning in terms of any one variable on its own. In the case of "Local Authority Housing" a district having, in extreme form, all the characteristics normally associated with council housing, such as a high proportion of children under fifteen and similar housing conditions, might have been classified as "Local Authority Housing" type even though there were no council tenants in it. This argument applies equally to all the variables used.

The "Stable Working Class" type and the "Local Authority Housing" type formed the fourth major band of districts in Inner London. They were broken up in some areas by the "Poor" type described previously. On the southern edge of Inner London they gave way to the final type identified as the "Almost Suburban" type (Type 6). These districts had a relatively high proportion of owner-occupiers and above average occupational status and housing conditions.

The map (Figure 1) shows the result of this sixfold classification of enumeration districts for the districts falling within the Greater London Borough of Camden. The intermixture of all types of districts shown on this map is fairly typical of Inner London as a whole. Detailed results for the whole of Inner London are to be published early in 1969 in Volume I of the *Third Survey of London Life and Labour*.

The typology of Inner London's enumeration districts, described earlier, was largely confirmed by a classification of all the electoral wards of Greater London. Electoral wards were classified into from two to six groups using only seven of the original variables. A sample analysis of the variation between all the enumeration districts of Greater London indicated that variation between wards would account for about one half of the total variation. Seven of the original variables were computed as input for the ward classification — the variables that best distinguished between the first few classifications of the enumeration districts of Inner London. These were:

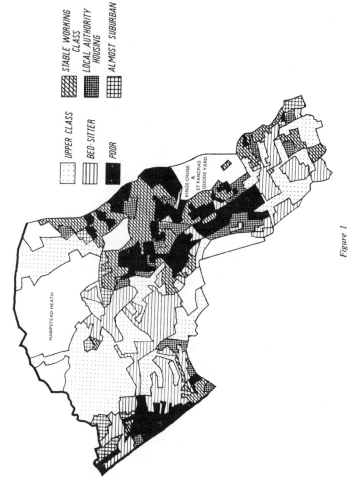

Figure 1

Six Types of Enumeration Districts in Camden Census 1961
The scale of the map is one inch to one mile.

Variable No.	*Description*
2	Per cent aged under 15
9	Per cent single adults
12	Per cent one- or two-person households
15	Per cent of all households overcrowded
18	Per cent of households sharing a dwelling
38	Per cent early school leavers
41B	Per cent males in unskilled manual occupations

Although the difference between means of Inner London and Greater London naturally affected comparison between the classifications the pattern in Inner London described previously was largely repeated. The central "cosmopolitan" block again occurred but with no distinction between the central core and the peripheral "Bed-Sitter" fringe; instead, the suburban areas of Outer London were divided into two types, a "Higher Status Suburban" type and a "Lower Status Suburban" type.

CONCLUSION

The data and the classification procedures used in this project do lead to a typology of London's subareas which is intuitively satisfying — the complexity of London is reduced to a meaningful pattern. But a true appreciation of this complexity is itself one of the rewards of the analysis. Stratification of areas cannot be satisfactorily achieved without recognizing that housing conditions and "transience," as well as occupation and schooling, play an important differentiating role. Once achieved, an optimum classification, which recognizes differences in all these respects and more, does not produce a geographically simple result. Although in the preceding summary, the location of different types of district has been described mainly in terms of the occurrence of substantial areas of a similar type, some parts of London are better described in terms of their heterogeneity and the mixture of all types of district within close proximity to each other. This is one of the aspects of London which, although apparent to the pedestrian on London's streets, has not previously been measurable on the large scale attempted here.

Appendix A

SELECTED MEAN CHARACTERISTICS OF SIX TYPES OF ENUMERATION DISTRICTS IN INNER LONDON, CENSUS 1961

		Enumeration District Type						All Inner London	
No.	Index Name	Type 1 Upper Class	Type 2 Bed-Sitter	Type 3 Poor	Type 4 Stable Working Class	Type 5 Local Authority Housing	Type 6 Almost Suburban	Mean	Standard Deviation
1.	% population under 5	4.0	4.2	9.8	7.8	6.9	6.0	7.0	2.6
2.	% population under 15	11.2	9.9	21.1	20.1	25.6	17.7	19.2	6.0
3.	% population 65 and over	14.2	11.1	9.8	12.2	9.1	14.5	11.8	4.0
6.	Female/male ratio, all ages	1462	1175	1030	1082	1059	1149	1123	237
7.	Female/male ratio, 25–44	1265	919	874	951	1066	1055	1005	226
8.	% women 20–24 ever married	22.7	26.1	60.6	63.6	43.4	53.1	50.9	20.2
9.	% adults single	40.0	47.8	29.0	25.2	25.4	24.9	28.7	8.6
11.	% one-person households	33.5	46.1	25.2	21.1	13.0	17.4	22.5	11.5
12.	% one- and two-person households	66.0	75.7	55.3	52.2	37.3	50.8	52.6	13.2
13.	% households of five or more persons	8.4	5.4	12.0	11.7	19.7	11.4	12.4	6.2
15.	% all households overcrowded	3.4	11.0	15.7	6.3	5.9	2.2	6.9	5.7
16.	No. of persons per room	0.65	0.81	0.92	0.77	0.89	0.63	0.78	0.14
18.	% households sharing dwelling	11.0	44.1	63.4	35.6	5.3	17.9	29.1	30.7
19.	% households sharing dwelling, stove, and sink	3.3	14.2	16.5	7.2	1.9	3.3	6.9	8.2

No.									
20.	% households sharing W.C.	17.2	48.4	59.3	36.6	7.8	19.1	30.4	23.6
21.	% households sharing dwelling, stove, sink, and W.C.	2.9	13.4	15.3	6.3	1.7	2.8	6.5	7.7
22.	% owner-occupiers	14.1	8.5	12.0	12.1	3.9	37.3	15.3	17.1
23.	% council tenants	4.9	3.3	6.6	13.3	74.6	8.8	21.2	30.9
24.	% private tenants, furnished accommodation	18.0	46.1	23.7	8.8	1.7	7.5	13.0	14.3
25.	% private tenants, unfurnished accommodation	54.2	38.0	55.2	62.1	16.2	43.3	46.0	25.8
28.	% born in India, Pakistan, and Ceylon	1.9	3.5	1.2	0.5	0.3	0.8	1.0	1.5
30.	% born in British Caribbean	0.4	1.6	6.8	2.2	0.3	1.0	2.1	3.6
32.	% born elsewhere outside British Isles and New Commonwealth	19.4	20.0	8.9	4.0	2.3	3.5	6.9	7.7
36.	% born in Ireland (both parts)	4.5	8.3	9.8	4.4	2.8	2.9	4.9	4.0
37.	% moved within year into local authority area	17.1	20.1	9.5	5.8	4.9	6.6	8.3	8.5
38.	% early school leavers	33.9	40.5	85.1	84.0	86.6	69.7	73.5	21.3
40.	% males in professional/managerial occupations	43.4	25.2	6.6	7.2	5.2	16.9	13.2	14.6
41.	% males in manual occupations	28.7	41.1	77.6	75.2	77.1	55.3	65.3	21.2
	Number of districts of each type	414	333	679	1423	832	888		4569
	Percentage of districts of each type	9.1	7.3	14.9	31.1	18.2	19.4		100

Appendix B

Variable Numbers and Titles

Variable No.	Variable Title
1.	Percentage of the population aged under 5
2.	Percentage of the population aged under 15
3.	Percentage of the population aged 65 or over
4.	Percentage of the population of pensionable age [(Enumerated males aged 65 or over and females aged 60 or over ÷ enumerated population all ages) × 100.0]
5.	Fertility ratio [(Enumerated population aged 0–4 ÷ enumerated females aged 15–44) × 1,000]
6.	Female/male ratio all ages
7.	Female/male ratio ages 25–44
8.	Percentage of women aged 20–24 who have ever been married
9.	Percentage of adult population that are single [(Enumerated population aged 15 or over that are single ÷ total enumerated population aged 15 or over) × 100.0]
10.	Number of dwellings per building
11.	Percentage of households containing one person
12.	Percentage of households containing one or two persons
13.	Percentage of households containing five or more persons
14.	Percentage of households containing five or more persons which are overcrowded [(Households present at census containing five or more persons who live at a residential density of over $1\frac{1}{2}$ persons per room ÷ total households present at census containing five or more persons) × 100.0]
15.	Percentage of all households that are overcrowded [(Households present at census with a residential density of over $1\frac{1}{2}$ persons per room ÷ total households present at census) × 100.0]
16.	Average number of persons per room
17.	Average number of rooms per dwelling
18.	Percentage of households sharing their dwelling
19.	Percentage of households sharing their dwelling, stove, and sink
20.	Percentage of households sharing or entirely without a W.C.
21.	Percentage of households sharing their dwelling, stove, sink, and sharing or without a W.C.
22.	Percentage of households owning their accommodation
23.	Percentage of households renting their accommodation from a Local Authority
24.	Percentage of households renting private furnished accommodation

Variable No.	Variable Title
25.	Percentage of households renting private unfurnished accommodation
26.	Percentage of one-person households containing one old person
27.	Percentage of two-person households containing two old people
28.	Percentage of the resident population born in India, Pakistan, or Ceylon
29.	Percentage of the resident population born in British Africa
30.	Percentage of the resident population born in the British Caribbean
31.	Percentage of the resident population born in the New Commonwealth (sum of variables 28, 29, and 30) [(Resident population stating their birthplace as India, Pakistan, Ceylon, British Africa, or the British Caribbean ÷ total population stating residence in England and Wales, or not stating usual residence) × 100.0]
32.	Percentage of the resident population born elsewhere outside the British Isles and the New Commonwealth [(Resident population stating birthplace as anywhere other than Great Britain, Ireland, India, Pakistan, Ceylon, British Africa, or the British Caribbean ÷ total population stating residence in England and Wales, or not stating a usual residence) × 100.0]
33.	Percentage of the resident population born anywhere outside the British Isles (sum of variables 28, 29, 30, and 32)
34.	Percentage of the resident population born in Malta (included in variables 32 and 33)
35.	Percentage of the resident population born in Cyprus (included in variables 32 and 33)
36.	Percentage of the resident population born in Ireland (both parts)
37.	Percentage of the population that moved into the local authority area within 12 months of census date
38.	Percentage of the population aged 15 or over that left school before the age of 16
39.	Percentage of the economically active population that are female
40.	Percentage of occupied and retired males who are employers or in professional or managerial occupations [(Occupied and retired males in socioeconomic groups 1, 2, 3, 4, and 13 ÷ total occupied and retired males in all socioeconomic groups) × 100.0]

Variable No.	Variable Title
41.	Percentage of occupied and retired males in manual occupations [(Occupied and retired males in socioeconomic groups 7–12 and 14–17 ÷ total occupied and retired males in all socioeconomic groups) × 100.0]
42.	Percentage of the economically active population working outside their local authority area of residence

Additional Variables Not Used in the Classification of Enumeration Districts

Variable No.	Variable Title
40A	Percentage of occupied and retired males who are employers or in managerial occupations [(Occupied and retired males in socioeconomic groups 1, 2, and 13 ÷ total occupied and retired males in all socioeconomic groups) × 100.0]
40B	Percentage of occupied and retired males in professional occupations [(Occupied and retired males in socioeconomic groups 3 and 4 ÷ total occupied and retired males in all socioeconomic groups) × 100.0]
41A	Percentage of occupied and retired males in skilled manual occupations [(Occupied and retired males in socioeconomic groups 8, 9, 12, and 14 ÷ total occupied and retired males in all socioeconomic groups) × 100.0]
41B	Percentage of occupied and retired males in unskilled manual occupations [(Occupied and retired males in socioeconomic groups 7, 10, 11, 15, 16, 17 ÷ total occupied and retired males in all socioeconomic groups) × 100.0]
43.	Percentage of occupied and retired males in intermediate and junior nonmanual occupations [(Occupied and retired males in socioeconomic groups 5 and 6 ÷ total occupied and retired males in all socioeconomic groups) × 100.0]
44.	Percentage change in population 1951–1961

15

NIGEL HOWARD

Least Squares Classification and Principal Component Analysis: A Comparison*

1. *GEOMETRICAL COMPARISON*

THERE IS A FUNDAMENTAL ANALOGY between the method by which the 4,500 enumeration districts of London Administrative County were classified into groups and the method of principal component analysis by which the principal factors of variation among the districts were discovered. To bring out this analogy, I shall discuss these two methods side by side.[1]

The data for both methods were the values of about 40 census variables for each of about 4,500 districts. These data may be displayed in a table, or matrix, with 4,500 columns and 40 rows. The number, say x_{ij}, in the ith row and jth column is the value of the ith variable for the jth district.

The object of principal component analysis is to summarize these data in a matrix with the same number of columns but fewer rows. That is, a smaller number of new variables is sought to express as much as possible of the diversity between districts expressed by the original variables.

The object of least squares classification is to summarize the data

* This paper is a part of the author's contribution to the *Third Survey of London Life and Labour*, organized by the Centre for Urban Studies, University College, London.

[1] See also R. N. Howard, "Classifying a Population into Homogeneous Groups," in J. R. Lawrence (ed.), *Operational Research and the Social Sciences* (London: Tavistock Publications, 1966); A. W. F. Edwards and L. L. Cavalli-Sforza, "A Method for Cluster Analysis," *Biometrics, 21* (June 1965).

in a matrix with fewer *columns* but the same number of *rows*. Let us regard the original data as giving the means of 4,500 groups of districts, each containing one district. Then we can say that we are seeking a smaller number of new groups, the means of which will express as much as possible of the diversity between the means of the original groups.

How this is done in each case may be illustrated geometrically — at any rate, in the two-dimensional case. Suppose that there are only two variables, perhaps a social-class index and a housing index, and only 16 districts. Then each district may, as in Figures 1 and 2, be plotted as a point in two-dimensional space.

Figure 1 illustrates the finding of the first principal component, that is, a single new variable in terms of which as much as possible of the original diversity between districts may be expressed. The new variable is represented by a line such that the sum of squares of distances from the points to the line is a minimum. In the figure, the sum of squares of lengths of the arrows drawn is minimized.

Figure 2 illustrates the partitioning of the population into two groups using least squares classification. The two groups are chosen so as to minimize the sum of squares of distances from any point to the mean of its group. Thus, again in Figure 2, where the means of groups are represented by crosses, the sum of squares of lengths of the arrows is minimized.

In each case the data are then summarized by giving for each district, not its actual position in space, but the position of the arrowhead drawn from it. In Figure 1 this makes it possible to characterize the

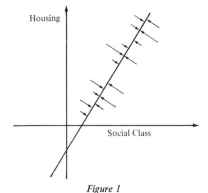

Figure 1

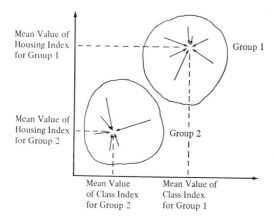

Figure 2

district by a value of just one variable — the position of the arrowhead on the line. In Figure 2, instead of sixteen positions in space, it becomes possible to give just two — the positions of the means of the groups.

These figures illustrate the problem in two dimensions. In m dimensions a principal component analysis seeks for p ($< m$) lines, which are at right angles to each other and thus define a p-dimensional subspace of the m-dimensional space in such a way that the sum of squares of the m-dimensional distances through which the points have to move when projected into the subspace is a minimum. This cannot be illustrated in two dimensions.

A p-fold classification, on the other hand, can be illustrated in two dimensions, though it should be imagined as taking place in m dimensions. A partition of n points into p ($< n$) groups is sought in which the sum of squares of all m-dimensional distances from the points to the means of their groups is a minimum.

It can be seen that the results will depend on the units in which the variables are measured along the axes. In fact, neither a principal component analysis nor a classification can be carried out without choosing not only a set of variables but also the units in which those variables are to be measured; and these choices must be made a priori.

This problem frequently arises in multivariate statistics, and it is often resolved by the decision to use *standardized* variables, which are measured in units of standard deviations from their means. This was what we decided to do. What should be emphasized is that this choice had to be made on intuitive grounds, a priori. It is natural that, in choosing the variables to be used, we should define the field of study in which we are interested. But if mathematical methods are to be used, we may have to make that definition very explicit. In particular, for component analysis or classification the definition must specify units for the variables chosen.

2. *MINIMIZATION OF VARIATION LOST*

Defining the *variation of a multivariable population* — one each of whose elements is described by the values of m variables — as the sum of the variations of all the variables,

$$nS^2 = \sum_{i=1}^{m} \sum_{j=1}^{n} (x_{ij} - \bar{x}_i)^2$$

(where $\bar{x}_i$ is the mean of the ith variable), we can say that both principal component analysis and least squares classification replace the original population by another that has less variation; and both seek to minimize the amount of the original variation that gets lost in the process. Geometrically, the variation that gets lost in each case is the sum of squares of the arrows illustrated in Figures 1 and 2; the variation retained is the variation of the population that replaces the original one, and that is the population of the points at the tips of arrows in Figures 1 and 2. In Figure 1 it is a population of n points on the line of the principal component; in Figure 2 it is a population of n points at the means of the two groups.

To verify these statements, we show that a general formula

Total variation = Variation lost + variation retained

does, in fact, hold in each case, and we derive the particular forms in which it holds. Then, working from the particular formula for each case, we show how the principal component problem and the classification problem are each solved by seeking to minimize the variation lost or, equivalently, to maximize the variation retained.

Clearly, there is a trivial solution for each problem by which all the original variation would be retained. If m axes at right angles, or n groups of elements each containing one element, were chosen (n being the original number of elements), then the variation lost would be zero. Moreover, the variation retained would in both cases increase (or, at least, never decrease) as p (representing the number of new variables or the number of groups) is increased. The question therefore arises: How should p be chosen? In both cases some analytical guidance can be obtained. But in both cases, the answer will also depend on how useful and interpretable the various sets of p variables or groups are found to be.

Essentially, in both cases a balance must be struck between simplicity in representing the data — for which p should be small — and detailed accuracy in doing the same — for which it should be large.

In both cases the mean point of the population of points which replaces the original population coincides with the original mean point. Thus in both cases, if $x_{ij}^{''}$ represents the value (of the original ith variable) which replaces x_{ij} (the original value of the original ith variable), then the formula mentioned earlier which gives the composition of the total variation becomes

$$\sum_{i=1}^{m} \sum_{j=1}^{n} (x_{ij} - \bar{x}_i)^2 = \sum_{i=1}^{m} \sum_{j=1}^{n} (x_{ij} - x_{ij}^{''})^2 + \sum_{i=1}^{m} \sum_{j=1}^{n} (x_{ij}^{''} - \bar{x}_i)^2$$

3. COMPARISON OF SOLUTIONS OBTAINED

The solution obtained for the classification problem suffers from two disadvantages compared to that obtained for the principal component problem.

A principal component solution replacing the original m variables with p $(< m)$ new variables involves the matrix

$$\{x_{ij}^{'}\} = \begin{bmatrix} x_{11}^{'} & x_{12}^{'} & \cdots & x_{1n}^{'} \\ x_{21}^{'} & x_{22}^{'} & \cdots & x_{2n}^{'} \\ \cdot & \cdot & & \cdot \\ \cdot & \cdot & & \cdot \\ \cdot & \cdot & & \cdot \\ x_{p1}^{'} & x_{p2}^{'} & \cdots & x_{pn}^{'} \end{bmatrix}$$

where the ith row gives the value of the ith new variable for each of the n points. Now this matrix gives not only the solution for p new variables but the solution for $1, 2, \ldots, p - 1$ new variables as well. For the solution for i $(< p)$ new variables is given in the first i rows. This means that many solutions are neatly comprehended in one.

By contrast, a solution that classifies the points into p groups involves the matrix

$$\{x'_{ij}\} = \begin{bmatrix} x'_{11} & x'_{12} & \cdots & x'_{1p} \\ x'_{21} & x'_{22} & \cdots & x'_{2p} \\ \cdot & \cdot & & \cdot \\ \cdot & \cdot & & \cdot \\ \cdot & \cdot & & \cdot \\ x'_{m1} & x'_{m2} & \cdots & x'_{mp} \end{bmatrix}$$

in which the jth column gives the mean values of each of the original variables for the jth group; this matrix does not, in general, have any columns in common with the matrix of p' ($\neq p$) columns which is given by the classification into p' groups.

The same phenomenon naturally appears if we introduce and compare the other two matrices given by the two solutions. The other matrix found by component analysis has p rows and m columns and gives the general definitions of all the p new variables in terms of the original m variables. (The ith such definition is of the form

$$x'_i = a_{i1}x_1 + a_{i2}x_2 + \ldots + a_{im}x_m$$

so that, in fact, the ith new variable is a linear function of the m original ones. From this definition, we may deduce each of the values in the ith row of the matrix $\{x'_{ij}\}$ given the matrix $\{x_{ij}\}$ which comprises the original data).

The matrix of definitions of all the p new variables is written

$$\{a_{ij}\} = \begin{bmatrix} a_{11} & a_{12} & \cdots & a_{1m} \\ a_{21} & a_{22} & \cdots & a_{2m} \\ \cdot & \cdot & & \cdot \\ \cdot & \cdot & & \cdot \\ \cdot & \cdot & & \cdot \\ a_{p1} & a_{p2} & \cdots & a_{pm} \end{bmatrix}$$

In the ith row this gives the coefficients occurring in the definition of the ith new variable. In this matrix, too, many solutions are comprehended. That is, the first i rows give the general definitions of the i new variables found when only i new variables are sought.

Contrast this matrix with the one obtained by a solution to the p-fold classification problem. This is a matrix with n rows and p columns in which the element δ_{ij}, occurring in the ith row and jth column, is defined by

$$\delta_{ij} = \begin{cases} 1 \text{ if the } i\text{th point is in the } j\text{th group} \\ 0 \text{ if not} \end{cases}$$

Thus the jth column gives the membership of the jth group, and in general it will not remain the same as p is varied. Thus, again, we cannot neatly summarize many solutions in one. (Here also, by the way, the matrix $\{x'_{ij}\}$ can be deduced from $\{\delta_{ij}\}$ together with $\{x_{ij}\}$.)

The other disadvantage suffered by a classification solution is that the method used to obtain it does not guarantee its over-all optimality. It guarantees only that it is *locally* optimal. That is, it finds a classification of the points into p groups such that, if any point in one group were transferred to another group, there would be a reduction in variation retained (or, equally, an increase in variation lost); but it does not guarantee that, by simultaneously exchanging sets of points between groups, the variation retained would not be increased. This may or may not be of much importance in practice, although it is easy to set up artificial examples in which it is very important. As far as it goes, our experience makes us hopeful.

To offset these disadvantages, a classification does have the advantage over a component analysis that the results are often easier to interpret. Note first of all that, whereas in component analysis one is more interested in the second matrix — the matrix $\{a_{ij}\}$ of definitions of the new variables — than in the first, in classification it is the other way round. The first matrix — of group means — tends to be of more interest than the second — the matrix of group memberships. The explanation is that in order to know what it means for a point to be in a certain group, we have to look at and interpret the means of the groups. However, to learn what it means for a point to have certain values of the new variables, we must interpret the definitions of the new variables.

Frequently the first interpretation is easier than the second. It is often easier to fit a concept to a group of elements for which one knows the mean values of certain variables than to interpret a variable defined as a weighted average of many other variables. Part of the reason for this may be that in interpreting group means it is possible to transform back to the original, natural units in which the variables were measured. But in interpreting a set of weights it is the relative size of any two weights which matters, and there are no natural units.

Finally, I must point out that classification provides a more "egalitarian" approach to certain social problems than does component analysis. Suppose we have measured, on certain objects, certain variables any of which might provide an "order of merit" for the objects. For example, one might have measured the various abilities of schoolchildren or the various statistics of industrial production of countries. The first component — the single new variable that absorbs as much as possible of the original variation — provides a general yardstick of "merit" for the objects. It is obviously justifiable to use it as such if the proportion of the variation it absorbs is high. If it is not, the alternative of classifying the objects into groups whose members score highly in different variables, without attempting to impose a general yardstick, might be better.

4. DUALITY RELATIONS

In Section 5 I shall show algebraically that there is a relationship of duality between least squares classification and a certain kind of restricted component analysis. It transpires that a least squares classification is simply a component analysis performed on the transposed matrix of "observations" $X^T = \{x_{ji}\}$ instead of the matrix $X = \{x_{ij}\}$, except that certain side conditions are added to this component problem. That is, the process of classification may be described as follows. Instead of regarding x_{ij} as representing the value of the ith variable for the jth element, we regard it as representing the value of a fictitious jth variable for a fictitious ith element. Then we perform a component analysis subject to these additional conditions:

1. Each fictitious variable shall have a nonzero coefficient in the definition of one and only one component.

2. The nonzero coefficients in the definition of a given component shall all be equal.

3. No component shall have only zero coefficients in its definition. (This assumes that the number p of components is fixed beforehand).

Conditions 1 and 3 correspond to the condition in the (nontransposed) classification problem that the elements be *partitioned* into p subsets. Indeed, let us recall the definition of a partition of a set S as a set of subsets of S such that

   i. Any two subsets are disjoint.
   ii. Together the subsets add up to S.
   iii. No subset is empty.

Thus we can easily see that Conditions 1 and 3 require the component analysis to determine a partition of the set of m variables into p subsets, the qth subset being the set of variables with nonzero coefficients in the definition of the qth component.

Condition 3 is, of course, unnecessary in the sense that, if a certain amount of variation can be retained using less than p subsets, at least the same amount can always be retained using p. I put it in for completeness, because it occurs in the definition of a partition.

Condition 2 corresponds, in the classification problem, to the fact that, of two elements in a group, one cannot be "more" in than the other. Each is either in or out. In the component problem it combines with Condition 1 to ensure that the problem of finding just the first component (solving the problem for $p = 1$) has only one trivial solution; this corresponds to the fact that there is only one trivial one-partition of a set of elements.

Condition 1 ensures that the axes of the p components found will be orthogonal. But, in fact, it says more. It says that any axis must be orthogonal to the axes of all the original variables except that which has a nonzero coefficient in its definition.

The *restricted* component problem, having these side conditions, is not of course as simple to solve as the ordinary unrestricted one. In fact, Conditions 1 and 2 are essentially logical "either-or" conditions; thus the problem is not amenable to ordinary calculus methods. This is why the classification problem, unlike the unrestricted component problem, can be solved by enumerative methods but cannot otherwise be solved in such a way as to guarantee global optimality. However, I shall prove a necessary condition for an optimal solution, and this can be enforced by iterative methods.

On the other hand, the components obtained by a restricted component analysis are defined in a much simpler way than those obtained by an unrestricted analysis. And this is perhaps the basic reason why classifications are easier to interpret.

Finally, these relationships of duality enable us to perform an "actual" restricted component analysis by performing a "fictitious" classification on the transposed matrix. The point of this would be to find components that are more easily interpretable than the ordinary principal components.

(Such a form of component analysis might seem to be of limited applicability because of Condition 2, which requires not only that the nonzero coefficients be equal in magnitude but also that they have the same sign. This, as it stands, means that a variable that would fit very well into a certain subset of variables is excluded simply because of its sign. In fact, however, there is no computational difficulty in simply disregarding the signs of variables, although here I shall not disregard signs, because to do so would obscure the duality relationships I am discussing.)

5. *ALGEBRAIC DISCUSSION OF DUALITY*

Suppose we are given a set of n elements each characterized by the values of m variables. The data may be represented in an $m \times n$ matrix

$$X = \{x_{ij}\}$$

as noted before. I shall write ξ_j for the jth column vector of this matrix — the vector of values characterizing the jth element — and x_i^T for the ith row vector — the vector of values of the ith variable. Thus

$$X = (\xi_1, \ldots, \xi_n) = \begin{bmatrix} x_1^T \\ \cdot \\ \cdot \\ \cdot \\ x_m^T \end{bmatrix}$$

(The superscript ^{T} is used to indicate transposition.)
Also I write

$$\bar{\xi} = \tfrac{1}{n} \sum \xi$$

for the vector of means of rows and

$$\bar{x} = \tfrac{1}{m} \sum x$$

for the vector of means of columns. Of course, $\bar{\xi}$ has a statistical and intuitive meaning as the vector of means of the variables, whereas $\bar{x}$ has not much meaning.

Consider first the *principal component problem*. I shall discuss this briefly, as it has often been discussed elsewhere. The problem is to find a matrix $V = (v_1, \ldots, v_p)$ and a vector h such that

$$\sum_{\xi} \left\{ (\xi - h)^2 - [V^T (\xi - h)]^2 \right\}$$

is a minimum subject to $V^T V = I$. Here the vectors v are any set of orthogonal unit vectors determining a p-dimensional subspace; h is the origin of the subspace; and the notation v^2, where v is a vector, is used for brevity to denote the inner product of v with itself.

The expression to be minimized is the sum of squares of arrows illustrated, for the case $p = 1$, in Figure 1. And when the matrix V has been found, the $p \times n$ matrix X' in which the n original m-vectors are represented (as closely as possible) by n p-vectors is

$$X' = (\xi_1' \ldots \xi_n') = V^T((\xi_1 - h) \ldots (\xi_n - h)).$$

An optimal value for h is $h = \bar{\xi}$. Let $\eta = \xi - \bar{\xi}$ and $g = h - \bar{\xi}$. Then the expression to be minimized

$$\sum (\eta - g)^2 - \sum [V^T(\eta - g)]^2$$

is always greater than or equal to

$$\sum \eta^2 - \sum (V^T\eta)^2$$

This is the form it takes when $h = \bar{\xi}$. Indeed, the difference between them is

$$\sum g^2 - \sum (V^T g)^2 = n g^T(I - VV^T)g$$

And if one writes V^* for an $m \times (m - p)$ matrix of orthogonal unit vectors in the $(m - p)$-dimensional subspace orthogonal to the p-space spanned by the vectors of V so that

$$(V|V^*)(V|V^*)^T = I$$

then

$$g^T(I - VV^T)g = g^T V^* V^{*T} g$$

and is nonnegative, being a sum of squares.

Hence, on setting the mean $\bar{\xi}$ equal to zero, the principal component problem becomes

$$\min. \sum \{\xi^2 - (V^T\xi)^2\}$$
$$\text{s.t.} \quad V^T V = I$$

The *restricted component problem* is the same problem, with the added restrictions on $V = \{v_{ij}\}$ that

    1. For all i, $v_{ik} \neq 0$ for one and only one k
    2. For all k, if $v_{ik} \neq 0$ and $v_{jk} \neq 0$, then $v_{ik} = v_{jk}$

These are restatements of Conditions 1 and 2 of Section 4. Condition 3 of Section 4 is already in the condition

$$V^T V = I$$

In full, the restricted component problem is

$$\min. \sum_{\xi} (\xi^2 - (V^T\xi)^2)$$

s.t.   1. $V^T V = I$
      2. For all i, $v_{ik} \neq 0$ for one and only one k
      3. For all k, if $v_{ik} \neq 0$ and $v_{jk} \neq 0$, then $v_{ik} = v_{jk}$.

The *dual restricted component* problem is the restricted component problem defined on the matrix X^T instead of the matrix X. Thus it is to find a matrix $V = (v_1 \ldots v_p)$ such that

$$\sum_x \{x^2 - (V^Tx)^2\}$$

is a minimum subject to the same three conditions as the primal problem. Here the x's are the rows of X (whereas the ξ's are the columns).

It is obvious that from any statement about the *primal* problem one can deduce a statement about the dual problem, simply by substituting x's for ξ's and m's for n's. Algebraically, this is completely trivial, for in this sense there is nothing about a matrix X which tells us that the columns correspond to elements and the rows to variables, rather than the other way about. However, statistically the two problems have quite different meanings; indeed, there is a problem — what does the dual problem mean?

The *classification problem* is to find a partition P of the set $\{\xi\}$ of columns of X into p subsets A such that

$$\sum_{A \text{ in } P} \sum_{\xi \text{ in } A} (\xi - \bar{\xi}_A)^2$$

is a minimum. Here $\bar{\xi}_A$ represents the mean vector of the vectors ξ which are in the set A, so that

$$\bar{\xi}_A = \tfrac{1}{n_A} \sum_{\xi \text{ in } A} \xi$$

where n_A is the number in the set A.

The *dual classification problem* is to find a p-partition of the set $\{x\}$ of rows of X such that

$$\sum_{A \text{ in } P} \sum_{x \text{ in } A} (x - \bar{x}_A)^2$$

is a minimum, where, if m_A is the number of rows in the set A,

$$\bar{x}_A = \tfrac{1}{m_A} \sum_{x \text{ in } A} x$$

The same considerations apply to this pair of dual problems. The *primal* problem is that of classification, described in Section 1, and has a straightforward interpretation. But what is the meaning of its dual problem? What statistical meaning, for example, has $\bar{x}_A$?

Actually, as I shall show, the dual restricted component problem is equivalent to the primal classification problem. Hence, by duality, the dual classification problem is equivalent to the primal restricted component problem.

Thus consider the dual restricted component problem. Since $\sum x^2$ is a constant, the problem is to maximize

$$
\begin{aligned}
\sum (V^T x)^2 &= \sum_x x^T V V^T x \\
&= \sum_x x^T (\sum_v v v^T) x \\
&= \sum_v v^T (\sum_x x x^T) v \\
&= \sum_v v^T X^T X v
\end{aligned}
$$

Now the conditions on V are that the set of permissible V's is in one-to-one correspondence with the set of all p-partitions P of the set $\{\xi\}$ of columns of X; the columns v of V correspond to the sets A in the corresponding partition P in such a way that the v, say v_A, corresponding to A is defined by

$$
v_A = \pm \frac{1}{\sqrt{n_A}} e_A
$$

where n_A is the number in the set A and e_A is a vector having a one in the jth position if ξ_j is in A, and a zero otherwise.

Hence the problem is to maximize

$$
\sum_{A \text{ in } P} v_A^T X^T X v_A = \sum_{A \text{ in } P} n_A \left(X \frac{e_A}{n_A} \right)^2
$$

over all p-partitions P of $\{\xi\}$. Since

$$
X \frac{e_A}{n_A} = \bar{\xi}_A
$$

this is to maximize over P

$$
\sum_A n_A \bar{\xi}_A{}^2
$$

Next,

$$
\sum_{\xi \text{ in } \{\xi\}} \xi^2
$$

which is a constant, decomposes into two terms as follows:

$$\sum_\xi \xi^2 = \sum_A \sum_{\xi \text{ in } A} \left[(\xi - \bar{\xi}_A) + \bar{\xi}_A \right]^2$$

$$= \sum_A \sum_{\xi \text{ in } A} (\xi - \bar{\xi}_A)^2 + \sum_A n_A \bar{\xi}_A{}^2$$

the cross-product term vanishing since

$$\sum_{\xi \text{ in } A} (\xi - \bar{\xi}_A) = 0$$

Hence, the problem is to minimize over P

$$\sum_{A \text{ in } P} \sum_{\xi \text{ in } A} (\xi - \bar{\xi}_A)^2$$

which is merely the classification problem.

This is proof of our assertions. Hence, instead of four problems there are two — restricted component analysis and classification. These are easily interpretable. The discussion may now be summarized and illustrated geometrically.

Restricted component analysis might also be called *dual classification* or *classification of variables*. Geometrically, it means that the given matrix X may be visualized either as n points in m dimensions or as m points in n dimensions. For example, the matrix

	(1)	(2)
[1]	1	−1
[2]	−3	3
[3]	2	−2

giving the results of observing the values of three variables for each of two elements and measuring the variables in units of deviation from their means, may be represented geometrically either as in Figure 3 or as in Figure 4.

The representation of Figure 3 is the same as that of Figures 1 and 2. The classification problem using this representation is illustrated in Figure 2. The dual classification problem, on the other hand, is the same geometrically as the classification problem if we use, instead, the representation of Figure 4. It is to group together points in space representing variables (instead of elements) so as to minimize the sum of squared distances from the points to the means of their groups; therefore, obviously, in the problem of Figure 4 the optimal classification into two groups would group together variables [1] and [3].

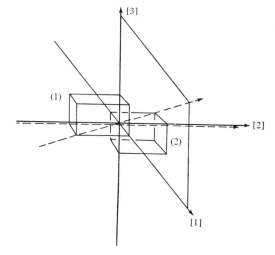

Figure 3

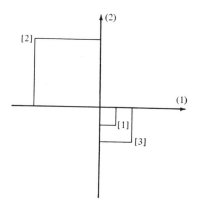

Figure 4

It is interesting that this process actually minimizes the sum of squared distances of points from certain orthogonal axes in the space illustrated in Figure 3. These axes pass through the origin; there is one axis for each group of variables; the direction cosines of an axis are equal and nonzero in the variables belonging to its group. The axes found by choosing the classification of variables.

$$\{[1], [3]\}, \{[2]\}$$

are shown by dotted lines in Figure 3.

16

FRANK L. SWEETSER

Ecological Factors in Metropolitan Zones and Sectors*

PROBLEM

THE USE OF FACTOR ANALYSIS as a method for discovering and generalizing the fundamental dimensions along which ecological areas are
differentiated has become commonplace. Depending on the investigator's
focus of interest, nations (Cattell, 1949), counties (Jonassen and Peres,
1960), cities (Hadden and Borgatta, 1965; Gittus, 1965), communes
(Piepponen, 1962; Janson, 1965) have been studied in this way. But
probably a majority of ecological factor analyses have been concerned
with the internal differentiation of cities and have used more or less
conventional demographic measures for census tracts or statistical areas
within single cities or metropolitan communities as input for the
analysis (e.g., Anderson and Bean, 1961; Bell, 1955; Grönholm, 1960;
Janson, 1966; Pedersen, 1965; Schmid and Tagashira, 1964; F. Sweetser, 1965*a*, 1965*b*, 1965c, 1966). In applications to data for statistical
areas within cities and metropolitan communities, factor analyses reduces the complexity of large correlation matrices for dozens of variables to a relatively few factors, which are then interpreted as the
fundamental dimensions of the community's ecological structure. Work
to date shows that the method does indeed produce useful summary
descriptions of the ecological structures of individual communities,

* This research has been supported by the Graduate School, Boston University,
and by a grant from the American Philosophical Society. Computations were done
in part at the Computation Center, Massachusetts Institute of Technology, and in
part at the Computation Center, Boston University.

413

with the few fundamental dimensions identified and related concisely to the numerous variables analyzed. Moreover, these studies offer the prospect that through comparative analysis clusters of factors found typically in one set of communities which differ systematically from clusters of factors found typically in another and distinct set of communities may be discovered. Thus a typology of commun ties, classified according to their ecological structure, may be developed. The development of such a typology for metropolitan communities in urban-industrial nations is the long-range objective of the writer's continuing research on aspects of metropolitan ecological structure. But before this goal can be reached, a number of procedural and technical problems must be solved (F. Sweetser, 1964; Janson, 1964). The present paper addresses itself to one such problem: the question of the relative stability of ecological factors. The approach taken is to view the metropolitan community first as a whole and then as divided into a number of zones and sectors and to perform factor analyses of a selected list of variables separately for the total metropolis, each of several zones, and each of several sectors. The pragmatic assumption is made that when factors from different total, zonal, and sector matrices show marked similarity in their profiles of factor coefficients, a stable dimension of ecological structure has been discovered. On the other hand, when similarity is less marked or is limited to only a few factor coefficients including the coefficients for the "defining variables" in terms of which the factor is interpreted, a condition of instability is assumed to exist. Both similarities and differences are of sociological interest, first, as revealing much about the patterns of residential area differentiation in different geographic sections of a particular metropolis and second, as providing a basis, through comparison of different metropolitan communities, for broader generalizations about types of ecological factors. Based on data from the writer's ongoing studies of the social ecology of metropolitan Boston and of the Helsinki metropolitan region, selected interzonal, intersector, and cross-national comparisons of factor profiles will be described as a basis for some tentative generalizations about types of ecological factors.

DESIGN

For *Boston*, thirty-four conventional ecological variables were computed from published and unpublished 1960 Census data for 441 census tracts in metropolital Boston. These variables are listed in Tables 1, 3, and 5 and are defined in Appendix A. "Metropolitan Boston" consists of the Boston and Brockton Tracted Areas as defined by the Census

Bureau. Tracts with very small or highly deviant populations and tracts added to the Boston tracted area between 1950 and 1960 were eliminated from the analysis (F. Sweetser, 1962b, p. 236). The total metropolitan community was divided into six zones and seven sectors in the original analysis, using housing type, population density, and clarity of ecological barriers as criteria of demarcation (F. Sweetser, 1962a, pp. 154–155). These zones and sectors are shown in Figure 1. For the purposes of the present analysis, the six zones were collapsed into three "broad zones," designated the inner, middle, and outer zones (F. Sweetser, 1965c). Thus, the total metropolis was divided into eleven geographic areas, as follows:

Broad Zones	Map Designation	Number of Census Tracts	
inner	zones 1 & 2	92 ⎫	
middle	zones 3 & 4	245 ⎬ total 441	
outer	zones 5 & 6	104 ⎭	
Sectors			
northeast	sector 1	79 ⎫	
north	sector 2	53 ⎪	total 433
northwest	sector 3	77 ⎪	(8 tracts of zone
west	sector 4	63 ⎬	1 not assigned
southwest	sector 5	42 ⎪	to any sector)
south	sector 6	77 ⎪	
southeast	sector 7	42 ⎭	
Total Metropolis		441	

It will be noted that the total metropolis includes all tracts in the analysis that zone and sector divisions cross-cut each other, but that the three zones are nonoverlapping, as are the seven sectors.

For *Helsinki*, thirty-three ecological variables were computed from published and unpublished 1960 Census data for 70 statistical areas in the City of Helsinki, and for 51 "metropolitan agglomerations" in the Helsinki Region outside the city limits. The variables are listed in Tables 2, 4, and 6 and are defined in Appendix B. The city statistical areas are described in F. Sweetser (1965a and 1966). "Metropolitan agglomerations" are nonadministrative urban settlements located in the Helsinki Region, having population densities of at least 58 per square kilometer (150 per square mile), and within, contiguous to, or within 2.5 kilometers of the continuous area of agglomerations centering on Helsinki. Figure 2 identifies the metropolitan agglomerations, and also shows the division of the total metropolis (the Helsinki Region) into three zones and three sectors. Figure 3 shows zone and sector divisions among statistical areas in the City of Helsinki. Because of the relatively small number of cases in the Helsinki Region—a total

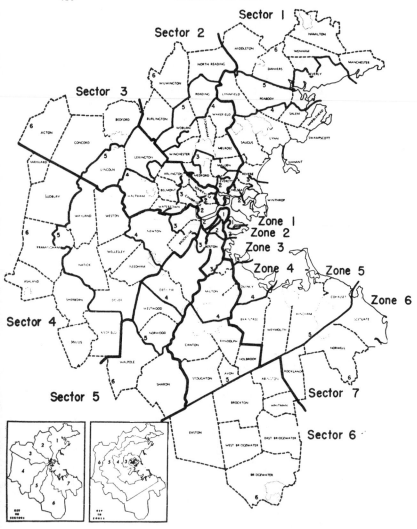

Figure 1

ZONES AND SECTORS OF METROPOLITAN BOSTON

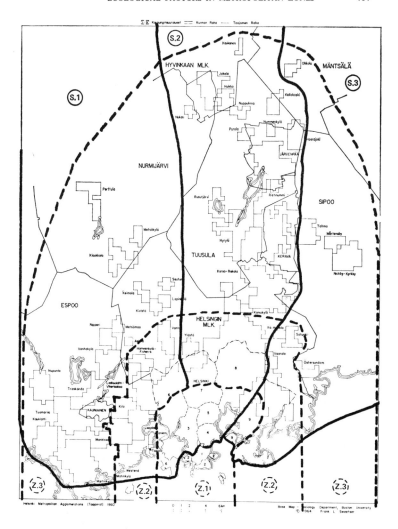

Figure 2
ZONES AND SECTORS, HELSINKI REGION

Figure 3
ZONES AND SECTORS IN CITY OF HELSINKI

of 121 statistical areas including agglomerations — division into zones and sectors was made so as to provide a reasonably large number of cases in each zone and sector while doing as little violence as possible to known demographic and social differences between areas. Even so, compelling facts of geography and population distribution made it impossible to retain an adequate number of cases in the east sector where there are fewer statistical areas than there are variables, as shown in the following table:

Zones	Map Designation	Number of Statistical Areas
inner	zone 1	41 ⎫
middle	zone 2	40 ⎬ total 121
outer	zone 3	40 ⎭
Sectors		
west	sector 1	45 ⎫ total 110 (11 areas
north	sector 2	46 ⎬ of zone 1 not in
east	sector 3	19 ⎭ any sector)
Total Metropolis		121

Data for the east sector are nevertheless included in Tables 2 and 4, since the factor profiles involved show reasonable consistency, in spite of the fewness of cases in the analysis.

Using these zone and sector divisions, eighteen different factor analyses were carried out: for Boston, total metropolis, three zones, seven sectors; for Helsinki Region, total metropolis, three zones, three sectors. Each was a principal component's analysis with 1's placed in the diagonals, and with varimax orthogonal rotations of appropriate numbers of factors — 7 for Boston matrices and 6 for the Helsinki matrices. The decision on numbers of factors to rotate was based on the modal number of factors having latent roots of unity or above in the several matrices for each community. The tally is as shown in the table. For both communities, rotated factors accounted for 80 per cent or more of the total variance in each matrix.

Number of Factors in Matrix with Latent Root at 1.0 or Above

Boston		Matrix	Helsinki	
6		total	6	
7		zone 1	6	
7		zone 2	7	
7		zone 3	6	Mode: 6
7	Mode: 7	sector 1	6	
7		sector 2	7	
6		sector 3	7	
7		sector 4	—	
6		sector 5	—	
7		sector 6	—	
6		sector 7	—	

PROCEDURE

No effort is made in this paper to analyze exhaustively the total of 119 thirty-three- or thirty-four-variable factor profiles produced by this design. Instead, certain factors of interest from the point of view of stability-instability are selected for comparison and analysis. A previous comparison of ecological factors in metropolitan Boston and the City of Helsinki showed that three types of factors were present in both communities: socioeconomic status factors, familism factors, and factors of residential status (F. Sweetser, 1966). The residential status factors were ill defined because of the absence of data on migration in Helsinki and on land use in Boston. Moreover, the variable list used in the present Helsinki Region analysis is more defective in this respect than the list of 42 variables previously used for the city itself; information available for *both* city statistical areas and the metropolitan agglomerations is somewhat limited. However, the other two types of factors found in both cities are thought to be *universal* in the sense that they may be expected to appear as fundamental dimensions of ecological structure in all metropolitan communities. Socioeconomic status factors and familism factors in zones and sectors of both communities are therefore examined (Tables 1, 2, 3, and 4).

The previous comparison also showed that there were a number of *special* factors, deriving from the particular sociocultural character of their respective national settings, in both Boston and Helsinki. These special factors included a number of ethnic factors (nonwhite, Irish middle class, Italian) in Boston and a factor called "career women" in Helsinki. Differences in ethnic homogeneity and in female labor force participation between Finland and the United States in general, and between Helsinki and Boston in particular, are thought to account for these differences. The special factors are usually less potent than the universal factors, as measured by their variance, and are also less consistently defined in the various zones and sectors. In order to illustrate these differences, the Irish middle-class factor as it appears in some of Boston's zones and sectors is examined (Table 5), and the career women factor, together with a "Swedish language" factor and a "ruralism" factor that emerged in some of the Helsinki matrices are presented in Table 6.

To summarize, in this paper we are concerned with the interzone, intersector, and cross-national stability of the following factors:

Universal factors
   Socioeconomic status
    SES in metropolis, zones, and sectors of Boston   Table 1
    SES in metropolis, zones, and sectors of Helsinki   Table 2
   Familism
    Familism in metropolis, zones, and sectors of Boston   Table 3
    Progeniture (young familism) in metropolis, zones, and
            sectors of Helsinki   Table 4

FINDINGS — UNIVERSAL FACTORS

Socioeconomic Status Factors in Metropolitan Boston

Table 1 consists of factor profiles of SES factors, one from each of the eleven Boston matrices. The table includes, in addition to factor coefficients for the 34 variables, the variance of each rotated factor (sum of the squared factor coefficients), the rank of the factor's variance in its own matrix, and the coefficient of congruence measuring the degree of similarity of each zone and sector SES factor to the metropolitan SES factor (Harman, 1960, pp. 256–259). In the body of the table, factor coefficients of .45 or above are enclosed in parentheses to indicate that these coefficients are large enough to merit special attention in interpreting the factor, since they mean that the factor accounts for at least one fifth of the variable's variance. In addition, italicizing and capitalization of variable names is employed, as explained in the footnotes to the table, to emphasize variables that load strongly and consistently on the several SES factors.

Examination of Table 1 shows that seven variables have factor coefficients of .45 or higher with appropriate signs — positive for high-status indicators and negative for low-status indicators — in ten of the eleven matrices:

20. Room crowding
21. Housing defects
22. Median family income
23. Low family income
30. Male professional and managerial occupations
33. White-collar occupations
34. 8 grades school plus

These seven variables include the conventional objective measures of socioeconomic status — housing, income, occupation, and education — and may be thought of as the defining variables for the SES dimension in Boston. In addition, it will be noted that the coefficients usually exceed .70, which means that the factor accounts for more than 50 per cent of the variable's variance and that the variable's loading on the SES factor is the highest in the matrix in question. An additional four

Table 1

SOCIOECONOMIC STATUS FACTORS, BOSTON, 1960:
METROPOLIS, ZONES, SECTORS
(Varimax Rotations of Principal Components Solutions)

*Variables***		*Total*	*Broad Zones*			*Sectors*						
No.	*Name*	*Metro.*	*Inner*	*Mid*	*Outer*	*1.NE*	*2.N*	*3.NW*	*4.W*	*5.SW*	*6.S*	*7.SE*
						Factor Coefficients for SES Factor in 11 Matrices (decimals omitted)*						
1.	Age 6–13 years	−10	00	−30	19	42	−01	−13	−07	16	08	18
2.	Age 14–17 years	−09	02	−07	17	00	−37	−09	23	07	16	−03
3.	Age 65 years plus	00	−20	22	−19	−26	09	19	00	−22	−30	−27
4.	Foreign born	−40	−03	−28	−26	(−75)	−15	(−65)	−18	(−46)	01	(−54)
5.	Foreign parentage	−12	20	00	−35	(−54)	−03	−25	−13	23	(46)	−37
6.	Irish stock	−11	−12	−06	−10	21	(−74)	−01	−36	−17	25	(−76)
7.	Italian stock	−39	−09	−31	−19	(−60)	02	−42	(−69)	00	−21	02
8.	Nonwhite	−30	−13	−25	−23	−23	−03	−22	−10	−33	−32	−20
9.	Sex ratio (single)	−30	−09	−40	−06	−36	−43	−18	−17	−26	(−48)	−29
10.	Fertility ratio	−26	−01	(−60)	−22	33	04	−22	−35	−09	−09	−03
11.	Detached dwellings	(54)	09	(48)	43	(86)	(68)	(65)	26	(79)	22	(86)
12.	Home ownership	(53)	26	44	40	(89)	(78)	(72)	19	(82)	42	(88)
13.	Women in labor force	−17	−01	−23	−44	−18	−28	−26	−35	−22	−16	−30
14.	Working mothers	−36	03	−32	(−56)	−07	(−48)	−24	(−47)	−40	−20	00
15.	Nonfamily	10	−19	33	03	−29	−30	03	14	−21	(−55)	−27
16.	Residential stability	−09	08	13	−21	−01	14	12	−14	(57)	09	05
17.	Intra-SMSA migration	−35	−15	(−55)	−09	−11	−31	(−62)	−01	(−78)	07	(−63)
18.	Inter-SMSA migration	40	02	(49)	28	23	24	21	15	04	−16	(74)
19.	New housing	40	14	24	34	(71)	(55)	38	08	(51)	17	(45)

20. ROOM CROWDING	(−80)	−36	(−72)	(−81)	(−65)	(−66)	(−83)	(−81)	(−80)	(−53)	(−78)
21. HOUSING DEFECTS	(−72)	(−56)	(−53)	(−71)	(−77)	(−79)	(−82)	(−50)	(−63)	(−85)	−43
22. MEDIAN FAMILY INCOME	(83)	33	(81)	(86)	(90)	(80)	(90)	(74)	(85)	(70)	(89)
23. LOW FAMILY INCOME	(−65)	(−49)	(−58)	(−56)	(−83)	(−93)	(−76)	−26	(−66)	(−79)	(−70)
24. *Auto to work*	(45)	(70)	30	−10	(90)	(86)	(57)	02	(69)	40	(83)
25. *Walk to work*	−42	−38	−32	−35	(−53)	(−80)	(−69)	−35	−41	(−86)	−20
26. *Commute*	42	(78)	34	20	42	(81)	(64)	08	(57)	24	(82)
27. *Males unemployed*	(−73)	(−68)	(−62)	(−71)	(−78)	(−90)	(−73)	−38	(−72)	(−81)	−32
28. *Males "at leisure"*	(−72)	−40	(−73)	(−62)	(−72)	(−58)	(−64)	(−67)	(−54)	−41	(−64)
29. *Employment in mfg.*	(−57)	18	(−68)	(−70)	−18	−15	(−76)	(−61)	−09	−05	−15
30. MALE PROF.-MGR. OCCS.	(94)	13	(95)	(89)	(70)	(79)	(83)	(93)	(89)	(50)	(92)
31. *Male cler.-serv. occs.*	−05	−07	01	20	−10	−40	02	07	−21	−13	(−58)
32. *College graduates*	(86)	06	(91)	(91)	(64)	(68)	(72)	(87)	(85)	41	(84)
33. WHITE-COLLAR OCCS.	(91)	11	(93)	(92)	(69)	(65)	(88)	(93)	(68)	(54)	(68)
34. 8 GRADES SCH. PLUS	(92)	34	(92)	(68)	(87)	(81)	(93)	(83)	(86)	(71)	(78)

Factor Variance and Congruence

Factor variance	9.31	3.14	9.16	8.27	11.15	10.94	10.79	7.15	10.06	6.57	11.0
Variance rank in matrix (1 = Highest of 7)	1	3	1	2	1	1	1	2	1	2	1
Congruence with metropolitan SES factor (Harman, 1960, formula 12.31)	—	.691	.969	.937	.886	.887	.972	.912	.902	.801	.866

* Factor coefficients of .45 or above are enclosed in parentheses: ( ).
** CAPITALIZATION indicates at least 10 factor coefficients for variable at .45 or above; *italics* indicate at least 10 factor coefficients for variable at .30 or above.

variables have factor coefficients of .30 or above (with appropriate signs) in ten or eleven of the eleven matrices:

25. Walk to work
27. Males unemployed
28. Males "at leisure"
32. College graduates

While not of so fundamental a character as the seven variables listed earlier, they solidly confirm the interpretation of the SES factors. With eleven of 34 variables so strongly loaded on these SES factors, the strength and importance of the SES factor is already clearly indicated. It is reinforced by the large factor variance of the SES factors in their respective matrices in all but the inner zone (see Table 1, bottom) and by the fact that the SES factor ranks first in variance in seven, and second in variance in three, of the eleven matrices.

Coefficients of congruence reinforce the impression of similarity among the factors of Table 1. In nine of ten comparisons, zone and sector SES factors are "very similar" to, or "congruent" with, the metropolitan SES factor (coefficients of congruence = .801 to .972). Again, the one exception is the SES factor in the inner zone, which is only "moderately similar" to the metropolitan SES factor.

A closer examination of the SES factor in the inner zone as shown in Table 1 will reveal that in addition to having conspicuously lower variance than the others in the table (ranking only third in importance in its matrix), this factor usually has decidedly lower factor coefficients for SES-defining variables than the others. The reason is not far to seek: ". . . there are, in fact, *two* SES factors in the inner zones. One of these is bipolar with familism. . . . Unitary in the wider metropolis, the SES factor divides into two factors in the urban core." (F. Sweetser, 1965c, p. 9.) The evidence for this conclusion is best seen by comparing directly the factor coefficients for SES-defining variables as they appear in the SES factor for the inner zone (Table 1) with the factor coefficients for the same variables in the familism factor in the inner zone (Table 3):

	Inner Zone Factor Coefficients	
SES-Defining Variables	*SES Factor*	*Familism (SES) Factor*
20. Room crowding	−.36	(.77)
21. Housing defects	(−.56)	.35
22. Median family income	.33	(−.47)
23. Low family income	(−.49)	.18
30. Male prof.-mgr. occs.	.13	(−.86)
33. White-collar occs.	.11	(−.83)
34. 8 grades sch. plus	.34	(−.68)

So far as these seven variables are concerned, it is evident that the inner-zone familism factor — if reflected — is more strongly a measure of SES than is the SES factor of Table 1. This is particularly notable in the loadings for the three occupational and educational variables which are very high for the familism (SES) factor of Table 3 but low or negligible for the SES factor of Table 1. It would appear from these data that, in the inner city, socioeconomic status as related especially to occupation and education is negatively associated with familism (child-rearing) but that there is a second dimension of SES also operating, principally in terms of housing defects and low family income, which is independent of familism, as the zero and near-zero loadings for variables 1 (age 6–13 years) and 10 (fertility ratio) on the inner-zone SES factor of Table 1 show.

As between zones and sectors, it may be noted in Table 1 that none of the ethnic variables (numbers 4–8) have factor coefficients of .45 or above on the metropolitan or zonal SES factors but that there are several such loadings on sector SES factors. Apparently, for the total metropolis and within zones, there are no strong correlations between measured aspects of ethnicity and the SES factor; but, within certain sectors, patterns of ethnic distribution are such as definitely to relate the ethnic character of residential areas to their socio-economic status.

Again, it may be noted, as shown by factor coefficients for variables 11 and 12 in Table 1, that home ownership and detached dwellings are more strongly associated with the status dimension in the total metropolis and in most of the sectors than in the three zones. The relationship is particularly weak in the inner zones. These differences are, no doubt, a direct consequence of the typical gradient in dwelling types from multiple dwellings in the core to detached houses in the suburbs: zones tend toward a degree of similarity in housing types, but the metropolis and the sectors show marked contrasts.

Socioeconomic Status Factors in the Helsinki Region

As in Boston, the SES factors in the metropolis and in the zones and sectors of the Helsinki Region are consistent and typically fairly strong. As is shown in the summary data at the bottom of Table 2, factor variances range from moderate to large, and the SES factors rank first or second in importance in five of the seven matrices. Congruence of zone and sector SES factors with the metropolitan SES factor range from "markedly similar" to "congruent" (.799 to .961). And the eight defining variables — for Helsinki, variables with factor coefficients of .45 or above in six or seven of the seven matrices — measure expected

Table 2

SOCIOECONOMIC STATUS FACTORS IN HELSINKI REGION, 1960:
METROPOLIS, THREE ZONES, THREE SECTORS
(Varimax Rotations of Principal Components Solutions)

Variables**		Total Metro.	Factor Coefficients, 33 Variables, 7 Matrices (decimals omitted)*					
			Zones			Sectors		
No.	Name		Inner	Middle	Outer	West	North	East
1.	Median age	25	01	30	24	39	05	(45)
2.	Age 0-4 years	-27	-06	-12	-18	-35	-25	(-48)
3.	Age 5-14 years	-12	00	-09	-24	-41	12	-39
4.	Preadolescent ratio	-26	-13	-07	-03	-16	-38	-23
5.	Middle-age ratio	-07	11	16	-12	-10	-11	-06
6.	Age 65 years plus	14	10	-04	06	05	22	38
7.	Proportion male	-43	-43	-36	-19	(-60)	-19	-14
8.	Swedish-speaking Finns	29	(81)	32	(54)	-03	18	(45)
9.	Married	-29	-18	-06	-07	-38	-14	(-66)
10.	Fertility	-21	05	-12	-15	-31	-16	-41
11.	Widowed and divorced	00	-35	-29	05	09	-10	24
12.	Nonfamily	19	-03	-05	18	39	-03	(62)
13.	Size of household	02	26	13	-20	-34	18	03
14.	ROOM CROWDING	(-76)	(-93)	(-88)	(-60)	(-71)	(-82)	(-93)
15.	LIVING SPACE	(74)	(89)	(85)	(62)	(66)	(84)	(90)
16.	Home ownership	10	17	40	-19	15	11	-04
17.	Women in labor force	22	-17	23	10	(65)	-17	05
18.	Dependence on agriculture	-01	-09	-11	-14	-14	20	-01

19. DEPENDENCE ON INDUSTRY	(−76)	(−83)	(−83)	(−54)	(−71)	(−60)	(−87)
20. DEPENDENCE ON SERVICES	07	(76)	(81)	(90)	(89)	44	(64)
21. Employers		(55)	−02	−04	−19	18	22
22. BLUE-COLLAR OCCUPATIONS	(−95)	(−84)	(−95)	(−63)	(−95)	(−86)	(−84)
23. 9 GRADES SCHOOL PLUS	(88)	(95)	(96)	(75)	(93)	(70)	(72)
24. Female higher education	(64)	(90)	(74)	−21	(78)	07	41
25. Population density (log)	26	−10	23	20	(58)	−10	−06
26. Public buildings	21	22	04	24	15	−19	39
27. Industrial buildings	−03	−23	03	−21	07	−27	16
28. Apartment house size	35	−05	(54)	01	(78)	−22	21
29. Detached dwellings	(−47)	−24	(−54)	−14	(−78)	02	−38
30. SMALL DWELLINGS	(−59)	(−69)	(−74)	(−57)	(−51)	(−62)	(−91)
31. New Housing	17	25	29	−20	27	−03	−19
32. *Housing defect–heat*	(−67)	(−64)	(−65)	(−73)	(−89)	−16	−39
33. HOUSING DEFECT-PLUMBING	(−70)	(−60)	(−75)	(−71)	(−92)	−20	(−49)

Factor Variance and Congruence

Factor variance	6.88	8.26	8.18	5.08	10.03	4.31	7.95
Variance rank in matrix (1 = Highest of 6)	1	2	1	3	1	4	2
Congruence with metropolitan SES factor (Harman, 1960, formula 12.31)	—	.893	.961	.860	.940	.799	.898

*Factor coefficients of .45 or above enclosed in parentheses: ( ).

**CAPITALS indicate coefficients of .45 or above in 6 or 7 matrices; *italics* indicate coefficients of .30 or above in 6 or 7 matrices.

aspects of housing, occupation, and education (no income data were available for Helsinki statistical areas):

14. Room crowding
15. Living space
19. Dependence on industry
20. Dependence on services
22. Blue-collar occupations
23. 9 grades school plus
30. Small dwellings
33. Housing defect–plumbing

One additional variable — housing defect–heat — loads at .30 or above in six of the seven matrices. As in Boston, a majority of the coefficients for defining variables are above .70, this shows that half or more of the variable's variance in the matrix is accounted for by the SES factor. Unlike Boston, however, none of the geographic subdivisions show a differentiation of the SES dimension into two distinct factors.

Helsinki SES factors in all three zones and in the east sector have loadings of .30 or higher for the ethnic variable (No. 8, Swedish language), though not in the metropolis or the west and north sectors. The loadings are especially large in the inner and outer zones (at .81 and .54, respectively) and arise from the marked concentration of Swedish-speaking Finns in certain of the higher-status statistical areas of the City of Helsinki, and from persistence of prevailingly Swedish-speaking agglomerations — often of higher status — in the outlying portions of the Helsinki Region. Generally, ethnic homogeneity characterizes Finland and Helsinki, in contrast to the typical ethnic heterogeneity of Boston and most other American metropolitan communities. In the City of Helsinki itself, as is shown in F. Sweetser (1963 and 1965b), there is no distinct ethnic (Swedish language) factor, although the association of Swedish-speaking Finns with higher-status areas is evident. Weak Swedish language factors (discussed later) appear in only two of the seven matrices for the Helsinki Region. This contrasts sharply with the three ethnic factors found repeatedly in Boston: Irish middle class (discussed later), nonwhite, and Italian (F. Sweetser, 1965c).

Table 2 also shows a slight tendency toward a negative association of familism and SES in both the west and the east sectors, as the negative signs and coefficients above .30 for variables 2 (age 0–4 years), 3 (age 5–14 years), 9 (married), and 10 (fertility) indicate; but none of these factors shows the clear bipolarity of SES and familism noted in

Boston's inner zone. As a final observation on SES factors in Helsinki's zones and sectors, it should be noted that detached dwellings (variable 29) loads negatively on SES in six of the seven matrices, and at substantial levels: $-.47$, $-.54$, $-.78$, and $-.$ 38 in four of them. This contrasts with the uniformly positive, and usually high, factor coefficients for detached dwellings in the Boston SES factor profiles (variable 11, in Table 1). The interesting fact that detached dwelling areas are associated with high SES in Boston and low SES in Helsinki is discussed in some detail in F. and D. Sweetser (1965).

Familism Factors in Metropolitan Boston

As the summary statistics at the bottom of Table 3 show, familism factors in Boston have high or moderately high factor variances, which rank either first or second among the factors in ten of the eleven matrices for metropolitan Boston and its zones and sectors, and third in the matrix for the south sector. Coefficients of congruence relating zone and sector familism factors to the familism — with the single exception of the measure for the familism ($-$SES) factor in the inner zone — are also generally high, ranging from .750 to .968 and showing marked similarity or congruence.

The character of Boston's familism factor as a dimension of child-centered familism is clear from the list of defining variables with appropriately signed loadings of .45 or above in ten or eleven of the eleven matrices:

1. Age 6–13 years
3. Age 65 years plus
10. Fertility ratio
15. Nonfamily

Two additional variables with ten or eleven factor coefficients at .30 or above further describe the factor as characterized by women at home, rather than in the labor force (variable 13), and by the presence of new housing (variable 19).

Variable 2, age 14–17 years, has factor coefficients ranging from .51 to .86 in seven of the eleven matrices, but this variable's loadings are below .30 for the outer zone and for three sectors: north, south and southeast. This circumstance is interesting for two reasons. First, it suggests a similarity, if not an identity, of the type of factor here described as "familism" with the factors of age composition discovered by other investigators (Hadden and Borgatta, 1965; Pedersen, 1965). As is evident from Table 3, dominant loadings in these factor profiles are

Table 3

FAMILISM FACTORS, BOSTON, 1960: METROPOLIS, ZONES, SECTORS

(Varimax Rotations of Principal Components Solutions)

Factor Coefficients* for FAM. Factor in 11 Matrices (decimals omitted)

No.	Name	Total Metro.	Broad Zones Inner	Broad Zones Mid	Broad Zones Outer	Sectors 1.NE	2.N	3.NW	4.W	5.SW	6.S	7.SE
1.	AGE 6-13 YEARS	(90)	(93)	(89)	(81)	(82)	(84)	(85)	(91)	(89)	(72)	(92)
2.	Age 14-17 years	(56)	(86)	(65)	15	(67)	17	(58)	(51)	(56)	23	25
3.	AGE 65 YEARS PLUS	(-80)	(-48)	(-75)	(-86)	(-84)	(-87)	(-79)	(-83)	(-83)	(-78)	(-75)
4.	Foreign born	(-68)	-02	(-72)	(-65)	-25	-37	(-56)	(-83)	(-53)	-47	(-68)
5.	Foreign parentage	-30	25	-24	-32	-04	-27	-13	(-49)	-02	-33	(-64)
6.	Irish stock	-14	15	-01	-23	-19	-23	-21	-27	-33	-07	-39
7.	Italian stock	-13	25	03	-08	24	07	02	08	15	04	-28
8.	Nonwhite	-12	01	-02	-26	12	-07	06	-15	-09	17	(60)
9.	Sex ratio (single)	04	-10	20	13	05	22	13	14	-13	00	08
10.	FERTILITY RATIO	(87)	(91)	(65)	(69)	(59)	(80)	(87)	(85)	(90)	(81)	(87)
11.	Detached dwellings	(66)	26	(64)	(80)	27	42	(55)	(83)	41	15	39
12.	Home ownership	(67)	(45)	(66)	(85)	32	35	(53)	(86)	35	15	29
13.	Women in labor force	(-70)	(-84)	(-56)	(-59)	-42	(-50)	(-69)	(-71)	-31	-18	(-65)
14.	Working mothers	-34	-24	-23	(-60)	-43	-11	-26	(-46)	-07	10	-17
15.	NONFAMILY	(-61)	(-87)	(-59)	(-61)	(-70)	(-72)	(-52)	(-67)	(-67)	-37	(-51)
16.	Residential stability	17	(78)	38	-18	11	-25	13	22	27	-12	-26
17.	Intra-SMSA migration	-05	16	-18	08	-10	21	14	-19	-08	02	13
18.	Inter-SMSA migration	-11	(-82)	-34	13	04	10	-17	-09	-23	18	27
19.	New housing	(75)	11	(72)	(73)	37	(63)	(76)	(91)	(66)	36	(82)
20.	Room crowding	32	(77)	35	29	(59)	(65)	36	14	44	(68)	(51)

	1	2	3	4	5	6	7	8	9	10	11
21. Housing defects	−20	35	−13	(−49)	−10	10	−20	(−48)	−05	13	−11
22. Median fam. income	16	(−47)	15	24	12	−11	09	27	16	−10	−07
23. Low family income	−26	18	−15	(−73)	−17	−02	−14	(−47)	−11	−04	16
24. Auto to work	(65)	(45)	(52)	(85)	10	41	(63)	(87)	(57)	12	35
25. Walk to work	(−45)	(−46)	−29	(−85)	(−46)	−20	−30	(−59)	−39	−21	−30
26. Commute	35	14	27	(65)	00	−03	00	(65)	(55)	13	33
27. Males unemployed	−22	28	−07	−43	−08	09	−11	(−65)	−24	−01	−03
28. Males "at leisure"	−32	16	−18	(−46)	−37	04	−11	−33	−40	07	−20
29. Employment in mfg.	30	(68)	16	−20	01	(64)	22	(54)	(74)	27	09
30. Male prof.-mgr. occs.	01	−33	−05	28	03	−07	−10	09	08	−39	11
31. Male cler.-serv. occs.	−40	(−87)	−19	−07	−32	(−69)	−27	(−55)	(−72)	−07	−12
32. College graduates	−07	(−83)	−08	15	−01	−13	−22	15	04	−40	13
33. White-collar occs.	−17	(−68)	−14	22	−12	(−47)	−21	−23	−38	−39	−05
34. 8 grades sch. plus	26		19	(63)	13	00	01	37	25	04	30

Factor Variance and Congruence

Factor variance	7.06	10.73	5.94	9.36	4.44	5.85	5.82	10.53	6.96	3.72	6.30
Variance rank in matrix (1 = highest of 7)	2	1	2	1	2	2	2	1	2	3	2
Congruence with metropolitan familism factor (Harman, 1960, formula 12.31)	—	.597	.968	.886	.874	.842	.962	.966	.919	.750	.847

*Factor coefficients of .45 or above are enclosed in parentheses: ( ).
**CAPITALIZATION indicates at least 10 factor coefficients for variable at .45 or above; *italics* indicate at least 10 factor coefficients for variable at .30 or above.

on age variables (variables 1, 2, and 3); and even variable 10, the fertility ratio, might be thought of as essentially a measure of age structure. Second, the failure of variable 2 to load at meaningful levels in four matrices has the effect of converting the general "familism" of the metropolis and the other zones and sectors into a special kind of familism, which might be labeled "young familism" or "progeniture." But in the City of Helsinki an earlier analysis showed that there (child-centered) familism typically differentiated into two factors, interpreted as "progeniture" and as "established familism" (F. Sweetser, 1965*b*). This differentiation of familism into distinct factors persists in the Helsinki Region, as indicated later and in Table 4.

Progeniture (Young Familism) Factors in the Helsinki Region

The earlier (42-variable) analysis of the City of Helsinki produced, not one, but three familism factors, described as "progeniture," "established familism," and "postgeniture" (F. Sweetser, 1965*b*, 1966). The same three familism factors also emerge in the set of seven matrices for the Helsinki Region. Taken together, these Helsinki familism factors are clearly dominant in each of the seven matrices under study. However, they are sometimes differentiated into distinct factors and sometimes merged with other factors, so that their complete elucidation would present a far more complex picture than can be presented here. Fortunately, *progeniture* emerges consistently in all seven matrices, as the factor profiles in Table 4 for Helsinki metropolis, zones, and sectors show. It is a distinct factor in six matrices and merges with the other two aspects of familism into a single factor in the seventh. This merged factor, in the inner zone, consequently takes on the character of a general familism factor of the sort more typical in Boston.

As with Boston's familism factors, the four defining variables for progeniture in Helsinki (variables with appropriately signed loadings of .45 or above in six or seven of the seven matrices of Table 4) accent age structure:

2. Age 0–4 years
4. Preadolescent ratio (proportion 0–4 among those 0–14 years of age)
5. Middle-age ratio (proportion 20–39 among those 20–64 years of age)
10. Fertility (ratio of children 0–4 to men age 20–49)

Three additional variables load on progeniture with appropriate signs at .30 or higher in at least five of the seven matrices: median age (variable

1,) nonfamily (variable 12), and new housing (variable 31). One of these additional variables also relates to age structure, strengthening the parallel previously suggested between these familism factors and the age-structure factors found by others; another, new housing, serves to accentuate the obvious similarity of Helsinki's progeniture factor with Boston's familism.

Perhaps the most interesting of the factor profiles in Table 4 is that for the inner zones, where additional high factor coefficients show that the dimension of progeniture here is also a dimension of established familism and (as a polar opposite requiring reflection of signs) of postgeniture. Two factor coefficients bring out the established familism aspect:

3. Age 5–14	(loading at .80)
9. Married	(loading at .90)

Three other high loadings, with signs reversed, show how the same factor could be reflected to stress the absence of youngsters along with older age and family decay:

6. Age 65 years plus	(loading at .89)	N.B.: Signs have been
7. Proportion male	(loading at − .65)	reflected from entries
11. Widowed & divorced	(loading at .83)	in Table 4

These are, of course, among the features of the "postgeniture" factor, described elsewhere as "indicating a late stage of familism overlapping the 'stage of the empty nest' and a later stage of retirement and senescence." (F. Sweetser, 1965b, p. 384.)

Entries at the foot of Table 4 show that the strength of the progeniture factor in the seven Helsinki Region matrices is quite varied, ranging from the strongest to the fifth strongest in variance rank. This is not surprising, in view of the differentiated character of the Helsinki familism dimension. However, coefficients of congruence relating zone and sector progeniture factors to the metropolitan progeniture factor are reasonably high, ranging from .687 to .952, indicating marked similarity or congruence of factors compared.

FINDINGS — SPECIAL FACTORS

Irish Middle-Class Factors in Metropolitan Boston

Ethnicity is clearly a fundamental dimension of Boston's ecological structure, as brought out elsewhere (F. Sweetser, 1965c; 1966). However, like familism in Helsinki, ethnicity as a type of ecological factor in Boston's zones and sectors differentiates into three distinct factors: nonwhite ethnic, Italian ethnic, and Irish middle-class factors. Moreover

Table 4

PROGENITURE (YOUNG FAMILISM) FACTORS IN HELSINKI REGION, 1960:
METROPOLIS, THREE ZONES, THREE SECTORS

| | | | Factor Coefficients, 33 variables, 7 Matrices (decimals omitted)* | | | | |
| *Variables*** | | Total Metro | Zones | | | Sectors | | |
No.	Name		Inner	Middle	Outer	West	North	East
1.	*Median age*	(−47)	(−93)	−25	−41	(−48)	(−59)	−44
2.	AGE 0–4 YEARS	(75)	(92)	(92)	(85)	(81)	(74)	(80)
3.	Age 5–14 years	24	80	00	−13	36	21	−09
4.	PREADOLESCENT RATIO	(72)	(57)	(84)	(83)	(75)	(63)	(82)
5.	MIDDLE-AGE RATIO	(67)	(86)	(62)	(63)	(72)	(64)	43
6.	Age 65 years plus	−20	(−89)	−15	−15	−10	−18	−27
7.	Proportion male	06	(65)	−37	−01	23	21	−03
8.	Swedish-speaking Finns	02	−32	10	−04	−04	−29	−05
9.	Married	34	(90)	39	27	43	28	23
10.	FERTILITY	(80)	(83)	(88)	(88)	(89)	(73)	(75)
11.	Widowed and divorced	−12	(−83)	09	−06	−08	−30	−16
12.	*Nonfamily*	−38	(−72)	−29	−22	(−47)	−39	−31
13.	Size of household	31	(72)	07	03	(52)	36	04
14.	Room crowding	15	06	13	(48)	43	−39	06
15.	Living space	−25	−30	−17	−43	(−47)	−12	−10
16.	Home ownership	02	05	30	−04	33	−08	11
17.	Women in labor force	−05	−02	38	05	−14	−32	21
18.	Dependence on agriculture	−12	07	13	−28	−13	−01	24
19.	Dependence on industry	15	08	12	16	17	40	19

20. Dependence on services	−05	29	−07	00	−12	−31	−27
21. Employers	−17	(−68)	−12	−27	−17	07	−02
22. Blue-collar occupations	04	−24	−12	29	12	27	04
23. 9 grades school plus	−07	13	08	−25	−15	−38	−09
24. Female higher education	−08	13	−21	−25	−25	−03	−08
25. Population density (log)	−34	(−54)	−22	−03	−30	(−68)	−13
26. Public buildings	−24	−28	−04	−11	−26	(−48)	25
27. Industrial buildings	−21	−13	05	−09	−04	−38	(60)
28. Apartment house size	−22	−42	(45)	07	−07	(−67)	20
29. Detached dwellings	09	11	−31	−02	10	(56)	−33
30. Small dwellings	10	−27	21	44	10	−15	08
31. *New housing*	39	(69)	32	(45)	(47)	05	22
32. Housing defect–heat	21	09	−07	01	15	(78)	−11
33. Housing defect–plumbing	19	12	−28	03	08	(81)	−21

Factor Variance and Congruence

Factor variance	3.56	9.84	4.16	4.12	4.78	6.52	3.45
Variance rank in matrix (1 = highest of 6)	4	1	5	4	3	1	3
Congruence with progeniture in metropolitan matrix (Harman, 1960, formula 12.31)	—	.833	.754	.868	.952	.793	.687

* Factor coefficients of .45 or above enclosed in parentheses: ( ).

** CAPITALS indicate coefficients of .45 or above in 6 or 7 matrices; *italics* indicate coefficients of .30 or above in 5, 6, or 7 matrices.

these distinct ethnic factors sometimes merge into a single — usually bipolar — factor and sometimes fail to appear in a given matrix. The over-all pattern of ethnic factors in the eleven metropolitan zone and sector matrices is too complex for analysis here. However, the factor profiles for the Irish middle-class factor as it appears in eight of the matrices will illustrate the ways in which special factors may vary among zones and sectors.

First a look at the summarizing data at the bottom of Table 5 will reveal that the eight Irish middle-class factors all have relatively low variances and rank from fourth to sixth in potency in their respective matrices, thus contrasting sharply in strength with SES and familism factors in Tables 1 and 3. These are evidently minor factors, as well as special factors. The congruence of the zone and sector Irish middle-class factors with the metropolitan Irish middle-class factors shows marked similarity for five matrices, but the factors in the inner zones and in the northeast sector are only moderately similar to the metropolitan factor.

With such low factor variance, it is to be expected that the number of defining variables will be few. Indeed, there are only two:

  6. Irish stock   (loading at .45 or above in 8 of
                                         8 matrices)

31. Male clerical-service employment (loading at .58 or above in 6 of
                                         8 matrices, and at .38 or above
                                         in 7 of 8 matrices

In addition, variable 29, employment in manufacturing, loads (negatively) at values above $-.45$ on three of the Irish middle-class factors. Where these negative loadings occur, of course, they reinforce the "middle-class" aspect of the factor.

Four of the factors shown in Table 5 are unambiguously Irish and middle-class, as shown by the facts that (1) both defining variables have higher loadings on this factor than on any other in their respective matrices; and (2) the coefficients for the two defining variables are the highest in the profile for the factor. These unambiguous Irish middle-class factors occur in the metropolis, the middle and outer zones, and the northwest sector.

Two of the factors of Table 5 seem Irish enough but lack a clearly defined middle-class aspect. In the northeast sector and the west sector, factor coefficients for the Irish stock variable are higher than for any other factor in the respective matrices; but coefficients for the second defining variable, male clerical and service occupations, are rather low, at .22 and .38, respectively. In the west sector, inspection of the factor profile (Table 5) suggests that here Irish ethnicity almost becomes a specific factor. However, since male clerical-service employment loads at .38 the factor may be thought of as retaining, at least weakly, a middle-class aspect.

In the northeast sector, variable 31 has the very low loading of .22 on the "Irish middle-class" factor. Thus the factor fails to qualify as "middle-class." Moreover, two other variables in the factor profile (Table 5) have factor coefficients above .50; variable 9, sex ratio, loads at −.72; and variable 13, women in the labor force, loads at .54. It would almost seem possible to interpret the factor as one of "single femaleness" or one of "career women." However, since the factor is more closely congruent with the Irish middle-class factor in the metropolis than any other factor in the matrix, and since the Irish stock variable has its highest-in-matrix factor coefficient for the factor, it has been included as an Irish ethnic factor in Table 5.

The two remaining factors of Table 5 (in the inner zone and the south sector) both have higher factor coefficients for variable 31 (male clerical and service occupations) than any other factors in their respective matrices. To this extent, they both exhibit a satisfactory "middle-class" aspect, although only in the south sector, where the loading is .74, would we call the interpretation unambiguous. But these two factors have the lowest coefficients for the Irish stock variable of any shown in the table, at .45 and .60, respectively. High enough to justify the interpretation of the factors as Irish middle-class factors, the coefficients nevertheless show that these ethnic factors account for only 20 per cent and 36 per cent of the variance in the distribution of Irish stock among Boston's census tracts. Thus the possibility is presented that other factors in the inner zone and the south sector may also account for meaningfully large proportions of the Irish stock variance. This is indeed the case. Two additional factors in the inner zone and one in the south sector have loadings of .45 or above for the Irish stock variable.

To consider the simpler case first, the south sector factor coefficient for Irish stock on the Irish middle-class factor of Table 5 is .60, and it is literally the highest in the matrix before rounding. But the matrix contains another factor with the following coefficients for the ethnic variables:

Variable	Factor Coefficient
4. Foreign born	−.07
5. Foreign parentage	(−.66)
6. Irish stock	(−.5968)
7. Italian stock	(−.74)
8. Nonwhite	(.76)

Table 5

Irish Middle-Class Factors, Boston, 1960:
Metropolis, Zones, Sectors
(Varimax Rotations of Principal Components Solutions)

	Variables**	Total	Broad Zones			Sectors						
No.	Name	Metro.	Inner	Mid	Outer	1.NE	2.N	3.NW	4.W	5.SW	6.S	7.SE
1.	Age 6–13 years	−08	−14	−07	−15	−02		−13	06		−16	
2.	Age 14–17 years	04	−25	00	−15	−16		−03	11		04	
3.	Age 65 years plus	16	(63)	−04	21	22		13	−24		13	
4.	Foreign born	−06	14	16	08	−26		−04	−02		18	
5.	Foreign parentage	02	−02	11	21	−20		32	−08		24	
6.	IRISH STOCK	(83)	(45)	(80)	(62)	(66)	***	(80)	(73)	***	(60)	***
7.	Italian stock	−44	−30	−13	−13	−32		−08	−20		−16	
8.	Nonwhite	−05	03	02	−13	−09		14	01		00	
9.	Sex ratio (single)	08	−04	−14	−13	(−72)		04	00		08	
10.	Fertility ratio	01	00	06	−08	09		04	07		−30	
11.	Detached dwellings	−17	02	−40	−09	−07		−38	−22		−14	
12.	Home ownership	−11	−05	−29	−03	−06		−14	−12		−14	
13.	Women in labor force	14	09	28	−02	(54)		24	08		04	
14.	Working mothers	−14	11	−10	−13	21		−07	−09		−27	
15.	Nonfamily	10	08	04	16	03		−03	00		19	
16.	Residential stability	08	03	−04	17	11		16	07		13	
17.	Intra-SMSA migration	13	(66)	07	16	−03		19	03		18	
18.	Inter-SMSA migration	−21	−37	−03	−32	−10		−23	−10		(−51)	
19.	New housing	−17	−35	−17	−10	−16		−22	−12		−18	
20.	Room crowding	06	−24	26	−14	−03		−10	43		−04	

21. Housing defects	-12	-07	06	-09	-32	-19	03	-21
22. Median family income	-08	-29	-08	00	00	-23	-09	17
23. Low family income	04	15	-01	-11	-05	-04	06	08
24. Auto to work	-28	-22	(-60)	-16	13	-22	-22	(-46)
25. Walk to work	01	07	-17	05	15	-33	05	05
26. Commute	-24	-17	-43	27	(-49)	28	-19	-08
27. Males unemployed	05	07	19	16	-09	16	24	-02
28. Males "at leisure"	05	(49)	03	30	-05	-16	-13	24
29. Employment in mfg.	(-48)	-25	(-56)	-29	09	-26	-28	(-88)
30. Male prof.-mgr. occs.	-14	-31	-12	-10	-04	-28	-22	11
31. MALE CLER.-SERV. OCCS.	(67)	(58)	(72)	(80)	22	(79)	38	(74)
32. College graduates	-12	-34	-04	-06	-04	-29	-06	24
33. White-collar occs.	23	12	18	12	13	-01	-02	(60)
34. 8 grades sch. plus	05	-09	-04	00	07	02	-08	04

Factor Variance and Congruence

Factor variance	2.04	2.66	2.67	1.80	2.12	2.44	1.42	3.22
Variance rank in matrix (1 = highest of 7)	5	5	4	5	6	4	6	5
Congruence with metropolitan I.M-C factor (Harman, 1960, formula 12.31)	—	.682	.857	.775	.509	.772	.789	.801

* Factor coefficients of .45 or above are enclosed in parentheses: ( ).

** *CAPITALIZATION*: variable has 6 or 8 (of 8) coefficients at .45 or above.

*** No I.M-C factor in this sector. Variable 6 (Irish stock) loads most heavily on SES in Sector 2 (negatively); on nonwhite in Sector 5 (negatively); and on SES in Sector 7 (negatively).

Evidently, this is a bipolar factor, which might be described as "non-white/foreign stock" because of the high positive loading for the non-white variable and the high negative loadings for foreign parentage, Irish stock, and Italian stock.

In the inner zone an analogous but more complex situation exists. Here, the Irish middle-class factor of Table 5 accounts for less of the variance of the Irish stock variable than either of two other factors. The character of these additional ethnic factors is shown by the following data on ethnic variables in this matrix:

Variables	Factor Coefficients (Reflected to Appropriate signs)		
	Irish Middle Class	Factor X	Factor Y
4. Foreign born	.14	(.87)	−.07
5. Foreign parentage	−.02	(.66)	(−.57)
6. Irish stock	(.45)	(−.50)	(−.48)
7. Italian stock	−.30	(.80)	−.18
8. Nonwhite	.03	−.21	(.86)
Factor variance	2.66	3.80	3.08

It is quite evident that factor X is a bipolar "Italian/Irish" factor. Identified as Italian by the high loading for Italian stock (.80), its bipolarity with Irish ethnicity is brought out by the substantial factor coefficient of −.50 for Irish stock. Similarly, factor Y is clearly a bipolar "nonwhite/Irish" factor. As in the south sector, inner zone Irish ethnicity as an ecological dimension is differentiated — this time into three distinct ethnic factors.

The three sectors of metropolitan Boston where no factor that could be classified as "Irish middle class" was found reveal two different patterns of loadings for the Irish stock variable. In the southwest sector, this variable repeats the pattern of the inner zone and the south sector in having its highest factor coefficient for the matrix (−.73) on a bipolar ethnic factor that is best interpreted as "nonwhite/foreign stock." In the north and the southeast sectors, however, Irish stock loads meaningfully only on the socioeconomic status factor, with coefficients at − .74 and − .76, respectively (see Table 1). In these two sectors, then, "Irishness" combines negatively with SES, but neither emerges as a distinct factor nor merges with another ethnic factor.

Swedish Language, Career Women, and Ruralism Factors in the Helsinki Region

The *Swedish language* factor (Table 6) is especially interesting because, as noted before, a prior search for a Swedish ethnic factor in the City of

Helsinki had failed (F. Sweetser, 1965*b*; 1966). Now, in the metropolitan Helsinki Region, such a factor emerges, matched by a closely similar factor (coefficient of congruence, .931) in the west sector. Defining variables for the Swedish language factor in both matrices include:

8. Swedish-speaking Finns	(loading positively)
14. Room crowding	(loading negatively)
15. Living space	(loading positively)

The factor evidently associates large proportions of Swedish speakers with more dwelling space. In other zones and sectors, there is no Swedish language factor; instead, the Swedish language variable loads most highly on a variety of other factors:

Matrix	*Swedish Language Variable Loads*
Inner zone	at .81 on SES (see Table 2)
Middle zone	at −.77 on career women (see Table 6)
Outer zone	at .54 on SES (see Table 2)
North sector	(dispersal of loadings, with none as high as .45)
East sector	at −.63 on a merged factor that combines career women and postgeniture

Even where it appears, the Swedish language factor is the weakest in the matrix, with very low factor variance, as is shown in Table 6 (bottom). It is evident that in 1960 in the Helsinki Region, language was no more than a very minor dimension of metropolitan ecological differentiation.

Career women factors of the Helsinki Region, the inner zone, and the middle zone are shown in the three central columns of Table 6. Examination of the table shows that there are considerable irregularities in the factor profiles, with high and low factor coefficients side by side for a number of variables. Yet for three variables, here considered to be the defining variables for the career woman factor, factor coefficients are the highest in the respective matrices:

17. Women in the labor force	(loading positively)
25. Logarithm of population density	(loading positively)
29. Detached dwellings	(loading negatively)

Two more variables are at .32 or above in all three profiles:

28. Apartment house size	(loading positively)
32. Housing defect–heat	(loading negatively)

Table 6

SWEDISH LANGUAGE, CAREER WOMEN, AND RURALISM AS ECOLOGICAL FACTORS: METROPOLIS, ZONES AND SECTORS OF HELSINKI REGION, 1960
(Varimax Rotations of Principal Components Solutions)

Factor Coefficients, 33 Variables, 7 Matrices (decimals omitted)*

| | Variables | Swedish Language | | Career Women | | | Ruralism | |
| | | Total Metrop. | West Sector | Total Metrop. | Inner Zone | Middle Zone | Outer Zone | North Sector |
No.	Name							
1.	Median age	04	09	22	25	−24	17	−12
2.	Age 0–4 years	−02	−06	−17	−10	02	−16	−03
3.	Age 5–14 years	−20	−12	(−68)	−21	−15	11	(51)
4.	Preadolescent ratio	11	04	27	03	11	−22	(−46)
5.	Middle-age ratio	−12	−24	08	01	(57)	(−45)	−39
6.	Age 65 years plus	15	19	−16	−09	−24	15	06
7.	Proportion male	03	−03	−28	−26	−21	−01	18
8.	Swedish-speaking Finns	(72)	(90)	−07	−20	(−77)	10	−35
9.	Married	−02	−06	−11	−10	−16	−23	−07
10.	Fertility	01	06	−40	−19	−26	04	20
11.	Widowed and divorced	−05	07	05	23	02	02	−20
12.	Nonfamily	−08	−10	42	(49)	29	11	−20
13.	Size of household	−04	01	(−73)	(−50)	−25	29	(53)
14.	Room crowding	(−55)	(−51)	06	26	28	−24	−10
15.	Living space	(46)	(45)	04	−13	−37	31	14
16.	Home ownership	−15	−19	−34	−12	−11	23	37
17.	Women in labor force	−34	−40	(73)	(85)	(74)	−23	−41

18. Dependence on agriculture	−09	−05	(−79)	−29	(−63)	(77)	(84)
19. Dependence on industry	−15	−12	01	−08	−11	−41	12
20. Dependence on services	02	01	(46)	21	41	−18	(−70)
21. Employers	04	04	(−85)	−08	(−76)	(83)	(83)
22. Blue-collar occupations	00	−09	01	−02	−02	(−47)	−18
23. 9 grades school plus	09	10	35	00	08	−24	(−45)
24. Female higher education	−03	17	−09	10	35	19	04
25. Population density (log)	−25	−36	(73)	(67)	(66)	(−86)	(−49)
26. Public buildings	02	−13	07	26	10	34	17
27. Industrial buildings	−16	−03	23	29	39	12	16
28. Apartment house size	(−45)	−22	(46)	(68)	(−58)	−21	−11
29. Detached dwellings	30	22	(−59)	(−81)	06	27	36
30. Small dwellings	−32	−30	26	(52)	19	−40	−22
31. New housing	−29	−31	09	13	19	−38	−10
32. Housing defect–heat	21	12	(−61)	−32	−43	34	(45)
33. Housing defect–plumbing	25	07	(−46)	−36	−27	22	22

Factor Variance and Congruence

Factor variance	1.98	2.13	5.78	4.03	4.66	4.02	4.42
Variance rank in matrix (1 = highest of 6)	6	6	3	3	3	5	3
Congruence with metropolitan factor	—	.931	—	.812	.783	−.690**	−.873**

* Factor coefficients of .45 or above enclosed in parentheses: ( ).

** Congruence with career women factor in Helsinki Region (Harman, 1960, formula 12.31).

In the east sector, a factor merging features of this career women profile with features of postgeniture (not shown in Table 6) is the most potent in the matrix and has a factor variance of 9.84. In the west sector, the career women configuration is almost completely merged with the SES factor shown in Table 2, as inspection of the high factor coefficients for the above five variables shows. It is notable that the merging is a "positive" one in the sense that higher socioeconomic status and higher levels for career women are combined. This is consonant with the original identification of the factor as it appeared in the 42-variable matrix for the City of Helsinki: "Not only working women but working women in the higher- rather than the lower-status white-collar occupations mark the factor." (F. Sweetser, 1965b.) Although detailed information on women's occupational status is lacking in the regional variable list, this positive merging of career women and SES is evidence that the original characterization can stand.

It will be noted that coefficients of congruence of the inner and middle zone career women factors at the bottom of Table 6 indicate at least marked similarity with the metropolitan factor and that these factors are of moderate strength, ranking third in factor variance in their respective matrices. It will be noted, too, that the metropolitan factor is to a degree a "merged" factor also; it includes appropriately signed high factor coefficients associated with postgeniture in variables 3 (age 5–14) and 13 (size of household). And, together with the career women factor in the middle zone, it has high loadings on the defining variables of ruralism (to be discussed next), though with opposite signs.

Two factors interpreted as *ruralism* are shown in Table 6 for the outer zone and the north sector. They derive their meaning essentially from high factor coefficients for three variables:

18. Dependence on agriculture	(positive)
21. Employers	(positive)
25. Logarithm of population density	(negative)

As just noted, the career women factors in the metropolis and in the middle zones have high factor coefficients for these same three variables, although with opposite signs. It is not surprising, therefore, that the two ruralism factors of Table 6, when tested for congruence against the metropolitan career women factor, turn out to be moderately similar or very similar on the basis of reflected signs (indicated by the negative values for the coefficient of congruence in Table 6). It is notable, however, that loadings of variable 17, women in the labor force, are not remarkably high for the two ruralism factors of Table 6, although they are negative, as would be expected (−.23 and −.41, respectively).

DISCUSSION AND CONCLUSIONS

Stability of Ecological Factors in Boston and Helsinki

It had been anticipated that the *universal* dimensions of metropolitan ecological differentiation as measured by factors derived from analysis of metropolis, zones, and sectors in Boston and Helsinki would prove to be more stable than the *special* factors, and this is indeed the case, although the data reveal a continuum from stability to instability of factors, rather than a clean-cut dichotomy. SES factors are consistently potent, as measured by the size and rank of their variances in nearly all of the eighteen matrices analyzed. They are also consistently congruent as compared across nearly all zones and sectors of both metropolises. Finally, they are very closely similar when compared cross-nationally between Boston and Helsinki. Even though the socioeconomic status dimension reveals a minor divergence from the usual pattern in the inner zones of Boston, where the dimension produces two distinct SES factors, the data warrant the conclusion that SES is a highly stable factor in interzone, intersector, and cross-national comparisons.

The universal dimension of familism, however, is less stable. In Boston it is manifest in most matrices as a powerful factor revealing a generally familistic age structure; but in the outer zone and in the north, south, and southeast sectors, it appears as a factor of young familism, or progeniture, without meaningful loadings for the adolescent ages (see Table 3, variable 2). In Helsinki, on the other hand, only one strong general familism factor emerges (in the inner zone). In other matrices, progeniture, established familism, and postgeniture factors are either fully differentiated into distinct factors or are merged with other factors. Collectively, these Helsinki familism factors are potent indeed, rivaling SES in strength in all matrices; but, individually, they may be rather weak, minor factors. Nevertheless, the progeniture factor appears in all the Helsinki matrices (as a distinct factor everywhere except in the inner zones) and shows marked similarity or close congruence across zones and sectors (Table 3). From these data, familism factors seem relatively stable in Boston and moderately stable in Helsinki. But, in general, the familism factors are best described as moderately stable in interzone, intersector, and cross-national comparisons.

The special, culturally bound dimensions of metropolitan ecological structure exhibit quite varying degrees of stability. In part, this is due to the fact that the special factors are often less potent than the universal factors and hence more subject to random statistical variation. But it is also to be attributed to the interactive relations of relevant variables in particular community settings. For example, the analysis of the Irish middle-class factors in Boston's zones and sectors showed that the ethnic dimension in that metropolis behaved statistically in much the same way as the familism dimension in Helsinki, producing three distinct ethnic factors (nonwhite, Italian, and Irish) in some matrices, which failed to appear, or merged in varying combinations, in other matrices. Yet strength was moderate and congruence with the metropolitan factor was often marked or close for zone and sector Irish middle-class factors. The special factors of career women and ruralism in Helsinki show similar permutations, and the weak Swedish language factor appeared in only two matrices. On the whole, the data support the generalization that these special factors are relatively unstable in interzone, intersector, and cross-national comparisons.

Technical (Formal) Classification of Metropolitan Ecological Factors

In previous papers, the writer has placed much emphasis on the invariance of factors in the domain of social ecology (F. Sweetser, 1965a; 1965b). But factorial invariance has two aspects: (1) in relation to the emergence of identical (congruent) factors from matrices based on different sets of variables for the same communities at the same point in time; (2) in relation to the emergence of identical (congruent) factors from matrices for either cross-sectional comparisons of different communities or longitudinal comparisons of the same community at different points in time. The first type of invariance has been tested in several ways, and seems well validated by the work of Schmid and Tagashira (1964) and F. Sweetser (1965a; 1965b). It is given further support by the close similarity of the factors derived for Helsinki from the present 33-variable analysis and those previously reported based on a 42-variable analysis (F. Sweetser, 1966).

The second type of "invariance," however, is really the quality of stability-instability we have just been examining. Clearly, only for the universal SES factor can such invariance be claimed. But the existence of a continuum of stability-instability among ecological factors does offer an empirical basis for the technical or formal classification of such factors which should also be a useful guide in their further analysis. Such a typology is suggested in the accompanying table.

A Technical Typology of Ecological Factors

Formal Types	Characteristics	Examples
(1) *Unitary factors*	(a) *Highly stabie* in intra- and intercommunity comparisons (b) *Potent*, with absolutely and relatively high variance (c) *Conceptually integrated*	SES factors (Boston and Helsinki zones and sectors)
(2) *Differentiating factors*	(a) *Moderately stable* (b) *Potent in combination only* (c) *Conceptually integrated*, i.e., measuring aspects of a single broad dimension	*Familism* factors in Helsinki *Ethnic* factors in Boston
(3) *Combinatory factors*	(a) *Relatively unstable* (b) *Weak as distinct factors* (may combine with potent factors) (c) *Conceptually distinct*, i.e., measuring a specific — and perhaps a minor — dimension	*Swedish language, ruralism,* and *career women* factors in Helsinki (Some) ethnic factors in Boston

While both differentiating and combinatory factors characteristically appear sometimes as separate factors and sometimes merged with other factors, the distinction between them on the basis of conceptual integration versus conceptual distinctness is thought to be valid in the present state of knowledge. Career women and ruralism factors in Helsinki (see Table 6 and previous discussion) could perhaps be thought of as differentiations of a conceptually integrated dimension of "urbanization"; but as described in our data, they appear to be conceptually distinct. Similarly, most Boston ethnic factors are differentiating factors; but, as noted earlier, Irish ethnicity shows combinatory tendencies by merging with SES in two of Boston's sectors. Perhaps further research will permit the reduction of the tripartite typology to a dichotomy: *unitary factors* and *differentiating/combinatory factors*. In the meantime, recognition of these formal distinctions among ecological factors should facilitate the analysis of metropolitan ecological structure.

Substantive Classification of Metropolitan Ecological Factors

Throughout this paper, ecological factors have been characterized as either "universal" or "special." The universal factors have been conceived as deriving from necessary societal and cultural features of urban-industrial societies and therefore present in *all* metropolitan communities in *all* such societies. The special factors have been presented as deriving from the distinctive social structures and normative systems of nations, regions, or local areas. Essentially, this distinction has been applied in cross-sectional comparisons of the ecological structures of Boston and Helsinki at a single point in time. When factors, or types of factors, were found to be matched in both communities, they were called "universal"; when factors or types of factors were found to be distinctively different in the two communities, they were called "special." A primary objective was to discover whether, as a preliminary contribution to the development of a typology of metropolitan communities based on their ecological structures, the analysis of Boston and Helsinki could support prototype descriptions of a "North American" and a "Scandinavian" type of metropolis. Previous comparison of the two total metropolises had produced a schematic summary of the substantively identified factors and types of factors in the two communities (F. Sweetser, 1966, Table 5). Now, a revision of that schematic listing is offered as a preliminary formulation of the two community types in the accompanying table.

Two Types of Metropolitan Ecological Structures

Metropolitan Type		Fundamental Dimension (Factor Type)
NORTH AMERICAN	Universal factors	⎧ Socioeconomic status ⎨ Familism/age structure ⎩ Residential/migrationst atus
	Special factors	Ethnicity
SCANDINAVIAN	Universal factors	⎧ Socioeconomic status ⎨ Familism/age structure ⎩ Residential/migration status
	Special factors	Career women

Residential/migration status as a type of ecological factor is discussed in detail in F. Sweetser (1965c and 1966); it has not been treated in this paper, as explained before, because the available data for the Helsinki regional analyses were insufficient to define the factor clearly. On the other hand, Swedish language and ruralism factors, which were discussed although relevant to the zone-sector analysis, were too weak and too sporadic to warrant inclusion as a feature of a generalized Scandinavian type of ecological structure.

This paradigm is broadly consonant (despite marked differences in method and detail; see F. Sweetser, 1965*a*) with the well-known Shevky and Bell schema (Shevky and Bell, 1955). It assumes the same sort of causal nexus between processes of city growth and ecological differentiation that has been part of the literature of social ecology for the last forty years (e.g., Burgess, 1925; Hoyt, 1939). As far as the universal factors are concerned, it accepts the Shevky-Bell argument that there are indeed fundamental dimensions of urban and metropolitan ecological structure arising out of the necessities of societal and cultural change in the process of industrialization-urbanization.

In one respect, however, the present formulation offers a radical departure from these earlier theories, which tend to be ethnocentrically bound to the particular manifestations of the process of urbanization in the United States. By introducing the dichotomy between the *universal* and the *special* dimensions of ecological structure, a theoretical position is established which facilitates recognition and description of types of ecological structures, as we have just seen. At the same time the theory recognizes that, while universal processes of industrialization-urbanization have their necessities, which produce the universal types of factors, they *also* allow considerable latitude for distinctive sociocultural features of national, regional, and local societies to influence ecological dimensions, thus producing special types of ecological factors. The ethnic mix in American cities, for instance, is a consequence of the whole history of the peopling of these cities, which, in turn, reflects the historic processes of industrialization, labor demand, and immigration (voluntary and forced) as they developed in the American milieu during the past three centuries. In contrast, Scandinavian cities are remarkably homogeneous ethnically; even in Finland, where there is a Swedish-language minority, the six centuries of Swedish domination prior to industrialization-urbanization on any considerable scale so thoroughly penetrated the Finnish institutional structure than no basic normative differences separate the Swedish-speaking and Finnish-speaking Finns today. It is no wonder that ethnic factors are fundamental in metropolitan ecological structure in America but unimportant in Finland.

To take another example, the presence of the special, career women factor as a fundamental dimension in Helsinki is certainly causally related to (*a*) the characteristically high participation of women in the labor force in Finland; (*b*) Finnish definitions of appropriate female occupational roles, manifested, for instance, in the cultural expectation that barbers and dentists will be women. We have ventured to generalize the career women factor from Finland to Scandinavia because of the belief that there is a common value set in the Scandinavian countries (with the possibln exception of Iceland) which is likely to produce analogous, if not identical, results in Sweden, Norway, and Denmark. Research now in progress in Stockholm, Copenhagen, and Oslo should effectively test this hypothesis (Gustafsson, 1964).

These two types of special factors, which in 1960 appear to be, respectively, the distinctive marks of North American and Scandinavian metropolitan ecological structures, are of additional interest because of the possibility that future developments may alter their exclusive character. The presence of large and growing numbers of foreign workers in Sweden *may* foreshadow the emergence of an ethnic factor or factors important at least in Stockholm's ecological structure. And the increasing participation of American women — especially married women and the mothers of young children — in the labor force *may* ultimately produce an important career women factor in American cities. Thus what are seen initially as special factors, peculiar to one nation or one region, may in time become more widespread. If the long-run evolutionary trend of industrialization-urbanization continues to move toward greater ethnic heterogeneity in metropolitan communities and toward broader labor force participation by women, it is even possible to imagine some ecological theorist in the twenty-first century classifying "ethnicity" and "career women" as universal factors in metropolitan ecological structure. For ourselves, we do not believe that world-wide societal and cultural standardization will quickly overwhelm persistent sociocultural differences in nations, regions, and local areas, and we therefore expect that special factors will continue to provide a useful means of distinguishing types of metropolitan ecological structures for a long time to come.

Modes of Ecological Differentiation

Elsewhere, the writer has suggested that one reason for the complexity of the factor structure which is observed when metropolitan communities and their parts are analyzed may be the existence of a number of different modes of ecological differentiation, which become interactive in the metropolitan community (F. Sweetser, 1965*c*). These modes of differentiation were described as:

1. Inner city (or *urban*)
2. Urban-suburban (or *metropolitan*)
3. *Rural-urban*

The conclusion was based on Boston's zones only, where, as we have noted in this paper, the inner zone SES and familism factors merge in a single bipolar factor, with a second SES factor differentiated, and the inner zone Irish middle-class factor differentiates from nonwhite and Italian ethnic factors. Confirmation of the hypothesis is found in the differentiation of Helsinki's career women factor from the ruralism factors in Helsinki's inner zone. The two types of factors elsewhere are partially merged. These data seem to show that urban cores in Boston and Helsinki may tend to be more fully differentiated than outlying zones. The finding conforms to Kish's hypotheses that degree of differentiation is inversely related to distance from the metropolitan center (Kish, 1954) and to the general hypothesis that one feature of urbanization is greater social differentiation. Thus the notion of a special mode of inner city ecological differentiation finds wider support.

Recognition that the metropolitan factor profiles of Tables 1–6 often differ in specific detail from those of any zone in both communities suggests that the idea of a core-suburban mode of differentiation (which is intuitively valid, in any event) has also an empirical basis.

Finally, the Helsinki materials (presented in Table 6) include two "ruralism" factors, defined primarily by economic dependence on agriculture, by low population density, and by the presence of large proportions of employers (independent farmers and small businessmen, one presumes) in the rural-urban fringe. Here, the suggestion of a rural-urban mode of ecological differentiation seems clear.

The evidence is not entirely clear, but it is at least highly suggestive, and it leads to one practical conclusion — that in the delimitation of metropolitan communities for factorial ecological analysis, careful attention ought to be paid to the outer boundaries chosen. Boundaries too narrow — geographically constrictive city limits, for example — may produce distortion through an overemphasis on the inner city mode of differentiation. Boundaries too wide — extended metropolitan regions, for example — may introduce unwanted effects of the rural-urban mode of differentiation. What is needed are studies of metropolitan communities with exterior boundaries drawn so as to reveal primarily the factors that operate in the urban-suburban mode of differentiation, without either of these kinds of distortion. The principle is easier to state than to practice, because of limitations on the availability of suitable data and the natural tendency to follow the line of least resistance and utilize someone else's delimitations of metropolitan areas or regions. But a fully objective comparative study of metropolitan ecological structures, whether interregional or cross-national, would appear to require that social ecologists develop some means of delimiting metropolitan communities on a uniform basis.

Appendix A

DEFINITIONS OF 34 VARIABLES DERIVED FROM CENSUS TRACT DATA, BOSTON, 1960[a]

1. Age 6–13 years	Percentage of population age 6–13 years (elementary school ages)
2. Age 14–17 years	Percentage of population age 14–17 years (high school ages)
3. Age 65 years plus	Percentage of population age 65 years and over (retirement ages)
4. Foreign born	Percentage of population foreign born
5. Foreign parentage	Percentage of population native born, of foreign or mixed parentage
6. Irish stock	Percentage of population of foreign stock (Ireland)
7. Italian stock	Percentage of population of foreign stock (Italy)
8. Nonwhite	Percentage of population nonwhite
9. Sex ratio (single)	Single males age 14 plus $\div$ single females age 14 plus $\times$ 100
10. Fertility ratio	Children under 5 years $\div$ females 15–44 years $\times$ 100
11. Detached dwellings	Percentage of housing units in one-unit structures
12. Home ownership	Percentage of occupied housing units occupied by owners
13. Women in labor force	Percentage of females age 14 and over in the labor force
14. Working mothers	Percentage of married couples with children under 6, wife in labor force
15. Nonfamily	Percentage of population in institutions or living as unattached individuals
16. Residential stability	Percentage of population age 5 and over in same house in 1955 as in 1960.
17. Intra-SMSA migration	Percentage of population age 5 and over which moved within SMSA from 1955–1960[b]
18. Inter-SMSA migration	Percentage of population age 5 and over which moved into SMSA from 1955–1960[b]
19. New housing	Percentage of housing units built from 1950 to 1960

20. Room crowding	Percentage of occupied housing units with 1.01 or more persons per room
21. Housing defects	Index based on lack of plumbing facilities or central heat
22. Median family income	Median family income (annual)
23. Low family income	Percentage of families with annual income under $3,000
24. Auto to work	Percentage of workers (transport known) traveling to work by auto
25. Walk to work	Percentage of workers (transport known) walking to work
26. Commute	Percentage of resident workers employed outside own "residential segment"[c]
27. Males unemployed	Percentage of civilian labor force males unemployed
28. Males "at leisure"	Percentage of males 14–65 years old not in school or in labor force[d]
29. Employment in mfg.	Percentage of employed workers in manufacturing industries
30. Male prof.-mgr. occs.	Percentage of employed males in professional and managerial occupations
31. Male cler.-serv. occs.	Percentage of employed males in clerical, sales, and service occupations
32. College graduates	Percentage of persons age 25 years and older with at least 16 years of school
33. White-collar occs.	The Shevky-Bell occupation standard score
34. 8 grades sch. plus	The Shevky-Bell education standard score[e]

[a] See also F. Sweetser, 1962b, pp. 232–235.

[b] Note that two SMSA's are involved, Boston and Brockton.

[c] Ten "residential segments" were delimited (F. Sweetser, 1962b, Figure 30-D, p. 160); "Commutation" does not necessarily mean travel from suburb to core but from segment to segment.

[d] Computed from unpublished Census "Special Table PH-2."

[e] These "standard scores" are defined in Eshref Shevky and Wendell Bell (1955), pp. 54, 55.

Appendix B

DEFINITIONS OF 33 VARIABLES DERIVED FROM CENSUS DATA FOR CITY STATISTICAL AREAS AND METROPOLITAN AGGLOMERATIONS, HELSINKI, 1960

1. Median age	Median age of total population[a]
2. Age 0–4 years	Percentage of population age 0–4 years
3. Age 5–14 years	Percentage of population age 5–14 years
4. Preadolescent ratio	Percentage of population under 15 years who are 0–4 years old

5.	Middle-age ratio	Percentage of population 20–64 years who are 20–39 years old
6.	Age 65 years plus	Percentage of population age 65 years and over[a]
7.	Proportion male	Percentage of population male
8.	Swedish-speaking Finns	Percentage of population speaking Swedish as principal language[a]
9.	Married	Percentage of population 15 years and older who are married
10.	Fertility	Number of children 0–4 years per 1,000 males 20–49 years[b]
11.	Widowed and divorced	Percentage of population 15 years and older who are widowed or divorced
12.	Nonfamily	Percentage of population 15 years and older in one-person households
13.	Size of household	Mean number of persons in households with two or more persons
14.	Room crowding	Number of persons per 100 rooms
15.	Living space	Number of square meters per person in dwellings
16.	Home ownership	Percentage of dwellings occupied by owners (including share-holders)
17.	Women in labor force	Percentage of females age 15 and older who are economically active (excluding those unemployed and seeking work)
18.	Dependence on agriculture	Proportion of total population economically dependent on agriculture (deciles)
19.	Dependence on industry	Proportion of total population economically dependent on manufacturing industry (deciles)
20.	Dependence on services	Proportion of total population economically dependent on services, including transportation, commerce, etc. (deciles)
21.	Employers	Percentage of economically active who are employers of labor
22.	Blue-collar occupations	Percentage of economically active who are manual workers
23.	9 grades school plus	Percentage of population age 15 and older who have passed middle school or student examinations
24.	Female higher education	Number of females who have passed student examination (for university admission) per 100 females who have passed middle school examination
25.	Population density (log)	Logarithm of number of persons per square kilometer
26.	Public buildings	Number of public buildings per 100 residential buildings
27.	Industrial buildings	Number of industrial buildings per 100 residential buildings
28.	Apartment house size	Number of dwellings per residential building

29. Detached dwellings	Percentage of dwellings in one or two dwelling buildings
30. Small dwellings	Percentage of dwellings with one or two rooms (including kitchen)
31. New housing	Percentage of dwellings built 1951–1960
32. Housing defect–heat	Percentage of dwellings lacking central heat
33. Housing defect–plumbing	Percentage of dwellings lacking flush toilet

[a] For city statistical areas, variables 1, 6, and 8 are for the combined Finnish-speaking and Swedish-speaking populations, comprising 99.3 per cent of total population in the City of Helsinki.

[b] The ratio of children to males was used to measure fertility because of the great excess of females in some statistical areas. See F. Sweetser, 1965a and 1965b.

REFERENCES

Anderson, T., and L. L. Bean (1961), "The Shevky-Bell Typology: Confirmation of Results and a Reinterpretation," *Social Forces, 40*, pp. 119–124.

Bell, W. (1955), "Economic, Family and Ethnic Status: An Empirical Test," *American Sociological Review, 20*, pp. 45–52.

Burgess, E. W. (1925), "The Growth of the City," in R. R. Park, E. W. Burgess, and R. D. McKenzie (eds.), *The City* (Chicago: University of Chicago Press), pp. 47–62.

Cattell, Raymond B. (1949), "The Dimensions of Culture Patterns by Factorizations of National Characters," *Journal of Abnormal and Social Psychology, 44*, pp. 443–569.

Gittus, E. (1965), "An Experiment in the Definition of Urban Sub-areas," *Transactions of the Bartlett Society, 2*, pp. 107–135.

Grönholm, L. (1960), "The Ecology of Social Disorganization in Helsinki," *Acta Sociologica, 5*, pp. 31–41.

Gustafsson, L. (ed.) (1964), Proceedings from the Conference about the ecological part of Project Metropolit at the Sociologiska Institutionen, Stockholm, July 15–17, 1964; mimeo. (Stockholm: University of Stockholm).

Hadden, Jeffrey K., and E. F. Borgatta (1965), *American Cities: Their Social Characteristics* (Chicago: Rand McNally).

Harman, H. (1960), *Modern Factor Analysis* (Chicago: University of Chicago Press).

Hoyt, H. (1939), *The Structure and Growth of Residential Neighborhoods in American Cities* (Washington: Federal Housing Administration).

Janson, C. G. (1964), Notes on assumptions concerning ecological variables in factor analysis: Working Paper for the Project Metropolit Conference on Ecological Research; mimeo. (Stockholm: University of Stockholm).

Janson, C. G. (1965), *Kommunklassificering* [Commune Classification]; mimeo. (Stockholm: Statens Institut för Byggnadsforskning).

Janson, C. G. (1966), *The Spatial Structure of Newark, New Jersey: Part I, The Central City*; mimeo. (Newark: Rutgers University).

Jonassen, Christen T., and S. H. Peres (1960). *Interrelationships of Dimensions of Community Systems: A Factor Analysis of Eighty-two Variables* (Columbus: Ohio State University Press).

Kish, L. (1954), "Differentiation in Metropolitan Areas," *American Sociological Review, 19*, pp. 338–398.

Pedersen, P. O. (1965), *An Empirical Model of Urban Population Structure: A Factor Analytical Study of the Population Structure in Copenhagen*; mimeo. (Copenhagen: The Technical University of Denmark).

Piepponen, P. (1962), "Suomen kuntien sosiaalisen rakenteen perustekijät" [Dimensions of Ecological Differentiation in Finnish Communes], *Yearbook of Population Research in Finland, 7*, pp. 34–46.

Schmid, C., and K. Tagashira (1964), "Ecological and Demographic Indices: A Methodological Analysis," *Demography, 1*, pp. 194–211.

Shevky, E., and W. Bell (1955), *Social Area Analysis* (Stanford: Stanford University Press).

Sweetser, F. (1962a), *Patterns of Change in the Social Ecology of Metropolitan Boston: 1950–1960* (Boston: Massachusetts Department of Mental Health).

Sweetser, F. (1962b), *The Social Ecology of Metropolitan Boston: 1960* (Boston: Massachusetts Department of Mental Health).

Sweetser, F. (1963), "Koulutustaso pääkaupungin eri alueilla" [Educational Status in the Statistical Areas of Helsinki], *Helsinki City Statistical Monthly Review, 14*, pp. 317–334.

Sweetser F. (1964) *Technical Problems in Factorial Ecology*: Working paper for the Project Metropolit Conference on Ecological Research; mimeo. (Stockholm: University of Stockholm).

Sweetser, F. (1965a) "Factor Structure as Ecological Structure in Helsinki and Boston," *Acta Sociologica, 8*, pp. 205–225.

Sweetser F. (1965b), "Factorial Ecology Helsinki, 1960," *Demography, 2*, pp. 372–385.

Sweetser. F. (1965c), *Factorial Ecology: Zonal Differentiation in Metropolitan Boston, 1960*; mimeo. (Chicago: Annual Meeting, Population Association of America).

Sweetser, F. (1966), Helsinging Ekologinen Erilaistuminen Vuonna 1960 [Ecological Differentiation in Helsinki, 1960], *Helsinki City Statistical Monthly Review, 17*, pp. 205–256.

Sweetser, F., and D. Sweetser (1965), "Omakotiasutus Helsingissä ja Bostonissa" [Detached Dwellings in Helsinki and Boston], *Asuntoreformi 2*, pp. 9–15, 52–53.

PART FIVE

Historical Dimensions of
Ecological Analysis

The ecological approach has one decisive advantage over the sample survey: it opens up possibilities of time-series analyses in historical depth. The bookkeeping machinery of most of the Western nation-states had been producing data for ecological analysis for at least a century by the time the sample survey entered the scene; the Gallup-Roper revolution hit the West as late as in 1936, and the possibilities of time-series analysis based on surveys are for most practical purposes limited to some period since the late forties. Even for this brief period the structure of the information collected through the use of sample surveys has proved much less stable than the structure of the official bookkeeping operations: the governmental statisticians have felt much more pressure than the commercial pollsters and the academic survey organizers to maintain stability in the categories and to establish indicators of change. This, of course, does not mean that the official data-gathering agencies have been particularly anxious to make life easy for the ecological analysts. There are many gaps in the series, there are changes in the boundaries of the territorial units, and there are various technical difficulties in the establishment of linkages across the many different bodies of accumulated data. Few of the data have been produced for the purposes the ecologist wants them for; to suit his needs they have to be reorganized and linked in ways never imagined by the original data collectors.

The political ecologists made their mark on the academic community by establishing systematic linkages between two sets of data files: the censuses and the election counts. Such linkages can be established diachronically as well as synchronically. The great thrust of Allardt's factor analysis of Finnish ecological variations lay in his ability to show how data for the early phases of politics in each local community still accounted for considerable shares of the variance in current party alignments. This is also what makes the development of the historical data archives of the Inter-University Consortium at Ann Arbor so promising; it will

457

allow a variety of diachronic analyses across such disparate data files as election statistics, censuses, religious enumerations, and land registers. But each such file will by itself alone allow methodologically challenging analyses of processes of change. This is the essential message of the two chapters by Converse and MacRae-Meldrum; they have worked out models for the analysis of variations in the patterns of change from one election to another over long periods of time and have shown how such data files from one single source can offer important clues in the development of hypotheses about processes of political alignment.

The easiest procedure in historical ecology is simply to punch onto cards the figures already tabulated in official publications. Once a few such sources have been linked over time, however, the ecologist will often want to push on to the recovery of unpublished counts and the generation of new statistical series from early registers. In organizing its file of historical electoral data by county, the Inter-University Consortium could not base its work on published tables; thus a great effort of data recovery had to be organized in each state by local historians. This is only one step away from the ultimate stage of data organization in historical ecology: the establishment of indicators of community structure through the processing of original data in registers and other standardized bookkeeping records. This can be done for early elections. John Vincent's work on the Poll Books *of Victorian England and Erik Høgh's analysis of Danish electoral registers during the period of open voting from 1849 to 1901 are outstanding examples. The procedure can also be used in reanalyzing early censuses: the original protocols are transferred to cards or tape to make fresh tabulations possible. This is essentially the strategy pursued by Emmanuel Leroy-Ladurie and his team at the* Centre de Recherches Historiques *in Paris; they are engaged in the computerization of the records of the French military archives and will, once the data have been organized, be able to study processes of change in traditional French society not only at the individual level but also at the level of the* commune. *The great French school of historical demographers have gone even further in the generation of data for the study of early developments. L. Henry and his colleagues have worked out techniques for the reconstruction of tables of fertility and mortality for the century* before *the first regular census; they have established samples of parishes and have tried to derive census-type information from the registers of christenings and burials. Laslett and his group at Cambridge have tried out a similar procedure for preindustrial England. The chapter at the end of Part Five offers a fascinating account of this work and spells out some of the possibilities of further development. Similar work is under way in other countries of Europe. Once such samples have been established, we shall know much more about the variations in the* situations de départ *in each region and will be able to carry out much more realistic analyses of the processes of cultural, social, and political transformation brought about through the growth of the economy and the strengthening of the central national institutions in each country.*

17

PHILIP E. CONVERSE

Survey Research and the Decoding of Patterns in Ecological Data

ACCIDENTS OF TRAINING, the swing of career lines, differential accessibility of research materials, and special capabilities of research institutes all often combine to produce the impression that the world of empirical social research is divided into two camps: the survey research specialists and the aggregate data specialists. And insofar as such specialization does exist, it is naturally a social imperative that the two camps be at intellectual war with each other!

Whatever grounds this observation may have had in the past, it now seems grossly inaccurate, if not downright amusing. Day-to-day specialization on one side or the other does exist, as a practical matter. At the same time it is self-evident to serious investigators of both breeds that neither data source taken alone is entirely satisfying. There are many exciting questions to be approached through aggregate data that can be confronted only ineffectively, if at all, with survey materials. And conversely, there are questions deftly answered by survey information that aggregated data comment upon only after a frightening series of inferential leaps or leave as a nest of complete indeterminacy. Thus, between them, the two types of data open up to us an extent of ground that neither taken alone would permit us to cover.

A far larger and more fascinating domain of problems, however, lies at the intersection of the two data bases: classes of inquiry that can best be pursued with joint or complementary use of aggregate and survey materials. Certainly such a tactic is necessary if we are to put to the test many of the things we have told ourselves over the years about the crucial theoretical significance of the interaction between the individual and his social microcosm, on the one hand, and broad systemic conditions, on the other. Work of this sort is well represented in this symposium. Yet this obvious example scarcely exhausts the types of investigations that may profit handsomely from joint exploitation of these data bases.

Another of these types of inquiry, and one that concerns us primarily here, attempts to work from the complementary strengths of both types of data to circumvent their respective weaknesses. One of the prime attractions of aggregate data is their richness in national variety and historical depth. Such scope gives analytic entrée into a range of systemic conditions — historical junctures, cultural and developmental differences — that survey data obviously cannot now match. A prime weakness of ecological materials lies in their aggregated, summary nature and the intrinsic ambiguities that spring from this fact. For any pattern of aggregate variation taken alone, it is typical that a number of plausible "models" of the underlying process that generated it can be imagined, and the aggregate information as traditionally treated provides little apparent leverage for a more satisfying diagnosis.

However, a close understanding of what we might call the "infrastructure" of the competing explanations through analyses of survey data even from a different time or place often serves to suggest further critical tests of the aggregate materials that may help to determine which process is the more plausible generator of the aggregate patterns. Sometimes survey materials will suggest ancillary or modifying variables that need to be brought to bear on the aggregate patterns. Sometimes understanding of the pattern in its disaggregated form suggests more incisive ways of organizing the aggregate data from a statistical point of view, to sharpen or purify the aggregate effects if indeed they have been generated in one way rather than another. In the most elegant cases, one may have a model or simulation of the suspected processes at an individual level. If such a model can faithfully reproduce the known survey effects while generating comparable gross aggregate patterns, one's power to decode the meaning of earlier aggregate materials is greatly enhanced. In some instances we may find that parameters important to the process as understood for the current period are known to have been quite different a century earlier (urbanization, education, population age structure, communication processes). Then with a satisfactory model it is an easy task to reset the appropriate parameters and discover whether the model can indeed reproduce the historical aggregate information.

Of course, such work can provide feedback in its turn to the design of survey instruments, specifications for critical data, suggestions for new analytic departures, and the like. Between the two data bases lies a two-way street, and we all shall profit from heavy traffic on it. It might be useful here to spend our time attempting to classify the kinds of traffic that could pass at various stages of an inquiry. I am more inclined to leave this a free matter and attempt instead to focus upon a concrete example of an analysis that has actually been carried out and has substantive interest of its own, while illustrating in transit the utility of information from sample survey work in the more intensive examination of historical aggregate data.

Indeed, I had originally chosen a subject for just such an illustrative analysis, to be based on the store of aggregate historical voting statistics which is accumulating at a rapid pace in the archives of the Inter-University Consortium for Political Research, based in Ann Arbor, Michigan. However, as time passed, it became clear that the materials I had expected to use would not be in manipulable format in time for this paper. Therefore, I have been obliged to use sketchier data than I had originally hoped, although I think they suffice perfectly well to suggest the logic of the operations conducted and to illustrate the interpretive role of survey research in such aggregate explorations. More important, just as analytic work with these data began, I received a copy of MacRae's and Meldrum's paper for this symposium and discovered that the problem I had decided to pursue — the use of sample survey insights to detect the occurrence and magnitude of critical elections in earlier American voting statistics — had already been tracked down with consummate skill.[1]

The latter problem could be transformed into an asset rather than a liability, since the MacRae and Meldrum paper could itself be used to exemplify the value of sample survey data in "decoding" patterns in historical aggregative material. Therefore, I shall first lay out briefly the primary model of the voting process which underlies the problem these authors have analyzed. I shall try in passing to point out the ways in which survey insights were helpful not only in motivating their inquiry but also in providing guidance along the way as to the most effective ways of organizing the aggregate materials in order to make them tell their story in most reliable and incisive form.

Then I shall proceed to develop from the same underlying model a quite different line of inquiry, although one which remains something

[1] Duncan MacRae, Jr., and James A. Meldrum, "Factor Analysis of Aggregate Voting Statistics," published in this volume, Chapter 18.

of a logical companion piece for the MacRae-Meldrum paper. This analysis will be pursued with the aid of illustrative aggregate data from the United States and France.

THE BASIC VOTING MODEL

Although survey research material on voting has been crucial in fleshing out the basic model we are employing here, some of the initial insights were emphasized by keen students of aggregate voting statistics. Most notably, V. O. Key became fascinated with the fact that voting returns over long periods of time tended to show long periods of relative stability, punctuated at rather rare intervals by large-scale shifts in fundamental political coloration of voting districts. This was neither a trivial nor a self-evident observation. The neophyte examining aggregate voting records over long periods of time might well not have noticed the fact, for, after all, such tabulations present quite a formidable sea of change. No election is quite like any other election, even for the same district, and the party division of the vote is always shifting this way and that from election to election. What attracted Key's attention was the fact that, although temporal variation in vote outcomes was ubiquitous across districts, such variation tended to have a rather clear center of gravity for any particular district; and short-term swings in actual elections returns could be seen as oscillations around this center of gravity. In other words, if a district seemed to cast most of its votes in the 40–45 per cent Democratic range over a period of time and then in a given election swung toward an unusual 55 per cent Democratic, it was far more likely to swing back toward the 40–45 per cent range in any subsequent election than it was to evolve onward into the 60 per cent Democratic range, or even to remain at 55 per cent. Occasionally, however, the center of gravity of a voting series for a district did appear to undergo a step change, with new oscillations beginning around the new level of partisanship. And most important, such step changes were not haphazardly distributed in time for districts but rather tended to occur for a large number of districts in the same election and then did not occur again for a considerable period of time. As we have seen, Key labeled these elections "critical elections" and commented upon their occurrence in American history.[2]

At the same time, survey research data were demonstrating that voters

[2] V. O. Key, Jr., "A Theory of Critical Elections," *Journal of Politics, 17* (1955), pp. 1–18.

often made significant distinctions between the party for which they had voted in a particular election and the party to which they felt a more abiding allegiance. Thus, for example, in 1952 General Eisenhower won the first substantial Republican majority for President that the nation had seen in 24 years; and political pundits began to write books prophesying a new era of Republican ascendance. Yet survey data from that year showed that the Eisenhower victory was due, not to masses of new recruits to the Republican faith, but rather to solid backing from traditional Republicans and large rates of defection on the part of citizens who told interviewers they continued to think of themselves as Democrats. It is no secret, of course, that these more basic expressions of loyalty turned out to be far more important as long-run predictors of voting decisions in the middle and late 1950's than the short-run flirtations with the Republicans.

Of course, the isomorphism between Key's observations about properties of voting trends and this kind of survey information was immediately clear. The short-term oscillations in voting series could be attributed to transient defections, recognized as such psychologically by the actors involved; and the center of gravity of such returns from a particular district would tend to represent the basic division of party loyalties elicited by survey measurements of "party identification." The stability of these identifications for individuals over time was to be heavily documented in survey studies in ensuing years. And "critical" or "realigning" elections (although none had been available for close study since survey research techniques had developed) would be ones in which voters not only crossed party lines in the sense of a short-term defection but underwent full-fledged conversion of loyalties as well.[3]

Since the time when these notions came into focus, more intensive work with sample survey materials has proceeded on all the fronts that the underlying model suggested. Factors governing the development and intensification of party loyalties were explored. Conditions facilitating or impeding short-term defections began to be systematized. Data collections associated with each election permitted a far more exact and direct measurement of the short-term forces producing defections in varying specific election races at different levels of office.[4]

Virtually all of this accumulating information can fruitfully be plowed back into a re-examination of American voting statistics from earlier

[3] A. Campbell, P. Converse, W. Miller, and D. Stokes, *The American Voter* (New York: Wiley, 1960). See especially Chapter 19.

[4] Donald E. Stokes, "Some Dynamic Elements of Contests for the Presidency," *American Political Science Review, 60:* 1 (1966), pp. 19–28.

eras for which no survey data are available. Perhaps the simplest and broadest lesson from the model is the fact that what registers as change in aggregate voting statistics — the swing of a vote division in a district from one election to another — can be of two radically different kinds: the short-term defection under the allure or repulsion of immediate stimuli as against more fundamental, long-range conversion. Furthermore, the fact that most electoral change is of the former, rather than the latter, kind in the United States has some critical implications for any interpretation of voting change in briefer periods. Historians attempting to understand the motivations prompting the electorate or portions of it in an election t_2 have long compared t_2 outcomes with the state of affairs at t_1, or the previous election, and supposed that an analysis of these changes and their social correlates would provide the nearest possible approach to an accounting of the dynamic forces driving voters in one party direction or another at the t_2 election. Yet, once it is clear as an actuarial fact that in the United States defection rather than conversion accounts for the vast bulk of electoral change, one implication of the model is that something approaching half of the change in vote proportions from one election to the next needs to be conceptualized not as the product of dynamic new short-term forces associated with the t_2 election but rather as the effect of a relaxation of short-term forces that were new and dynamic at t_1. For example, it can be shown that Protestants in the United States moved away from the Republican Party and toward the Democrats more vigorously than did Catholics at the time of the 1964 election (where the base line is the previous election). Should we interpret these aggregate patterns as telling us something of an unexpected set of short-term forces related to religious differences in the Goldwater-Johnson contest? No, of course not. These patterns have nothing to do with the election situation in 1964 per se but rather reflect the inevitable outcome given the relaxation of the forces peculiar to the 1960 election.

The model itself suggests a proliferating array of problems to be attacked with aggregate statistics, while lending guidance as to how those statistics should be treated statistically and ultimately interpreted. The MacRae-Meldrum paper involves a whole network of decisions about the organization of the data which such a model prompts. The averaging of time series to provide a stable base line; the introduction of an extremely minor office to minimize the error or "noise" in certain estimates that the large-scale defections associated with well-known candidate personalities can produce; the extraction at a point of the "traditional" component of the vote, in order to purify the variance being examined with respect to the immediate purposes of the inquiry: these and other steps reflect a thoughtful wedding between such a model and the gross variation in the aggregate statistics in their raw form. Indeed, the components of the vote are rendered explicit in item 6 of the section entitled "Basic Assumptions of the Method."[5]

Although clarification of the basic notions has already been an important contribution of survey research to the decoding of aggregate statistics, the contribution even on this specific set of points is continuing. Thus, for example, we are hoping that further work can improve on the methods for isolating the traditional component or political center of gravity of a district from variation due to short-term forces. It is clear that averaging a set of outcomes across several elections provides a much better estimate of the traditional component than would the results of any election taken alone. However, in terms of the model, the adequacy of this estimate hinges on the assumption that in any moderate run of time a district will have experienced a fairly balanced mix of pro-Republican and pro-Democratic short-term forces. This is demonstrably untrue in the recent period for which survey data are available. If, for example, one were to compute a center of gravity for various districts on the basis of their vote returns for the past four Presidential elections in the United States, the estimates might be reasonably good for a minority of heavily Catholic districts since, roughly speaking, these district have been subjected to two strong Democratic swings and two strong Republican ones. In strongly Protestant districts, however, such an average would suffer a substantial known bias since these districts have responded to three strong Republican swings and a single Democratic one. Attempting to improve the estimate by extending the time series and enlarging the sample of elections is not a reassuring solution since the longer the time base, the more severe the deception of population movement into and out of the district can become. In fact, even the twelve-year base our example assumes here would be treacherously long for some areas in the United States.[6]

Therefore we are currently involved in experimental work with survey and aggregate data from the 1950's, testing ways of working backward from aggregate returns to arrive at less biased estimates of the traditional component, based on even shorter segments of time than any averaging method can produce. We naturally are attempting to proceed in a

[5] MacRae and Meldrum, *op. cit.*

[6] One third or more of the 1964 electorate in Florida had migrated into that state since 1952, and the partisanship of the immigrants departs widely from that of the native population.

fashion that, although jointly confirmed by survey and aggregate data in the current period, could be extended back to periods for which the survey "crutch" becomes unavailable.[7]

The number of fascinating theoretical problems that can be handled in a much more meaningful fashion once the capacity to isolate short-term and traditional components from aggregate voting series is refined seems rather long. One brief example that may be of interest outside the American polity has to do with the progressive "deregionalization" or "nationalization" of electoral responses which is as apparent to even a cursory inspection of American historical statistics as it is in the voting statistics of many other nations over roughly the same period. There are obvious statistical tools for mapping out these trends over time in precise ways, and such a mapping, laid against other extant information on the development of mass national communication systems, could provide important information on the progressive integration of national polities in the modern period. However, in just such a problem as this, it would be of tremendous interest to treat election returns over the past century resolved into their two main components, for it is likely that the deregionalization of the short-term component, for self-evident reasons, has been leading the erosion of regionalism in the traditional component by 50–80 years. A mapping of these properties of the raw vote materials, without the components isolated, would give an "averaged" trend that would be thoroughly misleading.

VARIANCE PROPERTIES OF AGGREGATE VOTING SERIES

The MacRae-Meldrum paper focuses its attention on that portion of the model which involves the mean or central tendency of a series of votes over time, and it seeks to identify those infrequent points at which this central tendency shifted significantly. If the central tendency is one important property of a sequence of votes, its variance is another.

We have already spoken of short-term oscillations of a vote series around a (temporarily) fixed mean. It is clear, conceptually, that these oscillations might have quite different amplitudes for different populations, even though both populations were responding in the same general direction at the same time to the same set of short-term forces. In the American case, one population might swing 2 per cent to the Republican side in one election, and then 4 per cent to the Democratic side

[7] See "The Concept of a Normal Vote," Chapter 2 of A. Campbell, P. E. Converse, W. E. Miller, and D. E. Stokes, *Elections and the Political Order* (New York: Wiley, 1966).

in the next; another population might show a swing of 7 per cent Republican followed by a swing of 13 per cent Democratic in the same sequence of elections. If these differences in behavior persisted over any length of time, we might suspect that there were systematic reasons — that one population is for whatever reasons relatively unstable, responsive, or flexible, while the other is stable or rigid, the choice among adjectives depending primarily on how we may feel about the matter.

From many points of view, the variance property of the series is of just as great political significance as its central tendency. In the American system in the current period, for example, the central tendency of public preference favors the Democratic Party by several per cent, as it has for at least two decades and probably longer. The Democrats are in the majority, and the Republicans suffer minority status. This does not mean that Republicans have no hope of capturing the important nationwide office of the presidency from time to time; the system is a reasonably unstable or responsive one, and defections on a large scale are sufficiently plausible that, given favorable short-term forces, the Republican Party can manage a national majority. This responsiveness does not dim the significance of the fact that Democrats enjoy the majority, for that majority gives them a running start toward victory and assures them that they can capture the White House not only with neutral or favorable short-term forces but even with mildly unfavorable short-term forces as well (as was the case in 1960). Nonetheless, the fact of an underlying 54–46 majority has only limited significance, as Stokes has pointed out, unless we add some further information concerning the variance property of the voting system at the same time. That is, if the expected standard deviation of the vote were as large as 20 per cent, the minority party would face only 42–58 odds in any given election, whereas laboring under the same shortage of loyalists, its chances of victory would shrink to less than 3 in 100 — a rigid one-party state — were the expected standard deviation as small as 2 per cent. Thus the most important meaning of a basic majority is a joint function of the displacement of the mean from 50–50 and the variance of voter performance across a sample of elections.[8]

[8] See Donald E. Stokes, "Party Loyalty and the Likelihood of Deviating Elections," in *ibid.* Working from the variance shown by the American presidential vote over the past 65 or 70 years, Stokes estimated the probability of a Republican Presidential victory given a 54 per cent Democratic majority to be about .27. One assumes that the similarity between this figure and the proportion of administrations that the Republicans have indeed captured since the Democratic majority was forged at the time of the Great Depression — two administrations out of nine — is far from accidental.

Although the evidence is far more fragmentary, there is at least some reason to imagine that a high-variance voting population would be more susceptible, given a certain degree of crisis, to approaches from *ad hoc* parties mushrooming outside the traditional party system than would low-variance voting populations under the same objective pressures. In other words, a low-variance population seems more firmly anchored in the ongoing party competition than does a high-variance population. And it may well be that the notion of such a variance property is more readily transferred from the simplistic terms of the American two-party system to other multiparty polities than are questions of the central tendency of the vote and its relationship to the magic 50–50 watershed.

An interest in the variance property implicit in the model leads quite naturally to a consideration of differences in expressions of strength of party identification in sample survey work. In other words, we should certainly expect a population of adults indicating that they are strongly identified with one or another party to show a vote record over time with a lower variance in its party division than a population of adults who only felt vague "leanings" toward a party at the starting point. Furthermore, there is reason to believe that there are significant differences in the over-all level of allegiances between nations at any point in time, for the same nation at different points in time, and across certain predictable subpopulations of a given nation at any time. One of the fairly reliable findings in the latter category is that the strength of party allegiances grows with participation in the system; and for most mature systems, an elderly cohort of voters is likely to express far fewer equivocal allegiances to existing parties than does a cohort of younger voters. Working from sample survey information concerning these differential strengths of identification by age and the differential responses to the same short-term forces by strength of identification, we have simulated the behavior of a new cohort of American voters (ages twenty-one to twenty-four) and an elderly cohort (over seventy), bombarded by the same samples of short-term forces over a sequence of voting "trials."[9] The variance of the vote performances of the young is substantially greater than that of the oldest cohort.

The obvious conceptual relationship between strength of party identification, as it might be observed directly in sample surveys, and the variance properties of aggregate voting series opens the possibility

[9] The model bears some similarity to that discussed by McPhee in Chapter 5 of William N. McPhee and William A. Glaser, *Public Opinion and Congressional Elections* (Glencoe, Ill.: The Free Press, 1962).

that aggregate materials might be used to generate inferences concerning the underlying stability of partisan loyalties in historical populations for which survey data are not available, and hence to permit the reconstruction of the rates at which large-scale populations are socialized into new party systems. This is indeed the interest that we shall pursue in our pilot analysis to follow. However, it should be emphasized at the outset that enough is known of these matters not to expect any simple, one-to-one correspondence between the variance of a voting record over time and underlying strengths of partisanship. A correlation can indeed be expected and, *ceteris paribus*, a full correspondence. Yet we are already aware that a number of other conditions (some of which, like the rate of turnover of candidates presented to the public, represent "external conditions" and say little about the dispositions of the voter himself) can powerfully affect the variance of a voting record apart from the strength of identification of the voters, so that convincing detective work must await much more ambitious analytic efforts than we can bring to bear at this time.

Nevertheless, there is a sufficiently large number of questions abroad having to do with the stability of partisanship of differing populations that it seems worth presenting a pilot analysis here.

LONG-TERM PARTISAN STABILITY:
FRANCE AND THE UNITED STATES

One of these interesting questions has been on our collective agenda since the publication, in 1913, of André Siegfried's classic study of political behavior in the fourteen "western" departments of France.[10] While this rich work retains interest today in many substantive directions, one residue that the volume leaves in scholarly minds has to do with the remarkable stability of partisan tendencies over long periods of time on a geographic base in France.

This residual impression might be thought to stand somewhat at sixes and sevens to more recent work of both survey and aggregate types of French voting, which tend to comment on partisan instability and low levels of French identification with the major traditional parties. R. D. Masters has attempted a comparative investigation of stability of aggregate voting statistics in France, the United States, and Switzerland

[10] André Siegfried, *Tableau politique de la France de l'Ouest sous la Troisième République* (Paris: Armand Colin, 1913).

over the period from 1919 to 1958, and his index of mobility of the vote shows far higher values for France over this period than for either of the other two countries.[11] This impression of relative instability fits with deductions drawn from some treatments of sample survey data from postwar France.[12]

None of this newer work clashes with the Siegfried observations in any necessary way. Siegfried was dealing primarily with voting returns for the early years of the Third Republic, and it might easily be claimed that the trauma of two successive wars had served to shatter any bases of partisan stability that might have pertained in an earlier epoch. On the other hand, it might be argued instead that Siegfried's amazement at the stability of voting lines was mainly attributable to the expectations he had brought to the data; had he sat down for an intensive analysis of voting statistics from some other countries rather than France, his amazement might have been even greater.

There are other senses, too, in which the Masters article does not attempt to confront the Siegfried thesis. Masters operated on the grossest of all possible aggregate data: vote divisions summarized at the national level only, for each of the major elections during the period of interest in each of the three nations. The "index of mobility" is a simple first-order difference between the proportion of total national votes that a party received in one election (e_1) and in the next election of the same type (e_2). Such absolute differences are summed across parties to produce a total that describes over-all mobility across the pair of elections in question.

Although such first differences are indeed one of the most legitimate and accessible ways of expressing what we could call the short-term variability of the vote, in this comparative context they raise a number of methodological questions, while more or less escaping the main thrust of Siegfried's contentions. In the first instance it is apparent that the operation of summing differences across parties may have a radically different meaning for a system where ten or more party groupings can contribute to the total index for an election than for a system where

[11] R. D. Masters, "Une méthode pour mesurer la mobilité des attitudes politiques," *Revue Française de Science Politique, 10:* 3 (1960), p. 658.

[12] P. E. Converse and G. Dupeux, "Politicization of the Electorate in France and the United States," *Public Opinion Quarterly, 26:* 1 (1962), p. 1. MacRae elsewhere argues from postwar French survey data that interchanges of support between at least the stable traditional parties have been less than the comparable movement in the United States. See Duncan MacRae, Jr., *Parliament, Parties, and Society in France 1946–1958* (New York: St. Martin's Press, 1967), p. 240.

only two or three do.[13] Second, the restriction of the data to national-level totals bypasses the issue of internal geographic differentiation and its relative stability or instability. It would be possible, for example, for national totals to jump around quite wildly, with all component regions hewing to their same relative positions in the left-right spectrum.[14] This would be a type of instability, but one that would suggest potent underlying loyalties, combined with a certain freedom of short-term defection in a polity whose responses were relatively "nationalized." Third, the Masters' treatment is bound to the identity of specific parties over time rather than to the broad *tendances* or competing ideologies which successions of specific parties may represent over any long run in a sufficiently multiparty system. The Siegfried work is quite unequivocal on this point. The author was impressed by the proliferation of specific "etiquettes" that stood for election in the period and area that he studied, and the "astonishing stability" to which he refers is not that of the nominal party but rather that of the underlying ideological pre-dilection, whatever party names and short-term leaderships might float to the surface in various periods. And, finally, the primary measure used by Masters, dependent on the change between two successive elections, is addressed to change in the shortest-term sense (defections) and would tend to construe any phenomenon of a "return home" to one's basic party after a given defection as added proof of instability.[15]

---

[13] It should be noted that this problem does not wreak havoc with the broad con-clusions Masters draws, given the particular data presented. His index, averaged across elections, shows values of 39.0 for France and 16.2 for Switzerland, despite the fact that the number of parties contributing differences to each election total is about the same in the Swiss as in the French case. If one computes a per-party con-tribution to the index — the strongest correction one could conceivably require, and on several conceptual grounds *too* strong — then the index for the United States registers higher mobility than that shown for the French data in the major data dis-play. However, in this instance nonvoting is treated as a contribution to the index, and the large and regular fluctuations in turnout from Presidential to off-year Con-gressional elections in the United States add mightily to the magnitude of its mobility value, as Masters points out. Removing this effect by considering only the series of Congressional votes cast in Presidential elections reduces per-party United States value to about three fourths the magnitude of the comparable French figure. (The per-party value for Switzerland remains much lower than either.) See Masters, *op. cit.,* pp. 660–665.

[14] This is the property of American aggregate voting statistics which intrigued Louis Bean in his volume *How to Predict Elections* (New York: Knopf, 1948).

[15] One exception to this observation is the display of what Masters calls an index of cumulative mobility: the amount of change between the first election in the series and each successive election thereafter. It is with respect to this index that the French materials depart most radically from the Swiss and American in their suggestion of long-term as well as short-term instability. This index most closely approximates the

These remarks should not be taken as a critique of Masters, particularly as it is we who have introduced Siegfried into the discussion, and not Masters himself. What we wish to emphasize more than anything else is that terms like "change" and "instability" can have quite different referents and hence diagnostic operations for their discovery in aggregate statistics. It is our argument that models refined in survey analysis can be of great help in clarifying such distinctive referents.

We have already suggested that short-term variability of the kind that Masters taps, in at least a gross, national-level sense, is a symptom of weakness in underlying party identifications at an individual level. However, we should like to approach the problem from another angle, one that minimizes the influence of short-term variation in favor of long-term variation and in several other senses also fits the Siegfried perspective better.

Our procedure has in some ways been affected by the nature of the data readily available, and we might have handled the problem somewhat differently had we been able to start from more nearly raw voting statistics. The information on hand was contained in Goguel's *Géographie des Elections Françaises,* which presents in map form selected results from major French elections from 1870 to 1951, thereby sweeping back across most of the period covered by Masters and the period studied by Siegfried as well.[16] Because of the presentation in maps with eight or ten tinting gradations, the original metric information is destroyed, and the departments of the nation are, in effect, collapsed into ranks with multiple ties with respect to whatever voting variable may be at issue in the particular map.[17]

Moreover, there is a fair amount of "missing data" in that maps treating the same party of *tendance* are not provided for every major election, although there appears to be at least one map for every election. Finally, there is something of an "apples-and-oranges" problem, since the variable coded on some of the maps has to do not with the

---

manipulations of the data we shall use later, although it tends to require a "representativeness" of the first election in a series in a way that is unnecessary (Masters, *op. cit.,* pp. 668–670).

[16] François Goguel, *Géographie des élections françaises de 1870 à 1951,* Cahiers de la Fondation Nationale des Sciences Politiques No. 27 (Paris: Armand Colin, 1951).

[17] This collapsing has at least one beneficial side effect for our purposes. In view of the fact that the size of the intervals coded and the median rank were adjusted to leave something of a rectangular distribution, a primitive "normalization" has already been carried out which diminishes concern one might otherwise have about the differential effects of uniform class intervals on returns for large and small parties.

proportion of popular votes captured by a party or *tendance* but rather with the proportion of representatives elected for service in the Chamber of Deputies who were associated with the party or *tendance* in question.

On the other hand, as long as we make some effort to keep track of our apples and oranges, the data lend themselves to examination of Siegfried's thesis better than some data might, for reasons beyond the geographic base and the time depth. Despite the fact that in some instances, for some time periods, the data involve specific parties such as the Communists and the Socialists, the main maps from which our materials are drawn involve broader subjective codings of underlying *tendance,* whatever specific parties may have represented the *tendance* in the period. The most continuous data, and hence those which we shall use most, are presented for the Right and for the Extreme Left.

The parallel materials prepared for the United States are considerably more straightforward. The division of the popular vote between the major parties at the state level over the sequence of quadrennial Presidential elections from 1872 to 1960 formed the initial batch of data. These quantities were then collapsed into intervals or ranks, yielding distributions approximating those emerging from the French data as closely as possible.

In both cases, an intercorrelation matrix was formed, organized sequentially by election dates.[18] The United States matrix, being a pure and homogeneous one, was subsequently operated on in its initial form. The French matrix, involving quite a crossing of apples and oranges (different parties and measures of votes as opposed to proportions of seats), was largely discarded, with five more sparse submatrices being selected from it. These involved time correlations, over irregular lapses of time, between (1) proportion of seats for *La Droite*; (2) proportion of votes for *La Droite*; (3) proportion of seats for the Extreme Left; (4) proportion of votes for the Extreme Left; and (5) proportion of

---

[18] Because of the destruction of metric information, the correlation coefficients employed were tau-beta rank-order coefficients. The bivariate distributions underlying the coefficients are such that gamma coefficients (also generated by the computer program, but not used) depart only slightly from the tau-betas and in perfectly predictable ways; thus the general conclusions formed would differ in no particulars whatever had the gammas been used instead. As will be noted subsequently, some of the analytic machinery brought to bear presupposes Pearson correlation coefficients as a substrate, and with more adequate metric information available the product-moment coefficients would have been used. Once again, however, the correspondences between Pearson coefficients and the rank-order coefficients used are sufficiently straightforward for information of this kind that there need be little concern that the main comparative results are artifacts of the choice of coefficient.

votes for the Communist Party. Within each of these five matrices, the entries were pure in the sense of representing the same entity correlated with itself at another point in time.

These matrices resemble some that were involved in the MacRae-Meldrum paper; yet as we want to ask quite a different set of questions of them, we shall treat them in a radically different way.[19] For simplicity's sake, we shall proceed with the major part of the discussion referring to the more proper United States matrix (or any one like it) and postpone mention of the additional wrinkles that the French matrices imposed on us. We may think of this matrix as representing a surface that has contours into the third dimension, according to the relative sizes of the coefficients in different regions of the matrix. Given the kind of matrix we are dealing with here — organized by progressively larger time leaps — we would not be in much doubt as to what kind of surface in general we are likely to find. That is, we have the intuitive sense that many forces act over time to decay structured relationships progressively; and the longer the time that such forces operate, the greater the decay to be observed from any given temporal starting point. In other words, we would surely expect such an inter-correlation matrix to show the "simplex" form: a pitch like a roof, with the ridge running just off the main diagonal (the correlations between successive elections), sloping off progressively to a low point at the far corner of the matrix, where the correlations relate the most distant time points.[20] What is interesting to us is not the fact of the slope itself, which is nearly trivial, but the possibility of investigating the properties of the slope to arrive at more precise expressions concerning the rate of decay and its general form.

One simple way of proceeding is to consider all correlations in any given diagonal of the triangular matrix as repeated estimates of an underlying "true" value, representing the correlation between states for the particular lapse in time represented by that diagonal. In this light, it is a natural impulse to average these successive estimates in order to arrive at the best cross-sectional "slicing" of the roof, summarizing the

---

[19] Factor analysis would be a reasonable alternative at a point or two in the following inquiry, but we have refrained from using it in view of our interest in keeping some of the intermediate data organization explicit.

[20] More properly, perhaps, I should say these would be our expectations where the voting data are concerned. In some instances one would find matrices looking much more like a Chinese roof than a Western one, for example, with the $t_1 - t_5$ correlations generally greater than those for $t_1 - t_3$ or $t_1 - t_4$, and those for $t_1 - t_{10}$ generally greater than others intervening in time, all of which is a simple indicator of an underlying cyclical process.

general contour of the slope represented.[21] The number of estimates we have for each new diagonal diminishes progressively by one as we move outward from the main diagonal, so that our averages become less and less stable. However, with a matrix as large as that for the United States, we can cover time lapses as great as 70 years without falling below five estimates.

Such a single decay function, based on a diagonally averaged matrix and plotted as a function of the appropriate amounts of elapsed time, takes on additional interest when we recognize that comparable decay functions under various theoretically interesting limiting cases can be computed and laid against whatever our empirical materials generate. One such theoretical function can serve us as a kind of null model. This is the case in which information about the state of affairs at time t by itself is our best predictor of the state of affairs at time $t + 1$ and cannot be improved upon by importing information from $t - 1$, $t - 2$, or any other earlier states. In the vocabulary of Markov chains, the null model is that which fits the assumptions of a first-order chain. In correlation vocabulary, the null model is that in which (a) all correlations between successive time points $(r_{t, t+1})$ have the same value; and (b) all partials of the form $r_{1k \cdot 2, 3 \cdots (k-1)}$ can be said to vanish. This is a condition dear to the hearts of causal modelers, and it says essentially that whatever effects are transmitted across time from the first measurement to the kth measurement are transmitted completely through the intervening measured states. With all of these partials set to zero by assumption, then the correlation for any time lapse t_1 to t_k is readily computed as

$$r_{1k} = (r_{12})^k$$

and the appropriate decay function for the null model plotted.

Now this null model does not in itself represent anything we would want to call a stable or an unstable process, without further information. In particular, we should want to know the value of r_{12} governing the function in whatever special case we are treating. I would assume that if r_{12} were very large such as .95, we would consider the process much more stable than we would if the value r_{12} were found to be only .05, although, of course, decay functions could be plotted for either of these cases.

---

[21] The single function generated is formally very similar to the correlogram used by economists in connection with autocorrelation of time series data. See Maurice G. Kendall, *The Advanced Theory of Statistics,* Vol. II (London: Charles Griffin, 1948), Chapter 30.

However, the presence of background or higher-order partials, which our null model rules out, would suggest a further dimension or dimensions of stability not apparent in the single parameter, r_{12}. And, of course, the presence of such partials can rather radically alter the form of the decay function, progressively retarding it as they increase in magnitude. Indeed, for any r_{12} there exists a first partial $r_{13 \cdot 2}$ of what seems intuitively to be a remarkably modest size (i.e., the range .30–.47, for r_{12}'s from .50–.90), which is sufficiently large to render the decay function a horizontal line or independent of the elapsed time.

What would some nonzero partial mean substantively in the case of voting data correlated over time? The aggregated nature of the data, as usual, introduce some further ambiguities we must subsequently examine. However, let us suppose we are correlating successive votes over time for individuals in a system that operates along the lines suggested by our original model. That is, it is a system in which various short-term forces induce quite visible rates of defection in any given voting trial, although most participants have some underlying preference for one of the two parties. Thus while an individual may readily defect in one election and at considerably lower odds repeat his defection in a second election and still more rarely a third, there will remain a very strong "homing" tendency even when defection does occur. The correlation between any pair of successive elections will be reduced by the relatively "noisy" or largely uncorrelated defection phenomenon, but with additional elections, the underlying party fidelity will be manifested in the fact that r_{13} is greater than $(r_{12})^2$. This is another way of saying that there exists some nonzero partial $r_{13 \cdot 2}$, and the magnitude of that latter partial could be construed as some positive function of the strength and prevalence of the underlying trend toward continuity or stability, relative to the stability already manifest in r_{12}. Where the partial is actually zero, on the other hand, it would suggest the absence of any of the systematic "homing" tendency that is the essential feature of the defection phenomenon and the consequence of underlying party loyalties. That is, for a system of multiple parties ordered A through F, the absence of the partial indicates that if a voter has shifted his support from party C to party D over two elections, there is no unusual probability that he will return to party C in a third election, relative to the probabilities of remaining at D or passing on to E or F.

The existence of positive second-, third-, and higher-order partials in addition to the first partial would suggest that some systematic traces of "homing" tendencies may take two or even more elections to assert themselves. However, we would, of course, expect magnitudes to decline progressively as one moves to increasingly high orders of partials.

Now that we have considered some of the implications of these decay functions, let us turn to the data. In Figure 1 we have graphed the empirical functions generated by the United States and French matrices, and we have laid alongside these the decay function that would be associated with a comparable process in the null (zero-partial) case. It is apparent that both batches of data yield observations that are very well behaved, showing the expected decay form and clustering quite well along their respective functions. Most noteworthy is the fact that the two batches of data, while sharing a very similar r_{12} initial point, diverge completely and cleanly; thus there is certainly no problem of discrimination between them.

The French function departs systematically from the null model, with the rate of decay unquestionably being impeded by the existence of background partials suggesting a greater underlying stability over time than the simple r_{12} estimate would lead one to expect. Yet whatever these partials might be, it is obvious that they are even stronger in the American case and that rates of decay are impeded much more.

One may, in fact, take the smoothed curves of Figure 1 and calculate the progression of higher-order partials implied by the behavior of these functions. These data are presented in the second and third columns of Table 1 (the last column, "France B," will be considered later). In general, these computations tell us little beyond what is already apparent in Figure 1, although the squares of these partials would ordinarily (assuming data generated by product-moment correlations) suggest the additional proportion of variance accounted for, if we have knowledge not simply of the state of affairs in the next preceding election but of progressively earlier elections as well. The first two such squares for the United States are .068 and .033; for France they are .025 and .008.

In short, subject to various obvious caveats, these data suggest that in the longer run there is greater partisanship-*tendance* stability in the United States than in France. The list of caveats here is not dissimilar to that compiled for the MacRae-Meldrum paper. Perhaps most important is the fact that we are talking about rates of decay on a geographic base, and if the stability of the composition of the districts over the long period examined here were grossly different between the two countries, the differences in Figure 1 could arise in other ways than from variations in rates of individual political change. Thus, for example, if the French citizenry roamed en masse from department to department over this period, one might show apparently high rates of decay even if it were true that no Frenchman ever wavered in his political loyalty.

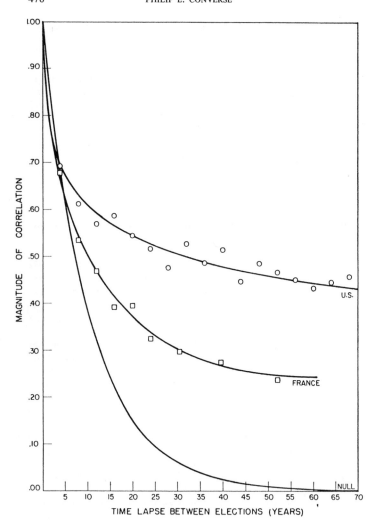

Figure 1

NULL AND EMPIRICAL DECAY GRADIENTS FOR FRANCE AND
THE UNITED STATES

Table 1

HIGHER-ORDER PARTIALS IMPLIED BY EMPIRICAL DECAY
FUNCTIONS OF FIGURE 1

Order of Partial	United States	France A	France B
First ($r_{13\cdot2}$)	.261	.159	.046
Second ($r_{14\cdot23}$)	.181	.092	.045
Third ($r_{15\cdot234}$)	.129	.062	
Fourth (etc. . . .)	.090	.042	
Fifth	.074	.027	
Sixth	.059	.046	
Seventh	.053	.031	
Eighth	.045	.026	

There is, however, no reason to suspect that conditions of geographic mobility are very disparate between the two countries.

It is true that the geographical units underlying the two batches of data are extremely disparate in average size, whether one deals in terms of population or area, the latter being conceivably important where rates of geographic mobility are concerned. However, examination of comparable matrices at finer geographic levels within the United States — scattered states of 80–120 counties, taken separately — shows no tendency for the estimated rates of decay to be greater than when gross data at the level of the states are considered; if anything, for the few states available, the decay rates look lower and hence even less like the French data. Thus there are no simple artifacts of unit size which account for the differences portrayed in Figure 1.

Nonetheless, the data of Figure 1 are arrived at through an averaging process that always throws away information, some of which may include sufficiently systematic variation to remain of theoretical interest. Therefore let us briefly consider some of the internal patterns that lead to the composite representation in that graph.

First and foremost, let us point out that the French observations of Figure 1 turn out to be somewhat sinful, having been born of the illicit union of apples and oranges. As observed earlier, purity was maintained up to a point. All of the matrices contributing correlations to the averaged estimates involved apple-apple or orange-orange relations, and no apple-orange impurities. However, when the data were averaged, purity became impossible to maintain. The preferable submatrices, based on vote proportions rather than proportions of seats won, had enough observations for brief lapses of time and constituted virtually all of the data points for the longest stretches of time but were too sparse for stable estimates (less than five observations) in the intermediate 20- to 40-year range. Hence, correlations concerning seats were added at this point to fill out stable estimates across the range of time intervals.

We can make a few tentative statements about the effect that the addition of seat proportions has on our decay function estimate of Figure 1. Where there are sufficient observations to compare the two data sources meaningfully — primarily over the first third of the slope — correlations based on seats tend to run lower than comparable correlations for vote proportions. The differences are typically not large — .06 to .08 — save in the first two observations. Elsewhere, there is a slight depressing effect exercised on the function by the inclusion of correlations based on seat proportions, although scarcely strong enough to account for the differences between the United States and French functions.

It is reasonable to assume that the correlations referring to seats tend to run lower because the measure is cruder and more inadequate than those referring to vote proportions. However, there is another interesting possibility. In isolating the decay functions originally, we had faced the question as to whether, in averaging data over a 70-year period, we might not be concealing significant temporal variation in the decay rate. We were not particularly concerned with the fact that a stray election here or there might yield a rather aberrant estimate, as this could be quite easily understood, and we were deliberately trying to bring into clearer focus the most general picture of the decay rate that could be constructed, short-term fluctuations aside. However, it was entirely possible that some major secular trend in the decay rate had been occurring over this period which our averages would conceal.

We had sufficient data to examine this possibility by splitting the time period into halves (pre- and post–World War I). Our a priori expectations were that if any noteworthy differences by era were to be found, they would not occur on the American side. Rather, they would show up in the French data and suggest that decay rates were most rapid in the early period — Siegfried notwithstanding — with something of a firming-up process occurring in the later stages. After all, the French voting system was essentially a new one in the 1870's, and there are theoretical grounds to suppose that a population becomes psychologically anchored in a firmament of democratic parties only as it has some experience with it over time. As of the 1870's the electorate had participated in the American system for well over a generation.

As expected, either half of the American matrix would have generated essentially the same function as that appearing in Figure 1. There are slight differences in the averages during the two eras, and these differences do not appear to be random. The values of the decay function in the 1872–1908 period are consistently a shade greater than those for the period 1916–1960.[22] However, we are talking here of differences that average less than .04 over all values where comparisons are reasonable (where there are at least five observations on both sides). Hence, we are quite satisfied that the results suggested in Figure 1 would not have been palpably different had we happened by chance on either of the shorter time intervals taken separately.

At first glance, our expectations were also fulfilled on the French side, for values from the earlier period are indeed visibly lower than those derived after World War I. If this were a genuine trend, it would be of great interest, since the direction of the trend is the opposite of the slight differences found on the American side. Unfortunately, the Goguel coding is such that measures referring to proportions of seats come almost exclusively from the period prior to World War I. Thus the decrements in values of .06–.08 are the same as those we have already examined in connection with the differences between seat-based estimates and vote-based ones. Ideally, we should be able to cast light on the matter by asking whether the vote correlations from the earlier period look more like the seat estimates of the same period or the vote estimates of the later period. If one were forced to make a choice, it does seem that the vote estimates from the early period look more like contemporaneous seat estimates (low) than like the later vote estimates. However, there are all of four vote-based correlations available from the earlier period, and they are scarcely conclusive. Therefore it seems wisest to leave the point a moot one until more adequate data can be mustered.

Perhaps what should be stressed is the fact that none of these variations — the slight absolute difference between periods on the American side or the larger difference between early seat-based estimates and later vote-based ones in the French data — is large enough to affect gross conclusions suggested by Figure 1. Differences in the estimated decay functions would be minimized by dealing with pure voting materials on both sides since 1916, and yet the two batches of data would remain very clearly discriminated from one another.

[22] For reasons to be mentioned later, the 1912 election was systematically eliminated from the analysis and from the data in Figure 1.

Indeed, there are sufficient initial observations in the pure voting materials from France to give good estimates of the beginning of the decay function (9 and 6 observations, respectively, for the first two mean values), and these first values would be .766 and .606, for these are the two points on which the seat-based estimates exerted their greatest depressing effect in Figure 1. If we took these as our estimates, rather than those of Figure 1, we would conclude that the French function started at a slightly higher point than the American (.77 rather than .70) but immediately declined below it at a precipitous rate. This would then suggest slightly less "noise" between adjacent pairs of elections in France, perhaps a result of the responsiveness of the American electorate to a sequence of rather disparate short-term forces from election to election. But acceptance of such a possibility carries with it a corollary, which is that the background partials in the French case would be considerably weaker than Figure 1 suggests. We have entered in column "France B" of Table 1 the values that would be appropriate for the beginning of the decay function as indicated by the pure-vote materials. In this case, the partials are trivial from the very beginning.

While the French data are too fragmentary for any more intensive analysis, the American materials readily sustain further dissection. As we have seen, a "split-half" test indicates that our decay estimates there do not depend heavily on the era for which the time series is drawn, in the period since 1870. However, the averaging of the initial matrix conceals contributions made by specific elections to the summary decay curve. We can now imagine a smoothed matrix, in which the entries along each diagonal are identical, and the average value for the diagonal. Such a matrix represents a set of "expected values," in an actuarial sense, for the American decay gradient. And the matrix that is the difference between this expected matrix and the observed matrix gives us a residual matrix highlighting the differential contributions of the various paired election correlations to the summary decay function. A negative entry means that the pair of elections involved taken alone would suggest a more rapid rate of decay of partisan structure than affirmed by the rest of the matrix. A positive value indicates abnormally slow decay or a heightened estimate of stability.

Once constructed, there are several alternate messages that the residual matrix might convey. The positive and negative values might show no particular pattern at all over the surface, indicating that while there is inevitable variability in the decay estimates, it is too unsystematic across time to be of interest. Or, again, there might be some clustering of negative values in the "early" or "late" portions of the matrix, although our split-half analysis has already ruled out this possibility. Finally, there might be some tendency for rows and columns associated with particular elections to show unusual proportions of negative or positive values. This would suggest that certain elections represented systematic instrusions on party stability, while other elections tended to underscore partisan stability.

Such a residual matrix in this case does show peculiarly consistent values associated with a small scattering of elections. The information can be summarized by taking algebraic sums along rows and columns associated with each election. When the set of elections are arrayed according to this summary value, the array is skewed, with few specific elections distinguishing themselves at the positive end of the distribution but with five elections standing out in a long negative tail of the distribution. These are the elections of 1872, 1896, 1912, 1928, and 1960. The presence of the election of 1912 in this set is not surprising, since it is an election involving the principal three-party race in the period being studied. There are sobering difficulties involved in treating the three-way vote proportions in a fashion conceptually parallel to the rest of the data. In other words, its deviant status represents more of a measurement problem than a substantive datum of interest.[23] Of the remaining four deviants, we see that two are the now-familiar realigning elections of 1896 and 1928. While our current analytic operations are less well calculated to single out realignments than the MacRae methods, which were tailored directly to this task, it is hardly surprising that moments of realignment should appear as contributing accelerated estimates of partisan decay to the over-all matrix.

What is interesting is that an election like that of 1960, known from sample survey data to have had relatively slight realigning properties, would also appear. Of course, 1960 and 1928 form a natural pair in the series of American elections, both featuring a Catholic candidate for President and vote returns that tore away from many of their traditional party anchors toward a heightened religious polarization, in a fashion particularly apparent on a gross geographic base. Yet this and other characteristics of the array — such as the failure of the next elections after the realigning ones to show either extreme or distinctive values — suggests that the elections singled out as deviant have properties that realigning elections share but that are not unique to such elections.

[23] For this reason, all of the data presented in this paper have been based on the matrix of Presidential elections from 1872 to 1960, with the data from 1912 excluded.

While no elections on the positive end of the array stand out as sharply as do those mentioned for the negative extreme, the three elections of the relatively quiescent 1880's all fall here. Of elections covered by postwar survey research, the largest positive value is shown for 1948, noted as a low-turnout, party-loyalty election.

Working from survey research materials, Campbell has associated surges in voting turnout with the entrance into the active electorate of individuals whose attachment to the standard parties is much weaker than that of more dutiful or experienced voters. Conversely, in an American election of relatively low turnout, voting tends to be left to the strongest party loyalists.[24] While realigning elections are typically "surge" elections in this sense, noteworthy surges are not necessarily accompanied by realignment.

If we classify the Presidential elections in our set according to their "surge" or "decline" properties by expressing the ratio of the turnout in each election to that of the average turnout among the eligible electorate in the next two preceding Presidential elections, we find a product-moment correlation of − .55 between the two arrays. The more marked the surge, the greater the negative contributions to the residual matrix; the more notable the decline, the greater the positive contributions to the matrix.

This is a very satisfying result, for it lends considerable weight to our general interpretation of the initial matrix and its implied decay gradients. That is, had we limited our averaging to those elections showing surge properties, we would have estimated the rate of decay to be more rapid than that depicted in Figure 1 and would have inferred weaker levels of partisan identification in the population. If, on the other hand, we had drawn our averages from those elections involving a relatively shrunken, hard-core electorate, we would have found slower decay rates and inferred a greater degree of partisan stability. Yet these differences in results would not have signaled any unreliability in our procedures, for we would, in fact, be looking at two different cuttings of the electorate. Sample survey evidence based on individual data indicates quite strongly that these two cuttings of the electorate would differ in their average level of partisan attachment in exactly this way.

Thus we come full circle, and we see that in averaging we have avoided dealing with either an abnormally swollen or a shrunken electorate and instead are representing in Figure 1 electorates of average size for

[24] Angus Campbell, "Surge and Decline: A Study of Electoral Change," *Public Opinion Quarterly, 25* (Fall 1960). pp. 397–418.

American Presidential elections. Had we turned our attention to off-year Congressional elections in an effort to avoid the strong short-term swings of the vote in Presidential elections, our comparisons with the French data would undoubtedly have been even more disparate. Yet we would be loading the dice in attempting to compare the more partisan two thirds of an "average American electorate" with an electorate of average size for French national elections. Most important, we have found the kind of interlocking evidence between sample survey evidence and patterns of variation in aggregate data which greatly enhances one's confidence that the aggregate information has been appropriately understood.

CONCLUSION

The contrasts between France and the United States that emerge from our pilot analysis are suggestive at best and will require further examination with aggregate data better suited to the task. Our major purpose was to illustrate the kind of role that survey evidence can play in stimulating inquiries with aggregate materials, in guiding their execution, and in helping to increase confidence in the inferences from results.

In this paper we have worked entirely with the structure of voting statistics, as did the MacRae-Meldrum paper, although to quite different ends. Many other kinds of worth-while analyses, each with unique goals, could be performed on the same limited base. Needless to say, there is no particular virtue in this narrowness, and in the long run we naturally shall want to conduct similar analyses introducing further social, demographic, and geographic variables. Growing data banks and increased computer power invite such activity.

At the same time, one cannot help being impressed at the variety of departures that can be taken with voting statistics alone. And such departures have an important function as a springboard to later and broader inquiries, for they investigate new ways of organizing aggregate data. They tend to generate a range of new dependent variables derived from the old, which are fruitful for further inquiries because their conceptual meaning is clearer than that of the raw statistics from which they are derived. Thus we are in a process of tool formation for a new era of exploitation of aggregate materials. In this process, accumulated knowledge from survey research can be a critical ingredient.

18

DUNCAN MACRAE, JR., AND JAMES A. MELDRUM

Factor Analysis of
Aggregate Voting Statistics

FOR TESTING HYPOTHESES over long historical periods, available records such as aggregate voting statistics have potentialities at least equal to those of demographic and economic data. A central question before us is to identify the important problems that can be investigated by means of these records and the methods appropriate to them.

This paper concerns one particular problem: identification of the changes in political issues in the two-party system of the United States over more than a century. It is only one of a wide variety of problems for which historical series of aggregate voting data are useful; these would also include the study of the effects of electoral systems on parties and factions, the spread of communication systems from the local to the national level, the importance of localism and fluid factions as against established parties, the estimation of individual decision processes from aggregates, the identification of geographically concentrated groups that exert political influence, the relation of political system and subsystem (such as federalism), and the characterization of the structure of political parties.

Common to all these problems is the fact that computer data processing has made possible their investigation on a large scale and in historical depth. But we must expect each problem to require a particular model or hypothesis that distinguishes it from others. The study of multipartyism, for example, requires an entirely different model from the one we shall discuss here.[1] It is our task to discover these diverse models and to fit them together.

Even when a widely applicable method such as factor analysis is used, it may have to be adapted in specific ways to the problem at hand. Thus we shall speak, not of factor analysis in general, but of a particular variant of that method designed to deal with voting in a two-party system where the parties have continuous existence over time, have stable groups of supporters, and undergo major realignments in their issue conflicts only once in about a generation. These changes of issues are important politically, since they reflect the increased access of new groups to power, they redefine the real constituencies of parties and of their elective officials, and they define "gateways"[2] that select and transform the issues of partisan debate.

THE "AL SMITH REVOLUTION" AND THE NEW DEAL: THE REORIENTATION OF 1928-1936

One instance of a lasting change of issues — the most recent one that has occurred in the United States — is that associated with the Presidential election of 1928. We shall use it to illustrate the method in concrete terms and then restate the underlying assumptions more systematically.

There are relatively few elections in the United States in which lasting reorientations of the voting public have occurred. Most Presidential elections have involved relatively uniform swings of states or counties toward one party or the other. Louis Bean summarized this phenomenon in his chapter title, "As Your State Goes, So Goes the Nation."[3] But the occasions when this uniform swing does not occur are of special interest because if the reorientations persist, they can mark the injection of new issues into national and state politics for a generation. Lubell noted the importance of the "Al Smith revolution," which preceded the "Roosevelt revolution";[4] and Key, naming these phenomena "critical elections," went on to show that Bryan's candidacy in 1896 marked an

[1] See M. J. Kesselman, *The Ambiguous Consensus: A Study of Local Government in France* (New York: Knopf, 1967), pp. 27–34.

[2] This term was introduced in B. R. Berelson, P. F. Lazarsfeld, and W. N. McPhee, *Voting* (Chicago: University of Chicago Press, 1954), p. 209.

[3] L. Bean, *How to Predict Elections* (New York: Knopf, 1948), Chapter 10. The following accounts of the reorientations of 1928 and 1896 are adapted from D. MacRae, Jr., and J. A. Meldrum, "Critical Elections in Illinois: 1888–1958," *American Political Science Review, 54* (September 1960), pp. 669–683.

[4] S. Lubell, *The Future of American Politics* (New York: Harper, 1952), p. 35.

earlier major reorientation of the electorate.[5] He defined a critical election as one in which "the depth and intensity of electoral involvement are high, in which more or less profound readjustments occur in the relations of power within the community, and in which new and durable electoral groupings are formed."[6]

In 1928, Alfred E. Smith became the first Catholic Presidential candidate of a major American party. He, and the issues he espoused, gave shape to new coalitions of voters, which were to coalesce after Franklin Roosevelt became President. These changes occurred not simply within the nation but also within the individual states. That Illinois reflected the reorientations of the nation in this respect — not merely in 1928 but earlier as well — can be shown very simply.

For this purpose we examine the shift in percentage of Democratic voters for each state or county from one election to the next and calculate the dispersion of the distribution of these shifts for each pair of elections. Distributions of these shifts have been presented by Butler and Rose for British elections; for the transition between 1951 and 1955, the dispersion of this distribution, as measured by its semi-interquartile range, was 0.97 per cent; from 1955 to 1959, 1.27 per cent; and from 1959 to 1964, 2.0 per cent.[7] These shifts are more uniform than those we shall report for the United States.

Graphs of the semi-interquartile range of this distribution for transitions between Presidential elections in the United States by states, and for Illinois by counties, are shown in Figure 1. For Illinois, as for the nation, there are principal peaks on the graph at the electoral transitions of 1892–1896 and 1924–1928, as well as one or more in the Civil War period. The curve for Illinois lies generally lower than that for the United States: even though smaller geographical units are used in the Illinois calculations, the shifts within the state are more uniform than those in the nation. In 1856 and 1928 the extent of reorientation in Illinois was about the same as that in the nation, while in 1896 it was considerably less.[8]

Thus for the study of these critical elections we can take Illinois as

[5] V. O. Key, Jr., "A Theory of Critical Elections," *Journal of Politics, 17* (February 1955), pp. 3–18.

[6] *Ibid.,* p. 4.

[7] D. E. Butler and R. Rose, *The British General Election of 1959* (London: Macmillan, 1960), pp. 236–237; D. E. Butler and A. King, *The British General Election of 1964* (London: Macmillan, 1965), p. 352.

[8] For evidence that Illinois participated only moderately in the 1896 reorientation, see H. C. Nixon, "The Cleavage Within the Farmers' Alliance Movement," *Mississippi Valley Historical Review, 15* (June 1928), pp. 22–23.

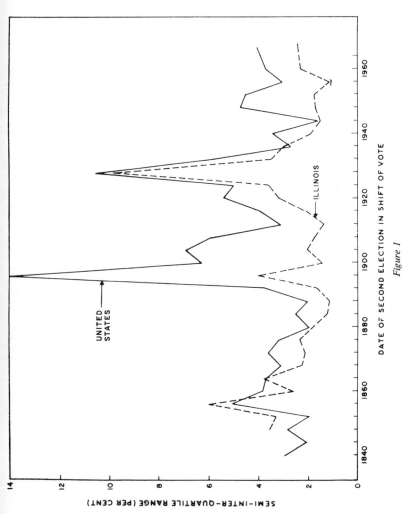

Figure 1

DISPERSION OF SHIFTS BETWEEN PRESIDENTIAL ELECTIONS

somewhat representative of the nation as a whole, though perhaps less so during the 1890's. Standing, as it does, between the Eastern urban and Midwestern farm interests, Illinois contains something of both political tendencies, and thus it showed swings in both directions even in a transition that was as strongly regional as that of 1896. Similarly, it reflected something of the South in the Civil War period. New England states, on the other hand, showed only over-all changes toward the Republicans in 1896, but not internal realignments such as appeared in the nation as a whole. Key notes that the 1896 election in New England "did not form a new division in which partisan lines grew more congruent with lines separating classes, religions, or other social groups."[9]

Key's notion of an election at which new and durable electoral groupings are formed requires examination of votes not only at successive elections but also at greater intervals. For a period within which only one such reorientation occurred, one would observe certain patterns of correlation between the votes in pairs of elections, calculated over subareas such as states or counties. All the elections before the reorientation would show high correlations with one another; all elections afterward would also be highly correlated; but any election before the critical transition would show a lesser correlation with any election afterward.

The problem of discovering two such groupings of elections is a special case of the general one faced by factor analysis or principal component analysis. Using these techniques, one might analyze the correlations between all possible pairs of elections in the period in question and try to find two clusters of elections, each of which reflected a quality of the vote distinct from the other. If there was a single critical election in the period, factor analysis would yield two closely correlated factors, each corresponding to a set of elections in a distinct interval.

Previous studies have shown that fluctuations in the social base of the vote in the United States normally involve only a relatively small fraction of the electorate, while a large fraction continues to vote according to geographical traditions.[10] Because a large fraction of the vote is traditional, even in periods of electoral reorientation, we should

[9] Key, *op. cit.,* p. 12.

[10] V. O. Key, Jr., and Frank Munger have pointed out the significance of traditional partisan alignments over periods of thirty years or more; this persistence appears to extend even across critical elections. See their "Social Determinism and Electoral Decision: The Case of Indiana" in E. Burdick and A. J. Brodbeck (eds.), *American Voting Behavior* (Glencoe, Illinois: The Free Press, 1959).

expect the two factors mentioned previously — for elections before and after the critical one — to be highly correlated. For this reason the reorientation involved in a critical election can be seen more clearly if the constant or "traditional" component of the vote is removed. This can be done by setting aside not only the average vote (such as percentage Democratic) in each election, as would ordinarily be done in calculating correlation coefficients, but also the average vote for each geographical subunit. Thus in Illinois, after subtracting the election average, we further correct the percentage Democratic for each county by subtracting that county's average residual percentage Democratic from all residual percentages for that county. The result is that the first principal component of what remains is a single dimension distinguishing (in positive and negative terms) between the opposing tendencies related to the critical election. If a critical election actually occurred in a given period, this would be revealed by the temporal pattern and magnitude of the loadings on this principal component; there would be a series of positive loadings followed in time by negative ones, or vice versa.

If this procedure is carried out, the results can be arranged in a rectangular matrix where each row corresponds to a county and each column to an election. The element in the ith row and jth column will then be

$$X_{ij} = D_{ij} - \bar{D}_{i\cdot} - \bar{D}_{\cdot j} + \bar{D}_{\cdot\cdot}$$

where

D_{ij} = the initial percentage Democratic for county i in election j

$\bar{D}_{i\cdot}$ = the mean percentage Democratic for county i over all the elections being considered

$\bar{D}_{\cdot j}$ = the mean percentage Democratic for all counties at a given election

$\bar{D}_{\cdot\cdot}$ = the over-all mean percentage Democratic (for all counties at all elections considered)

Let this data matrix be referred to as X and its transpose as X'. We then compute by "direct factor analysis" the first principal component of XX' and at the same time of $X'X$.[11] Loadings on these

[11] This procedure can be carried out by means of a FORTRAN program, DFA1, for the IBM 7094; the program and operating instructions are available at mailing cost from the Social Science Program Library, Computation Center, University of Chicago. References on the mathematics of the method are M. A. Woodbury, R. C. Clelland, and R. J. Hickey, "Applications of a Factor-Analytic Method in the Prediction of Biological Data," *Behavioral Science, 8* (April 1963), pp. 347–354; and P. Horst, *Factor Analysis of Data Matrices* (New York: Holt, Rinehart, & Winston, 1966).

components measure the extent to which various elections and counties, respectively, possess the quality that accounts for the maximum sum of squares in the matrix X. We shall refer to the county loadings as $u_1, u_2 \ldots, u_{102}$, and the election loadings as $v_1, v_2, \ldots$. To the extent that there was a critical election, we expect that x_{ij} will be approximated by a constant times the product $u_i v_j$, and that the time series v_j will be a step function.

Each entry in the data matrix is a percentage Democratic; third-party votes cannot be used within the framework we set (that is, use of raw election percentages rather than standard scores, and subtraction of county means as well as election means). The elections considered over this period are those for President, Governor, U.S. Senator, district Congressman, and Trustees of the University of Illinois.[12] The national and state-wide offices are chosen as involving candidates whose appeal was directed to a wide variety of audiences in Illinois and elsewhere. The vote for district Congressman is intended to reveal the sort of appeal made by a candidate who seeks votes more locally. The vote for Trustees is used as an indicator of the "depersonalized" vote — at least unrelated to the personalities of the candidates for that office.

To examine the period about 1928, the first principal component is computed for Illinois elections over the period 1914–1964. This period was chosen because it was believed to contain only one major reorientation; it is extended backward to include possible reorientations related to World War I and forward to 1964. The results of this computation consist of 97 loadings (v's) for the elections during this period, and 102 loadings (u's) on the same principal component for the counties of Illinois.

The loadings for elections in this period (v's) are shown in Figure 2. The scale of the loadings is adjusted so that the sum of squares of loadings on a given factor is equal to the corresponding eigenvalue of XX' or $X'X$.[13]

The variation of the first principal component with time shows the expected form, indicating a lasting reorientation; in the period prior to 1926, all loadings are lower than those of 1932 and after. This variation

---

[12] Sources for these data were the *Blue Book of the State of Illinois* (Springfield, biennial), and *Official Vote of the State of Illinois Cast at the General Election (date)*, compiled by the Secretary of State of Illinois (Springfield). In the elections of 1918 and 1920 the Democrats failed to nominate a Congressional candidate in one district; data for Trustees and Congressman-at-Large in the same year were substituted.

[13] This is a conventional procedure in factor analysis; see H. H. Harman, *Modern Factor Analysis* (Chicago: University of Chicago Press, 2nd ed., 1967), p. 140.

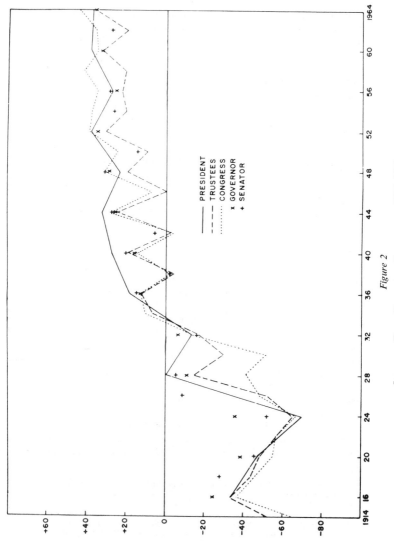

PRESIDENT
TRUSTEES
CONGRESS
× GOVERNOR
+ SENATOR

Figure 2

ILLINOIS: FIRST PRINCIPAL COMPONENT, 1914–1964

is unrelated to the over-all strength of the Democrats and Republicans during the period.

Factor analysis alone thus tells us that a lasting reorientation of the vote occurred, but it cannot tell just how the issues changed. Changes in the issues can be inferred from study of the campaigns themselves and of the socioeconomic and political characteristics of the counties that swung most in one direction or the other. It has been shown that the 1928–1936 reorientation in Illinois favored the Democrats most in urban areas that also favored the repeal of the Eighteenth (prohibition) Amendment and that those areas which moved relatively toward the Republicans were more rural and most opposed to relaxing the law regarding alcoholic beverages. Smith's Catholicism, though undoubtedly an important factor in 1928, had less effect in the longer run; the later consolidation of the Democratic Party's support, which Lubell called the "Roosevelt revolution," seemed more related to class and ethnicity than to religion. We therefore call a positive loading on this factor "New Dealism." And two splits in the Republican Party — in 1912 and 1924 — se₂m to have reflected dissidence in the same areas whose vote later tended to go over to the Democrats.

We can also see from Figure 2 that the votes for different offices behaved in different ways, especially during the period just before and after 1928. The candidacy of Al Smith in 1928 went far toward reorienting the Presidential vote, and some of the contests for Governor and Senator even ran ahead of the Presidential vote. On the other hand, the vote for Trustees, and especially that for Congress, lagged behind the Presidential vote in 1928 and 1930. This lag suggests that the capacity of a Congressman to adapt the meaning of his partisan affiliation to the political situation may stabilize the party vote for Congress, as it seems to for local offices as well.[14] On the other hand, the Trustee vote may reflect a limited association of straight ticket voting with local traditional party identification, even though the straight ticket is also affected by the personality at the head of the ticket.[15] Because these changes took place over several elections, we speak of a "critical period" rather than simply a critical election.

The generality of this reorientation may be shown by data for Michigan and New Hampshire, over a similar period, as in Figure 3.

---

[14] See V. O. Key, Jr., "Partisanship and County Office: The Case of Ohio," *American Political Science Review, 47* (June 1953), p. 526; M. Moos, *Presidents, Politics, and Coattails* (Baltimore: Johns Hopkins Press, 1952), pp. 13n., 110.

[15] See A. Campbell and W. E. Miller, "The Motivational Basis of Straight and Split Ticket Voting," *American Political Science Review, 51* (June 1957), pp. 293–312.

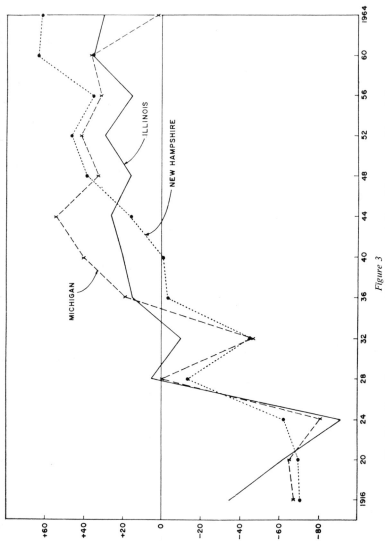

Figure 3

THE NEW DEAL REORIENTATION IN THREE STATES (adjusted for comparable scales)

In this case only thirteen Presidential elections are analyzed, but the patterns are much the same. Detailed comparative studies of a given reorientation in various states promise to provide useful details on issues, party structure, and social change at the state and national levels.[16]

BASIC ASSUMPTIONS OF THE METHOD

Having illustrated this method, we shall consider more precisely the conditions under which it can be used.

1. In its present form it is applicable only to two-party systems. One can, of course, condense a multiparty system into two hypothetical parties or "spiritual families" and study reorientations in the vote between two groups of this kind. But if we are really interested in realignments of votes among three or more parties, the problem is more difficult. Consider, for example, the British system and the problem of taking the Liberal vote into account. First, we should have to include in the data two sets of percentages for each election, that is, Labour and Liberal (the remainder, in percentage terms, being assumed to be Conservative). Then, we could no longer subtract the mean percentage for each election; we should have to do this separately for Labour and Liberal votes. It is as though we had two data matrices side by side, one for each of these two parties. If we analyzed them separately, we should be simply condensing them into hypothetical two-party systems in two different ways; this could be done with the Conservative vote as well. Analyzing them together, we should have to modify the procedure for subtracting area means. Moreover, we might expect more than a single principal component and thus confront the problem of preferred axes.

2. The electoral areas for which the aggregate data are available must not change their boundaries during the period under study. If a few boundaries change, one can compensate for this fact by combining areas into larger groupings that are constant over time; but a thorough redistricting can prevent this type of comparison of periods before and after it.

[16] The New Hampshire data are from A. Jeffrey, "Electoral Reorientation in New Hampshire: 1916–1964," M.A. thesis, University of Chicago, 1966, and are based on 234 townships. Those for Michigan are from unpublished research by J. D. Greenstone, based on 83 counties. The vertical scales for these states were corrected so as to be comparable with that for Illinois, in inverse proportion to the square root of the number of areal units studied.

3. The areas in question must be of the proper size and distribution to reflect the reorientation in question. If, for example, the reorientation is based on social classes, then the areas chosen must be small enough to differ from one another according to the residential patterns of social classes. If it is based on urban-rural distinctions, the areas must differ in this respect. If the reorientation realigns broad regions relative to one another, then the total sample of areas analyzed must extend substantially across these different regions. One shortcoming of our analysis of Illinois counties is that Cook County, which contains Chicago and includes a large proportion of the state's population, is counted as only a single unit. Differences in voting behavior and realignments within Cook County are thus not adequately revealed by this analysis.

4. It is assumed that the social and economic composition of the areas in question does not change radically over the period in question. Our procedure has been to compute values of the u's, or area factor loadings, and to compare them with census characteristics of the corresponding areas. But there is no provision in the analysis for change in these census characteristics. It is true that our method would reveal electoral reorientations among aggregates of persons that suddenly exchanged certain groups of members at a given time; but the normal processes of settlement, urbanization, suburbanization, and industrialization seem different in kind from those we are seeking. It is possible, however, that the steadily rising curve for New Hampshire in Figure 3 reflects an increasing social difference among townships.

5. The period of time chosen for analysis must include one and only one lasting reorientation of the electorate and a substantial number of elections both before and after that reorientation. For if the positive and negative factor loadings are not sufficiently represented in the data, the reorientation cannot be expected to emerge as a principal component. In turn, this principal component must be sufficiently predominant to preclude the problem of rotation to preferred co-ordinate axes. If there is more than one reorientation (as we shall see later for the Civil War period), or if the major reorientation is so weak as not to dominate other changes in the vote, then we can have correspondingly less confidence in our interpretation of the first principal component unless we can support it with other information. Thus the need to choose the proper period prevents the method from being purely "blind," unless the rotation problem can be solved.

6. If all the preceding conditions are satisfied, it is still necessary that for each geographic subarea studied the vote at a given election can reasonably be represented as the sum of several components:

a. A characteristic of the area in question, that is, a persistent division of the vote between the two parties considered (this may be related to party identification and the perpetuation of its distribution through socialization of children and adult in-migrants)

b. A short-run component associated with the dominant stimuli in individual elections, these stimuli being relatively uniform over the various subareas considered[17]

c. A component that varies in a similar temporal pattern for each geographical subunit, subject only to the condition that each subunit embodies this component multiplied by a (positive or negative) constant.

WILLIAM JENNINGS BRYAN AND THE REORIENTATION OF 1896

The same approach used to study the 1920's and their aftermath may also be applied to the 1890's. Starting with the Presidential election of 1888,[18] we may compute the first principal component for elections through 1922; the period 1914–1922 thus serves to bridge the two analyses. For the period 1888–1922, we obtain 57 v-loadings (for elections) and 102 u-loadings (for counties). The values of v are presented in Figure 4.

Again we observe that the expected transition in the signs of the loadings occurs at the year in which Key located a critical election — 1896, the year when Bryan was the Democratic candidate. But the mechanism of this reorientation is different from that of the 1920's. No significant role is played by Presidential third parties in the change; only about 3 per cent of Illinois voters supported Weaver on the People's ticket in 1892, perhaps because Altgeld's reform candidacy for Governor kept protest votes within the Democratic Party. Populist candidates were somewhat stronger in the Congressional elections of 1894, but Figure 4 does not suggest a significant amount of ticket-splitting as in 1924.

With respect to the votes for President, Congress, and Trustees, the 1896 reorientation is much simpler than that of 1928. The major

---

[17] This treatment is intended to parallel the concepts introduced in the work of the Survey Research Center at the University of Michigan. The concept of party identification appears in all their work. That of short-run stimuli is introduced in A. Campbell, "Surge and Decline: A Study of Electoral Change," *Public Opinion Quarterly, 25* (Fall 1960), pp. 397–418, reprinted in A. Campbell, P. E. Converse, W. E. Miller, and D. E. Stokes, *Elections and the Political Order* (New York: Wiley, 1966), Chap. 3.

[18] The first election at which a vote occurred for Trustees of the University of Illinois, this election was also selected in order to allow an interval before 1896.

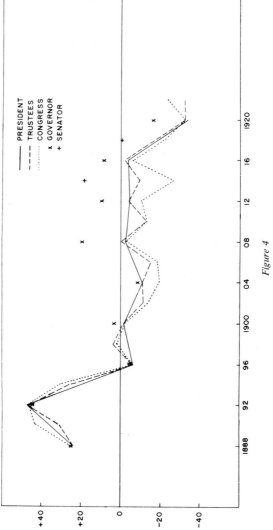

Figure 4

ILLINOIS: THE 1896 REORIENTATION

transition occurs between 1892 and 1896, and it occurs in much the same way for all the offices studied. Although the elections of 1894 anticipate this change, the magnitude of this anticipatory change is no greater than that of the changes from 1888 to 1892. Nor are there pronounced leads and lags of the votes for these three offices relative to one another; starting in 1904, the Congressional vote becomes more negative than other votes in its factor loadings, but not as much so as in Figure 2. One might almost say that there was a single critical election, rather than a critical period.

It is in the votes for Governor and Senator, starting in 1908, that the graph departs from the simple pattern that would correspond to a single critical election. The candidacy of Adlai Stevenson (the elder) for Governor in 1908 marks both an anticipation of "New Dealism" (matching the series of state-wide contests from 1914 on) and a re-collection of "Clevelandism" (Stevenson was Vice-President under Cleveland). But this series of deviant votes for state-wide offices starts twelve years after the initial critical election of 1896, rather than marking a stage in the transition.

We shall call the principal component for 1888–1922 "anti-Bryanism." This means that positive loadings in Figure 4 reflect an orientation of the Democratic vote toward Cleveland, rather than Bryan, while negative loadings reflect relatively greater support for Bryan and for Wilson. We choose to call the more urban aspect of this component "positive" for ease of comparison with "New Dealism" and with Figure 2.

The positive sides of these two reorientations — of 1896 and 1928 — are not, however, the same. Although their u's correlate $+.57$, there were distinct areas of Illinois that favored both Bryan and the New Deal (in the southern part of the state) and others that opposed both (the counties of German settlement). "Bryanism" also seemed associated with particular patterns of internal migration to Illinois prior to 1880. Areas where a high proportion of the population had come from the more southern states of Virginia, Tennessee, Kentucky, or Missouri tended to be high on "Bryanism," in contrast to the counties of northern Illinois, settled more from New England.

THE CIVIL WAR PERIOD

In the period before the Civil War, the American party system experienced more than a reorientation. For more than a generation national politics had concealed the growing divergence between North and South. A new wave of westward expansion reintroduced the issue of the status of slavery in the territories. The subsequent controversy affected every political organization in the nation. The Republican Party was formed in 1854; in the same period the Whig Party, the former major opponent of the Democrats, disintegrated. By 1856 the Republicans were in a position to wage an aggressive campaign, and the situation was favorable for a significant shift in political affiliations. The Democratic Party, while it persisted relatively unchanged in Illinois, divided nationally into Northern and Southern wings. In addition, two substantial minor parties, the American or Know-Nothing Party and the Free-Soil Party, rose to temporary success. Our analysis of the period is therefore complicated by the problems of a multiparty system.[19]

Preliminary investigation (see Figure 1) leads us to expect a reorientation in 1856, and we therefore extend our series as far back as we can before this time. It is not practical to go earlier than 1848, for before that time the rapid early settlement of Illinois was causing repeated changes in county boundaries, and the character of the settlement was less stable with regard to its presumed political traditions. A closer look at Figure 1 reveals a second peak for Illinois at 1864, and we shall indeed find that this year corresponded to a distinct reorientation.

For this period we use the Presidential vote together with the vote for State Treasurer in non-Presidential years, omitting years for which the data are inadequate. Factor analysis gave rise to two principal components, as shown in Figure 5. The first component shows a clear transition from positive to negative, but this occurs in 1864 rather than in the year expected from national voting, 1856. We thus consider the second component as well, and this comes nearer to our expectations, with a change of sign in 1856, the signs thereafter remaining negative until 1872. The curve for this component, however, shows an upward trend from 1858 on.

We thus confront several new problems in explaining these reorientations. We must account for the fact that the first principal component did not correspond to the major national reorientation of 1856 as expected. At the same time, we must try to choose a set of preferred axes among those that might be obtained by rotating the first two.[20]

---

[19] We simply use percentage Democratic in our analyses, grouping all other parties together. We omit the off-year elections of 1846, 1850, 1854, and 1874, in each of which one of the major parties was missing from at least ten counties in the voting statistics.

[20] This is a general problem of factor analysis; see Harman, *op. cit.,* Chapter 12.

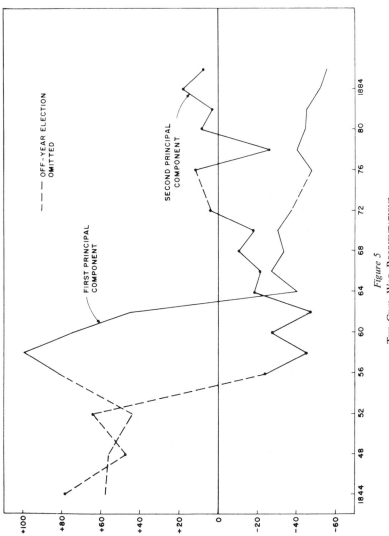

Figure 5

THE CIVIL WAR REORIENTATIONS

One method of choosing preferred axes is through inspection of the plot of the county loadings (u's). If we plot the county loadings in a two-dimensional space corresponding to these two principal components, we find that the distribution of loadings on the first differs from that on the second. On the first principal component, the ten highest loadings are all positive; all correspond to a contiguous group of counties in the southern tip of the state. The loadings on the second principal component, on the other hand, are symmetrically distributed about zero. This contrast could not be accentuated by rotating the two components, so we interpret them without further rotation.[21]

Closer investigation reveals that there was indeed an electoral reorientation in 1864, but it was restricted to southern Illinois; it was lasting, but not even state-wide in scope. A small number of counties swung to the Republican side in 1864 and remained there. These counties were contiguous and located largely in a single Congressional district. Before 1860 they had strong Southern ties and sympathies, and had consistently given overwhelming support to the Democratic Party. After the outbreak of hostilities, however, they rallied to the support of the Lincoln administration, and contributed high proportions of volunteers for the Union army.

Apparently instrumental in this shift was John A. Logan, who represented this district in Congress from 1859 to 1861. His political position at the start of the war was equivocal, but in the summer of 1861 he resigned his seat in Congress and accepted a commission as a general in the Union army. His former law partner and successor in Congress, William J. Allen, left no doubt concerning his Confederate sympathies; his opposition to the Lincoln administration was so strong that he was arrested and imprisoned during the war. In 1864 Allen was a candidate for re-election on the platform of the Peace Democrats. Several months before the election Logan was granted a leave to permit him to campaign for the Union ticket and for War Democratic candidates. The issue of loyalty to the Union was probably more clear-cut and dramatic in this contest than in any other in the nation. Logan's extensive and aggressive campaign was undoubtedly a strong factor in the reorientation of the vote in this area.[22]

---

[21] A Varimax rotation changed the axes by only 13 degrees.

[22] For documentation on these events, in addition to histories of the period, see *Illinois State Journal* (Springfield), July 7, October 26, November 15, 1864; J. G. Randall and R. N. Current, *Lincoln the President: Last Full Measure* (New York: Dodd, Mead, 1955), p. 240; and *Dictionary of American Biography*, Vol. I, pp. 213–214 (Allen).

The second component then corresponds more to the known national reorientation of 1856. On this component, many of the counties with positive loadings were in the northern part of the state, settled from New England, with abolitionist sympathies; the Free-Soil Party, favoring exclusion of slavery from the territories in the West, had previously been strong in this part of the state. In addition, the German-American vote also swung toward the Republicans on the slavery issue;[23] this was evidenced by a high positive loading for St. Clair County, in southwestern Illinois, across the Mississippi River from St. Louis, which had a considerable German population. The upward trend in the second component after 1860 requires closer study, as it seems to indicate a gradual weakening of the effects of the 1856 reorientation.

DISCUSSION

We have shown that in Illinois there were major and lasting reorientations of the party preferences of the electorate centering about the Presidential elections of 1928 and 1896 and that the former reorientation also appeared in Michigan and New Hampshire. In addition the Civil War period in Illinois saw two reorientations of the electorate, one local but pronounced, the other corresponding to a national change in voting alignments. By principal component analysis, we have been able to verify the existence of these reorientations and examine what population groups were involved in them, without selecting in advance certain counties or certain particular elections on which to make the test. Thus the method lends itself to a more general search for critical elections over a wider period of time.

At the same time this method enables us to examine the contribution of various elections in a "critical period" to a reorientation of the electorate and to see which contests for particular offices led, lagged, or departed from the more general trend. This detailed examination of particular elections and candidacies, made possible by the use of an electronic computer, brings into the analysis a greater degree of historical detail than would enter if we were concerned with the Presidential vote alone. It also suggests hypotheses about the nominating process in the states and state party structure, as contrasted with national nominations and parties. The part played by third parties in critical elections is also emphasized.

[23] See T. J. McCormack (ed.), *Memoirs of Gustave Koerner, 1809–1896* (Cedar Rapids, Iowa: Torch Press, 1909), Vol. 2, p. 21.

This analysis should not only throw light on Illinois politics but also suggest possible extensions and modifications of the method used. Some ways in which the method might be made more useful are as follows:

a. Studies of other countries, other states, and other geographical subdivisions can help to confirm or correct some of the hypotheses formulated about Illinois counties

b. Extension of the analysis to further principal components beyond the first, together with careful study of how these can be interpreted, may reveal other significant reorientations of the vote

c. Transformation of the variable "percentage Democratic" might be carried out to correct for the decreased variability of the percentage Democratic that necessarily results when it approaches zero or 100 per cent.

d. Regression analysis can be used to test directly hypotheses about population groups and the vote, which can be only explored and formulated with principal component analysis.

19

PETER LASLETT

Historical and Regional Variations
in Great Britain

THE PRESENT PAPER cannot properly comply with the excellent directive
of the organizers of the Evian Symposium that contributors, while
concentrating on issues of organization, theory, and method, should
"give a variety of concrete examples of analysis procedures and actual
findings." The reason is that the research project of the Cambridge
Group is only a few years old, and concrete results will have to be
worked out. We have as yet no quantitative, interregional comparative
results, though we hope to produce them soon.

One more preliminary remark must be made. In its initial stages the
Cambridge Group has been concerned with England from the middle
of the sixteenth to the middle of the nineteenth century and has generally
concentrated on the earlier part of this period. Therefore, nothing will
be said here about Scotland, Wales, or Ireland, and little about social
structure after the beginnings of industrialization.

THE PROGRAM OF THE CAMBRIDGE GROUP FOR
THE HISTORY OF POPULATION AND SOCIAL STRUCTURE[1]

The Cambridge Group is engaged in the following types of activity:

a. Aggregative analysis of the entries in English Parish Registers

[1] "The History of Population and Social Structure," an earlier account of the work
of this small research group, appeared in *The International Social Science Journal*,
17:4 (1965). I must emphasize that when the present article appears in 1969, it will
be almost three years out of date. Our research program has changed in many ways
in this interval, some of them of importance in regional comparisons within and

from the beginning of parochial registration in 1538 until the beginning of civil registration in 1837

b. Family reconstitution, in order to complete demographic details for selected parishes over the same period

c. Discovery and analysis of census-type documents earlier than 1841, when the English Census began to give adequate social structural information

d. Collection of ecological parameters for every parish for which demographic and social structural data are being recovered

e. Development of computer programs to carry out family reconstitution more speedily and with much greater versatility. This is progressing toward a general scheme of record linkage using a wide range of data other than the parish registers (poor law records, wills, etc.)

f. The preliminary stages of a nationwide study of the extent of literacy. The evidence will be the signatures in the parish registers back to 1754, when this practice started in England, and the records of ecclesiastical courts earlier than that period back into medieval times. These two sources will be supplemented by any other source that can be shown to be capable of yielding statistically reliable results

g. Correspondence with several hundred volunteer workers all over the country who are consulting local documents on behalf of the Group for the purposes specified, especially the counting of entries in parish registers, together with signatures and crosses.

h. Editing and publishing a series of works containing the results of the activities listed so far and presenting descriptions of historical demographic and social structural techniques.[2]

All these activities[3] are likely to show up historical regional variations of a quantitative ecological character. Progress made so far with the first four of them will be successively described.

---

between nations and cultural areas. A number of results have been published. It has not been possible to emend the present article to take account of these developments except in a very few particulars.

[2] Techniques relevant to activities *a, b, c,* and *d* are described in the first volume of an ongoing series entitled *An Introduction to English Historical Demography,* edited by E. A. Wrigley. It contains a contribution by him on family reconstitution, one by D. E. Eversley on aggregative analysis, another by Peter Laslett on the analysis of census-type materials before 1841, and one by A. Armstrong on census materials from 1841 on, published in February 1966. A volume describing techniques for the nineteenth century is in preparation. For literacy, see R. S. Schofield in J. Goody, ed., *Literacy in Traditional Societies* (Cambridge, 1968).

[3] It would be wrong to imply that this is the only work relevant to this Symposium going on in Great Britain. Scholars are engaged in the history of population and social structure at the universities of Leicester (where there is a professorship

AGGREGATIVE ANALYSIS OF PARISH REGISTERS, 1538–1837

By November 1968 there had been assembled at Cambridge monthly totals of registered baptisms, marriages, and burials for 425 out of some 10,000 parishes in England. These parishes have been selected for their size (over 750 inhabitants in 1801, the first Civil Census, but under 1,500), for their date of inception (at least as early as 1640), and for their continuity (no gaps lasting for more than a decade or so, except during the period of the Civil War and Commonwealth [Cromwell], 1640–1660). Though this collection probably represents less than 5 per cent of all parishes that registered baptisms, marriages, and burials during this period, we reckon that it contains a much greater proportion of all entries ever made. This percentage will rise further when figures from the 200 or more registers on which volunteers are still working are returned to us in Cambridge, and when we have found people willing to work on the 250 remaining registers that we listed in 1964 as suitable. The final proportion of parishes to be covered is something like 8 per cent. The sample at present available to us, large as it already is, has the following limitations:

a. The entries are subject to all the vagaries of underregistration because of carelessness, the presence of Dissenters and Roman Catholics, etc.

b. The method of selection previously noted is not one that would lead to a definable sample. In practice, it does seem (note no exact statement is possible) to follow roughly the distribution of population over the period but may be defective in Eastern England and must be in Southeastern England, where London dominates

c. The omission of urban parishes and those below 750 implies serious bias. This omission is not total, and we have acquired figures for a number of city communities since we began collection. But it appears that by selecting 750 as the lower limit, we may have cut off the whole lower half of the frequency distribution. It is entirely possible that the demography and social structure of smaller rural parishes had their own characteristics not necessarily the same as those of larger parishes even if these larger parishes were not urban

d. The lack of urban parishes severely limits its use for urban-rural comparisons

---

of local history, and where there is a Centre for Urban Studies), Nottingham, Sussex (where Dr. D. E. Eversley has gone from Birmingham), London (under Professor D. V. Glass), Kent, and other universities. In 1969 centers for initiating studies of this kind were being set up for Scotland at Edinburgh and for Ireland at Belfast.

Within these important limitations it is possible to make the following claim for this material for the purposes of historical regional comparison in England:

Every regional variation that consists in or can be correlated with the monthly numbers of baptisms, marriages, and burials registered by the priests of the Church of England between the early seventeenth (and perhaps back to the mid-sixteenth) to the early nineteenth century can in principle be examined in numerical terms.

The importance of this claim has to be judged in relation to the fact that this was the period of industrialization in England, the earliest country to be industrialized.

The work of calculating such regional variations, even the work of deciding whether the population was growing or declining over-all and at what period, has not yet been begun by the Cambridge Group. The sample of 5 per cent or more of the Parish Register entries is in our hands, but at the moment we are engaged in tackling the formidable statistical problems presented by the material, which is all in machine-readable form.

The variables that we intend to examine in relation to demographic fluctuation in English settlements include: area, height, distance from London, whether or not a market is present, whether or not the parish is maritime, status of parish (county town, parliamentary town, etc.), date of enclosure, farming (subdivided by pastoral, arable, mixed farming, market gardening, etc.), occupational structure (purely agricultural, agricultural with woolen industry, mixed industrial), type of industry other than textile, distribution of land, whether known to contain Roman Catholics or Dissenters, whether known to contain a seat or seats of nobility or gentry. This list may be extended even further, though certain items may not prove to be practicable. We are also considering some indication of the level of prices for each year, if possible a regional one, and perhaps indications of climate, war and peace, and so on.

In the present situation, therefore, only impressionistic answers can be made to questions about the contents of these data. I shall mention here only our first impressions of probable answers to simple historical questions, for we have concerned ourselves with these more than with historical regional cross comparisons. It seems likely that English population did increase over most of the country from the earliest time when we can get figures until the mid-seventeenth century. After that, there followed a very interesting period when population was static or in some places declining, at a time when the economic historians suppose that national income was rising and the first moves toward technological changes were being made. In the third or fourth decade of the eighteenth century, when the "take-off" was under way, the population seems to have been increasing rapidly almost everywhere, though there were areas of exception, and the baptism of bastards is, for the first time, a significant proportion of all baptisms.[4] This increase was intensified as industrialization proceeded, but quite early in the nineteenth century static or even declining population may have characterized areas untouched by industry.

The only cross comparison that I shall mention is not a regional but a national one. Meuvret, Goubert, and others have established beyond doubt that crises of subsistence could occur under particular regional conditions in seventeenth-century France, and the evidence is, to a large extent, just the simple figures we are discussing, correlations between sharp monthly fluctuations in registered baptisms and burials, though accompanied by indications of price rises and statements (made in the register books by the priests) about starvation. Our first cursory, unsystematic survey of this very large English sample seems to show that such crises of subsistence were virtually absent. Relatively mild versions of the classical French *crise de subsistance* can be observed in the mountainous regions of Northwestern England in the early 1620's, and quite clearly in the parish of Greystoke in Cumberland in 1623. But in England, the crucial question of regional variations in the relationship of population change to means of subsistence will have to be studied from less dramatic numerical indications — probably from statistical correlations involving monthly fluctuations of a less pronounced kind, the degree of maturity (child or adult), the sex of the victims, and indications of price levels for cereals and other foods and of economic expansion or contraction.

The following is a list of some of the possible local, regional, and historical variables that we should be able to examine from this sample, when it is suitably extended and refined.

   a. Food supply, level, tendency, and type of economic activity, in

---

[4] At least, since the sixteenth century. In Northwestern England (especially Lancashire) bastardy could rise higher in Elizabethan times than it ever did in the early days of industrialization, and the regional variations in this index are becoming one of the most interesting that we shall examine. Over this long period of time, illegitimacy levels in England appear to be correlated positively with *low* rather than *high* age at marriage. It has to be said in 1969 that the theory of the *crise de subsistance* discussed in the following paragraph is under criticism and revision in France.

their relation to indices of increase or decrease in population totals, fertility, nubility, mortality

b. Impact of contagious diseases as distinct from and as correlated with *a*

c. Effect of size of community, especially rapid increase recognizable as urbanization, on such demographic indices

d. Effectiveness of controls (ecclesiastical and general social) over sexual and other behavior revealed by such indices as seasonality of conception, seasonality of marriage, illegitimacy, and prenuptial pregnancy.

This list could, and no doubt will, be considerably extended. There are two further points to make here about aggregative analysis:

a. It provides essential extension, confirmation, and material for critical appraisal of the results of family reconstitution (see next section)

b. In general, along with family reconstitution, it makes possible the use of all the techniques of the social science of demography to determine regional variables in England as far back as the mid-sixteenth century.

FAMILY RECONSTITUTION

The whole process of family reconstitution has been carried out successfully for one English parish, that of Colyton in Devonshire, by Dr. E. A. Wrigley, cofounder of the Cambridge Group. We have available therefore at Cambridge exhaustive demographic detail, accurately reckoned and equal to or even exceeding the standards of contemporary demographic information, for something like a fifth of the families living in this one village from 1538–1837. These details include: age-specific fertility rates, mortality rates; age at marriage; expectation of life at various ages; size of completed families; age at birth of last child in completed families; and so on, all broken down into subperiods of some fifty years. Reports of the results of this study are now in progress from Dr. Wrigley himself, and copies of his first full-length article[5] will be available at the conference. This article

[5] E. A. Wrigley, "Family Limitation in Pre-Industrial England," *Economic History Review*, Second Series, *19*: 1 (April 1966), pp. 83–109. The methods used are not described in the article, and those interested may be referred to Wrigley's own contribution to *The Introduction to English Historical Demography, op. cit.*, and to his paper, read to the Third International Economic History Conference in Munich, 1965, entitled "Some Problems of Family Reconstitution Using English Parish

presents the figures for fertility and demonstrates the existence of family limitation during the period already referred to in the preceding section as peculiarly important for English development (and industrializing social development generally), that is, the period from the mid-seventeenth to the early eighteenth centuries. This is the earliest demonstrated example of family limitation affecting a whole preindustrial community, as distinct from a social group such as the nobility of a country.

The elaborate work of data preparation, done manually by volunteers, is complete for another Devonshire parish, Hartland; but though the *impression* given is that the figures may confirm those for Colyton, no result is yet available. Somewhat the same situation obtains for a very different and distant parish, Easingwold in the Vale of York. Recognizing the fundamental importance of checking the Colyton results against parishes of different economies as well as recognizing the absolute value of all such studies, the Cambridge Group is now undertaking, supervising, or encouraging similar projects — none as yet advanced as far as that for Hartland — at Banbury in Oxfordshire (a midland, hand-industry, and market center), St. Leonard's Shoreditch, London (for urban-rural comparison, the difficulties are formidable), and a group of parishes in Bedfordshire (very important so as to extend the proportion of analyzable families and to allow for migration).[6]

All the possible local, regional, and historical variables that were listed as suitable for study by aggregative analysis of parish registers can, of course, be examined for the small sample of parishes that will be reconstituted. But in these cases we shall be able to observe the variations in the actual behavior of individuals, which in the case of aggregative analysis is only very generally and vaguely indicated by changes in total per month or year. It can be recorded, as one more impression, that

Register Material." Dr. Wrigley makes plain his debt, and the debt of the Cambridge Group as a whole, to the French historical demographers for the method he has been using, and especially to Louis Henry and his colleagues at the Institut National d'Etudes Démographiques in Paris. (The results of the reconstitution at Colyton for fertility and life expectancy were published by E. A. Wrigley in *Daedalus*, Spring 1968.)

[6] Since the preceding was written, the prospect of rapid and efficient reconstitution of a long list of additional English parishes by the use of our computer program has transformed the situation. It remains true, however, that the condition of English registers must restrict our activities a great deal more than we should like. And we shall never be in the position of our colleagues in France with respect to this crucial undertaking.

where the aggregative figures for any community follow the very general historical pattern of population change in England, which was described earlier, the detailed demographic mechanism could be like that observed at Colyton, which has a demographic history between 1539 and 1837 of the "normal" type. It must be repeated that only by the combination of aggregative analysis and reconstitution can demography be put at the disposal of the historical study of regional variation.

Each parish will have its individual limitations and drawbacks, and none will yield certain classes of figures which social scientists would like to have. These include suicide rates, abortion rates, rates of still-births, and so on. But migration figures, as obtained by studying place of origin of marriage partners, will be available as a matter of course. Where the registers yield occupations (as they do at Banbury but, unfortunately, not consistently at Colyton or at Hartland), social mobility by marriage can be studied, as well as differential fertility, mortality, and migration by occupation.

DISCOVERY AND ANALYSIS OF CENSUS-TYPE DOCUMENTS FOR SOCIAL STRUCTURAL PURPOSES

It has already been pointed out that the comparative analysis of social structure from complete and official census material can be done only from 1841 onward.[7] The whole previous period, and this goes back further than the parish register era (indeed, it has no obvious historical limitation), can be examined only in documents of a similar kind made for a variety of purposes that were only seldom sociological. When work of this kind was first contemplated in the late 1950's and early 1960's, the general impression seemed to be that such documents were rare — so rare that they would yield very few statistically viable results and certainly not much in the way of regional, historical comparison.

This may, perhaps, still turn out to be the case. But the numbers and

[7] In fact, only the 1841 and 1851 census material seems to make possible the full analysis of the structure of families, households, and communities which we strive to obtain for earlier documents, and after 1861 the British census cannot·be inspected, because of the extraordinary hundred-year rule enforced by our Registrar General. Even the 1841 documents have formidable difficulties. It seems possible, then, that full historical examination of social structure, at least until late in this century, may be confined to the material mentioned in this article and footnote. At least, we shall soon be permitted to photograph census returns later than 1861, but with names of persons blocked out; thus all kinship analysis will be made impossible. It is unfortunate that the original material of recent postwar censuses in the country has apparently been destroyed. In England, therefore, the long-term possibilities for social structural history do not at the moment look good.

distribution in time and place of the documents represented by the collection of xerographs we are assembling at Cambridge are encouraging to us, and we find the results they yield very illuminating, particularly those of the regional comparative kind. The total is now about 170, with 44 from before 1699, 105 from 1700 to 1799, and 21 from 1800 to 1841, and we have no doubt that it will continue to grow, especially for the later period. They are, of course, very miscellaneous in their content and reliability, as well as in the amount of social structural analysis that they will bear. They come from 18 of the 40 English counties, but, as might be expected, there is considerable bunching by area and date.[8] It is not surprising that when it is a question of the accident of survival as well as of the attitude of the man making out the documents, very few of these 170 contain all the details that a sociologist interested in comparative ecology considers ideal. But six of them (one from the sixteenth, two from the seventeenth, three from the eighteenth century) contain something like the maximum possible information on every individual: age, sex, occupation, position in the household, and kin relationship. No less than 60 contain all these details except age.

The following are the more significant variables that can be discovered from the listings:[9]

Age structure
Distribution by sex
Occupational structure
Size of household
Size of sibling group
Proportion of households with kin
Proportion of households with servants
Proportion of servants in the community (with distribution by sex, in groups, and by age)

[8] A full discussion of this class of record and the types of occasion which gave rise to the documents being produced will be found in Peter Laslett's contribution to *An Introduction to English Historical Demography, op. cit.* The collection has grown since 1966, and an analysis of the hundred best listings is in preparation, together with an essay on "The Domestic Group in Pre-Industrial England" will be published in due course in a book entitled *Family and Community in Pre-Industrial England.* The complete figures from the ten best listings will be presented there as well.

[9] D. V. Glass, of the London School of Economics, has recently undertaken some work of the same character on a very important part of this material relating to London in 1695. See *London Inhabitants within the Walls* (London: London Record Society, 1966). Some material has already been published, though not yet analyzed in detail for social structural purposes, dating from the 1770's in the Western Islands of Scotland. We have been surprised at the apparent similarity of household structure there to that of England at the same time.

Proportion of households with resident children of mature age
(over sixteen)
Proportion of each age group married and single

It can therefore be stated that

*Every variable in the preceding list, and every other variable that could
be correlated with any one or any number of them which is of importance
for historical-regional analysis can, in principle, be recovered for this
growing sample of English communities before 1841.*

Once more, it must be said that the work of analysis has yet to proceed
to the stage where numerical cross comparisons can be published with
confidence. But we have already committed ourselves in public to the
following general assertions about this body of evidence. The mean size
of household in England in preindustrial times, and at least as far back
as the seventeenth century, lies between 4.5 and 4.8, showing no marked
tendency to vary with time.[10] In any one community and in the population at large the size of household varied directly with social status; the
higher the status, the larger the household. This variation is due almost
entirely to the distribution of servants between households, and servants
were something like 10 per cent or more of the total population. For the
rest, households consisted of the nuclear family[11] in all but 10 per cent
of the population surveyed, and the extended or multigenerational family
is rare in preindustrial England. The proportion and distribution of
servants, the size of the sibling group, and the numbers of mature
children resident in the parental household vary with occupational
structure and will probably be found to vary also with degree of
industrialization.

To these statements can now be added two further possibilities. The
first is that in England the tendency may have been for the "extended
family group" to become more rather than less common as industrialization and urbanization proceeded. Resident widowed grandparents,
visiting and lodging relatives, sharing of households between parents
and married children certainly seem to have become commoner after

[10] The points made in the text are examined in detail in the forthcoming publication referred to in the preceding footnote. In the sample of one hundred parishes,
multigenerational households make up on the average only 5.7 per cent of all households, and 11.7 per cent is the mean proportion of households with resident kin of
any kind.
[11] That is, the conjugal family with or without servants; one third of all households
had servants. The evidence confirms and gives historical extension to William J.
Goode's conclusions in *World Revolution and Family Patterns* (New York: The Free
Press, 1963).

the early nineteenth century. The second is that the nuclear family in England since medieval times, at least, may be correlated with what Hajnal has called the "European Marriage Pattern" (higher mean age of marriage, higher proportion of those never married)[12] and so may be contrasted with a tendency toward the extended family in Eastern and perhaps Southern Europe, Russia, India, and other parts of the world.

Though this material offers multiple opportunities for regional comparisons within England and Britain, we are once more interested in Continental and world comparisons, as well as in long-term historical comparison. Moreover, the demographic evidence already described ties in with the social structural evidence under discussion. It must be remembered that for evidence of the latter type, and to some degree the former type too, we have in England the great advantage of the work done in preindustrial times by contemporary political arithmeticians, especially that of Gregory King.[13]

REMAINDER OF WORK OF THE CAMBRIDGE GROUP AND CONCLUSION

To treat at similar length, even in the very superficial way that has been adopted here, the rest of the activities of the Cambridge Group which bear or will bear on historical interregional comparisons would require a great deal of work. It is obvious how the development of computer programs will increase the speed at which these results can be obtained. The cross comparisons of the material from the parish registers and the census-type documents that will then be possible will transform the subject. A body of theory and practice will also, we hope, come into being and eventually become standardized.

A word should be added about the mechanism of data gathering and preliminary processing in the field by volunteers. There are 260 men and women, living all over England, with whom we had (by 1966) made contact by circular letters, by organizational channels, and to some extent by the use of broadcasting. A tribute is perhaps due to the Third Programme of the BBC, which, with *The Listener* for the publication in print of its addresses, is an organ probably unique in any country.

---

[12] J. Hajnal, "European Marriage Patterns in Perspective," in David Glass and D. E. C. Eversley (eds.), *Population in History: Essays in Historical Demography* (Chicago: Aldine, 1965). See also Laslett in *The Listener*, February–March 1966.

[13] For an introduction (with references) and a superficial discussion of the value of these remarkable researches, see Peter Laslett's *The World We Have Lost* (New York: Scribner, 1966).

But the 165 local historians among our correspondents must have their equivalents in other European (or American or Asian) countries, and it is significant that their introduction to us has come through local history societies, archaeological or genealogical societies, archivists, or clergymen. University teachers have introduced 50 to us, and tutors in extramural adult education 20 more; only 25, perhaps an unexpectedly small proportion, are schoolteachers.

This body of volunteer correspondents is, as the reader must surely have recognized, a research tool of extraordinary value in this field, and we have been astonished by the speed with which we were able to bring it into being and with its flexibility when created. This is the only important contribution to methodology that, in these early stages of the work of the group, the present paper can claim. We are now beginning to use this research organ to study the issue of the history of the growth of literacy in England over the crucial generations of industrialization. When we also begin to analyze geographical mobility and occupational structure, all from parish registers and other locally available documents, we hope to extend greatly our available information in numerical and other forms for the purpose of regional historical comparison.

PART SIX

The Organization of
Ecological Data Archives

All the analyses presented in this volume are based on collections of data organized by some sort of locality. Some of these collections are simply private data files built up for some specific task of analysis; in certain cases the original file will remain as personal and inaccessible as the notes taken in the preparation of the research report; in others the file will sooner or later be incorporated with other files in a broader archive and placed at the disposal of qualified scholars for reanalysis and reinterpretation. The incentive to ''go public'' is markedly stronger in the case of ecological data than in the case of raw data from such costly research operations as tests or surveys. After all, most of the data in the majority of the existing ecological files are simply lifted out of already published official statistics, and there is no way of preventing other scholars from duplicating such efforts of data linkage. Obviously, this does not mean that scholars will be willing to spread their data indiscriminately to all comers; there are bound to be pressures to protect the original investments and to secure priority rights in the preparation of publications. But the trend is nevertheless quite clear: with the spread of high-level computer facilities to more and more research centers there is bound to be a mushrooming of efforts to assemble the long backlogs of ecological statistics on cards or tapes and to establish service-oriented archives of one variety or another.

The five chapters included in Part Six of this volume all deal in their various ways with the development of such archives. Warren Miller, already the elder statesman of the archival movement in the United States, reviews the experiences of the Inter-University Consortium in the field of ecological data. Dwaine Marvick and his co-worker Jane Bayes present information on the ways in which ecological data from official sources have been linked contextually with survey data in the

519

work carried forward at one of the most active of the local archives in the United States: the Falk archive at the University of California, Los Angeles. The next two chapters review experiences and discuss strategies in the organization of systematic files of ecological information for two countries with strong traditions of official bureaucratic bookkeeping: Germany and Austria. The chapter by Hartenstein and Liepelt is of particular importance because of their emphasis on the linkages of ecological data archiving with urban and regional planning. *This points to an exciting convergence in current trends of research: the social or political ecologist focusing on local variations within the total national territory finds himself increasingly attracted by the style of model construction and trend extrapolation characteristic of the physical planner and the regional scientist. There are important differences in the choice of territorial units, but the variables covered and the style of analysis tend to become increasingly similar. Most sociologists or political scientists who have made efforts to develop ecological data files have felt bound to stick to the smallest units of local administration, at least in the country-side; in the cities the tendency has been to focus on whatever is the equivalent of the census tract. To geographers and planners the interesting variations tend to occur at even lower levels of territorial aggregation: the Swedes are establishing a grid co-ordinate system for plotting census data, population movements, land use information, etc.; the Norwegians, the British, and the Americans are experimenting with similar systems; and the Germans hope to build up a block system with identifying co-ordinates. This is an exciting frontier of interdisciplinary research today — again a field where the International Social Science Council might serve an important function in linking national efforts and spreading technical know-how from the innovating to the less advanced centers. The final chapter, by the Argentinian sociologist Jorge Garcia-Bouza, helps to identify some of the important problems in extending the archival movement to the developing countries of Latin America. The International Social Science Council has been very much interested in promoting archival developments in all countries and regions where there are sufficient backlogs of ecological data worth reanalysis: major conferences on regional disparities and local variations in growth rates have been held in Buenos Aires in 1964 and in New Delhi in 1967 and will be followed up through concrete studies of the available data resources under contracts with UNESCO.*

20

WARREN E. MILLER

The Development of Archives for Social Science Data

ANYONE PROFESSIONALLY using modern techniques of social research can readily understand the growth of interest in social science data archives. Contemporary methodologies of social research have given renewed and increased attention to the use of large bodies of quantitative data. The addition of survey research to the existing portfolio of research methods now permits the creation of rich and complex sets of information that can be used in many ways by a variety of scholars. The prospect of elaborate combinations of different data collections opens still further possibilities for research of unmatched scope. At the same time, the technology for processing information by computers has made it possible to exploit masses of data with heretofore unimagined economy and efficiency. The researcher's appetite for data has been well matched by the computer's ability to manage and manipulate. And in addition to the newer developments in transmitting data by wire, data can now be readily reproduced and exchanged for the purpose of sharing the same data resources among an unlimited number of scholars.

If the technology of electronic data processing now provides a means of access to existing collections of data, the cost of independent and repetitious generation of data impels the scholar to try to use existing resources before mounting new data collections of his own. While survey research permits the collection of much valuable information in a single operation, the cost of a good piece of survey research is high and can be met only occasionally by the most fortunate researchers.

521

Organizing an extended set of election returns or consus reports for subsequent work with a computer may well be prohibitively expensive if a single piece of research must bear the entire cost. The demand for data resources of a scope and a quality commensurate with long-standing intellectual ambitions has grown as the creation of such resources has become technically feasible. Financial resources necessary to support significant social research have not grown at a comparable rate. Scarcity of funds to bear the cost of creating data resources has thus added impetus to the extended sharing of those data that do exist. Out of the need for data, the high costs, and the technical feasibility of sharing data has come the concept of a social science data archive.

RESEARCH CENTERS AS SITES FOR ARCHIVAL DEVELOPMENT

The history of modern archives of machine-readable social science data is so brief as to challenge immediate attempts at generalized description or commentary. Interest in these innovations by scholarly organizations has swelled astoundingly, but the number of such archives in actual operation is as yet very limited. Although we may envision a world-wide community of scholars and teachers sharing the world's entire store of data, our knowledge of the archival enterprise rests on our limited experience with the handful of archives actually existing.

From at least one perspective this is a curiously impoverished state of affairs. The essential components of an archive are few in number, only a subset of the components of a self-sufficient research installation and not substantially different from those of a single large research project. Indeed, more than one presently recognized archive came easily into being (if not into operation) with no addition of equipment or personnel beyond the complement already assembled for research purposes. Given a collection of data needed by distant colleagues and given a desire to respond to their requests for assistance, an internally oriented research operation can rapidly acquire the perspectives of an externally oriented data archive. If the research operation has been supported by an appropriately organized computer installation, the researcher's commitment to collegial co-operation may be stimulated by associates who appreciate the potential role of the computer in carrying out the tasks of data storage, processing, and retrieval so essential to an efficient data service organization. The tradition of intellectual exchange within an extended community of scholars makes the transition from a primary concern with one's own research needs to a co-ordinate concern with the research needs of others even more natural and swift.

We may expect this sequence of developments to be characteristic of many of the social science data archives of the future. This developmental mode not only has a certain naturalness about it but also gives some promise of optimal decisions in shaping archival policies and practices. In later stages of maturity, the archive is likely to become the concern of many interests other than those of the scholars who create the original state of supply and demand. Subsequent problems of maintaining the organization for its original purposes may be no greater than in other phases of academic life. And yet the orthodoxies of relevant administrative, technical, and financial interests are so much better established that subversion and diversion of energies for other ends may occur unless the founders of each archive firmly define the essential needs of scholarship and anticipate in some detail the implications of those needs for archival development.

Quite apart from organizational naturalness or necessity, the role of established research scholars in archival development is likely to increase for quite another reason. At least in the United States, it seems reasonable to expect that major research grants will more and more often depend on assurances that their intermediate product, data, will be used beyond the limits of the specific research being funded. Because of the inherent multiple utility of almost every large and complex data collection, some small awareness of the existence of service-oriented data archives will certainly lead to the stipulation that new data should be released for more general exploitation once the principal investigation and related objectives have been accomplished. Whether or not this view has already become a part of the thinking of foundation officers and granting agency personnel, a number of recent grants have supported applications that took the initiative in this regard. These requests held out the promise of eventual widespread use of data through archival dissemination as a dividend on the investment in the proposed research.

Everything mentioned thus far would forecast the rapid creation and growth of an extended set of social science data archives. Nevertheless, there are very few full-fledged archives actually in existence actively serving a constituency that extends beyond the limits of a single university. A somewhat closer view of the problems of creating, developing, and sustaining an archive may reveal some of the reasons for the gap between potential and performance.

FOUNDATIONS OF ARCHIVAL GROWTH

Although research scholars provide the impetus for archival development, they are reluctant to accept responsibility for specific archival
activities. Unless the creation of an archive promises to be the only way
of making a valued piece of research possible, most researchers are
profoundly uninterested in abandoning or diminishing their own work,
even temporarily, in order to become research administrators for other
people's research. In some ways this is as it should be. The scholar whose
foresight and imagination permit him to be excited by the promise of
archival development should remain unencumbered and free to devote
his imagination to scholarship. And yet if the individual decision always
favors the individual's immediate work, the collective result is a failure
of leadership. It is hard to fault any single decision that has left a
potential for archival development unrealized, but the cumulative effect
thus far has been to limit the number of places where interest in archival
development has passed beyond informal conversation and exhortatory
discussion.

In quite another way, reliance on a central role for the established
researcher provides a second limitation on establishing an archive.
There are relatively few instances in which an ongoing program of
research provides more than a beginning for an archive. Unless the
research program is so broad as to be relevant to hundreds of remote
scholars and students, it will most probably not justify a major capital
investment in the development of archival facilities. Consequently, a
serious commitment to the task of creating an archive usually requires
a concern with data and facilities far beyond one's own research interests. The voluntary extension into domains of reduced competence
and concern dilutes both enthusiasm and viability. The transition from
accumulating one's own research resources to making those resources
more widely available may be an easy, natural evolution guided by an
intimate knowledge of relevant professional and technical considerations; but if the new archive is to be maintained, permitted to take
advantage of new opportunities as they arise, and organized to respond
to new demands as they are made, the transition carries with it clear
implications for a continuing and growing involvement in a set of
problems increasingly remote from the point of departure, the concern
for one's own research.

The problems of archival administration may be fairly put in a single
question: What support is available to develop what organizations of
what sets of data to be acquired by whom from whom for what use by

whom, when, and with what support? The remaining comments select only a part of this set of quandaries for detailed attention.

THE ACQUISITION AND PROCESSING OF DATA

As soon as internal research objectives no longer define the boundaries of data acquisition, an archive must adopt a strategy for assigning priorities to future acquisitions. The strategy must balance the costs of acquisition, the costs of preparing data for machine handling, and the costs of responding to anticipated requests for the data against the probable volume and value of future use. The cost-use equation must at least balance for any acquisition; the margins by which expected values to users exceed expected costs to the archive may well determine the ideal priorities for expansion of the data base.

In concrete terms, however, each equation has many solutions. The cost of acquisition is likely to be the only fixed item, with the others more or less intricately and unpredictably interrelated. This is so because optimal use of the data may well depend on the variety of possible output, beginning with the simple ability to reproduce and redistribute the data as acquired. Beyond this beginning lies the broad question of how much of the cost of data analysis can, should, or must be borne by the constituents who use the archive's resources. With archives serving many constituents who command little or nothing in the way of access to the full power of today's big computers, the archive that does have such access must decide again and again whether an additional investment in data management systems development or computational routines or information retrieval is necessary or desirable as a means of increasing effective use of the data. For many would-be users there is no alternative. If the archive does not have a given capability, the data cannot be processed in the desired manner. If, at the same time, substantial numbers of scholars do have access to computer installations equivalent to that of the archive, the question changes but remains: How much of the cost that could be incurred by each of several users should be carried by the communal facility that is the archive?

As archival holdings grow in scope and complexity, a larger and larger set of potential capabilities must be assessed. The efficient management of data becomes an organizational problem totally different from the discrete problem of archive-user alternatives in processing a single set of data. But whatever the specific question — what information retrieval system for locating data, what standards of documentation, what means of optimizing the response to complex analysis problems —

the archive is uniquely concerned with using the best administrative and technological processes to enhance the value of data to a remote universe of potential users.

A preoccupation with the wants and abilities of others certainly should not divorce archival management from a deep concern with the frontiers of research and creative thought. Indeed, the future of archival development rests on the probability that first-rate scholars dedicated to professional and disciplinary excellence will recognize the strategic and crucial role the data archive will play in the future definition of intellectual concerns. Nevertheless, the responsibility for making wise use of scarce resources to facilitate other people's pursuit of selected lines of inquiry is not the same as making an independent decision as to one's own pursuit of research objectives.

The game of anticipating the future uses of data is by nature a perplexing game with many sets of rules. Wide experience and a certain rapport with the pioneers scouting the frontiers of research may provide insight into the substantive imperatives that should be allowed to shape the research of the future. On a somewhat less exalted plane, the decision to select some data rather than others, or to develop this capability for processing rather than that, may be limited if not controlled by boundaries established by fund-granting agencies; and the entire enterprise of archival development is so new that none of the large sources of financial support is really well prepared to make the independent decisions that will enhance one archival development and its lines of inquiry rather than another.

Whatever choices are now open, it seems certain that today's decisions will soon be judged by the reasonable criterion of tomorrow's use. It is hard to quarrel with the presumption that archives now absorbing hundreds of thousands of dollars in developmental funds should shortly be able to point to substantial quantities of first-rate research that could not have existed without the capital investment in archival resources. Of course, a well-established research tradition that can profit from a fuller, richer data base may, in one breath, promise an archive and its sponsor rich dividends, a safe investment, and steady returns over the years. On the other hand, the implicit reference to risk capital may be sufficiently apt to promise a mixed reward to the archival entrepreneur and a paucity of funds for any but the most assured venture in creating new research resources.

The necessary ubiquity of concern with a distant and dispersed universe of scholars who are an archive's constituency and reason for being further exacerbates an administrative problem common to almost all archives now in existence. Thus far, it is in the nature of a social science data archive to be a highly specialized facility. Geography, time, discipline, topic, and type of data variously define rather specific boundaries for each archive. Even the largest of the academic institutions now acting as more or less involuntary hosts to new archives contains only a minor fragment of the archive's potential constituency. Consequently, the task of institution building that confronts the organizers of a new archive is even more difficult than the normal task of creating a new resource within an established university.

None of the present archives came into being on the initiative of the administrative leaders of the host institutions. The research scholar seeking authority and financial support to create an archive has certainly been able to promise many advantages to his institution as a by-product of archival location. Nevertheless, these incidental advantages aside, the organizational perspective has necessarily been cosmopolitan rather than local. Because of the location of the potential users, the new facility is, in the sheer bulk of its activities, more a resource for others than a benefit to one's own staff and students. It seems fair to conclude that all of this has contributed to the present situation that finds each archive looking in vain to its parent institution for adequate support for developing and maintaining a significant role in the larger academic community.

In addition to these particular intellectual and administrative challenges to archival development, an additional complication is sometimes created by the staff responsible for data processing. The problem originates in the continuing evolution of computer technology. With *change* almost the hallmark of the world of computers, a good data-processing staff is well occupied in the search for better ways to accomplish set goals. The same good staff is also bound to be occupied with the innovations in technology that make possible new goals for computational, retrieval, and management abilities — abilities that may long remain underused by a constituency too unsophisticated to exploit them. Exotic data may remain outside the archive for lack of a champion; exotic data-processing capabilities are likely to be put forward with great enthusiasm by those whose work is the heart of the archival operation. In either instance, administrative imagination and vision may bring a valuable innovation to the attention of those who will put a new resource to brilliant use; lack of administrative restraint may permit an intriguing but virtually profitless diversion of funds.

All classes of developmental decisions must be made in response to existing, developing, or wisely anticipated needs of the community of users. The sheer existence of a set of data does not give it value; the existence of an elegant computer routine does not mean it will be used. Every aspect of an archive must be fashioned with a keen sense of the purpose and probability of its use. Until the resources available to social science are several magnitudes greater than they are now, it will be irresponsible to do any less.

ECOLOGICAL DATA AND SOCIAL SCIENCE ARCHIVES

The archive specializing in aggregative or ecological data seems in no way sharply different from the archive of survey data. There are, nevertheless, some differences of degree that are worth noting. For example, the strategy of acquisition for an archive of survey data should be somewhat more straightforward now and for the immediate future. Although very large quantities of data are now being generated by survey methods, only a small fraction promises to be of more than limited interest to the academic community. In the absence of any use-oriented criteria of value, there is a sufficient flood of survey, poll, and market research data to inundate a score of archives; but with even the most generous definition of probable value across the social science disciplines, the more pressing problem of the moment is actually the need for more and better collections of data. Moreover, even if other considerations dictate a rather indiscriminate acquisition of data of doubtful worth, the disciplined archive need process only selected collections for widespread use by its constituency.

There would seem to be no such relief in sight for the ecological archival effort. In country after country ecological data have been produced for scores of years, not simply during the past twenty years. There is little duplication among data collections, so the bulk cannot be reduced by selecting the better data — or by allowing an academic version of an inverse Gresham's Law to operate and wait for the good data to eliminate the demand for the bad. Moreover, the mass of quantified or quantifiable data in the public record — census data, election returns, governmental statistics, legislative records, and the like — often constitutes the single authoritative source of needed information.

A further definition of the necessary scope of ecological archival development is provided by the expanding set of probable users. Within a very few years the historian will join the sociologist and political scientist in force as an avid customer for archival goods. His movement into the ranks of the consumers of data will, however, only

accentuate the growing interest of those concerned with the large problems of national social, economic, and political development. With the
records of the past becoming the data base for a rapidly growing community of social science research scholars, the development of ecological
archives must assuredly contemplate an existing universe of data many
times larger than that available for survey archives.

This aspect of the problem of archival development is further complicated by the size of the subsets of data. Even the most impressive
archive of survey data will be an archive composed of data collections
that were created as discrete, limited collections — each with a clear
boundary enclosing a set of data that bulk much smaller than a single
series of ecological data. Although it is technically possible to set
restrictions on a set of ecological data to be added to an archive, it is
likely that each acquisition will necessarily be a larger set of data than is
characteristic of survey archives. Thus, from beginning to end, the
specification of a strategy for archival development seems more difficult
for the ecological archive. The alternatives are more numerous, the
demands are more universalistic, and the decisions must be made for
larger sets of data.

Beyond the question of scope, with the historical dimension so
prominent, lies a quite different problem created by contemporary
modes of using data. Although there may be no overriding necessity to
locate this problem in the ecological archive, it seems likely that much
support for the ecological archive will rest on the assumption that it will
make possible the creation of integrated data bases, mixtures of aggregative data and survey data so organized as to permit simultaneous use
in analytic schemes. The prospect is worth at least two passing comments. First, the technical problems are not simple. The ecological data
must be organized and documented, with both spatial and temporal
locations well established, in a manner that usually requires extended
work beyond the simple transformation of published material to a
machine-readable form. Where the nature of survey research anticipates
many of the requirements for archival data processing, the traditional
presentation of ecological data does little to anticipate many editorial
and data preparation steps necessary before the data can be merged
with other sets of information. Second, whoever bears the burden of
organizing data for use in an integrated data base bears unusual risks.
There is substantial agreement in select quarters that the integrated
data base holds infinitely great promise for imaginative and productive
research. In fact, few research scholars are well prepared to use such
a resource. Insofar as volume of use is the justification for the

developmental investment, investment in data organized in an integrated data base is a larger gamble than is investment in facilitating established research routines.

A third more or less unique problem of the ecological archive resides in the data source. A community of survey archives can be expected to exert significant influence on the population of data suppliers, particularly the academic researchers whose data are ultimately destined to be widely distributed for direct use by colleagues. Standardization of method and technique and a continued upgrading of the quality and utility of data can be expected, at least over time, as interaction among research scholars is promoted by shared interests in the archival pooling of data. Commercial suppliers of poll and market research data may be less susceptible to influence, but even there a growing set of common concerns bodes well for the future. The ecological archive, on the other hand, must usually deal with governmental agencies whose policy makers are more removed and whose operations are more securely established in a complex bureaucracy. Although the social bookkeeping of many nations provides a rich source of data for social research, the ability of the archival community to shape the generation of future data must be limited at best. Indeed, it seems that the initiation of ecological archive development finds the would-be archive more often in the position of supplicant, forced to demonstrate that national interests or agency interests will not be jeopardized by wider dissemination of data. In many instances, a variety of well-established policies relating to confidentiality for respondents who provided the original information sharply limits the access of the academic researcher. At least in the American context, many important contributions to ecological archival collections will become available only after the ponderous machinery of the data-gathering bureaucracies moves to more amiable postures of co-operation with the academic community.

As something of an innovation in social organization, the social science data archive is a part of the modern world but a challenge to many of its institutions. Where a scholar's capital once was measured in part by his access to information, it is now about to be measured more completely by his ability to use information. Where a university once became great by commanding the resources of scholarship, it may gain comparable recognition tomorrow by its ability to share those resources with sister institutions. The implications of the co-operative, inter-institutional, interdisciplinary network of social science data archives are extremely challenging. The realization of the idea, however, depends on the solution of many problems. The excitement that now grips the few who would create the archives must spread to the potential users, the suppliers, the financiers, and the administrators within whose bailiwicks the archives must find support. All of these contributors must move apace to a sophisticated understanding of the optimum relationships between them and this new inhabitant of the world of scholarly endeavor.

2I

DWAINE MARVICK AND JANE H. BAYES

Domains and Universes: Problems in Concerted Use of Multiple Data Files for Social Science Inquiries

IN THIS PAPER a number of disparate themes are explored and a number of preliminary research formulations described. An attempt is made to characterize the changing style and thrust of political behavior research. We have moved from a period when individual scholars worked alone, drawing mainly on ecological statistics, to a period when research teams collaborate in the tasks of gathering and analyzing relevant evidence, principally by using survey research methods. We are heading toward a period when multiple files of data will be invoked and computer-aided simulations will routinely be used to explore problems.

Survey research, with its emphasis on representative samples from large and heterogeneous universes, has been a powerful tool for political sociologists concerned with exploring the importance of attitudinal determinants of behavior. But it has been poorly suited to exploring the importance of context and process. The very methods by which samples are drawn from "universes" have tended to make it difficult to design survey research giving adequate attention to interaction patterns, sequence considerations, and other context-specific variables. Political phenomena occur in "domains" — that is, in organized social entities. Survey methods lift a panel of respondents "out of context" to form a representative "sample" of some larger universe. For the

533

research objectives in view, this is quite appropriate; for secondary analysis as part of a complex data base, the survey materials thus gathered too often lack the kinds of variables needed to fit a respondent into any quasi-realistic "domain," much less put him back into the actual context in which he lives.

The need to reintroduce context, sequence, and interaction as systematically considered dimensions of our research designs does not mean diverting attention from the subjective attitudinal dimensions emphasized by survey research. It means use of aggregate data — census materials, election returns, transaction statistics — to characterize the changing environment at the same time that it means use of records about individuals seen as participants in organized processes. It means that we need to be able to handle multiple data files.

Modern computers, with their capabilities for manipulating and transforming data, are well suited for modeling and simulation work and show promise for radically changing the ways in which social scientists use evidence. We need experimental modeling, on a large-scale basis, of political and social processes. Whole families of process models need to be compared in operation, using the same data base but varying the branching and decisional premises. The software capabilities currently exist, and the next generation of computer hardware should make data manipulations and simultaneous documentation of data transformations even easier.

What is also needed might be called computer calisthenics — enough planned exercise using the available configurations to acquire new habits of inquiry. In looking at the available data base for studying a social science problem, we need to be sensitive to at least four questions that have not routinely arisen heretofore: (1) On what terms of reference can two data files be interrelated? (2) What is the lowest possible level of "disaggregation"? (3) How can unambiguous identification of the various entities to which data records refer be maintained? (4) By what stages can interrelated data files be mobilized along time dimensions? In any work that seeks to make simulations or models of political processes, these problems probably will be handled in awkward ways for a long time.

For Los Angeles political behavior in recent years, the availability of both survey and ecological data files on comparable matters has permitted a number of *ad hoc* explorations of how they supplement one another as sources of evidence about the same political phenomena. After some further elaboration of the points just summarized, this paper will describe some results of those explorations.

THE THREE GENERATIONS IN THE HISTORY OF
QUANTITATIVE POLITICAL ANALYSIS

For certain purposes one may distinguish three generations of systematic inquiry into political life. The first may be said to have been preoccupied with contextual effects, the second with attitudinal determinants, and the third with sequence and interaction processes. The first relied heavily on aggregate data, the second on sample survey materials, and the third is attempting to use simultaneously more than one file of data relevant for describing behavior in a political domain.

The first generation is perhaps best exemplified by men like Harold Gosnell, André Siegfried, or V. O. Key. Their work stressed empirical patterns and trends that helped to characterize the history and politics of particular communities. They identified persistent geographic lines of cleavage, traced secular voting trends, showed how a locality's partisan ramparts could be flooded by national political tides, examined the erosion of political beliefs and the transformation of civic concerns by mass media and modern technology. They tended to stress contextual *effects* more than determinants; they attempted to gauge the tempo of emerging forces; they called attention to idiosyncratic factors. Perhaps their very sophistication about the subtleties of political life made them treat theoretical schematics gingerly, as likely to be overdrawn and implausible, even though *empirical* generalizations about political patterns and trends were quite acceptable.

During their period, largely prewar, census data and electoral statistics were the staple kinds of quantitative evidence available. Gradually a level of disenchantment came to prevail about what these data resources could be coaxed into revealing. By 1950, when W. G. Robinson published his well-known article on ecological fallacies, use of such data had already appreciably declined. Seen as an alternative to the survey approach, the use of aggregate data files by then had lost much of its appeal to political scientists interested in testing propositions about political behavior.

Second-generation work lost much of this earlier sensitivity to context. The postwar social science generation wanted to make explicit contributions to theory. It wanted to explore men's attitudes and beliefs. There was available a research technique — the sample survey — which probed hitherto inaccessible dimensions of political outlook with some precision. Methodological preoccupations centering around datagathering problems in applying survey techniques to publics, organizations, elites, and other human aggregates dominated the field.

Research was by no means cast in a single mold, but the concern with sampling methods was prominent. Paul Lazarsfeld and his Columbia associates employed community panel studies. Angus Campbell and his Michigan colleagues conducted national surveys. Heinz Eulau and his associates probed the lives of state legislators. Ithiel Pool, Herbert McClosky, Samuel Eldersveld, and others studied group leadership patterns. However different their contributions in focus and formula, a salient feature of this generation of scholars has been their willingness to confine research to the perspective secured by using a sampled universe.

The apprenticeship of social science to survey methodology during this second-generation period has created varied and voluminous data files, which are now sufficient to permit useful secondary analyses, historical trend inquiries, and simulations based on composite samples. The third generation is adding some distinctive components to the data base. A pragmatic (rather than doctrinaire) test of what constitutes an acceptable degree of data-gathering rigor seems increasingly to be employed, as field research is extended into underdeveloped areas, legislative arenas, top policy-making processes, opinion formation situations, or various intramural organizational settings. It is recognized that demanding the best sample, the most neutral interviewing, and the most carefully standardized questions might pose ideals that could frustrate purposeful inquiries. A complementary, rather than exclusive, attitude toward the relevance of documentary evidence and quantitative data is emerging, as the polemics over the behavioral persuasion cease to interest, or even frighten, members of the political science fraternity. Finally, a developmental, rather than static, pattern of inquiry is increasingly pursued. The agenda for research gives high priority to work that outstrips available data resources. The kinds of data available simply do not begin to meet the data requirements of system models.

These trends in current research methodology are linked to the growing attention to research problems arising when multiple data files are relevant. For a given entity, multiple data files might include opinion data, census material, voting figures, biographical statistics, tax levels, case loads, budget allocations, content analyses, sociometric rosters, and so on. The research ideal is to formulate problems that call for the concerted mobilization of these evidential resources rather than the artifactual elaboration of seemingly autonomous "planes" of political life, each discoverable in its own peculiar way — opinions by polling, interactions by observation, trends by transaction levels, recruitment by life histories. Much attention is given to modeling and simulation patterns.

Common today are references to the new computers — those configurations of machinery and circuits, of hardware and software — which will be big enough to permit simultaneous manipulation of numerous files. Some requirements or desiderata can be specified quite easily. *Automatic self-labeling* of the new data records and files which are generated at intermediate stages in a simulated process is desirable. Updated inventories of the entities, codes, and variables in each record of the relevant files need to be indexed, preferably by a *central dictionary* able to provide on-line knowledge of the available data base at intermediate stages as well as at the beginning of a multistage analysis. Even more esoteric would be *symbolic indexing capabilities*, such that computed cues could invoke key gambits and subsystems in a simulation problem at unanticipated stages in the process.

The current generation of computers (like the IBM 360 series) have memories that are sufficient, when augmented by cell disk and tape storage devices, to handle reasonably complex simulation problems. Moreover, various statistical processing and analysis software packages provide the essential capability. What is chiefly lacking in social science is experience and familiarity with the use of such resources. Few people have been working on the data manipulation and retrieval problems that arise when concerted use of multiple files is contemplated. Those who have been tend to move on to fresh complications and challenges as soon as the software package is debugged and ready for use. Too little actual research *use* is made of available concerted-analysis systems, yet the knowledge of how to apply such computer resources to a variety of relevant problems is likely to be gained only by a regimen of computer calisthenics.

THE ECOLOGICAL BASIS OF SURVEY SAMPLING

A review of the essentials involved in survey research is relevant to a discussion of multiple data files. Opinion survey techniques present the researcher with lengthy interview protocols, each containing an individual person's responses to variously framed questions. Taken as aggregates, each set of interviews constitutes a sample from a universe. Interesting questions about that universe can readily be posed, and adequate sampling and data gathering methods seem to promise that a representative cross section will provide a full profile of answers.

Selection of a representative sample apparently means systematic exposure to the relevant evidence. In approaching the business of sampling, the first task is to define the universe in terms that make possible the gathering of empirical cases. To sample a universe of disembodied ideas, actions, or characteristics is not possible; such things must be understood as aspects of human behavior. A universe must be reduced to people, groups, events, or records. In short, it must consist of tangible and discrete elements. Second, the universe to be sampled must be finite, even if arbitrarily so. The time span to be covered must be fixed. Place boundaries must be drawn. Channels of communication between researchers and the universe to be sampled must be devised. Third, the basic sampling units which constitute the tangible elements of a finite universe must be designated. One may wish to consider individual people, family or other group units, ten-minute periods of group discussion, or one-hour periods of observations to be the basic sampling units. In any case, a firm decision on this point also is necessary before a sample can be designed.

A sample is only a part — any part — of the universe in question. To get a representative sample, resting one's claim upon the impressive empirical substantiation of probability theory as used by modern science, one must seek to give every element in the universe the same chance of selection as every other element. A "representative sample" is a part of the "universe in question," so gathered that, according to probability theory, the likelihood is maximized that statements of a given precision *about the universe as a whole* based on sample information may be made with a known degree of confidence.

Such survey procedure when applied in social science inquiries presents at least two difficulties. It causes neglect of certain variables, notably those of context, and it fosters illusions about the distinctiveness of survey data which are not warranted by the way such data are currently analyzed.

First, people live in organized settings or "domains" within the larger universe sampled. In the individual's environment, interaction and sequence are often known to be coercive determinants of conduct. Yet these considerations are attenuated in survey research. Individuals are treated as the basic universe. In voting studies, those interviewed in a cross-section survey live in different communities and neighborhoods. They are stimulated by dissimilar campaign developments, despite mass-media communications. They face election day "choices" that are cast in particular terms by the conscious campaign efforts of local organized rival party groups — each trying to tailor the electioneering to the audience immediately at hand. Of course, when individual voters are chosen for inclusion in a sample, it is possible to ensure appropriate representation of many different types of voters, whether by quotas, area-selection methods, or random list choices. But each individual is lifted out of his habitat, both his mundane, nonpolitical round of activities and his occasional politicized moments. It seems clear that a marriage of survey data and ecological data is desirable in order to examine individual data in conjunction with evidence about the environmental complex from which, in each separate case, it was derived.

Second, it is necessary to consider the limitations of cross-tabular methods of analysis before concluding that survey data necessarily is distinctive, because the entities about whom inquiry is being made are individual persons. From the beginning, survey researchers have been unwilling to stop with statements about the sampled universe taken as a whole.

Sample surveys have not been viewed merely as aggregates of a special kind, deliberately created by the investigator. That one can secure "breakdowns" of the data by grouping the respondents into subcategories and separately tallying the frequency distribution on a particular variable for each subcategory has been made clear. Cross tabulations raise challenging analytical puzzles; technical terms such as partials and marginals, intervening and contingent variables, concept space, substructured typologies, and the like have been introduced to clarify the intellectual tasks involved.

With the flowering of multivariant analysis technology specifically for use with survey materials, the underlying similarity of many analytical problems encountered in using either ecological or survey data has been obscured. Multivariant analysis of survey data has been considered distinctive from aggregate data analysis, although both have been handled in closely analogous ways. It is, of course, true that ecological data do not permit the investigator to get close enough to the actors he is studying to analyze what motives and attitudes, skills, and living conditions link a given individual to his political conduct. Those who engage in ecological analysis have become highly sensitive to the danger of slipping from statements about how different kinds of areas behave to statements that refer to the behavior of the kinds of people one has in mind in characterizing the areas. When an area is composed overwhelmingly of the type in question, there is little doubt that the area's aggregate scores on other variables directly index individual behavior patterns. Conversely, when an area is characterized as containing few of the type in question, its aggregate scores are not likely to reflect the conduct of the minority component.

The danger in question is simply the analysis-of-variance problem in one of its aspects — that more difference within categories than between categories may prevail. As such it is not specifically a problem for ecological data, however troublesome it is to deal with such data and however sensitive about its relevance most analysts of aggregate data have become.

Covariance problems are pervasive also in multivariant analysis of survey data. Statistical developments in social science have begun to provide appropriate tests and procedures for evaluating categorical variables. Almost all cross-tabulation methods start by assigning individual respondents to categories. When the data warrant, it seems appropriate to claim, for example, that poorly educated conservatives tended to vote for Goldwater in larger proportions than did well-educated conservatives. A little reflection will remind us that this statement is based on a comparison of four-cell entities in a concept space:

	For Goldwater	Not for Goldwater
Well-educated conservatives	———	———
Poorly educated conservatives	———	———

Familiar questions arise. What other variables might be "masked" by education? Is the set of people here grouped together, namely "conservatives," really a proxy for an overlapping set — for example, Republicans? Is it really Goldwater, the man, for whom those people vote, or would they have voted for any alternative to Johnson appearing on the ballot? As one controls for the additional factors, the number of cases gets smaller. The idiosyncrasies of the individual respondents become troublesomely apparent. There is irony here. No doubt, it is useful and feasible to investigate empirically the warrant for all those tractable propositions about what "really" might be causing the data distributions in question that lend themselves to multivariant testing. But it is odd that data records that pertain to individuals are sanctified by that fact, although the way in which they are made to yield findings is often by treating them in multivariant categorical sets. An ecological domain is a useful concept when the variance within the geographic entity is no larger than the difference between comparable ecological areas. Many analyses of survey data group individuals into categories on the basis of multivariant conceptual indices that are as subject to the pitfalls of an "ecological fallacy" as are geographic indices. Those who seek to compare such ecological and multivariant categories risk coming to simplistic conclusions about complex phenomena. By focusing on "process" in time and space, ecological and multivariant categories become conceptual tools for exploring designated problems. The goal is not to identify single implicitly causal factors but rather to re-examine and redefine specific questions about ongoing processes in light of a given problem.

It is necessary on certain points to recognize that aggregate materials are distorted one step further than survey data. But the act of sampling is a distortion too in a different way. To a considerable extent, survey data are used in ways that involve analytical difficulties similar to those surrounding the use of ecological data. For many purposes survey data files can be treated as special kinds of aggregate data files. The incorporation and utilization of attitudinal materials in the same "mix" with demographic electoral, transactional, and similar aggregate statistics will clearly be facilitated by dispelling the illusion that survey data are distinctive, either in kind or in the way they should be analyzed.

The question can be turned around. How important is it for the full exploitation of survey data that they be linked to other kinds of data and exposed to the analytical subtleties of complex "modeling" inquiries into how processes work? It becomes evident that sequence and interaction, interdependence and experience itself are aspects of political life which are preserved only with difficulty and in attenuated form when individuals are studied "out of context." It is these very kinds of data — *sociometric links* within the same domain; *reciprocal commentaries* by people that they are using the same conventions, procedures, and facilities, not merely analogically similar ones; data on people with *backgrounds of common experience* in a particular setting, not merely one that is in some sense comparable — which become relevant when one seeks to mount a computer-aided simulation of political or social processes.

The true distinctiveness of survey data, in the sense that the data are concerned not with an "aggregate" but with an individual person, begins to be exploited in the following way. When individual respondents are entered as participants in the simulation process, they are juxtaposed against other equally complex individuals, are allowed to exchange views, are able to influence one another, are forced to respond to environmental changes, and are confronted with decisions that must conform to situationally prescribed rules and standards and that, once made, will significantly modify their previous store of experience and skill.

The crux of the problem is not to be found in distinctions between census data, survey data, voting data, marketplace data, or other kinds of evidence. Rather the question is the *comparability* of the data, the extent to which one has a basis on which one can interrelate facts about an individual to facts about his family, residential block, school district, the factory where he works, or the central business area where he shops.

Asking questions about comparability leads to the second problem: What level of concreteness, of specific character, is the best possible level, if a complex data base is given? What is the lowest feasible level of *disaggregation* that we are able to maintain? Data are available for land parcels, for blocks, and, of course, for much larger entities. Where interview materials exist or where statistics about individual performance can be found in public records, it is possible also to explore a problem in a sustained way in terms of individual persons.

Another aspect is location. One must develop methods of identifying geographic entities unambiguously and of specifying the uses made of structures and channels found in such entities, whether reference is to particular parcels of land or to areas of census tract size. This means that one must grapple with the problem of how to locate clearly — through time — which particular geographic area one has in mind. The complex and overlapping maze of political boundaries that surrounds a citizen consists of areal units that are ambiguously delineated, arbitrarily named, and distressingly impermanent. Yet this problem must be mastered as a prerequisite to successful computer-aided manipulation of multiple data files. Our Los Angeles experience indicates the feasibility of marrying demographic and electoral statistics by fitting precinct boundaries and allocating parts of precincts to different tracts when necessary. In the future, the possibility of using locational co-ordinates seems attractive. Electronic equipment presently exists with which to read into the computer numbers that refer to any area's quadrant position on a grid and which represent the latitude and longitude of points on its boundary.

Finally, the introduction of sequence considerations and time dimensions raises additional difficulties. The problem involves not only locating clearly whatever area one is analyzing but also studying the sequence of movement, the flow of people, the flow of resources, and the flow of information in that area. It involves doing so on different levels of generality, in terms of shifts from one party affiliation to another, from one legislative district to another, reportable for individuals, groups, and area aggregates that are in "nested" relations to one another, and doing so on a monthly, yearly, or longer time-period basis. In short, there are "flows" of all measures and sizes that must be studied by anyone interested in the information base on which a political or social process draws.

AN EMPIRICAL EXAMPLE: ANALYSES OF VOTING
IN LOS ANGELES

For more than ten years, a research program at the University of California has attempted to use the Los Angeles area as a natural laboratory for the study of political change. To this end, various aggregate and survey data files have been compiled: (1) electoral and demographic statistics; (2) materials on participation in campaigns and other party processes; and (3) public opinion data about Los Angeles as a whole and about several of its distinctive subcommunities.

In the so-called POLCEN data file, two kinds of data, election returns and census figures, have been brought together. The availability at UCLA of census data stored on magnetic tapes for each of the nearly 1,300 census tracts defined in the 1960 census of Los Angeles County has been paralleled since 1958 by the availability from the County Registrar of Voters of complete registration and voting figures for each of the over 12,000 election precincts within the county. To date, precinct records for the general elections of 1958, 1960, 1962, 1964, and 1966 have been obtained in the UCLA Political Behavior Archives.

To make comparable these two kinds of data, election returns and registration figures were generated by census tract units instead of by precincts. Generally a precinct is about one tenth the size of a census tract. This was done in our Statistical Laboratory by using a map overlay procedure. Census tract boundaries were drawn onto precinct maps as of a fixed reference date. Since precinct boundaries are constantly undergoing revision in response to population shifts and the administrative convenience of those in the County Registrar of Voters' office, more than one set of overlay maps had to be prepared and coded. To date, so-called PICT files (Precinct In Census Tract), which define each census tract in terms of its component precinct and partial precinct elements, have been completed, using September 1959 boundaries, September 1962 boundaries, and September 1964 boundaries.

In addition to the POLCEN file, various elite and cadre populations have been surveyed. So far, these include: (a) a three-wave panel interview study of virtually all campaign workers of both major parties who were found to be active in contrasting Los Angeles assembly districts during a factional primary, a partisan general election, and a nonpartisan municipal election period (1956–1957); (b) a twenty-city study of city councilmen (1959); (c) a twenty-city study of community leaders (1961); and (d) a survey of backgrounds and perspectives toward politics characterizing the members of the Democratic and Republican Party Central Committees of Los Angeles County (1962).

At the citizen level, several opinion surveys have been undertaken. These include: (a) a 1960 county-wide interview study of the political leadership within the Mexican-American community in Los Angeles; (b) a similar 1962 study within the Los Angeles Negro community; (c) a county-wide interview and questionnaire survey concerned with civil liberties and civil rights problems linked to the November 1964 election day choices (autumn 1964); and (d) a similar county-wide interview and questionnaire survey concerned with political participation and socialization patterns (summer 1965).

The availability of such comparable survey materials, census data, and electoral statistics about Los Angeles County enables the integration of disparate data files for analytical purposes. This can be extremely advantageous. Survey data taps attitudinal, socioeconomic, and political information in considerable detail and on an individual basis. Electoral and demographic data compiled by census tract are accurate and comprehensive in coverage but cannot provide the substantive or the subjective "depth" available in survey materials. Combining survey with aggregate materials should allow an investigator to emphasize the advantages and minimize the disadvantages of each type of data.

One way to illustrate the significance of context is to focus on political *process* within a type of geographic domain. The particular process of interest here is that of democratic citizen participation in political and civic affairs. To think of participation as a process is to include within the concept environmental, attitudinal, and social interaction patterns. Political participation then can be viewed as the process that relates the individual to a corporate unit. If such a definition is useful, then the type and intensity of participation mode should be related to the attitudes and interaction patterns linking the individual to any specified corporate entity. The following analysis attempts to identify and investigate the nature of such a relationship with specific reference to local governments as the corporate entities in question.

The data base for this exercise includes political and socioeconomic information for a random 5 per cent sample of the 1,300 census tracts in Los Angeles County. This information is available on the POLCEN file described earlier. In addition, this analysis draws upon 700 interviews obtained on a randomly selected basis within the same 5 per cent sample of census tracts. (It should be noted that the census material is that of 1960. The electoral statistics include the 1958, 1960, 1962, and

1964 elections, while the survey material was obtained during the summer of 1965.)

The first methodological problem involves linking survey and aggregate materials with specific reference to participation. For this task, we focus upon the total votes cast ratio, or the TVC ratio. For any election, the TVC ratio is equal to the number of votes cast divided by the major party registration for the tract in question. If used in an absolute sense, the TVC ratio can be averaged for a series of elections and used as a measure of geographic mobility. Second, the differences between TVC ratios for two consecutive elections may be used as an index of change in voting participation for the tract in question.

California laws governing the registration of voters are such that eligibility is maintained by voting at least once every two years. Hence, the registration totals are inflated by the inclusion, in a given tract, of those who have moved away at any time during a two-year span. In turn, this creates an artificially low TVC ratio for areas that have lost residents, since the total votes cast figure is divided by a deceptively large registration figure. Wherever this emigration effect is not operative, the TVC ratio should adequately represent the level of a tract's voting participation.

Empirically, then, how is geographic stability related to the TVC ratio for a given tract, and to what extent is this relationship independent of factors such as education and income? To investigate this problem, data for income, education level, and geographic stability were taken from the 1960 census. The percentages of registered Republicans and Democrats who voted in the 1958, 1960, and 1962 elections were averaged to give an average TVC ratio for each census tract being considered. Geographic stability was determined by using the 1960 census question asking whether the respondent lived in the same house in 1960 as he had in 1955. The number of affirmative answers divided by the number of people over five years of age in 1960, in each census tract, gave a "stability percentage" for that tract. The income factor is in terms of median family income for the census tract. Education is crudely measured in median years of education for each census tract.

With the average TVC ratio for each census tract as the dependent variable, stability, education, and income were used successively as independent variables, and their correlation with the average TVC ratio was then compared. The correlation coefficient for residential stability is $r = .5532$, at a significance level of $\sigma = .137$, $Z = .616$, making the correlation significant within three standard deviations. A scattergram shows that the relationship is more consistent for tracts with high

stability scores (over 25 per cent stable). The correlation coefficient for
the relationship between education and the average TVC ratio is very
similar: $r = .5349$ with a significance level of $\sigma = .137$, $Z = .589$.
Income also correlates with the TVC ratio to about the same extent as
stability and education level. The correlation coefficient and the
significance level are: $r = .587$, $\sigma = .137$, $Z = .629$. A plot of education
versus income shows that these two factors are highly correlated with
each other, as one might expect. The correlation coefficient and the
significance level are: $r = .76$, $\sigma = .137$, $Z = .87$. However, when
education is plotted against stability, the resulting scatter of points does
not suggest a regression line. The same is true for a plot of stability
versus income level. The conclusion is that stability is independent and
unrelated in any simple or direct way to education or to income with
respect to the average TVC ratio. Furthermore, it is clear that education
and income levels both vary in their relationship to the average TVC
ratio.

The figures for stability and either education or income can be used to
predict, with fair accuracy, the average TVC ratio for any tract.

The multiple linear regression formula for this prediction is[1]

$$Y_c = 47.44 + (.2495)X_1 + (1.43)X_2 + (.00008)X_3$$

where Y_c is the calculated average TVC ratio for the 1958, 1960, and
1962 elections in any given census tract in Los Angeles County; X_1 is the
ratio of those living in the same house in 1955 as in 1960 to the number
of people over five years of age in 1960, for the given census tract; X_2 is
the median education level in years of school completed for the census
tract, taken from the 1960 census; and X_3 is the median family income
for the given census tract.

This regression formula was computed with data for the 5 per cent
random sample of tracts used as the sampling base for an opinion survey
in the summer of 1965. With this formula, the calculated average TVC
ratio varied by ± 8 points for 91 per cent of the tracts when compared
with the actual average TVC ratios. When applied to a *different* 5 per cent
random sample of Los Angeles census tracts, the formula was accurate
in predicting the average TVC ratio within ± 8 points for 97 per cent
of the census tracts. Consequently, for a given education and income
level, the average TVC ratio can be a very accurate index of geographic
stability within a given census tract.

[1]See Paul G. Hoel, *Introduction to Mathematical Statistics* (New York : Wiley,
1954), pp. 129–132.

If a lower level of precision is accepted, the average TVC ratio can be used directly as an index of geographic stability. This is important because geographic mobility is a "contextual factor" that can now be predictably related to electoral statistics. This is a crucial step in the use of multiple data files because it provides some justification for using electoral statistics available at least every two years to update decennial census materials for the purpose of categorizing. Though the stability–average TVC ratio correlation may be spurious, it is quite reasonable for residential stability to be an important factor affecting political participation patterns, particularly in Los Angeles County, where approximately 39 per cent of the population had a different residence in 1955 than in 1960. Geographic areas characterized by high residential turnover levels impose contextual effects on both the newcomers and the long settled. Residential turnover is a property of the ecological entity as well as a fact about individuals and families. For most people, the adult participation roles they are periodically expected to perform are not any more demanding in Los Angeles than elsewhere. However, the extreme mobility of the population probably affects patterns of civic and political organization, participation, and leadership in cumulatively significant ways.

Using the TVC ratio to isolate changes in voting participation is rather tricky. Schematically, the relationship between possible changes in major party registration and possible changes in the TVC ratio from, say, 1958 to 1960 can be visualized in a matrix, like that shown in the accompanying diagram.

		Change in TVC Ratio 1958–1960		
		Increase	Same	Decrease
Change in Total Two Major Party Registration 1958–1960	Increase	A	B	C
	Same	D	E	F
	Decrease	G	H	I

Logic discloses that whenever the TVC ratio increases from one election to another two years later, voting participation must also increase (except for one marginal possibility). However, when the TVC ratio decreases or remains the same, participation in the later election may have been the same as two years before, or it may have decreased. Changes in the TVC ratio will not indicate which.

If we concentrate on increases in voting turnout from one election to the next, we could expect *increases* in all tracts when measuring the *difference* between off-year and Presidential year TVC ratios. Immigration cannot be adduced to explain such increases. Heightened interest in the election day choices would seem to be the principal factor determining the higher TVC score in a Presidential year.

Empirically, not all tracts exhibit such differences in electoral participation using this index of change. About 30 per cent of the Los Angeles sample survey tracts varied hardly at all in TVC ratio levels for consecutive elections. These we refer to as "steady state" *political domains*. At the other extreme, another 27 per cent showed increases of 10 or more percentage points for national over off-year election TVC ratios. These we call "vacillating" political domains. Between these extremes fall the rest of the Los Angeles sample survey tracts, with TVC ratio increases ranging from 2 to 9 percentage points. (Electoral statistics were not available for 11 of the original 67 census tracts.)

The TVC ratio derives from election statistics, generated for census tract units and spanning the period 1958 through 1964. As such, it serves as a bridge linking survey and census materials. First, the 1965 opinion survey results can be directly examined in light of 1960 demographic facts about the sampled tracts. Second, it is possible to interpret 1965 opinion patterns by reference to the 1958–1964 electoral change patterns of the tract areas. Because of the previously noted correlation between the electoral behavior of tract units and such 1960 census variables as residential stability, income level, and educational level, it is possible to make such comparisons and feel that any gross demographic changes making the 1960 census figures unreliable in 1965 have been adequately controlled by the TVC ratio classification. Basic ecological characterizations of the three types of "political domain" are presented in Table 1.

Interviews conducted in 1965, then, can be grouped according to the "political domain" in which the respondent lives. When this is done, our 1965 respondents are distributed as shown in Table 2. In comparing the three domains, note first that the population distributions by sex, age, and residential stability in each category are practically the same. More definite contrasts emerge when "steady state" and "vacillating" domains are examined on other counts. First, the proportion with at least some college education decreases from 55 per cent in "steady state" to 37 per cent in "vacillating" domains. Similarly, the proportion

Table 1

ELECTORAL AND ECOLOGICAL CHARACTERIZATIONS OF CONTRASTING LOS ANGELES POLITICAL DOMAINS

	Steady-State Domains (*N* = 17)	Mixed Areas (*N* = 24)	Vacillating Domains (*N* = 15)
Average TVC ratio, 1958 and 1962	80.25	76.28	73.00
Average TVC ratio, 1960 and 1964	81.21	82.94	85.53
1960 residential stability level (same abode as in 1955)	35.5%	38.6%	39.5%
1960 family income level	$8,309	$6,220	$5,966
Median years of school completed (persons 25 and older in 1960)	11.6	11.3	10.6

Table 2

SURVEY CHARACTERIZATIONS OF CONTRASTING LOS ANGELES POLITICAL DOMAINS (PERCENTAGES)

	Steady-State Domains (*N* = 213)	Mixed Areas (*N* = 218)	Vacillating Domains (*N* = 137)
1. Proportion female	51	48	54
2. Proportion over 40 years old	53	55	47
3. Proportion living at same address for six or more years, in 1965	35	35	32
4. Proportion with at least some college education	55	39	37
5. Proportion in white collar jobs	57	44	40
6. Proportion with 1965 family incomes over $10,000	44	32	21
7. Proportion married	82	72	65
8. Proportion who own their residence	83	59	39

engaged in white-collar occupations declines from 57 to 40 per cent, and the proportion with high incomes declines from 44 to 21 per cent. These economic and educational differences that were obtained by using survey materials correspond well to the domain descriptions according to 1960 census data displayed in Table 1. The population proportions in "steady state" and "vacillating" domains decline on two additional points: (1) the proportion married decreases from 82 to 65 per cent, which is an unusually sharp contrast to find on this variable; (2) the proportion of home owners falls even more precipitously, from 79 to 39 per cent.

These differentials may suggest analyses in terms of what social forces sustain different patterns of participation. Our concern here is with the attitudes and political participation patterns associated with residence in domains having markedly different levels of continuity in electoral participation. More specifically, what kinds of attitudes toward local political and civic affairs characterize individuals living in "steady state" as opposed to those residing in "vacillating" domains? A probing of this question illustrates the possibilities available in the use of *process* as a focus for analysis. Table 3 uses education as the test variable.

The first general observation concerning Table 3 is that the college-educated group in each category give very similar responses, indicating that domain makes little difference in their attitudes toward local affairs. Second, the non-college-educated group is not homogeneous in this sense, and the varying domains seem directly relevant.

More specifically, comparing people of different education levels living in the same type of domain suggests the importance of the political context. Consider first the "steady state" domain. On count after count, similar proportions of those with no college and those with college education said that: (1) they understood local issues fairly well; (2) they have sometimes tried to influence local government; (3) sometimes they might try to influence a local decision; and (4) they have felt that local police give them serious attention. Finally, in considering how to go about influencing a local government decision, those who said they would rely on the vote exhibit some educational differences, but the proportion who would turn to other individual modes of action is comparable.

Perhaps the most interesting finding to emerge is the extent to which educated people living in "vacillating" political domains mention group efforts as appropriate for implementing their political goals. In "vacillating" domains, nearly three times as many respondents with college education (56 per cent) as with no college education (20 per cent)

Table 3

ATTITUDES TOWARD LOCAL POLITICAL PROCESSES HELD BY RESPONDENTS OF CONTRASTING EDUCATIONAL STATUS LIVING IN DIFFERENT POLITICAL DOMAINS (PERCENTAGES)

	Respondents with Fuller Education			Respondents with Limited Education		
	Steady-State Domains (N = 118)	Mixed Areas (N = 85)	Vacillating Domains (N = 52)	Steady-State Domains (N = 93)	Mixed Areas (N = 133)	Vacillating Domains (N = 85)
1. Understand local issues at least fairly well	66	71	69	58	54	48
2. Sometimes have tried to influence local officials	42	42	44	29	17	14
3. Sometimes might try to influence local officials	66	63	67	58	46	32
4. Feels local police would give serious attention to his views	56	61	46	51	39	20
5. In trying to influence local officials would rely on voting	36	34	46	22	36	35
6. In trying to influence local officials would rely on individual actions other than voting	28	15	35	29	28	28
7. In trying to influence local officials would seek to use group methods	46	42	56	42	46	46

indicated that they would try to use group methods to influence local officials. The evidence in these data files cannot tell us whether this contrast reflects a lack of mutual neighborhood involvement or whether it reflects leadership among the educated in creating organizational structures presumably needed to compensate for or modify the character of the political domain itself.

Consider next the impact of a "vacillating" political domain. While well-educated people are apparently little affected by it, their neighbors with limited education respond to the ambiguous political scene by exhibiting discouragement and pessimism. Asked whether they understood local issues, only 48 per cent gave a positive response, compared with 69 per cent for their well-educated counterparts. On two other questions, the levels of positive orientation to local affairs indicated by those with limited education were more than thirty percentage points below those registered by their more fully educated neighbors.

SUMMARY

Initially, this research began with precinct information, census tract information, and interview materials gathered in a set of primary sampling units (psu's). The task of rendering precincts, tracts, and psu's comparable could not be avoided by any enterprise seeking to use these different sources of evidence to study a common problem. We have been concerned with the importance of being able to make concerted use of multiple data files to analyze political processes. Furthermore, we have tried to explore some of the intellectual puzzles involved in relating disparate data files to each other. Our focus has not been primarily on opinion data patterns, nor have we tried to classify respondents by census criteria. Rather our method has been to use electoral statistical patterns to classify people in terms of the political domains in which they participate.

Our findings show that educated people seem to be liberated from their environment. The neighborhood process characterized by vacillating electoral participation does not seem to affect the attitudes of educated people toward local political life. People with limited education, however, are considerably more vulnerable to the political processes that characterize their domain. In "steady state" domains, people of limited education on many counts express attitudes similar to their better-educated neighbors. This suggests that the political processes in these domains exhibit substantial integrative components. On the other hand, when people of limited education are found in "vacillating" domains, they often seem to lack both the ability and the will to participate in the local political process.

22

WOLFGANG HARTENSTEIN AND KLAUS LIEPELT

Archives for Ecological Research in West Germany

THERE HAVE always been archives, and there has always been the need to save documents from loss and destruction, to assemble paper from various sources at one place. Without archives, historians would be lost.

Data archives for the social and regional sciences is a novel phenomenon. Most social scientists today, who can do research without them, may have rather vague notions about their purpose. Indeed, there is little consensus even among the experts, and there have been shifts in their emphasis. The original function of data archives was copied from traditional archives: rescuing data that would otherwise be lost. In recent years, three needs that could be met by data archives have been articulated more clearly and will dominate the purely archival orientation: *research, training,* and *decision making.*

One of the more recent institutions in the field — DATUM[1] — reflects this new state of thinking.[2] Established in 1964 as a Documentation and Training Center in the Regional Sciences, it attempts to use data banks as instruments of urban analysis, regional planning, and advanced training.

DATUM must be seen within the institutional context of data gathering as well as urban research in West Germany. By looking both at this institutional context and at the specific effort DATUM has made to fit into it, some facets of general interest may become apparent.

---

[1] Dokumentations- und Ausbildungszentrum für Theorie und Methode der Regionalforschung, Bad Godesberg.

[2] Cf. "DATUM — A State of Aims" in *Social Science Information, 4*:3 (1965), pp. 187–190.

INTERESTS

As our concern is with ecological data and the kinds of uses to be expected from the systematic collection, storage, and manipulation of such data, there are three main types of interests involved here:

1. The regional scientist in a broad sense of the term, that is, the person engaged in the study of spatial phenomena, be it with emphasis on sociology, sociography, demography, economy, psychology, or political science

2. The producer of ecological data, that is, of information about people and their behavior, on the one hand, and the physical setting in which it takes place, on the other, and of information that can be located, that belongs to a place or moves between places

3. The person who is professionally engaged in the manipulation of the physical environment, particularly the urban and regional planner and the local decision maker

The relationship between these three professions has not been an altogether happy one in the past. Space, compared with time, has been a variable widely neglected in social and economic research. The interrelation between spatial and social structure, although of high relevance for the physical planner, has hardly been explored.

1. Social scientists have been only slightly interested in the physical environment or in the practical implications of their general findings for the planner; they have shown a strong preference for either surveys or census data and only recently have become aware of an approach that integrates the two.

2. Data producers have preferred the macro level and have not bothered with small units, partly because nobody asked for such information and partly because the handling of such large masses of data proved to be difficult.

3. Planners, with their typical background as designers, deal with the physical aspects of the city in their daily work but have difficulties in understanding changes and relationships they cannot see or draw. The kind of questions they put to the social scientist are not exactly those he has a ready answer for.

To be sure, much work and time and money have been invested in applied research during the last decade. But the practical and theoretical effect had been limited, for reasons that cannot be dealt with here. Lack of data has not been the primary problem. On the contrary, almost too much effort was sometimes directed toward the collection of data and their transformation (usually into a map).

The main point of this paper is that more use should and could be made of existing data, without the need to create one data center for the whole country.

FACTS

If the term "ecological data" refers to information aggregated for rather small units, such as communities, it would be hardly worth the trouble to collect and store this information at one place. Much of the work is already being done by the official census agencies. Later in this paper, it will be argued that a lower level of aggregation is desirable for many purposes.

Census activities follow the pattern of the administrative structure of the Federal Republic. There are 11 states (*Länder*); about 500 cities and counties (*Stadt- und Landkreise*), and about 25,000 localities and districts within the larger cities.

Although much more information is available on the level of the *Kreis* than of the locality, the amount of data gathered and published for communities is still impressive. Whereas the program is set up and co-ordinated by the federal Bureau of the Census, the eleven state offices are responsible for the publication and distribution of data below the *Kreis* level.[3]

The following groups of data are available for each of the 25,000 communities or city districts:

1. Social and demographic structure of the population
2. Employment
3. Economic structure
4. Commuting
5. Migration
6. Housing conditions
7. Election results

When working with these types of data their shortcomings will soon become evident. The material is abundant for the year of the census (the last one is 1960–1961) and poor for the years between censuses. Very

---

[3] The best survey on the census data available by smaller units is the *Quellennachweis regional-statistischer Ergebnisse,* ed. by the Statistische Bundesamt, Wiesbaden, in collaboration with the Statistische Landesämter, February 1966.

little is available for the prewar periods. In most cases, the analyst has to rely on published figures; working with the raw data or with cards or tapes is still the exception, partly for reasons of secrecy.[4] Because the data are kept, processed, and published at the eleven State Census Offices, and not always in an identical fashion, comparative research is not an easy job. Many questions cannot be answered with aggregated data for communities; for the time being, however, work at a level of aggregation below that is extremely difficult. And finally, only information that is part of the census programs or other official statistical activities can be found at the census offices. So far, no scheme has been developed to integrate materials from different sources.

Some of these problems could be solved by a research-oriented data center apart from or within the official agencies, but most of them would not. DATUM has sizable data collections (cards and tapes) on the community level, mostly from the 1961 Census. Its approach, however, is not to compete with existing institutions but to fill obvious gaps. As some of the limitations will be overcome in the near future, its activities are directed toward the 1970's rather than the 1960's. Therefore, it is worth having a brief look at the trends.

TRENDS

The most relevant changes in our context have to do with the techniques and tactics of data *production,* data *handling,* and data *utilization.*

Data Production

The General Census of 1970 is likely to differ from earlier ones in a number of ways:

1. The enumeration district used to be an oddly shaped, purely technical unit for which no data were available or asked for. At least in the larger cities, the new enumeration district will be identical with a block (that is, buildings surrounded by streets, with somewhere between 50 and 500 people), which at the same time is the lowest level of aggregation.

2. There is a general tendency away from publishing everything in books and tables but rather toward keeping data on cards or tape at the disposal of those who want them. This will become crucial in view of the

---

[4] The *Quellennachweis, op. cit.,* refers to published materials only and does not contain any information on card or tape.

sheer number of local units; there may be roughly 200,000 blocks in addition to the 25,000 communities.

3. The amount of information gathered has grown from census to census. It looks as if the next program will be a happy compromise between the need for continuity and the response to new demands from the practice of city planning.

This would mean more data on a smaller level of aggregation in a more manipulable form. This immediately raises the question of whether they will be used and manipulated.

Data Handling

The second trend has to do with the arrival of the computer in public administration. A number of larger cities already are using electronic data-processing equipment, mainly for the automation of certain branches of the administration; others have ordered or will soon order it. There are plans for some sort of local data banks that would hold administrative as well as census data. Before these data are aggregated on a higher level, such as the district or the communality, they can be stored either by street address or by block. Some of the cities have managed to obtain the 1961 and even the 1950 original data; most of them will try to keep a set of cards or tapes of the censuses to come.

Of particular interest for urban research, though largely neglected, are those data that are not part of a census or a specific survey but are, to use Rokkan's term, "process-produced," that is, generated by the daily processes of local administration — information on land use, population movements, car ownership, rent subsidies, etc. Data of this kind are collected for other purposes than analysis but constitute a rich source once the analyst has a chance to acquire them. Their main advantage is that they register changes at the moment when they occur.

In short, more and more data will be organized at the place where they are generated and where they are needed.

Data Utilization

During the last decade, there have been numerous studies in the field of urban development, carried out for the planning or some other department by outside institutions. Both university and nonuniversity institutions specialize in this field. These studies are somewhat random in their subjects and not altogether satisfying in their results.

There is a trend away from this custom. We can register a more systematic and long-range approach to city planning and regional development. The planning boards will be staffed more and more by people with a background in social science. First attempts are being made to use the computer and the data repositories for tasks beyond the mere automation of administrative procedures.

This is not general practice yet. The bureaucratic structure, the usual time lag between big cities and the smaller ones, and the lack of people trained in the use of data, methods, and machines will slow down the rate of progress possible with the computer. But it is certain that the situation in the 1970's will look quite different.

PERSPECTIVES

These trends should be taken into account when evaluating the prospects for systematic collection of "ecological" data. The DATUM approach, in the long run, aims at minimizing the costs and maximizing the benefits for public as well as research institutions. It starts from the assumption that it will be wiser, more practical, and more economical to support the growth and generation of existing data repositories than to establish some kind of "super archive."

The arguments in favor of such a decentralized solution may be briefly summarized:

1. *The smaller the unit of analysis, the greater is its utility for urban research.* Statistical studies today deal with data aggregated at the level of the community or — within larger cities — the district. Little can be said in favor of these units, which are large, oddly shaped, heterogenous in structure, and incongruent with natural areas, however defined. If data both on the physical and the social structure were to be assembled for a much smaller unit such as the block, these would be minor problems. It would then be possible to "construct" any area by accumulating data from several blocks until they show the size and shape desired, for example, of a specific market area, school district, polling district, or any other administrative unit.

2. *The sheer number of these units makes central storage and retrieval unfeasible.* At the present practice, data are available for about 25,000 local units (communalities or districts). Although bulky, such an array of information could be handled at one place, if necessary. If a block system was introduced, information for another 200,000 units would be gathered and asked for. It is, of course, technically possible to store the data from one census for all the blocks at one place, that is, the national Bureau of the Census, and keep them there forever. For all practical purposes, however, the data would not be accessible.

3. *The archive can grow only if it is located at a place where new information is generated.* If a unit such as the block is accepted as a meaningful and feasible level of aggregation, any additional data and their co-ordination with the original stock of information will enhance the value of the archive. Updating is one crucial issue; broadening the scope of the archive is another. Data repositories on the local level would profit from the fact that a community continuously produces new information. The main job is to organize the data flow. In the long run, census data are likely to constitute the most important, but not the most voluminous, section of the archive.

4. *Access to a local archive will be less restricted than to a central repository.* On the technical side, access could undoubtedly be facilitated within a decentralized scheme. As to the question of secrecy, experience has shown that it is much easier to work out a specific procedure for a specific problem (and finally acquire the data in a tolerable fashion) than to fight for a general policy of nonrestriction. There remains the problem of who will and can use a data center if there are a great many of them. One could argue that communication between archive and user would be smoother within a more centralized scheme. Whether this is the case depends on the quality of the reference system (cf. Point 10).

5. *The existence of local data archives will stimulate research.* This is obvious for the local planner and decision maker. Closer contact encourages more requests; more frequent communication will increase the quality of the request. If the archive is to be used not only for retrieval but also for analysis and projection, there is a chance that the local data archive may become an urban information system. The case is equally obvious for the person doing research on a specific locality or region. He will profit from a rich and well-organized data center; and the archive, in turn, will profit from the findings of his study. But even the social scientist not primarily concerned with ecological data and not familiar with the locality could take advantage of the local archive. At the very least, it would enrich survey practices by opening up new paths for "strategic" sampling.

6. *The distinction between the "ecological" and "survey" type of analysis or archive will become obsolete.* It might remain convenient to make the distinction on the level of data supply (public census agencies versus commercial survey outfits) and from a strictly methodological viewpoint. It will be hard to stick to it insofar as the nature of the data or the level of aggregation is concerned. Census policies already facilitate the use of individual data, for example, by providing analysts with a tape containing all the demographic variables for one per cent of the

population. The nature of "process-produced" data makes the distinction even more ambiguous. If archives are to become instruments of research, besides their storehouse function, any limitation as to the nature of the data will limit the potential use of the archive.

7. *The main distinction is between data banks defined by area and those defined by topic.* To put it crudely, one type of archive would comprise all information that could be located within a given area, without much regard for the kind of information; the other type would limit itself to the data relevant for a specific problem, the location of the data being one variable among others. In our context, such a "special-purpose data collection" could be concerned with topics such as occupational and residential mobility, traffic habits, urban renewal, or consumer behavior. It could be restricted in area as well, but its full potential lies in the fact that it would contain information from regions with different structure.

8. *Local data archives and special-purpose collections depend on each other.* The main consumers of a data archive defined by area will be local planners and decision makers as well as regional scientists interested in this particular area. The main consumers of the special-purpose collection will be regional or social scientists not satisfied with data taken out of one regional context. In many cases, the local archive can supply information on a specific problem that will then be included in the special-purpose collection, whereas the latter facilitates comparative research, produces findings of more general relevance, and supports the development of indices, typologies, computer programs, etc., which in turn can be used in the local data bank.

PREREQUISITES

Although the trends point in this direction, such a network of local archives communicating with one another and with central holdings will not come about and function automatically. To be sure, the whole scheme does not depend on the complete and simultaneous creation of local archives all over the country. It could function as a step-by-step operation, largely parallel to the introduction of electronic data processing into public administration.

Several other conditions, however, have to be fulfilled before such a configuration can work satisfactorily:

9. *The local data archives should be basically organized in a similar fashion.* A certain degree of similarity is secured by the standardized practices of census taking, by the rather uniform procedures in German

local administration, and by the technical requirements of central data management. The computer, once it is there, will set the rules of the game; among other things, it will make changes in format, labeling, etc., easier. In other words, a standard setup of all local archives would make research with them more convenient but is by no means a necessary (and realistic) condition.

10. *All the holdings must be documented at one central place.* The outside world, and the academic community in particular, will gain little from local repositories unless there is a quick and easy way of knowing where to find what. The same is true for the special-purpose data collections. The inventory must, in its most basic form, allow two kinds of approaches. Given a certain area and/or general topic, what kind of data will I be able to find? Given a specific kind of data, where will I be able to find it? In both cases, there should be detailed information on the storage media, level of aggregation, accessibility, exact location in space and time, etc. It is evident that such a reference system should be developed, kept, and updated at one central place in close collaboration with the data holders themselves. It must be easily reproducible and distributable.

11. *Programs for processing and analysis of data must be provided for.* It is one thing to set up an archive, or a network of archives, to guarantee access, and to provide for documentation. It is another thing actually to work with the archives. The enormous task of preparing routines for cleaning, updating, and setting up processing procedures and statistical programs should not and cannot be left to each archive individually. Part of the job remains with the immediate user: the city management, planning department, or research staff. What is needed, however, is a vehicle for communication among data banks, not so much for data but for programs. Such a central library should contain programs developed and tested elsewhere; it should evaluate them and integrate them into a system for statistical processing and analysis that is both flexible and consumer-oriented.

POSSIBILITIES

There can be no doubt that the possibilities for quantitative ecological research will be greatly enhanced once such a network of regional archives and means of communication between them exist. DATUM is convinced that the scheme is realistic and that it is worth the effort to make it operational.

From the discussion so far it is evident that DATUM has to proceed on four levels at the same time. These four activities are reflected in the organizational structure, which is described elsewhere.[5] In the long run, DATUM is expected to provide: (1) data, (2) information about data, (3) instruments of analysis, and (4) training.

Data Collections

For reasons elaborated in detail in this paper, little effort has been made to collect and store large masses of data. The main emphasis will be on data that are relevant to a specific problem but stem from different sources and are not normally accessible at the same time. The collections will thus be topical in the sense of Point 7 and will be part of ongoing research projects. The first DATUM projects have to do with questions of occupational and residential mobility and with social structure and social change in urban renewal areas.[6]

There are aggregated data that are of obvious relevance to these topics, such as census data on the structure of the labor or housing market. There are surveys especially designed to cover the problem. But beyond that, there are numerous other pieces of information that have to be located, pulled together, and related to other pieces of information. Many sample surveys, for instance, contain questions on first and present job, on location of home and firm, on recent moves. Instead of rescuing and storing complete studies, with the technical problems of transformation, formats, etc., DATUM will extract only the necessary information, make it as compatible as possible with other data, and bring it into a computer-manipulable form. These "special-purpose data collections," rather than the original data, can then be used effectively by the research community.

Documentation

As the purely archival functions of DATUM are played down somewhat, it becomes even more important to know where to find what and how (cf. Point 9). Data relevant for regional planning and research have to be documented centrally before any efficient communication between existing data collections can be realized. The coverage here should be as broad as possible and extend far beyond the research

[5] "Data on DATUM," paper presented at the Third ISSC Conference on Data Archives, London, April 1966.

[6] "Zum Forschungsprogramm von DATUM," Doc. No. 914/001 (Bad Godesberg: DATUM, May 1966), and "Soziale Prozesse in Sanierungsgebieten," Doc. No. 909/005 (March 1967).

topics. The main inventory (*Fundortkatalog*) should contain the following minimum information: kind of item; unit of reference (individual, household, building, firm, area, etc.); level of aggregation; location; date; type of survey or census; storage medium; other variables in the same document; accessibility.

Both the technical aspects and the problems of classification are still under discussion. There exist a number of useful schemes for inventorizing either official census data (which are highly standardized and present few problems) or survey data.[7] No serious attempt has yet been made to cover the great many nonofficial and semiofficial data. And no scheme has yet been developed applicable to data from different sources, census and survey alike. As DATUM will be working with a variety of data, the documentation program must be sufficiently wide in scope.

Systems Research

For concerted analysis of data of different origin, as is often the case in regional studies, there has to be a processing and manipulation system that contains a variety of programs and is highly flexible in use. In order to assess the merits of various approaches, DATUM has organized a Conference on Technical Aspects of a Regional Information System.[8] Special attention was given to SPAN (Statistical Processing and Analysis System), which was designed for regional analysis by Systems Development Corporation[9] and is now being remodeled for more general use in social and political research. DATUM has been invited to join these activities. On the one hand, a joint endeavor of this kind will make international communication much easier; on the other, it provides DATUM with an analytical tool that has already been operative in social and regional research.

Furthermore, it will eventually be used as a vehicle of communication between different data repositories. At this preliminary stage, DATUM functions as a consulting agency for the organization and design of local

[7] In the survey field, the Steinmetz Stichting, Amsterdam, has developed a classification scheme for an inventory of European holdings which applies not only to complete studies but to single items. The scheme is presently being tested on the survey data of the Institut für angewandte Sozialwissenschaft, from which the bulk of the DATUM survey material will come.

[8] The results of the technical conference are conveniently summarized in the final report by Dwaine Marvick, included in *Erster Bericht über DATUM*, Doc. No. 901/009 (Bad Godesberg: DATUM, September 1965).

[9] Cf. Vladimir V. Almendinger, *SPAN: A System for Data Management* (Santa Monica: Systems Development Corporation, 1964).

data banks. There exist well-established routines for the automation of certain administrative activities;[10] there is the widespread, if still somewhat abstract, belief that the goal is an "integrated" data-processing system; but there are only rudimentary notions of how long-range planning and policy decisions can be based upon an urban information system: how to find the relevant data, how to make them compatible and accessible, and how to manipulate them.[11]

Training

Public administration is a rather conservative and inflexible institution. Acceptance of a new technology and a new style of problem solving will be slow; but once it is accepted in principle, changes in organization and philosophy will be massive and thorough. It is extremely difficult, however, to adjust the personnel to these changes. There is a definite lack of people familiar with research methods, data handling, or computer techniques. Academic facilities hardly provide this kind of training. What is needed is a wide range of programs designed for different groups of people.

In its training program, DATUM[12] is going to concentrate on mainly two levels; there are other institutions that take care of other interests.[13] In a series of one-day conferences, leading planners and administrators will become acquainted with the general principles and problems of electronic data processing and its application in research and planning. The main emphasis will be on two-week seminars for younger people from planning departments, census offices, and research institutions. In these small workshops, the participants will be exposed to a case study, taken from one of the research projects, which gives them a chance to become familiar with the potential of an urban information system.

[10] For a number of years, the Kommunale Gemeinschaftsstelle für Verwaltungsvereinfachung, Cologne, has carefully studied these problems and made realistic proposals.

[11] The expectations of urban planning and urban research vis-à-vis local electronic data processing machinery have been discussed and formulated by a DATUM Conference in August 1965; see *Daten und Datensysteme für Stadtplanung und Regionalforschung,* Doc. No. 903/016 (Bad Godesberg: DATUM, January 1966).

[12] *Zum Fortbildungsprogramm von DATUM,* Doc. No. 907/003 (Bad Godesberg: DATUM, November 1965).

[13] The Verein für Kommunalwissenschaften, Berlin, plans a series of seminars for top management in public administration.

23

RODNEY STIEFBOLD

Ecological Data
on Austria

THIS PAPER seeks to summarize briefly recent Austrian experience in the generation and analysis of quantifiable data that are potentially relevant to the political scientist in performing computerized cross-national or cross-local comparative ecological analysis. The discussion will encompass not only academic research but also the relevant activities of commercial "data brokers," such as institutes for regional and urban planning and public opinion polling agencies. In the course of our discussion, we hope to indicate both the *obstacles* and the *opportunities* posed for data archiving and ecological research in Austria today — at precisely that point in time when fresh political winds are blowing (following dissolution of the twenty-year Great Coalition in April 1966) and creating new opportunities for social science research. That research and politics could be so closely connected may seem strange to the outsider; yet in this highly politicized, "segmentalized" society, social science research was for many years little more than a plaything of political party and interest group elites.[1]

GENERAL BACKGROUND

As several recent reports on historical trends and contemporary research activities in Austrian social science clearly demonstrate, Austria can claim a distinguished and innovative tradition of empirical

[1] Notable exceptions were the "Religious Sociography" studies sponsored by the Institut für kirchliche Sozialforschung in Vienna.

social-ecological research.[2] As early as the second half of the eighteenth century, government statisticians had assembled extensive data on the demographic, economic, and religious structure of communities throughout much of Austria-Hungary; this tradition of social, economic, and cultural cartography (or "social geography") has strongly influenced Austrian methods of data collection and handling down to the present day.[3]

Partly because of the development of Austrian "sociology" as metaphysical social criticism, partly because of traditional resistance by Austrian academic circles to the establishment of social science research centers within the universities, and partly, of course, because of the institutional advantages in data collection originally enjoyed by the territorial state, innovations in techniques of empirical ecological research typically emanated from official government statisticians. Thus the first data-based efforts to move analysis from variations at the level of proximal territorial units to variations at the level of individuals were made by government electoral statisticians in the late nineteenth and early twentieth centuries. Their technique consisted of drawing inferences about individual behavior from their observations of contrasting sets of juxtaposed maps and from simple statistical manipulations of aggregate data. By the 1920's the central statistical office had advanced to the analysis of primary data on some types of mass political behavior; the data were collected by means of colored ballots differentiating voters by sex.

Finally, in the early 1930's, Paul Lazarsfeld and his associates launched their pioneering studies on the social relations and attitudes of youth and unemployed workers in Marienthal, using a combination of primary data on personal attributes and behavior, derived contextual

[2] For reviews of Austrian traditions in social science, see L. Rosenmayr, "Austrian Sociology — Past and Present: Notes on Some Historical Trends and Present Activities," *Social Science Information, 4* (1965), pp. 85–101; L. Rosenmayr (with E. Kochkeis), *Sociology in Austria: History, Present Activities and Projects* (Graz: Koeln, 1966); F. O. Heyt and L. A. Vaskovics, "Soziologie in Oesterreich," in G. Eisermann (ed.), *Die gegenwärtige Lage der Soziologie, Beiträge zur Soziologie, 2* (Stuttgart: 1966); and F. O. Heyt and L. A. Vaskovics, "Sozialforschung und Soziologie in Oesterreich: Stand und Entwicklung seit 1945," *Koelner Zeitschrift für Soziologie and Sozialpsychologie, 18*:1 (1966), pp. 94–116. On recent developments see also Erich Bodzenta (ed.), *Soziologie und Soziologiestudium* (Vienna: Springer Verlag, 1966), pp. 110–119.

[3] Cf. R. Engelmann, "Die topographisch-statistischen Werke Oesterreichs," *Mitteilungen der Geographischen Gesellschaft in Wien, 69* (1927), pp. 273–282; and E. Arnberger, "Grundlagen und Methoden zur kartographischen Darstellung der Bevölkerungsentwicklung der letzten hundert Jahre in Oesterreich," *Mitteilungen der Oesterreichischen Geographischen Gesellschaft, 102* (1960), pp. 271–313.

data on individuals, and data on both global and aggregate attributes of the territorial setting.[4] But if Lazarsfeld's work promised new departures in sociological research, drawing on interview and survey data in conjunction with detailed ecological data, the promise was abruptly betrayed — in its Austrian setting — by the advent of National Socialism. Lazarsfeld and most of his colleagues left Austria, establishing in 1937 the Bureau of Applied Social Research at Columbia University in New York.

In many ways Austrian social science was set back nearly a generation by the events of the 1930's and 1940's. The major impediment to future ecological study was not so much in the production of data, although the constant realignment of territorial boundaries at all levels makes longitudinal analysis encompassing the thirties, forties, and even early fifties a tedious and virtually insuperable task. Rather, the principal obstacle lay in the severely restricted facilities for academic training and research and, concomitantly, in the paucity of serious analytical research undertaken and completed during that period. The strong influence of traditional approaches in the universities, the prejudice against new methods, the decimations of the Nazi and Dollfuss years and the intellectual and generational hiatus created by them, the manifold administrative and advisory tasks imposed on university professors, which left them little time for research, and widespread popular sentiment against attempts to study private attitudes or even "public opinion" for fear of attempted manipulation — all combined to produce a relatively inhospitable research environment.

To be sure, empirical sociology — but not political science — was gradually introduced into the university curriculum. The Social Science Research Center under Leopold Rosenmayr was established at the University of Vienna in 1954; the Institute for Empirical Sociology and Statistics under Johann Mokre opened in Graz in 1958; and in autumn of 1966 the College of Social and Economic Sciences in Linz matriculated its first students. Outside the universities a number of commercial and independent academic institutes, most of which are discussed elsewhere in this paper, began to provide limited facilities and training as early as 1952.

The paucity of facilities for training scholars and carrying out research projects utilizing quantified ecological data has hindered the development of Austrian research and methodological experimentation.

[4] M. Jahoda, P. F. Lazarsfeld, and H. Zeisel, *Die Arbeitslosen von Marienthal* (Vienna: 1933; 2nd ed., Allensbach and Bonn, Verlag für Demoskopie, 1960).

On the other hand, the mere availability of a sufficient range of usable raw data — not only on individual attributes and behavior but also for territorial units from the level of the commune (*Gemeinde*) and administrative county (*politischer Bezirk*) to the aggregate national level — ought to encourage rapid innovation in research as well as in methods of analysis.

AVAILABILITY AND TYPES OF DATA

Several types of organizations serving highly diversified commercial official, and academic clienteles are presently engaged in the generation of data relevant to ecological analysis. Among the most important, although not necessarily alone in their fields, are the following:

1. The Austrian Central Statistical Office. This produces a wide range of global and aggregate data for different territorial units.[5]

2. The Co-ordinating Center of the nine Provincial Statistical Offices. This operates within the Economic Section of the Lower Austrian Provincial Government. It collates finançial, demographic, social, cultural, and political data (both global and aggregate) for communes, counties, election districts, and provinces, and then it republishes the data in non-machine-readable form.[6]

3. Commercial research institutes, such as the Vienna-based institutes for regional (both rural and urban) research and planning and for basic economic research. These institutes maintain large staffs of experts in statistical geography, social ecology, and related disciplines. Each owns extensive data files, partly in punch-card form, consisting of both primary (global attribute) and aggregate data for territorial units.[7]

4. The statistical sections of the major economic interest groups and principal semipublic occupational chambers (*Kammern*). They compile data on individual party and group affiliations at different levels of society and polity.[8]

[5] Oesterreichisches Statistisches Zentralamt.

[6] Verbindungsstelle der Oesterreichischen Bundesländer, Amt der Niederoesterreichischen Landesregierung.

[7] Institut für Raumforschung und Raumplanung, Vienna, and Institut für Wirtschaftsforschung, Vienna.

[8] Space does not permit a comprehensive listing of these bodies. Suffice it to say that the major "private" economic interest groups in labor, business, and agriculture, as well as their principal semipublic chamber affiliates, are critically important "data-generators." They are probably more important than equivalent organizations in most other European societies because of the pervasive interlocking organization of Austrian social, political, and economic life. These organizations frequently

5. Commercial survey research organizations. There are three of these at the national level, all based in Vienna.[9]

6. Academic research institutes, such as the Social Science Research Center, at the University of Vienna, which has sponsored sociological and ecological studies on the family and youth, using sample surveys within small territorial units.[10]

The first three of these sets of organizations specialize in the production of primary or derived aggregate data for *territorial units*; the last three are concerned chiefly with the compilation of primary statistical information or survey research on the personal attributes or behavior of *individuals*.

Several shortcomings temper the utility of this fund of data:

1. While the development of sample survey data has become increasingly sophisticated over time (a problem in itself, since comparability with earlier surveys, particularly those by the nonprofit trade union-supported and Socialist-supported Social Science Studies Group, is difficult), surveys have been conducted relatively haphazardly in terms of both geographic areas analyzed and data collected. This is inevitable, for commercial survey research has been undertaken chiefly in response to the pragmatic momentary needs of the client, political parties, or their sponsoring interest asosciations.[11]

---

possess more "hard" data resources than relevant federal ministries. Perhaps the most extensive resources may be found in the Chamber for Workers and Employees, Vienna, Division on Education. (*Kammer für Arbeiter und Angestellte für Wien, Abteilung für Schul- und Bildungswesen*).

[9] Austrian Gallup Institute (*Oesterreichisches Gallup-Institut*); Dr. Fessel Institut für Markt- und Meinungsforschung; Institut für empirische Sozialforschung (IFES). In addition to these three commercial organizations, there are several others affiliated with parties or interest groups. The most important of these is the Social Science Studies Group (*Sozialwissenschaftliche Studiengesellschaft*).

[10] Sozialwissenschaftliche Forschungsstelle am Institut für Soziologie, University of Vienna. Other academic research institutes that generate similar types of data (contextual data on individuals) through the conduct of specific research projects are: Institute for Empirical Sociology and Statistics (*Institut für empirische Soziologie und Statistik*), University of Graz; Institute for Agrarian Politics and Sociology (*Institut fur Agrarpolitik und Agrarsoziologie*), Vienna; Institute for Advanced Studies and Scientific Research (*Institut für höhere Studien und wissenschaftliche Forschung*), Vienna.

[11] A compilation and discussion of polls conducted up to and including the 1966 parliamentary election, which marked the end of twenty years of coalition government in postwar Austria, will appear in a forthcoming book by Rodney Stiefbold, *Elections and the Political Order in Austria (1945–1966)*, Chapter 5 and Appendix I.

2. Another problem that severely compromises data usability is the inadequacy of many of the official Austrian census categories. For example, the census classification *Handel und Verkehr* includes transportation workers as well as merchants and bankers, while the term "salaried employees" refers simultaneously to salesgirls and managers of large industrial enterprises.

3. In addition to problems caused by the heterogeneity of socioeconomic groupings in the occupational statistics, another perplexing feature of official aggregate data is the failure of the Central Statistical Office to include in the publications on electoral statistics *Gemeinde* (commune) and other boundary changes that occur from one national parliamentary election to the next. These data can be found, but the process is often time-consuming and expensive. Nor are the occasional publications on boundary changes cross-referenced in electoral publications. Finally, these publications often are unavailable for a decade or more following issuance of official rating statistics, which considerably compromise the accuracy of many of the existing electoral studies of twentieth-century Austria.[12]

Nonetheless, despite different levels of sophistication in sampling and gathering, despite frequent failure of publications to specify problems encountered in delimiting precisely the territorial or aggregate individual sampling units, despite different levels of "hardness" of data, let alone "cleanliness" of available machine-formulated data — many of which problems persist elsewhere — the bulk of ecologically relevant data is probably comparable in usefulness to that produced in most other Western European countries.

A preliminary list and discussion appear in Stiefbold, "Politische Meinungsforschung in Oesterreich, 1954–1965," in Peter Gerlich, Georg Ress, and Rodney Stiefbold (eds.), *Die Nationalratswahl 1966* (Vienna: Verlag für Jugend und Volk, 1968).

The Austrian electoral system has had an interesting effect on the generation of survey research studies; the number of deputies allotted to specific election districts is computed on the basis of the number of citizens residing there (including minors); consequently, there is a premium on a good showing at election time in districts with high birth rates. Hence, there are a number of (highly classified) survey studies of small territorial units in high-natality western Austria. This subject is discussed further in Stiefbold, *Elections and the Political Order, op. cit.*, Chapters 3–5. The Austrian electoral system is described in Uwe Kitzinger, "The Austrian Electoral System," *Parliamentary Affairs, 12* (1959), pp. 392–404.

[12] An invaluable source for the period 1945–1961 is the Oesterreichische Statistisches, Zentralamt, *Gebiets- und Namensänderungen in der Verwaltungseinteilung Oesterreichs* (Vienna: Carl Ueberreuter Verlag, 1962). It also contains bibliographies of sources on boundary changes in the Austrian provinces since 1869.

DATA ARCHIVES FOR SOCIAL SCIENCE RESEARCH

None of the organizations mentioned earlier has archived more than its own studies (plus some official census and/or political data from federal government sources, depending on the organization's particular needs); indeed, some organizations have destroyed whole decks of punch cards from earlier years for lack of sufficient storage space or because the cards are not considered of commercial value.[13] A central data archive or co-ordinating body such as the American Inter-University Consortium for Political Research or the Roper center may be able to prevent such irretrievable losses in the near future.

But even if Austrians, in a new spirit of co-operative social science planning, should resolve the usual problems connected with data archiving, one major obstacle would remain: that of *access* to many of the most important studies. The declassification of data is a serious problem in many countries; in Austria it is a critical one, for large reservoirs of both aggregate and survey data were originally generated for political purposes by political parties, interest groups, or government ministries at various territorial levels. In such a sensitive society as Austria, where "hard" political, social, or economic data (even those easily obtainable from the Central Statistical Office) have often been regarded as a scarce, vitally important "resource," to be guarded jealously,[14] and a society in which general social, cultural, and political

[13] For example, the Austrian Gallup Institute conducted a number of electoral surveys in the early 1950's, some on the basis of small regional samples prior to provincial and communal elections, which it recently destroyed. It retained copies of the data "reports" only, which contain only the very few single-variable tabulations demanded at the time by the political interest group client.

[14] Publication of the first comprehensive work on contemporary Austrian elections and political sociology, *Wahlen und Parteien* (cited in footnote 15), provoked a storm of protest from both major political parties (the Socialist Party and the Austrian People's Party), which charged that the Institute for Advanced Studies in Vienna intentionally generated or reproduced data and documents that were deleterious to the parties' electoral interests. Both parties subsequently apologized and retracted the allegations; indeed, recent reviews in party-related publications have been appreciative and favorable. In fact, all primary materials reprinted were previously in the public domain, although many of the analyses were original. The initial reaction was part of a traditional syndrome that first began to dissipate in the period following the March 1966 parliamentary elections and the dissolution of the Great Coalition.

Interviews with party, interest group, and polling organization personnel turned up numerous instances in the past when party or group officials had commissioned surveys and/or aggregate data studies, ostensibly for electoral purposes, without ever using or even reading them. For one of the few published comments on the use, misuse, and nonuse of such material, see Otto Lackinger, "Die Wählerschaft unter

mistrust still casts long shadows over social "science" research, the problem of access can scarcely be overemphasized.

The inauguration in 1961 of the Institute for Advanced Studies and Scientific Research (IHS/Vienna), however, marked a positive step toward removing this barrier to social science research. The Institute, an independent academic center for advanced training and research in the social sciences, is supported by grants from the Ford Foundation, the Austrian Federal Government, and the Vienna municipal government. It was established, in part, to redress the existing research imbalances and supplement the teaching and use of social science methods in Austrian higher education.

The Institute maintains a complete array of unit record equipment for the processing and analysis of punch cards, and has recently completed installation of an IBM 1620 computer. Plans are being developed to acquire, process, store, and maintain machine-readable data and supporting documentation from a number of organizationally distinct Austrian data sources. IHS/Vienna plans to archive data from Austrian demographic, fiscal, agricultural, cultural, religious, and educational enumerations. It is also negotiating with relevant commercial organizations

---

der Lupe," *Politische Perspektiven,* November 1965. Indeed, the question of whether or not it is even *legitimate* to carry out such studies has been a subject of heated debate in the Socialist Party until very recently. Among many articles on this subject appearing in the Socialist bimonthly *Die Zukunft,* see especially that by Willi Liwanec, "Meinungsforschung und politische Arbeit," *23* (December 1965), pp. 5–7.

These taboos are rapidly disappearing, however. There has been a marked growth of serious public interest in politics, as well as an increase in the gathering and dissemination of information about politics; furthermore, incumbent political and social elites appear to be becoming more tolerant of the spread of both information and criticism. Several factors have abetted these developments:

1. The gain in political importance during the late coalition era of the nonparty press

2. Competition among several publishing houses (such as Molden, Herder, and Europa) for a newly discovered commercial "political interest" market

3. The writings of a number of bright, well-informed, and incisive political journalists, respected as "political scientists," who offer constructive criticisms of contemporary politics

4. The emergence of internal "technocratic" oppositions in each of the major political parties

5. Persistent, determined, and eventually highly effective reform mongering by leading publicists in the democratic center of the political spectrum

6. The enhanced political relevance and importance of old — and the establishment of new — nonparty, independent research institutes

7. The creation of the new College of the Social and Economic Sciences in Linz and the concomitant passage of new federal legislation designed to modernize social science curriculums in Austrian institutions of higher learning.

for establishment on its premises of a depository for public opinion surveys carried out in Austria.[15] For the time being, data will be archived only for the units for which it is available; later it will be converted, insofar as possible, to standard geographical units.[16]

Data-archiving plans are also currently under discussion by such diverse organizations as the Department of Sociology at the new College of the Social and Economic Sciences at Linz, the statistical offices of the federal provinces, working through their Co-ordinating Office, and an *ad hoc* group of political party officials and representatives of the three major polling organizations.

STRATEGIES OF ECOLOGICAL ANALYSIS

Since these problems of data organization and access do exist, what types of ecological research have been undertaken? Following Dogan and Rokkan,[17] one might identify several approaches to quantitative ecological research in contemporary Austrian social science, differentiating them by the following criteria:

1. *Level of analysis.* Are they interested primarily in variations among individuals, among territorial units, or within or among total social systems in small-scale territorial units?

2. *Purpose* or the direction of their explanatory efforts. Are they interested in description or explanation? In snapshots of a particular point in time or in the dimensions of change over time? And with what dependent variables are they primarily concerned?

---

[15] A first product of these plans, which have evolved organically in response to the Institute's needs for data for training purposes, was the three-volume collection of electoral documents, data, and analyses published under Institute auspices early in 1966: Rodney Stiefbold, Georg Ress, Arlette Leupold-Loewenthal, Walther Lichem, and Dwaine Marvick (eds.), *Wahlen und Parteien in Oesterreich: Oesterreichisches Wahlhandbuch* (Vienna: Oesterreichischer Bundesverlag/Verlag für Jugend und Volk, 1966).

[16] The smallest territorial unit of independent external representation in Austria is the commune (*Gemeinde*), but for some items — varying from census to census and from election to election — data are not tabulated below the level of the administrative county (*politischer Bezirk*). Moreover, the periodic boundary changes at the commune level and the relative stability of boundaries at the county level also favor the use of counties. *Gerichtsbezirke*, or court districts, have experienced even greater stability of boundaries, making them a third possible alternative for the primary archival units. For details on available data from election to election since 1869, see R. Stiefbold and R. Metzlar-Anderberg, "Austria," in S. Rokkan and J. Meyriat (eds.), *International Guide to Electoral Statistics*, Vol. I (Paris: Mouton, 1968).

[17] See pp. 3–11 of their Introduction to this volume.

3. *Type of data base utilized.* Are they interested in global and aggregate data for territorial units, survey and derived contextual data for individuals, or both simultaneously?

4. *Actual methods of analysis employed* in processing data at one level or the other.

In terms of the first three criteria, several partly overlapping but nonetheless distinct approaches can be distinguished. We might designate these different approaches as follows:

1. *Religious sociography*, an approach identified with the Institut für kirchliche Sozialforschung (IKS/Vienna) and its former director, Erich Bodzenta. This approach utilizes territorial aggregate data (or the original raw individual data in those cases where local authorities have preserved them and will permit their use for scientific research purposes) in an attempt to describe and explain variations in individual behavior, particularly with respect to individual participation in church-related activities.[18]

2. *Social ecology*, an approach identified with the Social Science Research Center and its director, Leopold Rosenmayr, with the work of Rosenmayr's student, Richard Gisser, with the Institute for Rural Sociology and its director, Ernst Lagler, with much of the work of Erich Bodzenta, and, finally, with some of the more recent studies sponsored by IKS/Vienna and directed by Laszlo Vaskovics. This approach is characterized by the combination of primary data on individual variations (from the raw, nonaggregated census data, interviews, or sample surveys), with detailed ecological analyses of the proximal contexts of such variations. It not only seeks explanations for current variations but also attempts to isolate sources and dimensions of change.

3. *Political ecology*, an approach identified with the studies of Herbert Tingsten, Robert Danneberg, and the Federal Statistical Office in the First Austrian Republic, and, among others, with Walter Simon, Otto Lackinger, and the Vienna Municipal Statistical Office in the Second Republic. Based on official aggregate census data, voting statistics, and local electoral registers, this approach involves the analysis of electoral turnout by categories of citizens differentiated by sex, age, and/or occupation, and the study of official tabulations of party votes by sex,

[18] Internationales katholisches Institut für kirchliche Sozialforschung, Abteilung Oesterreich, 1952–1962; since 1962, Institut für kirchliche Sozialforschung.

Methodological questions are discussed in Erich Bodzenta *et al.*, "Kirchliche Sozialforschung und Seelsorge; Berichte aus Oesterreich," *Der Seelsorger, 26* (1956); E. Bodzenta, "Forschungen in Oesterreich," *Social Compass, 6* (1959).

age, and/or occupation of voters. In each case the purpose is to describe variations in individual behavior by types of political locality (election districts, for example).

4. *Attitudinal ecology*, an approach identified with the polling institutes, particularly that of Karl Blecha. Based on community, provincial, or other regional sample surveys of the Austrian population, this approach has thus far involved the mere description of patterns of individual attitudes — but also, of course, of other forms of behavior for which the data provide evidence — within given localities.[19]

5. *Social geography*, an approach identified with Hans Bobek and Erich Arnberger. It consists in the production of detailed maps (in the style of the French schools of human and electoral geography) depicting environmental, demographic, social, economic, and political variations for official census-tract territorial units. Bobek has refined the strategy by development of commune typologies and the further production of maps for the typological units.[20]

6. *Regional and urban ecology*, an approach identified with Johannes Mokre and the Institute for Sociology and Statistics at the University of Graz, with the Institute for Regional Research and its director, Karl Stiglbauer, and with various social scientists and official statistical offices studying urban dwelling structures and patterns. This school focuses attention on territorial economic and social variables, not only for the purpose of describing unique local constellations but also to test general hypotheses about the consequences of variation and the sources of long-term change. Within this school, some urban ecologists

[19] Outstanding recent examples are Karl Blecha, *Die soziale Integration ehemaliger Bergarbeiter in Betrieben der Eisen- und Stahlindustrie* (Vienna: Institut für empirische Sozialforschung, 1966; volume one of a projected series entitled *Soziologische Diagnosen*); and Hans Strotzka, I. Leitner, G. Czerwenka-Wenkstetten, and S. R. Graupe, *Soziale Bedingungen psychischer Krankheit: Eine sozialpsychiatrische Feldstudie* (Vienna: Institute for Advanced Studies, 1966; mimeographed). Here we are distinguishing "attitudinal ecology" from other variants of ecological research, chiefly because of its specific choice of attitudes as dependent variables. However, to the extent that the survey researcher employs ecological data for proximal territorial units in which individual behaviors are being studied by means of poll data, this category overlaps both the first type of social-ecological research described previously and the work of those urban ecologists who, on the basis of mixed data types, analyze both ecological typologies of dwelling areas and differential individual behaviors across the different areas.

[20] Hans Bobek has edited the *Atlas der Republik Oesterreich* (Vienna: Kartographische Anstalt, Freytag-Berndt u. Artaria, 1962 ——). He has previously developed a very useful typology of ecological communities; see H. Bobek, A. Hammer, and R. Ofner, *Beiträge zur Ermittlung von Gemeindetypen* (Klagenfurt: Selbstverlag der Oesterreichischen Gesellschaft zur Förderung von Landesforschung und Landesplanung, 1955).

have occasionally worked with combinations of individual and territorial data for this purpose.[21]

This sketch identifies the principal ecological research traditions in
contemporary Austrian social science in terms of level of analysis,
purposes, and data bases. In terms of methods used in processing
available data, one can identify the following as the most typical and
frequently employed techniques:

1. The construction of simple typologies of available territorial units
and the straightforward contrasting of resultant distributions of aggregated individual behaviors

2. The construction of percentage indexes of selected behavioral
phenomena and the straightforward contrasting of their territorial
distributions

3. The comparison of paired maps contrasting territorial attributes
and aggregated behaviors, permitting visual cartographic correlations

In most cases more sophisticated statistical techniques, such as partial
or multiple correlation, or regression analysis, have not yet been used
in handling quantified ecological data. Moreover, most of the approaches cited previously are *descriptive*. They are concerned primarily
with describing concrete variations between territorial units or agglomerations of individual behaviors which they regard as essentially unique.
But an important core group — those identified earlier as social,
political, or urban ecologists — traditionally has been *comparatively*
and/or *developmentally* oriented. In some cases these analysts have been
concerned with the development of general propositions about the
consequences of variations in local community structures or in patterns
of behavior of particular groups of individuals; in other cases they have
attempted to construct general hypotheses about the sources and dimensions of change, and indeed they have developed a number of highly

---

[21] This approach to ecological analysis has a heavy planning bias; that is, it is
identified with official, goal-oriented efforts on the part of governmental and administrative authorities to discover past trends and prevailing patterns of territorial
economic and social life in order more effectively to anticipate and direct change.
Even when using individual data, regional and urban ecologists do so primarily in
order to characterize better the area(s) under study.

Finally, we should note that some of the publications of the private economic
interest groups and their semipublic chambers, as well as the *Monatsberichte* and
Beilagen of the Institute for Economic Research, belong in this category of approaches to ecological research in present-day Austria, despite the fact that they
usually base their analyses on data aggregated for large units — the provinces or
the national state.

sophisticated models of various part-processes of social change and modernization.

No doubt, the considerable *expertise* achieved by past and present Austrian social scientists in the manipulation of masses of ecological data by "traditional" methods has helped pave the way for a relatively rapid and smooth transition to the age of data processing by electronic computers. But what is urgently needed now is that high degree of bipartisan political co-operation which is absolutely necessary if younger Austrian social scientists are to have available even the minimum resources and independence requisite for that transition.

24

JORGE GARCIA-BOUZA*

The Future Development of Social Science Data Archives in Latin America

THE PRESENT REPORT lists the principal obstacles to the development of modern social science data archives in Latin America, discusses the individual and institutional resources that may be used to improve existing structures and to create new ones, and gives a set of general principles to guide the work of the Standing Committee on Social Science Data Archives of the ISSC in the area. A general plan of action is presented, together with a series of more specific steps.

PRINCIPAL OBSTACLES TO THE DEVELOPMENT OF SOCIAL SCIENCE DATA ARCHIVES IN LATIN AMERICA

Each continental area presents a different set of problems and prospects in the field of social science data archives. In the United States the main challenge is the development of technical and interinstitutional systems to maximize the availability and uses of existing large data bases, many of which are already located in research centers. The chief obstacles seem to be technical,[1] financial, and those derived from institutional jealousies and lack of co-operation.

I do not have a detailed knowledge of the situation in Europe, but I surmise that the problems there are a mixture of the same ingredients,

---

* Center for Social Research, Torcuata Di Tella Institute, Buenos Aires, Argentina.

[1] Including human reluctance to change techniques.

perhaps in different absolute and relative amounts, plus the resistances derived from *national* jealousies and lack of co-operation.

The development of social science data archives in Latin America faces all these obstacles, plus others which, although not totally absent in the United States or in Europe, are here much more critical. A partial list is the following:

1. Financial problems
2. Institutional isolation and misunderstanding
3. National isolation and mistrust
4. Lack of appropriate computing facilities and even of unit record equipment
5. Scarcity of well-trained data archive technicians, including programmers and other computer personnel
6. Poor communication facilities. This factor has to do with the technological and administrative substructure and is different from the institutional and national isolation and mistrust listed already (although it often reinforces both). Included here are high relative mailing costs, low quality of mail and telephone systems, high relative costs of air and surface travel and transportation, low quality and high relative cost of the available secretarial help, etc.
7. Higher relative costs and, hence, higher subjective value of the data for their producers. This factor makes for a highly possessive attitude on the part of many local social scientists (an attitude not totally absent in other continental areas)
8. Low level of training and "traditional" attitudes on the part of some Latin-American scientists and most local administrators — producers of data and/or decision makers as to their availability to the scientific community at large
9. Institutional instability in social science research and training, as well as political instability affecting the governmental agencies that produce and keep (or dispose of) many important sets of data
10. The effects of extracontinental interferences[2] and of the exploitative attitudes of some non-Latin-American social researchers, which reinforce the xenophobia and mistrust of the local ones.

This is not an unduly pessimistic view of things but rather a list of factors that have to be taken into consideration, as unavoidable facts of life, in any plans for the development of social science data archives in Latin America.

[2] As in the case of Project Camelot and similar ones; see I. L. Horowitz (ed.), *The Rise and Fall of Project Camelot* (Cambridge, Mass.: The M.I.T. Press, 1967).

INDIVIDUAL AND INSTITUTIONAL RESOURCES

On the other hand, some basic aspects of the situation permit us to plan from a more positive point of view. There is in Latin America a growing body of social scientists trained in modern techniques. Communications among them, although still unsatisfactory, are steadily increasing. Even though the institutional mortality is high, there is at present an increasing, albeit varying and shifting, number of modern and efficient research centers that may be used as the core of our effort to establish, develop, and upgrade social science data archives throughout the area.

Moreover, the rate of change and improvement in the field of social science in many areas of Latin America is often quite high, and situations that at first glance seem hopeless have a surprising capacity to change rapidly for the better. A good instance is the emergence of first-rate empirical research in several social sciences, such as economics, and of modern institutions of research and training in a number of countries where nothing of the kind existed ten to twelve years ago.

In Bogotá, Colombia, in October 1967, more than forty institutes of research in the social sciences have constituted the *Consejo Latinoamericano de Ciencias Sociales* (Latin-American Social Science Council).

SOME GENERAL PRINCIPLES FOR THE DEVELOPMENT OF DATA ARCHIVES

Our efforts in this area should be channeled, as much as possible, through Latin-American institutions. Whenever possible, these Latin-American centers should work within international or interinstitutional frameworks. The Latin-American Social Science Council is a good example of the desirable type of the multination, multi-institution, interdisciplinary setting.

We must always take into consideration the local peculiarities and differences, acting not at the "Latin-American" level, which in this area is nonexistent, but at the level of the region, the country, and even the discipline and the institution. Personal contacts are indispensable, especially in the initial stages of our work. Letters and printed materials should be used only as a complement to those person-to-person interviews and never as their substitute. We must impress everyone involved in our effort with the necessity for a maximum of tact, diplomacy, and consideration for local idiosyncrasies.

A strenuous effort should be made to avoid ever-possessive attitudes and negative competition among non-Latin-American institutions. On the other hand, our action in promoting social science data archives must be explicitly based on principles of open and symmetrical co-operation, redressing as much as possible the effects of technical and financial disparities between local and "outside" institutions and providing liberal access to data in every archive to all legitimate research centers.

As I said before, data are even more precious to Latin-American researchers than they are to Americans or Europeans. Many Latin Americans feel that they should get "something" when parting with a copy of their files or cards. Sometimes this will be the only way for our archives to obtain a significant body of data. Moreover, such require-ments may be justified as a means to support *further* research, the pro-duction of more data, etc. A list of some obvious items for such exchange should include funds for research, books, other data, fellowships (especially to train social science data archive technicians), and tech-nical advice and assistance. I shall come back later to some of these and related items.

At least in the initial stages of our progress, we should allow Latin-American data producers[3] to have exclusive rights to the use of their materials for longer periods than we would ordinarily deem reasonable in the United States or Europe. In many centers of Latin America there is a "possessive" tradition that we cannot just wish away; on the other hand, it is objectively true that local researchers, with far fewer financial, technical, and human resources and often with less training, need more time for their analyses.

A GENERAL PLAN OF ACTION

On the basis of these general principles, the main objectives of a realistic program will be, in an approximately sequential order:

1. To diagnose in a specific and detailed fashion the situation within each region, country, and discipline

2. To protect from destruction as many as possible of the existing sets of data

3. To improve the existing archival facilities and to create new national and/or regional archives

4. To develop new data sources and to incorporate new sets of data into the existing and new archives.

[3] Survey directors, social scientists, and researchers who have gathered some type of statistical or historical material, etc.

Our most pressing over-all need is information about existing situations. Each report should include: (1) a list of existing *sets of data*, their location, and the names of the persons and institutions that control the access to them and decide on their duplication and availability, etc.; (2) a list or directory comprising (and classifying) the available human and institutional *archival resources* that in each area constitute the most probable basis for national and/or regional archives; and (3) an appraisal of the particular *obstacles* to be confronted in each specific situation.

Research institutions in Latin America are much less stable than their counterparts in Europe or the United States. This does not mean that the institutions disappear; in most cases what happens is that the active scholars and administrators leave a center that has become unsuitable as a research environment or has suffered political persecution, and these same men create a different center in the same or another country. The first institution is downgraded, and there is risk of destruction for the data gathered and left behind.

The same risk is often present whenever an individual scientist leaves an institution. Quite often he has been there a "lone wolf," the only person in the organization interested in empirical research of a given type — or perhaps of any type — and when he leaves, his data are scattered and lost.

In other cases, a certain body of data is gathered, but because of the lack of appropriate training in the researcher and of an environment congenial to research, it is never analyzed and is subsequently destroyed. The governmental agencies that gather or produce important sets of data may also be affected by political instability. A change in government quite frequently means a change in the administration, the discontinuation of the series, and the probable loss of the existing data.

Whenever our diagnosis reveals the possible existence of situations equivalent to the ones previously described, we must try to protect, duplicate, and store the existing data. We may profit from the fact that more and more of the ongoing research in many countries of Latin America is being listed from its start (and even beforehand) in several up-to-date directories. We may offer researchers a chance to share the expense of punching their cards[4] in exchange for duplicate decks, together with the questionnaires and code books (in the case of surveys) or any other elements necessary to future users. Of course, this is only

---

[4] Like most other costs, these expenses are relatively higher in Latin America than in the United States or in Europe.

one example of the type of support that we can offer for acquiring a set of data and preventing its destruction. The only features that recommend it are: (*a*) that by offering to pay the cost of punching the cards, we put our hands on them at the earliest possible moment and avoid any subsequent vicissitudes they might suffer and (*b*) that the costs involved are minimal.

DEVELOPMENT OF EXISTING AND NEW ARCHIVES

Perhaps the hardest decision for us, to be made on the basis of our diagnostic report, is whether to wait until a wide enough consensus is obtained in a given country or region or to choose one of a few promising centers in each area and to concentrate in it our first efforts, trusting in some kind of "demonstration effect" to spread modern standards and techniques to the rest of the research and administrative agencies. I tend to favor the second alternative. This will mean the creation of "show-case" data archives in the most modern research institutions of Latin America. We shall then be able to organize seminars for top administrators from other centers within the region (or perhaps at a Latin-American level) so that they will have first-hand information about the advantages of the new systems, the support available for the upgrading of archival facilities provided minimal standards are met, etc.

For some time to come, the economic and technical problems of Latin-American archives will be those of rather small archives of heterogeneous material, including not only survey and ecological data but also historical data, etc. We could use any experience our European and American colleagues have had with similar problems.

A substantial part of the assessment of each regional or national area —which starts with what I have called the diagnostic report and develops into a continued effort to update information about the data situation in each discipline—must be devoted to locate potential, unused new sources of data. This will be coupled with an active program to gain access, gather, preprocess, and incorporate those new sets of data into existing or new archives.

Some of these programs may be included in ordinary research projects either as one of their main objectives or as an important by-product. In other cases, a special program will be needed, one that will not result immediately in analytical studies but will be devoted exclusively to gathering, cleaning, reclassifying, standardizing, and duplicating the new data. Since the indispensable financial and technical resources are especially scarce in the area, we shall have to support local institutions or interinstitutional consortia to realize these tasks and create, at a higher level — perhaps as a part of the Task Force on Social Science Data Archives of the Latin-American Social Science Council — a committee to assign priorities among different potential data sets.

Index of Persons

589

Index of Institutions

Geographical Index

Index of Subjects